THE DEVELOPMENT AND TREATMENT OF CHILDHOOD AGGRESSION

THE DEVELOPMENT AND TREATMENT OF CHILDHOOD AGGRESSION

EDITED BY

DEBRA J. PEPLER
York University

KENNETH H. RUBIN
University of Waterloo

LEA

LAWRENCE ERLBAUM ASSOCIATES, PUBLISHERS
1991 Hillsdale, New Jersey Hove and London

Lawrence Erlbaum Associates, Inc., Publishers
365 Broadway
Hillsdale, New Jersey 07642

Library of Congress Cataloging-in-Publication Data

The development and treatment of childhood aggression / edited by Debra J. Pepler, Kenneth H. Rubin.
p. cm.
A collection of papers and commentaries from the Earlscourt Symposium on Childhood Aggression held in Toronto, Canada in June 1988 as part of the Earlscourt Child and Family Centre's celebration of its 75th anniversary.
Includes bibliographical references.
Includes indexes.

1. Aggressiveness (Psychology) in children--Congresses.
I. Pepler, D. J. (Debra J.) II. Rubin, Kenneth H. III. Earlscourt Child and Family Centre. IV. Earlscourt Symposium on Childhood Aggression (1988 : Toronto, Ont.)
[DNLM: 1. Aggression--infancy & childhood--congresses. WS 350.8.A489 1988]
RJ506.A35.D48 1990
618.92'8582--dc20
DNLM/DLC
for Library of Congress 90-14018
CIP

ISBN 0-8058-0370-X

Printed in the United States of America
10 9 8 7 6 5 4 3 2

Contents

Foreword

Kenneth Goldberg, M.S.W.
Earlscourt Child and Family Centre

This book is a collection of papers and commentaries from the Earlscourt Symposium on Childhood Aggression held in Toronto, Canada in June, 1988 as part of the Earlscourt Child and Family Centre's celebration of its 75th anniversary. The Symposium reflected Earlscourt's commitment to link clinical practice to identifiable, research-based interventions that are known in the social sciences to be effective in the prevention and treatment of antisocial behavior in children. The education of human services professionals has typically failed to train them to work with specific client populations, opting instead to provide a generalist approach more typically grounded in theoretical assumptions and professional values than research and empirical studies. The symposium and this important book serve to fill this gap in professional education in the area of childhood aggression.

The problem of childhood aggression plagues those who wish to see an easing of the suffering that these children incur and inflict on others. The task of researchers and practitioners in this field has societal implications and considerable urgency. On a case-by-case basis, we will never reach all the children who might benefit from help, and without a scientific base to practice, we will never insure that those who do receive help receive effective treatments. Earlscourt is proud to mark its 75th anniversary by contributing to the dissemination of knowledge in this field and the advancement of a scientific approach to practice.

Childhood aggression must be understood multifactorially. Although there is no simple solution or cure-all to be applied to the problem of childhood aggression, the articles and commentaries gathered here represent substantial accomplishments in the advancement of an understanding of the plight of aggressive children and how best to ameliorate their often stressful, unpredictable, and painful situations.

Professionals in the field must guard against a pessimism toward the life prospects of aggressive children, which can lead to a nihilistic attitude towards services for these children and towards the children themselves. The Earlscourt Symposium on Childhood Aggression and this book allow for at least a cautious optimism that empirical research can have practical consequences for these children and their life prospects.

Earlscourt's 75-year history is a testament of community and government support for programs to help disadvantaged children. The Centre, originally known as Earlscourt Children's Home, has been sustained throughout its history by four generations of Wimodausis Clubs, a voluntary board of directors, and more recently the government of Ontario. Both the Ontario Ministry of Community and Social Services and the Social Sciences and Humanities Research Council of Canada contributed to the symposium. Their generous assistance is hereby acknowledged with much appreciation.

With so many of the presenters at the symposium staying throughout the 3½ days of presentations, commentaries, and discussion, the symposium became an intellectually stimulating experience that is seldom replicated. Reading this book will rekindle fond memories of the symposium for those fortunate enough to have attended it and will provide an opportunity for a much larger audience to share the symposium's deliberations. I thank our symposium co-chairpersons and the editors of this book, Debra Pepler and Ken Rubin, for their special contributions to the success of the Earlscourt Symposium on Childhood Aggression and for bringing its proceedings to print.

Introduction: Current Challenges in the Development and Treatment of Childhood Aggression

Aggressive children represent a special concern for society. A significant proportion of disturbed children referred to treatment centers evidence aggressive and disruptive behavior problems and hostile relationships with family members and peers (Kazdin, 1987; Patterson, 1982). These aggressive behavior problems are resistant to change and extremely difficult to treat; indeed, long-term benefits have seldom been demonstrated (Patterson, 1979; Kazdin, 1987). Aggressive behavior appears to persist both over time and across generations (Huesmann, Eron, Lefkowitz, & Walder, 1984; Olweus, 1978) and predicts maladaptive outcomes such as delinquency and hostility in the adolescent and adult years (Farrington, 1986; Huesmann, Eron, Lefkowitz, & Walder, 1984). The phenomenon is, therefore, significant and raises many critical questions. What are the origins of childhood aggression? What are the psychological costs of aggression? Can aggression be treated? When and how should it be treated?

The present volume represents an attempt by an esteemed group of researchers to address these questions. In the first section, different theoretical and empirical perspectives on the development of childhood aggression are presented (e.g., biological bases, socialization, and other family influences, social-cognitive influences and extra-familial/peer relational factors associated with childhood aggression). In the second section, implications of the above noted theoretical and research based perspectives are linked to the development of treatment programs for aggressive children and their families.

THE DEVELOPMENT OF AGGRESSION IN CHILDHOOD

Recent estimates suggest that 5.5% of children can be identified as having conduct disordered behavioral problems of an aggressive nature (Offord, Boyle, & Racine, Chapter 2). These behavioral patterns in childhood are stable and predictive of a wide variety of social and emotional difficulties in adulthood (Eron, Huesmann, & Zelli, Chapter 7; Farrington, Chapter 1). One such negative "outcome" of aggression that may serve to recycle the phenomenon across generations is inadequate parenting. Thus, it is known that inadequate or incompetent socialization by parents is predictive of childhood aggression (Patterson, Capaldi, & Bank, Chapter 6); furthermore, aggressive children appear to become incompetent parents (Serbin, Moskowitz, Schwartzman, & Ledingham, chapter 3). In order to interrupt this cross-generational cycle of aggression and hostility, it is important to determine the early behavioral markers or predictors of aggression as well as the familial and ecological influences that are likely to place young children at risk for aggression and its negative consequences.

There are some who believe that the early and consistent display of aggression is primarily the product of biological and/or genetic factors. Moreover, of those who do adopt a biological perspective, some believe that the course of aggression is set with minimal influence from the environment (Grennan, Mednick, & Kandel, Chapter 4). Others believe that a complex mix of familial and ecological factors conspire with biological factors to produce aggressive behavior in childhood (Bates, Bayles, Bennett, Ridge, & Brown, Chapter 5; Patterson, Capaldi, & Bank, Chapter 6). Clearly, the families of aggressive children differ from the norm and play a highly influential role in the development, maintenance, and/or decline of aggressive behavior (Eron et al., Chapter 7; Patterson et al., Chapter 6).

The negative fallout from aggression appears to be seen most clearly when the child is observed in extra-familial environments. Coercive antisocial behavioral patterns established at home generalize to negative interactions with peers and teachers as early as the preschool years. One apparent consequence of aggression in early childhood (and throughout the years of childhood) is peer rejection (Coie & Kupersmidt, 1983; Dodge, 1983; Rubin & Daniels-Bierness, 1983). As rejected-aggressive children grow up, they come to believe (perhaps accurately so) that their social worlds are hostile and biased against them (Dodge, 1986). Aggressive children appear to be less reflective and less willing and/or able to consider accurately the feelings, thoughts and intentions of others than are their normal peers. Furthermore, aggressive youngsters appear to have difficulty thinking about and acting through solutions to interpersonal dilemmas (Dodge, Petit, McClaskey, & Brown, 1986). These social-cognitive deficits may serve to reinforce or maintain the production of aggressive behavior in childhood. Thus, another cycle that requires intervention is that which begins with the premise that aggressive behavior results in peer rejection, peer rejection leads to the child's isolation by the peer group, then isolation and rejection preclude the child from the necessary social interaction experiences that foster the development of competent social cognizing (e.g., Rubin, LeMare, & Hollis, in press).

Finally, once established, the negative standing of aggressive children in the peer group appears to lead them to seek social support and reinforcement from those willing to provide such a comforting environment. Cairns and Cairns (Chapter 10) demonstrate that the support network of aggressive children is comprised usually of children who share their rejected status in the peer group. These delinquent and/or aggressive subcultures serve to perpetuate the cycle of hostility that began in the early years of childhood.

The bottom line is that the chapters in Section I of this volume tell a devastating tale. Aggression in childhood may be a product of a multiple and complex mix of forces. It leads to maladaptive extra-familial relationships and is accompanied by inappropriate means of thinking about the social world. Finally, aggression begets aggression as well as further aggression. The rejected, isolated youngster appears to cross generational lines to become the ineffective, incompetent parent. The incompetent parent is likely to raise an aggressive child, and so the story continues.

THE TREATMENT OF AGGRESSION IN CHILDHOOD

If aggression is the product of multiple forces, and indeed, if aggressive children come by their hostility in different ways (Rubin, Bream, & Krasnor, Chapter 9), then what can be done to solve the problem? It would not be inaccurate to suggest that for every apparent influence on aggression, there is a corresponding means of treatment. To deal with familial influences on aggressive behavior, interventions have been developed to modify the behaviors of the parents in relation to their aggressive children (Forgatch, Chapter 11; Forehand & Long, Chapter 12). School-based aggression and peer rejection are dealt with by interventions described by Kendall, Ronan, and Epps (Chapter 13); Pepler, Byrd, and King (Chapter 14); Coie, Underwood and Lochman (Chapter 15) and by Olweus (Chapter 16).

The reader will note, however, that most of the best interventions, if successful at all, appear to have the greatest influence over the *short* term. It may well be that our attempts to intervene have suffered from the same problems as have our attempts to explain the phenomenon—oversimplicity. For example, many interventions aimed at families of aggressive children fail to deal with issues of peer rejection and support. Interventions aimed at aggressive children's social cognitions and peer relations have often neglected the homes to which these children return. Finally, almost all intervention efforts have ignored the fact that there are many different pathways to the development and manifestation of aggressive behavior (Dodge, Chapter 8; Patterson et al., Chapter 6; Rubin et al., Chapter 9). The challenge within this volume has been to identify some of the pathways and processes traditionally implicated in the development of treatments for childhood aggression.

As noted above, we invited a highly esteemed cast of characters who have spent their very productive research careers studying the complex phenomenon of childhood aggression in order to contribute to this volume. Their current thoughts about the development and treatment of aggression are reflected in their chapters. We did not stop, however, with an uncritical acceptance of the state of the art. Instead, we invited other researchers in the field to provide critical commentaries of the chapters. It is the interaction between the information conveyed in the chapters and commentaries that we feel will stimulate major advances in the field.

We now have the responsibility for meeting some of the challenges presented in this volume with you, our reading audience.

Debra J. Pepler
Kenneth H. Rubin

REFERENCES

Coie, J. D., & Kupersmidt, J. B. (1983). A behavioral analysis of emerging social status in boys' groups. *Child Development, 54,* 1400–1416.

Dodge, K. A. (1983). Behavioral antecedents of peer social status. *Child Development, 54,* 1386–1399.

Dodge, K. A. (1986). A social information processing model of social competence in children. In M. Perlmutter (Ed.), Minnesota Symposium on Child Psychology (pp. 7–125). Hillsale, NJ: Lawrence Erlbaum Associates.

Dodge, K. A., Pettit, G. S., McClaskey, C. L., & Brown, M. M. (1986). Social competence in children. *Monographs of the Society for Research in Child Development* (Serial No. 213, Vol. 51, No. 2).

Farrington, D. P. (1986). Stepping stones to adult criminal careers. In D. Olweus, J. Block, & M. R. Yarrow (Eds.) *Development of antisocial and prosocial behavior* (pp. 359–384). New York: Academic Press.

Huesmann, L. R., Eron, L. D., Lefkowitz, M. M., & Walder, L. O. (1984). Stability of aggression over time and generations. *Developmental Psychology,* 20, 1120–1134.

Kazdin, A. E. (1987). Treatment of antisocial behavior in children: Current status and future directions. *Psychological Bulletin, 102,* 187–203.

Patterson, G. R. (1986). Performance models for antisocial boys. *American Psychologist, 41*:4, 432–444.

Patterson, G. R. (1982). *Coercive family process: A social learning approach, Vol. 3.* Eugene, Oregon: Castalia Publishing Co.

Patterson, G. R. (1979). Treatment for children with conduct problems: A review of outcome studies. In Feshbach, S., & Fraczek, A. (Eds.), *Aggression and behavior change: Biological and social processes.* New York: Praeger Publishing Co.

Rubin, K. H., & Daniels-Beirness, T. (1983). Concurrent and predictive correlates of sociometric status in kindergarten and grade 1 children. *Merrill-Palmer Quarterly,* 29, 337–351.

Rubin, K., LeMare, L., & Lollis, S. (1990). Social withdrawal in childhood: Developmental pathways to peer rejection. In S. Asher & J. Coie (Eds.), *Peer rejection in childhood.* New York: Cambridge University Press.

I

THE DEVELOPMENT OF CHILDHOOD AGGRESSION

Section 1: Descriptive and Predictive Studies of Childhood Aggression

1

Childhood Aggression and Adult Violence: Early Precursors and Later-Life Outcomes

David P. Farrington
Cambridge University

Farrington (1978) found that there was significant continuity in aggressiveness over time in a sample of London males. Teacher-rated aggressiveness at age 8 predicted self-reported violence at age 18. The extensive reviews by Olweus (1979, 1980, 1984a) show that these results are not untypical. In 16 surveys covering periods of up to 21 years, the average stability coefficient (correlation) for male aggression was .68. Further, this average stability coefficient decreased linearly with the time interval, according to the following equation:

$$y = .78 - .018x$$

(where y = stability coefficient and x = time interval in years). This chapter is not concerned with female aggression, but this also seems to be relatively stable over time (Olweus, 1981, 1984b). Olweus concluded that there were *relatively stable aggressive reaction tendencies within individuals.*

One of the most impressive and longest lasting studies of the continuity of aggressiveness was carried out by Huesmann, Eron, Lefkowitz, and Walder (1984). They followed up several hundred children from New York State, and found that peer-rated aggression at age 8 significantly predicted self-reported aggression at age 30 (for males, as in other studies quoted here). Similar results were reported by Eron and Huesmann (1984) and Eron, Huesmann, Dubow, Romanoff, and Yarmel (1987). Studies spanning shorter time periods have also reported significant continuity in aggression for males (e.g., Bachman, O'Malley, & Johnston, 1978; Moskowitz, Schwartzman, & Ledingham, 1985; Pulkkinen & Hurme, 1984; Stattin & Magnusson, 1984). The *first aim* of this chapter is to extend the analyses of Farrington (1978) up to the adult years (age 32) to investigate the degree of continuity in aggression from age 8 to age 32.

It is clear that early aggression also predicts later delinquency and crime, as the reviews by Loeber and Dishion (1983) and Loeber and Stouthamer-Loeber (1987) show. For example, Huesmann et al. (1984) found that peer-rated aggression at age 8 significantly predicted convictions up to age 30. In an impressive 40-year follow-up study in Massachusetts, McCord (1983) reported that aggressive adolescents were more likely to be convicted of index crimes than were nonaggressive adolescents. Also, in two studies in the mid-West of America, teacher-rated aggression significantly predicted juvenile delinquency and adult crime over periods of 8 years (Feldhusen, Aversano, & Thurston, 1976; Feldhusen, Thurston, & Benning, 1973) and 15 years (Roff, 1986; Roff & Wirt, 1984, 1985). In Chicago, Ensminger, Kellam, and Rubin (1983), and Kellam, Brown, Rubin and Ensminger (1983) reported that teacher-rated aggression in first grade significantly predicted self-reported delinquency 10 years later.

Early aggression also predicts later violent crime, as Farrington (1978) demonstrated. Similarly, in Finland, Pulkkinen (1983) showed that peer and teacher ratings of aggression at age 8 predicted violent offenses up to age 20; and, in Sweden, Magnusson, Stattin, and Duner (1983) reported that teacher-rated aggression at ages 10 and 13 predicted violent offenses up to age 26 (see also Magnusson, 1988). It is also clear that juvenile violent offenses predict adult violent offenses (e.g., Hamparian, Davis, Jacobson, & McGraw, 1985).

Little is known about other later-life outcomes of boys who are aggressive at an early age, although Huesmann, Eron, and Yarmel (1987) found that peer-rated aggression at age 8 significantly predicted low attainment (in reading, spelling, and arithmetic) at age 30. The *second aim* of this chapter is to investigate the later-life outcomes at age 32 of boys who were aggressive as children and adolescents (between ages 8 and 18).

Farrington (1978) discovered that the most important early precursor of aggression and violence was the harsh attitude and discipline of a boy's parents at age 8. Other important early precursors were low family income, parental criminality, poor parental supervision, separations from parents, high daring, and low intelligence, all measured at age 8–10. Similarly, McCord, McCord, and Howard (1963) found that, as children, violent delinquents tended to have parents who were in conflict, who supervised them poorly, who were rejecting and punitive, whose discipline was erratic, and who were aggressive, alcoholic, or convicted.

In her later follow-up, McCord (1977, 1988) again documented how violent parents tended to have aggressive sons.

The main problem in interpreting all these results centers on the issue of generality versus specificity in antisocial behavior. In a review of longitudinal research on violence, Farrington (1982) concluded that it was rare for offenders to specialize in violence. It was more common for offenders to commit a variety of different kinds of crimes, as the later review of specialization by Farrington, Snyder, and Finnegan (1988) also shows. Studies in Ohio (Hamparian, Schuster, Dinitz, & Conrad, 1978; Miller, Dinitz, & Conrad, 1982) and in Stockholm (Wikstrom, 1985, 1987) confirm that the majority of crimes committed by violent offenders are not violent. However, specialization seems to be more apparent in offenders aged over 40 (McCord, 1980; Peterson, Pittman, & O'Neal, 1962).

Farrington (1978) found that violent offenders tended to have committed more crimes than nonviolent offenders, and this result has been replicated in Copenhagen (Guttridge, Gabrielli, Mednick, & Van Dusen, 1983) and in Philadelphia (Piper, 1985). In general, violent offenders tend to be frequent or "chronic" offenders, and the probability of committing a violent offense increases with the number of offenses committed (Farrington, 1982). Hence, the difference between violent and nonviolent offenders may be quantitative, rather than qualitative, approximating the difference between more frequent and less frequent offenders. This may be why early aggression predicts chronic offending (Loeber & Stouthamer-Loeber, 1987).

The view that a general syndrome of antisocial behavior arises in childhood and continues into adulthood has been argued most persuasively by Robins (1979, 1983, 1986). She has repeatedly demonstrated that the *number* of types of conduct disorder shown in childhood predict the *number* of types of antisocial adult behaviors, rather than one specific type of child conduct disorder (such as aggression) predicting one specific type of adult antisocial behavior (such as violence; Robins & Ratcliff, 1978, 1980). Similarly, West and Farrington (1977) concluded that their research showed that a constellation of adverse childhood factors led to a constellation of deviant behaviors at age 18, including stealing, drinking, drug taking, sexual promiscuity, erratic work histories, reckless driving, and violence. They explained their results by suggesting that all these kinds of deviant behavior reflected a single underlying theoretical construct, which they termed *antisocial tendency.* This arose in childhood and continued into the teenage years, although its behavioral manifestations changed with age.

The key question is whether aggressive or violent behavior is merely one element of a more general antisocial tendency, or whether it reflects a more specific underlying violent tendency. The general continuity in antisocial behavior with age inevitably means that there will be continuity between child aggression and adult violence, and between child aggression and adult antisocial behavior. However, is it possible to demonstrate specific continuities involving aggression and violence that are different in some way from the general continuities? Loeber (1982, 1988) has consistently argued that overt aggressive behaviors are different in kind from covert nonaggressive acts, such as stealing, and that these two kinds of behaviors have different developmental pathways (see also Loeber & Schmaling, 1985a, 1985b).

One method of investigating this question is to compare aggressive and nonaggressive offenders. For example, McCord (1979, 1980) found that they were similar in having poor parental supervision, but different in that parental conflict and parental aggressiveness were more predictive of violence, whereas maternal affection and paternal criminality were more predictive of property crimes. Hogh and Wolf (1983) in Copenhagen showed that violent offenders had relatively low intelligence, and Wikstrom (1987) in Stockholm discovered that they were more likely to come from lower class families than other types of offenders. However, Farrington and West (1971) found few differences between self-reported violent offenders and predominantly nonviolent early delinquents.

If, indeed, violent offenders tend to commit more offenses than nonviolent offenders, it is only to be expected that these two groups will differ in childhood, adolescence, and adulthood. In order to disentangle qualitative and quantitative differences, the key question is whether violent offenders differ significantly from nonviolent offenders who have committed the *same* number of offenses, and this is the *third question* to be investigated in this chapter.

THE PRESENT RESEARCH

The present research is part of the Cambridge Study in Delinquent Development, which is a prospective longitudinal survey of 411 males. At the time they were first contacted in 1961–1962, they were all living in a working-class area of London, England. The vast majority of the sample was chosen by taking *all* the boys who were then aged 8 and on the registers of six state primary schools within a 1–mile radius of our research office. In addition to 399 boys from these six schools, 12 boys from a local school for the educationally subnormal were included in the sample, in an attempt to make it more representative of the population of boys living in the area. The boys were overwhelmingly White, working-class, and of British origin. Major results obtained in this survey have been reported previously (Farrington, 1989a; Farrington & West, 1981; West, 1969, 1982; West & Farrington, 1973, 1977).

The major aim in this survey was to measure as many factors as possible that were alleged to be causes or correlates of offending. The boys were interviewed and tested in their schools when they were aged about 8, 10, and 14, by male or female psychologists. They were interviewed in our research office at about 16, 18, and 21, and in their homes at about 25 and 32, by young male social science graduates. The tests in schools measured intelligence, attainment, personality, and psychomotor impulsivity, whereas information was collected in the interviews about living circumstances, employment histories, relationships with females, leisure activities, and offending behavior. On all occasions except at ages 21 and 25, the aim was to interview the whole sample, and it was always possible to trace and interview a high proportion. For example, at age 18, 389 of the 410 males still alive (94.9%) were interviewed.

In addition to the interviews and tests with the boys, interviews with their parents were carried out by female social workers who visited their homes. These took place about once a year from when the boy was about 8 until when he was aged 14–15 and was in his last year of compulsory education. The primary informant was the mother, although many fathers were also seen. The parents provided details about such matters as family income, family size, their employment histories, their child-rearing practices (including attitudes, discipline, and parental agreement), their degree of supervision of the boy, and his temporary or permanent separations from them.

The boys' teachers completed questionnaires when the boys were aged about 8, 10, 12, and 14. These provided information about the boys' troublesome and aggressive school behavior, their attention deficit, their school attainments, and their truancy. Ratings were also obtained from the boys' peers when they were in their primary schools, about such topics as their daring, dishonesty, troublesomeness, and popularity.

Searches were also carried out in the national Criminal Record Office in London to try to locate findings of guilt of the boys, of their parents, of their brothers and sisters, and (in recent years) of their wives and cohabitees. Convictions were only counted if they were for offenses normally recorded in this office, thereby excluding minor crimes such as common (simple) assault, traffic offenses, and drunkenness. The most common offenses included were thefts, burglaries, and unauthorized takings of motor vehicles. However, we did not rely on official records for our information about offending, because we also obtained self-reports of offending from the boys themselves at every age from 14 onwards.

This chapter reports data collected in the recent interview at age 32. Up to that age, 8 of the men had died, and 20 had emigrated permanently. Of the remaining 383 who were still alive and in the United Kingdom, 360 were interviewed personally (94.0%). Seven of the emigrated men were also interviewed, either abroad or during a temporary return visit that they made to the United Kingdom, making a total interviewed of 367. In addition, 9 emigrated men filled in self-completion questionnaires, and two cooperative wives of refusers filled in questionnaires on behalf of their husbands, in at least one case with the husband's collaboration and assistance. Therefore, interviews or questionnaires were obtained for 378 of the 403 men still alive (93.8%). For ease of exposition, this chapter refers to 378 men interviewed at age 32.

Summarizing, the Cambridge Study in Delinquent Development has a unique combination of features. Eight face-to-face interviews have been completed with the subjects over a period of 24 years, between ages 8 and 32. The main focus of interest is on delinquency, crime, and antisocial behavior. The sample size of about 400 is large enough for many statistical analyses yet small enough to permit detailed case histories of the boys and their families. Information has been obtained from multiple sources, including the subjects themselves, their parents, teachers, peers, and official records. Data have been collected about a wide variety of theoretical constructs at different ages, including biological (e.g., pulse rate), psychological (e.g., intelligence), family (e.g., discipline), and social (e.g., socioeconomic status) factors. The attrition rate is unusually low for such a long-term survey.

CONTINUITY OF AGGRESSION AND VIOLENCE

Measures of the aggressiveness of each boy at ages 8, 10, 12, and 14 were derived from the teachers' questionnaires. The measures at ages 8 and 10 were the least satisfactory. The aggressive boys at these ages were defined to be those who were difficult to discipline. This is not a very direct measure of aggression, although it has been used by other researchers (e.g., Stewart & de Blois, 1983). The aggressive boys at ages 12 and 14 were those whose teachers gave them most points for being disobedient, difficult to discipline, unduly rough during playtime, quarrelsome and aggressive, overcompetitive with other children, and unduly resentful of criticism or punishment.

Measures of aggressiveness at ages 16, 18, and 32 were derived from self-reports during the interviews at these ages. The aggressive youths at age 16 were those who most frequently admitted getting into fights, carrying and using weapons, and fighting police officers. The aggressive youths at age 18 were those who most frequently admitted getting into fights, starting fights, and carrying and using weapons. The most aggressive men at age 32 were those who admitted being involved in fights in the last 5 years. Fights were defined as incidents in which blows were struck, and fights in the course of work (e.g., as a police officer, prison officer, or security guard), and men who were victims of mugging were not counted.

Up to age 32, 153 men (37.2%) were convicted of a total of 683 crimes (average 4.5 each). In counting crimes, only one offense on each day of offending (the most serious) was included. This was to ensure that each offense occurred in a separate criminal event. Each crime usually corresponded to a separate conviction, because the 683 offenses corresponded to 613 separate convictions.

Of the 683 offenses, 85 (12.4%) were violent: 43 assaults (including wounding), 17 robberies, and 25 offenses of threatening behavior. Assaults had to be quite serious to be included in these figures, because minor assaults were not normally recorded in the Criminal Record Office. The remaining 598 offenses were nonviolent, although the crime of possessing an offensive weapon (17 cases) sometimes arose out of a violent incident. Of the 153 convicted men, 50 (32.7%) were convicted of at least one violent offense.

Table 1.1 shows the interrelationships between the measures of ag-

TABLE 1.1
Continuity of Aggression and Violence

		% A(N) on V2		
Variable 1	*Variable 2*	*V1 = Agg*	*V1 = Nonagg*	*Chi-Squared*
Agg 8–10	Agg 12–14	59.1 (93)	24.9 (317)	36.73***
Agg 8–10	Agg 16–18	40.4 (89)	26.7 (311)	5.63*
Agg 8–10	Agg 32	49.4 (79)	33.9 (298)	5.76*
Agg 8–10	Violence	20.4 (93)	9.8 (317)	6.66**
Agg 12–14	Agg 16–18	46.2 (130)	21.8 (271)	23.87***
Agg 12–14	Agg 32	47.2 (125)	32.1 (252)	7.48**
Agg 12–14	Violence	22.4 (134)	7.2 (277)	18.05***
Agg 16–18	Agg 32	54.5 (112)	30.0 (260)	18.99***
Agg 16–18	Violence	23.5 (119)	7.8 (282)	17.55***
Agg 32	Violence	22.9 (140)	5.1 (237)	25.33***
Agg 8–18	Agg 32	55.3 (94)	31.1 (283)	16.71***
Agg 8–18	Violence	28.2 (103)	6.8 (308)	30.92***

Notes:
*$p < .05$
**$p < .01$
***$p < .001$
Agg = Aggressive

gression and violence at different ages. The measures at ages 8–10, 12–14, and 16–18 are the same combined measures reported by Farrington (1978); the number of aggressive males identified was 93, 134, and 119, respectively, at these three ages. Just over one third of the males (140 out of 377 known, or 37.1%) were identified as aggressive at age 32. The number of convicted violent men is now nearly twice as many as in the previous analysis (50 as opposed to 27).

The figures in Table 1.1 show, for example, that about half (49.4%) of the most aggressive males at age 8–10 were still among the most aggressive at age 32, in comparison with about one third (33.9%) of the remainder, a statistically significant difference (chi-squared = 5.76, 1 df, $p < .025$, two-tailed; unless otherwise stated, all significance tests in this chapter are of this type). Similarly, 20.4% of the most aggressive males at age 8–10 were convicted of violence, in comparison with 9.8% of the remainder, a significant difference (chi-squared = 6.66, $p < .01$).

All the measures of aggression and violence were significantly interrelated, showing that there was significant continuity in aggressiveness from age 8–10 to age 32, and from child aggressiveness to adult criminal violence. The strongest relationships were generally between the measures that were closest in time. Relationships over long time periods, although statistically significant, were relatively weak. The difference between half of one group and one third of another does not indicate a very accurate prediction over time. Nevertheless, considering the rather poor measure of aggression at age 8–10 (being difficult to discipline), the fact that the measures came from different sources (teacher reports vs. self-reports), and the 20-year time interval, the degree of continuity is quite impressive.

The number of times that a male was identified as aggressive between ages 8 and 18 (out of the three measures) had some predictive power in regard to the aggression measure at age 32. About a quarter of the males who were nonaggressive at all three ages (8–10, 12–14, 16–18) were aggressive at 32 (45 out of 176, or 25.6%). This figure can be compared with 41.3% of 104 identified as aggressive at one age, 55.7% of 70 identified as aggressive at two ages, and 54.5% of 22 identified as aggressive at all three ages.

A combined measure of youthful aggression at age 8–18 was derived by contrasting the 103 males who were identified as aggressive at two or three ages with the remaining 308 (disregarding the fact that 11 were not known at one age). Table 1.1 shows, of course, that this combined measure was significantly related to both aggression at age 32 (chi-squared = 16.71, $p < .001$) and convictions for violence (chi-squared = 30.92, $p < .001$). The majority of convicted violent males (29 out of 50) were identified as aggressive in their youth. Criminal violence usually occurred at adult ages. Only three males were convicted of violence up to age 14, and only 19 up to age 18.

YOUTHFUL AGGRESSION AND LATER-LIFE OUTCOMES

Table 1.2 shows the relationship between youthful aggression and later-life outcomes at age 32. For example, as already mentioned, 37.2% of the men were convicted up to age 32, and this percentage (to the nearest whole number, for ease of presentation) is shown in the left-hand column of the table. Of the 93 boys identified as aggressive at age 8–10, 57.0% were convicted, in comparison with 31.2% of the remaining 317 known, a significant difference (chi-squared = 19.36, $p < .001$; indicated by three asterisks). Of the 134 boys identified as aggressive at age 12–14, 56.7% were convicted, in comparison with 27.8% of the remaining 277 (chi-squared = 31.09, $p < .001$). Of the 119 boys identified as aggressive

TABLE 1.2
Youthful Aggression Versus Later-Life Outcomes

		Aggression at Age:		
		8–10	*12–14*	*16–18*
Variable at Age 32	*(%)*	*% of A/NA*	*% of A/NA*	*% of A/NA*
Convicted	(37)	57/31***	57/28***	61/28***
Convicted last 5yr.	(11)	16/9	18/8**	18/8**
Chronic offender	(5)	14/3***	12/2***	14/2***
Not home owner	(52)	63/49*	62/47**	65/46***
Living in London	(52)	53/51	61/47*	65/46***
Doesn't agree with W/C	(8)	9/7	13/5*	10/7
Has struck W/C	(15)	22/12	21/11*	16/14
Not now employed	(12)	20/10*	16/10	17/10
Unemployed 10m+	(17)	25/15*	28/12***	27/13**
Heavy smoker	(27)	35/25	36/23**	35/24
Drunk driver	(53)	67/49*	63/48*	58/50
Heavy drinker	(20)	28/18	32/14***	33/14***
Taken marijuana	(18)	22/18	26/14**	29/14***
Self-report offender	(22)	29/21	33/17**	35/18***

Notes:
W/C = Wife or Cohabitee
A = Aggressive
NA = Non-aggressive
$*p < .05$
$**p < .01$
$***p < .001$

at age 16–18, 61.3% were convicted, in comparison with 28.0% of the remaining 282 known (chi-squared = 38.09, $p < .001$). As expected, therefore, all three measures of youthful aggression were significantly related to convictions. Aggression at ages 12–14 and 16–18 also significantly predicted convictions occurring in the 5 years up to the interview at age 32.

In this research, the "chronic offenders" were defined as the 22 men (5.4% of the sample) with at least nine offenses and at least eight separate convictions. They accounted for nearly half of the 683 offenses (45.7%). Table 1.2 shows that all three measures of aggression were significantly related to chronic offending. For example, 13 of the 93 aggressive boys at age 8–10 (14.0%) became chronics, in comparison with only 9 of the remaining 317 known (2.8%), a significant difference (chi-squared = 29.46, $p < .001$). The majority of eventual chronics, then, were identified as aggressive at age 8–10.

Just over half of the men (51.6%) were not homeowners at age 32, and all three measures of youthful aggression significantly predicted this. Similarly, just over half were still living in London. Generally, those who had moved out of London were upwardly mobile men moving to a better life in the leafy Home Counties surrounding London. The aggressive boys at ages 12–14 and 16–18 were significantly less likely to have moved out of London. However, youthful aggression did not significantly predict poor home conditions (e.g., dirty and damp) or high residential mobility (living at four or more addresses in the previous 5 years).

Most men (75.5%) were living with a wife or female cohabitee, and this applied equally to aggressive and nonaggressive boys. Similarly, youthful aggression did not significantly predict the minority of men (19.6%) who had been divorced or separated by age 32. However, the boys identified as aggressive at age 12–14 were significantly more likely than others to have struck their wife or cohabitee and to be not getting along very well with her.

All the measures of youthful aggression predicted long periods of unemployment at age 32 (of 10 months or more in the previous 5 years). Aggression at age 8–10 also significantly predicted current unemployment at age 32. However, youthful aggression did not significantly predict low take-home pay or a low socioeconomic status job.

Aggressive boys at age 12–14 significantly tended to be heavy smokers at age 32, smoking more than 20 cigarettes per day. In addition, aggression at ages 8–10 and 12–14 significantly predicted drunk driving (driving after consuming at least the equivalent of five pints of beer) in the previous 5 years. Of 66 drivers identified as aggressive at age 8–10, two thirds had driven while drunk, in comparison with less than half (48.8%) of the 246 remaining drivers at age 32, a significant difference (chi-squared = 5.98, $p < .025$). Aggression at ages 12–14 and 16–18 significantly predicted heavy drinking at age 32 (drinking at least the equivalent of 10 pints of beer in one session in the previous month).

Youthful aggression at ages 12–14 and 16–18 also significantly predicted marijuana use in the 5 years up to age 32, but not the use of other drugs, such as heroin or cocaine. Aggression also significantly predicted self-reported offending (admitting at least one of burglary, taking a vehicle, theft from a vehicle, shoplifting, vandalism, theft from an automatic machine, obtaining government benefits by fraud, or stealing checks or credit cards and obtaining money with them) in the previous 5 years. However, youthful aggression did not predict psychiatric disorder (as indicated by a score of 5 or more on the General Health Questionnaire).

SPECIFICITY OR GENERALITY IN VIOLENT OFFENDING

This was investigated by studying convictions for violence and for other offenses. As already mentioned, 50 of the 153 convicted men were convicted of violence. They committed a total of 85 violent offenses (an average of 1.7 each), but they also committed 263 nonviolent offenses leading to conviction (an average of 5.3 each). Only 7 of the 50 violent offenders had no convictions for nonviolent offenses. In view of the generality in antisocial behavior, it is only to be expected that the more antisocial people will commit more offenses and that they will therefore be more likely to include at least one violent offense in their criminal careers. This would be found even if different types of offenses were committed at random, with no tendency for specialization.

If there were complete generality in offending, the probability of committing a violent offense would increase with the number of offenses committed, and this was indeed found. Overall, 85 of the 683 offenses were violent (12.4%). Assuming that different types of offenses were committed at random (probabilistically), it might be expected that 12.4% of the 49 males who committed only one offense would commit a violent offense. Table 1.3 shows that the actual figure of 6 was close to the chance expectation of 6.1. Similarly, it might be expected that 23.3% of the 30 males who committed two offenses would commit at least one violent offense [a proportion 1 - (.876) squared]. Once again, the actual figure of 8 was close to the chance expectation of 7.0. The expected probability of committing at least one violent offense was very high for those who committed 9 or more offenses (82.6%).

Assuming complete generality in offending, it might be expected that 36.4% (55.7) of the 153 males would commit at least one violent of-

TABLE 1.3
Expected and Actual Number of Violent Offenders

		Violent Offenders			
		Expected		*Actual*	
No. of Offenses	*No. of Offenders*	*N*	(%)	*N*	(%)
1	49	6.1	(12)	6	(12)
2	30	7.0	(23)	8	(27)
3–4	23	8.2	(36)	9	(39)
5–8	28	15.4	(55)	12	(43)
9–20	23	19.0	(83)	15	(65)
Total	153	55.7	(36)	50	(33)

fense—quite close to the actual figure of 32.7% (50). On the other hand, if there had been a tendency to specialize in violent offending, the number of violent offenders would have been significantly fewer than expected, and each one would have committed more violent offenses (on average) than expected. However, a goodness-of-fit test showed that the actual numbers in Table 1.3 were not significantly different from the expected numbers (chi-squared = 1.83 with 5 *df,* N.S.). Therefore, it can be concluded that there was no detectable tendency for offenders to specialize in violent or nonviolent offending.

CHARACTERISTICS OF VIOLENT AND FREQUENT OFFENDERS

It is also possible to contrast the ideas of generality and specificity by comparing the violent offenders with nonviolent offenders who committed crimes equally frequently. The 50 violent offenders averaged 7.0 crimes each. The 38 nonviolent offenders who each committed at least three crimes committed offenses almost equally frequently on average (248 offenses, or 6.5 each). Assuming generality in offending, the frequent nonviolent offenders should be similar to the violent offenders in antisocial tendency, and hence similar in childhood, adolescent, and adult variables reflecting antisocial tendency. Assuming specificity in offending, the frequent nonviolent offenders should differ from the violent offenders. Both groups, of course, would always differ from the 65 occasional nonviolent offenders (who committed a total of 87 offenses, or 1.3 each) and the 258 unconvicted males.

Table 1.4 shows the percentage of each of the four categories of males (nonoffenders, nonviolent occasional offenders, nonviolent frequent of-

TABLE 1.4
Violent Offending Versus Childhood Factors

Variable at Age	*(%)*	*% of 258 NC*	*% of 65 NV, OC*	*% of 38 NV, FC*	*% of 50 VC*
Low family income 8	(23)	17	18	37**	44***
Poor housing 8–10	(37)	28	57***	50*	44*
Low social class 8–10	(19)	17	15	24	34**
Poor paternal job record 8–10	(13)	9	10	27**	26**
Large family size 10	(24)	16	28	45***	44***
Convicted parent 10	(25)	17	35**	39**	46***
Delinquent sibling 10	(11)	7	8	26***	24***
Behavior problem sibling 10	(38)	31	40	56**	57**
Poor parental behavior 8	(24)	20	19	44**	40**
Harsh parental att/disc. 8	(30)	26	18	50**	51***
Parental disagreement 8	(31)	24	33	55***	50***
Authoritarian parents 10	(24)	20	26	22	47**
Poor parental supervision 8	(19)	14	25	26	38***
Separated from parents 10	(22)	16	29*	32*	38***
Low parental int. in educ. 8	(17)	13	11	26	37***
Low nonverbal IQ 8–10	(25)	19	32*	37*	40**
Low verbal IQ 8–10	(25)	21	26	29	45***
High psychomotor impulsivity 8–10	(25)	20	32	37*	34*
Lacks concentration 8–10	(20)	16	19	34*	32*
High daring 8–10	(30)	20	40**	45**	52***
Doesn't care 8–10	(22)	14	28*	49***	40***
High laziness 8–10	(17)	12	16	39***	26*
High aggressiveness 8–10	(23)	16	30*	39***	38***
High troublesomeness 8–10	(22)	14	28*	47***	42***
High dishonesty 10	(25)	19	33*	32	42**
Vulnerable 8–10	(15)	7	17*	42***	38***
Predicted 8–10	(14)	6	17*	34***	32***

Notes:
*$p < .05$
**$p < .01$
***$p < .001$
(Significantly different from NC)
NC = Nonconvicted
NV = Nonviolent
OC = Occasional convicted
FC = Frequent convicted
VC = Violent convicted
att/disc. = attitude and discipline
int. in educ. = interest in education

fenders, and violent offenders) who possessed each of a number of childhood features. (For more details about all the variables listed in Tables 1.4–1.7, see the references to the study listed previously.) As an example, 93 of the 411 males (22.6%) came from low-income families at age 8, and this percentage (to the nearest whole number, for ease of presentation) is shown in the left-hand column of the table. Of the 258 nonoffenders, 17.4% came from low-income families, in comparison with 18.5% of 65 nonviolent occasional offenders, 36.8% of 38 nonviolent frequent offenders, and 44.0% of 50 violent offenders. Low income was significantly more common among the nonviolent frequent offenders (chi-squared = 6.64, $p < .01$) and among the violent offenders (chi-squared = 15.83, $p < .001$) than among the nonoffenders, and these significance levels are indicated by asterisks. Low income was not significantly more common among the nonviolent occasional offenders than among the nonoffenders.

Table 1.4 shows that *every one* of these childhood features measured at age 8–10 was more common among the violent offenders, who tended to come from poor housing, from lower-class families, from large-sized families, and to have fathers with erratic job records including periods of unemployment. They also tended to have convicted parents, delinquent older siblings, and siblings with behavior problems. Their parents had cruel attitudes, used harsh discipline, and tended to be in conflict with each other. Hence, their parents had poor parental child-rearing behavior, which was a combination of harsh parental attitude and discipline and parental disagreement. Their parents also expressed authoritarian child-rearing attitudes on a questionnaire, supervised them poorly, and had a low interest in their education, and they tended to have been separated from their parents for reasons other than death or hospitalization.

The violent offenders had significantly lower verbal and nonverbal intelligence than the nonoffenders. They also showed high impulsivity on psychomotor tests, were nominated by their teachers as lacking in concentration or as restless, and were said to be daring (in taking many risks) by peers and parents. Their teachers also said that they did not care about being a credit to their parents, that they were lazy in class, and that they were difficult to discipline (the measure of aggressiveness at age 8–10). They were also highly troublesome, according to peers and teachers, and highly dishonest, according to peers. They were also classified as "vulnerable" on one combined prediction scale including low family income, large family size, parental criminality, poor parental child-rearing behavior, and low intelligence, and predicted by another scale including indices of bad behavior and a deprived background (see Farrington,

1989b; Farrington, Gallagher, Morley, St Ledger, & West, 1988). However, the violent offenders were not significantly likely to be nervous or unpopular with their peers (not shown in Table 1.4).

Although the violent offenders were significantly deviant in many respects in childhood, so were the nonviolent frequent offenders, who also differed significantly from the nonoffenders on most of these variables. The biggest difference between the violent offenders and the nonviolent frequent offenders was in parental authoritarianism, with the violent offenders having more authoritarian parents. The nonviolent occasional offenders were less deviant. They differed significantly from the nonoffenders only in having poor housing, convicted parents, separations, low nonverbal intelligence, daring, an uncaring attitude, high aggressiveness, troublesomeness, and dishonesty, and in their scores on both prediction scales.

Table 1.5 shows the characteristics of the four groups of boys in adolescence (age 11–16). Once again, the violent offenders differed significantly from the nonoffenders in many respects. They were still living in large-sized families at age 14, and their parents were still in conflict with each other. However, they did not tend to come from low-income or lower-class families at age 14, to have parents with cruel, passive, or neglecting attitudes, or to be living in poor housing. Their fathers tended not to join in their leisure activities at age 12. They still had low nonverbal intelligence at age 14 (but not low verbal intelligence), and they were low on junior school attainment measures at age 11 and placed in low streams in their secondary schools at the same age. They tended to leave school at the earliest possible age (15) and to truant, but they did not tend to go to schools with high delinquency rates.

The violent offenders tended to smoke regularly before age 14, and to have had sexual intercourse for the first time under age 15. They had high self-reported delinquency and self-reported violence at age 14, and were significantly high on the aggressiveness measure at age 12–14. They tended to lack concentration and to be restless and daring at age 12–14, and they expressed hostile attitudes to the police at ages 14 and 16. They tended to be unemployed at age 16, but they were not particularly anxious (according to teachers) or nervous (according to parents).

As before, the nonviolent frequent offenders showed many of the same characteristics as the violent offenders. The biggest difference between them was that the nonviolent frequent offenders were significantly more likely to have parents with cruel, passive, or neglecting attitudes at age 14 (chi-squared = 4.61, $p < .05$). Again as before, the nonviolent occasional offenders were significantly deviant in only a few respects, notably in early school leaving, in attending a high delinquency

TABLE 1.5
Violent Offending Versus Adolescent Factors

Variable at Age	*(%)*	*% of 258 NC*	*% of 65 NV, OC*	*% of 38 NV, FC*	*% of 50 VC*
Low family income 14	(23)	22	18	30	26
Poor housing 14	(20)	17	25	19	29
Low social class 14	(32)	30	37	34	35
Large family size 14	(21)	15	24	41***	36***
Cruel parental attitude 14	(23)	22	10	53***	27
Parental disharmony 14	(18)	13	15	36**	43***
Father doesn't join in 12	(28)	24	20	40	52**
Low nonverbal IQ 14	(29)	23	31	46**	44**
Low verbal IQ 14	(23)	18	25	46***	30
Low junior attainment 11	(23)	16	26	51***	38***
Low streaming 11	(29)	24	29	45*	44**
Left school before 16	(61)	52	68*	84***	80***
High truancy 12–14	(18)	9	22*	39***	40***
High delinquency school 11	(21)	15	30*	42***	24
Regular smoking before 14	(17)	21	27	44**	41**
First sex before 15	(12)	5	11	36***	31***
High SR delinquency 14	(23)	14	27*	43***	52***
High SR violence 14	(26)	17	36**	35*	52***
High aggressiveness 12–14	(33)	22	43**	47**	60***
Lacks concentration 12–14	(14)	10	14	24*	30***
High restlessness 12–14	(21)	14	28*	29*	42***
High daring 12–14	(13)	8	17	18	28***
Hostile to police 14	(27)	20	25	35	54***
Hostile to police 16	(23)	14	22	49***	53***
High anxiety 12–14	(9)	7	9	21*	12
High nervousness 14	(28)	26	28	42	31
Unemployed 16	(22)	17	19	41**	36**

Notes:
*$p < .05$
**$p < .01$
***$p < .001$
(Significantly different from NC)
NC = Nonconvicted
NV = Nonviolent
OC = Occasional convicted
FC = Frequent convicted
VC = Violent convicted
SR = Self-Report

school, and in their high truancy, delinquency, violence, aggressiveness, and restlessness.

Table 1.6 shows the characteristics of the four categories of males at age 18, leading to similar conclusions. The violent offenders differed significantly from the nonoffenders in every respect except one; they did not have significantly low pulse rates (see e.g., Farrington, 1987b). The violent offenders had unstable job records, tended to be unemployed,

TABLE 1.6
Violent Offending Versus Teenage Factors

Variable at Age	*(%)*	*% of 258 NC*	*% of 65 NV, OC*	*% of 38 NV, FC*	*% of 50 VC*
Unemployed 18	(11)	6	19**	26***	18*
6+ jobs by 18	(20)	10	29***	50***	37***
Unstable job record 18	(24)	14	26*	56***	45***
Sacked by 18	(29)	20	32	50***	55***
Unskilled manual job 18	(16)	7	19*	31***	43***
Exams not taken by 18	(51)	39	60**	81***	76***
Poor reln. with parents 18	(22)	17	18	33*	45***
Tattooed 18	(9)	5	10	17*	24***
Low pulse rate 18	(26)	24	24	33	31
Hangs around 18	(16)	10	15	44***	27**
Group violence 18	(17)	10	23**	36***	31***
Anti-establishment 18	(25)	19	23	42**	45***
Pro-aggressive 18	(26)	22	29	31	37*
High sexual activity 18	(42)	32	55**	58**	69***
Heavy gambling 18	(22)	16	23	36**	45***
Heavy smoking 18	(27)	21	27	44**	41**
Heavy drinking 18	(20)	17	19	31	31*
Fights after drinking 18	(32)	24	45**	53***	43**
Drunk driver 18	(22)	15	29*	36**	37***
Marijuana user 18	(29)	22	26	50***	49***
Habitual drug user 18	(19)	14	16	31*	37***
High aggressiveness 16–18	(30)	18	38**	55***	56***
High SR delinquency 18	(25)	12	39***	56***	51***
High antisocial tendency 18	(28)	13	34***	67***	69***

Notes:
*$p < .05$
**$p < .01$
***$p < .001$
(Significantly different from NC)
NC = Nonconvicted
NV = Nonviolent
OC = Occasional convicted
FC = Frequent convicted
VC = Violent convicted
SR = Self-Report
reln. = relation

had already had several jobs and had been dismissed, and had unskilled manual jobs. In addition (not shown in Table 1.6), they had lower-class jobs according to the Registrar-General's scale of occupational prestige and had rarely spent as long as one year in any job, although they did not tend to have low take-home pay. They had rarely taken any examinations, had a poor relationship with their parents, and tended to be tattooed. They spent time hanging around on the streets, tended to get involved in group violence or vandalism, and expressed anti-establishment and pro-aggressive attitudes on a questionnaire.

The violent offenders were high on a combined scale of sexual activity that reflected a high frequency of intercourse, with a variety of different girls, starting at an early age. They tended to be heavy smokers and drinkers and were involved in fights after drinking. They tended to be drunk drivers and drug users and were high on measures of delinquency and aggressiveness. They were also significantly high on a combined measure of antisocial tendency.

Once again, the nonviolent frequent offenders were similar to the violent offenders in many respects. For example, about two thirds of both groups were high on the combined scale of antisocial tendency. Again, the nonviolent occasional offenders were less deviant, as shown by the fact that only one third of them were high on antisocial tendency.

Table 1.7 shows the characteristics of the four categories of males in adulthood at age 32. Again, the violent offenders differed significantly from the nonoffenders in most respects. The violent offenders tended to be living in London, to be living in poor home conditions, to have high residential mobility, and not to be homeowners. They were not particularly likely to be without a wife or cohabitee, nor to be divorced or separated; but they were in conflict with their wife or cohabitee, had struck her, and tended to have a child living elsewhere. They were not currently employed and had experienced long periods of unemployment, but they did not have low take-home pay or lower-class jobs. They went out frequently in the evenings and tended to be heavy smokers, heavy drinkers, drunk drivers, drug takers, and involved in fights. They tended to commit offenses, including theft from work but not tax evasion, but they were not high on psychiatric disorder, according to the General Health Questionnaire.

Again, the nonviolent frequent offenders were similar to the violent offenders in many respects. The biggest difference between them was that the nonviolent frequent offenders were significantly less likely to be involved in fights (chi-squared = 3.86, $p < .05$). The nonviolent occasional offenders were less deviant. They differed from the nonoffenders especially in heavy drinking, drunk driving, and fighting.

TABLE 1.7
Violent Offending Versus Adult Factors

Variable at Age 32	*(%)*	*% of 258 NC*	*% of 65 NV, OC*	*% of 38 NV, FC*	*% of 50 VC*
Not home owner	(52)	44	51	77***	73***
Living in London	(52)	45	63*	63	64*
Poor home conditions	(28)	24	27	36	43*
High residential mobility	(13)	10	14	20	24*
No wife or cohabitee	(24)	22	20	40*	22
Divorced or separated	(20)	14	27*	34**	27
Doesn't get on with W/C	(8)	3	9	24***	23***
Has struck W/C	(15)	10	15	29*	31**
Child elsewhere	(22)	12	21	50***	41***
Not now employed	(12)	8	7	31***	27***
Unemployed 10m+	(17)	10	17	43***	35***
4+ evenings out pw.	(17)	13	22	17	30*
Heavy smoker	(27)	19	36*	49***	40**
Drunk driver	(53)	44	73***	48	69**
Heavy drinker	(20)	10	31***	43***	39***
Taken marijuana	(18)	11	20	29**	48***
Taken other drug	(20)	5	8	23***	27***
Involved in fights	(37)	27	46**	49*	73***
Self-report offender	(22)	14	27*	40***	49***

Notes:
*p < .05
**p < .01
***p < .001
(Significantly different from NC)
NC – Nonconvicted
NV = Nonviolent
OC = Occasional convicted
FC = Frequent convicted
VC = Violent convicted
SR = Self-Report
W/C = Wife or Cohabitee

ARE VIOLENT OFFENDERS THE SAME AS FREQUENT OFFENDERS?

Over all 106 variables listed in Tables 1.4–1.7 or in the text, the average percentage of violent offenders possessing each feature was 40.5%, remarkably close to the average percentage of nonviolent frequent offenders (39.4%). Not surprisingly, these two percentages were not significantly different according to a paired t-test ($t = 1.17$). The average percentage of nonoffenders possessing each feature was 18.0%, and of nonviolent occasional offenders was 26.6%. All other group comparisons showed highly significant differences over these 106 variables (e.g., violent offenders vs. nonoffenders, $t = 21.45$, $p < .001$).

Although the average percentage of violent offenders possessing each feature was almost identical to the average percentage of nonviolent frequent offenders, it is possible that the two groups had a different pattern of relationships to the 106 variables. If so, it might be expected that the difference between the two percentages would have a variation greater than chance. On the null hypothesis, the standard deviation of the difference between a proportion p_1 in a sample N_1 and a proportion p_2 in a sample N_2 is the square root of:

$$\frac{p_1(1 - p_1)}{N_1} + \frac{p_2(1 - p_2)}{N_2}$$

With $p_1 = .405$, $N_1 = 46.8$ (average sample size for violent offenders), $p_2 = .394$, and $N_2 = 35.1$, this standard deviation came to .109.

If the null hypothesis (of no difference between violent offenders and nonviolent frequent offenders) is correct, about two thirds (68.6%) of differences between the two percentages should be of 11% or less, within one standard deviation. In fact, 81 out of 106 differences (76.4%) were within this range. Similarly, on the null hypothesis only 5% of differences should be greater than 1.96 standard deviations (21%), and only four out of 106 differences were of this figure or greater. The greatest differences between violent offenders and nonviolent frequent offenders were in cruel parental attitude at 14 (nonviolent frequent offenders 26% greater), authoritarian parents at 10 (violent offenders 25% greater), involvement in fights at 32 (violent offenders 24% greater), and drunk driving at 32 (violent offenders 21% greater). However, these differences are only what would be expected on the basis of chance variation. Overall, these tests indicate that *violent offenders and nonviolent frequent offenders are virtually identical in childhood, adolescent, and adult features.*

CONCLUSIONS

This study is, of course, limited in that it is based on about 400 urban working-class males from one place (London) born in one time period (mostly 1953). However, as the introduction shows, many of the results have been replicated with other samples in other countries. The violence committed by these males did not include the most extreme forms, such as homicide. The strengths of the study include its prospective longitudinal design, its low attrition rate over a long time period, and the fact that many different types of variables have been measured from several different sources.

This research demonstrates that there is significant continuity in aggression and violence from childhood to adulthood, spanning a time period of nearly a quarter century. It is also clear that boys who were aggressive in childhood or adolescence tended to be more deviant in adulthood: living in worse home circumstances, more in conflict with and violent towards their wife or cohabitee, more unemployed, heavier smokers and drinkers, more drunk drivers and drug takers, and committing more offenses (including violence). This continuity, however, is probably not specific to aggression and violence but is part of the general continuity in antisocial and deviant behavior from childhood to adulthood. This is why aggressive children have deviant lifestyles 20 years later as adults, and why aggression is transmitted from one generation to the next (Hucsmann et al., 1984). Violent offenders are essentially the most extreme offenders in frequency and seriousness.

It follows that *the causes of aggression and violence must be essentially the same as the causes of persistent and extreme antisocial, delinquent, and criminal behavior.* A great deal is known about these causes, which certainly include economic deprivation, family criminality, poor parental child-rearing behavior, and school failure (e.g., Farrington, 1986b, 1987a). For example, Table 1.4 shows that violent and nonviolent frequent offenders tended to be drawn from low-income, large-sized families in poor housing; that they tended to have convicted parents and delinquent siblings; that they were exposed to harsh parental discipline, parental disharmony, and separations from parents; and that they had low intelligence, high impulsivity, poor concentration, and high daring (the hyperactivity–impulsivity–attention deficit triad discussed at length by Farrington, Loeber, and Van Kammen, in press).

In order to prevent criminal violence and large numbers of other kinds of crimes, it is desirable to target these causal factors and early manifestations of antisocial tendency, such as child troublesomeness and aggression. Early social prevention programs, such as those reviewed by Farrington (1986a) and Burchard and Burchard (1987), may be more effective in reducing antisocial and violent behavior than later treatment or penal incarceration.

REFERENCES

Bachman, J. G., O'Malley, P. M., & Johnston, J. (1978). *Youth in transition, vol.6: Adolescence to adulthood.* Ann Arbor, MI: University of Michigan Institute for Social Research.

Burchard, J. D., & Burchard, S. N. (Eds.). (1987). *Prevention of delinquent behavior.* Beverly Hills, CA: Sage.

Ensminger, M. E., Kellam, S. G., & Rubin, B. R. (1983). School and family origins of delinquency: Comparisons by sex. In K. T. Van Dusen, & S. A. Mednick (Eds.), *Prospective studies of crime and delinquency* (pp.73–97). Boston: Kluwer-Nijhoff.

Eron, L. D., & Huesmann, L. R. (1984). The control of aggressive behavior by changes in attitudes, values, and the conditions of learning. In R. J. Blanchard & D. C. Blanchard (Eds.), *Advances in the study of aggression, vol.1* (pp.139–171). Orlando, FL: Academic Press.

Eron, L. D., Huesmann, L. R., Dubow, E., Romanoff, R., & Yarmel, P. W. (1987). Aggression and its correlates over 22 years. In D. H. Crowell, I. M. Evans, & C. R. O'Donnell (Eds.), *Childhood aggression and violence* (pp.249–262). New York: Plenum.

Farrington, D. P. (1978). The family backgrounds of aggressive youths. In L. Hersov, M. Berger, & D. Shaffer (Eds.), *Aggression and antisocial behavior in childhood and adolescence* (pp.73–93). Oxford: Pergamon.

Farrington, D. P. (1982). Longitudinal analyses of criminal violence. In M. E. Wolfgang, & N. A. Weiner (Eds.), *Criminal violence* (pp.171–200). Beverly Hills, CA: Sage.

Farrington, D. P. (1986a). Implications of longitudinal studies for social prevention. *Justice Report, 3(2),* 6–10.

Farrington, D. P. (1986b). Stepping stones to adult criminal careers. In D. Olweus, J. Block, & M. R. Yarrow (Eds.), *Development of antisocial and prosocial behavior* (pp.359–384). New York: Academic Press.

Farrington, D. P. (1987a). Early precursors of frequent offending. In J. Q. Wilson, & G. C. Loury (Eds.), *From children to citizens, vol.3: Families, schools, and delinquency prevention* (pp.27–50). New York: Springer-Verlag.

Farrington, D. P. (1987b). Implications of biological findings for criminological research. In S. A. Mednick, T. E. Moffitt, & S. A. Stack (Eds.), *The causes of crime* (pp.42–64). Cambridge: Cambridge University Press.

Farrington, D. P. (1989a). Later adult life outcomes of offenders and non-offenders. In M. Brambring, F. Losel, & H. Skowronek (Eds.), *Children at risk: Assessment and longitudinal research* (pp. 220–244) Berlin: De Gruyter.

Farrington, D. P. (1989b). Long-term prediction of offending and other life outcomes. In H. Wegener, F. Losel, & J. Haisch (Eds.), *Criminal behavior and the justice system: Psychological perspectives* (pp.26–39). New York: Springer-Verlag.

Farrington, D. P., Gallagher, B., Morley, L., St Ledger, R. J., & West, D. J. (1988). A 24-year follow-up of men from vulnerable backgrounds. In R. L. Jenkins & W. K. Brown (Eds.), *The abandonment of delinquent behavior: Promoting the turnaround* (pp.155–173). New York: Praeger.

Farrington, D. P., Loeber, R., & Van Kammen, W. B. (in press). Long-term criminal outcomes of hyperactivity–impulsivity–attention deficit and conduct problems in childhood. In L. N. Robins, & M. Rutter (Eds.), *Straight and devious pathways from childhood to adulthood.* Cambridge, England: Cambridge University Press.

Farrington, D. P., Snyder, H. N., & Finnegan, T. A. (1988). Specialization in juvenile court careers. *Criminology, 26,* 461–487.

Farrington, D. P., & West, D. J. (1971). A comparison between early delinquents and young aggressives. *British Journal of Criminology, 11,* 341–358.

Farrington, D. P., & West, D. J. (1981). The Cambridge study in delinquent development. In S. A. Mednick, & A. E. Baert (Eds.), *Prospective longitudinal research* (pp.137–145). Oxford: Oxford University Press.

Feldhusen, J. F., Aversano, F. M., & Thurston, J. R. (1976). Prediction of youth contacts with law enforcement agencies. *Criminal Justice and Behavior, 3,* 235–253.

Feldhusen, J. F., Thurston, J. R., & Benning, J. J. (1973). A longitudinal study of delinquency and other aspects of children's behavior. *International Journal of Criminology and Penology, 1,* 341–351.

Guttridge, P., Gabrielli, W. F., Mednick, S. A., & Van Dusen, K. T. (1983). Criminal violence in a birth cohort. In K. T. Van Dusen, & S. A. Mednick (Eds.), *Prospective studies of crime and delinquency* (pp.211–224). Boston: Kluwer-Nijhoff.

Hamparian, D. M., Davis, J. M., Jacobson, J. M., & McGraw, R. E. (1985). *The young criminal years of the violent few.* Washington, DC: National Institute for Juvenile Justice and Delinquency Prevention.

Hamparian, D. M., Schuster, R., Dinitz, S., & Conrad, J. P. (1978). *The violent few.* Lexington, MA: Heath.

Hogh, E., & Wolf, P. (1983). Violent crimes in a birth cohort: Copenhagen 1953–1977. In K. T. Van Dusen, & S. A. Mednick (Eds.), *Prospective studies of crime and delinquency* (pp.249–267). Boston: Kluwer-Nijhoff.

Huesmann, L. R., Eron, L. D., Lefkowitz, M. M. & Walder, L. O. (1984). Stability of aggression over time and generations. *Development Psychology, 20,* 1120–1134.

Huesmann, L. R., Eron, L. D., & Yarmel, P. W. (1987). Intellectual functioning and aggression. *Journal of Personality and Social Psychology, 52,* 232–240.

Kellam, S. G., Brown, C. H., Rubin, B. R. & Ensminger, M. E. (1983). Paths leading to teenage psychiatric symptoms and substance use: Developmental epidemiological studies in Woodlawn. In S. B. Guze, F. J. Earls, & J. E. Barratt (Eds.), *Childhood psychopathology and development* (pp.17–51). New York: Raven Press.

Loeber, R. (1982). The stability of antisocial child behavior: A review. *Child Development, 53,* 1431–1446.

Loeber, R. (1988). Natural histories of conduct problems, delinquency, and associated substance use: Evidence for developmental progressions. In B. B. Lahey, & A. E. Kazdin (Eds.), *Advances in clinical child psychology* (Vol. 11, pp.73–124). New York: Plenum.

Loeber, R., & Dishion, T. (1983). Early predictors of male delinquency: A review. *Psychological Bulletin, 94,* 68–99.

Loeber, R., & Schmaling, K. B. (1985a). Empirical evidence for overt and covert patterns of antisocial conduct problems: A meta-analysis. *Journal of Abnormal Child Psychology, 13,* 337–352.

Loeber, R., & Schmaling, K. B. (1985b). The utility of differentiating between mixed and pure forms of antisocial child behavior. *Journal of Abnormal Child Psychology, 13,* 315–336.

Loeber, R., & Stouthamer-Loeber, M. (1987). Prediction. In H. C. Quay (Ed.), *Handbook of juvenile delinquency* (pp.325–382). New York: Wiley.

Magnusson, D. (1988). *Individual development from an interactional perspective.* Hillsdale, NJ: Lawrence Erlbaum Associates.

Magnusson, D., Stattin, H., & Duner, A. (1983). Aggression and criminality in a longitudinal perspective. In K. T. Van Dusen, & S. A. Mednick (Eds.), *Prospective studies of crime and delinquency* (pp.277–301). Boston: Kluwer-Nijhoff.

McCord, J. (1977). A comparative study of two generations of native Americans. In R. F. Meier (Ed.), *Theory in criminology* (pp.83–92). Beverly Hills, CA: Sage.

McCord, J. (1979). Some child-rearing antecedents of criminal behavior in adult men. *Journal of Personality and Social Psychology, 37,* 1477–1486.

McCord, J. (1980). Patterns of deviance. In S. B. Sells, R. Crandall, M. Roff, J. S. Strauss, & W. Pollin (Eds.), *Human functioning in longitudinal perspective* (pp.157–162). Baltimore: Williams and Wilkins.

McCord, J. (1983). A longitudinal study of aggression and antisocial behavior. In K. T. Van Dusen, & S. A. Mednick (Eds.), *Prospective studies in crime and delinquency* (pp.269–275). Boston: Kluwer-Nijhoff.

McCord, J. (1988). Parental behavior in the cycle of aggression. *Psychiatry, 51,* 14–23.

McCord, J., McCord, W., & Howard, A. (1963). Family interaction as antecedent to the direction of male aggressiveness. *Journal of Abnormal and Social Psychology, 66,* 239–242.

Miller, S. J., Dinitz, S., & Conrad, J. P. (1982). *Careers of the violent.* Lexington, MA: Heath.

Moskowitz, D. S., Schwartzman, A. E., & Ledingham, J. E. (1985). Stability and change in aggression and withdrawal in middle childhood and early adolescence. *Journal of Abnormal Psychology, 94,* 30–41.

Olweus, D. (1979). Stability of aggressive reaction patterns in male: A review. *Psychological Bulletin, 86,* 852–875.

Olweus, D. (1980). The consistency issue in personality psychology revisited–with special reference to aggression. *British Journal of Social and Clinical Psychology, 19,* 377–390.

Olweus, D. (1981). Continuity in aggressive and withdrawn, inhibited behavior patterns. *Psychiatry and Social Science, 1,* 141–159.

Olweus, D. (1984a). Development of stable aggressive reaction patterns in males. In R. J. Blanchard, & D. C. Blanchard (Eds.), *Advances in the study of aggression, vol.1* (pp.103–137). Orlando, FL: Academic Press.

Olweus, D. (1984b). Stability in aggressive and withdrawn, inhibited behavior patterns. In R. M. Kaplan, V. J. Konecni, & R. W. Novaco (Eds.), *Aggression in children and youth* (pp.104–137). The Hague: Nijhoff.

Peterson, R. A., Pittman, D. J., & O'Neal, P. (1962). Stabilities in deviance: A study of assaultive and non-assaultive offenders. *Journal of Criminal Law, Criminology, and Police Science, 53,* 44–48.

Piper, E. S. (1985). Violent recidivism and chronicity in the 1958 Philadelphia cohort. *Journal of Quantitative Criminology, 1,* 319–344.

Pulkkinen, L. (1983). Finland: The search for alternatives to aggression. In A. P. Goldstein, & M. H. Segall (Eds.), *Aggression in global perspective* (pp.104–144). New York: Pergamon.

Pulkkinen, L., & Hurme, H. (1984). Aggression as a predictor of weak self-control. In L. Pulkkinen, & P. Lyytinen (Eds.), *Human action and personality* (pp.172–189). Jyvaskyla, Finland: University of Jyvaskyla.

Robins, L. N. (1979). Sturdy childhood predictors of adult outcomes: Replications from longitudinal studies. In J. E. Barrett, R. M. Rose, & G. L. Klerman (Eds.), *Stress and mental disorder* (pp.219–235). New York: Raven Press.

Robins, L. N. (1983). Continuities and discontinuities in psychiatric disorders of children. In D. E. Mechanic (Ed.), *Handbook of health, health care, and the health professions* (pp.195–219). New York: Free Press.

Robins, L. N. (1986). Changes in conduct disorder over time. In D. C. Farran, & J. D. McKinney (Eds.), *Risk in intellectual and psychosocial development* (pp.227–259). New York: Academic Press.

Robins, L. N., & Ratcliff, K. S. (1978). Risk factors in the continuation of childhood antisocial behavior into adulthood. *International Journal of Mental Health, 7,* 96–116.

Robins, L. N., & Ratcliff, K. S. (1980). Childhood conduct disorders and later arrest. In L. N. Robins, P. J. Clayton, & J. K. Wing (Eds.), *The social consequences of psychiatric illness* (pp.248–263). New York: Brunner/Mazel.

Roff, J. D. (1986). Identification of boys at high risk for delinquency. *Psychological Reports, 58,* 615–618.

Roff, J. D., & Wirt, R. D. (1984). Childhood aggression and social adjustment as antecedents of delinquency. *Journal of Abnormal Child Psychology, 12,* 111–126.

Roff, J. D., & Wirt, R. D. (1985). The specificity of childhood problem behavior for adolescent and young adult maladjustment. *Journal of Clinical Psychology, 41,* 564–571.

Stattin, H., & Magnusson, D. (1984). *The role of early aggressive behavior for the frequency, the seriousness, and the types of later criminal offenses.* Stockholm: University of Stockholm.

Stewart, M. A., & de Blois, C. S. (1983). Father–son resemblances in aggression and antisocial behavior. *British Journal of Psychiatry, 142,* 78–84.

West, D. J. (1969). *Present conduct and future delinquency.* London: Heinemann.

West, D. J. (1982). *Delinquency: Its roots, careers, and prospects.* London: Heinemann.

West, D. J., & Farrington, D. P. (1973). *Who becomes delinquent?* London: Heinemann.

West, D. J., & Farrington, D. P. (1977). *The delinquent way of life.* London: Heinemann.

Wikstrom, P-O. H. (1985). *Everyday violence in contemporary Sweden.* Stockholm: Swedish National Council for Crime Prevention.

Wikstrom, P-O. H. (1987). *Patterns of crime in a birth cohort.* Stockholm: University of Stockholm.

2

The Epidemiology of Antisocial Behavior in Childhood and Adolescence

David R. Offord
Michael H. Boyle
Yvonne A. Racine
McMaster University

Children with severe and persistent antisocial behavior comprise an important category of psychiatrically disturbed youth, treated or untreated (Robins, 1974). For example, in the community prevalence survey carried out in the Isle of Wight, (Rutter, Tizard, & Whitmore, 1970), almost three quarters of all the boys and about one third of all the girls who were considered to be psychiatrically disturbed were diagnosed as having conduct disorder. The rate of conduct disorder among 10- and 11-year-olds was 4.2% overall, with frequencies among boys and girls separately of 6.0% and 1.6%, respectively. The heavy burden of suffering attributed to this disorder results not only from the high frequency of the condition, but also because of two other reasons. First, children and adolescents with the disorder have impaired functioning in many areas of their lives, such as school and peer relationships (Offord & Waters, 1983). In addition, there is evidence that the childhood diagnosis portends serious psychosocial disturbances in adulthood for upwards of 40% of these youth (Robins, 1970; Rutter & Giller, 1983). Second, this condition imposes a heavy burden on society in the form of personnel and money committed to diagnostic and treatment efforts. The magnitude of the problem of serious and persistent antisocial behavior merits research efforts aimed at discovering effective prevention and treatment techniques (Offord & Reitsma-Street, 1983). An essential basis for these efforts is sound epidemiological data on the prevalence, distribution, and correlates of this disorder.

Recent reviews of community prevalence surveys of childhood psychiatric disorders, including conduct disorder, are available (Links, 1983;

Offord et al., 1987). The foremost epidemiological study of conduct disorder occurred on the Isle of Wight, a small island off the southwest coast of England (Rutter et al, 1970). The study has two major limitations. First, the population of the island is predominantly semirural with no large urban centers; and second, the data are restricted to 10- and 11-year-olds. These factors have limited the generalizability of the results to other, larger and more varied geographic areas and to a wider age span.

This chapter presents results on the epidemiology of conduct disorder from the Ontario Child Health Study (OCHS), a province-wide prevalence survey of emotional and behavioral problems, and other disordered health states, in children 4–16 years of age (Boyle, et al., 1987; Offord et al., 1987). The data presented in this chapter include information on the psychometric properties (internal consistency and relationship to clinical diagnosis, impairments, and need for treatment) of the measure of conduct disorder, prevalence rates of individual symptoms by age and sex categories, and of conduct disorder by age, sex, and urban–rural status. Also, results are presented on the relative contribution of different sources of data (respondents) to the diagnosis, the overlap of other psychiatric disorders with conduct disorder, and the relationships of selected correlates to conduct disorder in bivariate and multivariate analyses. Finally, information is presented on the utilization of mental health/social services, medical and school services, by children with conduct disorder, and on the major determinants of use of specialized mental health/social services by children with this disorder.

THE ONTARIO CHILD HEALTH STUDY (OCHS)

Setting

The OCHS was carried out in the Province of Ontario, a large and varied geographic area of 412,582 square miles, with a population of over 8.5 million persons, with almost 1.7 million of these being children between the ages of 4 and 16 in 1983.

Sampling

The sampling design and measurement of disorder of the OCHS have been covered in detail elsewhere (Boyle et al., 1987) and are summarized here. The target population included all children born between January 1, 1966 and January 1, 1979, whose usual place of residence was a household dwelling in Ontario. The survey excluded three groups of children representing 3.3% (55,100 of 1,687,200) of the population of children 4–16 years of age: those children living on Indian reserves (13,800); those in collective dwellings such as institutions (4,830); and those living in dwellings constructed after June 1, 1981 (Census Day) (36,500). The sampling unit consisted of all household dwellings listed in the 1981 Census of Canada. The sampling frame (source of subjects) was the 1981 census. The sample selection was done by stratified, clustered, random sampling from the census file of household dwellings (Statistics Canada, 1982).

The major strata for the survey were the four administrative regions of the Ontario Ministry of Community and Social Services (MCSS). Each MCSS region was divided into three strata based on the population as of the 1981 census; large urban areas with a population of more than 25,000; small urban areas varying in population from 3,000 to 25,000; and rural areas with populations less than 3,000. In large urban areas, a one-stage sampling procedure was used, with the sample selected randomly from all large urban areas within each MCSS region. A two-stage sampling procedure was used in small urban and rural areas. In the first stage, areas or clusters were selected; in the second stage, households were selected—both with known probability. Interviewers collected information from the female head of the household (parents), teachers, and youth 12–16. With the exception of school information (obtained by mail), all the data were collected during a home visit. The survey work was carried out by Statistics Canada, which is the federal government agency responsible for producing the census, the labor force survey, and other governmental reports. The survey was carried out during January and February of 1983. The participation rate among eligible households was high (91.1%), and the refusal rate was low (3.9%).

Measures

The survey investigated four childhood psychiatric disorders: conduct disorder, hyperactivity, and emotional disorders (neurosis) in children, 4–16; and somatization in adolescents 12–16 years of age. For measuring each of the four disorders, scales were developed comprised of problem behaviors (items) summed to form a score. DSM-III (American Psychiatric Association, 1980) criteria guided the selection of items for each scale. The item content for the emotional disorder scale was chosen to reflect elements of the DSM-III categories of overanxious disorder, affective disorder, and obsessive compulsive disorder. The Child Behavior Checklist (Achenbach & Edelbrock, 1981) furnished the basic pool of items for the scales. When items from the Child Behavior Checklist were felt not to describe adequately a particular criterion, additional items were generated. The resulting checklist was termed the Survey Diagnostic Instrument (SDI). Similar checklists were used for three sources: parents, teachers, and adolescents, 12–16. Checklist items applicable to a particular disorder were grouped to form a scale. Each item could be scored 0, 1, or 2, indicating responses of "never or not true," "sometimes or somewhat true," and "often or very true," respectively.

Checklist scale scores were converted to binary ratings of disorder based on their ability to discriminate best the presence or absence of a diagnosis made by a child psychiatrist. Separate thresholds were established for each data source or respondent assessment for the two age groups. The completion rate on the teacher form in the older age group was too low for measuring disorder. A 4- to 11-year-old child could have a disorder on the basis of one respondent (i.e., parent or teacher) or both respondents (i.e., parent and teacher). Similarly, a 12- to 16-year-old adolescent could have a disorder on the basis of one respondent (i.e., parent or adolescent) or both respondents (i.e., parent and adolescent). Children within each age group had to score below the thresholds on both respondents to qualify as *not* having a disorder.

In the case of conduct disorder, 15 items were used in the measure for the parent and youth forms and 12 were used for the teacher form (see Table 2.3). Statistic Canada omitted the items "steals things at home" and "steals from places outside the home" from the teacher form; and the rate of missing values for "running away from home" was so high that it also was excluded. For the 15-item scale, the scores could vary between 0 and 30; for the 12-item scale, between 0 and 24. For the 4- to 11-year-old age group, a threshold score of 9 was determined to be best, for both parents and teachers, for discriminating the presence or absence of a diagnosis of conduct disorder made by a child psychiatrist. The corresponding threshold scores for 12- to 16-year-olds for parents and youths were 8 and 9, respectively.

Definition of Variables

Impairments

1. Poor School Performance. Child is rated as currently performing in school either "not too well" or "not well at all." Parent responses are used for children 4 to 16.

2. Isolated Child. Child is rated as having no friends, or if the child has one friend, he or she does things with that child only one day a week or less. Parent responses are used for children 4 to 11; adolescent responses are used for youths 12 to 16.

3. Problems Getting Along. Child is rated as having frequent or constant problems getting along with one or more of family, teachers, and friends. Parent and teacher responses are used for children 4 to 11; parent and youth responses are used for the 12 to 16 age group. A positive response from either of the two respondents for each age group is sufficient to score the variable as present.

Need for Professional Help

This is rated as needing professional help for emotional or behavioral problems. Parent and teacher responses are used for children 4 to 11; parent and youth responses are used for adolescents 12 to 16. A positive response from either of the two respondents for each age group is sufficient to score the variable positively.

Correlates

All the correlate data are based on parental reports.

1. Sociodemographic

- Low income: total family income before taxes in preceding year (1982) was less than $10,000.
- Single parent: only one parenting figure currently in the house.
- Large sibship: four or more siblings, regardless of age, currently living in the home.
- Urban residence: urban areas are those with a population of more than 25,000. Rural area in this definition includes both small urban areas (population 3,000 to 25,000) and rural areas (population less than 3,000).

2. Family–Parental

- Family dysfunction: a score of 27 to 48 (range 12 to 48) on the 12-item General Functioning subscale derived from the McMaster Family Assessment Device (Byles, Byrne, Boyle, & Offord, 1988).
- Domestic violence: one parent hit partner at least once in the past 6 months.
- Parent hospitalized for "nerves": either parent ever hospitalized for nerves.
- Parent arrested: either parent was at some time arrested or charged with an offence other than a traffic violation.
- Parental excessive alcohol consumption: (a) dichotomous variable for bivariate analysis: either parent, on average, has more than

three drinks/day of alcoholic beverages in the past 6 months; (b) interval variable for multivariate analyses: a six-point variable indicating levels of alcohol consumption in the past 6 months. If data are available on more than one adult in the family for this variable, the responses of the adult with the greater consumption of alcohol were used.

3. Child

- Age: 4–11; 12–16.
- Sex: self-explanatory.
- Chronic medical illness: child has one or more illnesses or conditions that are usually chronic in duration (greater than 6 months).

Service Utilization

All the service utilization data are based on parental report.

1. Mental Health/Social Services Utilization (MH/SS). Child (4–16 years of age) was the focal point of a consultation in the preceding 6 months with staff from a mental health service (i.e., a mental health clinic, or private practitioner such as a psychiatrist, psychologist, or social worker), a social service (i.e., the Children's Aid Society or the Family Service Association), a service linked to the judiciary (i.e., the courts or after-care officer), or some other mental health/social/correctional service.

2. Ambulatory Medical Care (AMC). Child (4–16 years of age) was the focal point of a consultation within the last 6 months with staff from a hospital emergency room, a physician's office, or a hospital outpatient department or clinic. Routine pediatric care would be included, but dental care would not.

3. Special Education (SE). Child (6–16 years of age), at some time during his or her school career, had received special education or special teaching, full- or part-time, in a class for the perceptually handicapped, mentally retarded, emotionally or behaviorally disturbed, slow learner, or some other type of remedial education.

Statistical Analyses

To obtain the prevalence estimates of individual symptoms, and of conduct disorder by age and sex categories and urban–rural residence, responses were weighted to reflect the household probability of selection, its size, and the age and sex distribution of children (Boyle et al., 1987). All other analyses are based on actual (unweighted) responses (Offord et al., 1987). Because data on service utilization showed marked clustering within families, only one randomly selected child per family was used in these analyses (Offord et al., 1987). For the remaining analyses, all eligible children were included. The definition of emotional disorder based on the prevalence threshold was used for prevalence estimates; however, for the rest of the analyses, the threshold was raised (correlate threshold) to increase the likelihood that a child identified by the threshold was a case. For the bivariate analyses, x^2 with Yates' correction where appropriate was employed, and for the multivariate analyses, logistic regression was used (Dixon et al., 1983).

RESULTS

The data on the internal consistency of the scales used to measure conduct disorder in the OCHS reveal that for both respondents for each of the two age groups, Cronbach's alpha exceeds 0.70. The average inter-item correlation varies from a low of 0.15 for the parent scale for 4- to 11-year-olds to 0.20 for both the teacher scale for 4- to 11-year-olds and the parent scale for the adolescent age group. Table 2.1 presents data on the strength of agreement between psychiatrists' diagnosis and the checklist ratings, and the test–retest reliability of the checklist ratings over a 6- to 9-month interval. The strength of agreement was assessed using sensitivity, specificity, and *K* statistic (Cohen, 1960). *K* statistic is a valuable measure of agreement because it corrects for chance. As shown in Table 2.1, agreement between psychiatrists' diagnoses and the checklist approximations of conduct disorder are uniformly high for specificity. Estimates for sensitivity and values of the K statistic are in the moderate range.

The test–retest reliability of the checklist ratings of disorder was based on comparisons between the checklist responses collected 2 weeks before

TABLE 2.1
Agreement for Conduct Disorder Between Psychiatrists' Diagnoses and Checklist Assessments by Age; and Test–Retest Reliability of Checklist Assessments Over 6- to 9-Month Interval

		Checklist vs. Psychiatrist			*Test–Retest Reliability of Checklist*	
Age	*(n)*	*Sensitivity*	*Specificity*	*K*	*% Agreement*	*K*
4–11	(10)	0.62	0.99	0.68	93	0.35
12–16	(13)	0.45	0.96	0.39	94	0.54

the clinical assessments and checklist responses collected during the original survey (OCHS), 6 to 9 months earlier. Overall agreement exceeds 90% for both age groups.

Table 2.2 provides data on the pattern of impairments and need for professional help associated with the diagnosis of conduct disorder. Children, 4 to 11, with conduct disorder, compared to their peers without conduct disorder, are almost four times more likely to have poor school performance, over twice as likely to be rated as an isolated child, have problems getting along at almost ten times the rate, and have one or more impairments at five times the rate. In the older age group, adolescents with conduct disorder compared to their peers have almost four times the rate of poor school performance, over four times the rate of problems getting along, and an increase in excess of threefold for one or more impairments. Conduct-disordered and non-conduct-disordered youths, 12–16, did not differ in the frequency of their self-reports of being an isolated child. Lastly, conduct-disordered children of both age groups are significantly more likely to be seen as needing professional help compared to their peers. This is especially marked in the younger age group, where there is more than a sevenfold increase in the rate of needing professional help in conduct-disordered children compared to their peers.

Table 2.3 presents data on the prevalence of the 15 symptoms included in the definition of conduct disorder. Data are presented by sex for the two age groups and also by respondent, namely, parent and teacher for children 4–11, and parent and youth for children 12–16. Symptoms vary greatly in their prevalence, regardless of age, sex, or respondent. "Mean to other," "gets in many fights," "disobeys at school," and "lies or cheats" are examples of items that are commonly (usually

TABLE 2.2
Prevalence (per 100) of Selected Impairments and Need for Professional Help for Children 4 to 16 With and Without Conduct Disorder by Age

	Category[a]					
	4–11			*12–16*		
Variable	*CD*	*NCD*	*Significance*	*CD*	*NCD*	*Significance*
Impairments						
Poor School Performance	14.1	3.7	$p < 0.001$	22.8	5.8	$p < 0.00001$
Isolated Child	10.9	4.0	$p < 0.05$	3.5	2.4	p = n.s.
Problems getting along	65.7	6.7	$p < 0.00001$	53.8	12.3	$p < 0.00001$
One or more impairments	68.8	13.1	$p < 0.00001$	65.0	17.8	$p < 0.00001$
Need for Professional Help	62.5	8.5	$p < 0.00001$	74.2	43.8	$p < 0.01$

[a]CD = conduct disorder; NCD = no conduct disorder

TABLE 2.3
Prevalence (per 100)[a] of Symptoms of Conduct Disorder by Age/Sex Categories and by Respondent

	Age							
	4–11				*12–16*			
	Boys		*Girls*		*Boys*		*Girls*	
Symptoms	P[b]	T[b]	P[b]	T[b]	P[b]	Y[b]	P[b]	Y[b]
Aggressive Behavior								
Cruel to animals	2.2	1.6	0.5	0.1	2.7	10.2	1.2	9.1
Mean to others	15.0	21.8	10.7	9.6	15.0	44.2	9.2	38.5
Physically attacks people	7.2	18.1	4.5	4.4	6.9	12.3	2.9	7.1
Gets in many fights	22.4	30.9	8.5	9.8	19.7	29.5	9.6	21.0
Destroys own things	16.7	10.7	9.1	2.1	9.2	20.9	2.9	11.3
Destroys things belonging to others	13.2	10.6	6.3	4.4	9.8	14.3	3.8	7.6
Vandalism	0.3	2.9	0.1	0.6	1.8	9.2	0.2	4.6
Sets fires	1.5	0.8	0.2	0.1	1.6	6.4	0.1	1.9
Violation of Social Norms								
Disobeys at school	31.3	45.1	14.0	23.3	30.8	44.0	19.6	34.3
Cuts classes or skips school	0.6	2.1	0.3	1.8	7.6	14.9	6.2	18.4
Threatens to hurt people	4.9	13.1	4.1	4.0	8.1	28.8	5.1	18.1
Lies or cheats	28.0	23.4	21.8	12.1	26.0	34.8	21.2	33.6
Steals things at home	2.5	[c]	2.8	[c]	5.8	10.0	3.8	9.5
Steals from places outside the home	2.1	[c]	1.2	[c]	3.0	8.9	3.1	4.3
Runs away from home	0.8	[c]	1.1	[c]	1.9	3.3	2.4	4.3

[a]Prevalence estimates are a sum of the percentages of checklist responses "1" (sometimes or somewhat true) and "2" (often or very true).
[b]P = parent; T = teacher; Y = youth.
[c]These items were omitted from the teacher form.

between a tenth or a third of the time) checked as present; whereas "vandalism," "sets fires," and "runs away from home" all have low frequencies, especially based on parent and teacher reports. With few exceptions, and regardless of age or respondent, boys have a higher prevalence of these symptoms than girls. This is especially marked in parental reports of aggressive behavior in 4- to 11-year-olds. "Cuts classes or skips school" by youth report is the clearest example of a symptom where the frequency is higher in girls than boys (18.4% vs. 14.9%). In the age group 4–11, teachers report higher frequencies of the symptoms compared to parents in 8 of 13 instances among boys but in only 3 of 13 among girls. In general, the symptom frequencies, as reported by parents, do not alter appreciably from latency to adolescence except in the case of truancy, which rises dramatically in the 12–16-year age group. Lastly, it should be noted that, without exception, youth report higher symptom frequencies than parents. Moreover, in some instances the differences are marked. For example, "mean to others" and "threatens to hurt people" are checked approximately three times more often by youth than by parents.

Table 2.4 presents prevalence rates for conduct disorder by age and sex categories and by urban–rural residence. The rates vary from a high of 7.2% in urban boys, 4–11, to a low of 0.6% in rural girls, 4–11. The overall prevalence rate for children, 4–16, is 5.5% (not shown), with rates for boys and girls in that same age span of 8.1% and 2.8%, respectively (not shown). The overall urban and rural rates are 5.6% and 5.2%, respectively (not shown). In the younger age group, the rate is slightly higher in the urban compared to the rural areas, but this is reversed in the older age group. The diagnosis of conduct disorder is more common among boys regardless of their age or residency category. The boy:girl prevalence ratio is especially marked in 4- to 11-year-olds in rural areas, where it is 8.5 : 1. The increased boy:girl ratio in 4- to 11-year-olds, compared to the 12–16 year age group, is accounted for primarily by the relative excess of conduct-disordered boys 4–11 from the rural areas. It should be noted however, that a multivariate analysis (log linear analysis) reported in a previous paper (Offord et al., 1987) found that although age and sex were significantly related to the prevalence of conduct disorder, urban–rural residence was not. In addition, there was not a significant interaction between urban–rural residence and conduct disorder, nor was there a significant three-way interaction involving age, sex, and urban–rural residence.

Two important findings emerge when attention is focused on the patterns of individual respondents who identify children as having conduct disorder. First, there is a paucity of cases where the threshold scores are exceeded by more than one respondent. For instance, among boys in the 4- to 11-year-old age group, only 3 of 46 cases of conduct disorder

TABLE 2.4
Prevalence (per 100) of Conduct Disorder by Age/Sex Categories and by Urban–Rural Status

Age/Sex Category		*(n)*	*Urban*	*Rural*	*Overall*
4–11	Boys	(721)	7.2	5.1	6.5
	Girls	(721)	2.3	0.6	1.8
12–16	Boys	(608)	9.9	11.6	10.4
	Girls	(624)	3.6	5.2	4.1

were identified by both the parent and the teacher. Among girls in that age group, there were no pervasive cases (i.e., cases identified by both the parent and the teacher). In the older age group, over 80% of the cases of conduct disorder among the boys and almost 90% of the cases among the girls were identified by only one respondent. The second important point is that the pattern of respondents identifying conduct disorder varies by age. For example, in the younger age group, teachers identified over three quarters of the cases for both boys and girls. In the older age group, the boys themselves, compared to parents, identified 2.5 times more cases of conduct disorder. Older girls identified 1.7 times more cases than parents.

Co-morbidity, that is, the overlap of conduct disorder with other diagnoses measured in the OCHS, was found to be common. The largest overlap occurred between conduct disorder and hyperactivity in the 4- to 11-year-old age group. Here, almost 60% of children with a diagnoses of conduct disorder also received a diagnoses of hyperactivity. In the older age group, approximately one third of the children with conduct disorder were also seen as hyperactive. The overlap of conduct disorder with emotional disorder varied from a low of approximately one in six in adolescent boys to almost one in two in adolescent girls. Lastly, one in five of adolescent boys and over one in three of adolescent girls with a diagnosis of conduct disorder also had a diagnosis of somatization disorder.

Co-morbidity, in the case of conduct disorder, is so marked that, except for boys aged 12–16, the majority of cases of conduct disorder have one or more additional diagnoses. The overlap with one additional diagnosis is more marked in 4- to 11-year-olds, where approximately half the cases have one additional diagnosis. The corresponding proportion in the older age group is less than one quarter. The overlap with two other diagnoses is most obvious in conduct-disordered teenage girls, where over one third of them have two additional diagnoses.

Table 2.5 presents the bivariate relationships between selected correlates in the sociodemographic, family-parental, and child domains and conduct disorder. The strength of association in these relationships is indicated by the relative odds (R.O.). Among the sociodemographic correlates, low income has the strongest relationship with conduct disorder (R.O. = 4.0), followed by single parent and large sibship. Urban residence is not significantly related to conduct disorder. In the family-parental area, all the variables but parental excessive alcohol consumption are strongly (R.O. > 2.0) and significantly related to conduct disorder. Lastly, all three child variables are significantly related to the disorder, and the relative odds of two of them (male sex and chronic medical illness) exceed 2.0.

TABLE 2.5
Bivariate Relationships Between Selected Correlates and Conduct Disorder for Children 4 to 16

Correlate	*(n)*[a]	*Relative Odds*	*Significance*
Sociodemographic			
Low income	(187)	4.0	$p < .00001$
Single parent	(273)	2.2	$p < .001$
Large sibship	(465)	1.6	$p < .05$
Urban residence	(1668)	1.0	p = n.s.
Family-Parental			
Family dysfunction	(286)	2.9	$p < .00001$
Domestic violence	(54)	3.0	$p < .01$
Parent hospitalized for "nerves"	(152)	3.0	$p < .00001$
Parent arrested	(133)	2.5	$p < .002$
Parental excessive alcohol consumption	(105)	0.7	p = n.s.
Child			
Age 12–16	(1242)	1.7	$p < .01$
Male sex	(1346)	2.6	$p < .00001$
Chronic medical illness	(449)	2.1	$p < .001$

[a]Total $n = 2708$; it varies slightly for different variables because of missing data.

Although it is not shown in Table 2.5, comparisons of ordinal position were carried out for conduct-disordered and non-conduct-disordered children. Both groups were divided into four mutually exclusive categories: only child, youngest child, oldest child, middle child. The distribution of the children in two groups in these four categories was significantly different ($X^2 = 11.63$, $df = 3$, $p < 0.01$). Conduct-disordered children, compared to others, were more likely to be the oldest child (40.5% vs. 33.4%).

Table 2.6 presents the results of the logistic regression between the selected correlates included in Table 2.5 and conduct disorder. This analysis permits the determination of the strength of the relationship of each of the correlates and conduct disorder, controlling for the effects of the other variables. All the correlates were forced in, and interactions involving low income with the other variables competed for entry into the model. Only significant interactions ($p < 0.05$) were permitted to enter the model.

The results reveal that five variables have significant independent effects in predicting conduct disorder. The variable with the strongest independent relationship is family dysfunction (R.O. = 3.1), followed by parent hospitalized for "nerves," male sex and chronic medical illness,

TABLE 2.6
Strength of Association in Logistic Regression Between Selected Correlates and Conduct Disorder for Children 4 to 16

Correlate	*Relative Odds*
Main Effects	
Single parent	1.0
Large sibship	1.7*
Urban residence	1.0
Family dysfunction	3.1*
Domestic violence	1.8
Parent hospitalized for "nerves"	2.2*
Parental excessive alcohol consumption	(0.07)[a]
Male sex	1.9*
Chronic medical illness	1.9*
Interactions	
Low income by parent arrested	
(1) < $10,000	0.4
(2) > $10,000	3.2*
Age by low income	
(1) 4–11	3.7*
(2) 12–16	1.0

*$p < 0.05$
[a]Coefficient rather than a relative odds because the variable was not dichotomous but interval.

and large sibship. As would be expected from the bivariate analysis, urban residence and parental excessive alcohol consumption do not have significant independent effects in predicting conduct disorder. Two other variables, single parent and domestic violence, while having significant bivariate relationships with conduct disorder, do not have a significant independent effect in predicting the condition. Two interactions enter the model. The relationship between parent arrested and conduct disorder in significantly different as a function of level of income. The relationship is significantly stronger in families with incomes over $10,000 (R.O. = 3.2) than in those with incomes less than $10,000 (R.O. = 0.4). Indeed, parental arrest in low-income families does not have an independent significant relationship to conduct disorder; the relationship is, however, significant in the higher income families. That is, the relative odds of 3.2 is significantly different from 1.0 ($p < 0.05$). The second interaction involves age and low income. The strength of the relationship between low income and conduct disorder varies significantly as a function of age, being much stronger in the younger age group. Here, low income is significantly related to conduct disorder (R.O. = 3.7), but this is not so in the older age group (R.O. = 1.0).

The analysis in Table 2.7 is similar to that reported in Table 2.6, except that here the three other disorders (hyperactivity, emotional disorder, and somatization) are forced into the model. In all other respects the model to be tested is identical. The purpose of this analysis is to determine which variables are independently related to conduct disorder, controlling for the effects of both the other variables and the other psychiatric disorders. The results show that only three variables, large sibship, family dysfunction, and male sex now have a significant independent relationship to conduct disorder. Two variables (parent hospitalized for "nerves" and chronic medical illness in the child) no longer have independent significant relationships with conduct disorder. Their significant relationships with conduct disorder in the first model were accounted for in large part by the confounding effects of the other three disorders. These disorders were significantly related both to the variables

TABLE 2.7
Strength of Association in Logistic Regression Between Selected Correlates and Conduct Disorder, Controlling for Other Psychiatric Disorders, for Children, 4 to 16

Correlate	*Relative Odds*
Control Variables	
Hyperactivity	17.6*
Emotional Disorder	2.8*
Somatization	3.2*
Main Effects	
Single parent	1.0
Large sibship	2.4*
Urban residence	0.8
Family dysfunction	2.0*
Domestic violence	1.9
Parent hospitalized for "nerves"	1.7
Parental excessive alcohol consumption	(0.11)[a]
Male sex	1.9*
Chronic medical illness	1.3
Interactions	
Low income by parent arrested[b]	
(1) < $10,000	0.8
(2) > $10,000	3.8*
Age by low income[b]	
(1) 4–11	3.1*
(2) 12–16	1.2

*$p < 0.05$

[a]Coefficient rather than a relative odds because the variable is not dichotomous but interval.

[b]Both interactions are nonsignificant ($p > 0.5$).

in question and to conduct disorder. Table 2.7 shows, for instance, that all three disorders had strong independent relationships with conduct disorder. This was, as expected, especially marked for hyperactivity (R.O. = 17.6). Lastly, both interactions (low income by parent arrested and age by low income) are no longer significant. That is, the strata-specific odds ratios are no longer statistically significantly different from each other. However, "parent arrested" remains a significant predictor of conduct disorder in families with incomes greater than $10,000. Similarly, low income in the 4- to 11-year age group still has a significant independent relationship with conduct disorder.

Table 2.8 presents data on rates of service utilization for conduct-disordered and non-conduct-disordered children. Conduct-disordered children, compared to their peers of the same sex and age category, are two to four times more likely to receive mental health/social services (MH/SS) except in the case of adolescent girls, where the utilization rates are almost identical. Conduct-disordered adolescent girls, compared to other age/sex groups of conduct-disordered children, have an especially low rate of MH/SS utilization. For all groups but young girls, at least 50% of conduct-disordered children have been seen in the past 6 months by ambulatory medical care (AMC). In girls aged 4 to 11, the rate falls to a third. In the case of special education (SE), the rates of use are higher in conduct-disordered compared to non-conduct-disordered children for all age/sex categories except adolescent girls, where the rates are 7.1% and 12.9% respectively.

Table 2.9 presents the results of the logistic regression for selected variables and MH/SS. All variables listed in Table 2.9 were forced into the model, and all possible two-way interactions of conduct disorder with

TABLE 2.8
Service Utilization Rate (per 100) for Children 4 to 16 With and Without Conduct Disorder by Age and Sex

			Type of Service[a]					
			Mental Health/ Social Service		*Ambulatory Medical Care*		*Special Education*	
Age/Sex Category		*(n)*[b]	*CD* %	*NCD* %	*CD* %	*NCD* %	*CD*	*NCD*
4–11	Boys	(519)	15.6	5.7	50.0	62.3	21.2	17.3
	Girls	(499)	22.2	5.2	33.3	66.8	33.3	7.3
12–16	Boys	(366)	18.8	7.4	53.1	52.1	32.3	20.4
	Girls	(376)	7.1	6.0	50.0	46.9	7.1	12.9

[a]CD = conduct disorder; NCD = no conduct disorder.
[b]One child per family; n varies slightly for different variables because of missing data.

TABLE 2.9
Strength of Association in Logistic Regression Between Conduct Disorder, Selected Correlates and Rate of Utilization of Specialized Mental Health/Social Services[a]

Correlate	*Relative Odds*
Conduct Disorder	2.2*
Low Income	4.8*
Single Parent	1.2
Urban Residence	0.8
Age 12–16	1.2
Male Sex	1.2

[a]One child per family.
[b]$p < 0.05$.

other variables were candidates for entry. The results show that only two variables, conduct disorder and low income, have significant independent effects in predicting MH/SS (R.Os. = 2.2 and 4.8, respectively). Single parent, urban residence, age 12–16 and male sex were not significant independent predictors of MH/SS. None of the interactions entered the model.

DISCUSSION

The measure of conduct disorder used in the OCHS showed evidence of satisfactory psychometric properties and of being useful. The conduct disorder scale displayed adequate internal consistency for both age groups and for the different respondents. The measures of the strength of agreement between the checklist and psychiatrist diagnosis revealed that the relationship was stronger in the 4- to 11-year-olds than in the adolescents, but it was acceptable in both groups. Test–retest reliability after an interval of 6 to 9 months showed good stability in the adolescent age group and less, but acceptable stability, in the younger age group. Further, there was evidence, from the data on impairments, that children and adolescents identified as conduct-disordered had, with one exception, significantly greater rates of impairment than their peers. The exception was in the measure of isolation, where adolescents rarely described themselves as isolated. Lastly, the conduct-disordered group were viewed by respondents as being in need of professional help more often than their peers. Taken together, the data on the measure of conduct disorder provide good evidence of both internal and external validity.

Two findings stand out with regard to individual symptoms. First, the prevalence of many of these symptoms in a general population is quite high, reinforcing the belief that the occurrence of single symptoms should seldom be used as an indication of deviance (Offord, 1985). Second, the youths themselves consistently reported more antisocial symptoms than their parents. This finding is not in agreement with the literature, which suggests that children and adolescents will report more subjective symptoms than mothers, but mothers will report more behavioral symptoms than children and adolescents (Herjanic & Reich, 1982). However, these latter data are derived from interviews rather than from checklists. It may be that adolescents are more willing to report antisocial symptoms in a self-report compared to an interview format.

The overall prevalence of conduct disorder in this survey (5.5%) is similar to the rate reported in the Isle of Wight study for 10- and 11-year-olds (4.2%) but is slightly less than the prevalence noted in an Australian study (6.7%) that used the same methodology as the British study. This latter work also focused on 10- and 11-year-olds but included urban as well as rural areas (Connell, Irvine, & Rodney, 1982). The increased frequency in boys compared to girls is in agreement with the literature (Offord, 1985), but the markedly increased boy:girl ratio in younger children in rural areas has not previously been reported. The increased prevalence of conduct disorder in urban compared to rural areas in this study is slight and nonsignificant and certainly not nearly as marked as has been reported in the British studies. There, the rate of conduct disorder in an inner London borough was twice the rate reported for the Isle of Wight (Rutter et al., 1970; Rutter, Cox, Tupling, Berger, & Yule, 1975). One reason for this might be that the urban area in the British study was a poor inner-city area, whereas there was no such restriction in the urban areas included in the OCHS. Thus, it may be that the reported relationship between urban residence and conduct disorder is not a strong one once socioeconomic class is taken into account. The second reason centers on the different ages of the two samples. The British study was restricted to 10- and 11-year-olds, whereas the OCHS included adolescents. The literature suggests that conduct disorder in younger children is related to inner city areas, but such is not the case with regard to conduct disorder arising for the first time in adolescence (Rutter, 1981). In fact, in the OCHS, the prevalence of conduct disorder in adolescence was slightly greater in rural, compared to urban, areas.

The scarcity of conduct disorder identified by more than one source, though marked, was not unexpected. In the Isle of Wight study (Rutter et al., 1970), for instance, parents and teachers agreed on the presence of a psychiatric diagnosis in only 7% of cases. What was surprising was the finding in the OCHS that almost 8 of 10 young children with conduct disorder were identified by the teacher alone. In the Isle of Wight study, by contrast, parents and teachers identified equal numbers of disturbed children. These data suggest that most of the disorders of childhood, including conduct disorder, are situational in type. Perhaps conduct disorder should not be considered as one condition independent of source (respondent), but should be subdivided into parent-identified and other (teacher/youth)-identified disorder (Offord & Boyle, in press). The extent to which these subtypes are valid in terms of differences in etiology, family history, natural history, and response to treatment should be the focus of future work. Further, research is needed to determine the extent to which conduct disorder identified by two respondents is different along the lines outlined heretofore from conduct disorder identified by one respondent alone. For instance, boys who were reported to fight by both mothers and teachers were found to score higher on a variety of measures of antisocial behavior and to have families that were more seriously disturbed than boys who were reported to fight only in the home or only in the school (Loeber & Dishion, 1984). Similarly, differences along several dimensions have been reported between children who are judged as hyperactive in only one setting, home or school (situational), from those who were judged as hyperactive in both settings (pervasive) (Sandberg, Rutter, & Taylor, 1978; Schacher, Rutter, & Smith, 1981). The investigation of pervasive disorders will be difficult to carry out in a general population because of their rarity; a clinic population may be more appropriate.

The overlap of conduct disorder with other diagnoses illustrates the point that when child psychiatric diagnoses are formulated in such a way that overlap is permitted, then a child who has one diagnosis is likely to have more than one (Offord & Joffe, 1985). The large overlap between conduct disorder and hyperactivity has been noted previously (Offord & Waters, 1983). In the Isle of Wight study (Rutter et al., 1970), however, hyperactivity could not be diagnosed if another diagnosis were present, and thus it could not overlap with conduct disorder. In contrast, in the Isle of Wight, 39.3% (22 of 56) of antisocial boys and 35.7% (5 of 14) of antisocial girls had mixed disorders, indicating that in these children both antisocial and neurotic symptoms were prominent. The rate of overlap of emotional disorder with conduct disorder in the OCHS is similar to the British study for preadolescent girls (31.3%) but lower for young boys (18.6%). A major research issue with conduct disorder is the determination of the extent to which there are differences along etiologic, natural history, and treatment lines between conduct disorder when it occurs alone and when it is associated with other disorders. There is preliminary evidence, for instance, that indicates that when conduct disorder is associated with major affective disorder, successful treatment of the affective disorder results in improvement in the conduct disorder symptoms (Puig-Antich, 1982).

The results of the bivariate analyses reveal that there are a number of variables in the sociodemographic, family-parental, and child areas that are significantly related to conduct disorder. Only "urban residence" and "parental excessive alcohol consumption" were not significantly related to the condition. As noted earlier, the lack of relationship between urban residence and conduct disorder may be due to the fact that in the OCHS, the urban residences are not restricted to inner-city poor areas. The lack of relationship between excessive alcohol consumption of parents and conduct disorder was unexpected, because the literature suggests that alcoholism, particularly in the father, is a strong and consistent parental factor in increasing the child's risk for conduct disorder (Robins, 1966; Rutter & Giller, 1983; West, 1982). It may be that in this study the measure of the parental alcoholic factor is weak and could have been compromised by serious underreporting; or perhaps the relationship between parental alcohol consumption and conduct disorder is strong in clinical populations (Robins, 1966), or in particular geographic areas (West, 1982) but not in a large and varied community sample. The ordinal position data indicated that conduct-disordered children were more likely to be the oldest child in the sibship. This is in general agreement with the British work (Rutter et al., 1970), which found that "non-socialized" antisocial children showed a marked preponderance of eldest children over youngest children.

The results of the logistic regressions identify factors that have an independent role in predicting conduct disorder. Each correlate will be taken up in turn for the two logistic regressions. Large sibship size is significantly related to conduct disorder even after controlling for the effects of the other correlates and the other three psychiatric disorders. In the Isle of Wight study (Rutter et al., 1970), large sibship size was significantly related in the bivariate analysis to conduct disorder; and in the Cambridge study of delinquent development, large-sized families were found to be independently predictive of official delinquency in a sample of boys from a working class area in London (Farrington & West, 1981). The Cambridge study and another work (Wadsworth, 1979) reported that family size was associated most strongly with delinquency in low-income sections of the population. The OCHS data provide no support for this contention, in that there was no significant interaction between sibship size and low income. The mechanisms by which large family size has an effect on predicting conduct disorder are not well validated. They include the possibilities that large families stretch already inadequate family resources (Rutter & Madge, 1976), that they promote the contagion effect where antisocial behavior is transmitted from one child to another in the sibship (Jones, Offord, & Abrams, 1980; Robins, West, & Herjanic, 1975), or that the link is due to the association of large family size and educational backwardness (Rutter & Giller, 1983).

Family dysfunction is strongly related to conduct disorder independent of the influences of both the other correlates and psychiatric disorder. This correlate, as operationalized in the OCHS, attempts to measure the way families work together on the tasks that are essential to their viability as a social system. Examples of items are "planning family activities is difficult because we misunderstand each other" and "we are able to make decisions about how to solve problems." The scale has high internal consistency, and although it is positively related to both marital discord and domestic violence, it may be tapping a concept largely independent of these two variables (Byles et al., 1988). The measure of marital discord used in the OCHS, which focuses on patterns of the marital relationship short of physical violence, was not significantly associated with conduct disorder. Domestic violence was positively related to the condition in the bivariate analysis but not in the logistic regression, where its effect is probably taken up by family dysfunction. Male sex is the last main effect whose relationship to conduct disorder is independent of the correlates and the other three psychiatric disorders.

Parent hospitalized for "nerves" and chronic medical illness in the child both were independent predictors of conduct disorder controlling for the effects of other correlates. A major mechanism that has been suggested for explaining the relationship between parental mental illness and child psychiatric disorder is detrimental effect that parental illness has on family relationships (Rutter & Quinton, 1981; 1984). The OCHS data suggest that, although this may account for some of the relationship (the R.O. of 3.0 in the bivariate analyses is reduced to 2.2 in the logistic regression), a major portion of it is independent of this mechanism, because even in the presence of the effects of family dysfunction, parent hospitalized for "nerves" has a significant relationship to conduct disorder. However, the strength of the relationships of parent hospitalized for "nerves" and the child chronic medical illness are reduced to the statistically nonsignificant range when the effects of the other three psychiatric disorders are included. Thus, the relationship between these variables and conduct disorder is accounted for in an important way by the other disorders. In the case of chronic medical illness, for instance, data from the OCHS indicate that this correlate predicts all four psychiatric disorders, and, indeed, the strength of its relationship to conduct disorder is the weakest (Cadman, Boyle, Szatmari & Offord, 1987). For two variables, single parent and domestic violence, their significant relationship to conduct disorder in the bivariate analysis is taken up by other variables in the logistic regression. The literature is in agreement that single parent by itself is not strongly associated with conduct disorder but only when it co-exists with other variables, such as family dysfunction (Rutter & Giller, 1983). Parental excessive alcohol consumption was entered into the logistic regression as an interval variable to allow the usage of the full range of the responses available on the variable, and, as in the bivariate analysis, it was not a significant predictor of conduct disorder.

Parent arrested was a significant predictor of conduct disorder controlling for the effects of the other correlates and disorders *only* in families where the income exceeded $10,000. Parental criminality is reported in the literature to be a strong predictor of conduct disorder (Rutter & Giller, 1983), and, in the Cambridge study, it was an independent predictor of official delinquency across the somewhat restricted range of family incomes included in the sample (West & Farrington, 1977; Farrington & West, 1981). The OCHS data indicate that explanations of the mechanisms by which parental arrest leads to conduct disorder should not focus on the poorest families and should not be restricted to variables measuring family relationships, as the predictive effect of parental arrest in those families with incomes over $10,000 is independent of the effects of family dysfunction. Proposed mechanisms explaining the relationship between parental arrest and antisocial behavior in children have included genetic influences, greater police surveillance of criminal families, and imitation or copying of the parents' criminal behavior (West & Farrington, 1973; West, 1982; Rutter & Giller, 1983). The OCHS data indicate that the investigation of these mechanism must take into account that they operate primarily in families with incomes over $10,000.

Lastly, low income had a significant effect in predicting conduct disorder over and above the effects of the other correlates and the other disorders *only* in the 4- to 11-year-old age group. This provides further evidence suggesting that early onset conduct disorder is tied to poverty, but this is not so for conduct disorder among adolescents (Rutter, 1981). Conduct disorder arising in adolescence almost certainly has no significant relationship with low income.

The data on the distribution of the utilization of services raises two major points. First, any deliver system for conduct-disordered children that has as its goal reaching the majority of children with this disorder cannot rely exclusively on specialized MH/SS. Less than one of five children with conduct disorder received these services in Ontario within a 6-month period. Clearly, if it is to reach the children in need, the delivery system will have to include AMC, which sees between one third and one half of the conduct-disordered children every 6 months, and the school system, which services the vast majority of children (Offord et al., 1987). Second, conduct-disordered adolescent girls have a very different pattern of service utilization of MH/SS and SE compared to the other age/sex groups. In contrast to the other groups, they are no more likely to receive MH/SS than their non-conduct-disordered peers and are less likely to receive SE than their peers. The reasons for these findings are not understood and deserve further study.

Lastly, the results of the logistic regression on the predictors of use of MH/SS point out that both conduct disorder and low income have independent effects in explaining MH/SS use. In addition, the absence of significant inter-actions between conduct disorder and the other variables indicates that availability of MH/SS for conduct-disordered children does not vary significantly by income level, family status, place of residence, age, or sex. Thus, there are no particular subgroups (indicated by these descriptors) of conduct-disordered children who are relatively under- or over-services by MH/SS.

The data reported in this study have at least two major limitations. First, because of the large number of variables included in the study, there are restrictions on the thoroughness with which many variables are measured. Parental alcoholism is a prime example. Second, the data are cross-sectional, and thus the temporal relationship among variables cannot usually be determined. We have recently completed a 4-year follow up on the original 1983 OCHS cohort, which will be helpful in this regard. Longitudinal studies can address a major need in the field: that is data to determine which correlates are true risk factors, and information on the mechanisms through which they have their causal influence on conduct disorder. Such data would permit the formation of causal chains, which could form the basis of prevention efforts (Offord, 1982). The high prevalence of conduct disorder and the difficulty and expense of treating established cases make the search for effective primary prevention programs of central concern to workers in the field.

ACKNOWLEDGMENTS

This work was supported by the Ministry of Community and Social Services, Ontario, and the National Health and Research Development Program, Health and Welfare, Canada. It was carried out by the Child Epidemiology Unit, Department of Psychiatry, McMaster University, and the Child and Family Centre, Chedoke Division, Chedoke-McMaster Hospitals, Hamilton, Ontario.

REFERENCES

Achenbach, T. M., & Edelbrock, C. S. (1981). Behavioral problems and competencies by parents of normal and disturbed children aged four through sixteen. *Monograph of Society for Research in Child Development, 46*(Serial No. 188), 1–78.

American Psychiatric Association (1980). *Diagnostic and statistical manual of mental disorder* (3rd. ed.). Washington, DC: American Psychiatric Association.

Boyle, M. H., Offord, D. R., Hofman, H. G., Catlin, G. P., Byles, J. A., Cadman, D. T., Crawford, J. W., Links, P. S., Rae-Grant, N. I., & Szatmari, P. (1987). Ontario Child Health Study. I. Methodology. *Archives of General Psychiatry, 44,* 826–831.

Byles, J., Byrne, C., Boyle, M. H., & Offord, D. R. (1988). Ontario Child Health Study: reliability and validity of the General Functioning subscale of the McMaster Family Assessment Device. *Family Process, 27,* 97–104.

Cadman, D., Boyle, M., Szatmari, P., & Offord, D. R. (1987). Chronic illness, disability and social well-being: Findings of the Ontario Child Health Study. *Pediatrics, 79,* 805–813.

Cohen, J. (1960). A coefficient of agreement for nominal scales. *Educational and Psychological Measurement, 20,* 37–46.

Connell, H. M., Irvine, L., & Rodney, J. (1982). Psychiatric disorder in Queensland primary school children. *Australian Pediatric Journal, 18,* 177–188.

Dixon, W. J., Brown, M. B., Engelman, L., Frane, J. W., Hill, M. A., Jennrich, R. I., & Toporek, J. D. (1983). *BMPD Statistical Software.* Berkeley, CA: University of California Press.

Farrington, D. P., & West, D. J. (1981). The Cambridge study in the delinquent development (United Kingdom). In S. A. Mednick & A. E. Baert (Eds.), *Prospective longitudinal research: An empirical basis for the primary prevention of psychological disorders* (pp. 137–145). New York, Oxford University Press.

Herjanic, B., & Reich, W. (1982). Development of a structured psychiatric interview for children: agreement between child and parent on individual symptoms. *Journal of Abnormal Child Psychology, 10,* 307–324.

Jones, M. B., Offord, D. R., & Abrams, N. (1980). Brothers, sisters and antisocial behavior. *British Journal of Psychiatry, 136,* 139–145.

Links, P. S. (1983). Community surveys of the prevalence of childhood psychiatric disorders: A review. *Child Development, 54,* 531–548.

Loeber, R., & Dishion, T. J. (1984). Boys who fight at home and at school: Family conditions influencing cross-setting consistency. *Journal of Consulting and Clinical Psychology, 52,* 759–768.

Offord, D. R. (1982). Primary prevention: aspects of program design and evaluation. *Journal of the American Academy of Child Psychiatry, 21,* 225–230.

Offord, D. R. (1985). Child psychiatric disorders: prevalence and perspectives. *Psychiatric Clinics of North America, 8,* 637–652.

Offord, D. R. & Boyle, M. H. (in press). Ontario Child Health Study: Correlates of disorder. *Journal of the American Academy of Child and Adolescent Psychiatry.*

Offord, D. R., Boyle, M. H., Szatmari, P., Rae-Grant, N. I., Links, P. S., Cadman, D. T., Byles, J. A., Crawford, J. W., Munroe Blum, H., Byrne, C., Thomas, H., & Woodward, C. A. (1987). Ontario Child Health Study. II. Six-month prevalence of disorder and rates of service utilization. *Archives of General Psychiatry, 44,* 832–836.

Offord, D. R., & Joffe, R. T. (1985). Childhood depression. In W. G. Dewhurst & G. B. Baker (Eds.), *The chemotherapy of affective disorders: Theory and practice* (pp. 531–583). New York: University Press.

Offord, D. R., & Reitsma-Street, M. (1983). Problems of studying antisocial behavior. *Psychiatric Developments, 2,* 207–224.

Offord, D. R., & Waters, B. G. (1983). Socialization and its failure. In M. D. Levine, W. B. Carey, A. C. Crocker, & R. T. Gross, (Eds.), *Developmental-behavioral pediatrics* (pp. 650–682). Toronto: Saunders.

Puig-Antich, J. (1982). Major depression and conduct disorder in prepuberty. *Journal of the American Academy of Child Psychiatry, 21,* 118–128.

Robins, L. N. (1966). *Deviant children grown up.* Baltimore: Williams and Wilkins.

Robins, L. N. (1970). The adult development of the antisocial child. *Seminars in Psychiatry, 6,* 420–434.

Robins, L. N. (1974). Antisocial behavior disturbances of childhood: prevalence, prognosis and prospects. The E. J. Anthony, & C. Koupernick, (Eds.), *The child in his family: Children at psychiatric risk* (pp. 447–460). New York: John Wiley and Sons.

Robins, L. N., West, P. A., & Herjanic, B. L. (1975). Arrests and delinquency in two generations: A study of Black urban families and their children. *Journal of Child Psychology and Psychiatry, 16,* 125–140.

Rutter, M. (1981). The city and the child. *American Journal of Orthopsychiatry, 51,* 610–625.

Rutter, M., Cox, A., Tupling, C., Berger, M., & Yule, W. (1975). Attainment and adjustment in two geographical areas. I. The prevalence of psychiatric disorder. *British Journal of Psychiatry, 126,* 493–509.

Rutter, M., & Giller, H. (1983). *Juvenile delinquency: Trends and perspectives.* New York: Penguin Books.

Rutter, M., & Madge, N. (1976). *Cycles of disadvantage.* London: Heinemann.

Rutter, M., & Quinton, D. (1981). Longitudinal studies of institutional children and children of mentally ill parents. In S. A. Mednick, A. E. Baert, (Eds.), *Prospective longitudinal research: An empirical basis for the primary prevention of psychosocial disorders* (pp. 297–305). New York: Oxford University Press.

Rutter, M., & Quinton, D. (1984). Parental psychiatric disorder: Effects on children. *Psychological Medicine, 14,* 853–880.

Rutter, M., Tizard, J., & Whitmore, K. (1970). *Education, health and behavior.* London: Longman.

Sandberg, S. T., Rutter, M., & Taylor, E. (1978). Hyperkinetic disorder in psychiatric clinic attenders. *Developmental Medicine and Child Neurology, 20,* 279–299.

Schacher, R., Rutter, M., & Smith, A. (1981). The characteristics of situationally and pervasively hyperactive children: Implications for syndrome definition. *Journal of Child Psychology and Psychiatry, 22,* 375–392.

Statistics Canada. (1982). *1981 census directory.* Ottawa, Canada: Minister of Supply and Services.

Wadsworth, M. (1979). *Roots of delinquency: Infancy, adolescence and crime.* Oxford: Martin Robertson.

West, D. J. (1982). *Delinquency: Its roots, careers and prospects.* London: Heinemann.

West, D. J., & Farrington, D. P. (1973). *Who becomes delinquent?* London: Heinemann.

West, D. J., & Farrington, D. P. (1977). *The delinquent way of life.* London: Heinemann.

3

Aggressive, Withdrawn, and Aggressive/Withdrawn Children in Adolescence: Into the Next Generation

Lisa A. Serbin
Concordia University

Alex E. Schwartzman
Concordia University

Debbie S. Moskowitz
McGill University

Jane E. Ledingham
University of Ottawa

The Concordia Longitudinal Risk Project, begun in 1976, was designed to address the following question: What are the childhood behaviors and developmental paths that lead to major psychosocial problems in adolescence and adulthood? As our sample reaches its late teens to middle 20s, we are now beginning to address a second major issue: Are patterns of psychopathology transferred across generations, and, if so, can we identify the mechanism or socialization process from parent to child? In this report, we focus on the adjustment of socially atypical children during their adolescent years, and present preliminary results regarding the "transfer" of high-risk status from the girls in our sample who have now become mothers to their own young children.

BACKGROUND: PATTERNS OF AGGRESSION AND WITHDRAWAL

There is general consensus among investigators that aggression and social withdrawal constitute two major dimensions of childhood behavioral disturbance. Aggression, also referred to as conduct problems, unsocialized aggression, undercontrolled or externalizing behaviors, is broadly defined to include physical aggression, disruptiveness, and attention-seeking (Achenbach & Edelbrock, 1984; Quay, 1986). Social withdrawal, also referred to as inhibition, isolation, overcontrolled or internalizing behaviors, is defined to include avoidance, fearfulness, seclusiveness, timidity, shyness, and oversensitivity (Quay & LaGreca,

1986; Reznick et al., 1966; Rubin & Mills, 1988). In recent years, "aggression/withdrawal" has emerged as a third category of childhood behavioral pathology to describe children who are frequently aggressive *and* frequently withdrawn. There is evidence to suggest that this behavior pattern is clinically distinctive and is a possible risk marker for major forms of adult psychopathology, including schizophrenia-spectrum disorders (Ledingham, 1981; Milich & Landau, 1984; Schwartzman, Ledingham, & Serbin, 1985). The Concordia project was undertaken to examine the long-term effects of these three patterns of atypical social behavior in children.

The most developed literature on the relationship between childhood maladjustment and later outcomes in adulthood deals with aggressive behavior in boys. Numerous studies indicate that aggression in males is highly stable (Olweus, 1979). There is also ample evidence that aggression by boys is predictive of antisocial activity and criminal behavior as well as other negative outcomes in adolescence and adulthood (Cline, 1980; Eron, Lefkowitz, Walder, & Huesmann, 1974; Loeber, 1982; Magnusson, 1985; Robins, 1974).

There are relatively few studies of outcomes for aggressive girls. These studies indicate moderate stability for aggression and fewer negative outcomes for girls than for boys (Huesmann, Eron, Lefkowitz, & Walder, 1984; Olweus, 1979; 1981; Robins, 1986). One likely reason for the dearth of information about aggressive girls is that fewer girls than boys are identified as extremely aggressive (Fagot, 1984; Lyons & Serbin, 1986). The problem of insufficient numbers can be minimized, however, if we examine long-term consequences for girls who are considered extremely aggressive *relative* to other girls. This was the approach taken in the Concordia project.

The literature on stability and consequences of social withdrawal is considerably less developed and less consistent than it is on aggression. The prevailing view is that childhood withdrawal in itself is neither stable nor a predictor of later negative outcomes (Kohlberg, Ricks, & Snarey, 1984). Studies of the stability of childhood social withdrawal, however, have varied substantially in methodology, a factor that may explain the variability of results (Moskowitz, Schwartzman, & Ledingham, 1985; Olweus, 1981; Rubin, Hymel, & Mills, in press). In addition, the conclusions of these studies are based largely on findings obtained from follow-ups of small samples of clinic-referred withdrawn children (Quay & La Greca, 1986). Clinical studies are subject to socioeconomic and gender sampling biases that limit the generality of their results (Dohrenwend & Dohrenwend, 1969; Eme, 1979). In studies that have followed children sampled from the community, there is contrasting evidence that childhood social withdrawal is stable (Bronson, 1966; Moskowitz et al., 1985;

Wiggins & Winder, 1961), and may well be a risk factor for later anxiety disorders (Kagan, Reznick, Clarke, Snidman, & Garcia-Coll, 1984; Rubin et al., in press).

Relatively little is known about the stability and consequences of the aggressive/withdrawn pattern of behavior in children. Reports of a precursor pattern of aggression and withdrawal, however, appear consistently throughout the literature on the characteristics of preschizophrenic adjustment, despite marked differences in methodology among investigations (Mednick & Schulsinger, 1968; Michael, Morris, & Soroker, 1957; Robins, 1972; Watt, Stolorow, Lubensky, & McClelland, 1970). In addition, there is evidence that risk for substance abuse and delinquency is particularly elevated in children who are both shy and aggressive (Kellam, Ensminger, & Brown, 1987; McCord, 1987). The fact that the aggressive/withdrawn pattern encompasses a broad spectrum of behavioral disturbance raises the possibility that aggressive/withdrawn children are particularly vulnerable to a broad spectrum of major mental health problems.

To summarize, the research literature led us to expect that aggressive children, particularly boys, would be troubled as adolescents. Specifically, we expected relatively poor intellectual and academic competence, a high incidence of family-related problems, and a high incidence of contact with mental health professionals and with law enforcement agencies relative to other children. We expected a similar but more pronounced profile of negative characteristics for aggressive/withdrawn children. We were less clear as to what to expect for withdrawn children. We assumed that whatever the negative sequelae of childhood social withdrawal in adolescence, the effects would not be as apparent as those associated with childhood aggression.

We were also concerned with the lack of information about aggression and withdrawal as predictors for girls. The fact that girls have been omitted or underrepresented in most of the available studies indicated to us that we would need to take a different approach to constructing the design of our longitudinal study. Instead of selecting children on the basis of referrals for emotional or behavioral problems, we decided to take a "community based" approach, selecting extremely aggressive and/or withdrawn children from a large, unscreened population of school children. Further, we deliberately arranged that children would be rated relative to children of their own sex, rather than to the group as a whole. In this way, we were able to ensure that we would find the most aggressive and withdrawn girls, relative to the norms for the female population, and thus ensure a sufficient sample of females in each of the groups of interest. With this sample, which is 50% female, we could approach the issues of prediction of later psychopathology for girls, and we could also examine specific patterns of outcome that are most typical of the female population.

PROJECT DESIGN

The project began with the screening in 1977 and 1978 of 4,100 children in grades 1, 4, and 7, whose modal ages were 7, 10, and 13 years, respectively. The screening procedure yielded a pool of 1,774 research subjects for follow-up study. They comprised three groups judged by their classmates to exhibit a marked pattern of aggressive behavior ($N = 198$), withdrawn behavior ($N = 220$), or both aggressive and withdrawn behavior ($N = 239$), and a control sample of 1,117 students rated as nondeviant by their peers. Thus, the basic statistical design identified three independent factors for univariate and multivariate analyses: Behavior patterns (4) × grade levels (3) × sex (2). The selection of children in three grades separated by 3 years permitted the study to provide both cross-sectional and longitudinal data. This design allowed for the extension of the data collection stage into the period of risk for major psychopathology in adulthood so that childhood patterns associated with later psychiatric disorders could be readily identified.

The decision to use peer nominations as the criterion measure of aggression and withdrawal was prompted by a number of advantages that this procedure has to offer. The researcher gains access to the unique relationship and perspective shared by the actual participant-observers of peer social interactions (Smith, 1967). Childhood peer relations have been found to be associated with psychopathology in adulthood (Kohlberg, LaCrosse, & Ricks, 1972; Parker & Asher, 1987). There is also evidence that peer opinion is a more potent predictor of adult maladjustment than are teacher and clinician ratings (Cowen, Peterson, Babigian, Izzo, & Trost, 1973; Roff, 1970). This may be so not only because of the unique perspective of peers, but also because there are many more of them than teachers or clinicians who are doing the evaluating, thereby increasing the power of the assessment procedure. Finally, peer assessment instruments contain specific and simply couched behavioral descriptions for which convergent validity data can be collected through direct observation of children's social interactions and for which remediation programs can be targeted.

Separate equal-sized samples of girls and boys were included in the study, for several reasons. First, there is evidence (c.f. Lewine, 1981) that the course of development of major psychiatric disorders is different for the two sexes, especially regarding patterns of social interaction. Second, we wanted to ensure a sufficient sample size of female subjects for complete analyses of prediction patterns. As mentioned earlier, there have been problems in identifying an adequate number of aggressive girls for follow-up study in other longitudinal investigations. Third, independent selection and sampling of female subjects guaranteed that these subjects would be classified according to norms that were socioculturally appropriate for females.

The Selection Criterion Measure

At the beginning of Phase I of the study, we administered a French translation of the Pupil Evaluation Inventory (PEI), a peer nomination instrument (Pekarik, Prinz, Liebert, Weintraub, & Neale, 1976) to 4,100 Francophone children in 152 classrooms. The PEI contains 35 items that load on three factors: aggression (items such as "those who always get into trouble" and "those who are mean and cruel to other children"), withdrawal (items such as "those who are too shy to make friends easily" and "those who often don't want to play"), and likability (items such as "those who help others" and "those who everybody likes"). Each class was asked to nominate those boys or girls in the class who best fit the description of each item on the questionnaire. Boys and girls were rated by both male and female classmates in separate administrations. The total number of nominations received from all classmates for each child was calculated separately for items loading on the aggression factor, the withdrawal factor, and the likability factor. Total nomination scores for each factor were subjected to a square root transformation to reduce skew, and converted to *Z* scores for each sex within each class to remove the effects of sex differences in baseline rates of aggression and withdrawal and the effects of differences in class size on total scores.

Only *Z* scores on the aggression and withdrawal factors contributed to the selection of target subjects. Children with a score on the aggression factor equal to or exceeding the 95th percentile cutoff and a score on the withdrawal factor below the 75th percentile cutoff were designated as aggressive. Similarly, children with a withdrawal score equal to or exceeding the 95th percentile and an aggression score less than the 75th percentile were designated as withdrawn. Those children whose scores were above the 75th percentile on both aggression and withdrawal formed the aggressive/withdrawn group. Control subjects were those children whose scores fell below the 75th percentile and above the 25th percentile on both aggression and withdrawal. Computing *Z* scores within each sex and classroom meant that *Z* scores, and thus procedures for selection of target subjects, were relative with respect to the sex, classroom, and grade level of the child. Thus, girls selected as aggressive

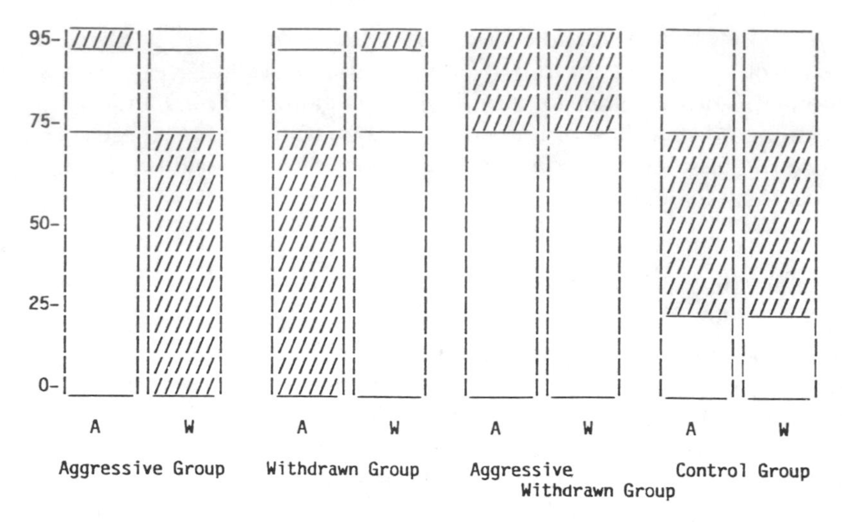

FIG. 3.1. *Criteria for Selection for Each Group:* Percentile Score

targets could have substantially lower raw scores on aggression than boys in the aggressive group who had identical *Z* scores. Similarly, specifying the *Z* score cutoffs for target subject selection did not guarantee that raw score cutoffs for aggression and withdrawal were equivalent across grades and classrooms. The advantage of this procedure is that it established cutoffs that were specific to the context of the sex and grade level of the child, and thus took into account age and sex appropriate norms of behavior, norms that are not easily specifiable a priori from raw scores.

RESULTS FOR PHASE II: THE ADOLESCENT PHASE

In this section, we summarize the results of the study to date. All findings reported hereafter are statistically significant. In Phase I (1976–1981), we found evidence that the aggressive/withdrawn children were an unusual group. They were described as immature by teachers and parents; their intelligence and school achievement test scores were low; their social judgment and motor development were immature; and they displayed cognitive-attentional deficits. On 3-year follow-up, there was a high incidence of school failure and special class placement in this group. The aggressive children also fared poorly in school achievement despite adequate intellectual ability. The withdrawn children were not low on intelligence but presented a mixed picture in terms of school achievement.

In Phase II (1982–1985), when the children were in their teens, we examined in more detail their social competence, problem behaviors, intellectual ability, motor ability, attentional deficits, school achievement, contact with helping agents, and family characteristics. Information was collected from provincial medical records, a day of testing at the university, and a visit with the family. Medical records (in grouped form so that the individual identity of cases remained confidential) were obtained for 95% (N = 1,677) of the sample. We were also able to test approximately 25% of the sample at the university and in their homes. The rates of retrieval for each of the peer classification groups were approximately the same within each of the sources of data.

Intelligence

Approximately 6 years after initial identification, members of a subsample of the original pool were individually assessed at the university on six subtests of the WISC-R or the WAIS-R (if they were 17+ years of age). The aggressive children obtained significantly lower test scores than the control group, and the children who had been identified by peers as aggressive/withdrawn continued as in Phase I to show significantly below average intellectual performance as adolescents.

Problem Behaviors and Social Competence

The target children completed the Youth Self-Report form of the Child Behavior Checklist (CBCL; Achenbach & Edelbrock, 1983). The aggressive and the aggressive/withdrawn youths reported significantly more problems of the externalizing type than the control youths. Members of all three deviant groups saw themselves as low on social competence relative to the control group. The aggressive/withdrawn youths perceived themselves to be significantly lower than the control individuals on total social competence (Moskowitz & Schwartzman, 1989).

Medical and Psychiatric Problems

Medical records were obtained from the Régie de l'Assurance-Maladie du Québec (RAMQ) for the years 1981 through 1984, by the end of which period the children were 13 to 20 years of age. These records were obtained in denominalized form; that is, the identity of individual cases remained unknown except for the individual's sex, classification group, and age group. It was possible to extract four measures from the case records: (a) frequency of assessment leading to a psychiatric diagnosis, (b) frequency of assessment leading to a nonpsychiatric medical diagnosis, (c) frequency of psychiatric treatment, and (d) frequency of nonpsychiatric medical treatment.

These data indicated that the aggressive group had the most psychiatric and nonpsychiatric medical problems. This group was receiving more psychiatric assessment and services and more nonpsychiatric medical treatment and services than the other peer classification groups. They were more than twice as likely as controls to have received psychiatric treatment. The aggressive females were receiving the highest rate of nonpsychiatric medical treatment, more than the other groups of adolescent girls and more than the aggressive males. They had more gynecological problems than other females (Moskowitz & Schwartzman, 1989). The withdrawn group and the controls were similar on the indices of psychiatric and medical contact, with one notable exception. Withdrawn females had the highest incidence of abortions among the groups; they were more than twice as likely as control females to have had an abortion (Moskowitz & Schwartzman, 1989).

Parent Factors

As part of the Phase II follow-up, parents were asked to describe their children as adolescents. Mothers and fathers received high or low ratings on Positive Expressed Emotion and Negative Expressed Emotion (Wynne & Gift, 1978), two measures that were based on an audiotaped 5-minute speech sample provided separately by each parent. Significantly more adolescents who had been peer-identified as socially atypical in childhood received negative criticisms from their mothers than did those previously identified by peers as socially normative; and significantly more adolescents identified as aggressive/withdrawn in childhood received negative criticisms from their mothers than did those adolescents who had been originally identified as either aggressive or withdrawn. There were no differences among the groups in the proportions receiving positive comments from mothers or negative comments from fathers, but significantly more fathers of socially atypical children than control children offered positive comments. Finally, the children of highly critical mothers were less socially competent than other adolescents (Beaudet & Schwartzman, 1987).

The relation of parents' emotional adjustment, marital adjustment, and overt expression of marital hostility to the psychosocial adjustment of their adolescent children was also examined (Back, 1988). The parent measures included the Symptom Checklist-90 to assess psychopathology;

the Short Marital Adjustment Test (SMAT; Locke & Wallace, 1959); and the O'Leary-Porter Scale of Overt Marital Hostility (OPS; Porter & O'Leary, 1980). These results indicated that marital maladjustment and overt marital hostility were associated with childhood aggression in both boys and girls. The degree of emotional disturbance in the parent, whether mother or father, was also associated with both the male and female adolescent's level of emotional disturbance.

These findings attest to the predictive value of peer opinion in identifying children who are likely to be in psychosocial difficulty. All three groups who were identified by childhood peers as socially deviant had problems as children and were continuing to have problems as adolescents.

The profile of the aggressive child in adolescence that emerges from these results is consistent with the picture of long-term negative effects that has been well documented in the research and clinical literature on childhood aggression in males. The skills that are critical for educational and occupational advancement are adversely affected in both aggressive boys and aggressive girls. This factor in itself potentiates the likelihood of socioeconomic disadvantage and its psychosocial penalties in adulthood. These adolescents are more likely to be contending with troubled parents in marital conflict and to be having behavior problems that bring them to the attention of mental health professionals. In addition, the results highlight the link for girls in particular between aggression in childhood and physical health problems in adolescence.

Our results present a more complex picture of withdrawn children as adolescents. There was little to distinguish them from their socially normative peers. They did not differ in intelligence, in behavior problems, and in referrals for psychiatric services. Yet they perceived themselves as low in competence, and more of them than their normative peers received negative criticism from their mothers. These data are consistent with findings reported by Rubin et al., (in press). The withdrawn child appears vulnerable to pessimistic self-evaluation that is fueled or reinforced by negative maternal feedback in adolescence. These factors in combination may lead to anxiety and depression in adulthood. Our current follow-up assessment should provide information on the vulnerability of withdrawn children to clinical levels of anxiety and depression in the early adult years. Whether the unexpected high incidence of abortions in our sample of withdrawn females reflects self-negating and approval-seeking attitudes towards men also merits further study.

Probably the most prominent and surprising feature of the follow-up data on aggressive/withdrawn children is the contrast between a profile of continuing immature intellectual, motor, and socioemotional development in adolescence on the one hand, and an unremarkable record of family problems on the other. We expected that a behavior pattern that encompasses two major dimensions of childhood social deviance would be associated with a history of pronounced family difficulties. It is possible that the family measures used in the study are not sufficiently sensitive to the more covert stressful aspects of family interaction that may foster or relate to an aggressive/withdrawn behavioral style in childhood. Alternatively, the data are consistent with the assumption that the aggressive/withdrawn behavior pattern reflects immature neurobiological development more than the impact of a stressful family environment as the primary source of adaptational difficulty. The pattern was not only far less common but also less stable among older members of the sample (Ledingham, 1981; Moskowitz et al., 1985). Whether or not the assumption is correct, the few older children who continue to display frequent aggression and frequent social withdrawal constitute an unusual group who may be particularly susceptible to major mental disorders in adulthood. Future follow-ups of the aggressive/withdrawn group should enable us to determine whether its older members are at an especially elevated level of psychiatric risk.

To summarize, these results indicate that children who are perceived by peers as aggressive, withdrawn, or frequently aggressive and withdrawn are likely to have problems as adolescents. Boys who are aggressive are more likely than other boys to become aggressive adolescents performing poorly at school and receiving psychiatric services. Girls who are aggressive are more likely than other girls to be performing poorly at school, receiving psychiatric services, and having medical treatments. Children who are withdrawn may be contending with self-esteem issues and a lack of self-confidence as adolescents. Children who are both aggressive and withdrawn are likely to have problems in adolescence that reflect low competence and poor coping skills across a broad spectrum of developmental challenges. Family problems appear to be particularly relevant to the adaptational difficulties of aggressive children.

THE NEXT PHASE: LATE ADOLESCENCE AND EARLY ADULTHOOD

In the current phase of the study, our subjects, now in their late teens to middle 20s are being assessed for outcome in a variety of spheres: academic, occupational, marital/family, health services, social welfare services, contacts with the justice system, and diagnoses of psychiatric illness, antisocial personality disorders, and substance abuse. In this phase, we will be especially interested in sex differences in outcome patterns.

To date, one of the most striking sex differences we have found concerns criminal behavior (again, all results reported hereafter are statistically significant). Although Phase II data indicated that aggressive girls were similar to aggressive boys in showing poor school achievement, our most recent data on the oldest cohort (Moskowitz, Crawley, & Schwartzman, 1989) indicate that the aggressive males are far more likely to commit a criminal offence, with a rate of 45.5% having appeared in court, than are the aggressive females, with a rate of 3.8% (this compares with rates of 10.8% for control males and 1.8% for control females). Similar sex differences were found for the other two deviant groups, with rates of 3.8% for withdrawn males and 1.8% for withdrawn females, and 26.1% for aggressive/withdrawn males as compared with 10.1% for aggressive/withdrawn females. If the girls in our sample are having psychosocial problems, these do not typically take the form of criminal behavior.

Because of their pattern of poor school achievement and poor coping skills, we currently hypothesize that the girls in our deviant groups may be at high risk for early pregnancy and school drop out, and may have difficulty acquiring adequate parenting skills or providing a stable, supportive home environment for their young children. Medicare data, as of 1987, indicate very high birth rates (two to three times higher than the general population) for all groups in our sample. Teen pregnancy carries its own risk for mothers and young children, which, combined with our deviant groups' likelihood of psychopathology and psychosocial problems, gives these young women and their children a very high risk index. As we study these issues, we will be alert to specific patterns presented by girls in the three deviant groups, and also to identifying "buffer" factors that predict positive outcomes for girls with a high-risk background.

We are currently conducting a pilot project that focuses on the parenting behavior and home environments created by the women in our sample who have become mothers, and on early developmental outcome for their children. Results to date, utilizing a very small sample of 13 mothers and children from the "high risk" groups and 12 control families, indicate that the mothers in the deviant groups are indeed likely to provide less adequate stimulation and home environments for their children (McAffer, Serbin, & Schwartzman, 1988). Directly relevant to their role as parents, the High Risk group showed significantly lower emotional and verbal responsivity to their children on the Home Observation for Measurement of the Environment (HOME; Caldwell & Bradley, 1979), and also provided significantly fewer appropriate play materials for their children. Concerning the children of these young mothers, we found that significantly more children of mothers in the High Risk group failed items at their age level on the "personal/social" scale of the Denver Developmental Screening Test (DDST; Fankenberg, Dodds, & Fandal, 1973).

In sum, although these results are based on a very small preliminary sample, they do support our hypothesis that the women in the high risk groups are likely to have difficulties as parents, and indicate that their children may be showing early signs of psychosocial difficulties. Over the next 3 years, we hope to extend these findings to a much larger sample, including over 300 women from the sample and their young children. With this larger sample, we will be able to identify specific parenting and developmental patterns associated with early classification of the mother as aggressive, withdrawn, or aggressive/withdrawn.

We also hope to be able, via path analysis, to identify the specific process that occur when risk for psychosocial problems is transferred from mother to child. That is, we want to identify the specific factors, such as extent of maternal psychopathology, family educational and economic status, stress, and social support that intervene between childhood status and negative versus positive outcome for these women as parents. We are also interested in the specific ways these women socialize their children, again to identify possible "buffer" variables that may protect offspring coming from a high-risk background from poor outcomes. As the offspring of our sample grow older, we will also be examining their patterns of social behavior to see if they repeat their parent's early classification as aggressive and/or withdrawn.

CONCLUSION

It is clear from the results of the Concordia Risk Project to date that early patterns of aggression and withdrawal signal the likelihood of a variety of psychosocial problems in adolescence. Further, the need to include female subjects in studies of socially deviant behavior, using appropriate norms to identify atypical girls, is clear. Aggressive and withdrawn girls not only present a picture of high risk, they also seem likely to play a central role in the early socialization of psychopathology in the next generation.

At this stage, the Concordia Risk Project is entering its most exciting phase. We will soon be able to examine the paths from childhood aggression and withdrawal to outcome in early adulthood. We will also begin to address the issue of whether children who are socially deviant grow up to become the parents of another high-risk generation. Most important, we hope to identify the specific processes that lead to negative outcomes, and, conversely, to identify those factors and experiences that may buffer or protect individuals coming from a high-risk background from negative outcomes. In this way, the "life cycle" of psychopathology may be better understood and effective preventive interventions for high risk children explored and implemented.

ACKNOWLEDGMENTS

The research described in this chapter was supported by grants from the Conseil Quebecois de la Recherche Sociale of the Ministry of Health and Social Services of Quebec, the F.C.A.R. of the Ministry of Education of Quebec, and the National Health Research and Development Program of the Department of Health and Welfare, Canada. Many individuals have contributed to the collection, management, and analyses of the data set of the Concordia Longitudinal Risk Research Project since its beginnings in 1976. We acknowledge in particular the contributions of Joseph Beltempo, Punam Bhargava, Keith Marchessault, Valerie McAffer, Denise Morin, Linda Prenoveau, Geoffrey Selig, and Claude Senneville. We are grateful to the Commission des Ecoles Catholiques de Montreal and the Regie d'Assurance Maladie du Quebec for their help. We are most indebted to the participants of the study. Correspondence concerning this manuscript should be sent to Lisa A. Serbin, Centre for Research in Human Development, and Department of Psychology, Concordia University, 1455 De Maisonneuve West, Montreal, Quebec, Canada H3G 1M8.

REFERENCES

Achenbach, T. M., & Edelbrock, C. S. (1983). *Manual for the child behavior checklist and revised child behavior profile.* Burlington: University of Vermont.

Achenbach, T. M., & Edelbrock, C. S. (1984). Psychopathology of childhood. *Annual Review of Psychology, 35,* 227–259.

Back, M. A. (1988). *Psychopathology and marital discord in parents of socially deviant children.* Unpublished doctoral dissertation, Concordia University, Montreal, Quebec.

Beaudet, J., & Schwartzman, A. E. (1987, June). *Parental affective attitudes and children's atypical social behaviors.* Paper presented at the Annual Meeting of the Canadian Psychological Association, Vancouver, British Columbia.

Bronson, W. C. (1966). Central orientations: A study of behavior organization from childhood to adolescence. *Child Development, 37,* 125–155.

Caldwell, B. M., & Bradley, R. H. (1979). *Home observation for measurement of the environment.* Little Rock: University of Arkansas at Little Rock.

Cline, H. (1980). Criminal behavior over the life span. In O. Brim & J. Kagan

(Eds.), *Constancy and change in human development* (pp. 641–674). Cambridge, MA: Harvard University Press.

Cowen, E. L., Peterson, A., Babigian, H., Izzo, L. D., & Trost, M. A. (1973). Long-term follow-up of early detected vulnerable children. *Journal of Consulting and Clinical Psychology, 41,* 438–446.

Dohrenwend, B. S., & Dohrenwend, B. P. (1969). Social class and the relations of remote to recent stressors. In M. Roff, L. Robins, & M. Pollack (Eds.), *Life history research in psychopathology* (pp. 170–185). Minneapolis: University of Minnesota Press.

Eme, R. F. (1979). Sex differences in childhood psychopathology: A review. *Psychological Bulletin, 86,* 574–595.

Eron, L. D., Lefkowitz, M. M., Walder, L. O., & Huesmann, L. R. (1974). Relation of learning in childhood to psychopathology and aggression in young adulthood. In A. Davids (Ed.), *Child personality and psychopathology* (Vol. I, pp. 53–88). New York: John Wiley & Sons.

Fagot, B. I. (1984). The consequents of problem behavior in toddler children. *Journal of Abnormal Child Psychology, 12,* 385–395.

Frankenburg, W. K., Dodds, J. B., & Fandal, A. W. (1973). *Denver development screening test, manual workbook for nurses and paramedical personnel.* Denver: University of Colorado Medical Center.

Huesmann, L. R., Eron, L. D., Lefkowitz, M. M., & Walder, L. O. (1984). The stability of aggression over time and generations. *Developmental Psychology, 20,* 1120–1134.

Kagan, J., Reznick, J. S., Clarke, C., Snidman, N., & Garcia-Coll, C. (1984). Behavioral inhibition to the unfamiliar. *Child Development, 55,* 2212–2223.

Kellam, S. G., Ensminger, M., & Brown, C. H. (1987, April). *Early behavioral responses of children to school: The importance of shy, aggressive, and other behaviors to later outcomes in the life course.* Paper presented at the Biennial Meeting of the Society for Research in Child Development, Baltimore, MD.

Kohlberg, L., LaCrosse, J., & Ricks, D. (1972). The predictability of adult mental health from childhood behavior. In B. D. Wolman (Ed.), *Manual of child psychopathology* (pp. 1217–1283). New York: McGraw-Hill.

Kohlberg, L., Ricks, D., & Snarey, J. (1984). Childhood development as a predictor of adaptation in adulthood. *Genetic Psychology Monographs, 110,* 94–162.

Ledingham, J. E. (1981). Developmental patterns of aggressive and withdrawn behavior in childhood: A possible method for identifying preschizophrenics. *Journal of Abnormal Psychology, 9*(1), 1–22.

Lewine, R. J. (1981). Sex differences in schizophrenia: Timing or subtypes? *Psychological Bulletin, 70,* 681–693.

Locke, H. J., & Wallace, K. M. (1959). Short marital-adjustment and prediction tests: Their reliability and validity. *Marriage and Family Living, 21,* 251–255.

Loeber, R. (1982). The stability of antisocial and delinquent child behavior: A review. *Child Development, 55,* 1431–1446.

Lyons, J. A. & Serbin, L. A. (1986). Observer bias in scoring boys' and girls' aggression. *Sex Roles, 14*(5/6), 301–313.

Magnusson, D. (1985). Adult delinquency in the light of conduct and physiology at an early age. *Reports from the Department of Psychology, University of Stockholm, 63,* 1–18.

McAffer, V., Serbin, L. A., & Schwartzman, A. E. (1988, June). *The intergenerational transmission of high risk status.* Paper presented at the Canadian Psychological Association Annual Conference, Montreal, Canada.

McCord, J. (1987, June). *Aggression and shyness as predictors of problems: Another view.* Paper presented at the Biennial Meeting of the Society for Research in Child Development, Baltimore, MD.

Mednick, S., & Schulsinger, F. (1968). Some premorbid characteristics related to the breakdown of children with schizophrenic mothers. In D. Rosenthal & S. S. Kety (Eds.), *The transmission to schizophrenia* (pp. 267–292). New York: Pergamon.

Michael, C. M., Morris, D. P., & Soroker, E. (1957). Follow-up studies of shy, withdrawn children II: Relative incidence of schizophrenia. *The American Journal of Orthopsychiatry, 27* (2), 331–337.

Milich, R., & Landau, S. (1984). A comparison of the social status and social behavior of aggressive and aggressive/withdrawn boys. *Journal of Abnormal Child Psychology, 12*(2), 277–288.

Moskowitz, D. S., Crawley, M., & Schwartzman, A. E. (1989, August). *Adult criminal activity among adolescents who were aggressive or withdrawn.* Paper presented at the meeting of the American Psychological Association, New Orleans, LA.

Moskowitz, D. S., & Schwartzman, A. E., (in press). Life paths of aggressive and withdrawn children. In D. Buss & N. Cantor (Eds.), *Personality psychology in the 1990's.* New York: Springer-Verlag.

Moskowitz, D. S., Schwartzman, A. E., & Ledingham, J. E. (1985). Stability and change in aggression and withdrawal in middle childhood and early adolescence. *Journal of Abnormal Psychology, 94*(1), 30–41.

Olweus, D. (1979). Stability of aggressive reaction patterns in males: A review. *Psychological Bulletin, 86,* 825–875.

Olweus, D. (1981). Continuity in aggressive and withdrawn, inhibited behavior patterns. *Psychiatry and Social Sciences, 1,* 141–159.

Parker, J. G., & Asher, S. R. (1987). Peer relations and late personal adjustment: Are low-accepted children at risk? *Psychological Bulletin, 102,* 357–389.

Pekarik, E. G., Prinz, A. J., Liebert, D. E., Weintraub, S., & Neale, J. M. (1976). The pupil evaluation inventory: A sociometric technique for assessing children's social behavior. *Journal of Abnormal Child Psychology, 4*(1), 83 97.

Porter, E., & O'Leary, K. D. (1980). Marital discord and childhood behavior problems. *Journal of Abnormal Child Psychology, 8,* 287–295.

Quay, H. C. (1986). Classification. In H. C. Quay & J. S. Werry (Eds.), *Psychopathological disorders of childhood (3rd ed.)* (pp. 1–34). New York: John Wiley.

Quay, H. C., & LaGreca, A. M. (1986). Disorders of anxiety, withdrawal, and dysphoria. In H. C. Quay & J. S. Werry (Eds.), *Psychopathological disorders of childhood (3rd ed.)* (pp. 73–110). New York: John Wiley.

Reznick, J. S., Kagan, J., Snidman, N., Gersten, M., Bank, K., & Rosenberg, A. (1986). Inhibited and uninhibited children: A follow-up study. *Child Development, 57,* 660–680.

Robins, L. N. (1972). Follow-up studies of behavior disorders in children. In H. C. Quay & J. S. Werry (Eds.), *Psychopathological disorders of childhood (2nd ed.)* (pp. 483–513). New York: Wiley.

Robins, L. N. (1974). *Deviant children grown up.* Huntington, NY: Robert E. Krieger Publishing Company.

Robins, L. N. (1986). The consequences of conduct disorder in girls. In D. Olweus, J. Block, & M. Radke-Yarrow (Eds.), *Development of antisocial and prosocial behavior: Research, theories, and issues* (pp. 385–414). New York: Academic Press.

Roff, M. (1970). Childhood antecedents of adult neurosis, severe bad conduct, and psychological health. In M. Roff & D. F. Ricks (Eds.), *Life history research in psychopathology,* (Vol. 1, pp. 131–162). Minneapolis: University of Minnesota Press.

Rubin, K. H., Hymel, S., & Mills, R. S. (in press). Sociability and social withdrawal in childhood: Stability and outcomes. *Journal of Personality.*

Rubin, K. H., & Mills, R. S. (1988). The many faces of isolation. *Journal of Consulting and Clinical Psychology, 56,* 916–924.

Schwartzman, A. E., Ledingham, J. E., & Serbin, L. A. (1985). Identification of children at risk for adult schizophrenia: A longitudinal study. *International Review of Applied Psychology, 34,* 363–380.

Smith, G. (1967). Usefulness of peer ratings of personality in educational research. *Educational and Psychological Measurement, 24,* 967–984.

Watt, N. F., Stolorow, R. D., Lubensky, A. W., & McClelland, D. C. (1970). School adjustment and behavior of children hospitalized for schizophrenia as adults. *American Journal of Orthopsychiatry, 40*(4), 637–657.

Wiggins, J. S., & Winder, C. L. (1961). The peer nomination inventory: An empirically derived sociometric measure of adjustment in preadolescent boys. *Psychological Reports, 9,* 643–677.

Wynne, L. C., & Gift, T. (1978, April). *Brief speech samples as an analogue of expressed emotion.* Paper presented at the National Mental Health Workshop on Methods for the Study of Intrafamilial Stress in Schizophrenia, Washington, D.C.

Commentary

Aggression, Prosocial Behavior, and Gender: Three Magic Words But No Magic Wand

R. E. Tremblay
University of Montreal

This discussion of the first three chapters deals with three issues. First, a question of semantics: What do we mean by "childhood aggression"? Second, a question of focus: Should we limit ourselves to the study of maladjusted children's negative behaviors? Third, a question of gender: Why has so much attention been given to male aggression and so little to female aggression?

Aggression is a word that is part of everyday language and appears misleadingly unambiguous. The Oxford dictionary defines aggression as an unprovoked attack or assault. Generally, in our field, we give a broader definition to aggression when we talk of "childhood aggression." It is important that some thought be given to how broad or narrow that definition should be kept if aggression is to be a useful concept for research, prevention, and treatment. Offord, Boyle, and Racine, in the Ontario Child Health Study (see chapter 2), chose to use the term "conduct disordered" children rather than "aggressive children"; on the other hand, in the Concordia Longitudinal High Risk Project (see chapter 3) and the Cambridge Study in Delinquent Development (see chapter 1), children were categorized as aggressive or nonaggressive. If we limit ourselves to these labels, we get the impression that the Concordia and the Cambridge studies are closer to this book's focus on aggression than is the Ontario Child Health Study. But, a close look at the content of the items used to measure behavior in each study gives a different picture. In the Ontario Child Health Study, 7 of the 15 conduct disorder items describe physically aggressive behaviors (see Table 2.4). On the other hand, The Pupil Evaluation Inventory (Pekarik, Prinz, Liebert,

Weintraub, & Neale, 1976) "aggression" scale, used in the Concordia study, contains only two clear physical aggression items (those who start a fight over nothing; those who say they can beat everybody up) out of the 20-items scale[1]; similarly, the items used to classify an individual as aggressive in the Cambridge study contained few clear physical aggression items when the boys were aged 8 to 14 (see chapter 1, page 10). The Concordia and Cambridge studies are far from being the only studies that use a "loose" definition of aggressive behavior. In our own longitudinal study (Tremblay, Charlebois, Gagnon, & Larivée, 1986) of what we first chose to call "aggressive" kindergarten boys and now tend to call "disruptive" kindergarten boys, we used the Preschool Behavior Questionnaire's "aggressive" factor to identify our "aggressive" subjects. In this widely used scale (Moller & Rubin, 1988; Tremblay, Desmarais-Gervais, Gagnon, & Charlebois, 1987) only four of 13 items clearly tap physically aggressive behaviors. The same streched definition of aggression is observed in the extensively used Child Behavior Checklist (Achenbach, 1978). Of 23 items on the aggression scale, only 3 items are clearly descriptive of physically aggressive behaviors.

To summarize, many (if not most) studies of "childhood aggression" are relying on aggression scales that are externalizing scales (Achenbach & Edelbrock, 1978) or disruptive behavior scales (American Psychiatric Association, 1987), containing few aggressive behavior items. This semantic "laissez-faire" may be an important handicap in our efforts to understand the development and the prevention of children's maladjusted behavior. We need to take a closer look at the differences between aggressive children, oppositional children, rejected children, inattentive children, hyperactive children, and others. More rigorous operational definitions could probably lead to better developmental studies, but its most important benefit would certainly be in the clinical sphere. Many of our failures in successfully helping these children could stem from our inability to adequately identify their behavior problems before treatment, by using scales that are misnomers.

My second question asks: Should we limit ourselves to the study of

---

[1]The other 18 items are: Those who can't sit still; those who try to get other people in trouble; those who act stuck-up and think they are better than everyone else; those who play the clown and get others to laugh; those who tell other children what to do; those who always mess around and get into trouble; those who make fun of people; those who do strange things; those who bother people when they are trying to work; those who get mad when they don't get their way; those who don't pay attention to the teacher; those who are rude to the teacher; those who act like a baby; those who are mean and cruel to other children; those who give dirty looks; those who want to show off in front of the class; those who exaggerate and make up stories; and those who complain that nothing makes them happy.

maladjusted children's negative behavior? The answer, obviously, depends on why we are studying these children. If we are strictly describing the prevalence of conduct disorder in a population, we can probably limit ourselves to measuring that behavior. However, I argue that, even then, the measurement of adaptive behavior could help in deciding which individual is a "case" and which is not. For those who are interested in predicting future maladjustment or planning prevention and treatment, I argue more strongly that we need to assess adaptive as well as maladaptive behaviors.

In recent years there has been an increase of interest in prosocial behaviors. At first glance, one might guess that prosocial behaviors are the reverse side of the coin from aggressive or antisocial behavior. There are not many researchers who have measured prosocial and aggressive or antisocial behaviors in the same children. Some studies have found no correlations between these two concepts, others have found positive correlations, and still others have found negative correlations (Radke-Yarrow, Zahn-Waxler, & Chapman, 1983). In each case where there was a correlation, the level was moderate (from 0.2 to 0.3). This indicates that children who are high on an aggression score (whatever that may mean) are not all low on a prosocial scale. This should be fairly obvious from observational studies of children's behavior. It is quite clear that the actual aggressive or coercive behaviors of highly aggressive children are still only a fraction of their total behavior and that there is considerable variability of prosocial behavior within groups of "aggressive" children (Strayer, Noel, & Leclerc, 1989; Tremblay, Charlebois, Gagnon, & Larivée, 1989).

Eron and Huesmann (1984) reported that the prosocial behavior of boys at age 8 was significantly associated with aggression, educational attainment, and ego development at age 30, even after controlling for aggression at age 8. In our longitudinal study of disruptive boys in kindergarten, the data show similar results. We created two groups of disruptive boys where one boy from each group had identical scores on the disruptive scale but opposite scores on the prosocial scale. In one group, all the boys had a prosocial score above the 70th percentile (based on the normative group); in the other group, all the boys had a prosocial score below the 30th percentile. This gave us two groups of disruptive boys, one judged highly prosocial, and the other judged not prosocial. No differences were found between these two groups on a measure of anxiety in kindergarten. Three years later, at age 9, the two groups of boys were assessed by their teachers and their mothers. Results showed (Tremblay, Vitaro, Gagnon, Piché, & Royer, 1989) that the nonprosocial disruptive boys, compared to the prosocial disruptive boys, were rated significantly more disruptive by mothers and significantly more anxious by teachers. These results, with those of Eron and Huesmann, indicate that the prognosis for disruptive prosocial boys is more optimistic than for nonprosocial disruptive boys.

To relate this approach to the category of aggressive/withdrawn children used in the Concordia study, I categorized our disruptive-anxious kindergarten boys into two categories, those below the 30th percentile on the prosocial scale (the nonprosocial) and those above the 30th percentile (the prosocial group). The results show (see Fig. A.1) that 3 years later (at age 9) the nonprosocial-anxious-disruptive boys' school adjustment was much worse than that of the prosocial-anxious-disruptive boys. Sixty-three percent of the former were held back in grade or in special programs, compared to only 29% of the latter. It is quite clear that amongst the disruptive-anxious boys, those who are also prosocial are at much less risk of future school maladjustment. These results are a good indication that the assessment of adaptive behaviors, when we are interested in children's maladjustment, should help to formulate more accurate prognoses and plan more adequate interventions. The use of categorical approaches, as exemplified by the Concordia study (as well as by the Cambridge and Ontario studies) are also promising signs for clinicians who tend to think in terms of categories rather than multiple linear relations. A number of publications in recent years (Hinde & Dennis, 1986; Loeber & Dishion, 1983; Magnusson, 1988; Tremblay,

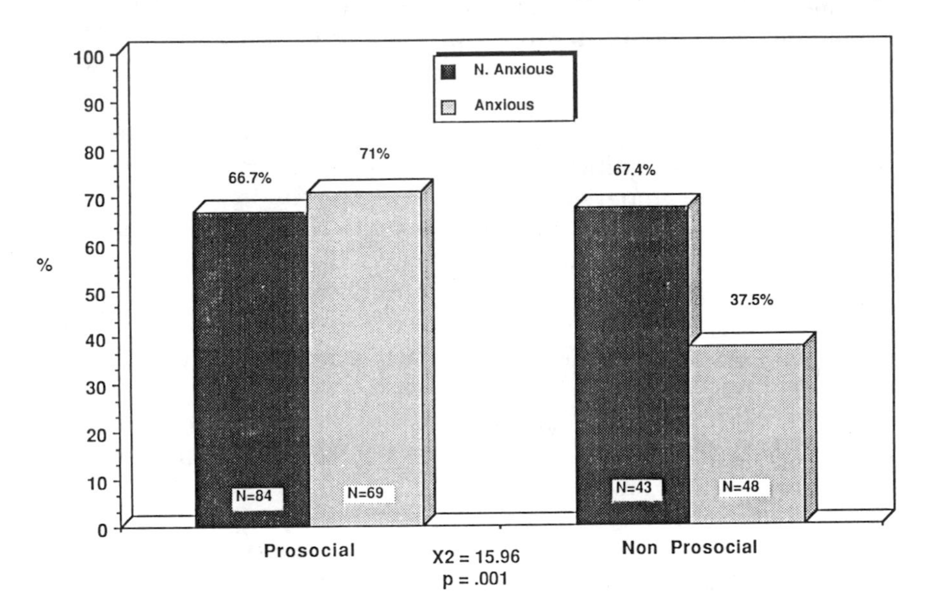

FIG. A.1. Four categories of Age 6 Disruptive Boys in Regular 3rd Grade at age 9

LeBlanc & Schwartzman, 1988) have proposed that categorical analyses may be more adequate than linear analyses for clinicians who have to make decisions for individual cases. If we measure with greater care what we intend to measure, it is likely that we will be able to create categories of subjects that are "pure" forms of a given maladjustment; then we should be in a better position to develop and assess specific treatments for specific behavioral pathologies.

My last point addresses the question: Why has so much attention been given to aggressive males and so little to aggressive females? The statistics presented in chapter 2 from the Ontario Child Health Study show again that girls are rated by teachers and mothers as much less conduct-disordered than boys. However, these statistics must be looked at from a broader perspective. The attempt to treat all these conduct-disordered, aggressive, disruptive, delinquent, criminal males is a very costly enterprise, and it has not been very successful (Dumas, in press; Farrington, Ohlin, & Wilson, 1986; Kazdin, 1987). Eron (1980) proposed that we try to socialize boys the way we socialize girls, because the latter have fewer problems with aggressive behavior. Although I agree with Eron that we should encourage boys to develop "socially positive qualities," I doubt that boys should be brought up as girls are, mainly because most boys are relatively well adjusted and the truly persistent antisocial males are a minority. The Cambridge study (Farrington, this volume) and others (Wolfgang, Figlio, & Sellin 1972; LeBlanc & Fréchette, 1979) have shown that approximately 6% of boys commit 50% of crimes. These boys were brought up in highly deprived families (Tables 1.4, 2.10, 2.11; see also Kolvin, Miller, Fleeting, & Kolvin, 1988) where it is quite difficult to help parents socialize their children (Dumas & Wahler, 1983), let alone socialize them the way middle-class girls are socialized.

I think that it is time that conduct-disordered girls get their share of the attention from scientists and clinicians (this comes from someone who is involved in a long-term longitudinal study of aggressive boys!). The Concordia study shows that conduct-disordered girls are much less at risk of committing a criminal offense (3.2%) than are conduct-disordered boys (42%), but they are more likely than other girls to become adolescent mothers, single parents, to have higher levels of psychiatric symptomatology, to be less competent mothers, and to have children with early signs of psychosocial difficulties. Our own data (Tremblay, Charlebois, & Gagnon, 1989) show that conduct-disordered boys in kindergarten (compared with non-conduct-disordered boys in kindergarten) are likely to have mothers who had their first child during adolescence or in their early 20s. Robins, West, and Herjanic (1975) showed that mothers who had been delinquents during adolescence had more daughters and sons who became delinquents. Robins (1986) also reported that conduct disorder for girls was a "good predictor" of later internalizing disorders, major depression, phobia, dysthymia, and obsessive compulsive disorder.

The Ontario Child Health Study statistics on self-reported conduct disorder in adolescent girls are also quite revealing. First, the number of girls who report conduct disorder is two to four times the number reported by parents. Second, when boys' reports are compared to girls' reports, the differences between sexes is greatly reduced. Finally, only 7% of the conduct-disordered adolescent girls, compared to 19% of the conduct disorded boys, are receiving mental health or social services. The gap is even greater for special education (7% vs. 32%).

The neglect of conduct-disordered girls is evident in scientific publications as much as in service delivery. To get larger *n*'s for statistical analyses, investigators either study only boys or pool boys and girls together and call them "children." We pay more attention to boys' conduct disorders and antisocial behavior, I believe, not because it is more frequent, but because it is generally more intense and disruptive and "here and now." However, we forget that the less intense, less disruptive, conduct-disordered girls quickly become mothers who start a new generation of highly disruptive conduct-disordered boys. From a research point of view, we need to start large longitudinal studies of conduct-disordered girls. From a prevention and treatment perspective, we need to think a few years ahead and realize that conduct-disordered girls, much more than conduct-disordered boys, are at risk of being the main—often only—parent figure for their children. If we are to break the reproductive cycle of social maladjustment, I propose that we will get better results by increasing the attention and energies we give to conduct-disordered girls. We have, however, some hard work to do, for there does not appear to be any magic wand available.

REFERENCES

Achenbach, T. M. (1978). The child behavior profile: 1. Boys aged 6–11. *Journal of Consulting and Clinical Psychology, 46,* 478–488.

Achenbach, T. M. & Edelbrock, C. S. (1978). The classification of child psychopathology: A review and analysis of empirical efforts. *Psychological Bulletin, 85* (6), 1275–1301.

American Psychiatric Association (1987). *Diagnostic and statistical manual of mental disorders* (3rd revised edition). (DSM-III). Washington, DC: American Psychiatric Press.

Dumas, J. E. (in press). Treating antisocial behavior in children: Child and family approaches. *Clinical Psychology Review.*

Dumas, J. E., & Wahler, R. G. (1983). Predictors of treatment outcome in parent training: Mother insularity and socioeconomic disadvantage. *Behavioral Assessment, 5,* 301–313.
Eron, L. D. (1980). Prescription for reduction of aggression. *American Psychologist, 35,* 244–252.
Eron, L. D., & Huesmann, L. R. (1984). Cognitive-processes and the persistence of aggressive behavior. *Aggressive Behavior, 10,* 243–251.
Farrington, D., Ohlin, L. E., & Wilson, J. Q. (1986). *Understanding and controlling crime, toward a new research strategy.* NY: Springer Verlag.
Hinde, R. A., & Dennis, A. (1986). Categorizing individuals: An alternative to linear analysis. *International Journal of Behavioral Development, 9,* 105–119.
Kazdin, A. E. (1987). Treatment of antisocial behavior in children: Current status and future direction. *Psychological Bulletin, 102(2),* 187–203.
Kolvin, I., Miller, F. J. W., Fleeting, J., & Kolvin, P. A. (1988). Social and parenting factors affecting criminal offense rates: Findings from the Newcastle thousand family study (1947–1980). *British Journal of Psychiatry, 152,* 80–90.
LeBlanc, M., & Fréchette, M. (1979). *La délinquance cachée à l'adolescence* [Self-reported delinquency of adolescents]. Montréal: Groupe de Recherche sur l'Inadaptation Juvénile, Université de Montréal.
Loeber, R., & Dishion, T. (1983). Early predictors of male delinquency: A review. *Psychological Bulletin, 94(1),* 68–99.
Magnusson, D. (1988). *Individual development from an interactional perspective.* (Paths through life, Vol. 1). Hillsdale, NJ: Lawrence Erlbaum Associates.
Moller, L., & Rubin, K. H. (1988). A psychometric assessment of a two factor solution for the preschool behavior questionnaire in mid-childhood. *Journal of Applied Development Psychology, 9,* 167–180.
Pekarik, E. G., Prinz, R. J., Liebert, D. E., Weintraub, S., & Neale, J. M. (1976). The pupil evaluation inventory. *Journal of Abnormal Child Psychology, 4,* 83–97.
Radke-Yarrow, M., Zahn-Waxler, C., & Chapman, M. (1983). Children's prosocial dispositions and behavior. In P. H. Mussen (Ed.), *Handbook of child psychology* (vol. 4, 4th ed.) (pp. 469–545). New York: Wiley.
Robins, L. N. (1986). The consequences of conduct disorder in girls. In D. Olweus, J. Block, & M. Radke-Yarrow (Eds.), *Development of antisocial and prosocial behavior* (pp. 385–414). New York: Academic Press.
Robins, L. N., West, P. A., & Herjanic, B. L. (1975). Arrests and delinquency in two generations: A study of Black urban families and their children. *Journal of Child Psychology and Psychiatry, 16,* 125–140.
Strayer, F. F., Noel, J. M., & Leclerc, D. (1989). Le développement et la socialisation des activités agonistiques en milieu préscolaire. In R. E. Tremblay (Eds.), *Le développement de l'agressivité.* Manuscript submitted for publication.
Tremblay, R. E., Charlebois, P., & Gagnon, C. (1989). La prédiction de troubles du comportement chez les garçons de maternelle: primauté de caractéristiques personnelles de la mére sur celles du pére. Manuscript submitted for publication.
Tremblay, R. E., Charlebois, P., Gagnon, C., & Larivée, S. (1986, July). *Prediction and prevention of juvenile delinquency in early childhood: The Montréal longitu-*

dinal study. 11th International Congress of the International Association for Child and Adolescent Psychiatry and Allied Professions, Paris.

Tremblay, R. E., Charlebois, P., Gagnon, C., & Larivée, S. (1988, July). *The predictive power of prosocial behavior for disruptive and non-disruptive kindergarten boys.* Paper presented at the VIIIth Biennial World Meeting of the International Society for Research on Aggression. Swansea.

Tremblay, R. E., Desmarais-Gervais, L., Gagnon, C., & Charlebois, P. (1987). Factor structure of the preschool behavior questionnaire: Stability between sexes, ages, socioeconomic classes and cultures. *International Journal of Behavioral Development, 10,* 467–484.

Tremblay, R. E., LeBlanc, M., & Schwartzman, S. E. (1988). The predictive power of first grade peer and teacher ratings of behavior and personality at adolescence. *Journal of Abnormal Child Psychology, 16(5),* 571–583.

Tremblay, R. E., Vitaro, F., Gagnon, C., Piché, C., & Royer, N. (1989). A prosocial scale for the preschool behavior questionnaire: Concurrent and predictive correlates. Manuscript submitted for publication.

Wolfgang, M. E., Figlio, R. M., & Sellin, T. (1972). *Delinquency in a birth cohort.* Chicago: University of Chicago Press.

Section 2: Dispositional Factors Associated with Childhood Aggression

4

Congenital Determinants of Violent and Property Offending

Patricia Brennan
Sarnoff Mednick
Elizabeth Kandel
University of Southern California

This chapter examines whether adolescent and adult criminal behavior is partly determined by factors already in place at the time of birth. We review the research on genetic influence and find evidence of hereditary transmission of criminal behavior, but only for property offending. We also consider the research on prenatal and perinatal factors and find evidence that these factors predict criminal behavior, but only for violent offending. In short, this chapter suggests that biological predispositions for criminal behavior do exist and that they take a different form for property and violent offending.

SPECIALIZATION

Before we try to understand the role that congenital factors play in violent and property offending, we must first consider whether these types of offenders actually exist. If property crime and violence are acts that *all* criminal offenders are equally likely to commit, then it could be said that specialization in these types of offending does not exist. If specialization does not exist, then there would be no reason to study the etiology of property and violent offending separately. On the other hand, if specialization does exist for these two types of criminal behavior, then studies that fail to distinguish between them may lose information. For example, critical information on unique histories that may predispose individuals to violent offending may be ignored if all criminal offenders are studied as one population.

Many investigators have addressed the question of specialization (Bursik, 1980; Klein, 1980; Phillpotts & Lancucki, 1979; Wolfgang, Figlio, & Sellin, 1972), and their conclusions have varied considerably. One major reason for this variation appears to be the differing definitions that are applied to the term *specialization*. For example, Wolfgang et al. (1972) have defined specialization as two contiguous offenses of the same type; they find no evidence for its occurrence at greater than chance levels. Phillpotts and Lancucki utilized a broader definition of specialization—a higher percentage of a single type of offending during a criminal career than would be expected to occur by chance alone—and found that it *does* exist.

We suggest that specialization exists if first-time violent offenders are more likely than previously *nonviolent* offenders to commit future violence, and if first-time property offenders are more likely than nonproperty offenders to commit future property crime. This method of assessing specialization has been applied to a fully ascertained birth cohort of 31,436 men born in Copenhagen, Denmark from January 1, 1944 to December 31, 1947 (Guttridge, Gabrielli, Mednick, & Van Dusen, 1983).

In Fig. 4.1, the percentage of offenders with subsequent violence whose first offense was violent is compared to the percent of offenders with subsequent violence whose first offense was nonviolent. This comparison is made for groups of offenders with equal numbers of total arrests. For the group with two to three arrests, no difference is seen between the rate of future violence for offenders with a violent first offense and offenders with a nonviolent first offense—in fact, very little future violence is observed at all. This finding makes sense, given the low

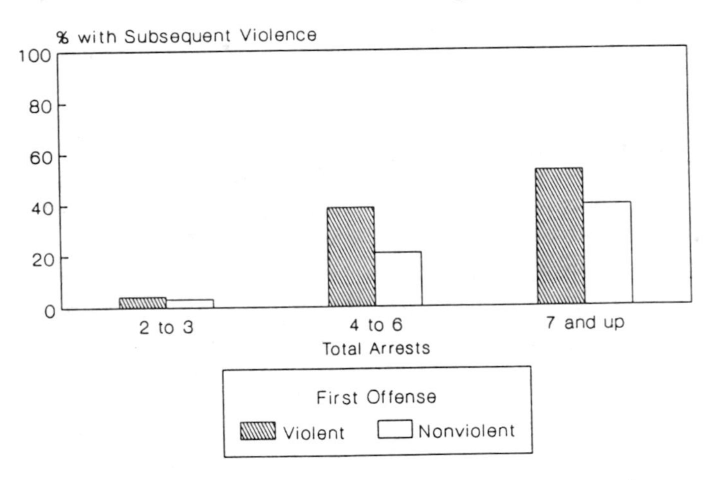

FIG. 4.1. Future violence of offenders categorized by first offense.

base rate of violent offending and the small number of total arrests for this group. For the groups with four to six arrests and seven or more arrests, however, a higher percentage of offenders with a violent first offense than offenders with a nonviolent first offense go on to commit future violent crimes. Note that this difference and all reported differences in this chapter are statistically significant.

In Fig. 4.2, the percentage of offenders with future violence whose *second* offense was violent is compared to the percentage of offenders with future violence whose second offense was nonviolent. Again, the same effect is observed. Offenders who *have* committed a violent offense are more likely to commit future violence than offenders who have *not* been previously violent. A similar finding was observed for property offending. These results suggest that some offenders are more likely than others to commit certain types of crime—to "specialize" in violent or property offending.

The existence of specialization suggests that certain individuals have some enduring personal characteristics that predispose them to property or violent offending. We can now consider whether congenital factors—inherited traits and perinatal experiences—contribute to these predispositions.

GENETIC INFLUENCES

Three methods of study—family, twin, and adoption—can be utilized to assess the effect of genetic influences on criminal behavior. Robins' (1966) classic family study revealed that one of the best predictors of antisocial behavior in boys is the criminal arrest record of their fathers.

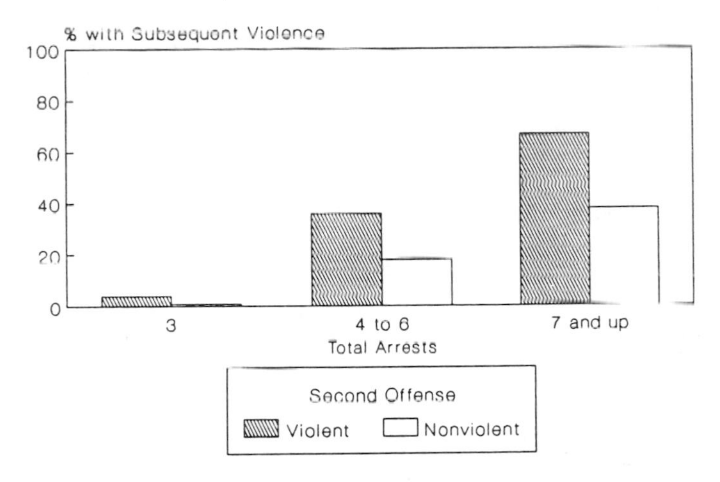

FIG. 4.2. Future violence of offenders categorized by second offense.

This type of finding cannot be considered definitive evidence of a genetic influence, as the father also plays a role in the child's *social* environment; most family studies are limited in this manner.

The objective of twin studies is to compare twins who are genetically identical (MZ) with twins who are not (DZ) in order to assess the role that genetic factors play in criminal behavior. A review of twin studies (Mednick & Volavka, 1980) reveals that MZ twins have a much higher concordance rate for criminal behavior than do DZ twins. In the best designed and largest of these studies, Christiansen (1977) reported a 35.2% pairwise concordance rate for male MZ twins and a 12.5% concordance rate for male DZ twins. This suggests that a genetic influence for criminal behavior does exist. Unfortunately, separate analyses were not done for property and violent crime. Moreover, some have suggested that the twin data may be questionable evidence of genetic influences because identical twins are not only more similar genetically but also are treated more similarly by their family and friends.

Adoption studies are better able to separate hereditary and environmental influences on behavior. For example, if the biological son of a severely criminal father is adopted at birth by a noncriminal family and that son becomes severely criminal, this may be seen as evidence (with appropriate controls) that the criminal father passed on to his son a biological characteristic that predisposed both men to criminal acts.

We studied the entire cohort of all 14,427 nonfamilial adoptions in Denmark from 1924 to 1947 (Mednick, Gabrielli, & Hutchings, 1984). The conviction rates of the identified members of this cohort are shown in Table 4.1.

The conviction rates for the biological fathers and their adopted-away sons are much higher than than those of the adoptive fathers. Moreover, most of the criminal adoptive fathers were one-time offenders; male

TABLE 4.1
Conviction Rates of Completely Identified Members of Adoptee Families

Family Member	Number Identified	Number Not Identified	Conviction rate by number of convictions			
			0	1	2	>2
Male adoptees	6,129	571	.841	.088	.029	.049
Female adoptees	7,065	662	.972	.020	.005	.003
Adoptive fathers	13,918	509	.938	.046	.008	.008
Adoptive mothers	14,267	160	.981	.015	.002	.002
Biological fathers	10,604	3,823	.714	.129	.056	.102
Biological mothers	12,300	2,127	.911	.064	.012	.013

adoptees and their biological fathers were more heavily recidivistic. Although the conviction rates of the women in this study were much lower, they appear to follow the same pattern as the males.

These data have been examined in a manner similar to the cross-fostering model used in behavior genetics. Females were not included in this analysis because of their low levels of conviction. Male adoptees with noncriminal biological fathers and criminal adoptive fathers were found to have evidenced a 14.7% conviction rate, which is not very different from the 13.5% rate observed for adoptees with noncriminal biological and noncriminal adoptive fathers. Thus, if the biological father is not convicted, adoptive father convictions are not associated with an elevation in adoptee convictions. Those male adoptees whose biological father was convicted and whose adoptive father was not evidenced a 20% conviction rate, quite a bit higher than the rates observed in the aforementioned groups. The highest percentage of criminal convictions (24.5%) was observed for adoptees with criminal biological and criminal adoptive fathers. These data seem to support the assumption of partial genetic etiology of criminal behavior.

In this same cohort, when the percentage of adoptive males convicted is plotted against the number of biological parent convictions, a positive near-linear relationship is noted (see Fig. 4.3). In order to simplify interpretation, all cases where adoptive parents have been convicted were excluded from this figure and the analyses from the adoption cohort presented after this point.

As can be seen from Fig. 4.3, biological parents with three or more

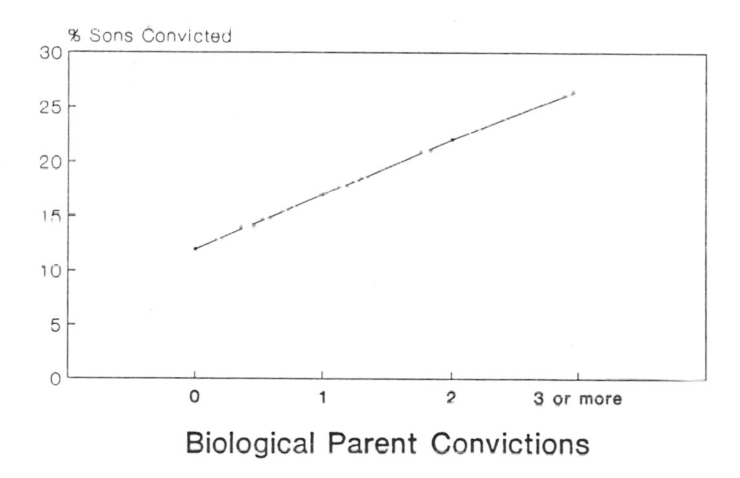

FIG. 4.3. Adoptive male convictions by biological parent convictions.

convictions have sons that are convicted at twice the rate of biological sons of nonoffenders.

This genetic effect appears to be stronger in cases where the biological parents are chronic offenders. As Table 4.2 reveals, the proportions of both low and high rates of criminal offending *increase* as a function of the level of the recidivism in the biological parents. About 25% of the adopted-away sons of chronic offenders become criminal offenders themselves.

As this chapter is concerned with the role that genetics plays in the unique histories of property and violent offenders, it is necessary to separate these two types of offenders in the analysis of the adoption data. In Fig. 4.4 we have plotted the percent of male adoptee *violent* and *property* offenders against biological parent convictions. Adoptee violent offenders may also have committed property crimes; however, no property offenders committed violent crimes.

As the figure reveals, a significant relationship exists between parents' convictions and property offending. A significant relationship does not exist for violent offending. In fact, the slight degree of relationship for violence in Fig. 4.4 disappears if the property crimes of the offenders are partialled out.

There has been one analysis of data from the adoption cohort that found biological parents' characteristics to be associated with adoptee violence (Moffitt, 1984). If one biological parent (typically the father) was frequently convicted and the other biological parent (typically the mother) was admitted to a hospital with an antisocial psychiatric diagnosis, then the adopted-away son was more likely to evidence violent offending. This may be a genetic effect, or it may be a result of the biological (antisocial) mother's poor health habits during pregnancy (alcohol, drugs, poor nutrition), which changed the development of the fetus' brain. This leads us directly into the next section, in which we consider evidence linking obstetrical factors and criminal behavior.

TABLE 4.2
Proportions of Offending in Male Adoptees by Level of Crime in Biological Parents

Number of Male Adoptee Convictions	*Number of Biological Parent Convictions*			
	0	*1*	*2*	*3 or More*
Nonoffenders	.87	.84	.80	.75
1 or 2 convictions	.10	.12	.15	.16
3 or more convictions	.03	.04	.05	.09
# of adoptees	2492	547	233	419

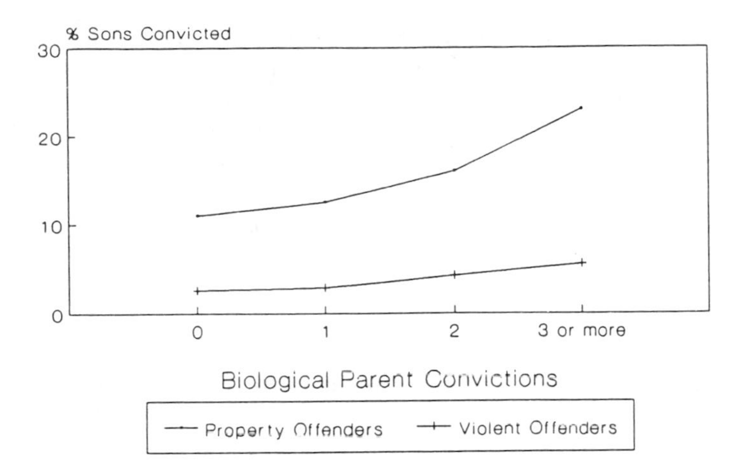

FIG. 4.4. Property/violent offenders by biological parent convictions.

OBSTETRICAL FACTORS

In 1861, W. J. Little observed that "the act of birth does occasionally imprint upon the nervous and muscular systems of the nascent infantile organism very serious and peculiar evils" (p. 343). It was not until 1934 that Rosanoff and his coworkers (Rosanoff, Handy, Rosanoff-Plesset, & Brush) suggested that adult behavioral deviance (schizophrenia) might be a consequence of perinatal events. Pasamanick, Rodgers, and Lilienfield (1956) studied the effect of obstetrical complications on behavior disorders in children. They found a significant relationship between such behavior disorders and prematurity, neonatal seizures, and pregnancy complications. Mungas (1983) noted a similar relationship between perinatal factors and violence in a sample of neuropsychiatric patients. Litt (1971) studied perinatal disturbances in a birth cohort of 1,944 individuals in Denmark born between January 1, 1936 and September 30, 1938. He discovered that perinatal trauma predicted impulsive criminal offenses that were ascertained at age 36. Birth factors do seem to be related to later behavioral deviance.

In contrast to genetic predisposition, the relationship between perinatal factors and criminal behavior seems to be particular to violent offending, rather than property or other, less serious types of offending. In 1977, Lewis and Shanok reported nonsignificant differences between delinquents' and nondelinquents' perinatal histories. Later, they compared nonincarcerated delinquents with incarcerated delinquents (who were significantly more violent), and discovered a positive relationship between more serious offending and perinatal difficulties (Lewis, Shanok, & Balla, 1979). These results are consistent with those that we obtained in a Danish perinatal project studying the long-term consequences of pregnancy, delivery, and neonatal difficulties (Mednick, Pollack, Volavka, & Gabrielli, 1982). When we observed delinquent *property* offenders as a unique population, we found that their medical, physical, and neurological progress in the pregnancy, delivery, and neonatal period was significantly *better* than that of nondelinquents. On the other hand, the *violent* delinquents in this cohort were found to have significantly *worse* one-year physical status and neurological status than the nondelinquents.

Utilizing 216 subjects from a Danish birth cohort, we have recently begun to study the effects of delivery complications on adolescent and adult criminal behavior. Delivery complications were recorded at birth and included such occurrences as weak labor, forceps extraction, and duration of labor for more than 3 days. A weighted score of complications was employed, and the median score was used to split subjects into two groups—those with high numbers of delivery complications and those with low numbers of delivery complications. Figure 4.5 presents the percentages of nonoffenders, property offenders, one-time violent offenders, and multiple violent offenders with *high* numbers of delivery complications.

As can be seen from this figure, only 46.9% of the nonoffenders, 29.1% of the property offenders, and 55.6% of the one-time violent offenders had high numbers of delivery complications. In contrast 80%, (a significantly higher percentage) of the multiple violent offenders evidenced high numbers of delivery complications. Again, we have evidence for a biological predisposition to violence caused by perinatal diffi-

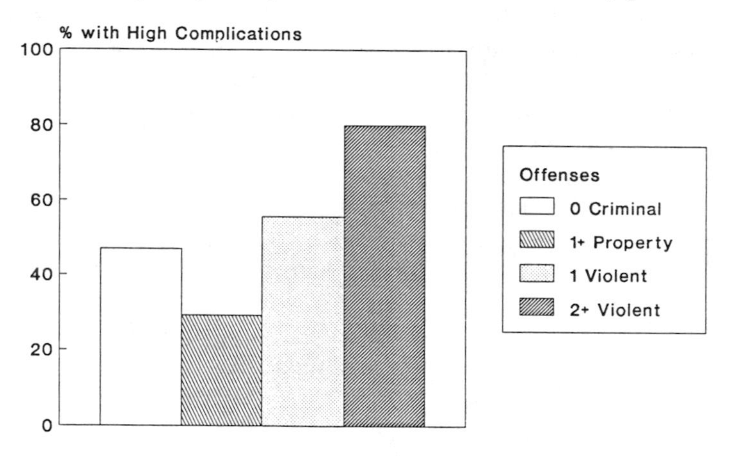

FIG. 4.5. Delivery complications and violent and property offending.

culties. We also note the useful distinction between one-time violent offenders and multiple violent offenders. Our data suggest that perinatal complications may predict specifically to persistent violent offending, rather than a single uncharacteristic outburst of violence.

We have studied one other index of obstetrical difficulty, in addition to delivery complications, in its relationship to violent and property offending. That index is minor physical anomalies (MPAs). Obstetrical difficulties may be massive, leading to the death or serious malformation of the fetus. Pregnancy complications may also produce less severe disturbances in the development of the fetus, evidenced externally only by MPAs. For example, consider the development of the ears. The ears start low on the neck of the fetus and gradually drift into their accustomed positions. If a teratogenic event or substance interferes, the development may be slowed or stopped and the ears' drift upward may end prematurely, resulting in low-seated ears—an observable MPA. Disturbances that cause MPAs might also cause unobservable anomalies in concurrently developing organs, including the central nervous system. We have utilized a count of MPAs as an index of such hidden anomalies.

Employing longitudinal data for a Danish birth cohort of 265 subjects, MPAs at age 12 were studied in relation to criminal offenses recorded by age 21. Although MPAs were not related to property offending, a strong positive relationship was discovered for violent offenders with more than one arrest for violence. Figure 4.6 presents the data for violent offending and MPAs. As can be seen, 33% of the subjects with no violent offending and 45% of the subjects with only one violent offense have high numbers (above the median) of MPAs. A significantly higher percentage (70%) of the subjects with two or more violent offenses have high numbers of MPAs.

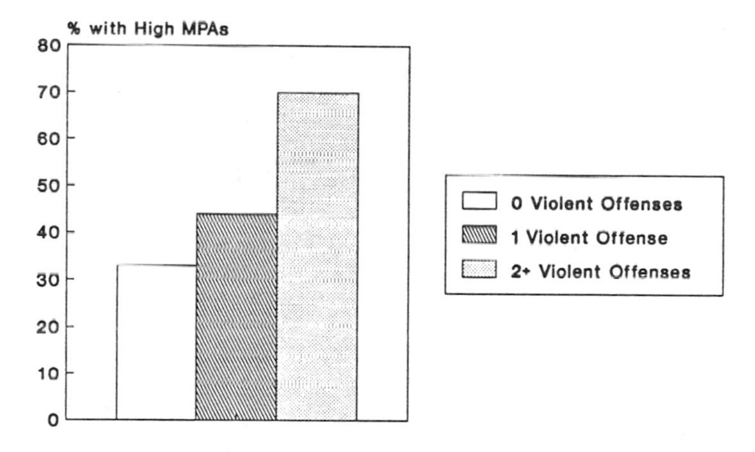

FIG. 4.6. Minor physical anomalies by number of violent offenses.

It should be noted that most of the subjects with only one arrest for violence had been charged with disorderly conduct, one of the least serious types of violent crime. In addition, those multiple violent offenders with *lower* numbers of MPAs had also been arrested only for disorderly conduct. Thus, these results are consistent with those of other studies that have found a relationship between obstetrical factors and serious, repetitive violent offending.

Aggressive behavior at very young ages has been found to be highly predictive of aggressive behavior in adolescence and adulthood (Olweus, 1979). Such a finding suggests that factors leading to aggression may be set in place very early in life. In this chapter, we suggest that perinatal factors may play a causal role in repetitive violent offending. Neurological dysfunction may be the mediating factor in this process. Perinatal difficulties have been found to be directly related to brain damage evidenced later in life (Nichols & Chen, 1981). Brain damage, in turn, may be at the basis of poor impulse control in emotionally laden situations, and subsequent increases in violent criminal behavior (Nachson & Denno, 1987).

IMPLICATIONS FOR TREATMENT AND PREVENTION

Both the existence of specialization and the unique predictive findings for violent and property offending suggest that different "types" of offenders exist. If this is so, then it seems plausible that quite different treatments might be suitable for these different types of delinquents. Further research that examines the unique characteristics of these offender types would be useful in developing specific treatment programs for them.

Our findings suggest that genetic, prenatal, and perinatal factors play a significant role in the prediction of criminal behavior. If this is so, then prevention programs may be designed on the basis of this information. For example, children found to be at "high risk" for violence (due to poor perinatal histories) could be placed in special programs designed to foster impulse control. Programs such as these may put a stop to delinquent behavior before it begins.

REFERENCES

Bursik, R. J. (1980). The dynamics of specialization in juvenile offenses. *Social Forces, 58,* 851–864.

Christiansen, K. O. (1977). A preliminary study of criminality among twins. In

S. A. Mednick & K. O. Christiansen (Eds.), *Biosocial bases of criminal behavior* (pp. 89–108). New York: Gardner Press.

Guttridge, P., Gabrielli, W. F., Mednick, S. A. & Van Dusen, K. T. (1983). Criminal violence in a birth cohort. In K. T. Van Dusen & S. A. Mednick (Eds.), *Prospective studies of crime and delinquency* (pp. 211–224).

Klein, M. W. (1980, August). *Cafeteria-style delinquency: Evidence and implications.* Paper presented at the meeting of the Society for the Study of Social Problems.

Lewis, D. O., & Shanok, S. S. (1977). Medical histories of delinquent and nondelinquent children: An epidemiological study. *American Journal of Psychiatry, 134,* 1020–1025.

Lewis, D. O., Shanok, S. S. & Balla, D. A. (1979). Perinatal difficulties, head and face trauma, and child abuse in the medical histories of seriously delinquent children. *American Journal of Psychiatry, 136,* 419–423.

Litt, S. M. (1971). *Perinatal complications and criminality.* Unpublished doctoral dissertation, University of Michigan.

Little, W. J. (1861). On the influence of abnormal parturition, difficult labours, premature birth and asphyxia neonatorum on the mental and physical condition of the child, especially in relation to deformities. *Transactions of the Obstetrical Society of London, 3,* 293–344.

Mednick, S. A., Gabrielli, W. F. & Hutchings, B. (1984). Genetic influences in criminal convictions: Evidence from an adoption cohort. *Science, 224,* 891–894.

Mednick, S. A., Pollack, V., Volavka, J. & Gabrielli, W. F. (1982). Biology and violence. In M. E. Wolfgang & N. A. Weiner (Eds.), *Criminal violence* (pp. 21–80). Beverly Hills: Sage.

Mednick, S. A. & Volavka, J. (1980). Biology and crime. In N. Morris & M. Tonry (Eds.), *Crime and justice: An annual review of research: Vol. II* (pp. 85–158) Chicago: University of Chicago Press.

Moffitt, T. E. (1984). *Genetic influence of parental psychiatric illness of violent and recidivistic criminal behavior.* Unpublished doctoral dissertation, University of Southern California.

Mungas, D. (1983). An empirical analysis of specific syndromes of violent behavior. *Journal of Nervous and Mental Disease, 171,* 354–361.

Nachson, I., & Denno D. (1987). Violent behavior and cerebral hemisphere dysfunctions. In S. A. Mednick, T. E. Moffitt, & S. A. Stack (Eds.), *The causes of crime: New biological approaches* (pp. 185–217). New York: Cambridge University Press.

Nichols, P. L., & Chen, T. (1981). *Minimal brain dysfunction: A prospective study.* Hillsdale, NJ: Lawrence Erlbaum Associates.

Olweus, D. (1979). Stability of aggressive reaction patterns in males: A review. *Psychological Bulletin, 86,* 852–875.

Pasamanick, B., Rodgers, M. E., & Lilienfield, A. M. (1956). Pregnancy experience and the development of behavior disorders in children. *American Journal of Psychiatry, 112,* 613–618.

Phillpotts, G. J., & Lancucki, L. B. (1979). *Previous convictions, sentence and reconviction.* London: Her Majesty's Stationery Office.

Robins, L. N. (1966). *Deviant children grown up.* Baltimore: Williams and Wilkens.

Rosanoff, A. J., Handy, L. M., Rosanoff-Plesset, I., & Brush, S. (1934). The etiology of so-called schizophrenic psychoses. *American Journal of Psychiatry, 91,* 247–286.

Wolfgang, M., Figlio, R. M., & Sellin, T. (1972). *Delinquency in a birth cohort.* Chicago: University of Chicago Press.

5

Origins of Externalizing Behavior Problems at Eight Years of Age

John E. Bates
Kathryn Bayles
David S. Bennett
Beth Ridge
Melissa M. Brown
Indiana University

This chapter concerns a longitudinal study of the development of children's social adjustments. The research focuses on common problems of childhood adjustment, including difficulties as seen by parents, elementary school teachers, and peers.

Previous models of social development tended to rely on relatively simple, causal mechanisms. Learning or behavioral models emphasized conditioning processes; psychodynamic models emphasized complex affective and mental processes. In both kinds of model the parental behavior dimensions of love rejection and dominance–submission were the primary causal factors. For example, children's aggressiveness toward peers and defiance toward teachers were thought to result from parental neglect or rejection and harsh discipline (e.g., see review by Hetherington & Martin, 1979).

More recently, theories of the origins of children's social competency have been increasingly complex systems models. The behavioral and psychodynamic models have been incorporated in the systems models, rather than discarded, and newer concepts about psychobiological processes have been added. There is still an emphasis on parental behaviors as causal factors (e.g., see Patterson, 1986), but not so exclusively. Parental behaviors, important as they may be, are seen as themselves subject to other influences. They are part of a dynamic, transactional system in which biological, psychological, and sociological factors are all intertwined. Qualities of parenting are themselves partly determined by child behavioral dispositions and external, environmental stresses on the family. For example, child aggressiveness and defiance are seen as the culmination of a complex process involving parental neglect and harshness that are functions of parental predispositions (e.g., depression; Patterson, 1982), of child predispositions (e.g., tendency to be coercive; Lee & Bates, 1985), and of stressors such as losing a job.

A further complication in the modern systems models is their emphasis on the likely importance of moderator variables, that is, specific conditions in which a hypothetical causal process will and will not operate. The best, most extensively studied example is child gender: Linkages between early experiences and later behavioral and cognitive competencies differ for boys and girls. Most striking is the evidence that boys' behavioral adjustments are more adversely affected by family stress, especially parent–parent conflict, than those of girls (Emery, 1982; Hetherington, 1989; Rutter & Garmezy, 1983). However, except for this finding, there are not many good empirical examples. There are many plausible interactions between variables across development, few replications of the ones that have been noted, and conceptual difficulties in the statistics used to evaluate interactions between correlated predictors usually used in this kind of research (Viken, manuscript in progress). The newest of the systems models emphasize the dynamic, emerging nature of the phenomena of development; they emphasize the chaos (Gleick, 1987) in nature, and warn that prediction of some long-term outcomes is not likely to be possible (Thelen, in press). One wonders if the search for predictable antecedents to child behavioral adjustment differences is futile.

There is no question that the interactive, nonlinear-type models currently offer the description of the developmental process that is richest and most in tune with our clinical theories and experiences. However, for the present, there has been inadequate exploration of even the simpler, linear models against which the nonlinear models must be judged. The theoretical and measurement foundations for specific nonlinear models are weak. In past analyses, we have evaluated a wide range of possible interaction effects, with a relatively low yield (e.g. Bates, Olson, Pettit, & Bayles, 1982). In the current study, we focus mainly on the simple, linear effects models, but we do analyze boys' and girls' data separately.

One further moderator variable with important implications for research strategy is normal range versus extreme group sampling. Rutter (1983) has noted that processes operating in extreme samples, such as socioeconomically distressed families, may be different from those operating in normal samples. Assuming that disproportionate numbers of children with behavioral and academic problems come from that small percent of multiproblem families who so greatly challenge social service agencies, a good research strategy would be to study the developmental process in such families (e.g., see Erickson, Sroufe, & Egeland, 1985; Renken, Egeland, Marvinney, Mangelsdorf, & Sroufe, in press). It seems unlikely, however, that such families would account for the largest proportion of adjustment problems in the population as a whole, especially when the full range of problems, from moderate to extreme, is considered. For the sake of more general models and, ultimately, more widely useful prevention recommendations, studies should be done on nonclinical, non-high-risk populations, too.

THE BLOOMINGTON LONGITUDINAL STUDY

Basic Design. The longitudinal study described here was designed as a multivariate, follow-through study on a generally normal sample, in a medium-sized town (approximately 50,000). Socioeconomic levels of the participants ranged from poor, working class to affluent, upper–middle class, but were predominantly comfortable working class to middle–middle class. The sample cannot address the role of squalid housing, malnutrition, and highly chaotic family relationships, but it has the advantage of being fairly representative of the range of conditions experienced by most children in our society. There were 168 families recruited when the children were 6 months of age. The sharpest decline in participation was at the first follow-up: At 13 months, the *N* was 139. Since then, sample sizes have ranged from about 90 to 120, depending on the particular follow-up and resources to pursue families who had moved or were reluctant to participate. Analyses have shown that there has not been differential loss of the lower-functioning families.

Temperament Measures. From the outset, there has been a special emphasis on the construct of temperament, the most frequently cited biological factor in systems models. We took special care to develop meaningful measures and concepts of temperament relevant to the question of how behavior problems develop, especially the concept of difficult temperament, introduced by Thomas, Chess, and Birch (1968). The sample was designed to depart from normality in one way—more difficult and easy and fewer average infants were included. The parts of the sample in each category were, respectively, 29%, 31%, and 40%. Bates (1987; in press) and Bates & Bayles (1984) have presented some of what we have concluded from our temperament work. Mother perceptions of infant temperament were collected on the Infant Characteristics Questionnaire (ICQ; Bates, Freeland, & Lounsbury, 1979) at 6 months of age, and on age-adjusted forms of the ICQ at 13 months and 24 months. For construct-validation purposes, other temperament questionnaires were collected at various points, including the McDevitt & Carey (1978) Behavioral Style Questionnaire at 7 years. Observational indexes of temperament were also collected.

Questionnaire Measures of Child Adjustment. Parent and teacher questionnaire measures of child behavior problems and positive social adjustment have been pivotal in the research. Despite their limitations, they are the most practical basis for any wide-scale screening, and caregiver perceptions are, in fact, the main bases for natural designations of psychopathology versus adjustment. At 3 years, mothers completed the Preschool Behavior Questionnaire (PBQ; Behar, 1977). At ages 4–8 years, mothers completed the Child Behavior Checklist (CBCL; Achenbach & Edelbrock, 1983), which primarily assesses behavior problems, but also some positive competencies. At ages 6 and 8 years, teachers completed the teacher form of the CBCL. At 8 years, mothers rated children on the Home Behavior Scale (HBS), a questionnaire newly developed to assess competencies in positive social roles and other activities in greater detail than the pre-existing, pathology-oriented questionnaires.

Other Measures. Although the questionnaire measures of temperament, behavior problems, and other forms of social competency were crucial, it was important to establish a network of validation around these measures. Consequently, we have looked at many other variables describing the process of development. We used not only questionnaires but also naturalistic and standardized observations, with both highly objective, molecular codes and more impressionistic ratings. The specific variables in the general domains were chosen to represent theoretically interesting, empirically supported concepts, as well as a few hunches based on clinical experience. There was no single, guiding framework for selecting variables, unless one wants to call the systems model a theory. Eclecticism seemed the most prudent strategy. Not every measure was used in the current analyses, but the major domains are listed here so the reader can have a more complete overview of the project:

1. *Mother–child interaction* at home was observed in two, 3-hour periods at 6 months and at 24 months, and one 3-hour period at 13 months. Molecular behavior codes were factor analyzed and summarized in reliable, stable composites. Along with various sequential indexes, these home observation scores have been extensively validated (Bates et al., 1982; Lee & Bates, 1985; Olson, Bates, & Bayles, 1984; Pettit & Bates, 1984).

2. In the second of the two waves of subjects, at age 13 months, *attachment security* was assessed in the standard Ainsworth strange situa-

tion paradigm (Ainsworth, Blehar, Waters, & Wall, 1978). The attachment classifications have been well validated (Frankel & Bates, in press; Kiser, Bates, Maslin, & Bayles, 1986; Maslin & Bates, 1988).

3. *Child cognitive abilities* were assessed via the Bayley (1969) scales of mental development at 6, 13, and 24 months, and via the Peabody picture vocabulary test at 24 months and 6 years (Dunn & Dunn, 1981). Another kind of social-cognitive ability, envisioning solutions to interpersonal problems, was assessed via the Spivack and Shure (1974) Preschool Interpersonal Problem Solving test at 6 years and the Rubin (1980) Social Problem Solving Test-Revised at 8 years.

4. *Child self-control and task orientation* were assessed at 6 and 8 years in a set of laboratory tasks (see Olson, Bates, & Bayles, 1989), including walking and drawing lines slowly, coloring shapes in the presence of interesting toys and "gifts," and the Matching Familiar Figures Test (Kagan, Rosman, Albert, & Phillips, 1964).

5. *Mother personality* was assessed via Jackson's (1974) Personality Research Form at 6 months and a short form of the MMPI at 3 years.

6. *Family stress and coping* were measured via interviews with the mother at 6 months and 6 years and via the Spanier (1976) scale of marital adjustment at 3 and 6 years.

Prior Findings

Based on the lack of any preeminent theory, the existing empirical literature, and the expected limitations of reliability and validity of the measures, one would expect that links between measures would be mostly of a small order. Therefore, we felt that a narrow-focus strategy of analysis would yield mostly null or tenuous results, and we adopted the strategy of searching more broadly to increase the chances of detecting significant linkages.

Fishing Expeditions. There are some dangers in the broad-scale strategy of data analysis. Our work has been sometimes criticized as a "fishing expedition." When used by critics, the term implies a lack of theory-driven hypothesis testing, with the danger of being fooled by spurious results. There are scientific advantages to narrowly focused tests of hypotheses, and there are real dangers in accepting post hoc explanations. Furthermore, when one considers a large number of statistical relationships simultaneously, one can exceed human information organizing capacity and end up with a fairly meaningless jumble. If one does find confirmation in the data for a limited set of hypotheses, that certainly does add to one's confidence in the model generating the hypotheses. However, there has never been a test of anything approaching a full systems model. And the fact that certain statistical relationships have been found does not mean that others are not still latent in the data.

We do recognize the dangers, but still do not see "fishing expeditions" or "hunting trips" so negatively. What is the implicit, opposing metaphor? Is it gardening? Should we be putting out seeds of known types in well-prepared ground and then harvesting what was expected all along? The current state of theory and the sparse data base seem more suited to the hunting/fishing metaphor. Some of the most relevant prior conclusions (trophies of previous years' fishing trips) in the Bloomington Longitudinal Study are briefly listed hereafter.

Temperament. We have developed and explored the meanings of several short scales of infant and toddler temperament. Many identify us with the position that temperament questionnaires need to be regarded as social perceptions (Bates, 1980), but fewer understand well what we mean by that: Social perceptions have both objective and subjective meanings. Each of these meaning components has empirical support, and it is generally clear that the subjective elements in mother reports do not overshadow the objective elements (Bates & Bayles, 1984). Moreover, the research has shown an impressive degree of continuity in differentiated perceptions. For example, infants' temperamental *difficultness,* as we have defined it via factor analyses, primarily refers to frequent and intense displays of negative emotion, whereas *unadaptability* refers to negative reactions to new people and situations, and these two factors remain distinct across ages 6 to 24 months. A third, early-appearing, temperament-like dimension showing the same kind of continuity is *resistance to control* of activity, as indexed by perceptions of the child such as ignoring "no-no."

Early Cognitive/Verbal Competence. Intelligence has often been found to have a concurrent relationship with acting-out problems in children (Rutter & Garmezy, 1983). IQ- and related deficits could be both causes and effects of developmental psychopathology. Our previous findings agree with other research in suggesting that individual differences in intelligence develop in the context of positive maternal involvement with the infant and toddler, which is partly predictable by social class (Olson, Bates, & Bayles, 1986). The current phase of the study can ask what consequences early intelligence might have.

Control Issues. Difficult temperament, even measured at 6 months of age, but especially when measured at 24 months, predicted relatively frequent *negative control* interactions at age 24 months. The difficult children got into positions of possible trouble more often than other children but did not actually complete more trouble acts, and their mothers issued more initial and repeated prohibitions and warnings and used more physical restraint. Difficult group dyads were also higher than average or easy child dyads on *conflict sequence* indexes, in which the child engaged in some trouble behavior, the mother sought to control it, and the child resisted that control through ignoring, repeating the action, or expressing negative emotion (Lee & Bates, 1985). This pattern is interpreted as a possible representative of the emergence of the kind of coercive interaction style that Patterson (1982) has found prevalent in aggressive children.

Dyadic Problem Solving. At 24 months, we videotaped mother–toddler interactions in the Matas, Arend, and Sroufe (1978) tool problems for the last wave of subjects. As described by Frankel and Bates (in press), the major factor in observed behavior, *discordant task interaction,* indexed levels of child anger, noncompliance, aggression toward the mother, nonenthusiasm, and time off task, and mother unsupportiveness and low-quality assistance. Many of these variables individually and the factor as a whole were predicted by attachment insecurity assessed at 13 months. The factor was also predicted by the relative absence of positive involvement observed in the home at 6 and 13 months, especially for dyads with boys.

Behavior Problems at 3 Years. Mothers' temperament reports predicted their behavior problem reports at age 3 years, and in a differentiated fashion. Unadaptability predicted the PBQ Anxious scale. Resistance to control of activity predicted the PBQ Hostile and Hyperactive scales. And difficultness predicted all three types of problems. This pattern is discussed more extensively in the section on the 8-year follow-up. Home observation measures generally did not predict mother behavior problem scores, although there were some links between conflict sequences at 2 years and mother perceptions of behavior problems a year later. Child cognitive competency, contrary to expectation, did not predict 3-year behavior problems as seen by the mothers. High problem scores as rated by secondary caregivers (including preschool teachers, regular babysitters, and close relatives other than the fathers) were slightly (i.e., to a modest degree of correlation) predicted by low scores on the early cognitive development tests and by low positive involvement observed in mother–child interactions. Attachment security did not predict behavior problems at 3 years. Details of these findings can be found in Bates, Maslin, and Frankel (1985) and Bates, Pettit, and Bayles (1981).

Behavior Problems at 5 and 6 Years. Mother temperament reports at ages 6–24 months predicted their later reports of behavior problems on the CBCL, especially for boys, in a differentiated fashion similar to that seen at age 3. PBQ Anxious scores predicted CBCL Internalizing scores, and PBQ Hostile predicted CBCL Externalizing. In addition, early home observation of relative absence of positive involvement predicted higher levels of both internalizing and externalizing problems, especially among girls. Attachment security did not predict the behavior problem indexes (Bates & Bayles, 1988).

FOLLOW-UP AT EIGHT YEARS

Here, we describe the age-8 problem and competency outcomes of the children in the Bloomington Longitudinal Study, as well as the origins of a few of those outcomes. The age-8 follow-up is particularly important for two reasons. First, research generally agrees that individual differences at this age in psychopathology, especially conduct problems, are fairly representative of subsequent characteristics (e.g., Kohlberg, LaCrosse, & Ricks, 1972). Second, the assessments at this age were more extensive than any of our previous follow-ups. Measures included not only checklist descriptions of the children by parents, but also teacher reports and peer sociometrics. And not only did we assess problem behaviors, but we also made a special effort to assess positive social behaviors.

There were several, more particular issues concerning the origins of the children's outcomes. Were early mother temperament reports still predictive even 7 or 8 years later? If so, were they predictive in the same, well-differentiated way as they were at ages 3–6? Would the behavior problems at ages 3–6 predict behavior at age 8 in a differentiated fashion, analogous to the differentiation in mother perception antecedents of 3- and 6-year behavior problems? Would a more impressive role for early intelligence emerge at age 8 than had been seen at earlier outcome assessments?

Before we could find meaningful answers to the question of antecedents, we had to ask about the nature of the outcome variables: Were perceptions of the child by parents convergent with those of teachers, peers, and laboratory testers? Should we think of positive social competencies and behavior problems as independent dimensions or as alternate poles of a single dimension? Depending on the nature of the links among the outcomes, it was possible that there would be different antecedents of mother, teacher, and peer indexes of child problems and positive competencies.

Outcome Domains

To see meanings in the outcome measures beyond their surface content, we examined intercorrelations among the many outcome measures, ultimately through principal components analysis. The first analyses allowed consolidation of the list of variables. For example, there were high correlations between teacher reports of academic performance at years 7 and 8, even though the teachers were different at the two follow-ups; so these measures were averaged prior to inclusion in the principal components analysis. The principal components analysis shown in Table 5.1 suggests that the set of 29, somewhat condensed outcome variables can be summarized further in four dimensions.

I. Academic-social Competence

First is a broad dimension of social and academic competence measured at school. One of the factor's central loadings was for a teacher variable called "academic progress," which summed teacher Achenbach questionnaire ratings including academic performance, how much the child is learning, and how hard the child is working (averaged across follow-ups at 7 and 8 years). The factor was also defined by teacher ratings of conduct (summing ratings of happiness and appropriateness of behavior, not averaging across ages). Consistent with these loadings, more detailed ratings of the child's conduct, on the teacher CBCL internalizing and externalizing behavior problem scales (averaging years 7 and 8), load negatively on the factor. Mother academic reports also load highly, which shows some convergence between teacher and mother views. The first dimension also includes peers' ratings of how much they like to play with the child and nominations of the child as being one of their best friends. Finally, the dimension has a significant but nondiscriminating loading for ratings of task orientation in the laboratory tasks.

It was not surprising to see convergence among the teacher's ratings of child internalizing and externalizing behavior, academic competence, and peer status, although one might have expected a more noticeable bifurcation between behavioral adjustment and academic competence. However, we were surprised to see the peer ratings loading with the academic indexes. Bivariate correlations between peer and academic scores were in the .30 to .45 range, suggesting that the convergence is of a modest order, even though significant. It is intriguing to speculate on how the relationship emerges: Does it reflect a generally competent child, meeting both academic and social demands of school (vs. the opposite pattern)? Or do children see academically competent pupils as better prospects for friendship? Or do both happen?

TABLE 5.1
Factor Loadings for Principal Components Analysis of 7- and 8-Year Child Outcome Variables

Variables	*Factor Loadings*			
Factor I. (18.1% of total variance)	*I*	*II*	*III*	*IV*
1. Academic progress, teacher (7&8yr)	*.83*	−.11	.00	.19
2. Externalizing behavior, teacher (7&8yr)	*−.80*	.01	.20	.19
3. Academic status, mother (8yr)	*.74*	.00	.32	.14
4. Happy, appropriate beh., teacher (8yr)	*.70*	−.10	−.04	.11
5. Happy, appropriate beh., teacher (7yr)	*.64*	.00	−.16	.04
6. Avg. "like to play" rating, sociom. (8yr)	*.62*	−.08	.06	.06
7. Academic status, mother (7yr)	*.60*	−.02	.26	.22
8. Internalizing behavior, teacher (7&8yr)	*−.58*	.08	−.07	.25
9. "Best friend" nominations, sociom. (8yr)	*.55*	−.19	.03	.00
10. Task orientation, laboratory (8yr)	.28	.12	.11	.28
Factor II. (12.5%)				
1. Internalizing behavior, mother (7&8yr)	.11	*.82*	−.08	−.06
2. Externalizing behavior, mother (7&8yr)	−.10	*.78*	−.09	−.01
3. Difficult, mother, BSQ, (7yr)	−.10	*.76*	.04	.20
4. Unadaptable, mother, BSQ, (7yr)	−.07	*.58*	−.39	.22
5. Task orientation, mother, BSQ, (7yr)	.25	*−.49*	.11	.21
6. Low threshold, mother, BSQ, (7yr)	−.06	*.49*	.07	.10
7. Cooperative/compliant, mother, HBS, (8yr)	.01	−.44	.44	−.09
8. Positive peer relations, mother, HBS, (8yr)	.29	−.43	.07	−.43
Factor III. (8.1%)				
1. Social involvement, mother (8yr)	.08	−.08	*.68*	.11
2. Creative/engaged, mother, HBS, (8yr)	−.10	−.20	*.61*	.19
3. Sociable/affectionate, mother, HBS, (8yr)	.07	−.13	*.56*	−.35
4. Social activities, mother (8yr)	.32	.15	*.51*	−.07
5. Social activities, mother (7yr)	.33	.19	*.48*	−.04
6. Extraverted/sociable, laboratory (8yr)	−.20	−.07	*.38*	−.02
Factor IV. (5.9%)				
1. Flex./relevancy, problem solving (8yr)	−.10	.00	.07	*−.68*
2. Social involvement, mother (7yr)	.11	−.03	.49	.52
3. Proportion of agonistic solutions, problem solving (8yr)	−.10	−.12	.33	−.44
4. Rhythmicity, mother, BSQ, (7yr)	−.06	−.22	.26	*−.42*
5. Number of solutions, prob. solving (8yr)	−.00	−.02	.13	.16

Note: Discriminating loadings are underlined. Principal components analysis, varimax rotation, 4-factor solution with pairwise deletion of missing values. First four factors accounted for 44.7% of total variance. Initial eigenvalues greater than 1.0 (first 10 factors): 5.25, 3.63, 2.35, 1.72, 1.62, 1.57, 1.50, 1.16, 1.14, 1.09. *N*s ranged from 87 to 128 in the correlation matrix, with 43 subjects contributing data for all variables. Mother and teacher ratings are from the Achenback CBCL unless otherwise noted.

II. Maternal Perception of Personality/Adjustment

The second outcome is best defined by the internalizing and externalizing composites of the mother CBCL (averaged across years 7 and 8) and a difficultness composite (negative mood and intensity) that we extracted from the McDevitt and Carey (1978) Behavioral Style Questionnaire. The BSQ is a measure of the 9 Thomas-Chess temperament dimensions. It was administered to the mothers at age 7. The factor also includes two other BSQ indexes created by us, including unadaptability (the adaptability and the approach scales) and, loading negatively, task orientation (based on Keogh, 1986: distractability, activity, and persistence). The BSQ low threshold (for response to stimulation) score also helped define the factor. Two subscales of the Home Behavior Scale (HBS), completed by mothers at age 8, Cooperative-Compliant and Positive Peer Relations, had substantial negative loadings on the second factor, consistent with the overall content of the factor, but also had similar-sized loadings on other factors. Overall, the factor suggests that mothers' perceptions of their children's acting-out, anxiety, and temperament-like behaviors covaried.

III. Active Engagement

The third component suggests an independent dimension of social competence, primarily as perceived by the mother. It is defined by mother report on the CBCL of the child's social involvement at 8 years, two Home Behavior Scale composites, Creative-Engaged (reflecting the child's ability to fill free time with worthwhile activities and to play creatively) and Sociable-Affectionate (reflecting the child giving affection and gifts, telling parents about activities, and exchanging phone calls with friends), and CBCL indexes of involvement in hobbies and other activities at 7 and 8 years. It is also defined by our ratings of sociability or extraversion in the laboratory visit at 8 years. The factor also has a substantial, nondefining loading for level of social involvement at 8 years.

IV. Social Cognition

Finally, the fourth component groups social cognition indexes from the object-acquisition scenarios of the Social Problem Solving Test-Revised. Most central is a composite of relevancy of solutions and flexibility (offering different kinds of solutions in successive "attempts" to solve the problem). Proportion of agonistic solutions and total number of solutions also load to a modest degree on the factor. Finally, the loading for the BSQ rhythmicity scale suggests that children who do not go to sleep immediately at night and who eat between regular meals are somewhat more likely to do poorly on the social cognitive problem-solving task. Among other post hoc explanations, this linkage may reflect chronic sleep deficit (Bates, in press; Weissbluth, in press).

Implications. What do the principal components tell about the meanings of the outcome measures? First, there is a high degree of independence in how mothers and teachers perceive the same child in terms of presence or absence of behavior problems. This converges with prior findings (Achenbach & Edelbrock, 1986). Can this relative independence be ascribed simply to rater variance? No, because the peer assessments of the child's likeability converge with the teacher ratings of behavior problems and academic characteristics, and so do mother ratings of academic status. We would ascribe the independence more to situational effects. A second implication of the components analysis is that there is evidence that levels of problem behaviors and positive competencies vary independently, although perhaps only in the perceptions of mothers. Mothers can see their children as high in behavior problems without necessarily seeing them as low in creativity and positive, active engagement with people and things. Third, a similar point can be made about cognitive problem-solving skills. The relationships among the outcome variables suggest that the child who does well in listing varied and relevant solutions to hypothetical problems of getting another child to share a toy may or may not be correspondingly low in behavior problems as seen by the mother. The child also may or may not be correspondingly high in ratings of competence and popularity by teacher and peers. This is not to say that there is absolutely no relationship between these variables, just that it is quite small if there is any. In short, it appears that there are relatively distinct facets in children's adjustments at 7–8 years of age in our sample. It is possible that these different facets have different paths of development.

Antecedents

The current chapter focuses on the antecedents of only one of the outcome domains: mother ratings of behavior problems. This is a logical first choice, because parent perceptions are the most crucial in designating psychopathology. Success in school is also relevant to evaluations of development, however, and as shown earlier, is relatively independent of mother ratings. Therefore, for the sake of enhancing further the meaning of the maternal rating outcome, via contrast, the chapter also briefly describes the important antecedents of a composite measure of the child's competence in school.

Antecedents of Mother Ratings of Child Psychopathology

Psychopathology Outcome Indexes. Although the internalizing and externalizing summary scales of the CBCL load on the same factor in the outcome domain analyses reported previously, we decided to keep them as separate targets. This was done for theoretical reasons, given the previously mentioned evidence of somewhat separate developmental paths for the two kinds of disorder. For the analyses reported, 7- and 8-year CBCL scores were averaged together. Because of the aggression focus of this book, we also did preliminary analyses on individual scales of the CBCL, including the aggression scale, but viewing the aggression scale by itself did not reveal much more than the more aggregated externalizing scale. Also because of the book's focus, we present mainly the data on antecedents of externalizing. The origins of internalizing are briefly summarized, too, however, because they shed extra light on the meaning of the externalizing scores.

As discussed previously, in general, mother and teacher perceptions of child psychopathology did not converge. However, when the concurrent correlations were examined separately for boys and girls, there were some interesting departures from the general finding: When mothers described their sons as high in internalizing, the teachers were somewhat more likely to describe them as low in externalizing problems, $r(65) = -.27$, $p = .03$. Perhaps this reflects fearful boys being less likely to be rough and overexuberant at school. When mothers described their daughters as high in externalizing, the teachers tended to agree, $r(51) = .29$, $p = .03$. Perhaps this suggests that a girl's externalizing behaviors are more consistent across settings.

Antecedent Indexes. We now turn to the search for antecedents of the mother-perceived behavior problem outcomes of boys and girls. The future behavior problems of the 8-year-old are not marked by neon lights in the early record, but there are a few, discernable clues even in the first 2 years. We selected a set of plausible predictors from 11 sets of antecedent variables: (a) mother perceptions of temperament (3 major, cross-age composites, plus the variables from 6, 13, and 24 months separately correlated with the separate 7 and 8-year outcomes, as a finer-grain check on possible temperament roots); (b) mother perceptions of behavior problems (7 scores); (c) teacher CBCL at age 6 (2 scores); (d) positive involvement measures from the home observations at 6–24 months (18 scores); (e) dyadic problem solving at 24 months (the main factor, Discordant Task Interaction) and attachment security at 13 months, both collected only for the latter part of the sample; (f) negative control and conflict measures from the home observations (14 scores);

(g) child cognitive development tests from 6 months to 6 years (5 scores); (h) mother personality scales selected from those given at 6 months and 3 years (9 scores); (i) child self-control tests at 6 years (3 scores); (j) cognitive social problem-solving test at 6 years (2 scores); and (k) family SES and marital stress assessed at 6 months and 6 years (10 scores). In what follows, we consider how these 11 different antecedents predicted outcomes at 7–8 years, with boys' and girls' outcomes considered separately. In each of the following tables of results for externalizing problems, the significant predictor correlations (two-tail test) are listed for each predictor domain. In cases where a particular measure had shown a significant link to a related measure in analyses at the 6-year follow-up, and the present correlation was in the same direction and general range of size of the previous one, we have listed the correlation in the table even if it is not significant. This is relevant only for the temperament, positive involvement, and negative control domains.

Boys' Externalizing. The antecedents detected for boys' acting-out problems were nearly all indicators of early problems of control. Table 5.2 shows that earlier externalizing-type behavior problems predicted later externalizing. Because levels of internalizing and externalizing symptoms tend to covary, we computed partial correlations between early and later externalizing, controlling for the later internalizing score. The results suggest that there is continuity in mother perception of externalizing specifically, not simply in generalized behavior problems. As shown in the "Mother PBQ & CBCL" section of the table, in all instances the partial correlation remained significant. The reverse partial, correlating early internalizing with later externalizing, controlling for later internalizing, reduced the correlation to nonsignificance in all instances.

Some variables listed under "Temperament" predicted externalizing, too. The pattern suggests that difficultness at 6 months had a slight bit of power to predict the later externalizing, and so did resistance to control at 13 and 24 months. This pattern is consistent with the patterns found in previous follow-ups, even though the correlations were not quite as strong. We first measured resistance to control at 13 months of age. It could signify a constitutionally based, child trait of resistance to control of active exploration, or it may signify a relationship pattern established through inept parental control. Whatever the actual blend of child and parent causes, it is striking that resistance to control could have even modest predictive value when measured so early in development.

Difficult temperament did not just predict externalizing; it also predicted internalizing (as mentioned in the later summaries of results for internalizing), as had been true at previous follow-ups. How might diffi-

TABLE 5.2
Antecedents of Boys' Externalizing

Predictor Domains / *Specific Correlations*						
Temperament (*N* = 55–59)		*Positive Involvement* (*N* = 55–72)		*Negative Control* (*N* = 55–60)		*Dyadic Problem Solving* (*N* = 18–29)
Difficult(6m7y)	.22			Non-restrict.	−.33*	
Difficult(6m8y)	.31*					
Resist Control(13m7y)	.35*					
Resist Control(13m8y)	.24					
Resist Control(24m7y)	.26+					
Resist Control(24m8y)	.36*					
Mother PBQ & CBCL (*N* = 48–65)		*Teacher CBCL* (*N* = 27)		*Cognitive-Verbal* (*N* = 45–72)		*Self-Control* (*N* = 45)
Hostility(3y)	.31*,[a]					
Externalizing(5y)	.34*,[b]					
Externalizing(6y)	.68***,[c]					
PIPS (*N* = 45)		*Mother Personality* (*N* = 65–71)		*Stress/SES* (*N* = 42–72)		
Relevancy ratio	−.30*	Pt Anxiety	.54***			
		K Defensive	−.49***			
		Social Desirab.	−.35**			

Notes: Some not-quite-significant *r*s tabled where they are conceptually predictable and where they are in same direction as 6-yr follow-up results.

[a] Partial *r*, controlling for Internalizing. Zero-order $r = .47$.

[b] Partial *r*, controlling for Internalizing. Zero-order $r = .58$

[c] Partial *r*, controlling for Internalizing. Zero-order $r = .82$

***p .001, **p .01, *p .05, ^{+}p .10. Two-tailed tests.

cult temperament, operationally defined as tendency to express negative emotions, be linked to both externalizing and internalizing problems? There may actually be two separate reasons for negative emotionality (e.g., Bates, 1987). One is tendency to be easily distressed. This is analogous to the anxiety tendency, and hypothetically it would predict later internalizing better than externalizing, if we could operationally isolate this component. The second component is coercive demand for social stimulation, which could be due to innate traits of sociability, need for producing environmental effects, aggressiveness, or a response to sleep deprivation stress (Bates, in press). Such a trait has been observed in clinical cases of externalizing problems in older children (Bates, in press). Hypothetically, the social demand component should predict externalizing better than internalizing.

Only one mother–child interaction measure, ratings of restrictive, punitive control at 24 months, predicted boys' externalizing. This converges with the links between early mother perceptions of control problems and later externalizing, from an independent vantage. However, the current findings do not repeat the 6-year follow-up results, in which a pattern of positive involvement indexes predicted later externalizing. Perhaps, just as temperament's links to problem outcomes appear to have faded from 6 to 8 years, so too have the links from early mother–child interaction. This may reflect limited continuity in characteristics of the relationship, probably due in part to limited reliability of the measures. Even if some form of continuity is assumed, it may be that the variables assessed at the early ages have decreasing impact on the adjustment of the child, and other variables have increasing roles. For example, qualities of interactions with father, sibs, and peers probably have increasing influence as the child moves into middle childhood. Attachment security did not predict externalizing.

As can be seen in the "Mother Personality" section of the table, mothers' self-descriptions of negative and nondefensive traits preceded later ratings of child externalizing. The more the mother had described herself as anxious and not presenting a defended, socially desirable self, the more she described her son at 8 years as having externalizing behavior problems. The simplest interpretation of these correlations is response bias—some mothers see both self and others in a negative fashion, whereas others are biased to see self and others in a positive light. This explanation cannot be dismissed, but it probably is not the only way in which maternal personality is involved in the development of children's psychological adjustment. We know from previous analyses that mother indexes commonly interpreted as bias factors can also correlate with quite objective descriptors of child characteristics, such as vocabulary development (Bates & Bayles, 1984). So, we think that the mother characteristics may also play some direct roles in child development; for example, as suggested by clinical experience, anxious, negative mothers are low in positive parenting and prone to fall into coercion traps.

One of the social-cognitive problem solving indexes, the proportion of solutions that were relevant to the problem, predicted later lack of externalizing problems in boys. Based on prior literature (e.g. Rubin & Krasnor, 1986) we had expected some low-level correlations between problem-solving skill and a variety of other indicators of adjustment. However, the link showed up only in the area of boys' externalizing perceived by the mother, and there only faintly. The current analyses are only the first of a number of planned analyses, but the general lack of relationships so far makes us consider the possibility that the measures of social problem solving collected at 6 years were no longer reflective of individual differences in the problem-solving domain by the time of the later assessments. It is also possible that the problem-solving measures were somehow inappropriate for 6-year-old children.

Externalizing problems seen by boys' mothers were not predicted by teacher ratings on the CBCL at 6 years, by the tests of cognitive development, by the self-control measures in the 6-year laboratory tests, or by the stress indexes. In summary, boys' externalizing was predicted to a modest degree by early difficult temperament and resistance to control, observed negative control, and mother personality, and to a somewhat stronger degree by acting out behavior problems from age 3 to 6.

Girls' Externalizing. A girl's rating on externalizing problems at 8 years was, like a boy's, best predicted by earlier ratings of similar traits, including behavior problem scores from ages 3 to 6 and, to a lesser degree, temperament indexes from the first 2 years (see Table 5.3). As with the boys, partial correlations controlling for the internalizing outcome showed that early externalizing-type problems were specifically predictive of the externalizing outcome, not just problems in general. One difference from the boy group is that girls' hyperactivity at age 3 predicted externalizing, as would be expected because hyperactivity is usually regarded as in the externalizing domain. (For boys, not only was hyperactivity's prediction of externalizing not significant, it actually predicted internalizing to a slight, but significant degree.)

In the domains of observed mother–child interaction, there were a few correlations that confirmed the prior finding that positive involvement predicts the absence of externalizing problems, and discordant interactions during the age 2 tool tasks (unsupportive mother, angry, unenthusiastic child), predicted the presence of problems. Considering just the positive pole of these correlations, the process producing the obtained linkage might reflect some degree of continuity in positive

TABLE 5.3
Antecedents of Girls' Externalizing

Predictor Domains *Specific Correlations*							
Temperament (*N* = 49)		*Positive Involvement* (*N* = 41–56)		*Negative Control* (*N* = 43–52)		*Dyadic Problem Solving* (*N* = 20–26)	
Difficult(6m7y)	.22	Affec. Contact(6m)	−.32*	Conflict/warn	.25	Discord	.60**
Difficult(6m8y)	.31*	HOME Respons.(6m)	−.21				
Resist Control	.29*,[a]						
Mother PBQ & CBCL (*N* = 32–50)		*Teacher CBCL* (*N* = 17)		*Cognitive-Verbal* (*N* = 31–54)		*Self-Control* (*N* = 31)	
Hostile(3y)	.44***,[b]						
Hyperactive(3y)	.30*,[c]						
Externalizing(5y)	.51***,[d]						
Externalizing(6y)	.61***,[e]						
PIPS (*N* = 31)		*Mother Personality* (*N* = 50–53)		*Stress/SES* (*N* = 25–56)			
		Pd Psychopathic	−.30*				
		K Defensive	−.24+				

Notes: Some not-quite-significant *r*s tabled where they are conceptually predictable and where they are in same direction as 6-yr follow-up results.

[a] Partial *r*, controlling for Internalizing. Zero-order $r = .36$. (Predictor is composite of 6 and 13 mo. and outcome is composite of 7 and 8 yr.)

[b] Partial *r*, controlling for Internalizing. Zero-order $r = .56$.

[c] Partial *r*, controlling for Internalizing. Zero-order $r = .40$.

[d] Partial *r*, controlling for Internalizing. Zero-order $r = .67$.

[e] Partial *r*, controlling for Internalizing. Zero-order $r = .81$.

$^{***}p < .001$, $^{**}p < .01$, $^{*}p < .05$, $^{+}p < .10$. Two-tailed tests.

involvement and positive resolution of conflict in the mother–child interactions, as well the ontogenetically accumulating emotional and social skill benefits that such interactions can be assumed to produce. There were more predictive variables in these domains for the girls than for the boys, but, even for the girls, the relevance of individual differences in mother–infant interaction appears slighter at 8 than it had been at 6. The modest size of the correlations suggests caution: Interaction qualities in infancy are clearly not crucial to the later development of behavior problems, even if they do have *some* predictive value.

The domain of mother personality also had a few, slight correlations with the outcome, analogous to findings in the boy group, but reflecting a more tenuous linkage. Girls' externalizing problems were not predicted by teacher reports at 6 years, by cognitive development tests, by self-control indexes, by social problem solving, or by the stress measures.

In summary, girls' externalizing problems were predicted to a modest degree by early difficultness and resistance to control, by the absence of positive involvement, and by mother personality, and to a moderate degree by discordant mother–toddler problem-solving interactions and the acting-out type of behavior problems from age 3 to 6.

Boys' Internalizing. In brief summary, boys' internalizing scores were predicted to a very slight degree by infant and toddler difficultness and unadaptability temperament scores and observed negative control, to a modest degree by negativity of mother self-description, and to a stronger degree by mother ratings of anxiety-type behavior problems in years 3–6. A series of partial correlations corresponding to those described for externalizing problems produced homologous results: Early markers of internalizing were differentially predictive of internalizing; they were not simply predictors of perceived pathology in general. There may be a constitutionally based tendency toward anxiety, starting with a negative reaction to novelty (unadaptability) and ultimately taking the form of anxiety-based behavior problems, such as social withdrawal (Bates, 1987; Kagan, Reznick, & Snidman, 1986).

Girls' Internalizing. The findings for girls' internalizing were generally similar to those for boys. In brief, girls' internalizing was predicted tenuously by early difficult temperament and unadaptability, to a modest degree by the absence of positive involvement and the presence of mother negative control as well as negative maternal self-ratings, and to a stronger degree by internalizing behavior problems at ages 3 to 6. Partial correlations produced the same kind of evidence for the specificity of internalizing predicting internalizing, and not predicting externalizing, as was found for boys. Once again, the attachment security variable did not predict the outcome. However, just as for girls' externalizing outcomes, discordant interactions in the dyadic problem-solving task at age 2 predicted internalizing problems. The domains of 6-year teacher CBCL, cognitive development, self-control, social problem solving, and stress did not produce any significant predictions of girls' internalizing, just as was so for the boys.

General Comment. Considering the antecedents of mother-perceived behavior problems, in both girls and boys, the main generalization from the present data is that there are clearly differentiated antecedents for externalizing and internalizing in earlier mother perceptions of the same kind of disorder versus adjustment. This is particularly striking, considering the relatively high overlap between the two kinds of behavior problem outcomes. Less striking, but still interesting, is the finding that there are some roots of later perceived behavior problems of both types in observed qualities of mother–child interaction as early as the first and second years. The particular variables that predict vary with the particular problem outcome and the sex of the child. It appears from the overall pattern of findings, however, that more positive involvement and less negative control have some linkage to later mother perceptions of the relative absence of problem behaviors.

One interesting nonfinding is the lack of any apparent family stress antecedents of maternally perceived behavior problems. We would have especially expected some low-order correlations between marital stress indexes and boys' externalizing behavior problems, based on both the literature (e.g. Rutter & Garmezy, 1983) and on the correlation we found between the overall mother report on the dyadic adjustment scale at 3 years and concurrent mother report on the PBQ Hostile scale, $r(65) = -.30$.[1] Actually, however, the prior findings have not been that strong, especially in nonclinical populations (see O'Leary, 1984). Perhaps, then, we should not be surprised that our stress indexes did not predict perceived psychopathology.

Antecedents of School Competence

The pattern of antecedents of school competence were rather different from those of maternally perceived behavior problems. School competence was defined as a composite largely based on the first principal

---

[1]At age 3 years, mothers' ratings of overall marital satisfaction on a composite of subscales of the Spanier Dyadic Adjustment Scale were not significantly correlated with their perceptions of any kind of problems in girls, but fathers' ratings of satisfaction were associated with hostile problems in boys as perceived by either mother or self, and with each kind of problem in girls as perceived by mother or self.

component, thus including the teacher ratings of academic competencies and behavior problems (both externalizing and internalizing) and peer sociometrics. The peer indexes were standardized within classrooms to control for variation between classrooms in general levels of liking among the children. What follows is only a brief summary of the results.

Boys' School Competence. The most consistently predictive type of antecedent of boys' school competence was positive involvement. Five positive involvement observation composites from 6–24 months had significant, modest correlations with the outcome: These were mother verbal stimulation, teaching, positive control, mutually affectionate interactions, and maternal involvement. Both mother and teacher ratings of externalizing at 6 years were modest, but significant predictors of relatively low competence at 8 years, as would be expected. There were also a few modest, positive predictions of school competence from types of antecedents that had no links to the mother perception outcomes, including cognitive verbal development at 2 years, self-control at 6 years, and social-cognitive problem-solving at 6 years. There were no predictions from some domains that did have links to the mother perception outcomes, including temperament and mother personality.

Girls' School Competence. As in the boys' group, higher levels of girls' school competence were predicted by higher levels of positive involvement between the girls and their mothers at ages 6 months and 13 months. However, to a slightly greater degree than for the boys, the variables that predicted are all more indicative of the educative rather than the affectional component of the positive involvement domain, pertaining to direct stimulation of conceptual and verbal development (see Bates et al., 1982). Negative control was also a predictor of school competence. Where mothers of girls had been less restrictive and punitive and the girls less often doing troublesome things and reacting negatively to mother control after nonobvious trouble, the girls tended, somewhat, to be rated well by teacher and peers.

The other predictors of girls' school competence resemble the list for boys, but there were a few interesting differences. One difference between boy and girl antecedents was that for girls the mother 3-year PBQ Anxious scale predicted higher levels of school competence, whereas for boys the predictive index was the perceived absence of acting-out problems at 6 years. Perhaps a girl who shows more anxiety in the preschool years is more responsive to the social and academic demands of school. More in line with our initial concepts, the cognitive-motor inhibition factor in the self-control battery at 6 years predicted school competence in a positive direction. This repeated the finding for boys, to a stronger degree. Another interesting difference between girls' and boys' antecedents concerned which of the Preschool Interpersonal Problem Solving test indexes predicted school competence: For girls it was the proportion of aggressive solutions, with fewer aggressive solutions predicting greater competence, whereas for boys it was the proportion of relevant solutions. Perhaps this is a function of boys tending to give more aggressive solutions and a consequent decrease in meaningful variance in that index for boys. However, this cannot be the full answer, because the sex difference on agonistic solutions was slight (9% of solutions agonistic for boys and 5% for girls, $t(82) = 1.41$, $p = .16$).

Finally, whereas the only stress/SES domain indicator of boys' school competence was social class, for girls, social class did not predict, and marital stress did. Marital satisfaction as rated by the mother at 6 years predicted competence positively, and an index of occurrence plus recency of divorce predicted negatively, to a slight degree. The observed contrast between boys and girls in sensitivity to marital discord is the opposite of what we might have expected from the literature (Rutter & Garmezy, 1983; Emery, 1982). However, most of the literature has concerned conduct problem outcomes. Perhaps the school competence index of the current study is fundamentally different from the previous, conduct disorders indexes.

CONCLUSION

How do the current data, combined with previous results, support or challenge the extant models of developmental psychopathology? A common way to depict such models is with boxes and arrows. There is usually an outcome box with multiple antecedent boxes. Our results suggest that it would make sense to draw multiple, rather independent, outcome boxes. We found one basic, coherent adjustment dimension among our various school indexes, including both externalizing and internalizing scores. However, mother reports were largely independent of the school indexes. Among the mother reports there were at least two dimensions. The principal components analysis showed that mothers' ratings of behavior problems were relatively orthogonal to their ratings of active engagement, a set of socially positive child traits. The behavior problem factor contained both externalizing and internalizing scales. Even though these scales are generally thought of as separable dimensions, as assessed in this and many other studies, they are considerably overlapped (Achenbach & Edelbrock, 1983). However, longitudinally, our results show that the dimensions do follow separable threads of continuity. To be comprehensive, a model should not treat adjustment at age 8 as a monolith.

What antecedent boxes should the model have? The pattern of results throughout the past 7 years of follow-up assessments supports a box for temperament: (a) consistent differentiation in the continuity of maternal perceptions of difficultness versus unadaptability versus unmanageability, (b) replicated findings of external validity for the mother ratings, despite having a subjective element too, (c) links between difficult temperament and measures relevant to coercive mother–child interaction, (d) links between unadaptable temperament and anxiety/ internalizing problems, and (e) links between very early resistance to control and later aggression/externalizing. Of course, our results do not in themselves constitute support for a biological basis of temperament and behavior problems; however, the pattern is consistent with it, and this is perhaps the most generalized support to date for such a model. It must be reemphasized, also, that the temperament antecedents have grown very weak as predictors of behavior problems by 8 years of age, even though traces are still present. Another child characteristic often modeled as having biological roots and a role in the development of adjustment is child cognitive competency. In the present study, there are some modest links between cognitive competency indexes and later school competence, but only tenuous evidence for it playing a role in mother-perceived behavior problems. Overall, then, there remains plenty of variance to be accounted for by experiential factors.

The hypothetical factor of experience most emphasized in the Bloomington Longitudinal Study, as in most conceptual models, was the mother–child relationship. There was not a differentiated pattern of roots of behavior problems in the observed relationship in the first 2 years, but there were some connections. Many of these links involved variables that can be construed as positive maternal involvement predicting fewer behavior problems as well as greater competence at school. We interpret these linkages as being due primarily to prevention of problem behaviors and the fostering of socially valued behaviors, especially communicative competence. This is based on the continuity in maternal positive involvement measures over ages 6 to 24 months and the apparent role of positive involvement in the development of communicative competence (Olson et al., 1984, 1986). The process of positive involvement probably concerns affective as well as cognitive development, for example, the child learning to feel positive versus negative about self and others in addition to learning social skills. However, the data so far do not allow us to separately evaluate the roles of cognitive and affective experiences, if indeed they can ever be separated. Other relationship links involved measures of negative or reactive control. These links could also involve both relatively direct teaching of social competencies (e.g., use of coercion to resolve conflicts) and affective conclusions (e.g., generalized defensiveness).

As a general comment on the findings from 3 to 8 years, we have found fewer links between adjustment and negative control antecedents than the prior, mostly nonlongitudinal literature had led us to expect, and we found more links with positive involvement antecedents than expected. This applies to mother ratings, teacher and other secondary-caregiver ratings, and peer ratings. In overview, the evidence justifies one and perhaps two boxes for mother–child interaction antecedents. Positive involvement and negative control were relatively independent dimensions up to age 2, but they may have converged in their extensions to the future relationship (see Pettit & Bates, 1989). Based on the standard systems models, we assume that the early relationship qualities would achieve predictiveness both via simple continuity in interaction qualities to the later ages and via the impact that early interactions have on development. To date, our findings do not address this assumption. Nor do the findings address the question of how child characteristics, such as manageability, influence parenting qualities.

Most likely, other antecedent boxes will be found, even if not in this study. For example, although we have not found a clear role for family stress (except perhaps among the girls), most models include a box for stressful conditions and events, and there have been some supporting findings, especially in more extremely stressed samples than the present one.

However, assuming for the moment that we have identified the key antecedent and outcome boxes, how should those boxes be linked? According to the predominant models, simple, linear arrows will probably not suffice. For example, a process by which difficult temperament might be linked with later aggressive behavior disorder could involve the interaction of a child constitutional tendency to be demanding of social responsiveness interacting with parental tendencies to be depressed or otherwise unresponsive to mild initiation attempts by the child, and consequently, coercive process and system-maintaining cognitive and affective biases. Theoretically, in such an interactive model, if one of the elements changes, then the outcome will be changed. But it will be very difficult to evaluate the model empirically, assessing accurately and controlling for all the relevant parameters, including the child and parent personalities, changes over time in their personalities, and external social supports and stressors, such as qualities of particular teachers and peers. Some relevant parameters have not even been assessed in rudimentary ways, such as individual differences in how parents or teachers respond to the recognition of incipient behavior problems in a child. The current results are linear, except for comparison of girls' and boys' development, and much simpler than the general model. However, by showing some lines of continuity, the results do increase the clarity of basic elements of the system, and thus represent a small step toward eventual analysis of a more complex model.

What practical implications do the findings have, especially for efforts to understand and treat childhood aggression disorders? First, we can recommend the continued search for early antecedents. The data provide hope that this search might succeed, and that it may therefore be eventually possible to develop effective techniques to prevent the great damage that aggressive behavior disorders do to individuals and society. Second, it appears increasingly justifiable to include temperamental qualities in formulating the development of behavior problems. Temperament concepts might imply useful interventions (Bates, in press), such as guiding the parents of a difficult-demanding child in shaping socially appropriate behaviors to meet the presumed basic need, or such as changing the child's bedtime to reduce a sleep deficit. And they might also provide a basis for a more benign and strategically effective reframing of the child's behavior problem. Finally, the results remind us that individual differences in development are multifaceted. Just because a child is doing poorly in one facet, such as parentally perceived behavior problems, it should not be assumed that the other facets are following suit. The child may actually be adapting well to the social and academic demands of school, and may be creatively and positively engaged in many activities around home and the neighborhood. Recognition of the fuller pattern of strengths and problems will probably lead to more effective clinical intervention.

ACKNOWLEDGMENTS

Our research was partially supported by NIMH grants MH28018 and MH38605. Many individuals have played key roles in the collection and analysis of data over the 10 years of this project, but special gratitude is due Dr. Sheryl L. Olson for her many substantive contributions, and to the families who have so generously served as the subjects of this research.

REFERENCES

Achenbach, T. M., & Edelbrock, C. (1983). *Manual for the Child Behavior Checklist and Profile*. Burlington: University of Vermont.

Achenbach, T. M., & Edelbrock, C. (1986). *Manual for the Teacher's Report Form and teacher version of the Child Behavior Profile*. Burlington: University of Vermont.

Ainsworth, M. D. S., Blehar, M. C., Waters, E., & Wall, S. (1978). *Patterns of attachment*. Hillsdale, NJ: Lawrence Erlbaum Associates.

Bates, J. E. (1980). The concept of difficult temperament. *Merrill-Palmer Quarterly, 26*, 299–319.

Bates, J. E. (1987). Temperament in infancy. In J. D. Osofsky (Ed.), *Handbook of infant development* (2nd ed.) (pp. 1101–1149). NY: Wiley.

Bates, J. E. (1989). Applications of temperament concepts. In G. A. Kohnstamm, J. E. Bates, & M. K. Rothbart (Eds.), *Temperament in childhood.* Chichester: Wiley.

Bates, J. E., & Bayles, K. (1984). Objective and subjective components in mothers' perceptions of their children from age 6 months to 3 years. *Merrill-Palmer Quarterly, 30* (2), 111–130.

Bates, J. E., & Bayles, K. (1988). The role of attachment in the development of behavior problems. In J. Belsky & T. Nezworski (Eds.), *Clinical implications of attachment* (pp. 253–299). Hillsdale, NJ: Lawrence Erlbaum Associates.

Bates, J. E., Freeland, C. A. B., & Lounsbury, M. L. (1979). Measurement of infant difficultness. *Child Development, 50,* 794–803.

Bates, J. E., Maslin, C. A., & Frankel, K. A. (1985). Attachment security mother–infant interaction and temperament as predictors of behavior problem ratings at age three years. In I. Bretherton, & E. Waters (Eds.), *Growing points of attachment theory and research: Monographs of the Society for Research in Child Development* (Serial No. 209) (pp. 167–193).

Bates, J. E., Olson, S. L., Pettit, G. S., & Bayles, K. (1982). Dimensions of individuality in the mother–infant relationship at six months of age. *Child Development, 53,* 446–461.

Bates, J. E., Pettit, G. S., & Bayles, K. (1981, April). *Antecedents of behavior problems at age three years.* Paper presented at convention of Society for Research in Child Development, Boston.

Bayley, N. (1969). *Bayley Scales of Infant Development.* New York: Psychological Corp.

Behar, L. B. (1977). The Preschool Behavior Questionnaire. *Journal of Abnormal Child Psychology, 5,* 601–610.

Dunn, L. M., & Dunn, L. (1981). *Peabody Picture Vocabulary Test—Revised.* Circle Pines, MN: American Guidance Service.

Emery, R. (1982). Interparental conflict and the children of discord and divorce. *Psychological Bulletin, 92,* 310–330.

Erickson, M. F., Sroufe, L. A., & Egeland, B. (1985). The relationship between quality of attachment and behavior problems in pre-school in a high-risk sample. In I. Bretherton & E. Waters (Eds.), *Growing points of attachment theory and research. Monographs of the Society for Research in Child Development, 50* (Serial No. 209, pp. 147–165).

Frankel, K. A., & Bates, J. E. (in press). Mother–toddler problem solving: Antecedents in attachment, home behavior and temperament. *Child Development.*

Gleick, J. (1987). *Chaos: Making a new science.* NY: Viking.

Hetherington, E. M. (1989). Coping with family transitions: Winners, losers, and survivors. *Child Development, 60,* 1–14.

Hetherington, E. M., & Martin, B. (1979). Family interaction. In H. C. Quay & J. S. Werry (Eds.), *Psychopathological disorders of childhood* (pp. 247–302). New York: Wiley.

Jackson, D. N. (1974). *Personality Research Form Manual.* Goshen, NY: Research Psychologists Press.

Kagan, J., Reznick, J. S., & Snidman, N. (1986). Temperamental inhibition in early childhood. In R. Plomin, & J. Dunn (Eds.), *The study of temperament: Changes, continuities and challenges* (pp. 53–65). Hillsdale, NJ: Lawrence Erlbaum Associates.

Kagan, J., Rosman, B. L., Albert, J., & Phillips, W. (1964). Information processing in the child: Significance of analytic and reflective attitudes. *Psychological Monographs, 78,* (1).

Keogh, B. K. (1986). Temperament and schooling: Meaning of "goodness of fit"? In J. V. Lerner & R. M. Lerner (Eds.), *Temperament and social interaction in infants and children* (pp. 89–108). San Francisco, CA: Jossey-Bass.

Kohlberg, L., LaCrosse, J., & Ricks, D. (1972). The predictability of adults' mental health from childhood behavior. In B. B. Wolman (Ed.), *Manual of child psychopathology* (pp. 1217–1284). New York: McGraw-Hill.

Kiser, L. J., Bates, J. E., Maslin, C. A., & Bayles, K. (1986). Mother–infant play at six months as a predictor of attachment security at thirteen months. *Journal of the American Academy of Child Psychiatry, 25,* 68–75.

Lee, C., & Bates, J. (1985). Mother–child interaction at age two years and perceived difficult temperament. *Child Development, 56,* 1314–1326.

Maslin, C. A., & Bates, J. E. (1988). *Individual differences in attachment security: Antecedent, concurrent, and subsequent indicators in mother–infant interaction.* Unpublished manuscript.

Matas, L., Arend, R. A., & Sroufe, L. A. (1978). The continuity of adaptation in the second year: Relationship between quality of attachment and later competence. *Child Development, 49,* 547–556.

McDevitt, S. C., & Carey, W. B. (1978). The measurement of temperament in 3–7 year old children. *Journal of Child Psychology and Psychiatry, 19,* 245–253.

O'Leary, K. D. (1984). Marital discord and children: Problems, strategies, methodologies, and results. In A. Doyle & D. S. Moskowitz (Eds.), *Children in families under stress. New Directions for Child Development, No. 24* (pp. 35–40). San Francisco: Jossey-Bass.

Olson, S. L., Bates, J. E., & Bayles, K. (1984). Mother–infant interaction and the development of individual differences in children's cognitive competence. *Developmental Psychology, 20,* 166–179.

Olson, S. L., Bates, J. E., & Bayles, K. (1986). Mother–child interaction and children's speech progress: A longitudinal study of the first two years. *Merrill-Palmer Quarterly, 32,* 1–20.

Olson, S. L., Bates, J. E., & Bayles, K. (1989). Predicting long-term developmental outcomes from maternal perceptions of infant and toddler behavior. *Infant Behavior and Development, 12,* 77–92.

Patterson, G. R. (1982). *Coercive family process.* Eugene, OR: Castalia.

Patterson, G. R. (1986). Performance models for antisocial boys. *American Psychologist, 41,* 432–444.

Pettit, G. S., & Bates, J. E. (1984). Continuity of individual differences in the mother–infant relationship from 6 to 13 months. *Child Development, 55,* 729–739.

Pettit, G. S., & Bates, J. E. (1989). Family interaction patterns and children's behavior problems from infancy to 4 years. *Developmental Psychology, 25*(3), 413–420.

Renken, B., Egeland, B., Marvinney, D., Mangelsdorf, S., & Sroufe, L. A. (in press). Early childhood antecedents of aggression and passive-withdrawal in early elementary school. *Journal of Personality, 57,* (2), 257–281.

Rubin, K. H. (1980). *The Social Problem Solving Test—Revised.* Unpublished manuscript, University of Waterloo, Canada.

Rubin, K. H., & Krasnor, L. R. (1986). Social cognition and social behavioral perspectives on problem-solving. In M. Perlmutter (Ed.), *Minnesota symposia on child psychology* (Vol. 16, pp. 1–68). Hillsdale, NJ: Lawrence Erlbaum Associates.

Rutter, M. (1983). Statistical and personal interactions: Facets and perspectives. In D. Magnusson, & V. Allen (Eds.), *Human development: An interactional perspective* (pp. 295–319). New York: Academic Press.

Rutter, M., & Garmezy, N. (1983). Developmental psychopathology. In P. H. Mussen (Ed.), *Handbook of child psychology* (4th ed., vol. IV, pp. 775–911). New York: Wiley.

Spanier, G. B. (1976). Measuring dyadic adjustment: New scales for assessing the quality of marriage and similar dyads. *Journal of Marriage and the Family, 38,* 15–28.

Spivack, G., & Shure, M. B. (1974). *Social adjustment of young children.* San Francisco: Jossey-Bass.

Thelen, E. (in press). Dynamical systems and the generation of individual differences. In J. Colombo & J. W. Fagan (Eds.), *Individual differences in infancy: Reliability, stability, and prediction.* Lawrence Erlbaum Associates.

Thomas, A., Chess, S., & Birch, H. G. (1968). *Temperament and behavior disorders in children.* New York: New York University Press.

Weissbluth, M. (1989). Sleep-loss stress and temperamental difficultness: Psychobiological processes and practical considerations. In G. A. Kohnstamm, J. E. Bates, & M. K. Rothbart (Eds.), *Temperament in childhood.* Chichester, England: Wiley.

Commentary

Bad Seeds and Vile Weeds: Metaphors of Determinism

Allan Cheyne
University of Waterloo

Beyond the issues, theories, and evidence that researchers have to offer there are values, expressed in images or metaphors, that transcend the specifics of any or all particular research projects. Sometimes these metaphors inspire us, sometimes they anger us and, perhaps most often, they simply slip into our modes of thought without reflection. We define our world, set agenda, and carry them out according to the metaphors we accept (Lakoff & Johnson, 1980). Thus, there is a metaphysical tariff on the goods and services imported from research that applies to one's self-image and one's image of others. With its history of positivistic striving, it is scarcely surprising that most of the images of psychology are highly deterministic. Hence, my commentary is not only methodological but also hermeneutical, in the sense that there is a close reading of the authors' text to determine its metaphors and values (e.g. Palmer, 1969; Weinsheimer, 1985).

The guiding metaphor in chapter 4, by Brennan, Mednick, and Kandel, is based on an old folk image of the "bad seed." The bad seed notion is elevated as a "biological factor," but the deterministic image is the same. The notion behind this "biosocial theory" (Mednick, 1977a) is that the bad seed produces poor ANS functioning and, hence, certain critical deficiencies in learning and, ultimately, defective socialization and criminality. Thus, these bad seeds have a strong "predisposition" to grow into deviant and pathological "vile weeds" that are the direct and efficient "causes" of crime. The underlying explanatory strategy of projects guided by the bad seed metaphor is to discover "origins" of deviance.

In chapter 5, Bates, Bayles, Bennett, Ridge, and Brown consider some of the sequelae of differences in perceptions of temperament in infancy. Although they struggle to invoke a new image, that of systems, they are functionally guided in their methods and goals by essentially the same metaphor; but with an emphasis on the growth of the vile weed rather than on the origins of the bad seed. The strategy of projects guided by the vile weed metaphor is to seek out continuities of development that reveal the persisting effects of early deficits as well as to discover the impact of untoward events along the way.

RAIDING THE ARCHIVES

Brennan, Mednick, and Kandel (in chapter 4) tell their "origins" story by describing explorations in the vastness of bureaucratic archives containing extensive information on people born in Denmark between 1924 and 1947. It is important to note here that the archives may be employed in a variety of ways. They may be explored with a discovery heuristic, or used to test well-formed hypotheses, or employed as a scientistic warrant to proclaim an "irrefutably" demonstrated truth.

Archives have long been thought to be the repositories of great truths. The examination of archives has further been thought to give one warrant for proclaiming one's beliefs, hypotheses, convictions, and so on as revealed truth. One of the earliest scientistic uses of archives was made by John Taylor in the 1850s (Gardner, 1957). He reported his conclusions in his monograph, "The Great Pyramid: Why was it built? And who built it?". Taylor was able to demonstrate that the Great Pyramid was a very central feature of God's plan. The warrant for this claim was that its structure contained, among other things, many mathematical truths (e.g., the pyramid's height divided by twice the side of its base, gives a fairly close approximation of π). According to Gardner, Taylor's research was replicated and extended in the 1860s when Charles Piazzi Smyth discovered that the entire history of the world, past and future, had been recorded in the internal passages of the Great Pyramid. By measuring the inner passages of the great pyramid in biblical "cubits," and the appropriate "pyramid inch," one may uncover an account of the "significant events" of the earth's history. Gardner (1957) commented:

> It is not difficult to understand how Smyth achieved these astonishing scientific and historical correspondences. If you set about measuring a complicated structure like the great pyramid, you quickly have on hand a great abundance of lengths to play with. If you have sufficient patience to juggle them about in various ways, you are certain to come out with many figures which coincide with important historical dates or figures in the sciences. Since you are bound by no rules, it would be odd indeed if this search for Pyramid truths failed to meet with considerable success. (p. 178)

Although the statement that Smyth was "bound by no rules" may be something of an overstatement, it points up the basic problem of zealots armed with irrefutable truths running amok among the indeterminate possibilities of archives. Smyth certainly was unconstrained in the arbitrariness of his unit of measurement. Nobody knows what a pyramid inch or a cubit is any more than we know the unit of measurement of "deviance" or "law abidingness." Smyth assumed that the pyramid inch was close to the Anglo-Saxon inch and presumably adjusted the measure until the results "came out right," presumably by some informal iterative method of bootstrapping.

Another crucial liability of the pyramidologists was the *vagueness* of their omnibus theories (e.g., that the "important" events of history and "significant" facts of science were somehow recorded in the great pyramid). Here we have a research project in which (a) nothing *specific* is predicted and (b) almost everything in *general* is predicted. This leads to the curious result that whatever is found was predicted and whatever is not found was not specifically predicted and hence cannot call the omnibus theory into question. Thus, the "hard core" of the research program is insulated in a manner perhaps unimagined by sophisticated falsificationists. This is one reliable way to generate "irrefutable" evidence. Booth (1983) has made a distinction between attempting to understand texts and "raiding" texts. The same might be said of the use of archives. Hence, I refer to this as the problem of the "Empiricist Raiders of the Lost Archives."

It is rather easy for us to see through the speculative empiricism of Taylor and of Smyth, because their accounts do not have a ring of plausibility for us. We do not share their cultural and metaphysical horizons. Their stories are, prima facie, absurd in our world and so we expect and readily accept accounts of their logical errors. Yet, though we may construct more plausible stories for ourselves from our archives, we are subject to the same logical errors. The vastness of modern bureaucratic archives matches or surpasses that of the ancient pyramids. The latitude for selection of material, measures, and analytic techniques may be taken to suggest that we may be no more, and possibly less, constrained in our analysis of archival records than were the pyramidologists. In science or augury there is no a priori guarantee that the entrails of bureaucracies will be inherently more informative than the entrails of chickens.

This is not to argue that archival data are not useful, but that they have potential for illusion as well as for enlightenment. Their richness may be as much a source of deception as of information. Without clear goals and a theoretical framework, one inevitably becomes lost in a confusing morass. Yet that framework must be such that it can be altered, informed, enlarged, or even destroyed by the evidence extracted from the archives. One must be scrupulous in pursuing supplementary analyses to check on alternative explanations. Unfortunately, the archives are often inadequate to deal with most of the interesting alternatives.

OVERVIEW OF CHAPTER 4

Mednick (1987) has argued for the reasonableness of seeking biological "causes" of crime. He has accused some of his opponents of emotionally and politically motivated prejudice against biologism. It does, however, take a certain passion, not to say hubris, to claim that one's research and that of one's colleagues "*irrefutably* support the influence of heritable factors in the etiology of some forms of antisocial acts" (Mednick, 1987, p. 6, italics added). This assertion, and its form, suggest a certain lack of openness (unless heritability is to be interpreted so broadly as to be meaningless) to alternatives and to the possibility that one *may* be wrong. After all, it is in the nature of a scientific claim to be, in principle, refutable. It may be compelling. It may be convincing for the moment. But it must be constantly open to refutation. In fairness, it must be pointed out that "environmentalists" are not above being equally absolutist in their claims for "final answers" on their side (e.g. Futterman & Allen, 1988).

The structure of chapter 4 and its authors' argument is fairly straightforward:

1. The basic speculation (hypothesis?) is that criminal behavior may have some biological basis.
2. The authors present evidence and arguments for a degree of specialization in antisocial behavior.
3. There is a speculation that different specializations may be influenced differently by biological factors.
4. It is argued that adoptees have higher conviction rates when records show that their biological fathers have had convictions than when their biological fathers have had no convictions. Based upon subsequent analysis, this claim is subject to several unanticipated and unexplained limitations: (a) it holds for convictions for property offenses but not for violent offenses, (b) the finding is largely if not entirely accounted for by cases in which biological fathers have multiple convictions, and (c) it holds only for male adoptees.
5. There is a reported positive correlation between the *rates* of conviction for male adoptees and those of their biological fathers.
6. The authors also argue that those who are convicted of violent offenses have evidence of high rates of birth complications and minor physical anomalies.

The Dangers of Vagueness

The vagueness of the omnibus biological theory is seriously problematic and is not reduced by the introduction of the specialization issue. At first glance, it appears that this refinement of the dependent variable (into property and violent crime convictions) might have made the biological claims more specific. However, quite the contrary, the distinction provided much more latitude, for there were no predictions offered about which of the two forms of convictions was the more "biologically determined." Thus, although the authors examined "specific" types of convictions, nothing specific was predicted, but what was found has now become evidence for the omnibus biological theory, and what was not found is not held to count against it. This reveals a most unrelenting confirmation bias in the research program. Moreover, there has been no admission of a constriction of the presumptive generality, nor any sharpening of the vagueness, of the underlying theory. The persisting vagueness of the theoretical claims allows so much discretionary power that they can easily evade disconfirmation. Such theories can no more be resolved empirically than can the more explicitly metaphysical questions of the scholastics.

The property offense/violent offense distinction is the centerpiece of the chapter. Was there any a priori rationale for this? Or was this a hunch that "paid off"? Or was it an ad hoc and serendipitous finding? These distinctions are critical to the logic of induction. A priori hypotheses corroborated by even the weak method of null-hypothesis testing have a different status, in establishment social science, than post hoc explanations. In the absence of explanation, one must speculate that, in the spirit of opportunistic empiricism, the distinction was investigated because it was readily available and easily accessible in the archives. In any case, it seems that some attempt should be made at developing an explanation of this finding and going beyond the, by now, extensive restatement of the finding (e.g., Mednick, Gabrielli, & Hutchings, 1983, 1984; Mednick, Moffitt, et al., 1983; Mednick, Pollock, Volavka, & Gabrielli, 1982). The failure, in the present case, to make the hypothesis more specific and to live with the consequences is particularly disturbing, because the obvious a priori prediction, which the authors make no attempt to come to terms with, is that violent crimes would be more biologically heritable than nonviolent crimes. Indeed, it is difficult to imagine what would serve as grounds for predicting a biological basis for property offending. Certainly, none are provided. On the contrary, there is not even a post hoc rationale offered. Thus, where Buikhuisen & Mednick (1988) have claimed that this adoption study has "proven to be difficult to attack methodologically" (p. 6), they should rather have admitted that the results thereof appear to have proven equally resistant to meaningful interpretation.

What Theories Have Been Disconfirmed?

The boast of Buikhuisen and Mednick notwithstanding, the quasiexperimental design of the adoption study is inherently unsound as a test of biological effects. For example, the more convictions the biological fathers of the adoptees had the more likely it is that they were individuals from social classes, backgrounds, and districts of lower status (e.g., Mednick, Moffitt, et al., 1983, Table 5). To the extent that adoption agencies succeed in matching the social background of the adoptive parents to that of the child, the more likely the adoptees will end up living under the same social conditions as did their biological parents. This is also evident in the same data set, even to the point of evidence of matching adoptive and biological fathers on conviction rates (see Kamin, 1985). In general, however, the adoptive fathers are strikingly unlike the biological fathers in some rather critical ways. The adoptive parents have been specifically selected in order to qualify as adoptive parents. This is evident in the low rates of adoptive father convictions (6.2%) compared to the biological fathers (28.6%), biological mothers (8.9%), their adoptive sons (16.6%) and even male adoptees for whom neither the biological nor the adoptive father have convictions (13.5%) (chapter 4 of this book; Hutchings & Mednick, 1977; Mednick, Gabrielli, & Hutchings, 1985). *Virtually any theory that considers the foregoing complexities of the adoptive paradigm must perforce predict that the adoptees' rates of convictions will be intermediate between those of biological and adoptive parents and that there must be some correlation between conviction rates of biological fathers and of their sons.*

The critical issue, however, is not whether a particular theory could be corroborated by these data but whether any theory could be falsified by them. Null hypothesis testing, at best, yields only a very weak corroboration of theory because almost any but the most trivial theory can survive such tests (e.g., Meehl, 1967). These weaknesses were exacerbated in the present case by the combination of imprecise theories and a problematic quasiexperimental design. Because no available theory can make precise predictions for such a design, few theories can be eliminated, and none can receive any meaningful corroboration. The only theory that has been rendered at all doubtful by any of these results is an unstated biological theory of violent crime, because it is the one theory that might have plausibly and incorrectly predicted a higher degree of concordance between adoptees and their biological fathers for violent crimes than for property crimes.

In earlier reports Mednick, Gabrielli, and Hutchings (1983, 1984) attempted to make a test, via a cross-fostering analysis, to compare the impact of biological and adoptive fathers on adoptee's criminal convictions. The analysis, however, was rendered useless as a test of theory by virtue of some severe limitations of their quasiexperimental design. In these analyses, adoptees' conviction rates were better predicted by biological fathers' conviction rates than by adoptive fathers' conviction rates. However, we know that the effect for biological fathers is almost entirely due to multiple convictions and especially to multiple recidivism. Multiple recidivism (whatever it may be taken to index) is 13 times greater for biological fathers than for adoptive fathers, that is, multiple recidivism is *extremely* rare in adoptive fathers. Hence, the biological/adoptive classification is almost perfectly confounded by the recidivism variable, rendering the cross-fostering analysis profoundly misleading. It is absurd to pretend that one could possibly assess the impact of adoptive fathers on adoptees with regard to criminal convictions when relevant variation has been so severely restricted.

On the Similarity of the Results for Men and Women

Brennan, et al. report that the results for women appear to follow the same pattern as for the males. In fact, the patterns are the same only in the trivial sense that in both cases the conviction rates for adoptees were intermediate between those of biological and adoptive parents of the same sex. It is clear from Table 4.1 in that male adoptees' conviction rates were roughly equidistant from those of their biological fathers and those of their adoptive fathers. Female adoptees, in contrast to the males and contrary to the claim of Brennan et al., are much more like their adoptive mothers in their conviction rates (see Table 4.1). Female adoptees are clearly much more like adoptive mothers than biological mothers in terms of their conviction rates for each level of number of convictions. This is a very different pattern than that which is evident for male adoptees. There appears to be a "glossing" of details that complicate interpretation and interfere with an unambiguous biological message.

Vulnerability and Labelling Effects

Adoptive sons for whom neither biological nor adoptive fathers had convictions have much higher conviction rates (13%) than do nonadoptees (8%) (Mednick, Gabrielli, & Hutchings, 1983). It seems likely that the circumstances preceding and following adoption very much put the young male at risk for subsequent conviction independently of paternal conviction rates. Now adoption is clearly an omnibus variable that combines an array of stressors. These will likely vary as a function of the social background of the adoptees. The adoptive parents may well be affected by their knowledge of these background factors. Hutchings and Mednick (1977) have argued that their findings cannot be explained by this "stigmatization" through labelling based on the biological father's criminal reputation per se, because even when the adoptive parents could not have known about the biological parents' convictions (i.e., when they had not occurred prior to adoption) the same effects were obtained. However, from this account we know that the adoptive parents did receive background information on the adoptees. We also know that this information is extensive, especially with regard to parental criminal convictions (Hutchings & Mednick, 1977). Some of this information may have been correlated with future convictions (e.g., early arrests that did not lead to convictions). This may explain why there was a closer relation between convictions of adoptees and their biological parents based on the data of police records than based on in-court convictions (Mednick, Mednick, Gabrielli & Hutchings, 1985). In any case, differential stigmatization or labelling has hardly been ruled out as a possible confound.

"Having a Line"

The authors of chapter 4 take some effort to demonstrate a degree of "specialization" of offenses. The rationale given for considering specialization is that its very existence suggests that certain individuals have some enduring *personal* characteristics that predispose them to property or violent offending. This necessarily follows only if one is committed to a psychologism that posits a sort of inverted Rousseau-like model of an ignoble savage operating as an isolated individual. However, crime is a form of social activity (Becker, 1963) and sometimes entails elaborated and well-integrated networks of career criminals (Sutherland, 1937; Waldo, 1983) as well as much interrelatedness between the deviant culture and the wider society (Prus & Irini, 1980). Thus, it seems that career criminals are not merely driven to their recidivism by some primordial criminal urge but are sometimes skilled criminals who approach their work "with some degree of pride, discipline and rationality" (Roebuck & Windham, 1983; p. 22). The specialization of such people may no more reflect nontrivial biological characteristics than specialization in carpentry or bricklaying. Some activities deemed illegal in our society entail mechanical, organizational, and social skills (Letkemann, 1973) that often require informal on-the-job apprenticeships within a social network. Thus, *limited* (see Letkemann, 1973) specialization, especially for property crime, makes very good sense in a sociocultural context for crime but less so within a biological context. Career criminals usually deal in commodities because they are simply trying to make a dishonest living. Thus, if adoptees from families living in a subculture of criminal careers are recruited back into the fold, it will be for the purposes of profit and will lead to conviction for property crime. It is naive to assume that adoption inevitably severs all ties to extended families.

Major and Minor Anomalies

Having been presented with an apparent, albeit unacknowledged, disconfirmation of the biological hypothesis of violent crime, the authors consider hypotheses of prenatal (unspecified) and perinatal (delivery complications) effects on future criminal convictions. The independent variable, minor physical anomalies (MPAs) assessed at 12 (sic) years of age, used to index prenatal complications is a very indirect and nonspecific one. MPAs are neither an invariant result of prenatal and perinatal difficulties nor are they uniquely associated with these. Hence, they are far from uniquely indexing prenatal and perinatal problems.

Nonetheless, the authors do report significant associations between the incidence of delivery complications and *both* property *and* violent convictions. Unexpectedly and inexplicably, individuals convicted of property crimes were found to have *fewer* delivery complications! However, individuals convicted of violent crimes tended to have a greater incidence of both delivery complications and minor physical anomalies. Brennan et al. suggest that this is because MPAs may index other "hidden anomalies" of an antisocial nature. Sadly, MPAs also index a variety of anomalies that are not well "hidden" at all. MPAs are associated with a variety of problems, including chromosomal anomalies (Holmes et al., 1972), genetic defects (Smith, 1970), mental retardation (Jakab, 1982), hyperactivity (Quinn & Rapoport, 1974) and, most obviously, *major* physical anomalies and handicaps (Holmes et al., 1972). Thus, there is an indefinitely large number of practical hypotheses regarding intellectual, social, and physical problems, also potentially "indexed" by MPAs, that may be associated with violent crime. It might prove prudent for the investigators to explore such hypotheses before entertaining too seriously subtle neurological and psychological hypotheses, such as impulse control, ANS recovery time, or insensitivity to punishment.

What Are the Implications?

Let us grant, for a moment, a simple-minded "biological" determination of crime. What form might it take? There may, under the biological hypothesis, be a variety of physical characteristics that could be inherited under the general hypothesis and that may, in one culture or another, be related to criminal behavior, for entirely historical, social, economic, and cultural reasons (e.g., tradition, economic exploitation, racism, etc.). These may also be different from one culture to another. Yet, the biological hypothesis would be corroborated by Mednick in every culture, *but for different social reasons in each.* The techniques of Mednick and colleagues would give the impression of cross-cultural uniformity in a biological effect. However, this impression would be incorrect, because their methods do not and can not specify the nature of the "biological factor." Thus, it is difficult to grasp the point of this research even if the simple-minded biological hypothesis were true.

I conclude my discussion of chapter 4 by returning to the opening theme of the deterministic metaphor. Mednick (1979) has suggested that individuals who have been identified "should then be followed until *this serious criminal behaviour has manifested itself*" (p. 48, italics added). The notion of "manifestation" suggests teleological unfolding of a latent preexisting entity which is simply brought out into the open (Harré, 1988). The extent to which Mednick's text is guided by this hypostatization of latent criminality is revealed by the labelling of *children* as "criminals" who, *as adults,* were convicted of criminal offenses (Mednick, 1977b). It is a sobering thought that individuals convicted of criminal offenses must live with the label for many years subsequent to their offense, but it seems especially unfair that the label be applied retroactively to one's childhood. This simplistic instantiation of a socially defined legal construct as a sort of internal biological time-bomb contributes more to a justification of "criminal" stereotypes than to a clarification of the functional and organic relationships entailed in understanding or preventing crime.

COMMENTARY ON CHAPTER 5

As pointed out in the introduction, the search for continuities of development is guided by a slightly different metaphor than is the project that seeks to find the congenital *origins* of deviance. The stated goal of the project reported in chapter 5 is to understand the development of psychopathology in the early years of life. The immediate goal of the chapter was to explore the correlation between mothers' perceptions of early child temperament (in the first 2 years) with reports of later child adjustment. The latter reports included the Behar Preschool Behavior Questionnaire (completed by the mothers), the Achenbach Child Behavior Checklist (completed by the mothers), and the Home Behavior Scale (also completed by the mothers). There were also observational measures of the children's behavior (with their mothers) as well as later teacher and peer ratings. Bates et al. have been scrupulous in the detail they have provided about the characteristics of the participants in their study as well as about the measures employed in the analysis. This detail reveals the central role that the mothers played in this work; as parents, as participants, as context for the children's actions, and as informants about themselves and about their children.

For the most part, Bates *et al.* are also scrupulous about making reference to maternal "perceptions," especially with regard to temperament. They do persist, however, in referring to children's externalizing and internalizing problems as though they were somehow less based on maternal perceptions. Moreover, Bates and Bayles (1988) argued that "because . . . the objectivity of the mother's perception of the child is not overshadowed by subjective biases (Bates & Bayles, 1984; Pettit & Bates, 1984), we are not inclined to reduce this continuity in mother's descriptions to mere method variance" (p. 291). These sentiments are echoed in the conclusions of chapter 5. I strongly agree that to attribute such findings to "subjective bias" and "mere method variance" is unjustifiably dismissive of the validity of mothers' interpretations and judgments. However, Bates and colleagues accept and reinforce a contemporary polarization in which there is, on the one hand, an "objective reality"[1] about the child's development, ultimately discoverable by "objective" methods. Against this is set a hypothetical "subjective bias" of maternal fantasy. In this view maternal, teacher, and peer measures are all biased or distorted with regard to an underlying "construct" (cf. Patterson, 1986). Hence, maternal reports are taken to be valuable only to the extent they can be made to surmount an inherent subjectivity to enable positive science to derive constructs that are perspicuous mirrors of an objective reality. An alternate interpretation of maternal reports is captured in the interactionist term *perspectival* (Blumer, 1969; Mead, 1934). In this view, a mother's report is intersubjective and interpretive. One of the consequences, and indeed, the functions of interpretation is to lend coherence and continuity to the sequence of successions that is our lived experience. A mother's reports may incorporate many of the important dynamic processes of her child's development. There are alternatives to the reduction of maternal insights to mere "subjectivity," on the one

[1]In chapter 5, Bates and colleagues eschew reality but retain objectivity! Although the authors were reluctant to equate mothers' perceptions with "reality," they continue to claim an objective component. It is not clear whether or not they actually claim that mothers' perceptions of temperament can "tap temperament as an inborn, biologically based construct." It is also unclear what is the intended ontological status of an inborn "construct." Perhaps it is something psychologists are born with as part of their nomological network.

hand, or, on the other, to treat them as a "windowpane" (Gusfield, 1976) on the child's "objective" development. A perspectival view would not necessarily lead one to expect that mother and teacher ratings would strongly "converge" but, in fact, represent different perspectives on the child in different contexts. It would, however, lead one to expect a good deal of coherence in any one perspective. I suggest that the researchers' interpretation gains more purchase than they admit or realize from the coherence lent to the overall patterning of results by the extensive use of the perspective of the mothers as the source for both predictor and outcome variables. Merely demonstrating modest convergence of mothers' perspectives with those of observers, teachers, or peers does not demonstrate, by the methods used, that it is some "objective component" of the mothers' perspectives that shows continuity over time. However, it may be useful to appreciate the continuity of the mother's perspective on the development of the child. Much of what the practitioner has to operate with is other people's perspectives on the child, and it is probably useful to consider these *as perspectives* and to be reminded that one's knowledge of a child as client, for example, is also a perspectival one.

Quasiarguments and Pseudoempiricism

Bates et al. begin their chapter with a comment that older models "tended to rely on relatively simple causal mechanisms" for explaining aggression, for example, via "parental behavioral dimensions." They argued that contemporary approaches must look to complex systems models and feel that their own work is guided by such thinking. In the end, however, they admit that the investigation of such systems theories lies in the future and merely conclude that their data show "some lines of continuity. . . [hence] increase the clarity of basic elements of the system, and thus represent a small step toward eventual analysis of a more complex model." (Chapter 5, p. 116) These claims sound very much like those of simple-minded models of the past and the promise of a future systems integration remains as vague at the end as at the beginning of the chapter. Moreover, upon closer examination, even the modest claims of this conclusion may be found to be overstated. Interpreting selected correlations, as mini-quasiexperimental tests of hypotheses, from large data sets has always been beset by problems and has led many an investigator astray. Bates and colleagues are aware of the problems associated with what they frankly refer to as a "hunting trip." (Chapter 5) While they proudly speak of their "trophies from previous seasons",[2] (Chapter 5) they are aware of the

[2]Bates et al. prefer the hunting metaphor to the more conventional fishing metaphor. A rhetorically sounder strategy might have been to evoke the image of the *naturalist* gathering specimens rather than that of a hunter collecting trophies.

dangers of making too much of spurious results. However, there is also the danger of making too much of nonspurious results. One particular problem encountered in wading through masses of data and attempting to explain post hoc findings, that I think has not been much noted, is that investigators can sometimes deceive themselves that they have refuted, or at least weakened, alternate explanations to one they prefer. This error is, I suggest, an inevitable outcome of an honest but misguided process of interpretation of isolated correlations in a complex data set. Investigators need to make some interpretation of data because models are constructed of concepts, not of raw correlations, but there is great potential for self-deception in this. Consider the finding reported by Bates and colleagues that the more mothers saw themselves as "needing to be aggressive" the more they saw internalizing problems in their sons. The authors immediately note that "the simplest interpretation of these correlations is response bias." They then go on to admit that "this explanation cannot be dismissed, but it probably is not the only way [to explain the correlation]." It is a curious way of dismissing a confound to suggest that it is probably not the only one! Actually, this is part of quite a clever but probably unconscious rhetorical strategy in which the confound is presented first and then the preferred explanation is offered as a counterproposal to the obvious confound. The counterproposal (the preferred explanation) was that maternal characteristics may play direct roles in child development, for example, by the quality of care the mother gives the child. Such "abductions" set up the reader for the general conclusions at the end of the chapter that, in agreement with "general models," antecedents of adjustment and competence can be seen in "qualities of interaction" between mother and child. Two points should be emphasized here. First, this is an argument in appearance only. The authors said nothing that would cast doubt on the response bias explanation. The apparent argument is mere hand waving. The ostensive point in discussing alternative explanations is to alter their plausibility and acceptability. The authors' text does nothing of the sort.

Second, because the speculations are discussed in the context of an empirical finding, even though it cannot be brought to bear on the issue of the warrantability of competing claims, there is an appearance of an empirical warrant for one's preferences. The authors' statement that they "think" their interpretation is supported by their research is logically and empirically vacuous. Yet, occurring in the context of a significant correlation in a large empirical study, it is all too easy for authors and readers to come away with the feeling that there is at least some vague and tenuous support for preferring one explanation over alternatives when there is none at all. The chapter is replete with references to the authors' "preferred interpretations" of correlations, all of which appear to gain a modest degree of plausibility through merely contingent association with empirical correlations that in no way selectively "support" them. We are participating against our better judgment in the construction of a model based on a kind of "truth by association" rhetoric, in spite of the caution and best intentions of the authors.

A similar nonargument occurs with regard to the transformation of correlational findings to explicitly causal questions. Bates and colleagues do not fall into the trap of *explicitly* arguing causality from correlational data. Yet we find immediate elisions from correlations (e.g., that earlier positive involvement between mother and child predicts later problems and competencies) to the question, in the following sentence, of *how* positive involvement might *contribute* to these outcomes. There is absolutely no empirical warrant for assuming the causal state of affairs that the question assumes. However, the introduction of the "how" question does assume the causal state of affairs and, in posing the question, the authors implicitly express confidence in the warrantability of the assumed causal state of affairs. To be fair, Bates et al. do subsequently list a variety of alternate possible explanations. Unfortunately, as the authors admit, there is nothing in their results that provides any substantial clues that would increase or decrease the plausibility of any of them. I hasten to add that I do not find Bates and colleagues' preferred opinions and arguments at all implausible. In fact, they are so plausible that they scarcely need extensive tables of correlations to make them seem so.

CONCLUDING REMARKS

In the two projects reviewed herein, I have attempted to illustrate how the investigators have argued their way through a tenuous nomological network, performing a series of "experiments" as part of an integrated research program, "*without ever refuting or corroborating so much as a single strand of the network*" (Meehl, 1967, p. 114). I fear that these studies are far from unique. Much research in psychology may be empirical in name only. The possession of data appears to serve primarily to give one warrant to speak and to speculate and it might be a useful exercise to determine how much of what is said is warranted by the accompanying empirical data and how much would be as reasonable and compelling without it.

REFERENCES

Bates, J. E., & Bayles, K. (1984). Objective and subjective components of mothers' perceptions of their children from age 6 months to 3 years. *Merrill-Palmer Quarterly. 30,* 111–130.

Bates, J. E., & Bayles, K. (1988). The role of attachment in the development of behavior problems. In J. Belsky & T. Nezworski (Eds.), *Clinical implications of attachment* (pp. 253–297). Hillsdale, New Jersey: Lawrence Erlbaum Associates.

Becker, H. S. (1963). *Outsiders: Studies in the sociology of deviance.* New York, NY: Free Press.

Blumer, H. (1969). *Symbolic interaction.* Englewood Cliffs, NJ: Prentice-Hall.

Booth, W. C. (1983). *The rhetoric of fiction* (2nd ed.). Chicago, IL: University of Chicago Press.

Buikhuisen, W., & Mednick, S. A. (1988). The need for an integrative approach in criminology. In W. Buikhuisen & S. A. Mednick (Eds.), *Explaining criminal behavior: Interdisciplinary approaches* (pp. 3–7). Leiden: E. J. Brill.

Futterman, A., & Allen, G. (1988). Genetics, race, and IQ: A Final answer to an old question [Review of *Education and class: The irrelevance of genetic studies of IQ*]. *Journal of the History of the Behavioral Sciences, 24,* 402–406.

Gardner, M. (1957). *Fads and fallacies in the name of science.* Boston, MA: Dover.

Gusfield, J. (1976). The literary rhetoric of science: Comedy and pathos in drinking driver research. *American Sociological Review, 41,* 16–34.

Harré, R. (1988). Wittgenstein and artificial intelligence. *Philosophical Psychology, 1,* 105–115.

Holmes, L. B., Mack, C., Moser, H. W., Pant, S. S., Halldórsson, S., & Matsilevich, B. (1972). *Mental retardation: An atlas of diseases with associated physical abnormalities.* New York: Macmillan.

Hutchings, B., & Mednick, S. A. (1977). Criminality of adoptees and their adoptive and biological parents: A pilot study. In S. A. Mednick & K. O. Christiansen (Eds.), *Biosocial bases of criminal behavior* (pp. 127–141). New York, NY: Gardner Press.

Jakab, I. (1982). *Mental retardation.* Basel: Karger.

Kamin, L. J. (1985). Criminality and adoption *Science, 227,* March, p. 983.

Lakoff, G., & Johnson, M. (1980). *Metaphors we live by.* Chicago: University of Chicago Press.

Letkemann, P. (1973). *Crime as work.* Englewood Cliffs, NJ: Prentice-Hall.

Mead, G. H. (1934). *Mind, self, and society.* Chicago, IL: University of Chicago Press.

Mednick, S. A. (1977a). A biosocial theory of the learning of law abiding behavior. In S. A. Mednick & K. O. Christiansen (Eds.), *Biosocial bases of criminal behavior* (pp. 1–8). New York, NY: Gardner Press.

Mednick, S. A. (1977b). Part IV—Factors predictive of asocial behavior: A prospective study (with L. Kirkegaard-Sorensen & J. Loeb). In S. A. Mednick & K. O. Christiansen (Eds.), *Biosocial bases of criminal behavior* (pp. 227–273). New York, NY: Gardner Press.

Mednick, S. A. (1987). Introduction: Biological factors in crime causation: The reactions of social scientists. In S. A. Mednick, T. E. Moffitt, & S. A. Stack (Eds.), *The causes of crime: New biological approaches* (pp. 1–6). Cambridge: Cambridge University Press.

Mednick, S. A. (1979). Biosocial factors and primary prevention of antisocial behavior. In S. A. Mednick & S. G. Shoham (Eds.), *New paths in criminology:*

Interdisciplinary and intercultural explorations (pp. 45–53). Lexington, MA: D. C. Heath.

Mednick, S. A., Gabrielli Jr., W. F., & Hutchings, B. (1983). Genetic influence in criminal behavior: Evidence from an adoption cohort. In Van Dusen, K. T. & Mednick, S. A. (Eds.), *Prospective studies of crime and delinquency* (pp. 39–56). The Hague: Kluwer-Nijhoff.

Mednick, S. A., Gabrielli Jr., W. F., & Hutchings, B. (1984). Genetic influences in criminal convictions: Evidence from an adoption cohort. *Science, 224*, 891–894.

Mednick, S. A., Gabrielli Jr., W. F., & Hutchings, B. (1985). [Response to critics]. *Science, 227*, 984–989.

Mednick, S. A., Moffitt, T. E., Pollock, V., Talovic, S., Gabrielli, Jr., W. F., & Van Dusen, K. T. (1983). The inheritance of human deviance. In D. Magnusson & V. L. Allen (Eds.), *Human development: An interactional perspective* (pp. 222–242). New York, NY: Academic Press.

Mednick, S. A., Pollock, V., Volavka, J., & Gabrielli Jr., W. F. (1982). Biology and violence. In M. E. Wolfgang & N. A. Weiner (Eds.), *Criminal violence* (pp. 21–80). Beverley Hills, CA: Sage.

Meehl, P. E. (1967). Theory testing in psychology and physics: A methodological paradox. *Philosophy of Science, 34*, 103–115.

Palmer, R. E. (1969). *Hermeneutics: Interpretation theory in Schleiermacher, Dilthey, Heidegger, and Gadamer.* Evanston, IL: Northwestern University Press.

Patterson, G. R. (1986). Performance models for antisocial boys. *American Psychologist. 41*, 432–444.

Pettit, G. S., & Bates, J. E. (1984). Continuity of individual differences in the mother–infant relationship from 6 to 13 months. *Child Development, 55*, 729–739.

Prus, R., & Irini, S. (1980). *Hookers, rounders, and desk clerks: The social organization of the hotel community.* Salem, WN: Sheffield.

Quinn, P., & Rapoport, J. (1974). Minor physical anomalies and neurological status in hyperactive boys. *Pediatrics, 53*, 742–747.

Roebuck, J. B., & Windham, G. O. (1983). Professional theft. In G. P. Waldo (Ed.), *Career criminals* (pp. 13–29). Beverley Hills, CA: Sage.

Smith, D. (1970). *Recognizable patterns of human malformation.* Philadelphia, PA: W. B. Saunders.

Sutherland, E. (1937). *The professional thief.* Chicago: University of Chicago Press.

Waldo, G. P. (1983). *Career criminals.* Beverley Hills, CA: Sage.

Weinsheimer, J. C. (1985). *Gadamer's hermeneutics: A reading of Truth and Method.* New Haven, CN: Yale University Press.

Section 3: Familial Factors Associated with Childhood Aggression

6

An Early Starter Model for Predicting Delinquency

G. R. Patterson
D. Capaldi
L. Bank
Oregon Social Learning Center
Eugene, Oregon

The early starter model describes the family matrix that provides for the direct training of antisocial behavior in young boys. We believe that reinforcement for aggression is provided directly in the interaction among family members. The antisocial behaviors then generalize from home to other settings, leading to social failures that in turn contribute to the long-term maintenance of the child in the antisocial process. The findings relating to this are briefly reviewed. In this chapter, the general hypothesis that is tested is that antisocial behavior assessed at Grade 4 is prototypic and predictive of delinquent behaviors occurring at Grades 7 and 8. Longitudinal data from the Oregon Youth Study (OYS) are presented that examine this connection.

The formulation that family members inadvertently provide reinforcers for antisocial behavior and fail to provide effective punishment for transgressions is in marked contrast to the major sociological theories of delinquency. From one of these perspectives, family interactions are only *indirectly* implicated in the training for antisocial behaviors (Elliott, Huizinga, & Ageton, 1985). Elliott and his colleagues emphasized the direct training for antisocial behavior as taking place in the context of the deviant peer group. Family variables are presented as weak determinants for which individuals become involved in the deviant peer group.

In contrast to this position, a social learning perspective assumes that the home-based training for antisocial acts takes place *before* the deviant peer group process begins. We hypothesize that the emergence of the deviant peer group as a measurable entity in preadolescence adds little to the predictive power of early antisocial behavior in identifying delinquents. In the present report, structural equation models are used to examine the contributions of latent constructs for antisocial and for deviant peer involvement to account for variance in a construct measuring delinquent behavior. We also assume that by mid- to late adolescence the deviant peer group does make a unique and significant contribution to prediction; at that time, family variables will make a smaller one.

The review by Patterson, DeBaryshe, and Ramsey (1989) suggests that there may be two major paths to delinquent behavior. One path is the early starter model detailed in the present report. The boys who follow this path begin their antisocial training in the home early on (around ages 4 to 9). The problem behaviors are accompanied by massive social skill deficits. These boys seem to be at significant risk for status as chronically offending delinquent adolescents *and* for careers as antisocial adults.

The second path, defined by the late starter model, is quite different in several important respects. The boys are not identified as problem children during the elementary grades. They are at least marginally skilled in peer relations and academics. For them, the process begins in early adolescence. At this point, their parents' marginal family-management skills are disrupted by forces such as divorce, unemployment, substance use, illness, or by the normal perturbations that accompany their son's shift into pubescence. The resulting disruptions in parental supervision create a situation in which the child can become heavily involved in the deviant peer group. The training and support provided by the deviant peer group leads the youth to become involved in delinquent activity. Late starters do not begin offending until age 15 or later.

The age of the child at the initiation of the process is the key variable that differentiates these two paths; the age at which the antisocial process is initiated determines the magnitude of accompanying social skill deficits. Presumably, if the antisocial process is initiated during Grades 1 through 3, it hinders the child's learning of peer relational and academic skills. If the antisocial process does not begin until Grade 6, 7, or 8, then there is a good chance that the youth has already acquired some modicum of social skills before the training for antisocial behaviors begins.

We assume that the early starters are at significantly greater risk than the late starters, both for chronic offending during adolescence and for careers as antisocial adults. The late starters are at less risk for both, presumably because their higher level of social skills (work and relational) make them *more likely to drop out of the antisocial process.*

The OYS now has data collected at Grades 4 and 6 for two cohorts of families living in the highest crime areas of a medium-sized metropolitan area. Police records were also available for Grades 7 and 8. These data sets are used to examine the various hypotheses about the early starter model. The pivotal assumption is that assessing the model at Grade 4 will provide the basis for predicting which boys will become involved in delinquent acts prior to age 15. We also examine the possibility that measures of academic skill deficiency assessed at Grade 4 will provide significant predictions above those made by assessing the antisocial trait alone.

Subsequent studies will test the late starter model. If the model proves useful, we can then proceed to examine the relation of the early and late starter models to chronic offending and adult antisocial careers.

Chronic Offenders

One of the key assumptions made here is that the early starter model may account for a substantial number of adolescents who become chronic offenders. This section briefly outlines the findings relating to chronicity and the central role it plays in the design of prevention programs.

The Philadelphia cohort studies made several important contributions to our understanding of the delinquency process (Wolfgang, Figlio, & Sellin, 1972; Wolfgang & Tracy, 1982). One such contribution was the identification of a subgroup of delinquent offenders who had five or more arrests. These *chronic offenders* accounted for 52% of all juvenile arrests in Cohort I and 61% in Cohort II. Of the total sample, 6% of Cohort I and 7% of Cohort II were chronic offenders; about 18% of the *offenders* were chronic. The general findings were replicated in two studies. Shannon (1980) showed that 6% of his cohort were involved in 51% of the police arrests; Farrington (1983) found that 6% were involved in 49% of the convictions.

The Philadelphia cohort studies also demonstrated that the likelihood of repeating offenses was an exponential function (Wolfgang et al., 1972). The data showed that the more arrests a youth experiences, the greater the likelihood of a future arrest. For example, the likelihood of a second arrest given the first was .54; the likelihood of a third given the second was .65, and a fourth given the third, .72. The progression seemed to asymptote at about .8. Other investigators have reported very similar values.

The possibility that only a small group of boys needs to be targeted for early intervention or prevention is an appealing notion. Some scholars have proposed identifying these offenders and prolonging their period of incarceration as one means of reducing crime rates in the nation (Blumstein, Cohen, & Nagin, 1978). The other—and to the present writers the more appealing—idea is that successful prevention would be most cost effective if focused on the subgroup of boys identified as being most at risk for becoming chronic offenders. Even a moderately effective intervention could significantly reduce community crime rates if it could be initiated during the elementary grades.

There is no single definition of the term *chronic offender*. Evidence from self-report studies strongly suggest that using police arrests to define chronicity is undoubtedly accompanied by high false negative errors (Farrington, Ohlin, & Wilson, 1986); that is, many youths who commit high rates of serious offenses are not caught. For example, the large-scale survey study by Dunford and Elliott (1984) showed that based on self-reports, 86% of career offenders (5 or more crimes committed) had no arrests at all. For the subgroup of 23 boys reporting 20 of more index crimes, the ratio of occurrence of index crimes to arrests was 40 : 1.

Adult Career Offenders. The chronic juvenile offender costs society a great deal, but the cost is even greater if the process continues into adulthood. Careers as adult antisocial offenders lead to the involvement of a larger number of social agencies, both in the justice and in the mental health communities (Caspi, Elder, & Bem, 1986; Robins & Ratcliff, 1980).

A follow-up of a subgroup of the Philadelphia cohort at age 25 showed that about 39% of the juvenile offenders went on to become adult offenders (Wolfgang, 1977). For juveniles with three offenses, the likelihood of adult offenses was .46 (11% of them had three or more adult offenses); for those juveniles with five or more offenses, the likelihood was .66. The findings are in rough agreement with those from the retrospective study by Robins and Ratcliff (1978–1979). They found that roughly half of the extremely antisocial juveniles became antisocial adults.

The longitudinal study in Marion County, Oregon, (Polk, 1974) also showed that 56% of the juvenile offenders committed offenses (official records) after leaving high school. Polk pointed out that the adult career offender was significantly more likely to have been a juvenile who had committed higher rates of serious crimes.

Robins and Ratcliff (1978–1979) found that 70% of antisocial adults had been antisocial children. In an earlier report, Robins (1974) asserted that *no* adult sociopaths began their careers after the age of 18.

Early Starters. There are two interrelated hypotheses that emerge in the empirical literature for early starters (Patterson, Reid, & Dishion, in press). First, there is the frequency–seriousness hypothesis, which suggests that severity and seriousness of delinquent behavior are probably a manifestation of frequency. The child or adolescent who is engaged in very high rates of trivial antisocial behaviors is therefore at greater risk for engaging in more serious, but lower baserate, antisocial behavior. The second hypothesis asserts that early forms of antisocial behavior are prototypic of adolescent delinquent behaviors. In the present context, high frequencies of antisocial behavior measured in the elementary grades should correlate significantly with frequencies of adolescent crimes, including index crimes. In a very real sense, juvenile behaviors such as disobedience, fighting, and stealing are thought to be prototypic of adolescent crimes.

Given the assumption that most police contacts are fortuitous affairs (Dunford & Elliott, 1984; Hood & Sparks, 1970), those who engage in high rates of antisocial behavior should be at greater risk for their first police contact at an early age. Although there is perhaps no consensus on this matter, we assume that those who have their first police contact prior to age 15 are at greatest risk for both chronic juvenile offending and for a career as an adult offender.

Polk (1974) noted that most delinquents committed their first offense at age 16. Wadsworth (1979) found that recidivists had a mean age of 13.6 years for the first indictable offense, as compared to a mean age of 15.6 for the one-time offender. In keeping with the hypothesis, the follow-up study by Osborne and West (1978) found that 61% of those who committed their first offense before age 14 were reconvicted before age 25. This is in contrast to a reconviction rate of 36% for those with a first conviction in their late teens. A study cited by Tolan (1987) also showed that the age of first arrest was one of the best predictors for later arrest. In that study, the self-report data showed that early age of onset significantly predicted later delinquent behavior that was more frequent and more serious.

In their 1978 analyses, Osborn and West identified the following variables measured at age 10 that predicted recidivist offenders: very poor parenting, large family, father or siblings convicted at least twice, exceptional troublesomeness as rated by teachers, and an IQ of 83 or less. Recidivists were defined by two convictions prior to the 19th birthday and a further conviction before the 24th birthday. Blumstein, Farrington, and Moitra (1985) developed an elegant model using this and other data sets for the prediction of persisters and desisters.

Extremely antisocial boys who are identifiable in the elementary school grades are more profoundly disrupted socially and are at significant risk for both early starting and recidivist offending as adolescents. In keeping with the prototypic hypothesis, Robins (1966) noted that antisocial patterns typically begin early, often before the age of 10. She also noted that the greater the variety, frequency, and seriousness of childhood antisocial behavior, the greater the risk for adult antisocial behavior. West (1980) also provided data showing that if *both* the Grade 3 and 4 teachers identified the boys as "troublesome," then the risk for adolescent delinquent offenses was .42.

Farrington (1987) cited three studies showing significant relationships between teachers' ratings of aggressivity in Grades 1 and 2 and adolescent delinquency. In those studies, the proportions of adolescent delinquents previously rated by teachers as aggressive ranged from 45% to 83%. As noted earlier, we assume that youths trained to be antisocial in the home generalize the training to the school and community.

It is interesting to note in this connection that Offord, Sullivan, Allen, and Abrams (1979) found that early-starter delinquents tended to have been more hyperactive than late starters. The early start and the high frequency of prototypic antisocial behaviors place them at risk of becoming the first to be apprehended by the police.

The Oregon Youth Study Sample

The analyses reported in this subsection were based on a sample of two cohorts of Grade 4 boys ($N = 206$) and their parents. A cohort sequential design (Baltes, 1968; Schaie, 1965) was used for this research, with two successive birth cohorts of Grade 4 boys being sampled to permit the replication of results. The sample was selected from schools in the higher crime areas of a medium-sized metropolitan area and, thus, had a higher chance of involvement in delinquency than was average for the area. Of the target sample, 74.4% agreed to participate in the study. The details of the recruitment procedures are described in Capaldi and Patterson (1987).

The two cohorts ($n = 102$, $n = 104$) looked very similar on all major variables. Most of the sample was low income and blue collar; during the first year of the study (a recession year), one third of the sample received welfare. The demographic characteristics of the sample and the analyses describing the constructs are in Capaldi and Patterson (1989) and Patterson et al. (in press).

Each of the families participated in roughly 23 hours of assessment at Grade 4 and again at Grade 6. The assessment battery included observations in the home, questionnaires to parents and target children, videotaped family problem-solving situations, interviews, teacher ratings, peer nomination, achievement and intelligence tests, and brief telephone reports by parents and child. Records of police contacts and self-reported delinquent acts were collected each year beginning at Grade 4.

A strenuous effort was made to see that the constructs used in the structural equation models are all defined by heteromethod, heteroagent reports (i.e., by more than one method or more than a single agent). The procedures for combining different types of data to define a construct are discussed in Patterson and Bank (1986, 1987). The details of the itemetric analyses, the factor analyses, and the distributions for indicators and constructs used in the present study are detailed in Capaldi and Patterson (1989).

FORMULATION FOR THE EARLY STARTER MODEL

Differences among theories about delinquency become most apparent when the focus is on *how* the child or adolescent learns to perform antisocial acts. There seem to be two general sets of answers to this question.

The *Hobbesian view,* which is tacitly espoused by the established churches and both Freudian and social control theorists, is that the individual is naturally evil. If left to their own devices, all individuals would behave in an antisocial manner. From this perspective, each family and each society sets about the task of helping each child achieve internal controls. As a result, antisocial acts are performed only within acceptable limits. By definition, then, the appearance of delinquent or antisocial behavior is the result of a breakdown in internalized moral and social controls.

An alternative view, the *social interactional perspective,* is that certain specifiable reactions from the parent will produce a toddler who displays stable patterns of coercive behaviors and noncompliance (Martin, 1981). Similar contingencies maintain the performance of these behaviors in older children as well (Patterson, 1982). Treatment consists of *changing the contingencies* supplied by family members for antisocial and prosocial behaviors. The descriptor for these kinds of aversive exchanges among family members is *coercion.* This term describes the process by which the child is trained to employ aversive behaviors to terminate aversive intrusions by other family members.

Coercion Model: Family Training

It is assumed that coercive exchanges are the key ingredient in setting the early starter process in motion. Once it begins, it seems to move through a sequence of three stages: (a) The child shows clearly identifiable antisocial behaviors (e.g., fighting, temper tantrums, disobedience, stealing); (b) the child is rejected by the normal peer group; and (c) the child fails in school. The coercion model purports to explain how these things come about (Patterson, 1982; Patterson et al., in press).

As the child passes through each stage, he or she is placed at increased risk of continuing on to the next one. At each stage, there is an increase both in the spectrum of antisocial behaviors *and* in accompanying skill deficits. The details of these stages are presented in Patterson et al. (1989) and discussed in Patterson (1986).

As shown in Fig. 6.1, the early starter path is initiated by poor family-management practices, particularly unskilled discipline. Analyses of the details of parent–child interaction sequences showed that parent efforts to discipline often served to actually *strengthen* the child's coercive behaviors rather than weaken them (Patterson, 1982).

In these dysfunctional families, the interaction of family members provides specific training in aggression at a microsocial level. Analyses of the hundreds of social exchanges occurring in clinical and normal samples showed rich schedules of reinforcement for coercive child behaviors (Patterson, 1982; Snyder, 1977; Snyder & Patterson, 1986). Although

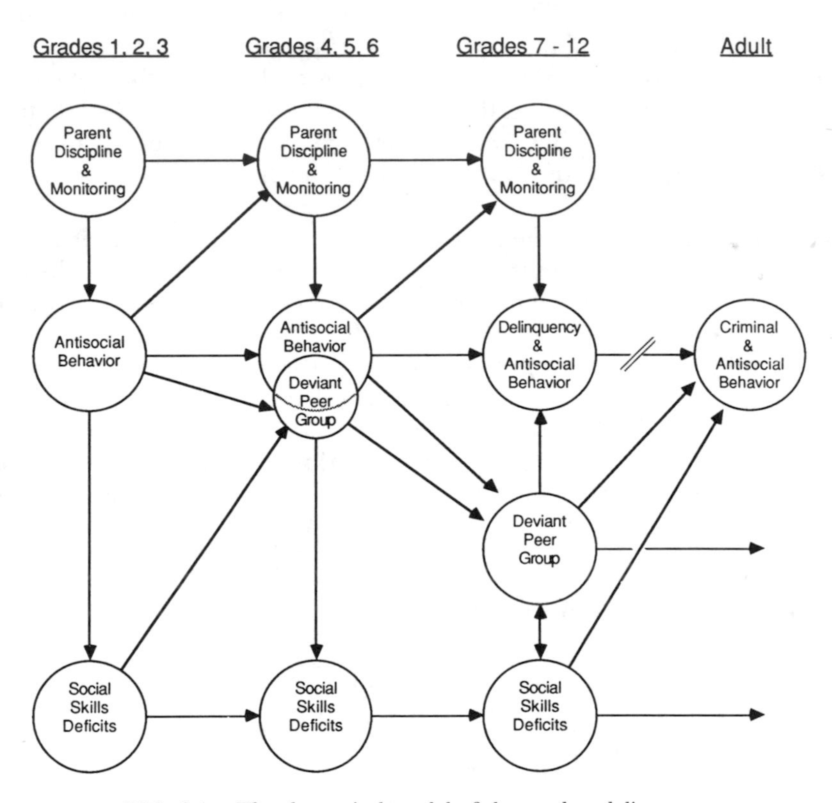

FIG. 6.1. The theoretical model of the road to delinquency.

positive reinforcement for coercive child behavior occurs (Snyder, 1987), the key contingencies are thought to be negative reinforcement. In this arrangement, a family member intrudes with an aversive behavior such as nagging or scolding. The child reacts coercively and the family member then reacts in a neutral or even positive manner and often withdraws. The data collected thus far suggests that, for normal families, about 14% of the child's coercive behaviors produce this sequence of contingencies, compared with 22% for boys in clinical samples.

The experimental and correlation studies summarized in Patterson (1982), replicated in Snyder (1987) and Snyder and Patterson (1986), showed that negative reinforcement contingencies significantly strengthen coercive child behaviors.

It is easy to see that a key requirement for family training in antisocial behavior is that the child live in a highly coercive family. This would maximize the likelihood that he or she could learn coercive behaviors as a means of adapting to the social environment. The accompanying hypothesis would be that *all* members of families referred for treatment of antisocial children are likely to be significantly more coercive than are corresponding members of normal families.

Table 6.1 summarizes the data comparing three samples observed for three sessions in their homes. The two clinical samples were referred for treatment. The data collected during the intake interview showed that the social aggressor sample engaged in *overt* antisocial behaviors but did not steal. Those in the stealer sample were selected because they engaged in clandestine antisocial behavior (e.g., stealing, lying, fire setting) but did not engage in high rates of overt antisocial behavior. It can be seen that members of antisocial families engaged in the highest rates of

TABLE 6.1
Coercion Levels by Family Members

Family members	*Social aggressor*	*Stealer*	*Normal*	*F value*	*Duncan*
Target Child	.90	.65	.17	25.12**	SA-ST-N
	(34)	(37)	(36)		
Mother	.87	.89	.45	11.51**	SA&ST-N
	(34)	(37)	(37)		
Father	.68	.50	.34	4.51*	SA-N
	(14)	(25)	(26)		
Siblings	.66	.53	.31	5.00*	SA-N
	(31)	(33)			

Note. The figures in parentheses are *N*s.
$*p < .01$
$**p < .001$
Source: Patterson (1982).

total aversive behavior (TAB), and those from normal families the lowest. It is obvious that aggressive boys live in aggressive families. The comparisons of clinical to normal samples have been replicated by Snyder (1977).

As the training in coercion progresses, the child's performance escalates from coercive behaviors of little significance (e.g., noncompliance, whining, talking back) to more intense, higher amplitude behaviors (e.g., temper tantrums, hitting). An accompanying hypothesis is that as the training continues, the child is increasingly likely to be engaged in low baserate, more serious antisocial acts (from temper tantrums and fighting to stealing and fire setting). Patterson et al. (in press) have reported findings from cross-sectional data consistent with the requirements for such a transitive progression.

There is evidence that the effects of the basic training in the home generalize to the school. Ramsey (1989) collected multiple indicator measures defining antisocial behavior for a subsample from the OYS sample. The indicators defined antisocial behavior as it occurred in the home (observation data, parent report, child telephone report). A year later, when the boys were in Grade 5, indicators were collected in school (discipline contacts, observation of peer interaction, teacher ratings, classroom observation). The findings strongly supported the hypothesized generalizability across settings (and time) for the latent constructs assessing antisocial behavior. The path coefficient was .71 ($p < .01$).

Failures in Peer Relations

The hypothesis here is that children's antisocial behavior causes two forms of massive social failure, both of which are crucial to their later development. One failure involves the peer group, and the other involves academic skills.

From nursery school through the elementary grades, the peer group defines a uniquely important segment of the social environment for the child. In addition to teaching a range of subtle social skills (Youniss, 1980), the peer group gradually develops a clearly defined code of acceptable and unacceptable behavior. Children with odd social behaviors, or even those differing in physical appearance, are either neglected or rejected. A majority of the antisocial boys are found in the rejected group. For example, French (1987) reported that half of the rejected boys in his sample were aggressive, and two thirds of all aggressive boys were rejected.

Two experimental manipulations have established that the correlation most likely reflects a causal relation in which the aversive behaviors and the lack of social skills produce the rejection (Coie & Kupersmidt, 1983; Dodge, 1983). These studies suggest that only a few hours of interaction are required in order for the newly introduced antisocial child to be assigned to this social limbo.

The reactions of peers may play several important roles in this process. For example, rejection has been shown to be the major determinant for preadolescent depressed moods (Patterson, 1988; Patterson, Reid, & Dishion, 1989). K. Dodge (in personal communication, October, 1988) has noted that the studies in his laboratory show that about one third of the aggressive boys are *not* rejected by normal peers, and he has hypothesized that these nonrejected aggressive boys may be the ones who drop out of the coercion process (i.e., they constitute many of our false positive errors in prediction from early antisocial to adolescent delinquency).

Dodge's idea of the nonrejected aggressive boy dropping out may relate to the fact that peer relations seem to have a *lagged* effect on later antisocial behavior, as shown by Patterson and Bank (1989). In that study, peer rejection at Grade 4 significantly contributed to antisocial behavior at Grade 6, relative to the stability for that trait. It seems, then, that in the short run, aggressive behavior leads to rejection, but in the long run peer rejection may function as a determinant of who drops out and who stays in the antisocial process.

School Failure. The easy tolerance and lack of expectations for achievement that characterize the nursery school give way to regular evaluations in the elementary grades. This poses a problem for the coercive child; the very core of the antisocial trait is *noncompliance.* The reason for the failure in the classroom is straightforward. It is assumed (given normal intelligence) that academic achievement is determined primarily by time on task in the classroom and on homework assignments in the home. Because the antisocial child spends less time on task than other children, it follows that he or she is at increased risk for academic failure.

Data collected at Grade 4 were used to examine the hypothesis that concurrent levels of antisocial behavior would correlate with measures of peer rejection and academic failure (Patterson, 1986). The findings showed strong paths from antisocial behavior to both of these constructs. Dishion (1988) has considerably extended these findings in demonstrating that child antisocial behavior in Grade 4 is strongly related to failed peer relations 2 years later. Patterson et al. (in press) showed that antisocial behavior at Grade 4 correlated with academic failure at Grades 5 and 6.

Classroom observation studies (e.g., Cobb & Hops, 1972; Walker,

Shinn, O'Neill, & Ramsey, 1987) have shown that antisocial children were on task in the classroom about 20% less than normal children. The findings from the longitudinal study by Tremblay (1988) have provided even stronger support for the role of antisocial behavior as a cause for academic failure. In his at-risk sample, 38% of the children rated as aggressive by kindergarten teachers were failing in school 3 years later. The likelihood of later school failure for the subgroup of aggressive children whose parents received parent training was 20%.

These massive social failures lead to frequently recurring depressed moods. Data from the combined Grade 4 OYS cohorts were used to model these relationships in Patterson et al. (in press). Failed peer relations made the largest contribution to the boys' dysphoric moods; the effect of academic failure on depression was mediated by its impact on peer relations. The model accounted for 50% of the variance in parents' and observers' ratings of children's depressed moods. The model has recently been replicated for a sample of preadolescent boys from recently separated families (Patterson, 1988).

Each new stage in this process may function as a positive feedback loop that contributes to the long-term maintenance of the child in the coercion process (Patterson et al., in press). Thus far, the hypothesis has been tested only for the Peer Relations and the Self-Esteem constructs. In the modeling study using OYS longitudinal data, Patterson, Bank, and Stoolmiller (1990) showed that the Peer Relations construct measured at Grade 4 served as a significant feedback loop to later antisocial behavior. Low self-esteem did not serve this function.

EMPIRICAL STUDIES OF THE EARLY STARTER MODELS

This section summarizes the information from a sequence of four structural equation models. The models were designed to test the hypothesis that there is a significant path from juvenile forms of antisocial behavior measured at Grade 4 to delinquency measured through Grades 7 and 8. Another set of the models was designed to test the relative contribution of the Deviant Peer construct measured at Grade 6 to predicting delinquency measured through Grades 7 and 8. Data are also presented to test the hypothesis that youngsters with more extreme scores on the Antisocial construct assessed at Grade 4 would be at greater risk for recidivism than would intermediate- or low-risk boys. Finally, the hypothesis that the more extreme-risk boys will have committed their first police offense at an earlier age is tested.

Predicting Delinquency From Grade 4

Both self-reported delinquency measured at Grade 7 (Elliott, Ageton, Huizinga, Knowles, & Canter, 1983) and official records of police contacts for Grades 4 through 8 were used to define the Delinquency construct. An itemetric analysis was used for the self-report items to identify those that formed an internally consistent scale for this age group.

Only the data for Cohort I are used for this analysis. the court records showed that 20% of this group had had at least one police contact; 11% had committed two or more offenses. Given an average age of 14, the prevalence rate compares favorably to the study by Polk (1974). His survey of 14 high schools in Oregon showed that by age 18 about 25% of the boys had at least one police offense; as he noted, the comparable figure for Caucasians from the Philadelphia cohort studies was 29%.

The convergent and discriminant correlation matrix is summarized in Table 6.2. It includes the intercorrelations among the indicators for the following constructs: Antisocial Behavior, Peer Relations, and Academic Achievement measured at Grade 4, and Delinquency measured at Grades 7 (self-report) and 8 (police records).

The convergence among the indicators for each construct seemed generally to be quite high. The mean correlation was .50 for Peer Relations, .29 for Antisocial Behavior, .61 for Academic Achievement, and .36 for Delinquency. The correlation of .36 between self-report and official records is very close to the gamma of .30 reported by Burcart (1977) as an average based on his review of studies in sociology.

Bentler's (1985) EQS program was used for the modeling analyses. The hypothesized model requires direct paths from all three Grade 4 constructs to later delinquency. In addition, it was thought that Antisocial Behavior would influence both Peer Relations and Academic Achievement, although the data for all three of these constructs were collected at approximately the same time.

A measurement model was fitted first. All four constructs were allowed to covary with one another, and several indicator residuals were set to covary as follows: The method variance represented in the three teacher-as-agent indicators was isolated in the three corresponding residual covariances. Three other pairs of residuals were covaried: (a) peer nominations of peer relations and teacher Child Behavior Checklist on achievement; (b) observed child aversive behavior at home and parent reports of their sons' antisocial behavior; and (c) observed child aversive behavior at home and performance on tests at school. One additional covariance parameter—child self-reported antisocial behavior from the interview with his later report on the Elliot—was included.

TABLE 6.2
Convergent and Discriminant Correlation Matrix for Peer Relations, Achievement, Antisocial, and Delinquency Constructs (Listwise N = 91)

		Negative Peer Relations		Child Antisocial				Academic Achievement			Delinquency	
		Peer Nomination	Teacher CBC	Parent report	Child phone	Observer report	Teacher CBC	Teacher CBC	School tests	WRAT: Reading	Elliott Self-report	Court records
	(Standard Deviation)	(.7703)	(.5589)	(.85342)	(.6672)	(.9973)	(.7053)	(.7521)	(.6685)	(.7149)	(.5224)	(.6657)
Negative	Peer nomination	1.00										
Peer Relations	Teacher CBC	.499	1.00									
	Parent report	.304	.294	1.00								
Child	Child phone	.065	.215	.251	1.00							
Antisocial	Observer report	.183	.167	.429	.067	1.00						
	Teacher CBC	.449	.705	.485	.330	.193	1.00					
Academic	Teacher CBC	-.519	-.471	-.299	-.174	-.163	-.553	1.00				
Achievement	School tests	-.364	-.220	-.228	.157	-.341	-.327	.685	1.00			
	WRAT: Reading	-.224	-.125	-.083	-.153	-.161	-.247	.488	.667	1.00		
Delinquency	Elliott Self-report	.149	.275	.388	.524	.117	.385	-.096	-.088	-.026	1.00	
	Court records	.309	.418	.351	-.010	.012	.460	-.223	-.068	-.035	.362	1.00

The measurement model recreated the covariance matrix rather well: $\chi^2(32) = 32.60$, $p = .39$, BBN = .921, BBNN = .992. At Grade 4, the intercorrelations among constructs were substantial; negative Peer Relations correlated .72 with the Antisocial construct and −.47 with Academic Achievement. The Academic Achievement and Antisocial constructs correlated −.52. In keeping with the a priori model, both the Antisocial (.69) and Peer Relations (.59) constructs correlated very well with later delinquency. The correlation of −.17 between Academic Achievement and Delinquency is in the expected direction, but its magnitude suggests that this feature of the a priori model will not be supported. As the boys enter middle adolescence, the time in which the greatest density of adolescent law violations exists, the magnitude of the achievement–delinquency relationship is expected to increase substantially. For example, the review by Hawkins and Lishner (1987) showed that school failure was one of the best predictors of recidivism among first offenders.

The a priori model stipulated that there would be significant paths from the Antisocial construct to both the Peer Relations and the Academic Achievement constructs at Grade 4 and that all three of these constructs would be directly related to later delinquency. This model showed a good fit to the data: $\chi^2(32) = 33.50$, $p = .394$. In addition, the model accounted for a surprisingly high 57% of the variance in the Delinquency construct. Nevertheless, there were several difficulties that led us to search for a better model. Neither of the paths for the two maintenance constructs (Peer Relations and Academic Achievement) were significant. In addition, the matrix manipulations converted a *negative* bivariate correlation between Academic Achievement and Delinquency to a *positive* path! We also determined that very small increments (from −.17 to −.30) in the magnitude of the Academic Achievement–Delinquency correlation would shift the value of the path to approximately zero. It seemed, therefore, that this particular path in the initial model was an artifactual one. Furthermore, when alternative paths were tested among the three constructs with data collected at Grade 4, almost all variations produced a similar fit.

The obvious alternative model has covariances among the three Grade 4 constructs, but only the direct path from Antisocial to Delinquency. The fit of this model was adequate: $\chi^2(33) = 37.25$, $p = .280$. The amount of variance accounted for was 46%. This more restricted model, though acceptable, was not entirely satisfactory either. It was obvious that the attenuated model ignored a good deal of relevant information contained in the covariance matrix.

Within the EQS (Bentler, 1985) framework, nonstandard or specific paths can be designated from any independent variable to any dependent variable, or between any two dependent variables. For example, all error terms are, by definition, independent variables (uniqueness plus noise) and therefore may have specific paths to other dependent variables, latent or measured. All measured indicators are dependent variables and therefore may have specific paths to other dependent variables, latent or measured.

There were two potential paths that seemed of interest. The first was the correlation of .52 between the child telephone interview at Grade 4 and self-reported delinquency several years later! In that the early report only correlated .01 with later police records, the least that one can say is that the child is consistent in his self-reports, even though these early reports have little predictive validity. This effect was modeled in the previously mentioned models as an error covariance term, but because the sequence of measurement rules out backwards in time causation, this term was converted to a path. Figure 6.2 shows how the model was altered to include a specific path that reflects this thread of information.

The second theme is reflected in the correlation of .42 between earlier teacher reports of peer relations and later court records for delinquency. Indicator loadings were quite stable throughout the series of analyses described. When these two specific paths were added to the attenuated model, there was a significant improvement in the fit of the model. The resulting model is shown in Fig. 6.2. As shown there, the direct path from the Antisocial construct accounts for about 44% of the common variance on the Delinquency construct. Notice that the teacher ratings with a factor loading of .80 serve as the marker variable for the Antisocial construct.

The path coefficients from earlier measures of peer relations and academic achievement measured to later delinquency were nonsignificant. We interpret this to mean that the contribution of disrupted peer relations to later delinquency is indirect. At this age, it is primarily mediated by antisocial behavior. The findings do not support the hypothesis that social skill deficits contribute directly to maintenance, at least not during the interval from Grade 4 to Grade 8. We believe that the skill deficit constructs will play a significant role during late adolescence, when most delinquent youth begin to drop out of the process.

The findings offer strong support for the continuity hypothesis. Antisocial behaviors measured at Grade 4 do indeed seem to be prototypic for later delinquent behaviors. The findings also suggest that teacher ratings may serve an extremely important function in early identification of at-risk samples. The court record data to be collected this fall will provide a basis for replicating the model using Cohort II data.

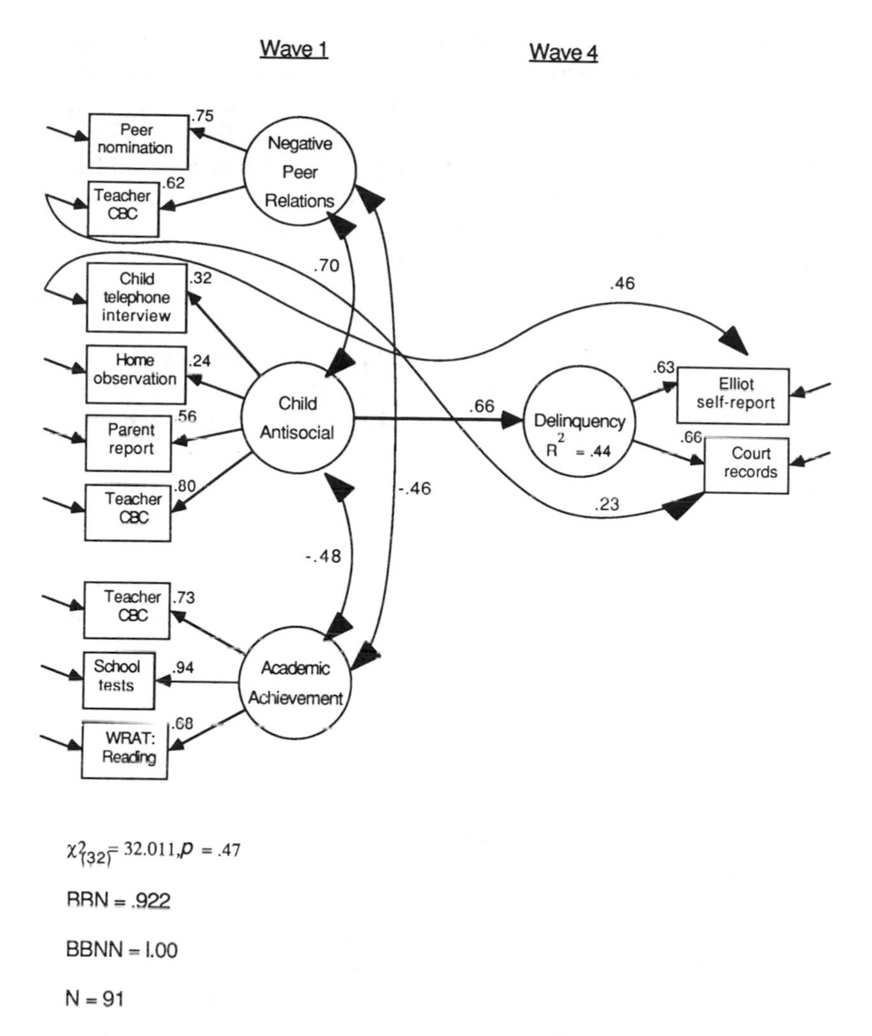

$\chi^2_{(32)} = 32.011, p = .47$

BBN = .922

BBNN = 1.00

N = 91

FIG. 6.2. The early starter path at Grade 4 (Cohort 1).

The Contribution of the Deviant Peer Group

According to Patterson et al. (1989), the function of the deviant peer group is thought to be very different for early and late starters. Presumably, the late starters become heavily involved during adolescence. Findings by Elliott and Menard (1988) have shown that the maximum exposure to deviant peers markedly increased at about age 15 or 16 and continued at a high level through age 18. These studies do not answer the question of exactly when boys come under the strong influence of deviant peers in their daily commerce with the social environment; taking all these findings together, our best guess is sometime after age 12 and before age 15. Elliott and Menard suggested that there may be several strata within the deviant peer group, each characterized by varying densities of delinquent youth but such that almost all adolescents have some contact with groups containing delinquent members. As noted earlier, one of the prime products of involvement in such groups is thought to be a short burst of delinquent activity, after which the youth drops out of the process.

We believe that during preadolescence, antisocial boys constitute the primary constituency for the emerging deviant peer group. In adolescence, its membership will be expanded to include youth who are not considered antisocial but who are experimenting with drugs and alcohol and rebelling against school and adult authority. At ages 10 and 12, a latent construct assessing involvement with deviant peers would *not* be expected to make unique contributions to predicting later delinquency beyond what could be made using just the construct for antisocial behavior measured at the same point in time. Our studies suggest that at this early juncture, the Antisocial and Deviant Peer constructs seem to be almost equivalent terms; that is, almost all boys who are involved in the deviant peer group are antisocial.

To test these assumptions, data were used from the assessment of the Antisocial and Deviant Peer constructs made at Grade 6. What is of particular interest is the intercorrelation of these two constructs and the correlation of each with the Delinquency construct. As a matter of interest, we also included the assessment of the Antisocial construct at Grade 4 to determine what its relation would be with later measures of both antisocial behavior and deviant peer association.

The correlations for the convergent and discriminant validities are presented in Table 6.3. A measurement model specifies which indicators load on which constructs; it also makes the general assumption that all constructs are significantly intercorrelated. In the present case, this would mean that early (Grade 4) and late (Grade 6) measures of antisocial behavior, late measures of deviant peer involvement, and later measures of delinquency would *all* intercorrelate. The findings for the measurement model are summarized in Fig. 6.3.

Although there is a good fit of the model to the data, the *very* high magnitude of correlations among all constructs is immediately apparent. As stipulated by the early starter model, there is a very high correlation (.93) between the latent constructs of Antisocial Behavior and Deviant Peer Association measured at Grade 6. The magnitude of this correlation strongly suggests that multicolinearity would make it impossible to

TABLE 6.3
Convergent and Discriminant Correlation Matrix for Two Models
(Listwise N = 88)

		Monitoring			Antisocial Behavior[1]			Achievement			Antisocial Behavior[2]				Delinquency		Deviant Peers		
		Child int'view	Interv. impress	Parent report	Parent int'view	Child phone	Obser-vation	Teacher CBC	WRAT	Test scores	Parent int'view	Child phone	Teacher CBC	Obser-vation	Self-report	Court records	Child int'view	Parent int'view	Teacher CBC
	S.D.	.573	.776	2.252	.838	.657	[illegible]	.752	14.11	1.322	.891	3.104	.907	1.260	.529	1.323	.472	.705	.880
Monitoring	Child int'view	1.00																	
	Intv'wer imp.	.379	1.00																
	Parent report	.132	.288	1.00															
Antisocial Behavior	Parent int'view	-.182	-.213	-.261	1.00														
	Child telephone	-.155	-.230	-.193	.305	1.00													
	Observation	-.120	-.248	-.112	.368	[illegible]	1.00												
Achievement	Teacher CBC	.271	.384	.131	-.269	[illegible]	[illegible]	1.00											
	WRAT	.250	.293	.149	-.145	[illegible]	-.231	.509	1.00										
	Test scores	.265	.392	.069	-.189	[illegible]	-.302	.679	.725	1.00									
Antisocial Behavior	Parent int'view	-.224	-.228	-.206	.785	[illegible]	[illegible]	-.297	-.071	-.141	1.00								
	Child telephone	[illegible]	-.258	-.305	.350	[illegible]	.091	-.392	-.375	-.356	.404	1.00							
	Teacher CBC	-.156	-.352	-.083	.375	.305	.070	-.466	-.156	-.247	.565	.383	1.00						
	Observation	[illegible]	-.242	-.034	.361	.205	.243	-.222	-.147	-.182	.339	.121	.331	1.00					
Delinquency	Self-report	-.022	-.191	[illegible]	.384	.546	[illegible]	-.081	-.037	-.070	.347	.429	.451	.380	1.00				
	Court records	[illegible]	-.128	-.002	.318	.012	[illegible]	-.204	-.080	-.027	.521	.189	.504	.165	.356	1.00			
Deviant Peers	Child int'view	[illegible]	-.338	-.237	.221	.162	[illegible]	-.336	-.230	-.264	.352	.641	.391	.034	.394	.243	1.00		
	Parent int'view	[illegible]	-.296	-.116	.452	.073	.165	-.251	-.124	-.206	.657	.350	.434	.222	.262	.507	.385	1.00	
	Teacher CBC	-.272	-.393	-.157	.422	.267	[illegible]	-.514	-.341	-.365	.525	.376	.760	.243	.317	.342	.332	.399	1.00

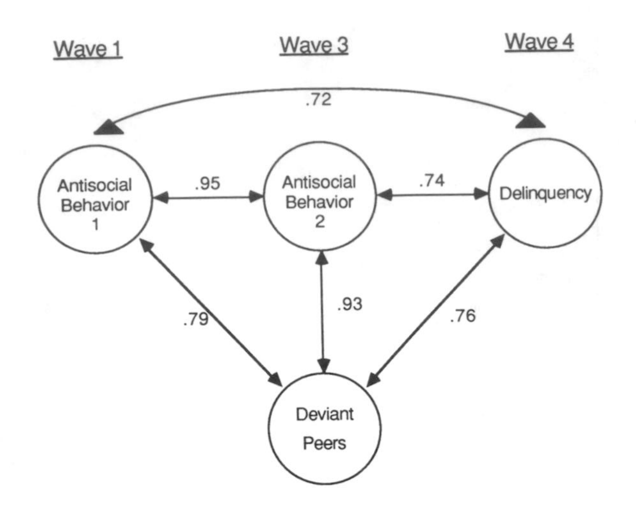

$\chi^2_{(32)} = 37.27$

$p = .240$

BBN = .907

BBNN = .974

Listwise $N = 89$

FIG. 6.3. Measurement model for the relative contribution model.

partial out the unique contribution of the Deviant Peer construct to predicting later delinquency (Pedhazur, 1982). Indeed, when attempts were made to include both constructs, such models proved to be unworkable.

Dishion, Patterson, and Skinner (1988) showed that the convergence among teacher, parent, and child indicators for a Deviant Peer construct at age 10 was borderline. As shown in Table 6.3, however, the convergence was quite strong at age 12. They inferred from their findings that, at this early stage, the deviant peer group was just emerging as a phenomenon and was, therefore, difficult to measure properly. This interpretation is consistent with the findings previously discussed.

It was a matter of some interest to explore further the possibility that the Deviant Peer and Antisocial constructs measured at Grade 6 might each make some uniquely interesting contribution to understanding later delinquency. For this reason, separate models were constructed that tested two possible early starter models. Both of them began with Antisocial Behavior measured at Grade 4. In the first model, the path moves from there to the Deviant Peer construct measured at Grade 6 and then to delinquency. In the second, a chronicity model, the path moves to a reassessment of Antisocial Behavior measured at Grade 6 and then to delinquency.

Both models also included assessment of Monitoring (i.e., supervision) and Academic Achievement constructs measured at Grade 4. This decision was based on findings from a previous study showing that both variables contributed significantly to deviant peer involvement in early adolescence (Patterson & Dishion, 1985).

The findings from the structural equation models for deviant peers are summarized in Fig. 6.4. The path coefficient of .63 gives strong support for the hypothesis that early forms of antisocial behavior are significantly related to later involvement in a deviant peer group. This finding neatly replicates the early analyses of a different sample by Snyder, Dishion, and Patterson (1986). The path coefficient of .70 between lagged measures of deviant peer involvement and later delinquency also replicates the findings from the longitudinal studies by Elliott et al. (1985). As hypothesized, monitoring was predictive of deviant peers (−.40), although the Achievement construct would make a direct contribution to involvement with deviant peers.

The deviant peer model accounts for a respectable 49% of the variance in the measure of delinquency, although the fit of the model to the data was marginal: $\chi^2(68) = 88.34, p = .049$. Residuals covaried included the Elliott with each of three Grade 4 indicators (child telephone interview on antisocial behavior, observed child antisocial behavior, and number of hours per day with son), court record with parent reports of son's association with deviant peers (at Grade 4), and school tests with parent reports of son's antisocial behavior (at Grade 4). An alternative model that added a direct path from Antisocial Behavior at Grade 4 to later Delinquency did not account for any additional variance and was rejected.

The intercorrelations among the constructs used in the second model are summarized in Table 6.3. The data set was based on assessments at Grades 4 and 6 for Cohort I.

The model summarized in Fig. 6.5 is labeled the "chronicity model" because it describes boys who are extremely antisocial at two points in time. The assumption is that such boys would be at greater risk for delinquency than would boys described as antisocial at only one point in time. As expected, there is a significant path (.47) from the Antisocial Behavior construct measured at Grade 6 to later delinquency. It is particularly interesting to note the significant path coefficient (.40) from the measure of Antisocial Behavior in Grade 4 to later delinquency; this

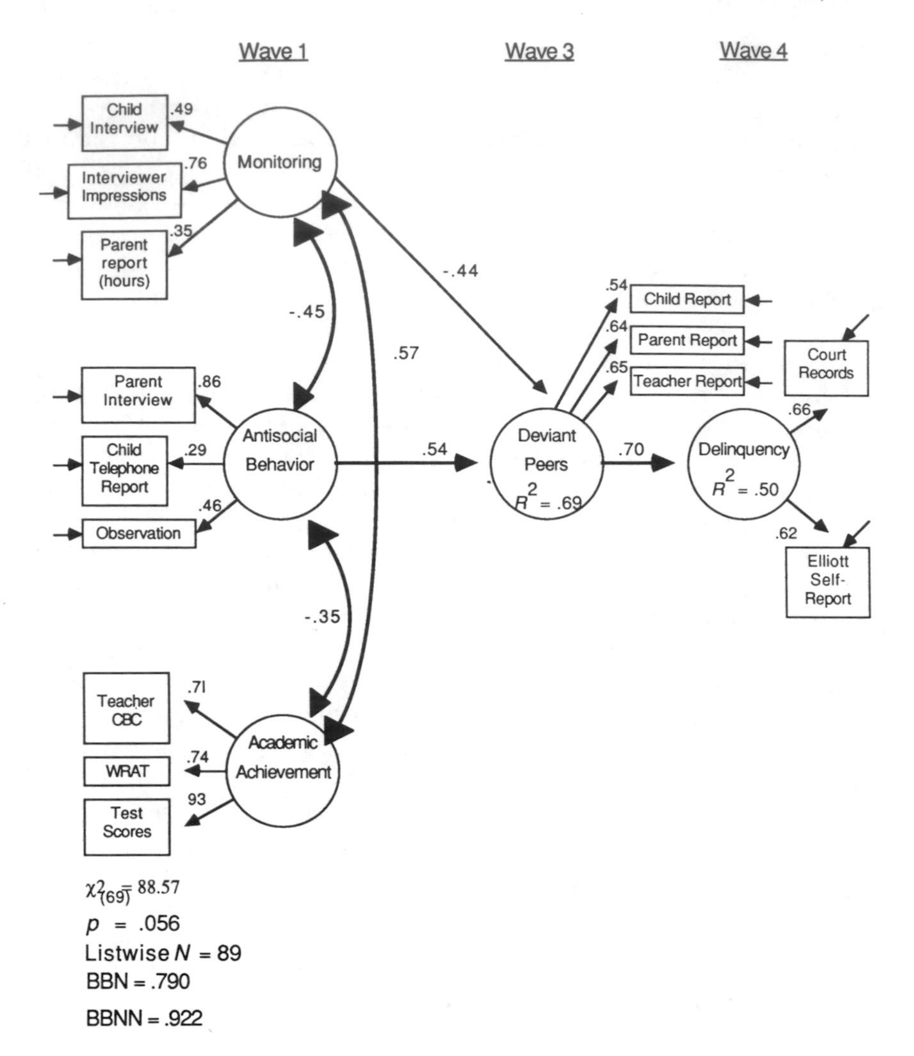

FIG. 6.4. The deviant peer model for delinquent behavior (Cohort I).

emphasizes the fact that antisocial behavior at Grade 4 makes *both* a direct and an indirect contribution to later delinquency. In a prediction study, this would suggest that the second assessment gate for a multiple-gating design (Loeber, Dishion, & Patterson, 1984) might include a search of the school records during the prior year in order to build an Antisocial construct score similar to the one suggested by Ramsey (1989).

The a priori model fit the data adequately: $\chi^2(77) = 87.1$, $p = .20$. Note that the path from parent Monitoring to later Antisocial Behavior reaches statistical significance in this model. The fact that the model

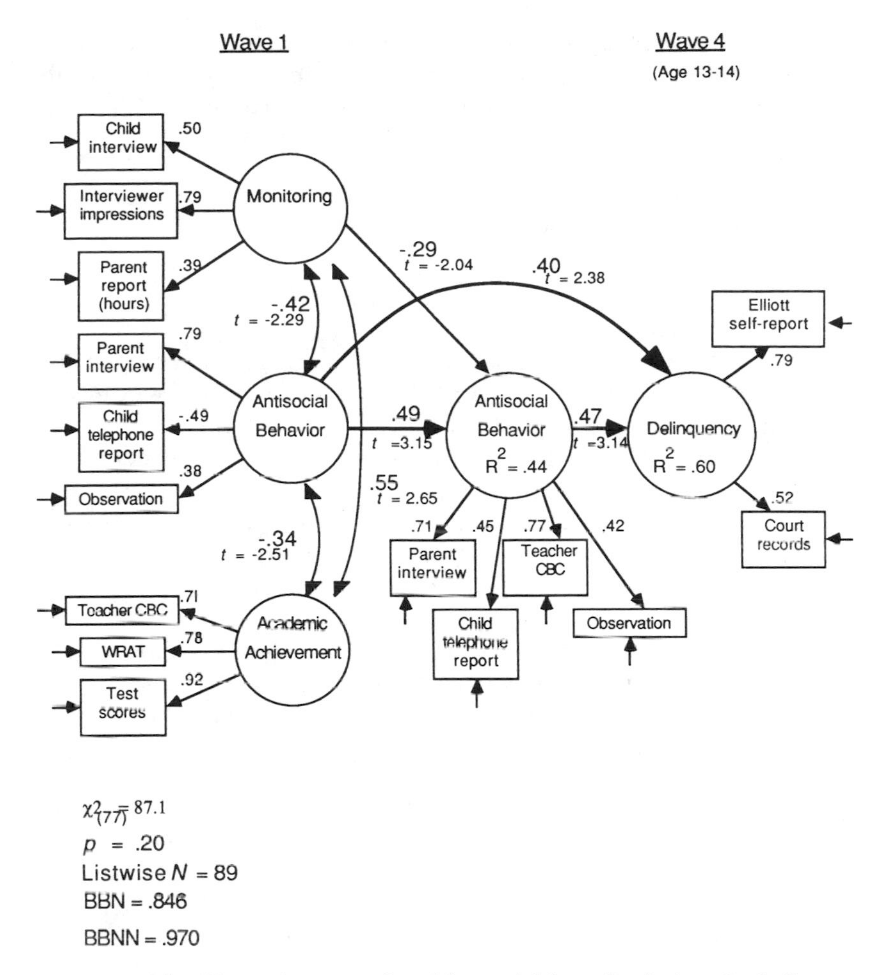

FIG. 6.5. The early-starter chronicity model from Grade 4 to Grade 7 (Cohort I).

accounted for 60% of the variance in the Delinquency construct is also noteworthy. Residuals covaried in this model include those from parent reports of child Antisocial Behavior for Waves 1 and 3, and teacher reports (Child Behavior Checklist) of boys' Antisocial Behavior for Waves 1 and 3. In addition, the residual from the Elliott was covaried with both the Wave 1 child telephone interview on Antisocial Behavior and the parent telephone interview on Monitoring; the court record residual was covaried with both the parent and teacher reports of the boys' Antisocial Behavior at Wave 3.

It remains to be seen just what the contribution of the Deviant Peer construct might be at middle or late adolescence. As noted earlier, the expectation is that it is the socially unskilled early starter who remains involved with the deviant peer group during late adolescence. Presumably, it will be this combination of factors that determines risk for adult career offending.

Recidivists and Early Offenders

The findings presented thus far are certainly consistent with the formulation for the early starter model. Nevertheless, a rigorous test must await the completion of the longitudinal study, when it will be possible to evaluate the efficacy of the early and late starter models. As an interim evaluation, one might think of the different levels of antisocial scores as varying in the fit they would provide for predictions about delinquent behavior. For example, boys with more extreme scores on Antisocial Behavior at Grade 4 would be at greater risk than boys with lower scores for both recidivism and younger age at first police offense.

To test these hypotheses, both cohorts were divided into three risk groups according to their score on the Antisocial construct assessed at Grade 4. The top quartile were designated as being at extreme risk, the next quartile as at moderate risk, and the lower half at low risk. The first hypothesis tested was that the three at-risk groups would differ significantly on general measures of child adjustment, parent family-management skills, and parent pathology.

Table 6.4 summarizes the findings. Multivariate analyses of variance were run separately for the boys, parents, and family-management variables. The omnibus statistics (Pillai-Bartlett trace) were significant for all three Manovas ($p < .001$). In general, the children and parents in the extreme-risk group showed the most distress, and those in the least-risk group showed the least.

Examination of the univariate *F*s revealed that the extreme-risk boys were more maladjusted in all six areas of child adjustment. Their parents' retrospective ratings showed them to be difficult preschoolers; the multiagent-multimethod constructs showed them to be significantly involved with deviant peers, less socially skilled, more prone to academic failure, more depressed in moods, and more likely to be rejected by peers. They were also characterized by significantly less effective monitoring and discipline practices.

The scores assessing parent functioning showed a rather surprising pattern of results. The parents of moderate-risk boys might best be characterized as antisocial, depressed, and stressed. On the other hand, the parents of the extreme-risk boys seemed to be characterized by lower social status and depression.

TABLE 6.4
Comparisons Among Three Risk Groups

Boys' Variables	*Extreme Risk* *N = 51*	*Moderate Risk* *N = 50*	*Low Risk* *N = 104*	*F value*
		Child Adjustment		
Early difficulties	.66	.14	−.40	.001
Deviant peers	.73	.24	−.48	.001
Social skills	−1.06	−.21	.62	.001
Academic skills	−.48	−.04	.29	.001
Depression	.72	.14	−.42	.001
Peer relations	−1.06	−.06	.55	.001
Pillias (2,202) = 14.82 ($p < .001$)				
		Family Management		
Monitoring	−.32	−.21	.26	.01
Discipline	−.64	−.09	.37	.001
Pillias (2,203) = 11.87 ($p < .001$)				
		Parent Dispositions		
Socioeconomic status	−.28	−.11	.20	.05
Depression	.20	.29	−.25	.01
Stress	.19	.45	−.33	.001
Drug use	.22	.37	−.28	.001
Antisocial behavior	.03	.34	−.19	.01
Pillias (2,202) = 4.08 ($p < .001$)				

The findings are consistent with the hypothesis that extreme-risk boys are less well adjusted and must also cope with less skilled parents. The extreme-risk boys seem to experience more social disadvantage, whereas the moderate-risk boys seem to be products of antisocial parents.

The next hypothesis tested concerned the expected differences among the groups in recidivism and age at first offense. The official records collected when the boys were entering Grades 8 and 9 showed that 51% of the extreme-risk group had an arrest, compared to 29% for the moderate-risk group and 7% for the low-risk group. The likelihood of committing two or more offenses was .31 for youths in the extreme at-risk group; the comparable likelihoods for the moderate- and low-risk groups were .10 and .00 respectively. The findings offer strong support for the hypothesis that at Grade 4 the extremely antisocial boys are at greater risk for recidivism.

The mean dates of first offense showed that the extreme-risk group committed their first offenses at around age 10 or 11, on the average 1.5 years earlier than the moderate-risk group and 1.8 years ahead of the low-risk group. These findings are consistent with the hypothesis that extremely antisocial boys in Grade 4 are at greater risk for committing their first offenses at a younger age.

DISCUSSION

The empirical literature suggests that the 15th birthday may serve as a reasonable place to distinguish between early- and late-starting offenders. Because the vast majority of Cohorts I and II are not yet 15, it is too early to test the late starter model. Even so, it was expected that the police offense data available when the boys were ages 13 and 14 should provide a fit to the a priori model for early starters. It was gratifying to see that this was indeed the case. The antisocial behavior of the boys when assessed at Grade 4 made significant predictions to future delinquency. It should be noted, however, that 3–4% of the boys had committed offenses prior to the assessment at Grade 4. More precise estimates of predictive efficiency will require that this effect by partialed out.

There is a suggestion from one of the models that an estimate of chronicity measured at two points in time might account for some additional variance in predicting later delinquency. This is a notion that we intend to pursue further.

The efforts to model the contributions of the Deviant Peers construct at age 12 suggest that, although the construct is definable, it overlaps in *function* with the contribution made by the Antisocial construct. The deviant peer group certainly plays a key role for the older adolescent and the antisocial adult. The question is *when* this function becomes salient; evidently not by age 12.

The analyses also suggested that boys with the more extreme scores on Antisocial Behavior at Grade 4 were not only more maladjusted, but came from more distressed families than did boys with intermediate or low risk scores. As predicted, boys with more extreme scores did indeed have first police offenses at a younger age and were at greater risk for recidivism.

The findings are generally consistent with the early starter model. The crucial data will be those that demonstrate that early starters are at greater risk than late starters for chronic offending, as tested when the boys are age 18 or 19. Our hunch is that the early starters will eventually be shown to carry a strong heritable component, as well as lower social status, as factors contributing to the antisocial behavior.

The idea behind the notion of two paths to delinquency is that one path (that of the early starter) leads to chronicity and continuance to adult careers, whereas the other (the late starter path) leads to early dropout from the process. The findings in this chapter are consistent with these ideas but do not constitute a rigorous test. In a sense, this chapter describes a research strategy for a project that is at its midpoint. The data are illustrative but do not constitute the rigorous testing that is eventually required before the two paths can be accepted.

ACKNOWLEDGMENTS

An earlier draft of this manuscript was presented at the *Earlscourt Conference on Childhood Aggression*, June, 1988, Toronto, Canada. The writers gratefully acknowledge the support provided by MH 37940 and HD 22679 for the collection and analyses of these data. The artistry in the figures reflects the talents of Will Mayer, and the mathematical skill required for the analyses was the responsibility of Mike Stoolmiller. We owe a special debt to our colleagues at the Center; each of them critiqued an earlier draft of the manuscript and followed up their comments with an insightful seminar on the topic. We also wish to thank Katie Douglass for the careful editing of the final manuscript.

REFERENCES

Baltes, P. B. (1968). Longitudinal and cross-sectional sequences in the study of age and generation effects. *Human Development, 11,* 145–171.

Bentler, P. M. (1985). *Theory and implementation of EQS: A structural equations program.* Los Angeles: BMDP Statistical Software.

Blumstein, A. D., Cohen, J., & Nagin, D. (Eds.). (1978). *Deterrence and incapacitation: Estimating the effects of criminal sanctions on crime rates.* Washington, DC: National Academy of Sciences.

Blumstein, A. D., Farrington, D., & Moitra, S. (1985). Delinquency careers: Innocents, desisters, and persisters. In M. Tonry & N. Morris (Eds.), *Crime and justice: An annual review of research* (vol. 6, pp. 187–219). Chicago: University of Chicago Press.

Burcart, J. M. (1977). *Measuring delinquency through self-report instruments: A bibliographic essay.* Unpublished manuscript.

Capaldi, D. M., & Patterson, G. R. (1987). An approach to the problem of recruitment and retention rates for longitudinal research. *Behavioral Assessment, 9,* 169–177.

Capaldi, D. M., & Patterson, G. R. (1989). *Psychometric properties of fourteen latent constructs from the Oregon Youth Study.* New York: Springer-Verlag.

Caspi, A., Elder, G. H., & Bem, D. J. (1986). *Moving against the world: Life course patterns of explosive children.* Unpublished manuscript.

Cobb, J. A., & Hops, H. (1972). Effects of academic survival skill training on low achieving first graders. *Journal of Educational Research, 12,* 43–51.

Coie, J. D., & Kupersmidt, J. B. (1983). A behavioral analysis of emerging social status in boys' groups. *Child Development, 54,* 1400–1416.

Dishion, T. J. (1988). *The family ecology of boys' peer relations in middle childhood.* Manuscript submitted for publication.

Dishion, T. J., Patterson, G. R., & Skinner, M. L. (1988). *Parent monitoring and peer relations in the drift to deviant peers: From middle childhood to early adolescence.* Manuscript submitted for publication.

Dodge, K. A. (1983). Behavioral antecedents: A peer social status. *Child Development, 54,* 1386–1399.

Dunford, F. W., & Elliott, D. S. (1984). Identifying career offenders using self-reported data. *Journal of Research in Crime and Delinquency, 21,* 57–86.

Elliott, D. S., Ageton, S. S., Huizinga, D., Knowles, B. A., & Canter, R. J. (1983). *The prevalence and incidence of delinquent behavior: 1976–1980. National estimates of delinquent behavior by sex, race, social class, and other selected variables.* (National Youth Survey Report No. 26). Boulder, CO: Behavioral Research Institute.

Elliott, D. S., Huizinga, D., & Ageton, S. S. (1985). *Explaining delinquency and drug use.* Beverly Hills, CA: Sage.

Elliott, D. S., & Menard, S. (1988). *Delinquent behavior and delinquent peers: Temporal and developmental patterns.* Unpublished manuscript.

Farrington, D. P. (1983). Offending from 10 to 25 years of age. In K. T. Van Dusen & S. A. Mednick (Eds.), *Prospective studies of crime and delinquency* (pp. 17–37). Boston: Kluwer-Nijhoff.

Farrington, D. P. (1987). Early precursors of frequent offending. In J. Q. Wilson & C. C. Loury (Eds.), *From children to citizens: Vol. 3. Families, schools, and delinquency prevention* (pp. 27–50). New York: Springer-Verlag.

Farrington, D. P., Ohlin, L. E., & Wilson, J. Q. (1986). *Understanding and controlling crime: Toward a new research strategy.* New York: Springer-Verlag.

French, D. (1987, June). *Peer relations and child adjustment.* Seminar presented at Oregon Social Learning Center, Eugene.

Hawkins, J. D., & Lishner, D. M. (1987). Schooling and delinquency. In E. H. Johnson (Ed.), *Handbook on crime and delinquency prevention* (pp. 179–221). New York: Greenwood.

Hood, R., & Sparks, R. (1970). *Key issues in criminology.* London: Weidenfeld & Nicolson.

Loeber, R., Dishion, T. J., & Patterson, G. R. (1984). Multiple gating: A multistage assessment procedure for identifying youths at risk for delinquency. *Journal of Research in Crime and Delinquency, 21,* 7–32.

Martin, J. (1981). A longitudinal study of the consequences of early mother–infant interaction: A microanalytic approach. *Monographs of the Society for Research in Child Development, 46*(3, Serial No. 190).

Offord, D. R., Sullivan, K., Allen, N., & Abrams, N. (1979). Delinquency and hyperactivity. *Journal of Nervous and Mental Disorders, 167,* 734–741.

Osborn, S. G., & West, D. J. (1978). The effectiveness of various predictors of criminal careers. *Journal of Adolescence, 1,* 101–117.

Patterson, G. R. (1982). *A social learning approach to family intervention: III. Coercive family process.* Eugene, OR: Castalia.

Patterson, G. R. (1986). Performance models for antisocial boys. *American Psychologist, 41,* 432–444.

Patterson, G. R. (1988). *A replication of a model for preadolescent boys' depressed moods.* Unpublished manuscript, Oregon Social Learning Center, Eugene.

Patterson, G. R., & Bank, L. (1986). Bootstrapping your way in the nomological thicket. *Behavioral Assessment, 8,* 49–73.

Patterson, G. R., & Bank, L. (1987). When is a nomological network a construct? In D. R. Peterson & D. B. Fishman (Eds.), *Assessment for decision* (pp. 249–279). New Brunswick, NJ: Rutgers University Press.

Patterson, G. R., & Bank, L. (1989). Some amplifying mechanisms for pathologic process in families. In M. Gunnar & E. Thelen (Eds.), *Systems and development: The Minnesota Symposia on Child Psychology* (Vol. 22, pp. 167–209). Hillsdale, NJ: Lawrence Erlbaum Associates.

Patterson, G. R., Bank, L., & Stoolmiller, M. (1990). The preadolescent's contributions to disrupted family process. In R. Montemayor, G. R. Adams, & T. P. Gullotta (Eds.), *From childhood to adolescence: A transitional period?* (pp. 107–133). Newbury Park, CA: Sage.

Patterson, G. R., DeBaryshe, B. D., & Ramsey, E. (1989). A developmental perspective on antisocial behavior. *American Psychologist, 44*(2), 329–335.

Patterson, G. R., & Dishion, T. J. (1985). Contributions of families and peers to delinquency. *Criminology, 23,* 63–79.

Patterson, G. R., Reid, J. B., & Dishion, T. J. (in press). *Antisocial boys.* Eugene, OR: Castalia.

Pedhazur, E. J. (1982). *Multiple regression in behavioral research: Explanation and prediction* (2nd ed.). New York: Holt, Reinhart, & Winston.

Polk, J. (1974). *Teenage delinquency in small town America* (Research Report No. 5). Washington, DC: National Institute of Mental Health Center for Studies on Crime and Delinquency.

Ramsey, E. (1989). *Generalization of antisocial behavior in boys from home to school.* Unpublished manuscript, Oregon Social Learning Center, Eugene.

Robins, L. N. (1966). *Deviant children grown up: A sociological and psychiatric study of sociopathic personality.* Baltimore: Williams & Wilkins.

Robins, L. N. (1974). Antisocial behavior disturbances of childhood: Prevalence, prognosis, and prospects. In E. J. Anthony & C. Koupernik (Eds.), *The child in his family: Children at psychiatric risk* (vol. 3, pp. 447–460). New York: Wiley.

Robins, L. N., & Ratcliff, K. S. (1978–1979). Risk factors in the continuation of childhood antisocial behaviors into adulthood. *International Journal of Mental Health,* 7(3–4), 96–116.

Robins, L. N., & Ratcliff, K. S. (1980). Childhood conduct disorders and later arrest. In L. N. Robins, P. Clayton, & J. Wing (Eds.), *Social consequences of psychiatric illness* (pp. 123–157). New York: Brunner/Mazel.

Schaie, K. W. (1965). A general model for the study of developmental problems. *Psychological Bulletin, 64,* 92–107.

Shannon, L. W. (1980, November). *Assessing the relationship of juvenile careers to adult criminal careers.* Paper presented at the conference of the American Society for Criminology, San Francisco, CA.

Snyder, J. J. (1977). Reinforcement analysis of interaction in problem and non-problem families. *Journal of Abnormal Psychology, 86,* 528–535.

Snyder, J. J. (1987, June). *Learning and family interaction.* Paper presented at the Second Annual Summer Institute of the Family Research Consortium, Santa Fe, NM.

Snyder, J. J., Dishion, T. J., & Patterson, G. R. (1986). Determinants and consequences of associating with deviant peers during preadolescence and adolescence. *Journal of Early Adolescence, 6,* 29–43.

Snyder, J. J., & Patterson, G. R. (1986). The effects of consequences on patterns of social interaction: A quasi-experimental approach to reinforcement in natural interaction. *Child Development, 57,* 1257–1268.

Tolan, P. H. (1987). Implications of age of onset for delinquency risk. *Journal of Abnormal Child Psychology, 15,* 47–65.

Tremblay, R. (1988, June). *Some findings from the Montreal studies.* Paper presented at the Earlscourt Symposium on Childhood Aggression, Toronto, Ontario, Canada.

Wadsworth, M. E. J. (1979). *Roots of delinquency: Infancy, adolescence, and crime.* Oxford, England: Robertson.

Walker, H. M., Shinn, M. R., O'Neill, R. E., & Ramsey, E. (1987). A longitudinal assessment of the development of antisocial behavior in boys: Rationale, methodology, and first-year results. *Remedial and Special Education, 8*(4), 7–16.

West, D. J. (1980). *Followup data from the Cambridge studies.* Seminar presented at the Oregon Social Learning Center, Eugene.

Wolfgang, M. E. (1977, September). *From boy to man—from delinquency to crime.* Paper presented at the National Symposium of Serious Juvenile Offenders, Minnesota Department of Corrections, Minneapolis.

Wolfgang, M. E., Figlio, R., & Sellin, T. (1972). *Delinquency in a birth cohort.* Chicago: University of Chicago Press.

Wolfgang, M. E., & Tracy, P. E. (1982). *The 1945 and 1959 birth cohorts: A comparison of the prevalence, incidence, and severity of delinquent behavior.* Paper presented at the Conference on Public Danger, Dangerous Offenders, and the Criminal Justice System, Kennedy School of Government, Harvard University, Cambridge, MA.

Youniss, J. (1980). *Parents and peers in social development: A Sullivan-Piaget perspective.* Chicago: University of Chicago Press.

7

The Role of Parental Variables in the Learning of Aggression

Leonard D. Eron
L. Rowell Huesmann
Arnaldo Zelli
University of Illinois at Chicago

In a number of studies, parents' child-rearing styles have been related to the aggressive behavior that children display outside the home, especially in school, as well as to their antisocial behavior as adolescents and adults. In two large-scale longitudinal investigations, conducted in different areas of the United States and in four other countries with 6- and 8-year-old children, parental rejection of the child, punishment for aggression by the child, and lack of identification of the child with the parent were related independently both to contemporaneous behavior in school and to adult behavior. However, regression analyses seem to indicate that the parent behaviors were more likely a response to the aggression of the child than an instigation to aggression by the child. The best predictor to adult aggression and antisocial behavior was the extent of child aggression, regardless of parental behavior.

A rapidly accumulating body of data suggests that aggression, as a characteristic way of solving interpersonal problems, usually emerges early in life. Each individual seems to develop a characteristic level of aggressiveness early on, which remains relatively stable across time and situation. One of the first explanations that comes to mind is that aggression must be constitutionally or genetically determined. To a certain extent, this may very well be the case. We ourselves have data demonstrating the consistency of aggressive behavior over three generations (Huesmann, Eron, Lefkowitz, & Walder, 1984; Eron, Huesmann, Dubow, Romanoff & Yarmel, 1987). However, over and above whatever equipment the infant is born with, aggression as a way of interacting with other persons is learned, as we and others have demonstrated, from a developing youngster's interactions with the environment. The most significant part of that environment, for the vast majority of children, is the parents. Parents teach children aggression by the models of behavior they present, the reinforcements they provide for aggressive behavior, and the conditions they furnish in the home that frustrate and victimize the child. In this chapter, we focus on the contribution that parents make to the characteristic aggressive responding of their children.

Among the parent variables that have been implicated in the etiology of aggression are inconsistent parental disciplinary practices (McCord, 1979; Patterson & Stouthamer-Loeber, 1984) parental disharmony (Farrington & West, 1971; Wadsworth, 1979), parental rejection (Olweus, 1980), harsh punishment (Andrew, 1981); father absence (Hoffman, 1971); parental modeling (Neapolitan, 1981; West & Farrington, 1973); lack of parental supervision, (Farrington, 1983); and family history of antisocial behavior (Osborn & West, 1979; Robins, West, & Herjanic, 1975).

Recent theoretical formulations have stressed the importance of a child's cognitive capacities and information-processing procedures in the learning of aggressive behavior (Dodge, 1980; Dodge & Somberg, 1987; Huesmann, 1986; Huesmann & Eron, 1984). The theories have differed in terms of exactly what is learned, whether attitudes, perceptual biases, response biases, or scripts, and programs for behavior. Our own formulation stresses the importance of scripts for social behavior that serve as cognitive representations of personality traits (Huesmann & Eron, 1989). In any case, however, learning is hypothesized to occur both as a result of one's own behaviors and the environment's response to those behaviors (i.e., enactive learning) and/or as a result of viewing the behavior of others in the environment (i.e., observational learning). For example, under certain conditions a child's exposure to others behaving aggressively will increase the chances that a child will respond to frustration and victimization with aggression. However, the transformation of the child's initial aggressive behavior into habitual aggressive behavior may depend as much on the responses of the child's environment to the aggression, the continuance of precipitating factors, and the convergence of other causal factors as on the initial exposure to violence.

Parents can provide critical input into both the enactive and observational learning processes. The parents' aggressiveness, punitiveness, and rejection serve both as reinforcements and as models of behavior for children to observe and incorporate into their own behavioral repertoires, especially when children observe the rewards that such behaviors provide. Furthermore, children's cognitive processes may well be influenced by the parents' own cognitive processes; for example, parents who view the world as hostile are apt to have children who view the world as hostile. In addition, parents can intervene to reinforce their children's aggressive and prosocial responses differentially, to moderate their children's exposure to aggressive scripts, and to convince their children that the violent solutions to social problems that they are observing or utilizing are not realistic or adaptive. Such interventions would reduce the likelihood that the children would encode the aggressive scripts that they see, or utilize the aggressive scripts that are encoded. Equally important, parents can intervene to help their children learn prosocial scripts that will compete with aggressive scripts as guides for behavior (Eron, 1986).

We have had the opportunity to investigate the influence of parental variables on the development of aggressive behavior in the growing child in two large-scale longitudinal studies. In the first study, begun in the Spring of 1960 in a semirural county of New York State, we followed 632 children out of a total of 875 studied when they were in the third grade to age 30 in the summer of 1981. During the first phase of the study, in 1960, we had also interviewed the subjects' parents. The most notable result of this study was the finding that early childhood aggression, as observed in school, is correlated with adult antisocial and criminal behavior. The best predictor to later aggression was early aggression. The second study consisted of 3-year longitudinal investigations that we conducted between 1977 and 1983 in five countries—the U.S.A., Australia, Finland, Poland, and Israel. The focus of this study was the relation between television habits and the development of aggressive behavior. Indeed, we found such a relation in all five countries. However, in both of these longitudinal studies, we also found significant relations with parent variables that seemed to exacerbate or mitigate the relation of these and other independent variables to concurrent and/or subsequent aggressive behavior.

It is our purpose in this chapter to integrate the findings of both studies so as to gain a comprehensive understanding of the processes through which parental behavior and attitudes can lead to the learning of aggressive behavior in children.

MEASURES

We refer to three measures of parent behavior that have figured prominently in our previous writing: rejection, punishment for aggression, and identification. In the long-term study, these data were collected from the parents just once, when the subjects were 8 years old. In the 3-year study, the data were collected from the parents at the start of the investigation when half of the subjects were 6 years old and half of them were 8 years old and then again at the end of the study. This was the same in all the countries except Israel, where no parent data were collected, and in Poland, where parent data were collected only in the first phase of the investigation.

Rejection was operationalized as the number of changes in the child's behavior and characteristics (not including aggression) desired by the parent, for example, Do you think *NAME* wastes too much time? Are you satisfied with *NAME'S* manners? There were 10 such items. That parent was considered accepting of the child who indicated that his or her needs were satisfied by the child: "I like you the way you are."

Punishment for aggression was defined as rewards and punishments of various intensities administered by parents contingent upon the child's aggressive behavior. The scale itself consisted of 24 items having to do with likely responses of the parents to four kinds of aggressive behavior on the part of their children, two dealing with aggression toward the parent and two with the aggression toward other children. Two specific punishments at each of three levels of intensity were assigned to each of the four items, for example, if *NAME* were rude to you, would you:

1. Tell him/her I will give you something you like if you act differently.
2. Wash out his/her mouth with soap.
3. Remind *NAME* of what others will think of him/her.
4. Say, "Get on that chair and don't move until you apologize."
5. Tell *NAME* that young men (ladies) don't do this sort of thing.
6. Spank *NAME* until he/she cries.

The Identification measure of the child with his or her parents was a difference score between the child's and parent's self-ratings on a series of 18 bipolar adjectives having to do with expressive motor behavior, such as eating, walking, talking, and so forth. The less discrepancy between the child's score and that of either parent, the closer the identification with the parent was assumed to be. Thus, identification was operationalized as perceived similarity in expressive behavior. Because this measure correlated highly with measures of confession and guilt over being naughty, we also interpreted this identification measure as an indication of internalization of parental standards for behavior.

In the 3-year longitudinal study, the same type of discrepancy procedure was used to measure identification. However, discrepancy was measured by comparing the subject with his or her mother on nine items concerned with fantasy behavior, television realism, and television viewing[1]. The rejection and punishment measures in the 3-year study were identical to those in the longer (22-year) study.

The dependent aggression measures in the 22-year study included a concurrent peer nomination measure at age 8; two measures of aggression taken 10 years later, peer nominations and self-rating on the MMPI scales $F + 4 + 9$ (Huesmann, Lefkowitz, & Eron, 1978); and 10 measures of aggression and criminality compiled 22 years later, including self-ratings, ratings by subject's spouse, and data obtained from the Criminal Justice Division regarding number and seriousness of arrests and convictions.

The dependent aggression measures in the 3-year study included peer ratings at the initial phase of the study as well as in the second and third phase of data collection one year apart.

RESULTS

Because we had data obtained independently from both mothers and fathers of the subjects, it was possible first of all to determine how well the way in which they evaluate their interactions with their children agree. Intercorrelations of parental measures are presented in Table 7.1 for both the 22- and the 3-year study. It is obvious that there is considerable agreement between mothers and fathers in how they evaluate their interactions with their children. It is also apparent that the three parental variables are reasonably independent of each other, although there is some agreement between the way individual parents evaluate one variable and the way they evaluate the other two, suggesting that there may be some carryover. However, parents agree with one another on a given variable more than they agree with themselves on the three variables. There is also remarkable similarity between the correlations obtained in both studies. Thus, it is unlikely that there is a significant carryover or halo effect from one variable to another. Further, in a series of factor analyses, the three parent variables were found to load heavily on separate factors (Eron, Walder, & Lefkowitz, 1971).

The correlations in Tables 7.2 & 7.3 indicate that there is a moderate amount of communality between the information provided us by the parents of our subjects in the first phase of the study and the multiple

[1]The reason for the change was that the items related to expressive motor behavior were not included in the interview for the 3-year study. The identification measure for the 3-year study was adapted by Laurie Miller (1988). The items used for this post hoc derived measure were all items that were common to the mother and child interviews.

TABLE 7.1
Intercorrelations of the Parent Variables

	M Rej	*M Pun*	*Low M Ident*	*F Rej*	*F Pun*
	22-Year Study (N = 535)				
Mother Rejection					
Mother Punishment	.19**				
Low Mother Identification	.06	.19**			
Father Rejection	.45***	.13⁺	.06		
Father Punishment	.07	.35***	.22**	.14⁺	
Low Father Identification	.00	.16*	.53***	.07	.19*
	3-Year Study (N = 380)				
Mother Rejection					
Mother Punishment	.24***				
Low Mother Identification	.05	.07			
Father Rejection	.63***	.16*	.06		
Father Punishment	.16*	.42***	.16*	.21*	
Low Father Identification	.04	.22*	.48***	.15*	.05

***$p < .001$
**$p < .01$
*$p < .05$
⁺$p < .10$

TABLE 7.2
Correlations Between Parent Variables and Aggression Measures—
22-Year Study
Female Subjects

	Rejection		*Punishment*		*Low Identification*[x]		*Sum of Rej, Pun, Id*	
Aggression Measure	*r*	*N*	*r*	*N*	*r*	*N*	*r*	*N*
Age 8								
Peer-Nominated Aggression	.28***	229	.30***	229	.20**	187	.43***	187
Age 19								
Peer-Nominated Aggression					.20*	127		
MMPI Aggression			.18*	155				
Age 30								
No. of Arrests	.16*	175						
No. of Convictions	.16*	175						
Seriousness of Arrests	.18*	175					.15⁺	144
Violence of Crimes	.13⁺	175						
Actual Punishment of Child							.27*	58
Imagined Punishment of Child	.14⁺	171	.25***	171	.23**	137	.35***	137
Self-Rated Aggression			.13⁺	171			.18*	137

[x]low identification = Mother + Father

TABLE 7.3
Correlations Between Parent Variables and Aggression Measures—
22-Year Study
Male Subjects

	Rejection		*Punishment*		*Low Identification*[x]		*Sum of Rej, Pun, Id*	
	r	*N*	*r*	*N*	*r*	*N*	*r*	*N*
Age 8								
Peer-Nominated Aggression	.19***	306	.23***	306	.24***	274	.36***	274
Age 19								
Peer-Nominated Aggression			.14+	166	.14+	153	.15*	153
MMPI Aggression	.20**	166					.17*	153
Age 30								
MMPI Aggression	.16*	161	.17*	161			.19*	145
No. of Arrests			.21***	284	.12*	252	.21***	252
No. of Confictions			.25***	284			.20***	252
Seriousness of Arrests			.13*	284	.14*	252	.11+	252
Violence of Crimes			.12*	284	.13*	252	.16**	252
Actual Punishment of own Child			.34**	54				
Imagined Punishment of Child			.18*	164				
Frequency of Spouse Abuse					.34**	70		
History of Spouse Abuse			.20+	80	.21+	70	.21+	70
Self-Rated Aggression			.23**	164	.16	148	.24**	148

[x]Low identification = Mother + Father

measures of aggression and antisocial behavior obtained from and about the subjects themselves some 22 years later. The final column in the tables presents the correlation of the sum of the three standard scores on each of the antecedent variables with the criterion variables. Considering the length of time between the two data collection phases and the different sources of information for antecedent and consequent variables, the findings are quite remarkable. The same order of correlation between parent variables and school aggression was obtained in the cross-national study. Rejection and punishment by parents were at least moderately related to how aggressive the children were in school in all four countries (Huesmann & Eron, 1986).

One might wonder whether the correlations between the parent variables and the child's aggression are due to a single child-rearing factor or whether each parent behavior relates independently to aggression. The data from both studies suggest the latter explanation. As the regressions in Figs. 7.1 and 7.2 show, the parent variables generally predict aggression independently of each other.

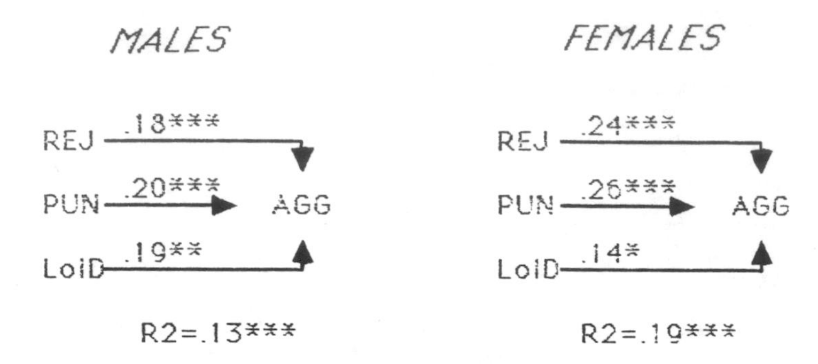

FIG. 7.1. Synchronous regressions relating parent behaviors to child aggression in the 22-year study.

Table 7.4 shows the mean aggression scores of all those subjects in the 22-year study whose parents scored above or below the median on all three parent variables. One should note that for males the means are at least marginally significant on all of the major aggression measures. For females, the difference on "imagined punishment of child" is particularly significant. (See section on Punishment ahead for description of measure of "imagined punishment of child.") Those scoring above the median on all three variables should be the youngsters most at risk for developing antisocial behavior patterns before reaching adulthood; and indeed, on the average, each of the male subjects in the above the median group has had at least one arrest before age 30. In the below-the-median group, the subjects are eight times less likely to have been arrested, and only one in five actually had such a record.

These data seem to indicate that parents do indeed have an important impact on whether or not their children will, in the future, engage in the type of antisocial behavior that can bring them into conflict with the law, their peers, and their own family members. However, as we noted in the beginning of this chapter, the best predictor to aggression of the subjects as adults was how aggressive they were as children. When we examined the probable causal effects of these parent variables, measured when our subjects were 8 years old, on the various indices of aggression as adults, controlling for how aggressive they were at age 8, much to our surprise we found that for boys the probable causal effect vanished on all adult measures. For girls, however, some interesting causal effects remained. The more harshly girls were punished for aggression at age 8, the more harshly did they punish their own children, the more abusive were they toward their spouses, as reported by their spouses, and the more prone

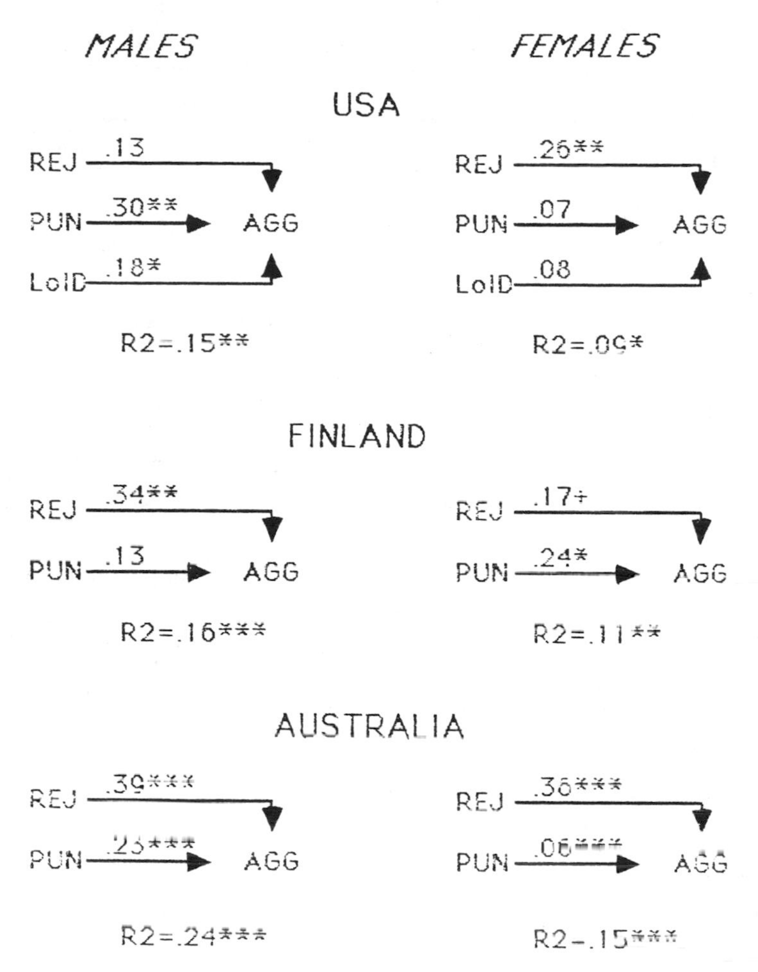

FIG. 7.2. Synchronous regressions relating parent behaviors to child aggression in the 3 year study.

were they to respond with aggression and violence in many situations according to self-ratings.

Turning to the 3-year study, Table 7.5 presents the correlations between each of the three parent variables in the first year and peer-nominated aggression in each of the 3 years of the study. Scores on each of the variables were converted to standard scores and the three parent variables were summed, as shown in the last column of the table, giving an indication of total parental impact on the development of aggression. The correlations between the sum of the three variables and aggression

TABLE 7.4
Mean Aggression Score of Subjects Whose Parents Scored Above or Below The Median on All Three Parent Variables in 22-Year Study

	Females			*Males*		
Aggression Measure	*Above*	*Below*	*t*	*Above*	*Below*	*t*
Age 8						
Peer-Nominated Aggression	16.30	3.94	3.64***	21.03	8.24	3.76***
Age 19						
MMPI Aggression	175.36	179.14	.50	196.25	178.10	2.20*
Age 30						
MMPI Aggression	165.57	161.04	.63	182.79	164.92	2.01+
No. of Arrests	.11	.00	1.73+	1.69	.21	1.83+
No. of Confictions	.06	.00	1.18	.89	.08	1.78+
Imagined Punishment	28.57	10.00	2.62***	33.57	17.78	2.06*
Self-Rating Aggression	33.36	16.00	1.16	100.00	3.69	3.70**

were somewhat higher for both boys and girls than when each of the variables was considered by itself. Thus, the sum seems to be a good indication of the effect of parent behaviors on the development of aggression.

Indeed, Table 7.6, which presents correlations summed for all years in which measurements were taken, indicates a correlation of .50 for boys

TABLE 7.5
Correlations Between Parent Variables at Time 1 and Aggression Measures 3-Year Study

Aggression Measure	*Year*	*N*	*Rejection*	*Punishment*	*Low Identification*	*Sum of Rej, Pun, Id*
			Females			
Peer-Nominated Aggression	1	286	.17**	.17**	.04	.24***
Peer-Nominated Aggression	2	250	.13*	.18**	.09	.22***
Pear-Nominated Aggression	3	213	.19**	.11	.17*	.27***
			Males			
Peer-Nominated Aggression	1	263	.26***	.28***	.13*	.37***
Peer-Nominated Aggression	2	233	.13*	.28***	.13+	.33***
Peer-Nominated Aggression	3	202	.17*	.17**	.07	.25***

***$p < .001$
**$p < .01$
*$p < .00$
+$p < .10$

TABLE 7.6
Relation of Parent Variables Measured at years 1 & 3 to Sum of Aggression Measures at Years 1, 2, & 3

	Rejection		*Punishment*		*Low Identification*		*Sum of Rej, Pun, Id*	
Aggression Measure	*r*	*N*	*r*	*N*	*r*	*N*	*r*	*N*
Girls' Aggression	.31***	137	.08	137	.12	108	.30***	108
Boys' Aggression	.26**	140	.35***	140	.22*	119	.50***	119

and .30 for girls, both highly significant, between the parent variables we measured and the appearance of aggressive behavior in school. This is of exactly the same order as the estimated stability of aggression derived from the 22-year study (Huesmann et al., 1984). Those stability figures were .50 for boys and .35 for girls.

Thus, it seems from the 3-year study, at least, that some parental behaviors are indeed important in determining whether children will develop aggressive habits that can place them in conflict with society. This is the case because it has been demonstrated elsewhere that these very school behaviors that we have shown to be related to parental practices are themselves predictive of adult antisocial behavior (Huesmann et al., 1984). However, because they are related, this does not mean, as we all know, that the parental practices are causing the aggressive behavior. Perhaps parental rejection and punishment are reactions to the aggressive behavior that the youngster originally displays, and lack of identification then results from the aversive nature of the interaction between parent and child.

Rejection

When the rejection scale was constructed, 30 years ago, we were concerned with this very question of parental rejection versus child rejectability—that is, was rejection of the child less a characteristic of the parent than it was of the child? There are certain children who might just be rejectable because of some inherent or early-appearing deficit or behavior that would make it unlikely that others would be attracted to them or approve of them. This belief was supported at that time by the high correlation found in pilot studies between rejection by the mother and father (r = .64) and between rejection by the parents and rejection by peers (r = .35 for mothers and .20 for fathers) as well as between rejection by parents and aggression in school (r = .40 for mothers and .31 for fathers). Therefore, a number of items were added to the scale of parent rejection in order to tap the parent's emotional reaction in response to the child's undesirable behavior. The revision did not alter the obtained relation to school aggression, strengthening our conviction that the original 10-item scale reflected the parent's behavior more than the child's behavior.

Rejection by peers was measured at the time by one item on the peer nomination inventory, "Who do you wish was not in your class at all?", which was later eliminated from the peer nomination procedure for ethical reasons and also because, in a factor analysis, this item loaded heavily on a general aggression factor (Walder, Abelson, Eron, Banta, & Laulicht, 1961). In both the 22- and 3-year studies, we did ask two popularity questions, "Who are the children you would like to have for your best friends?" and "Who would you like to sit next to in class?" Indeed, in both studies, we found negative correlations between popularity among peers, as indicated by this measure, and rejection by parents. Further, the correlation between mother and father rejection, in the 22-year study, as indicated in Table 7.1, was .45, and it was .63 in the 3-year study. Although the rejection measures used in the two studies were the same, the 3-year correlations were not quite as high as in the earlier study; however, they still clearly indicate that children rejected by their parents tend also not to be accepted by their peers. Correlations range from −.14 to −.27 for girls, and from −.21 to −.30 for boys between rejection by parents and popularity among peers. Further, in the 22-year study, there seems to be an incremental effect in the relation to aggression as peer rejection is added to parental rejection. Table 7.7 includes the mean aggression score of those children rejected only by peers, only by parents, by both peers and parents, and by neither parents nor peers. For boys as well as girls, those rejected by both their peers and their parents have a somewhat higher mean score. What is most interest-

TABLE 7.7
Mean 3rd-Grade Aggression Scores of Subjects Above Median on Rejection in 22-Year Study

Rejection By	*Females*		*Males*	
	Mean Score[1]	*N*	*Mean Score*[1]	*N*
Parents	6.25	39	15.39	64
Peers	10.73	61	17.50	90
Peers + Parents	13.96	6	18.26	69
Neither Parents nor Peers	4.83	88	9.13	104

[1] Mean score of all those subjects above the median on rejection by the group or groups indicated.

ing, however, is the exceptionally low mean score on aggression of those scoring below the median on both parent and peer rejection. The overall significance for this table is $F\ (3,252) = 10.14, p < .0001$ for girls and $F\ (3,323) = 8.06, p < .0001$ for boys.

In Tables 7.8 and 7.9 we present longitudinal regression predictions of adult aggression in our 22-year study from parenting behaviors when the subject was 8 years old. From these regressions, we can see that early rejection of the child is related significantly to several adult measures of aggression.

These data, however, still leave us with the question of whether rejection by the parent perhaps sets up an emotionally frustrating situation at home, which leads the child to act out aggressively in school, or whether the youngster's unacceptable behavior leads to rejection by the parent. We could not answer this question with the 22-year data because we had a measure of parental rejection only at one time—at the beginning of the study. However, in the 3-year study, we were successful in obtaining parent interviews at both the initial and final phases of the study, and it was possible to distinguish between these possibilities (Huesmann & Eron, 1986). In the United States, early aggression for boys is a significant predictor for later rejection even after effects of parents' early rejection are partialled out. However, the converse is not true. Early rejection is not predictive of later aggression once initial aggression is partialled out. Thus, parental rejection seems to be more a response to child aggression than a cause of aggression in the United States sample.

TABLE 7.8
Regression Prediction of Aggression Measures from Parent Variables—
22-Year Study
Female Subjects

	Standardized Coefficients for Age 8 Predictors				
Criterion	*Rejection*	*Punishment*	*Low Identification*	R^2	*N*
Age 8					
Peer-Nominated Aggression	.24***	.26***	.14*	.19***	186
Age 19					
Peer-Nominated Aggression	.10	.00	.21*	.05+	126
Age 30					
No. of Arrests	.16+	.04	.10	.03	143
No. of Confictions	.19*	.08	.12	.05	143
Seriousness of Arrests	.33*	.06	.11	.13	35
Violence of Crimes	.32+	.03	.06	.10	35
Actual Punishment of own Child	.16	.23+	.01	.10	57
Imagined Punishment of Child	.09	.26**	.19*	.13***	136

TABLE 7.9
Regression Prediction of Aggression Measures from Parent Variables—22-Year Study
Male Subjects

	Standardized Coefficients for Age 8 Predictors				
Criterion	*Rejection*	*Punishment*	*Low Identification*	R^2	*N*
Age 8					
Peer-Nominated Aggression	.18**	.20***	.19**	.13***	273
Age 19					
MMPI Aggression	.19*	.04	.02	.04+	152
Age 30					
MMPI Aggression	.10	.17*	.03	.05+	144
No. of Arrests	.05	.22***	.08	.06**	251
No. of Confictions	.01	.26***	.06	.08***	251
Violence of Crimes	.01	.13	.23+	.09	61
Actual Punishment of own Child	.01	.38**	.23	.15+	47
Imagined Punishment of Child	.00	.15+	.06	.03	147
Frequency of Spouse Abuse	.22*	.12	.38**	.17**	69
Self-Rating of Aggression	.04	.23**	.12	.08**	147

In Finland, as in the United States, rejection is more predictable from aggression than vice versa, supporting the idea that rejection of children by their parents is more a response to their childrens' aggressive behavior than an instigation to aggression. In Poland, the analysis could not be done because just one wave of parent data was collected there. Only in Australia is rejection a significant predictor of later aggression even when early aggression is controlled.

Punishment

The effect of punishment on antisocial aggression is quite independent of the effect of rejection, as indicated in the multiple regression in the 22-year study (Tables 7.8 & 7.9). For female subjects, parental punishment makes an independent contribution to aggression at age 8 as well as to two measures of aggression obtained from the subjects at age 30. At that time, all subjects were asked to imagine how they would respond if they had an 8-year-old child who engaged in a variety of aggressive behaviors, the very same questions their parents were asked 22 years earlier. This was the measure of *imagined punishment.* Those subjects who indeed had children of that approximate age were also asked what they actually did in response to such behaviors. This was the measure of *actual punishment.* Thus, punishment of the subjects by their parents, measured 22 years earlier, related to the variation in both of these aggression measures independently of rejection. For males, parental punishment seemed to be an even better predictor of aggression than for females, relating independently not only to 8-year-old peer-nominated aggression and to the two age-30 measures of aggression that were significant for females, but also to two age-30 measures of self-rated aggression as well as to the number of arrests and convictions for criminal behavior. Punishment by parent also was marginally related to peer-nominated aggression 10 years later and to spouse abuse, as reported by spouse, 22 years later.

In the 3-year study we found bivariate correlations between punishment and aggression of similar magnitude as with rejection and the same relation between early and later aggression and early and later punishment. Furthermore, as with rejection, early aggression was a significant predictor of later punishment, even after effects of early punishment were partialled out. However, early punishment was not predictive of later aggression once early aggression was partialled out. Thus punishment also seems to be more a response to aggression than a cause of aggression. Similar results were obtained in Finland and Australia for both boys and girls.

Identification

Low identification with parents for females (Table 7.8) related only to peer-nominated aggression at age 8 and 19 and to imagined punishment of child at age 30. For males (Table 7.9) there were significant independent relations only for concurrent aggression at age 8 and frequency of spouse abuse 22 years later. There was a marginally significant relation to violence of crimes committed.

In the 3-year study in which a different measure of identification was employed (Miller, 1988), when aggression over the three phases of the study and identification at the first and last phase were correlated, low identification correlated significantly with aggression only for boys (Table 7.6). Thus, in both the 3-year and the 22-year studies, low identification seems to be a more important variable for boys than it is for girls.

However, regression analyses revealed interesting information about the direction of the relation when predicting from first-year low identification to third-year aggression as well as from first-year aggression to third-year low identification. For girls, low identification with mother in the first year significantly predicts to child aggression in the third year with aggression in the first year partialled out, but there were no similar effects for boys. For boys, on the other hand, early aggression predicts to later low identification with early identification partialled out. There was no similar effect for girls (Miller, 1988). Thus, it appears that aggression in boys must be very aversive to parents, leading to rejection, harsh punishment, and perhaps, because of the aversive quality of these parental behaviors directed at children, to low identification with the parents.

It may be recalled that in the earlier study, as described elsewhere (Eron, 1987), we had found that low identification was an important mediator in the relation between punishment and aggression for boys. This finding bears repeating here. For boys who were highly identified with their fathers, punishment that the father administered for aggressive behavior by the child tended to inhibit aggression. However, if boys were not highly identified, any punishment the fathers administered seemed to exacerbate the aggression. Further, we found in that study that children tended not to identify with highly aggressive parents, and as long as a youngster identified with one parent, whether mother or father, he or she tended not to be aggressive.

The interaction of punishment and identification highlights the importance of a child's cognitions in determining whether or not he or she will use aggression as an interpersonal problem-solving tactic. A child who identifies with a parent, that is, who has incorporated the standards of the parent, probably interprets punishment as an appropriate response to bad behavior. Such a child probably attends to the standards set by the parent rather than the nature of the punishment used to enforce those standards. However, the unidentified child who has not incorporated those standards interprets the parents' punitive behavior as a way of forcing someone to comply with an arbitrary set of rules. In the latter case, the instigatory quality of the interaction becomes more important than the expected inhibitory nature of the punishment, and the lesson learned is "you get what you want by beating up on other persons."

DISCUSSION

What is the significance of these results in helping us understand how parents influence their children's behavior? On the surface, they seem to suggest that individual differences in parental child-rearing styles have very little effect on the development of aggression, at least after the age of 6. With some exceptions, the parental differences seem to be more a function of differences in the children's aggression than causes of the children's aggression. This is not at variance with other studies relating aspects of child rearing to later measures of personality (McCrae & Costa, 1988; Plomin, Loehlin, & DeFries, 1985; Scarr, Webber, Weinberg, & Wittig, 1981). Nevertheless, a number of aspects of the data suggest that the picture is more complex than this. First, harsh parental punishment of some girls clearly seems to make it more likely that they will behave aggressively towards those close to them when they are adults. Second, there are trends in some subsamples that suggest that excessive punishment and rejection do indeed stimulate greater aggression (e.g., in Australian boys). Third, it is clear that the relations between aggression and the different child-rearing variables are not explained by a single factor or else they would not have independent relations with aggression in multiple regression analyses. These child rearing practices do seem to have their individual effects.

We have been arguing for some time that individual differences in childhood aggression are primarily learned. We view social behavior as controlled by scripts that are learned at a very young age and become very resistant to change, promoting stability of aggressive behavior over time. The current data suggest that such learning must take place even before age 6 if these parental factors are to have much of an effect, because they certainly do not have much of an effect after age 6. Furthermore, the lack of a relation from earlier parental rejection and punishment to later aggression over the 22 years of our study may reflect the statistical aggregation of several different learned responses to parental rejection and punishment. Although we could not find any variable that seemed to mitigate or exacerbate the effects of rejection and punishment, there may well be some that were not measured by us. For example, whereas some severely punished children may encode scripts for aggressive behavior based on the observed punishments, others may see how ineffective the punishment actually is in changing their own behavior and therefore may not encode such scripts. Aggregated data from these two groups of subjects, thus, would reveal little evidence for an effect of punishment on aggression. Similarly, it may be that aggression is only one of the ways in which children react to rejection. Some children may withdraw from rejecting parents and rejecting peers and shun social contacts altogether. Again, aggregated data would reveal no relation. This seems to argue for more studies of highly selected groups of subjects followed for a number of years, or even individual case studies (see, e.g., chapter 9, this volume).

One piece of data in support of the notion that different processes are operating in different children is the enhanced results that obtain when children who score at the upper end on all the child-rearing measures are compared to those scoring high on only one. If the same processes were responsible for placement of these children at the higher end of rejection, punishment, and lack of identification, then one would not expect any greater aggression among those who score highly on all three than among those who score highly on only one. The rejected children, who also do not identify with their parents and who are harshly punished, may be those very children for whom few alternatives are possible except aggression. And, indeed, they are the most antisocially aggressive individuals over the 22-year span.

However, if aggression is a learned behavior and is learned primarily within the home, evidence for this must come from studies done with children before the age of 6. By the time youngsters are 6, patterns of aggressive behavior seem so well established that they persist into adulthood despite what must be a wide variety of environmental contingencies and events, including varied parental child-rearing practices and other interpersonal behaviors.

ACKNOWLEDGMENTS

Over the years this research has been supported by research grants to L. D. Eron from the National Institute of Mental Health and the Office of Child Development, to L. R. Huesmann from the National Institute of Mental Health, and by contract to M. M. Lefkowitz from the Office of the Surgeon General.

REFERENCES

Andrew, J. M. (1981). Delinquency: Correlating variables. *Journal of Clinical Child Psychology, 10,* 136–140.

Dodge, K. A. (1980). Social cognition and children's aggressive behavior. *Child Development, 53,* 620–635.

Dodge, K. A., & Somberg, D. (1987). Attributional biases in aggressive boys are exacerbated under conditions of threat to self. *Child Development, 58,* 213–224.

Eron, L. D. (1986). Interventions to mitigate the psychological effects of media violence in aggressive behavior. *Journal of Social Issues, 42,* 155–169.

Eron, L. D. (1987). The development of aggressive behavior from the perspective of a developing behaviorism. *American Psychologist, 42,* 435–442.

Eron, L. D., Huesmann, L. R., Dubow, E., Romanoff, R., & Yarmel, P. W. (1987). Aggression and its correlates over 22 years. In D. H. Crowell, I. M. Evans, & C. R. O'Donnell (Eds.), *Childhood aggression and violences* (pp. 249–262). New York: Plenum Publishing Co.

Eron, L. D., Walder, L. O., & Lefkowitz, M. M. (1971). *The learning of aggression in children.* Boston: Little, Brown.

Farrington, D. (1983). Offending from 10 to 25 years. In K. T. Von Desen & S. A. Mednick (Eds.), *Prospective studies of crime and delinquency* (pp. 17–37). Boston: Kluver-Nijhoff.

Farrington, D. P., & West, D. J. (1971). A comparison between early delinquents and young aggressives. *British Journal of Criminology, 11,* 341–358.

Hoffman, M. L. (1971). Father absence and conscience development. *Developmental Psychology, 4,* 400–406.

Huesmann, L. R. (1986). Psychological processes promoting the relation between exposure to media violence and aggressive behavior by the viewer. *Journal of Social Issues, 42,* 125–139.

Huesmann, L. R., & Eron, L. D. (1984). Cognitive processes and the persistence of aggressive behavior. *Aggressive Behavior, 10,* 243–252.

Huesmann, L. R., & Eron, L. D. (1986). *Television and the aggressive child, a cross national comparison.* Hillsdale, NJ, Lawrence Erlbaum Associates.

Huesmann, L. R., & Eron, L. D. (1989). Individual differences and the trait of aggression. *European Journal of Personality, 3,* 95–106.

Huesmann, L. R., Eron, L. D., Lefkowitz, M. M., & Walder, L. O. (1984). The stability of aggression over time and generations. *Developmental Psychology, 20,* 1120–1134.

Huesmann, L. R., Lefkowitz, M. M., & Eron, L. D. (1978). Sum of the MMPI Scales F, 4, and 9 as a measure of aggression. *Journal of Conssulting and Clinical Psychology, 46,* 1071–1078.

McCord, J. (1979). Some child rearing antecedents of criminal behavior in adult men. *Journal of Personality and Social Psychology, 37,* 1477–1486.

McCrae, R. R., & Costa, P. T., Jr. (1988). Recalled parent–child relations and adult personality. *Journal of Personality, 56,* 417–434.

Miller, L. (1988). *The relations among child identifications with mother, television viewing habits and child aggression.* Unpublished master's thesis, University of Illinois at Chicago.

Neapolitan, J. (1981). Parental influences of aggressive behavior: A social learning approach. *Adolescence, 16,* 831–840.

Olweus, D. (1980). Familial and temperamental determinants of aggressive behavior in adolescent boys: A causal analysis. *Developmental Psychology, 16,* 644–660.

Osborn, S. G., & West, D. J. (1979). Conviction records of fathers and sons compared. *British Journal of Criminology, 19,* 120–123.

Patterson, G. R., & Stouthamer-Loeber, M. (1984). The correlation of family management practices and delinquency. *Child Development, 55,* 1299–1307.

Plomin, R., Loehlin, J. C., & De Fries, J. C. (1985). Genetic and environmental components of "environmental" influences. *Developmental Psychology, 21,* 391–402.

Robins, L. N., West, P. A., & Herjanic, B. L. (1975). Arrests and delinquency in two generations: A study of Black urban families and their children. *Journal of Child Psychology and Psychiatry, 15,* 125–140.

Scarr, S., Webber, P. L., Weinberg, R. A., & Wittig, M. A. (1981). Personality resemblances among adolescents and their parents in biologically related and adoptive families. *Journal of Personality and Social Psychology, 40,* 885–898.

Wadsworth, M. (1979). *Roots of delinquency: Infancy, adolescence, and crime.* New York: Harper and Row.

Walder, L. O., Abelson, R., Eron, L. D., Banta, T. J., & Laulicht, J. H. (1961). Development of a peer rating measure of aggression. *Psychological Reports, 9,* 291–334 (monograph supplement 4-49).

West, D. J., & Farrington, D. P. (1973). *Who becomes delinquent? Second report of the Cambridge study in delinquent development.* London: Heinemann.

Commentary

Expanding the Perspective on Contributing Factors and Service Delivery Approaches to Childhood Aggression

Ray DeV. Peters
Queen's University &
Beechgrove Children's Centre

Family influences, particularly parenting influences, on the social and emotional development of children have played a central role in social learning theories of childhood and adolescent aggression for many years (Bandura & Walters, 1959; 1963; Sears, Maccoby, & Levin, 1957). No one has contributed more to research and theory in this tradition during the past three decades than Leonard Eron and Gerald Patterson. In the previous two chapters, these two outstanding scientists and their colleagues presented findings from recent longitudinal studies that were designed, in part, to provide further insights into the nature of parental influences on aggressive children. This commentary highlights some of the interesting findings from their work and then discusses implications of this research for intervention approaches to the problems of aggressive and antisocial youth.

PATTERSON, CAPALDI, AND BANK

Beginning with a pioneering study in 1967 (Patterson, Littman, & Bricker; 1967) Gerald Patterson and his colleagues at the Oregon Social Learning Centre have made enormous contributions to the literature on childhood aggression and antisocial behavior. Patterson's coercion model (Patterson, 1982; Patterson, DeBaryshe, & Ramsey, 1989) is concerned with explaining how some young children learn to engage in antisocial behaviors (fighting, temper tantrums, and noncompliance) as a result of poor family management practices by parents. Patterson,

Capaldi, and Bank contend that, by learning these antisocial forms of interpersonal behaviors, and concomitantly failing to learn more prosocial forms of behavior in the family setting, antisocial children are at increased risk for two forms of subsequent massive social failure, both crucial to their later development. One failure involves rejection by the normal peer group due to the child's use of antisocial behaviors, such as aggression or temper tantrums, in peer interactions and lack of appropriate social skills. The second failure entails school factors, resulting from the child's noncompliance with normal classroom activities and lack of adherence to reasonable teacher expectations. This academic failure can further reinforce the rejection by normal peers and lead to further rejection of the authority of the teachers by the child. According to Patterson and his colleagues, peer rejection may also be an important causal factor in the development of depression, dysphoric mood, and poor self-esteem in school-aged boys.

In chapter 6 of this book and in another recent paper (Patterson et al., 1989), Patterson expands his developmental model of antisocial behavior by positing that normal peer-group rejection and academic failure during middle childhood leads to the child's commitment to a deviant peer group and thereby to delinquency during adolescence. To summarize, Patterson's current model of the developmental progression for antisocial behavior emphasizes: (a) the contribution of poor parental discipline and monitoring during "early childhood" to the development of child conduct problems, (b) conduct problems leading to rejection by normal peers as well as academic failure during "middle childhood," followed by, (c) commitment to a deviant peer group and subsequent delinquency in late childhood and adolescence. The strategy for building and testing this model is described in more detail in a previous publication (Patterson, 1986). A key ingredient is the use of structural equation modelling procedures within the context of longitudinal studies.

In chapter 6, Patterson, Capaldi, and Bank report preliminary findings from a prospective longitudinal study of delinquency from a cohort of 104 boys beginning when they were in Grade 4. Using both self-report and court records of delinquency when the boys were in Grade 7, Patterson et al report the results of structural equation modelling in which they assessed the predictive contributions to delinquency of three constructs measured when the boys were in Grade 4: (a) *Parental Monitoring,* (b) *Academic Achievement,* and (c) *Antisocial Behavior.* The results of the analysis, presented in Fig. 6.3, suggests that although parental monitoring and academic achievement were both associated with concurrent antisocial behavior in Grade 4, the only construct that was predictive of delinquency in Grade 7 was antisocial behavior in Grade 4. An unexpected finding was that neither poor parental monitoring nor poor academic achievement in Grade 4 was associated with Grade 7 delinquency. The reasons for these unexpected results are not discussed by Patterson et al., nor do they explain why measures of family management practices other than parental monitoring, or measures of peer rejection at Grade 4, were not included in the analyses. Given the importance of parental discipline and peer relationships in the theoretical model described previously, it will be extremely interesting to see the results of structural equation models that include these concepts in subsequent reports.

As is true of so much of Patterson's writings, chapter 6 is replete with interesting ideas and tantalizing data. If there is one criticism that can be made about the chapter, it is that it is, at times, overwhelming, with a mixture of theory, empirical findings, and conceptual models coming at the reader at a dizzying rate. Given the past history of Patterson and his colleagues, it is expected that, as further results from this longitudinal study become available, our understanding of developmental contributions to the emergence of delinquency, both in early starters (or unsocialized delinquents) and in late starters (socialized delinquents) will be strengthened.

ERON, HUESMANN, & ZELLI

The large-scale longitudinal study of aggression begun by Eron and his colleagues in 1960 has been extremely influential in the current understanding of the stability of aggression from the early primary-school years to young adulthood. In chapter 7, Eron, Huesmann, and Zelli present results from a series of shorter longitudinal studies covering the age of 6–10 years carried out in five different countries. The main focus of the results from the shorter longitudinal investigations was to determine the relationship between three aspects of parent behaviors (rejection, punishment for aggression, and identification) and peer-rated aggression over the 3-year period.

Although there are many interesting results reported in chapter 7, the most salient for the present discussion is the finding that, in general, the various parenting behaviors were unrelated to peer-rated aggression after initial aggression ratings were statistically removed via a regression analysis. The reverse, however, was not true; that is, the ability of initial ratings of aggression to predict subsequent aggression was unaffected by statistically removing initial ratings of parental behaviors. The interpretation that Eron et al make of these findings is that, after 6 years of age, peer-rated aggression is causally independent of differences in parenting behaviors. These latter differences are viewed as a *response* to the aggression of the child rather than a stimulus for its expression. According to Eron et al, it is the child's aggressive behavior that influences parents' punishment and rejection, rather than vice versa.

Several concluding statements from chapter 7 warrant repetition in this regard:

> We have been arguing for some time that individual differences in childhood aggression are primarily learned . . . The current data suggest that such learning must take place even before age 6 if these parental factors are to have much of an effect, because they certainly do not have much of an effect after age 6. (p. 185)

It will be interesting to see whether future reports from the Oregon Youth Study replicate Eron et al.'s finding that parental discipline practices may be more appropriately viewed as a result than a cause of aggressive behaviors in children during middle childhood. Eron et al.'s findings are not inconsistent with Patterson's developmental model, which posts that parent socializing practices have their greatest impact during "early childhood" (presumably younger than 6 years of age), whereas during "middle childhood" academic failure and peer rejection are seen as the predominant influences on the maintenance and expression of antisocial behaviors. Also, Patterson has repeatedly emphasized the reciprocal nature of the parent–child dyad, viewing the parent as both the "architect and victim" of the child's coercive behaviors. By middle childhood, the parents of aggressive children may be more victims than architects.

The possibility of relatively weak parental influence on children's antisocial behaviour during the primary school years presents an interesting paradox in light of recent reviews of the literature on the treatment of childhood conduct problems (e.g., Kazdin, 1987; McMahon, 1987). Although such reviews point to the lack of procedures that have proven effective with large percentages of antisocial youth, the treatment approaches that hold the greatest promise for children between the ages of 4 and 11 are those that deal directly with parental discipline and family management practices. Perhaps a reason why such procedures have not proven more effective is that although extensive attention is given to parent training and family concerns, peer relationships and academic performance are typically ignored. A strong implication of Eron et al.'s findings, as well as Patterson's developmental model, is that during middle childhood, treatment approaches for antisocial behavior need to explicitly address peer and academic difficulties.

In addition to the search for more effective treatment approaches, another issue concerns the epidemiology of the problem. As discussed by Offord, Boyle, and Racine in chapter 2 of this book, the prevalence of conduct disorders in children is considered to be between 5–10%. Offord also reports that less than 20% of the conduct-disordered children in his study had received any form of mental health or social service assistance in the previous 6 months. Offord's findings were based on a large-scale epidemiological study in the Canadian province of Ontario. Similar conclusions about the low percentage of children with mental health problems who receive professional attention in the United States have recently been documented (Sax, Cross, & Silverman, 1988). Given this state of affairs, even if treatment procedures were much more effective, the impact of such procedures on the overall prevalence of antisocial behavior disorders in children would be minimal. The same situation exists for other forms of childhood disorders, including hyperactivity, anxiety, and depression.

THE PREVENTION APPROACH

Such considerations have led some professionals to conclude that greater attention must be directed toward efforts to *prevent* the development of conduct problems in children rather than the present, almost exclusive concern with treating the problems after they have become well established. It has been said by Dubos (1959) that ". . . no major disease in the history of mankind has been conquered by therapists and rehabilitation methods alone, but ultimately only through prevention" (p. 4). Such an analysis seems particularly germane to antisocial behavior.

Patterson, Capaldi, and Bank (chapter 6) comment on the potential value of preventing adolescent delinquency by first identifying those children who, at a young age, are known to be at risk for developing subsequent delinquency and then implementing preventative interventions with those at-risk children. As Patterson et al rightly point out, such an "*at risk*" prevention strategy requires prediction tools that will keep false negative and false positive prediction errors to a manageable level. The approach that Patterson et al. suggest is actually "early intervention" or "secondary prevention," because it is based on identifying and intervening with problems early in an attempt to prevent more serious problems from developing. A major challenge in early intervention approaches is to develop a cost-efficient screening mechanism that will allow for the effective early identification of a large percentage of individuals who are manifesting the problem. "Primary prevention" refers to approaches that attempt to intervene with at-risk individuals *before* any problem is manifested. With primary prevention, the ability to accurately determine who is at risk for a particular problem—in this case, antisocial behavior and/or adolescent delinquency—becomes crucial. Unless factors exist that are extremely highly correlated with the subsequent appearance of the problem condition, primary prevention initiatives need to be directed toward a very large percentage of the population in order to include enough true positives to make an impact on the prevalence of the problem, or else directed at only those individuals who are at extremely high risk, in which case many who will eventually develop the problem are not included (Chamberlain, 1984).

THE HEALTH PROMOTION APPROACH

An additional and quite recent approach to prevention, namely "health promotion," is worthy of note. Consider, for example, current programs that are designed to prevent heart disease. Many such programs are directed towards all members of a community, not just those who have been identified as being "at risk" for heart diseases. Efforts are directed toward improving diets, increasing physical exercise, and decreasing tobacco, alcohol, and drug use in all individuals.

One major objective of this "health promotion" approach is to reduce the prevalence of particular types of health problems/diseases, such as heart disease and lung cancer. However, an additional objective includes increased vitality and energy and improved feelings of well-being and physical fitness. Thus, such physical health promotion programs may be said to have dual objectives: (a) decreasing or preventing disease ("adding more years to one's life") and (b) increasing or strengthening healthy life styles ("adding more life to one's years").

It is interesting to consider the potential value of adopting a health promotion approach in the area of children's mental health problems in general, or antisocial, conduct problems specifically. Research discussed in this book indicates that family, peer, school, and media influences are all important in the development of and maintenance of childhood aggression. *The failure of conduct-disordered children to learn prosocial skills and attitudes is viewed as central to the problem.* In fact, many current approaches to the treatment of aggressive children are predominantly concerned with developing and strengthening child competences (e.g., compliance with reasonable adult requests, self-control, positive peer relationships, and problem-solving skills), as a means of decreasing antisocial behaviors. In this sense, treatment approaches have a dual goal similar to the health promotion programs described earlier: decreasing social and emotional problems in children while increasing psychosocial competence. The major limitation is that the current service delivery system permits the dissemination of these treatment procedures, no matter how effective, to only a small percentage of those children and families for whom the procedures are designed.

In this context, mental health promotion and primary prevention programs may be of considerable value (Peters, 1988). The objectives of such programs would be consistent with current treatment approaches: (a) to promote psychosocial competence and prosocial attitudes and (b) to prevent the development of behavioral and emotional difficulties. Such programs would be designed to reach all children, with activities and materials appropriate to their developmental level. Parents, teachers, and health/social service workers would be actively involved in developing and implementing the programs.

A BROADER PERSPECTIVE FOR SERVICE DELIVERY

It is important to emphasize that children's mental health and promotion programs are not meant to replace treatment approaches; *au contraire!* Such programs can be seen as the front line of mental health service where fostering the social and emotional development of all children is the objective. In addition to the potential for increasing the mental health of children and reducing or preventing the development of behavioral and emotional problems, children's mental health promotion programs provide an excellent infrastructure for identifying and intervening with problematic children and their families at a very early stage. As mentioned before, a practical limitation of implementing early intervention programs is the difficulty in screening the entire population to identify problems. Mental health promotion programs have the capability of allowing such screening in a highly efficient and cost-effective way.

The addition of early intervention, primary prevention, and promotion programs to the children's mental health system would provide a continuum of care, a much broader service system that may be better able to deal with the current needs of children and their families. Is this perspective a realistic one? Is it not somewhat naive to expect the introduction of new programs in a time of shrinking government resources and extensive waiting lists at existing children's mental health facilities?

The reality is that many promotion, prevention, and early intervention programs already exist in North America, and there is a growing interest and commitment to these approaches. An excellent example is provided by "family support and education programs" (Kagan, Powell, Weissbourd, & Zigler, 1987). These programs are directed toward the prevention, rather than the treatment, of mental and physical health problems, and they provide support and services with the goal of promoting optimal development in young children and their families. Family support programs are often designed to reach all families with young children in a particular community, and they usually include one or more of the following activities: (a) parent education, (b) joint parent–child activities focusing on child development and family relationships, (c) information and referral to other community services, (d) home visits to hard-to-reach families, and (e) health and nutrition education for parents and developmental/health screening for infants and children (Weissbourd & Kagan, 1989). This approach to dealing with children and families has recently begun to attract widespread attention from state and provincial governments (Peters, 1988; Weiss, 1989).

Another example of community-wide approaches is the growing number of school-based programs for the prevention of drug and alcohol abuse, teenage pregnancy and sexually transmitted diseases (especially fuelled by concerns about AIDS), and mental–emotional problems. Although these programs have targeted different outcomes for their prevention efforts, an emphasis on promoting the development of psychosocial competencies, particularly social awareness and social problem-solving, communication, assertiveness, decision making, and coping are increasingly being included in most programs for children across the entire school-age range (Bell & Battjes, 1985; Elias & Clabby, 1988; Long, 1986; Price, Cowan, Lorion, & Ramos-McKay, 1989; Quest International, 1988).

More research into the effectiveness of family support and primary prevention programs such as these is sorely needed and presents many challenges (Bell & Battjes, 1985; Steinberg & Silverman, 1987; Zigler & Black, 1989). The same is certainly true of efforts to develop more effective treatment procedures for use with conduct problems in children (Kazdin, 1987). However, closer cooperation and awareness of these varied approaches has tremendous potential for aiding in the critical struggle to deal more effectively with antisocial values and behavior in our society.

REFERENCES

Bandura, A., & Walter, R. H. (1959). *Adolescent aggression.* New York: Ronald.

Bandura, A., & Walters, R. H. (1963). *Social learning and personality development.* New York: Holt, Rinehart & Winston.

Bell, C. S., & Battjes, R. (Eds.). (1985). *Prevention research: Deterring drug abuse among children and adolescents.* U.S. Department of Health and Human Services Publication No. (ADM) 85-1334. Washington, DC: U.S. Government Printing Office.

Chamberlain, R. W. (1984). Strategies for disease prevention and health promotion in maternal and child health: The "ecologic" versus the "high risk" approach. *Journal of Public Health Policy,* June, 185–196.

Dubos, R. (1959). *The mirage of health.* Garden City, NJ: Doubleday.

Elias, M. J., & Clabby, J. F. (1988). Teaching social decision making. *Educational Leadership,* March, 52–55.

Kagan, S. L., Powell, D., Weissbourd, B., & Zigler, E. (Eds.). (1987). *America's family support programs.* New Haven: Yale University Press.

Kazdin, A. E. (1987). Treatment of antisocial behavior in children: Current status and future directions. *Psychological Bulletin, 102,* 187–203.

Long, B. L. (1986). The prevention of mental–emotional disabilities: A report from a National Mental Health Association Commission. *American Psychologist, 41,* 825–829.

McMahon, R. J. (1987). Some current issues in the behavioral assessment of conduct disordered children and their families. *Behavioral Assessment, 9,* 235–252.

Patterson, G. R. (1982). *A social learning approach: 3 coercive family process.* Eugene, OR: Castalia.

Patterson, G. R. (1986). Performance models for antisocial boys. *American Psychologist, 41,* 432–444.

Patterson, G. R., DeBaryshe, B. D., & Ramsey, E. (1989). A developmental perspective on antisocial behavior. *American Psychologist, 44,* 329–335.

Patterson, G. R., Littman, R. A., & Bricker, W. (1967). Assertive behavior in children: A step toward a theory of aggression. *Monographs of the Society for Research in Child Development, 32,* 1–43.

Peters, R. DeV. (1988). Mental health promotion in children and adolescents: An emerging role for psychology. *Canadian Journal of Behavioural Science, 20,* 389–401.

Price, R. H., Cowan, E. L., Lorion, R. P., & Ramos-McKay, J. (1989). The search for effective prevention programs (and what we learned along the way). *American Journal of Orthopsychiatry, 59,* 49–58.

Quest International (1988). *Skills for adolescence.* Granville, OH: Author.

Sax, L., Cross, T., & Silverman, N. (1988). Children's mental health: The gap between what we know and what we do. *American Psychologist, 49,* 800–807.

Sears, R. R., Maccoby, E. E., & Levin, H. (1957). *Patterns of child rearing.* New York: Harper.

Steinberg, J. A. & Silverman, M. M., (Eds.) (1987). *Preventing mental disorders: A research perspective.* U.S. Department of Health and Human Services Publication No. (ADM) 87-1492. Washington, DC: U.S. Government Printing Office.

Weiss, H. B. (1989). State family support programs: Lessons from the pioneers. *American Journal of Orthopsychiatry, 59,* 32–48.

Weissbourd, B., & Kagan, S. L. (1989). Family support programs: Catalysts for change. *American Journal of Orthopsychiatry, 59,* 20–31.

Zigler, E., & Black, K. P. (1989). America's family support movement: Strengths and limitations. *American Journal of Orthopsychiatry, 59,* 6–19.

Section 4: Social-Cognitive and Peer Relational Factors Associated with Childhood Aggression

8

The Structure and Function of Reactive and Proactive Aggression

Kenneth A. Dodge
Vanderbilt University

Consider two different aggressive boys. They are fictitious, but each might be considered a prototype, based on examination of case records of children classified as violent and emotionally disturbed in a novel treatment program in the state of North Carolina.

The first boy, Billy, is 12 years old and has been arrested four times for vandalism, theft, and similar offenses. He is reported to be a major behavior problem in school. He is a bully among peers, in that he regularly coerces other boys into deferring to him. He teases peers, threatens them, dominates them, laughs at them, and starts fights with them. Billy would most likely fit criteria as socially rejected (highly disliked and not at all liked by peers). His background is fairly underprivileged. His father has been in and out of prison, and he has grown up in a "tough" neighborhood, without close monitoring or guidance from adults.

The second boy, Reid, is also 12 years old. He has been arrested for assault on his teacher. One day following her ridicule of him for failing an exam, he pulled a knife on her in the school parking lot and cut her in the arm. He is also considered highly aggressive and socially rejected among peers, but he doesn't seem to start fights as much as he escalates conflicts and can't avoid them. He overreacts to minor provocations and is viewed as volatile and short-tempered. Nobody wants to get too close to Reid because he might strike at any time. During the case manager's inquiry into this boy's background, it was determined that he had been abused physically as a young child.

Both of these boys are socially rejected and aggressive toward peers; yet, they seem to be quite different from each other. The first boy uses aggression in a *proactive* way to meet his goals. The second boy seems more *reactive,* angry, and volatile. The first boy is troubling *to* others, whereas the second is troubled *by* others.

This chapter draws out the distinction between reactive and proactive aggression. Numerous aspects of these two types of behavior will be considered, including theory, topography, individual differences, social correlates, legal implications, processes and mechanisms, etiology, and intervention.

THEORY

Beginning with Greek philosophers such as the Stoics and Seneca, it has been popularly held that aggression and anger are instinctive reactions that are part of the nature of human beings (Averill, 1982). The groundwork for the modern version of this view was laid by the 17th-century philosopher Thomas Hobbes (1651/1969) who argued that children are naturally disposed toward reacting violently to aversive events, so external forces must be imposed to try to stop these angry reactions. William James (1890) similarly argued that aggressive instincts are ready to erupt at any time. The opposite perspective was advanced by the social philosopher John Locke (1690/1913), who argued that the child is born with a *tabula rasa,* or blank slate. Anything is possible, from murder to intimacy, depending on how the environment reacts to the child's behavior. These two views prevail even today, in the forms of the two dominant theories of aggression: the frustration–aggression model and the social learning theory.

One of the most important reasons for distinguishing between reactive and proactive aggression is the potential for resolving this theoretical debate. It is curious that these theories of aggression have emphasized either the reactive or proactive aspects, but not both. The frustration–aggression model posited by Dollard and colleagues (Dollard, Doob, Miller, Mowrer, & Sears, 1939) and refined by Berkowitz (1962, 1978) holds that aggression is a hostile, angry reaction to perceived frustration. In fact, according to Berkowitz, "*aggression* and *hostility* are synonymous terms" (1962, p. xii). The goal of aggression is to defend oneself or to inflict harm on the source of the frustration. The empirical emphasis of this formulation is on the instigators of the aggressive reaction, such as goal blocking, heightened anger, threat, crowding, and frustrated expectations. These instigators are formulated either as innate precipitants of an aggressive drive response or as stimuli to a classically conditioned response.

The other major theoretical formulation is the social learning theory of Bandura (1973, 1983). This theory postulates that aggression is an acquired instrumental behavior that is controlled by external rewards. Empirical work in this tradition has emphasized a search for the incentives for aggressive behavior and is impressively epitomized in the early findings of Patterson, Littman, & Bricker (1967) in observational studies on the school playground and more recently in observations of family process by the group at the Oregon Social Learning Center (Patterson, 1982). Bandura (1973) highlighted the distinction between these two theories by noting that frustration–aggression theories "generally give disproportionate attention to aversively motivated aggression . . . Incentives also constitute important impellers of action. A great deal of aggression is prompted by its anticipated benefits. Here, the instigator is the *pull* of expected success, rather than the *push* of aversive treatment" (p. 57, italics added). The learning theory underlying this perspective is obviously operant conditioning.

It should be noted that even these theorists seem to recognize the validity of the opposing theory. Each theory acknowledges both the instigative and the incentive aspects of aggressive motivation. Berkowitz (1983) recognized that reinforcements might alter the strength of an aggressive display, and Bandura (1983) hedged by acknowledging that his theory applied to only "a great deal" of aggression. Patterson's (1982) model is more complex than simple operant reinforcement, in that aggressive behavior is strengthened not by overt positive outcomes but by the removal of a negative stimulus. Thus, both reactive and proactive elements are present in his theorizing. Although this debate continues, it is proposed here that the theoretical resolution might come not from a single formulation that incorporates both instigative and incentive aspects, but by a theory that recognizes that aggressive behaviors come in multiple forms. The reactive aggressive behaviors described by Berkowitz (1962) are different phenomena than the proactive aggressive behaviors described by Bandura (1973). These behaviors differ in structure, topography, function, processes, mechanisms, and etiology.

TOPOGRAPHY

There have been numerous attempts by ethologists to classify types of aggressive behavior based on topographical features of the behavior itself. Psychobiologists (e.g., Moyer, 1976) have suggested that there are as many as a dozen types of aggression, but the major distinction made by Lorenz (1966), Reis (1974), and Scott (1972) has been between *affective aggression* and *instrumental aggression*. The former is characterized by intensive patterned autonomic activation, "hot-blooded" anger or fear responses, frenzied, menacing attacks, defensive postures in response to threat, and a feeling of release, relief, and fatigue afterward. Instrumental aggression, on the other hand, is characterized by little autonomic activation or irritability, but is highly organized and "cold-blooded" and appetitive in function (the goal usually being feeding or territoriality). The behavior is patterned and directed toward the promise of a reward. Consider the distinctions made between two types of aggressive behavior in domestic cats, as described by Moyer (1976):

> . . . the topography of behavior (i.e., the motor patterns) in predatory attack by the cat is quite different from a type of aggression which has been

> called "affective." The former involves relatively little emotional display. The cat does not hiss or growl, but slinks close to the floor and makes a silent, deadly attack on the rat. In "affective" aggression, however, there is evidence of pronounced sympathetic arousal. The back arches, the tail fluffs out, the animal hisses and growls, and may attack in a flurry of scratching and biting. (p. 224)

In contrast to the evidence for these subcategories in animals, relatively little evidence has accumulated to substantiate these differences in humans. Hartup (1974) has identified two types of aggression in children, based on the target of the act itself. Instrumental aggression consists of grabbing, pushing, or shoving another in order to obtain an object, such as a toy. The aggression itself is incidental to the main goal, acquisition of the object. Hostile aggression, on the other hand, is person-directed, in that the goal is to hit, and hurt, another person. Whereas this distinction has strong reliability, we are less sure of its functional validity, in that one might conceive of person-oriented aggression that has instrumental value and object-oriented aggression that is displayed in reactive anger. On the other hand, Hartup has made the perceptive insight, supported by data (Blurton-Jones, 1967; Dawe, 1934), that nonsocial object acquisition is the primary type of aggression displayed in infancy and early childhood, whereas as children get older, more of their aggression tends to be personally-directed as a part of interpersonal conflict. Averill (1982) described reactive aggression in some detail, and noted a distinction between acceptable reactive aggression and unacceptable reactive aggression. Acceptable reactions are those that are perceived by society to be measured responses in accord with some unreasonable provocation, such as when a boy responds to being hit by hitting back. It is a sad but insightful comment that our society accepts some forms of anger and aggression, as long as it follows particular rules of degree and appropriateness. Unacceptable reactions are those that are clearly overreactions to some instigation that is either nonexistent or minor. An example would be a boy who beats up a peer who has mildly teased him. Rule (1978) is another theorist who has suggested that the distinction between hostile and instrumental aggression is informative. Within the instrumental category, Rule has suggested a further distinction between personally motivated aggression and socially motivated aggression. Socially motivated aggression is destructive behavior in service of a socially appropriate goal, such as defending one's country in war or pushing another person out of the way of an automobile. Even though the question of morally acceptable aggression is an interesting one, it has little relevance to the present concern with socially deviant boys and girls, and so it will not be discussed further.

In our own observations of boys engaged in free-play with peers in laboratory settings (Dodge, Coie, Pettit, & Price, 1990), as well as in playground settings (Price & Dodge, 1989), distinctions can be made along a continuum of the severity of aggression, as well as according to types of aggression. The first distinction has been between rough play and overt aggression. This distinction is a fairly reliable one, as indicated by interobserver agreement. The distinction also has validity, in that socially rejected boys have been found to engage in greater rates of overt aggression than average boys, but the two groups do not differ in rates of rough play (Dodge, et al, 1990). The distinction between rough play (called "rough and tumble") and overt aggression has also been noted by Humphreys and Smith (1987) who found as well that rough and tumble play is not related to negative sociometric status. This distinction is important because it tends to refute the notion that aggression can be identified merely by high-rate behavior (Blurton-Jones, 1967; McGrew, 1972; Walters, 1964). Within the overt aggression category, distinctions can be made between angry-reactive behaviors and non-angry-proactive behaviors. This distinction can be made reliably in observations of children, and it is proposed that it has theoretical and functional value as well. These labels have strong resemblance to hostile and instrumental aggression, but they place emphasis on both the instigation to the behavior and its incentives. In children, reactive aggression is displayed as anger or temper tantrums, with an appearance of being out of control. Proactive aggression occurs usually in the form of object acquisition, bullying, or dominance of a peer.

The validity of this distinction has also been demonstrated by the display of these behaviors within the context of dyadic peer relationships. In recent observations, Dodge, Price, Coie, and Christopoulos (in press) identified some peer dyads in which each partner displayed a high rate of aggression toward the other and disliked each other, as if these boys were in constant conflict with each other (called high-conflict dyads). Also identified were other dyads in which one boy repeatedly aggressed toward the other, but this aggression was not reciprocated. The aggression was distributed asymmetrically. It is interesting to note that 82% of the aggression displayed by the highly aggressive member of these asymmetric dyads was proactive aggression, in the form of bullying and victimization. On the other hand, almost half (45%) of the aggression in the high-conflict dyads was reactive aggression. It does seem that proactive aggression is coercive behavior observed in one boy's domination of a peer, whereas reactive aggression occurs in the context of a negatively affectively-charged, high-conflict relationship.

In conducting these observations, the authors noticed that the distinction between reactive and proactive aggression is often one of relative emphasis. That is, it is sometimes the case that a reactive behavior has a proactive goal, for example, when a boy gets angry to communicate to a peer that he will not submit to domination. Also, proactive behaviors sometimes are delayed reactions to an earlier episode, such as when a boy picks on a younger peer after being teased by another peer. All behaviors have aspects of reaction and proaction, in that one can make guesses regarding the precipitants as well as the functions of all behaviors. At the extremes, the distinctions are clearly noted by topographical features, such as the presence or absence of anger or the apparent functional value. At the borders, the distinctions are less reliable. This problem does not negate the validity of the qualitative distinction, however, any more than dusk would negate the difference between day and night.

INDIVIDUAL DIFFERENCES

Researchers have been concerned not only with the observation and understanding of single acts of reactive and proactive aggression, but also with individual differences in the display of these behaviors. The identification of individual differences is important for the study of personality correlates of these behavioral tendencies, as well as for an understanding of their mechanisms of action and the discovery of their etiologies. The rates of these behaviors are known to be significantly stable over short periods of time, such as across 5 days of peer play (Dodge et al., 1990). This stability suggests that reliable individual differences might be detectable.

In an effort to document these individual differences, Dodge and Coie (1987) developed a teacher rating instrument that listed both reactive and proactive aggressive behaviors. An example of a reactive item is this: "When this child has been teased or threatened, he or she gets angry easily and strikes back." An example of a proactive aggression item is this: "This child uses physical force to dominate other kids." This instrument was administered to teachers of 259 third- through sixth-grade boys in Indianapolis, IN, and 339 first- and third-grade boys in Durham, NC. Internal consistencies of the scales were found to be quite high in both samples, with median within-scale item correlations of .67 and higher, suggesting strong convergent validity. The cross-scale correlations are not as high, suggesting some discriminant validity as well. The eigenvalues for the second factor are not up to standard levels of acceptability, however, making this conclusion an equivocal one. On the other hand, the factor loadings are more clear in indicating that certain items load heavily on the reactive factor, whereas others load more heavily on the proactive factor. These findings give a mixed picture of the validity of the distinction between reactive and proactive aggression. Because of the mixed picture, the scales were recently administered to a new sample of teachers of 103 boys and girls in kindergarten classrooms, as well as to their mothers and fathers (Dodge, unpublished data). Confirmatory factor analyses were used to test the adequacy of a two-factor model of aggressive behaviors. With each of the three informants, the two-factor model was found to yield a high degree of goodness-of-fit. The aggregated findings thus seem strong enough to warrant a look at the social correlates of these behaviors.

SOCIAL CORRELATES

The first question that one might address is the evaluation that peers give of these different kinds of behaviors. It is known that rates of overall aggressive behavior are correlated quite negatively with social preference by peers and are the single most frequently cited reason for disliking a peer (Asher & Hymel, 1981; Coie, Dodge, & Coppotelli, 1982). Recently, Price and Dodge (1989) sought to determine whether both reactive and proactive aggressive behaviors are equally negatively evaluated. The subjects were 70 kindergarten and first-grade boys. The measures included peer sociometric scores for social preference and mean play ratings (1 to 5 scale), teacher rating scores for reactive and proactive aggression, and rates of reactive and proactive aggression as observed directly on the playground. Because the teacher ratings of the two types of aggression were so positively correlated ($r = .80$), a strategy of partialling out the effect of one construct when analyzing the association between the other construct and peer evaluations was adopted. In so doing, additional evidence for validity of these constructs was found, in that the teacher ratings and direct observations correlated more positively within constructs than between constructs. It was also found that at this young age, peer evaluations were more closely associated with reactive aggression than proactive aggression. That is, peers disliked boys who engaged in high rates of reactive aggression, but they did not necessarily dislike boys who were proactively aggressive. The correlations varied slightly across the two age levels, with proactive aggression being more negatively evaluated at the older age than the younger age. Using direct observations in play group settings, Dodge and Coie (1987) have found a similar trend, in that reactive aggression was consistently associated with peer disliking, but proactive aggression came to be negatively evaluated only among older boys.

The next step (Dodge & Coie, 1987) was to learn more about the behavior of boys who behave aggressively in reactive versus proactive ways. Boys were identified who were socially rejected and either (a) proactively aggressive; (b) reactively aggressive; (c) both proactively and reactively aggressive; or (d) nonaggressive, but still rejected. For comparison, a fifth group of sociometrically average boys were also identified. Peer nominations for various aspects of behavior were used to generate behavioral profiles of these groups. It was found that all three aggressive rejected groups were similarly disliked by peers, again supporting the finding that by age 9 both reactive and proactive aggression are disliked by peers. The proactively aggressive group was viewed as most disruptive to the peer group. On the other hand, this proactive group was also viewed as having the strongest leadership qualities and as having the strongest sense of humor. Again, these findings support the validity of the distinction between these types of aggression and give an indication that peers evaluate reactively-aggressive rejected boys in uniformly negative ways, whereas the boys who are proactively aggressive but refrain from reactive aggression are viewed in more mixed ways.

LEGAL ASPECTS

A slightly different picture emerges from an analysis of the legal aspects of homicide. It is interesting that legal systems have distinguished between proactive and reactive violent behavior since the time of the ancient Greeks (McDowell, 1978). In current systems, there is a distinction between voluntary manslaughter and first-degree murder. The former has been referred to as a "crime of passion," committed in a frenzied reaction to some provocation, almost always by an acquaintance. First-degree murder, on the other hand, is committed with "malice aforethought," meaning that the killing is premeditated and has been committed while the individual is capable of cool reflection. A higher proportion of murders are directed toward a stranger than is true for manslaughters. Manslaughter is far more frequent than murder and is treated much more leniently. There are numerous defenses that an individual can claim for manslaughter, and the usual sentence if convicted is either probation or a few years in prison, in contrast with life in prison for first-degree murder.

Within the voluntary manslaughter category, it is interesting to note the possible mitigating circumstances that have been accepted in courts of law. These circumstances have parallels in peers' evaluations of a child's aggressive behavior and in adults' treatment of aggression in children. In Medieval times, mitigating circumstances did not absolve an individual from his or her crime. A man who killed an attacker would be convicted of homicide in the same way that the attacker could be convicted. The only leniency, if it could be called such, afforded to the defender was that, although both the attacker and the defender would be dealt with by capital punishment, the defender would be executed more humanely. That is, the defender would be killed quickly by the sword, whereas the attacker would be tortuously broken on the wheel (Averill, 1982).

With English Common Law came a recognition of mitigating circumstances. There were two grounds for mitigation, the suddenness of the action and evidence that there was no malice aforethought (no premeditation). The concept was that a crime could be mitigated if it was committed only in reaction to a provocation, rather than proactively in cold blood. Suddenness and lack of premeditation were evidence of the reactive nature of the crime. The unmitigated crime came to be known as murder and was subject to death, whereas mitigated homicide came to be known as manslaughter and was subject to only one year in prison and branding of the thumb (Averill, 1982).

An important development for modern legal systems came with the M'Naghten Rules in 1843 (Gendin, 1973). With these guidelines, there was a shift from concrete extenuating circumstances to a more general principal that mitigation could occur if it could be determined that there was a defect of reasoning or a disease of the mind. This was the first time that the notion of impairment was recognized as mitigating factor.

The English Homicide Act of 1957 spelled out aspects of English Common Law and articulated the notion that sometimes impassioned acts occur in otherwise reasonable persons (Averill, 1982). An important aspect of this act was the notion of temporary uncontrolled anger. The United States Model Penal Code of 1974 acknowledged a similar concept, as well as the notion that extreme mental disturbances could lead to violence.

All of these legal systems have endorsed the concept that reactive violence can be mitigated if four conditions are present; (a) the provocation that instigated the act is sufficiently strong to make an otherwise reasonable person react violently; (b) it has to be demonstrated that indeed the individual is acting in the heat of passion, that is, with an "absence of design to cause death" (*People v. Lewis*, 1953); (c) there is an insufficient cooling time for the individual to get over the initial provocation; and (d) there must be a causal path from the provocation and the passion to the crime (Averill, 1982). Of course, one important question left unanswered is just how great a provocation is necessary to justify homicide. Most jurisdictions have ruled that the crime must be proportional to the provocation. So death, or threat of death, would be the minimal provocation to justify homicide. On the other hand, there is the law of the state of Texas, which in 1936 held that a provocation involving the insulting of one's female relative is sufficient grounds to excuse homicide (Averill, 1982)!

In sum, the two kinds of mitigations that have excused reactive violence in our legal courts have involved the concepts of passion and pathology, both of which come from the same Latin root *pathos*. The similarity between anger and madness is just as striking.

MECHANISMS AND PROCESSES

Neural Mechanisms. In developing a theory of subtypes of aggression, one must consider the processes and mechanisms through which reactive and proactive aggression occur. Because the evidence in favor of distinct paths for these two behaviors is strongest in the study of neuroanatomical function, this is a reasonable starting point. It has long been known that electrical stimulation of portions of the midbrain and limbic system, particularly the hypothalamus and the amygdala, can lead to an emotional reaction of rage as well as indiscriminate fighting (Afifi & Bergman, 1980; Guyton, 1981). Likewise, lesioning of these centers often leads to reductions in aggression. Interestingly, experimental studies by Karli (1978) and others (Adams & Flynn, 1966; Panksepp, 1971) have suggested that stimulation and lesioning of different areas have quite specific and differential behavioral effects on rats and cats. For example, stimulation of the medial hypothalamus leads to defensive posturing, hissing, and attack in response to the slightest provocation; in contrast, stimulation of the lateral hypothalamus leads to a highly oriented, prolonged search for prey and quiet biting behavior. Also, the septal lesioned rat will demonstrate hyperactivity and aggressive responses to aversive stimuli, whereas it will not increase search for prey (Karli, 1978; Miley & Baenninger, 1972). On the other hand, lesioning the centromedial region of the amygdala will reduce previously reinforced mouse-killing predatory behavior in the rat, but will not affect aggressive responses to threat (Karli, 1978). It seems that the mechanisms most likely involved in aggressive behavior that is affective are those that increase hyperactivity and implicate aversiveness regions of the brain. In contrast, regions that involve appetitive functions and reward centers seem to be associated with proactive forms of aggression. Whether the proactive forms of aggression studied in rats (such as predation) generalize to the proactive forms of aggression in children (such as bullying) is, of course, unclear. R. Cairns (personal communication, June, 1988) has speculated that because predation is interspecies aggression, it might not generalize to intraspecies aggression in children. Other forms of intraspecies aggression in rats (such as dominance and unprovoked attacks) might generalize, however.

Social Information Processing Mechanisms. At a different level of analysis, cognitive mechanisms have also been implicated in aggressive behaviors, in this case in children (Dodge, 1986). A range of social information processing biases and deficits has been associated with heightened aggressive behavior (see reviews by Dodge, 1986, and Rubin & Krasnor, 1986). To understand the processes through which these biases lead to aggression, it is helpful to understand the sequence of processing steps that an individual passes through in response to an environmental stimulus (Dodge, 1986; Rubin & Krasnor, 1986). When presented with a social cue, such as a provocation by a peer or a group of peers engaged in a fun game, a child first encodes this information through sensory reception and perception. The child then mentally represents those cues as threatening or benign through the application of rules acquired in socialization, and may experience emotions such as fear, anger, or a desire for pleasure. The child then engages in a response search, in which one or more behavioral responses are accessed from long-term memory. These responses are evaluated as acceptable or unacceptable, and one is selected for enactment.

Patterns of bias or deficiency at each of these stages of processing have been correlated with aggressive behavioral tendencies in children (Dodge, 1986). Specifically, aggressive children demonstrate biased attention and encoding of hostile stimuli (Dodge & Newman, 1981; Strassberg & Dodge, 1987), intention-cue detection errors (Dodge, Murphy, & Buchsbaum, 1984), hostile attributional biases (Dodge, 1980; Nasby, Hayden, & dePaulo, 1979; Slaby & Guerra, 1988), inadequate response search and problem solving (Asarnow, 1983; Dodge, Pettit, McClaskey, & Brown, 1986), and biased response evaluation in the form of expectations of favorable outcomes for aggression (Crick & Ladd, 1987; Perry, Perry, & Rasmussen, 1986). Often, however, these correlations are weak in magnitude and do not account for large portions of variance in aggression. It is also the case, however, that these studies have relied on rates of overall aggressive behavior and have not differentiated between reactive and proactive aggression. It is hypothesized that processing patterns at each of these steps might be more strongly associated with one type of aggression than the other, and that the indiscriminate combination of these aggressive behaviors has obscured the actual relation.

The mechanisms implicated are as follows. Problems at early stages of processing, such as hypervigilance to hostile cues, hostile attributions regarding minor provocations, and unwarranted fear responses, are hypothesized to lead to overreactive, defensive aggressive responses. On the other hand, a child who accurately perceives others' intentions but has a limited and biased response repertoire, and who evaluates the outcomes of behaving aggressively in positive ways may be likely to employ aggressive tactics proactively in instrumental ways. Finally, a child who accurately perceives the environment and who appropriately accesses and attempts a nonaggressive response, but who has problems with this enactment, may engage in what we might call accidental aggression.

These hypotheses obviously open a field of inquiry, one that has only recently begun. To date, one set of studies has been completed, testing the hypothesis that errors in intention-cue detection and hostile attributional biases are related to reactive aggression but not proactive aggression. Dodge and Coie (1987) presented boys from five different status groups (reactive, proactive, combined, nonaggressive-rejected, and average) with tasks designed to assess these aspects of processing provocation cues. The cues were presented on videorecords. Children were asked to watch short vignettes and then to interpret the intent of the peer provocateur in the videorecording. As hypothesized, only the two groups of reactively aggressive boys demonstrated relative inaccuracies in interpreting peers' cues. The proactively aggressive boys were no less accurate than the nonaggressive groups of children. Similarly, the two reactively aggressive groups of boys demonstrated strong tendencies to attribute hostile intentions to the peer in ambiguous circumstances, whereas the proactively aggressive group did not differ from average. These findings provide further validation of the distinction between the two types of aggression and suggest different mechanisms of action. The complementary relevant hypotheses from the information processing model, namely that favorable evaluations of the outcomes of aggression will be associated with proactive, but not reactive, aggression, have also been supported (Crick & Dodge, 1988).

ETIOLOGY

If these types of aggression have different neural and cognitive mechanisms, then it is also possible that they have different etiologies and developmental courses. Numerous theories have been generated regarding the etiology of aggressive behavior, and hundreds of studies have been conducted of the socialization origins of patterns of aggression, but no studies have examined differential origins for the two types of aggression (Parke & Slaby, 1983).

The origins for reactive aggression are proposed to be as follows. Because this behavior involves anger, fear, and hyperactivity to threatening stimuli, early experiences that promote these affects will most likely be the source of chronic reactive aggression. Early chronic life-threatening danger (such as growing up in a ghetto or a war zone) should lead to hypervigilance. Trauma in the form of a lost loved one should disrupt any sense of security. Being the object of violence, in the form of physical abuse, should also enhance hypervigilance, fear, and rage reactions (Hamburg & van Lawick-Goodall, 1978). On the prophylactic side of reactive aggression, one must consider the role that attachment relationships play in the development of feelings of security and the potential for empathy and accurate understanding of others (Rutter, 1981). These feelings and skills are the basis of learning to refrain from reactive aggression. Thus, poor early relationships, particularly privation or isolation from early intimate relationships and the presence of others who are inconsistent, should lead one to be prone toward angry aggression.

Proactive aggression, in contrast, should have its origins in a different constellation of experiences. These experiences are ones that enhance the child's repertoire of aggressive tactics, limit the child's repertoire of competent nonaggressive tactics, and lead the child to evaluate the outcomes of aggressive behavior in positive ways. The following experiences are most likely implicated. A child who has been exposed to high rates of violence on television, in the neighborhood, or among family members, will develop a large repertoire of aggressive responses. When these responses are endorsed either explicitly or implicitly by the environment, the probability is even greater that they will be easily accessible in problematic situations. That is, they will be at the top of the memory storage bin, ready to be called into action. Thus, parents who teach their children to value aggressive heroes such as Rambo and to hit back when pushed around will be likely to have children who develop proactive aggressive behaviors. It is important to point out that these parents rarely explicitly teach their child to be proactively aggressive; they feel that they are teaching appropriate *reactive* aggression. Nonetheless, the exposure and endorsements are hypothesized to lead to the employment of proactive aggressive behaviors in problematic situations. On the prophylactic side, children who are exposed to competent role models will broaden their repertoire of nonaggressive, assertive responses. In contrast, the lack of these models will amplify the salience of incompetent aggressive responses in one's repertoire. Finally, proactive aggression is hypothesized to grow out of operant reinforcement and family social learning of the kind described by Patterson (1982).

The hypothesized etiology for proactive aggression may seem to overlap heavily with that hypothesized for reactive aggression. Thus, the child who has been exposed to violence among other family members might be the victim of violence as well. Likewise, parents who endorse aggression might well employ it with their child. However, it is not necessary that independent or mutually exclusive developmental tracks be hypothesized for reactively aggressive and proactively aggressive children, as these two forms of behavior are positively correlated. Still, a theory emphasizing the distinctions between these behaviors must highlight the differences in their etiologies. The major differences are as follows. It is hypothesized that a history of trauma, abuse, deprivation, and insecure attachment relationships will lead to hypervigilance and active aggressive behavior; on the other hand, a history of coercive training (in Patterson's terms) and observation of and experience with successful aggressive tactics will lead a child to access aggressive responses and to evaluate them favorably, resulting in proactive aggression.

INTERVENTION

The final topic to be covered here is the implication of this formulation for intervention with aggressive children. Treatments for aggressive behavior problems have typically focused on one or more of the following aspects of the aggressive child: (a) the overt behavior itself, (b) social cognitive aspects of the child's functioning, (c) and the child's relationships with significant others. For example, Patterson's intervention (1982) is clearly a splendid example of a primarily behavioral approach. Spivack and Shure's (1974) social problem solving skills training and Lochman and Curry's (1986) anger-control training are more social cognitively oriented. Psychodynamic approaches (Keith, 1984) and attachment theories (Belsky & Nezworski, 1988) emphasize the importance of the child's relationships with others.

Since these approaches are often implemented without regard to the type of aggressive behavior being targeted, it is probable that their impact is not as specific or as strong as it might be. The three approaches can be used to treat either reactive or proactive aggression, but their effects will be strongest if they are implemented in different ways. Consider first the treatment of a highly reactively aggressive child, such as Reid, the boy described at the beginning of this chapter. Because Reid is so overly focused on the threatening cues in his environment, a behavioral treatment might emphasize repeated presentation of nonthreatening cues. These cues are discriminative stimuli for aggressive responses, so if they are avoided, the boy might not react violently. Concretely, this means that if Reid reacts strongly to embarrassment, one might try to avoid these situations for him. If these situations cannot be avoided completely, one might redirect his attention to other aspects of the environment, by changing the topic of conversation or introducing other tasks at key moments. Reid's social-cognitive problems lie in his inaccurate reading of others' intention cues, and his tendency to overattribute hostility to others in provocation situations. Treatment might consist of training him in social role-taking or in understanding others' thoughts and feelings. Since overreactive anger is a major problem, anger-control training may be critical. Finally, establishment of a strong relationship with Reid may be critical to his treatment. Children like Reid are hypothesized to be lacking in close interpersonal relationships with significant others such as parents. It is hypothesized that the normal way in which children acquire a tendency to attend to, understand, and take into account others' intentions is through an important early interpersonal relationship, in which the child may learn reciprocity, cooperation, and communication of feelings. In such a relationship, Reid may be exposed to another person who attends to his feelings, so he may come to imitate this characteristic. Unfortunately, the patterns of reactive anger displayed by this child are self-perpetuating (Dodge, 1980), so the prognosis may be poor. Sobering reality limits the optimism of treatment at this time.

The proactively aggressive child may have a better prognosis. His problems seem more straightforward. Consider Billy, the bullying child described earlier. The treatment of choice for Billy may involve consistent punishment of aggressive behaviors, and reinforcement of nonaggressive responses in problematic situations. Social-cognitive interventions might focus on social problem-solving training, in order to enhance Billy's repertoire of competent, nonaggressive alternatives. Billy evaluates the outcomes of aggression in overly favorable ways, so another cognitive intervention might focus on teaching him that aggression has its negative consequences and that nonaggressive alternatives may meet his needs more adequately. It does not appear that the interpersonal relationship between the therapist and Billy is critical to treatment, so this aspect of treatment is not likely to be emphasized.

Of course, the interventions described here are overly simplistic and are too broad to serve as a manual for action. The efficacy of these treatments has not been tested in reactively and proactively aggressive children, but this task will lie ahead.

ACKNOWLEDGMENTS

The material in this chapter was presented at the Earlscourt Symposium on Childhood Aggression, June 15–18, 1988, Toronto, Ontario. The author acknowledges the support of a Research Career Development Award (No. K04 HD00806) from the National Institute of Child Health and Human Development and Grant No. 38765 from the National Institute of Mental Health.

REFERENCES

Adams, D., & Flynn, J. P. (1966). Transfer of an escape response from tail shock to brain-stimulated attack behavior. *Journal of the Experimental Analysis of Behavior, 9,* 401–410.

Afifi, A. K., & Bergman, R. A. (1980). *Basic neuroscience.* Baltimore: Urban and Schwarzenberg.

Asarnow, J. R. (1983). Children with peer adjustment problems: Sequential and nonsequential analyses of school behaviors. *Journal of Consulting and Clinical Psychology, 51,* 709–717.

Asher, S. R., & Hymel, S. (1981). Children's social competence in peer relations: Sociometric and behavioral assessment. In J. D. Wine & M. D. Smye (Eds.), *Social competence* (pp. 125–157). New York: Guilford.

Averill, J. R. (1982). *Anger and aggression: An essay on emotion.* New York: Springer-Verlag.

Bandura, A. (1973). *Aggression: A social learning analysis.* Englewood Cliffs, NJ: Prentice-Hall.

Bandura, A. (1983). Psychological mechanisms of aggression. In R. G. Green & E. I. Donnerstein (Eds.), *Aggression: Theoretical and empirical views* (Vol. 1, pp. 101–140). New York: Academic.

Belsky, J., & Nezworski, T. (Eds.) (1988). *Clinical implications of attachment.* Hillsdale, NJ: Lawrence Erlbaum Associates.

Berkowitz, L. (1962). *Aggression: A social psychological analysis.* New York: McGraw-Hill.

Berkowitz, L. (1978). Whatever happened to the frustration–aggression hypothesis? *American Behavioral Scientist, 32,* 691–708.

Berkowitz, L. (1983). The experience of anger as a parallel process in the display of impulsive, "angry" aggression. In R. G. Geen & E. I. Donnerstein (Eds.), *Aggression: Theoretical and empirical reviews* (Vol. 1., pp. 103–134). New York: Academic.

Blurton-Jones, N. G. (1967). An ethological study of some aspects of social behavior in nursery school. In D. Morris (Ed.), *Primate ethology.* London: Weidenfeld and Nicolson.

Coie, J. D., Dodge, K. A., & Coppotelli, H. (1982). Dimensions and types of social status: A cross-age perspective. *Developmental Psychology, 18,* 557–570.

Crick, N. R., & Dodge, K. A. (1988). *Social information processing mechanisms of reactive and proactive aggressive behavior in children.* Unpublished paper, Vanderbilt University, Nashville, TN.

Crick, N. R., & Ladd, G. W. (1987, April). *Children's perceptions of the outcomes of social strategies: Do the ends justify being mean?* Presented at the biennial meeting of the Society for Research in Child Development, Baltimore, MD.

Dawe, H. C. (1934). An analysis of two hundred quarrels of preschool children. *Child Development, 5,* 139–157.

Dodge, K. A. (1980). Social cognition and children's aggressive behavior. *Child Development, 51,* 162–170.

Dodge, K. A. (1986). A social information processing model of social competence in children. In M. Perlmutter (Ed.), *Minnesota symposium in child psychology,* (Vol. 18, pp. 77–125). Hillsdale, NJ: Lawrence Erlbaum Associates.

Dodge, K. A., & Coie, J. D. (1987). Social-information processing factors in reactive an proactive aggression in children's peer groups. *Journal of Personality and Social Psychology, 53,* 1146–1158.

Dodge, K. A., Coie, J. D., Pettit, G. S., & Price, J. M. (1988). Peer status and aggression in boys' playgroups: I. Developmental and contextual analyses. *Child Development.*

Dodge, K. A., Murphy, R. R., & Buchsbaum, K. (1984). The assessment of intention-cue detection skills in children: Implications for developmental psychopathology. *Child Development, 55,* 163–173.

Dodge, K. A., & Newman, J. P. (1981). Biased decision making processes in aggressive boys. *Journal of Abnormal Psychology, 90,* 375–379.

Dodge, K. A., Pettit, G. S., McClaskey, C. L., & Brown, M. M. (1986). Social competence in children. *Monographs of the Society for Research in Child Development, 51* (2, Serial No. 213).

Dodge, K. A., Price, J. M., Coie, J. D., & Christopoulos, C. (in press). On the development of aggressive dyadic relationships in boys peer groups. *Human Development.*

Dollard, J., Doob, L. W., Miller, N. E., Mowrer, O. H., & Sears, R. R. (1939). *Frustration and aggression.* New Haven, CT: Yale University Press.

Gendin, S. (1973). Insanity and criminal responsibility. *American Philosophical Quarterly, 10,* 99–110.

Guyton, A. C. (1981). *Textbook of medical physiology.* Philadelphia: W. B. Saunders.

Hamburg, D. A., & van Lawick-Goodall, J. (1978). Factors facilitating development of aggressive behavior in chimpanzees and humans. In W. W. Hartup & J. de Wit (Eds.), *Origins of aggression* (pp. 57–83). The Hague: Mouton.

Hartup, W. W. (1974). Aggression in childhood: Developmental perspectives. *American Psychologist, 29,* 336–341.

Hobbes, T. (1969). *Leviathan.* Cambridge, England: Cambridge University Press. (Original work published 1651)

Humphreys, A. P., & Smith, P. K. (1987). Rough and tumble, friendship, and dominance in school children: Evidence for continuity and change with age. *Child Development, 58,* 201–212.

James, W. (1890). *Principles of psychology* (Vol. 2). New York: Holt.

Karli, P. (1978). Aggressive behavior and its brain mechanisms (as exemplified by an experimental analysis of the rat's mouse-killing behavior). In W. W. Hartup & J. De Wit (Eds.), *Origins of aggression* (pp. 85–98). The Hague, Netherlands: Mouton.

Keith, C. R. (1984). Individual psychotherapy and psychoanalysis with the aggressive adolescent. A historical analysis. In C. R. Keith (Ed.), *The aggressive adolescent: Clinical perspectives* (pp. 191–208). New York: Free Press.

Lochman, J. E., & Curry, J. F. (1986). Effects of social problem-solving training and self-instruction with aggressive boys. *Journal of Clinical Child Psychology, 15,* 159–164.

Locke, J. (1913). *Some thoughts concerning education.* London: Cambridge University Press. (Original work published 1690)

Lorenz, K. (1966). *On aggression.* New York: Harcourt.

McDowell, D. M. (1978). *The law in classical Athens.* Ithaca, NY: Cornell University Press.

McGrew, W. C. (1972). *An ethological study of children's behavior.* New York: Academic Press.

Miley, W. M., & Baenninger, R. (1972). Inhibition and facilitation of interspecies aggression in septal-lesioned rats. *Physiology and Behavior, 9,* 379–384.

Moyer, K. E. (1976). *The psychobiology of aggression.* New York: Harper and Row.

Nasby, W., Hayden, B., & DePaulo, B. M. (1979). Attributional bias among aggressive boys to interpret unambiguous social stimuli as displays of hostility. *Journal of Abnormal Psychology, 89,* 459–468.

Panksepp, J. (1971). Aggression elicited by electrical stimulation of the hypothalamus in albino rats. *Physiology and Behavior, 6,* 321–329.

Parke, R. D., & Slaby, R. G. (1983). The development of aggression. In P. H. Mussen (Ed.), *Handbook of child psychology* (4th Ed.), *Vol. 4. Socialization and personality processes* (pp. 547–642). New York: Wiley.

Patterson, G. R. (1982). *Coercive family process.* Eugene, OR: Castalia.

Patterson, G. R., Littman, R. A., & Bricker, W. (1967). Assertive behavior in children: A step toward a theory of aggression. *Monographs of the Society for Research in Child Development, 32,* (5, Serial No. 113).

People v. Lewis, 123 N.Y.S.2d 81 (1953).

Perry, D. G., Perry, L. C., & Rasmussen, P. (1986). Cognitive social learning mediators of aggression. *Child Development, 57,* 700–711.

Price, J. M., & Dodge, K. A. (1989). Reactive and proactive aggression in childhood: Relations to peer status and social context dimensions. *Journal of Abnormal Child Psychology, 17,* 455–471.

Reis, D. J. (1974). Central neurotransmitters in aggression. In S. H. Frazier (Ed.), *Aggression* (Research publications, Association for Research in Nervous and Mental Disease, *Vol. 52,* pp. 119–148). Baltimore: Williams and Wilkins.

Rubin, K. H., & Krasnor, L. R. (1986). Social-cognitive and social behavioral perspectives on problem solving. In M. Perlmutter (Ed.), *Cognitive perspectives on children's social and behavioral development. Minnesota Symposia on Child Psychology, Vol. 18,* (pp. 1–68). Hillsdale, NJ: Lawrence Erlbaum Associates.

Rule, B. G. (1978). The hostile and instrumental functions of human aggression. In W. W. Hartup & J. de Wit (Eds.), *Origins of aggression* (pp. 121–142). The Hague: Mouton.

Rutter, M. (1981). *Maternal deprivation reassessed.* New York: Penguin.

Scott, J. P. (1972). Hostility and aggression. In B. Wolman (Ed.), *Handbook of genetic psychology.* Englewood Cliffs, NJ: Prentice-Hall.

Slaby, R. G., & Guerra, N. G. (1988). Cognitive mediators of aggression in adolescent offenders: 1. Assessment. *Developmental Psychology, 24,* 580–588.

Spivack, G., & Shure, M. B. (1974). *Social adjustment of young children: A cognitive approach to solving real-life problems.* San Francisco: Jossey-Bass.

Strassberg, Z., & Dodge, K. A. (1987, November). *Focus of social attention among children varying in social status.* Presented at the meeting of the Association for the Advancement of Behavior Therapy, Boston, MA.

Walters, R. H. (1964). On the high-magnitude theory of aggression. *Child Development, 35,* 303–304.

9

Social Problem Solving and Aggression in Childhood

Kenneth H. Rubin
Linda A. Bream
University of Waterloo

Linda Rose-Krasnor
Brock University

SOCIAL PROBLEM SOLVING AND AGGRESSION IN CHILDREN

The importance of understanding the development of aggression cannot be understated. Of all the child behavior disorders, aggression appears to have the most far-reaching social and psychological implications. The most important of these implications is the long-term stability of the phenomenon. As the reader may have noted in earlier chapters, aggressive behavior is highly stable from childhood through adolescence. Stability of aggression is reported as high not only among North American youth (Moskowitz, Schwartzman, & Ledingham, 1985), but also in Britain (Farrington, 1978) and Scandanavia (Olweus, 1979); furthermore, the phenomenon is stable seemingly regardless of how it is assessed (i.e., whether through teacher ratings, peer assessments, or behavioral observations).

Perhaps as important as the stability of aggression are its concurrent and predictive correlates. For example, from very early in childhood, aggression is associated causally with the development and maintenance of negative peer reputations and peer rejection (Dodge, 1983; Rubin & Daniels-Beirness, 1983). Furthermore, aggressive children appear to be at high risk for the development of antisocial and other adjustment problems in adolescence and adulthood (see Parker & Asher, 1987, for a recent review).

Given that aggression is highly stable and potentially harmful to both the aggressor and to his or her victims, it behooves us to explore the potential causes of this malevolent behavior. Once identified, it is anticipated that treatment programs, drawn from demonstrated causes, will be developed to ameliorate problems associated with and causal of aggression in childhood.

Causes and Correlates of Childhood Aggression

Needless to say, it is beyond the scope of this chapter to review the literature on the causes and correlates of childhood aggression; the interested reader is referred instead to recent reviews by Parke and Slaby (1983) and Shaffer (1987). Nevertheless, it is useful to outline briefly those factors that have been implicated in the development of aggression in childhood.

First, there are those who suggest a biogenetic origin to aggression. Thus, aggressive behavior is thought, by some, to derive primarily from genetically inspired variations in temperamental and physical characteristics (see Cairns, 1979, for a review). Second, some psychologists believe that aggression is a learned phenomenon that is reinforced, directly and indirectly, by parents, peers, the media, as well as by others in the child's social milieu (e.g., Patterson, this volume). Those who support this theory of causal influence believe that aggression begets aggression, and that vicious, coercive cycles of interpersonal violence can be predicted when aggression is negatively reinforced or modelled by significant others. Third, some psychologists believe that certain social conditions serve to evoke aggressive displays. One of the most devious social conditions is that which elicits a seemingly intolerable degree of frustration; in turn, frustration, when left unchecked, can lead to aggression (Dodge, 1980). Fourth, and most recently, aggression has been thought to result from deficits and breakdowns in the ways that children process information emanating from their social environments (e.g., Dodge, 1986; Rubin & Krasnor, 1986).

By and large, it is probably the case that all four causal factors serve to elicit, reinforce, and maintain the production of aggressive behavior in children. Indeed, it is likely that these factors interact in an insidious fashion to produce highly aggressive behavior in children. Yet it is often the case that proponents of the various theories extant pit their biases against each other in efforts to find the single, most powerful explanatory truth concerning the cause of hostility and aggression. Consequently, one of our purposes in writing this chapter, is to suggest that some aspects of some theories and explanatory variables work best for some, but not all children; that is, there is no single, theoretically driven cause that will account for all the variance in any attempt to explain the aggressive behaviors of individual children. To make this point clear, we begin by outlining one theory and how it has been implicated in the study of childhood aggression. In the section that follows, we provide an overview of our theory and those of others concerning social information processing and social problem solving. We then examine data demonstrating that this particular theory, in its varied forms, may be useful in accounting for the hostile behaviors and negative reputations of some, but certainly not all, aggressive children.

Information Processing and Social Problem Solving in Childhood

By the time the typical North American and European child is 3 or 4 years old, she or he has probably experienced many formal and informal group interactive experiences. Certainly by kindergarten age, virtually all such youngsters will have spent countless hours in the company of extra-familial children and adults.

During the course of these experiences, children are likely to regularly encounter a wide variety of dilemmas. Some of these problems are primarily physical, such as keeping one's balance on a skateboard or coloring between the lines. Other everyday problems are predominantly cognitive, such as calculating how many more allowances it will take to buy a new skateboard. However, some of the most complex and interesting problems are primarily interpersonal in nature. Convincing someone to allow the use of his or her precious skateboard or persuading a parent to provide a loan for the purchase of a new skateboard are two examples of these social dilemmas.

We think that an individual's social competence can be defined within a problem solving framework (Krasnor & Rubin, 1981; Rubin & Krasnor, 1986). In this approach, *social interaction* is considered to be comprised of a series of goal-directed, other-oriented acts, and *social problem solving* is broadly construed as the process of achieving social goals.

Some common social goals include joining an ongoing group activity, gaining access to objects or information, and obtaining assistance. A variety of potential strategies may be available for achieving one's social goals. For example, the goal of acquiring a desired toy from a peer may be achieved by asking, crying, grabbing, physically attacking the possessor, waiting, or soliciting help from an adult. The selection of a strategy may be based upon factors such as prior experience, ease of performance, projected likelihood of success and the social acceptability of each potential strategy. Some goals may be target specific (e.g., getting invited to Josh's birthday party); others may be nonspecific to a given person (e.g., getting someone to help with a flat bicycle tire). Some goals may concern the present (e.g., getting Randy to stop teasing); others may have a longer-term perspective (e.g., becoming Rebecca's friend).

Within this orientation, we define *social competence* as the ability to achieve personal goals in social interaction while simultaneously maintaining positive relationships with significant others. This emphasis on effectiveness in social interaction has been repeatedly apparent in the social skills literature (see Rubin & Krasnor, 1986, for a review). As such, it is consistent with theorists who have stressed mastery and effectance as critical aspects of competence and adaptation (e.g., Harter, 1980).

This functional approach toward social competence suggests a model which borrows heavily from the cognitive problem solving and information processing literatures. In recent years, a number of researchers have adapted these frameworks to explain social behavior (e.g., Dodge, 1986, this volume; Spivack & Shure, 1974). We present our general model of the social problem solving process in Fig. 9.1 (adapted from Rubin & Krasnor, 1986).

The model identifies a number of points for assessing a child's social skills. At the level of *individual acts,* these assessment points include the relative distribution of social goals and targets, the child's perception and understanding of task relevant information (e.g., others' intentions and emotions; the relative status of the target[s]), the number and quality of available strategies, and the selection of appropriate and effective strategies. At the level of *social effects,* assessment points include the social outcomes of the child's attempts as well as others' judgments of the child's strategic choices. At the level of behavioral *sequences,* assessments of the child's responses to failure are relevant. These sequential dimensions typically have been measured in terms of persistence and flexibility as well as escalation and de-escalation progressions (e.g., Krasnor & Rubin, 1983). Other important assessment areas may include the child's own affect and the quality of the child's relationship with the social target.

Children's social problem solving behaviors have generally been examined by observing in relatively unconstrained situations (e.g., Krasnor & Rubin, 1983; Rubin & Borwick, 1984; Rubin, Daniels-Beirness, & Bream, 1984), as well as in situations in which problem solving is "manipulated" by the experimenter (e.g. Putallaz & Gottman, 1981). In both contexts, behavioral evidence of preferred strategies, social effectiveness, and flexibility have been related to peer status and/or teacher ratings of social competence (Putallaz & Gottman, 1981; Rubin & Krasnor, 1986).

Studies of social problem-solving behavior in the natural setting, however, have been much less common than studies of how children *think* about solving their interpersonal dilemmas. We have labelled much of

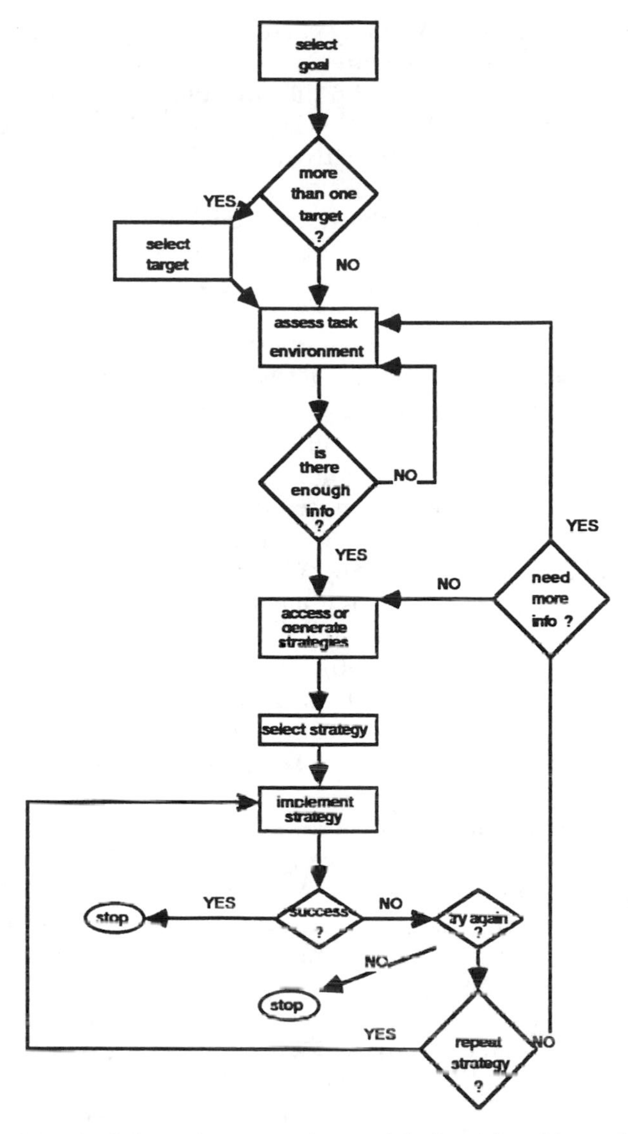

FIG. 9.1. An information processing model of social problem solving (adapted from Rubin & Rose-Krasnor, 1986).

this latter line of research as "hypothetical–reflective" because hypothetical problem situations are presented to children in an attempt to measure their ability to think through or "reflect" about a response (Rubin & Krasnor, 1986). Although studies of hypothetical–reflective social problem-solving have become increasingly popular, the scope of investigation has been surprisingly narrow. The great majority of studies has focussed on describing children's strategy repertoires, elicited in response to social goals defined by the investigator. In the widely used Preschool Interpersonal Problem Solving Test (PIPS), for example, the child is asked to generate alternative strategies to solve (a) a peer-oriented goal in which a child seeks to obtain a toy in the possession of another child, and (b) an adult-oriented goal in which a child seeks to avoid a mother's anger after property damage (Spivack & Shure, 1974). Other goals used commonly in tests of hypothetical–reflective strategy generation have included initiating friendship (e.g. Gottman, Gonso, & Rasmussen, 1975; Renshaw & Asher, 1983), providing help to a needy other (Ladd & Oden, 1979), soliciting help from a peer (Rubin, Moller, & Emptage, 1987), and resolving peer conflict (Selman, 1980).

Hypothetical–reflective assessment of social problem solving components, other than strategy generation and selection, has been relatively rare. A few researchers have attempted to examine children's goals (Renshaw & Asher, 1983); strategy sequencing after failure has also been assessed (Rubin & Krasnor, 1986). One programmatic series of hypothetical–reflective studies that has gone well beyond the simple examination of strategy generation and production is the work by Dodge and his associates (e.g., Dodge, 1980, 1986). One of Dodge's major contributions has been the elegant manner with which he has demonstrated that the child's assessment of the task environment is likely to predict his or her choice of problem solving strategies. For example, in some of his studies, Dodge has presented children with hypothetical scenarios in which a peer performs a potentially provocational behavior that has some type of negative outcome for them. The scenarios are worded in a manner that leaves the intentions of the peer provocateur ambiguous. Dodge (1980) has shown that when children assess the environment and come to the conclusion that the negative outcome was caused by deliberately hostile intentions, they are highly likely to suggest agonistic, retaliatory strategies. When the peer's actions are judged as having resulted from benign intent, children's suggested strategies are unlikely to be agonistic.

Applied interest in hypothetical–reflective methodologies has been justified largely by a hypothesized connection between social problem-solving cognitions and behaviors. It has been assumed generally that the strategic responses to hypothetical problems posed in an interview reflect those actions that would be displayed in response to similar problems in the natural setting. Furthermore, it has been suggested that the ways in which children assess hypothetical task environments can allow a prediction of their choices of strategic responses in "real-life" settings. For example, children who, in an interview, indicate that a negative outcome was caused maliciously and intentionally when, in fact, intentionality was ambiguous, are thought to be those who in "real life" tend to misinterpret intentionality and strike out against their peers (Dodge, 1986). As such, it has been predicted that children's aggressive behaviors are mediated, in part, by the ways that they think about their social worlds; that is, children's enactment of aggression is often mediated by an inappropriate "reading" of the task environment, feelings of anger or hostility in reaction to the assessment of the task environment, and the selection of agonistic strategies from the cognitive repertoire. In the following section, we examine these hypothesized links between social problem-solving cognitions and children's aggression.

Social Problem-Solving, Social Information Processing, and Aggression

The link between hypothetical–reflective thought and aggressive behavior has been of interest to researchers throughout the past two decades. Much of the early work was given to the study of the numbers and types of solutions children offered in situations that varied with regard to the social goals. As such, these early studies dealt with those aspects of our social information processing model that concerned the child's goals and his or her generation and selection of strategies to meet those goals.

In the first programmatic set of studies on this topic, Spivack and colleagues (e.g., Spivack & Shure, 1974) indicated that children identified by teachers as aggressive generated fewer solutions to hypothetical dilemmas involving peer and parent conflict. For goals that involved the acquisition of objects or access to desired activities, Rubin and Clark (1983) found that preschoolers rated by teachers as aggressive offered as many relevant solutions as their non-aggressive counterparts to hypothetical problems; however, the aggressive youngsters were more likely to suggest agonistic or bribe strategies and less likely to offer prosocial strategies to the set of hypothetical problems.

More recent studies of elementary schoolers have produced somewhat similar results. Rubin, Moller, and Emptage (1987) found that children rated as aggressive by their teachers had social information processing difficulties at varying levels of the theoretical model and that these difficulties varied given the child's particular social goals. For example, with regard to object possession dilemmas, aggressive grade 1 children were not less likely to produce fewer strategies than their nonaggressive agemates; however, their choice of particular solutions did vary from the norm. Aggressive children were more likely to suggest bribe and affect manipulation as strategies and were less likely to offer the possibility of prosocial strategies. With regard to the goal of friendship initiation, aggressive youngsters not only produced fewer relevant strategies overall, but they had a higher proportion of bizarre/ abnormal strategies and offered fewer invitations to potential friends than did the nonaggressive children. Furthermore, when informed by the interviewer that the initial strategy would not work, aggressive children were less able to provide alternate methods to resolve the social dilemma. As such these children could be described as less cognitively flexible than their nonaggressive counterparts. Finally, with regard to the goal of seeking help from another, aggressive youngsters were more likely to suggest strategies that involved commanding their targets ("You better help.") or using bizarre/abnormal strategies and were less likely to offer prosocial strategies such as asking politely.

In a study of grade 2 to 6 children, Walters and Peters (1980) found that teacher rated aggressive boys did not produce quantitatively fewer relevant solutions to goals involving object possession, peer group initiation, and the resolution of peer provocation; however, the quality of their solutions deviated from the norm in different ways across the three different types of dilemmas. For example, across all problems, aggressive boys were the most likely to suggest aggressive solutions as a *first* response. This finding suggests the primacy of an aggressive response across social situations. Aggressive boys were also more likely to seek help from others (adults) when asked how they would go about initiating a friendship, and they were more likely to suggest physically aggressive strategies in response to peer provocation.

The studies described above concern the social problem solving concomitants of teacher rated aggression. According to Deluty (1981), peer identified aggressive elementary school children are more likely than nonaggressive children to suggest more aggressive solutions in hypothetical situations involving the resolution of peer conflict. In this study, aggressive children did not differ from others concerning the overall number of solutions offered. Finally, in a recent analysis of data from the Waterloo Longitudinal Project, we have discovered that in both grades 1 and 2, peer nominated aggressive children are less likely to offer prosocial solutions and more likely to suggest bribery as resolutions to object acquisition dilemmas; they are also more likely to suggest abnormal/bizarre resolutions to friendship initiation dilemmas (e.g., "I'd buy him a belt."; "I'd sneak into her room at night.").

Taken together, these studies suggest that for certain goals (e.g., object acquisition; the resolution of peer conflict; friendship initiation), aggressive children, from the preschool through elementary school years, are more likely than their nonaggressive age-mates to suggest that they would employ agonistic or other, non-normative strategies to deal with interpersonal dilemmas. Interestingly, the breadth of their cognitive repertoires (as assessed by the number of suggested alternatives) do not appear lacking except, perhaps, during the preschool years. As such, one conclusion that can be drawn from the literature is that intervention efforts should center on the quality of the child's strategic response choices and not necessarily increasing the numerosity of solutions.

Given the above described findings, it would appear reasonable to ask why it is that aggressive children offer agonistic solutions to hypothetical–reflective interviews concerning solutions to their interpersonal dilemmas. One answer may derive from research that has concerned the assessment of the task environment. According to Dodge (1986; this volume), children can interpret social situations and interactions in ways that are biased and/or deficient. Such misguided and potentially inaccurate perceptions may predict the strategies children choose to resolve their interpersonal dilemmas. For example, if a child has not received an invitation to a classmate's party, he or she may conclude that this negative consequence was intentional. The attribution of negative consequences to hostile, malevolent intent may evoke anger and ultimately the selection of an inappropriate, aggressive solution to the dilemma (e.g, physically attack the party-giver).

Interestingly, Dodge (1986; this volume) has demonstrated that aggressive children *do* misperceive the intentions and/or thoughts of others in their social milieus. Thus, when negative circumstances befall them and when the intentions of the provocateur are clearly ambiguous, aggressive children are more likely than their nonaggressive peers to insist that the negative circumstances were caused by malevolent intent. One consequence of this biased perception is that aggressive youngsters are likely to react with hostility when they believe they have been intentionally harmed.

The cycle of violence that aggressive children find themselves in may be exacerbated by the ways in which their age-mates interpret their intentions in socially provocative situations. For example, Dodge (1986; this volume) has found that when negative circumstances of ambiguous intent are experienced by nonaggressive youngsters, and when the perpetrator is an aggressive child, negative, hostile intentions are attributed to the provocateur. This negative attribution is much less likely to occur when the provocateur is a nonaggressive child. Needless to say, when hostile intentions are attributed to a social "outcome", nonaggressive children are more likely to respond with aggressive solutions than when the attribution is one of benign intent. Thus, not only do the biased perceptions of aggressive children mediate their hostile behavioral reactions to provocation, but the biased perceptions of their nonaggressive peers about them also are likely to draw aggressive youngsters into negative interchanges (Dodge & Frame, 1982).

In summary, it seems clear from the above review, that aggressive children from as early as the preschool years are more likely to attempt to achieve some social goals by means of aggressive, hostile or bizzare/abnormal behaviors. It seems also as if the aggressive strategies chosen to meet their social goals are mediated by a biased perception of the social milieu. It should be noted, however, that data supportive of the links between various points in the information processing model have been assessed only through the use of hypothetical–reflective interview methods. Surprisingly, we are aware of no studies in which the social goals, the means by which these goals are achieved, the relative success rates of the chosen strategies, and the subsequent responses to failure (e.g., persistence, flexibility; Rubin & Krasnor, 1986) have been examined observationally for aggressive children. Are the social *goals* of aggressive children different from those of their non-aggressive counterparts? For example, are they more likely to attempt to acquire objects in the possession of a playmate or to stop the ongoing activities of a playmate than their less aggressive peers? Are the *strategies* chosen by aggressive youngsters to meet their social goals more directive and agonistic than those of their less aggressive peers? Are the *outcomes* of their strategic choices more likely to be successes or failures than those of their nonaggressive age-mates? Finally, how is it that aggressive youngsters *respond to failure?* Are they more likely to be inflexible and to continue using the original strategy that resulted in failure? Are they more likely to give up in the face of failure? These and other questions served as starting points for the studies described herein.

STUDY 1: AGGRESSION AND SOCIAL PROBLEM SOLVING AS ASSESSED IN NATURALISTIC SETTINGS

In the first study, we examined the relations between peer assessments of childhood aggression and social problem-solving behaviors and cognitions. This multifaceted approach allowed us to trace, in a single data set, almost all points in our information processing model.

The first set of analyses tested the relations between peer assessed aggression and the distribution of observed social goals. We expected that aggressive children would be observed to have more disruptive and confrontative social goals (e.g., stopping a peer's ongoing activity) than their less aggressive counterparts. The second set of analyses concerned the distribution of social strategies. For the hypothetical dilemmas, it was expected that aggressive children would suggest more aggressive and disruptive strategies than their less aggressive peers (*strategy generation* and *selection*). It was expected also that aggressive children would be observed to employ more aggressive strategies (*enactment*) to meet their social goals. The final set of analyses concerned the *outcomes* of children's social encounters. Given that aggression is often associated with peer rejection (e.g., Dodge, 1983; Rubin & Daniels-Beirness, 1983), and given that rejection has been taken as an index of social failure, it was predicted that peer assessments of aggression would be associated with high frequencies of interactive failure following strategy generation.

Participants. Fifty-four third- and fourth-grade children from an elementary school in Southern Ontario were group administered a peer assessment of social reputation. Forty of these children (20 boys and 20 girls) were randomly selected to participate in a second phase of the study involving behavioral observations. The 40 children ranged in age from 102 to 126 months (M = 112.32 mos, SD = 6.41 mos).

Peer Assessments. All children were administered the Revised Class Play (Masten, Morison, & Pellegrini, 1985). Children were requested to nominate classmates who would best fit each of 30 behavioral descriptors. Subsequently, nominations received from same-sex peers were used to compute each of three factor scores for each child following procedures outlined by Masten and colleagues (1985): sociability–leadership, aggression–disruption, and sensitivity–isolation. For each summary score, the number of nominations received by each child was standardized within class and gender groups to permit appropriate comparisons. Higher scores were indicative of stronger peer perceptions of the identified behavior in each case. For purposes of this report, only the aggression–disruption scores were reported.

Hypothetical Social Problem Solving. Children's abilities to generate alternate solutions to social dilemmas were assessed using a modified version of the Open Middle Interview (Weissberg, Gesten, Rapkin, Cowen, Davidson, Flores de Apodaca, & McKim, 1981). In this individually administered test, same-sex peer story characters are faced with four social problems: (a) getting to take the school gerbil home for the weekend when a classmate also wants it; (b) stopping other children from teasing; (c) getting a turn on a bicycle ridden by a peer; and (d) alleviating a peer's anger after losing his/her toy.

The children were asked what the story character could do or say to solve the specific social problem. After the child generated a first strategy, she/he was asked what the story character could do or say if the first strategy had resulted in failure. The interviewer probed for additional strategies until the child could produce no further alternatives.

Eight content categories were coded: (a) help-seeking ("Tell the teacher."); (b) non-confrontation ("Go away."); (c) physical aggression ("Hit him."); (d) verbal aggression ("Call him names."); (e) compromise ("Let's share."); (f) bargaining ("I'll give you a dollar."); (g) verbal assertion ("Tell her to get off."); and (h) direct action ("I'd stop the bike.").

Observed Social Problem-Solving. Children were randomly paired into 20 same-sex, same-grade dyads for a 10-minute videotaped session to assess social problem-solving goals, strategies, and outcomes. The children were brought to a small school room and were asked to construct a single animal from blocks scattered on a table in front of them. They were told that a photograph would be taken of their animal at the end of the session to assess how well it was built. The children were also told that the session would be videotaped.

Observational data were coded for social problem-solving attempts, defined as socially oriented behaviors that were directive and initiated by the focal child. Attempts were categorized according to criteria drawn from Krasnor & Rubin (1983).

Strategy. Strategies included: (a) statements that expressed personal need or desire ("I want that."); (b) direct imperatives ("Give me that."); (c) imbedded imperatives ("Would you help me?"); (d) suggestions ("Wanna do a giraffe?"); (e) conditional statements including bribes and threats ("If you don't help, I won't be your friend."); (f) descriptive statements ("The blue one is over here."); (g) claims ("It's mine."); (h) orienting acts (show, point); (i) agonistic acts (hit, grab); (j) affiliative acts (hug); and (k) callings ("Hey, Jim.").

Goals. Goal categories were: (a) stop action (stop or redirect peer's behavior); (b) self-action (obtain permission to act); (c) object acquisition (gain sole possession or use of an object); (d) gain attention; (e) seek information; and (f) give and obtain affection. *Successful outcomes* were defined as attempts followed by compliance within a 10 second period. *Partial compliance* was scored when attempts ended in bids for clarification or in partial compliance. *Failures* were coded when attempts were not followed by compliance within a 10 second period (Krasnor & Rubin, 1983).

Reliability was assessed by an independent coding of 10 randomly selected 3-minute segments from the 20 videotapes. Percent agreement for the judgment of social problem solving attempts was 90.0% based on 164 attempts. Reliability for the observed strategies ranged from 67% to 94% (for categories with frequencies > 5), Cohen's $K = .82$, $z = 34.00$. For goals, percent agreement ranged from 65% to 100%, $K = .84$, $z = 16.13$. Percent agreement for success, partial success, and failure outcomes were 76%, 64% and 82% respectively, $K = .78$, $z = 10.37$.

Results of Study 1

Aggression and Social Goals. The relation between patterns of social goals and peer nominated aggression was tested in a multiple regression analysis. Age and sex were entered first into the regression equation as control variables, followed by the relevant sets of observational data as predictor variables. Age and sex were nonsignificantly related to peer assessed aggression. The distribution of goals significantly predicted peer nominated aggression, F (8, 31) = 2.48, $p < .05$, increasing R^2 from .06 to .39.

In order to control the number of statistical tests, the relation between specific predictor variables and peer assessed aggression was examined only when the variance added by the entire data set was at a trend level of significance or better. Partial correlations controlling for age and sex were used to assess the relation between specific predictor variables and the criterion since they were judged to be more stable and more meaningfully interpreted than the beta weights. The analyses revealed that children assessed by peers as highly aggressive attempted significantly more attention ($r = .33$, $p < .01$) and stop action ($r = .40$, $p < .01$) goals than those viewed as less aggressive.

Aggression and Social Strategies. The relation between responses on the hypothetical–reflective social problem solving test and peer assessed aggression was likewise tested using multiple regression procedures controlling for age and sex. As before the control variables were not predictive of aggression. In a first analysis the control variables were followed by the addition of the total number of strategies and the average number of strategies offered in response to the interview. These data tapped that level of competence that we identify as the strategy repertoire. These two quantitative measures did not add significantly to the prediction of aggression.

A similar regression analysis in which the frequencies of qualitatively different strategies was added to the equation following the entry of control variables revealed a marginal association with aggression, F (11, 28) = 2.03, $p < .06$, resulting in an R^2 increase from .06 to .44. Partial correlations revealed that physically aggressive strategies were positively associated with peer assessed aggression, $r = .50$ $p < .01$, as was bargaining, $r = .31$, $p < .03$.

A multiple regression analysis using the *observed* strategy patterns as predictors indicated that peer assessed aggression could be reliably predicted, increasing R^2 from .05 to .54, F (11, 28) = 3.00, $p < .05$. Partial correlations revealed that four strategies were significantly predictive of aggression: agonistic acts, $r = .45$, $p < .01$; callings, $r = .45$, $p < .01$; statements, $r = .33$, $p < .02$; and orienting acts, $r = .28$, $p < .05$.

Aggression and Observed Outcomes. Partial correlations were calculated to assess the relations between aggression and observed success, partial success, and failure, controlling for age and sex. A significant positive relation was found between percent success and aggression, $r = .30$, $p < .04$, and a significant negative relation was found with percent partial success, $r = -.30$, $p < .04$.

Discussion of Study 1

Our data revealed consistent relations between aggression and each of the information-processing steps we investigated herein. For example, significant relations were obtained between peer nominated aggression and children's choice of social goals, the selection of strategies to meet their goals (as measured by responses to hypothetical–reflective scenarios), the implementation of strategies (as assessed by our observations of strategy usage), and social problem-solving outcome.

Beginning with social goals, we found that the most highly aggressive children were more likely to attempt to stop the activities of their dyadic partners or to redirect their partner's attention to themselves or to other features of the playroom. Both of these goals may be considered disruptive, especially in a situation in which the children were supposed to be completing a required task. Thus, the predicted relation between aggression and intrusiveness was obtained.

With regard to the selection of strategies, the data supported previous research in which aggressive children have been found to suggest more physically aggressive strategies to resolve hypothetical social dilemmas (e.g., Dodge, 1986). Furthermore, they were also more likely to suggest bargaining; this strategy often involved offering an enticement for compliance. These data are interesting for two reasons. First, they suggest that agonism is a highly salient response in the cognitive repertoire of aggressive children. That this is the case is supported by the finding that aggressive children not only were more likely to *suggest* aggression as a means to meet their social goals, but also by the observation that they were more likely to *use* aggression to meet their social goals in natural settings. Second, it is noteworthy that, for all children, the two least frequently offered solutions to the hypothetical–reflective scenarios were physical aggression ($M = 1.77$) and bargaining ($M = .05$); these *M*s may be contrasted with those for verbal assertions ($M = 5.92$), help-seeking ($M = 3.95$), compromise ($M = 3.32$) or nonconfrontation ($M =$

3.25). Thus, just as it is the case that rejected children tend to select social strategies that deviate from peer group norms (Ladd & Oden, 1979), this appears to be true for aggressive children. Needless to say, aggressive children are also highly at risk for peer rejection (Dodge, 1983).

As mentioned earlier, highly aggressive children were more likely to employ agonistic strategies as well as callings and orienting acts than their less aggressive counterparts. These strategies are likely to disrupt the ongoing behaviors of their peers and, more importantly, the production of a higher frequency of agonistic strategies indicates that their peers' perceptions of them as aggressive were accurate.

Finally, with regard to the outcomes of their strategic attempts, our expectations were disconfirmed; children perceived as aggressive were reinforced at rather high levels by their peers. These data support earlier reports by Patterson (e.g., Patterson, Littman, & Bricker, 1967) that preschool aggression is highly reinforced. Thus, although agonistic strategies may not be socially acceptable, they are nevertheless relatively effective. Consequently, the strategies employed by aggressive children may be resistant to modification attempts founded on social acceptability arguments.

More recently, Patterson (1979) has suggested that aggressive behaviors are maintained by negative reinforcement and that they function primarily to terminate the aversive behaviors of their peers. Interestingly, in this study, peer assessed aggression was associated with the frequent incidence of stop action goals; that is, aggressive children often sought to terminate the activities of their peers and they did so with much success. If the aggressive children had perceived their peers' behavior to have been underscored often by malevolent intent (as Dodge, 1986 has reported), our data would support Patterson's contention.

In summary, we have found that the social goals, the strategies selected and enacted to meet these goals, and the outcomes of these strategic attempts differentiated aggressive children from their non-aggressive counterparts. These data, drawn from traditional hypothetical–reflective interview procedures as well as from behavioral observations help round out the picture concerning the social problem-solving cognitions and behaviors of aggressive children. Like all other published reports of this ilk, however, our data serve only to allow conclusions to be drawn about the skills and deficits of aggressive children *in general*. As such, it may be that many practitioners can be misled somewhat concerning the social-cognitive and behavioral difficulties that the *particular* aggressive youngsters who have been referred to them may be experiencing; treatment programs suggested by general findings may be inappropriate for many aggressive children. To make this point more salient, we present, in Study 2, case study profiles of four extremely aggressive fourth-grade children.

STUDY 2: CASE STUDIES OF THE SOCIAL PROBLEM-SOLVING PROFILES OF FOUR CHILDREN

Is it the case that most aggressive children share similar social, cognitive, and social–cognitive profiles? From our perspective, the response is obvious; life is far more complex than generalizations about data lead us to believe. Consequently, it would be naive for us to conclude that most aggressive children are alike. We draw our own conclusions from data gathered as part of The Waterloo Longitudinal Project, a study that began in the early 1980s in an effort to examine the stability and the consequences of social withdrawal and peer rejection in childhood (e.g., Rubin & Mills, 1988). In some years of data collection, teacher ratings and peer assessments of aggression were obtained. The case studies presented herein were drawn from the grade 4 data corpus.

In fourth grade, all participants in The Waterloo Longitudinal Project ($n = 109$) were administered the Revised Class Play (Masten et al., 1985), a peer assessment of social behavior. The aggression–disruption factor is of particular interest herein. For this factor, the number of nominations received by each child was standardized within class and gender groups in order to permit comparisons across classrooms differing in size and gender composition.

All fourth-grade teachers were asked to complete the Preschool Behavior Questionnaire (Behar & Stringfield, 1974), a measure designed to identify socio-emotional problems in young children. Recent research has demonstrated that this 30-item scale yields two reliable factors in the elementary school years (Moller & Rubin, 1988). The first factor, *externalizing,* consists of items descriptive of hostile-aggressive and impulsive-distractible behaviors; the second factor, *internalizing,* consists of items descriptive of fearfulness, anxiety, and social solitude. Each child received a total score for those items that loaded on each of the two factors.

From these data, we identified those children whose (a) aggression–disruption scores on the Revised Class Play and whose externalizing scores on the teacher rating scale were one standard deviation above their respective means and (b) whose sociability–leadership and isolation–fearfulness scores on the Revised Class Play and whose internalizing scores on the teacher measure fell at or below their respective means. Four highly aggressive children were so identified, two boys and two girls.

In addition, all fourth-grade children were administered a hypothetical–reflective measure of social problem solving and half of the sample (including all four target children) was observed in dyadic interaction for two 15-minute play sessions.

Measures

Social Problem Solving Interview (SPSI). The SPSI was administered to all children during a single individual interview session. Children responded to three hypothetical stories in which they were to imagine being the recipient of a negative outcome produced by a peer or peers. In all cases, the intentions of the peer(s) were ambiguous. The three stores involved (a) *physical provocation* (being hit in the back with a ball); (b) *verbal provocation* (being laughed at when unable to catch someone in a game of tag); and (c) *peer rejection* (not being invited to a classmate's birthday party).

Each child was asked to project either a positive or negative expected outcome to the social dilemma, to describe the actor's intentions, to infer either accidental or purposeful intent to the actor, and to suggest possible responses to the situations.

Children's responses to the expected outcome question ("Do you think that there will be a problem between you and the other kids(s)?") were coded as either positive or negative. The proportion of outcomes for which the child indicated that there would be a problem served as one dependent measure.

Children's responses to the open-ended intent questions ("Why do you think she/he did that?") were coded along an attributional dimension of perceiver responsibility. This attributional dimension involved consideration of the degree to which the child viewed the actor as responsible for the outcome described. Children's responses were coded as falling into one of the following five categories:

1. *Full blame*—the outcome is viewed as resulting because of purposeful or intentional motives (e.g., "He hit me just to be mean.");
2. *Partial blame*—the actor is primarily but not exclusively responsible for the outcome;
3. *External constraints*—the actor's responsibility is minimized because of third party constraints, situational constraints, or the child's own behavior (e.g., "Maybe his mom wouldn't let him invite any more kids.");
4. *Reinterpretation of intentionality*—the negative act or the the actor's motives are reinterpreted in such a way that the outcome is no

longer perceived as negative (e.g., "He didn't mean to hurt me; it was just an accident."); and

5. *Denial*—the negative act or the impact of the act is denied by the child (e.g., "She didn't really do that.").

For purposes of the present study, we examined the proportion of responses that could be coded as full blame.

Children's responses to the forced choice intentionality question ("Do you think that she/he did that on purpose or do you think it was an accident?") were coded as accidental or purposeful. The proportion of responses coded as intentional served as the dependent variable.

Finally, suggested behavioral solutions were coded into one of five categories: *Avoidance* (the child leave the scene; remains on the scene but does nothing); *prosocial* (the child either takes the blame or remains benevolent in the face of the negative outcome); *gain information* (the child attempts to get more information about the cause of the outcome); *confrontative* (the child confronts the actor in a non-hostile manner); and *adult intervention.* The proportions of each response choice served as dependent measures.

Social Problem Solving Observations. An observational taxonomy described earlier by Rubin and Krasnor (1986) was used to examine the children's interpersonal problem solving skills. First, 50 children were selected from the full sample to participate in two 15-minute observational sessions. Each child was paired with a same-sex, same age play partner who was not a member of his or her class. The four highly aggressive youngsters were each paired with a nonaggressive, "normal" play partner.

Both observational sessions took place in a laboratory playroom equipped with games, dolls, Transformers, paper and markers. In the first 15-minute session, the children were informed that they could play as they wished. In the second session, the toys were first placed in a corner of the playroom and the children were requested to sit at a small table and work together to construct an airplane or spaceship out of Lego blocks. A picture of these objects was provided the children in an effort to provide them with a choice of desired "outcomes." This cooperative construction session ended after eight minutes and the children were then allowed to engage in free play for seven additional minutes.

Each of the play sessions was videotaped from behind a one-way mirror. The children's interpersonal problem solving behaviors were subsequently coded using a taxonomy developed by Rubin and colleagues (e.g., Rubin & Borwick, 1984; Rubin & Krasnor, 1986). Social goals, strategies, outcomes, and strategies following initial failure were noted.

Goals were classified as elicit action, stop action, gain partner's attention, object acquisition, joint action, and requests for information. Strategies were coded as direct requests (commands), indirect requests (including imbedded imperatives and suggestions), conditional statements (bribes and threats), and agonistic acts. Outcomes of requests were coded as successful, partially successful, failures, and failure to wait for the partner's response. Finally, after a strategy failed, children's behaviors were coded as rigid re-request (re-use of the original strategy), modification of the original strategy, and no further response (including giving up and solving the problem by the self). Reliability coefficients (Cohen's Kappa) based on independent codings of 10% of the data ranged from .67 to .91 for goals, strategies, outcomes, and follow-up strategies.

Results of Study 2

Given the literature concerning the information processing difficulties of aggressive children, we expected that the four most highly aggressive participants in the fourth grade-cohort of The Waterloo Longitudinal Project would exhibit uniformly similar interpersonal problem solving profiles. More specifically, we predicted that they would be more likely to expect a problem to ensue following a hypothetical negative outcome, that they would blame the protagonist for the outcome and suggest that the provocative act was intentionally motivated. Following the literature on the choice of solutions to hypothetical social dilemmas, the four children were predicted to suggest more aggressive and fewer avoidant and prosocial solutions than the norm for their age group. During interaction with a nonaggressive peer, we expected the aggressive children to have more stop action and attention getting goals, to use more direct request, agonistic and bribe strategies, and to be quite successful in attaining their goals relative to their nonaggressive counterparts.

The social problem solving profiles of the four most highly aggressive children are contrasted with the norms provided by the entire sample of Tables 9.1, 9.2, and 9.3. As the reader can see, it is quite clear that the children differed in some respects from the norms and in most respects from each other. From the hypothetical–reflective interview, the two children who best fit the caricature for aggressive children were both girls, Carol and Tiffany. This finding, in and of itself, was surprising given that the literature on aggression is dominated by reports concerning males only (e.g., Dodge, 1986). Both Carol and Tiffany were more likely than the normative sample to blame the provocateur for the negative outcome and to attribute the outcome to hostile, malevolent intent. Their suggested solutions to the interpersonal dilemmas were most likely

TABLE 9.1
Case Studies Means and Standard Deviations:
Hypothetical–Reflective Measure

	Michael	Chuck	Tiffany	Carol	Norms (n = 109) M	SD
Expect a Problem	1.00	1.00	3.00*	1.00	.87	.87
Blame Other	.00*	1.00	2.00*	2.00*	.90	.78
Purposeful Act	1.00	2.00*	3.00*	3.00*	1.02	.90
Solutions (proportions)						
Aggressive	.00	.00	.67*	.67*	.08	.17
Adult Intervention	.00	.33*	.00	.33*	.05	.13
Avoidant	.33	.00*	.33	.00*	.46	.32
Confrontative	.00	.00	.00	.00	.19	.26
Prosocial	.67*	.67*	.00	.00	.23	.29

**At least 1 SD* above/below *M*

TABLE 9.2
Case Study Means and Standard Deviations
for Observation Session 1: Free-Play

Variable	*Michael*	*Chuck*	*Tiffany*	*Carol*	*Norms (n = 48) M*	*SD*
Total Requests	78*	9	38*	5	22.41	15.75
Strategies						
ppn direct	.64*	.33	.32	.40*	.26	.14
ppn indirect	.32*	.67	.68	.60	.64	.27
ppn bribe	.01	.00	.00	.00	.01	.04
ppn agonistic	.03	.00	.00	.00	.03	.15
Outcomes						
ppn success	.27*	.78	.63	.80	.60	.24
ppn failure	.68*	.22	.24	.20	.25	.16
ppn other	.05	.00	.13	.00	.15	.17
Follow-Up						
rigid	.20	.00**	.33*	.00*	.14	.12
modify	.51*	.50**	.16	.00*	.26	.18
give up/self solve	.29	.50	.51	1.00	.60	.42
Goals						
elicit action	.07	.22**	.08	.00*	.12	.10
stop action	.01	.00	.00	.00	.05	.09
object acq.[a]	.09	.00	.08	.00	.05	.15
attention	.65*	.22	.30	.60*	.22	.19
joint action	.06*	.00**	.00*	.00*	.15	.09
information	.12*	.56	.54	.40	.41	.26

[a]acq. = acquisition
* = at least 1 *SD* above/below *M*

TABLE 9.3
Case Study Means and Standard Deviations for Session 2: Constructive Task

Variable	*Michael*	*Chuck*	*Tiffany*	*Carol*	*Norms (n = 48)*	
					M	*SD*
Total Requests	35**	14	12	7**	14.52	7.15
Strategies						
ppn direct	.17	.21	.17	.29*	.19	.13
ppn indirect	.83	.79	.83	.71	.81	.18
ppn bribe	.00	.00	.00	.00	.00	.00
ppn agonistic	.00	.00	.00	.00	.00	.00
Outcomes						
ppn success	.43	.50	.92**	.57	.55	.19
ppn failure	.49**	.21	.08**	.43	.28	.20
ppn other	.08	.29**	.00	.00	.07	.11
Follow-Up						
rigid	.06	.00	.00	.00	.07	.14
modify	.59**	.33	.00	.00	.29	.21
give up/self solve	.35	.67	1.00	1.00	.66	.54
Goals						
elicit action	.06	.14	.08	.00	.14	.12
stop action	.00	.00	.00	.00	.04	.06
object acq.[a]	.03	.07	.00	.00	.06	.08
attention	.23	.07	.08	.43**	.13	.12
joint action	.03	.14	.17	.00**	.19	.17
information	.65	.58	.67**	.57	.43	.24

[a]acq. = acquisition
*.5 *SD* above/below *M*
**1 *SD* above/below *M*

to involve agonistic actions. The two boys, on the other hand, were more likely than the norm to suggest prosocial solutions, a finding opposite to that which was expected. Only Chuck indicated that the negative outcomes were caused primarily by hostile intentions; Michael never blamed the provocateur for the negative outcome, another response that deviated from the norm in the opposite direction than was expected!

From these interview data, one would predict that the children who would best fit the profile for aggressive children during the play sessions would be the two girls, Tiffany and Carol; if cognitions mediated behavior, the child least likely to fit the behavioral profile for aggressive children was Michael. A glance at Table 9.3 reveals how the tempo for Session 2 may have been set initially by the focal children's behavior in Session 1. In Session 1, one child partially fit the expected pattern for aggressive youth, Michael. This child was more likely than the norm to make social requests and to issue commands. Yet, in contrast to our expectations, most of his requests resulted in failure and when he chose to follow-up on these failures he was more likely than the norm to produce modified strategies. The primary goal of his social requests was to call attention to himself. Furthermore, he was less likely than the norm to attempt to join the play partner in a shared activity (joint action goals). In short, the one child who least fit the social-cognitive profile for aggressive children was the most likely to resemble the behavioral profile for that group.

Examination of Table 9.3 provides information concerning the cross-situational consistency of behavior. The data described in Table 9.2 are taken from a 15-minute free-play session, whereas those data described in Table 9.3 are drawn from an 8-minute cooperative constructive task. Once again in this second session, Michael issued more requests than was the norm for the comparison group and once again he experienced a higher proportion of social failures despite his seemingly more acceptable behavior (proportionally fewer commands than in Session 1). Needless to say, play partners have good short-term memories and the child who reacted negatively to the receipt of many commands in an earlier social interactive experience *may* have been negatively predisposed to the authoritarian play partner in the subsequent session. Interestingly, this child appeared less concerned than was the norm in trying to join the play partner in the cooperative endeavor (fewer joint action goals).

For Michael then, it appears as if an overbearing, authoritarian and somewhat egocentric (many attention getting goals) behavioral demeanor in Session 1 paved the pathway to a negative social experience in Session 2. Yet, one would have been hard-pressed to predict the observational outcome from the social-cognitive interview. But what about Tiffany, the most social-cognitively hostile child? It appears as if this child shared but a few of Michael's behavioral characteristics. In Session 1, she shared her male counterpart's higher than normal level of requestive behavior; a prediliction that may be interpreted by others as reflecting a social overbearingness. However, despite her verbosity, her strategies resembled those of the normal comparison group as did the outcomes of her social requests. When Tiffany's strategies failed, however, unlike Michael, she was more likely than the norm to use inflexible, rigid follow-up strategies. Like Michael, she was less likely than the norm to initiate requests to play cooperatively with the play partner; she did not, however, appear to call undue attention to herself.

In Session 2, Tiffany appeared normal, almost to a fault. She issued requests that were neither more numerous nor more commandeering, and, indeed, they were more successful than those of her normal counterparts. Her social goals were directed at cooperation at a normal level and it appeared as if the only deviation concerned her seeking information more often than was the norm. For Tiffany then, the non-structured free-play environment appeared somewhat more socially difficult for her than the structured cooperative-construction session. By and large, however, this highly aggressive child who evidenced stereotypical social-cognitive deficiencies was not observed to deviate from the norm in many ways.

Finally, in Session 1, both Chuck and Carol were less rigid in issuing re-requests; Chuck was more likely to modify his failed requests and Carol was less likely than the norm to modify her original requests. Both children were more likely than the norm to give up following initial requestive failure. Only Carol was more likely to use commands. As with the other two children, their social goals were rarely directed toward cooperative joint action and were more likely to call attention to themselves (in the case of Chuck). In many ways, the behavioral profile for Chuck, an aggressive male, resembled that of Tiffany, a female, for Session 2. His behavior, in the cooperative structured situation appeared normal in almost all respects. Carol, on the other hand, remained less socially directive.

Discussion

The divergent patterns of behavior and cognitions shown by the four children suggest at least three major issues for further consideration. The first issue concerns the "meaning" of teacher and peer assessments of aggressiveness. The second issue focusses on expectations of consistency within and between cognitive and behavioral domains. The third issue concerns implications for treatment and intervention.

Each of the four children subjected to our case studies was selected as highly aggressive on the basis of the same criteria consisting of teacher ratings and peer nominations of aggression. Yet, an examination of the case study data revealed few overall similarities between the children. It is certainly the case that the identification procedures are valid to the extent that they have correlated with a variety of adjustment indices such as sociometric status, academic performance and behavior. Yet, little is known about the actual criteria peers and adults use to evaluate others or about the cognitive processes used to make these evaluations. Cairns and Green (1979), for example, have suggested that judges make ratings of individuals by averaging behaviors across different situations and instances, while adjusting for unusual circumstances (e.g., temporary stress, illness). This process of cognitively averaging may give ratings the quality of consistency and generality; however, it does not yield the type of specific causal or frequency information obtainable from direct observations. Cairns and Green thus argue that direct observations and judges' assessments do not produce the same types of information and, consequently, are not predictable from each other. Nevertheless, both sources of information are valuable and useful in their own ways.

We do suggest, however, that data derived from hypothetical–reflective interviews provide a distinct and valuable third source of information concerning children's aggressiveness. The non-overlapping nature of these information sources in the case studies highlights either a need to sample all three areas or a need to carefully consider those factors most germane to the construct of aggression. Should we be most concerned for children with high rates and/or intensities of observed aggression, about those who others perceive as aggressive, about those who misinterpret the intentions of others and who suggest hostile solutions to hypothetical dilemmas, or about those children who meet more than one of these criteria? Our current knowledge base of data and theory does not provide any clear answers to this question.

The second issue raised by the case studies concerns the degree of consistency expected not only within the cognitive and behavioral domains, but also between them. It appears that none of the theories of aggression outlined in the first pages of this chapter would lead researchers to expect strong consistencies in behaviors or cognitions across settings or between cognitions and behaviors.

From a learning theory perspective, inconsistency between cognition and behavior should be a common occurrence. In part, this predicted inconsistency emerges from the theoretical distinction between learning and performance. Nonaggressive strategies, for example, may be in the cognitive repertoire of an individual (that is, they may have been learned) but because of a lack of motivation they may not be exhibited in behavior (that is, not performed). This motivational deficit may emanate from not having experienced, directly or indirectly, positive reinforcement for using nonaggressive social strategies. In addition, situational specificity of reinforcement history and stimulus cues may provide good reason for predicting context-based inconsistencies within the behavioral domain. For example, in our case studies, Tiffany and Michael seem to illustrate this pattern of inconsistency within the behavioral domain; few behaviors showed similar patterns in the free play and block building sessions. Social-learning theory, however, provides little guidance in understanding consistencies or inconsistencies within the cognitive domain.

Social-cognitive approaches to the study of childhood aggression present a somewhat different set of expectations and, as such, do help explain inconsistencies in cognitions. Sequential and discrete processing steps form the basis of the information processing framework (e.g., Fig.

9.1). If this differentiated view of cognition is correct, children should *not* demonstrate uniform performance within the cognitive domain. For example, the perception that a negative outcome was caused purposefully as opposed to accidentally should lead to different strategic choices to deal with the social dilemmas.

The social-cognitive approach would also help explain variations in observed behavior; the cognitive selection of one strategy over another is presumed to predict the enactment of the selected strategy. Unfortunately, just as the means by which aggressive children are identified tend to average across different events, times, and places, so too do our inferences concerning children's social-cognitive capacities. Thus, it is generally assumed that children who, during interviews, misread cues of intentionality and suggest the employment of aggressive strategies to resolve social dilemmas are those who, when observed in the natural setting, will display more than the average amount of hostility and agonism. It is important to note, however, that the situations described in the hypothetical–reflective scenarios are rarely, if ever, similar to those situations in which the children are observed. Indeed, we know of no study in which social problem solving cognitions and behaviors are related as they are expressed in identical social settings. This methodological incompatibility may well explain why there were very few expected matches between cognition and behavior in our case studies. It does not explain, however, why in at least two of the cases, there was no match between social-cognition and the more general assessments of teacher-rated and peer-nominated behavior.

The third explanation for the development of aggression offered in the introduction involved dispositional or temperamental factors. At first glance, temperament explanations of behavior seem to suggest strong consistency within and between cognitive and behavioral domains. Recent research, however, has emphasized the context-dependent nature of temperamental effects. A relatively impulsive child, for example, might be less likely to show problems in a well specified, structured task than in an unstructured open-ended one (a pattern shown by Tiffany). In addition, the lack of a connection between cognition and behavior can be explained by the link between affective arousal and temperament. For example, it is known that dispositionally inhibited children are easily aroused in novel, mildly stressful social situations (Kagan, Reznick, & Snidman, 1987). These children may have a well developed, adaptive social-cognitive repertoire and yet, in the face of reality, may not be able to apply their knowledge in an effective manner. The temperament approach, like the social-learning approach, fails to address the possibility of inconsistencies within the cognitive domain.

In summary, our examination of the major theoretical explanations of aggression reveals gaps in the consideration of consistency. Each theory provides incomplete coverage of the relations within and between the cognitive and behavioral domains. As such, much work is required to address these issues of consistency both at a theoretical as well as an empirical level of analysis.

Finally, the third issue raised by the case study data concerns implications for intervention and treatment. In general, the data suggest markedly different interventions for each of the four children. For example, the hypothetical–reflective assessments indicated that both girls, Tiffany and Carol, might benefit from some form of social-cognitive intervention based on an information processing perspective. Yet, the behavioral profiles revealed substantial differences between the two girls. Tiffany was verbose and highly directive, whereas Carol was less directive. In actuality, Carol's behavior showed evidence of social passivity (few requests, much attention seeking, a high likelihood of giving up after an unsuccesful request). Indeed, from the larger corpus of longitudinal data from which these case-by-case analyses were derived, Carol deviates significantly from the norm (by at least one standard deviation) on measures of depression (higher than average), self-perceived social competence, attractiveness, and general self-worth (lower than average), and both height and weight (smaller and lighter than average). On the other hand, supplementary data concerning Tiffany reveal higher than average scores on self-perceived social competence, physical attractiveness, and general self-worth. Thus, both the behavioral and the supplementary data demonstrate clearly that these two girls with similar social-cognitive profiles and similar assessments of aggression, are extremely different from each other.

Given these data, it may be that the identification of Tiffany and Carol as aggressive was accurate but that the source of the assessments varied. It is conceivable, for example, that Carol was involved in aggressive interchanges at school because she was a target or victim of the hostile overtures of others. As such, she would fit Olweus' (1981; see also Olweus' chapter in this volume) portrait of a victimized child and her interpretations of ambiguously caused, negative social outcomes as motivated by hostility may, in fact, have been accurate. Tiffany, on the other hand, may have been the prototypical bully who successfully victimizes others and thinks better of herself for her successes. Her self-aggrandizing cognitions mirror earlier findings that hostile/aggressive children often report perceiving their own competencies in an inaccurate, perhaps overblown fashion (Rubin & Cohen, 1986). On the basis of these data, it would appear as if very different interventions would be required for these two aggressive girls who seem to have similar social-cognitive difficulties.

Turning to the boys, it might be appropriate to advocate a social-cognitive intervention for Chuck. Yet, as with Carol, our supplementary data reveal him to have extremely negative self perceptions of his social skills, his attractiveness, his general self-worth, and also his physical prowess. Chuck reported higher than average loneliness, and interestingly, he is extremely large physically relative to the norms for his age group (14 lb. heavier than the group average). Thus, like Carol, this seemingly quiet child may be a victim rather than an instigator of hostility.

Michael demonstrated normal hypothetical–reflective responses. Behaviorally, however, this child was highly assertive; he issued a request at the average rate of 5 per minute across Sessions 1 and 2! Furthermore, he continued to be socially assertive throughout the sessions despite his receiving a high proportion of noncompliant responses. Additional data revealed that Michael's self perceptions did not match his behavioral efficiency. He had extremely high regard for his own social competence, physical attractiveness, and general self-worth. Because Michael does not appear to recognize his own social failures or others' negative evaluations of and responses to him, he could best be characterized as cognitively egocentric. Thus, some form of social-cognitive intervention may be appropriate for this child. His treatment should probably include a strong component based on building accurate interpretation of social information and/or role-taking abilities.

In conclusion, we have attempted to demonstrate that meaningful relations between aggression, social cognition, and social behavior do not necessarily mean that all *individually targeted* aggressive children neatly fit the profiles derived from *correlational* data sets. Thus, as we indicated earlier, life is clearly complex; it is far more complex than researchers often make it out to be. Perhaps more importantly, life (and the causes and correlates of aggression) is too complex to allow practitioners to accept, "lock, stock, and barrel," any one set of pre-packaged intervention programs. The essential message we hope to convey in this chapter is a simple one. The future treatment of aggression must, of necessity, take on an interdisciplinary, multifaceted approach: one that involves the cognitions, motives, behaviors, and life circumstances of the focal child as well as of his or her significant social environment of peers, parents, and teachers.

ACKNOWLEDGMENTS

The material presented in this chapter was presented at The Earlscourt Symposium on Childhood Aggression, June 15–18, 1988, Toronto, Ontario. The studies described in this chapter were supported, in part, by a grant from Health and Welfare Canada to author Rubin, and by a grant from the Social Sciences and Humanities Research Council of Canada to author Rose-Krasnor. Study 1 described herein was presented earlier by Rose-Krasnor at The Annual Meeting of the Canadian Psychological Association, Winnipeg, June 1983. Preparation of this chapter was aided by a Killam Research Fellowship to author Rubin.

REFERENCES

Behar, L., & Stringfield, S. (1974). A behavior rating scale for the preschool child. *Developmental Psychology, 10,* 601–610.

Cairns, R. B. (1979). *Social development: The origins and plasticity of interchanges.* San Francisco: Freeman.

Cairns, R. B., & Green, J. A. (1979). How to assess personality and social patterns: Observations or ratings? In R. B. Cairns (Ed.), *The analysis of social interactions: Methods, issues, and illustrations.* (pp. 209–226). Hillsdale, NJ: Lawreance Erlbaum Associates.

Deluty, R. (1981). Alternative thinking ability of aggressive, assertive and submissive children. *Cognitive Therapy and Research, 5,* 309–312.

Dodge, K. A. (1980). Social cognition and children's aggressive behavior. *Child Development, 51,* 162–170.

Dodge, K. A. (1983). Behavioral antecedents of peer social status. *Child Development, 54,* 1386–1399.

Dodge, K. A. (1986). A social information processing model of social competence in children. In M. Perlmutter (Ed.), *Minnesota Symposium on Child Psychology.* (pp. 77–126). Hillsdale, NJ: Lawrence Erlbaum Associates.

Dodge, K. A., & Frame, C. L. (1982). Social cognitive biases and deficits in aggressive boys. *Child Development, 53,* 620–635.

Farrington, D. P. (1978). The family backgrounds of aggressive youths. In L. Hersov, M. Berger, & D. Shaffer (Eds.), *Aggression and antisocial behavior in childhood and adolescence.* Oxford: Plenum.

Gottman, J. M., Gonzo, J., & Rasmussen, B. (1975). Social interaction, social competence, and friendship in children. *Child Development, 46,* 709–718.

Harter, S. (1980). A model of intrinsic mastery motivation in children. In W. A. Collins (Ed.), *Minnesota Symposia on Child Psychology.* Hillsdale, NJ: Lawrence Erlbaum Associates.

Ladd, G. W., & Oden, S. L. (1979). The relationship between peer acceptance and children's ideas about helpfulness. *Child Development, 52,* 171–178.

Kagan, J., Reznick, J. S., & Snidman, N. (1987). The physiology and psychology of behavioral inhibition in children. *Child Development, 58,* 1459–1473.

Krasnor, L., & Rubin, K. H. (1981). The assessment of social problem solving skills in young children. In T. A. Merluzzi, C. R. Glass, & M. Genest (Eds.), *Cognitive assessment* (pp. 452–478). New York: Guilford Press.

Krasnor, L., & Rubin, K. H. (1983). Preschool social problem solving: Attempts and outcomes in naturalistic interaction. *Child Development, 54,* 1545–1558.

Masten, A. S., Morison, P., & Pellegrini, D. (1985). A revised class play method of peer assessment. *Developmental Psychology, 21,* 523–533.

Moller, L. C., & Rubin, K. H. (1988). A psychometric assessment of a two-factor solution for the Preschool Behavior Questionnaire in mid-childhood. *Journal of Applied Developmental Psychology, 9,* 167–180.

Moskowitz, D. S., Schwartzman, A. E., & Ledingham, J. E. (1985). Stability and change in aggression and withdrawal in middle childhood and early adolescence. *Journal of Abnormal Psychology, 94,* 30–41.

Olweus, D. (1979). Stability and aggressive reaction patterns in males: A review. *Psychological Bulletin, 86,* 852–875.

Olweus, D. (1981). Child-to-child violence: Bullying among school-boys. In N. Cantwell (Ed.), *Children and violence* (pp. 97–131). Stockholm: Akademilitteratur.

Parke, R. D., & Slaby, R. G. (1983). The development of aggression. In E. M. Hetherington (Ed.), *Handbook of child psychology, Vol. 4, Socialization, personality, and social development.* (pp. 557–641). New York: Wiley.

Parker, J. G., & Asher, S. R. (1987). Peer acceptance and later personal adjustment: Are low-accepted children "at risk"? *Psychological Bulletin, 102,* 357–389.

Patterson, G. (1979). A performance theory for coercive family interaction. In R. Cairns (Ed.), *The analysis of social interactions.* (pp. 119–161). Hillsdale, NJ: Lawrence Erlbaum Associates.

Patterson, G., Littman, R. A., & Bricker, W. (1967). Assertive behavior in children: A step toward a theory of aggression. *Monographs of the Society for Research in Child Development, 35* (No. 5).

Putallaz, M., & Gottman, J. M. (1981). An interactional model of children's entry into into peer groups. *Child Development, 52,* 286–294.

Renshaw, P., & Asher, S. R. (1983). Children's goals and strategies for social interaction. *Merrill-Palmer Quarterly, 29,* 353–374.

Rubin, K. H., & Borwick, D. (1984). Communicative skills and sociability. In H. E. Sypher & J. L. Applegate (Eds.), *Communication by children and adults: Social cognitive and strategic processes.* Beverly Hills, CA: Sage publications. (pp. 152–170).

Rubin, K. H., & Clark, M. L. (1983). Preschool teachers' ratings of behavioral problems: Observational, sociometric, and social-cognitive correlates. *Journal of Abnormal Child Psychology, 11,* 273–285.

Rubin, K. H., & Cohen, J. S. (1986). The Revised Class Play: Correlates of peer assessed social behavior in middle childhood. In R. J. Prinz (Eds.), *Advances in Behavioral Assessment of Children and Families, Vol. 2 (pp. 179–206).* Greenwich, CO: JAI Press.

Rubin, K. H., & Daniels-Beirness, T. (1983). Concurrent and predictive correlates of sociometric status in Kindergarten and Grade 1 children. *Merrill-Palmer Quarterly, 29,* 337–351.

Rubin, K. H., Daniels-Beirness, T., & Bream, L. (1984). Social isolation and social problem solving: A longitudinal study. *Journal of Consulting and Clinical Psychology, 52,* 17–25.

Rubin, K. H., & Krasnor, L. R. (1986). Social-cognitive and social behavioral perspectives on problem solving. In M. Perlmutter (Ed.), *Cognitive perspectives on children's social and behavioral development. The Minnesota Symposia on Child Psychology (Vol. 18)* (pp. 1–68). Hillsdale, NJ: Lawrence Erlbaum Associates.

Rubin, K. H., & Mills, R. S. L. (1988). The many faces of withdrawal in childhood. *Journal of Consulting and Clinical Psychology, 6,* 916–924.

Rubin, K. H., Moller, L., & Emptage, A. (1987). The Preschool Behavior Questionnaire: A useful index of behavior problems in elementary school-age children: *Canadian Journal of Behavioural Sciences, 19,* 86–100.

Selman, R. (1980). *The growth of interpersonal understanding.* New York: Academic Press.

Shaffer, D. (1987). *Social and personality development.* New York: Brooks-Cole.

Spivack, G., & Shure, M. (1974). *Social adjustment of young children.* San Francisco: Jossey-Bass.

Walters, J., & Peters, R. D. (June, 1980). *Social problem solving in aggressive boys.* Paper presented at the Annual Meeting of the Canadian Psychological Association, Calgary.

Weissberg, R. P., Gesten, E., Rapkin, B. D., Cowen, E., Davidson, E., Flores de Apodaca, R., & McKim, B. J. (1981). The evaluation of a social problem solving training program for suburban and inner-city third grade children. *Journal of Consulting and Clinical Psychology, 49,* 251–261.

10

Social Cognition and Social Networks: A Developmental Perspective

Robert B. Cairns
Beverley D. Cairns
University of North Carolina at Chapel Hill

Our aim in this chapter is to review the links between social cognition in aggressive children and the social networks in which they are embedded. Following some comments on the developmental perspective, we examine the solutions it provides to three nuclear questions on aggressive patterns, namely:

1. Are the perceptions of aggressive children and adolescents more distorted—or more accurate—than those of nonaggressive peers?
2. Do children behave aggressively because of their social affiliations; or, alternatively, are they aggressive because they have been alienated and rejected by the social system?
3. Extremely aggressive behaviors in childhood are associated with aggressive problems in adolescence and they are predictive of other serious problems in living (e.g., school dropout, suicidal behavior). Why do some highly aggressive children show configurations of both internalizing and externalizing problems in later development?

Each of these issues is important in its own right, and each has stimulated at least minor controversy. They are considered together in this chapter because a developmental analysis suggests that the answers are interrelated. We begin with a brief account of the developmental perspective and some implications for understanding aggressive behavior.

DEVELOPMENTAL LEVELS AND AGGRESSIVE PATTERNS

Levels of Analysis Unfolded

The developmental model has its foundation in the social-cognitive theory of J. M. Baldwin (1897/1902), and the developmental psychobiology of T. C. Schneirla (1966) and Z. Y. Kuo (1967), with modern systematic statements provided by Bronfenbrenner (1979), Cairns (1979), Gottlieb (1976), Magnusson (1988), and Sameroff (1983). Although the statements differ among themselves in important ways, they agree on two assumptions fundamental to the developmental perspective, namely: (a) social behavior patterns are determined by multiple factors, and they should not be divorced from the ontogenetic and social contexts in which they normally occur; and (b) the scientific understanding of social patterns requires a holistic, integrated view of the person over time. The developmental perspective thus holds that the factors that influence social behaviors are fused and coalesced in development: they do not "interact" or maintain their separate identities in the child or adolescent.

These assumptions have strong methodological implications, as Magnusson (1988) has cogently observed. Accordingly, the preferred developmental research design is longitudinal, and the preferred developmental measurement model is ecologically appropriate and multilevel. Multilevel measurement requires the simultaneous assessment of individual factors, interindividual interactions, social networks, internetwork relations, and cultural–ecological–economic conditions. An example of a multilevel measurement model is shown in Table 10.1. On the left side are the levels of behavioral organization. On the right side are ways in which each level may be "unfolded," or opened for further analysis. Unfolding is necessary in order to look precisely at the subsystems that operate within each level.

At first blush, the simultaneous consideration of the multiple levels of analysis may seem to hopelessly complicate the problem and render a careful scientific analysis of social behavior impossible, and that occurs even before the levels are "unfolded." We argue that just the opposite is the case. In our view, an explicit recognition of the complexity of the task and the simultaneous operation of different levels of influence must precede a thoughtful appraisal of simplifying assumptions. Accordingly, we first illustrate some issues raised by a multifactor, multilevel analysis for understanding aggressive behavior, then examine two developmental assumptions which could simplify the empirical task.

TABLE 10.1
Levels of Analysis and Levels Unfolded

Levels of Analysis	*Levels of Analysis Unfolded*
Individual	Neurobiological Morphological Temperament Behavioral organization Cognitive organization Social role
Interindividual	Intraindividual organization and constraint Interindividual similarities and accommodation
Network	Homophily: "Birds of a feather" Intracluster reciprocity Developmental dynamics within clusters Social status and rejection
Inter-Network	Linkages between familial and peer systems: conflicts and commonalities Changes in peer network affiliations over time
	Changes in familial network
Cultural-Ecological	Economic and societal constraints upon families and individuals Contributions to behavior (e.g., gender role, aggression) and status (e.g., drop-out, career)

Individual Dispositions. Some of the unclarity in analyses of aggressive behavior concerns the operation of subsystems within the individual. For instance, the operation of cognitive–social processes addresses two subsystems at the individual level; namely, the linkage between conceptual formulations about other persons and behaviors in relation to those persons (e.g., Dodge, 1986; Rubin, Bream, & Rose-Krasnor, this volume). But that is only part of the story at the individual level. For example, emotional factors are strongly implicated in aggressive behaviors. They stimulate affective outbursts of rage and anger, and they contribute to enduring temperamental differences of sullenness, dysphoria, and/or hostility. Further, morphological and biosocial factors can play a nontrivial role in stimulating and inhibiting aggressive behaviors. Pharmacological studies and experimental analyses have strongly implicated neurobiological and genetic factors in aggressive expression (Cairns, 1979, reviewed relevant information in humans and nonhuman mammals).

Each of these subsystems at the individual level must be considered in terms of its own organization, and in its relation to other subsystems. To this point, research on aggression has tended to be limited to one or two systems—such as cognition and behavior or neurochemistry and behavior—and their interrelations.

Interactions. The systems analysis of Patterson (1982) has focused on the powerful effects of dyadic interchanges in the family in the support and control of aggression in young children. Earlier, Patterson and his colleagues published an influential set of studies on dyadic interchanges among nursery school children (Patterson, Littman, & Bricker, 1967; see also Cairns & Scholz, 1973, and Hall & Cairns, 1984). Similarly, Raush (1965) investigated the aggressive interchanges of disturbed and normal children, and found high levels of reciprocity in that aggression begets aggression. Studies of adult interchanges, such as violent exchanges between police officers and offenders, indicate that interactions can indeed escalate in intensity and hostility (Toch, 1969). Parallel instances of dyadic influence have been identified in diverse domains, from drug usage in adolescents (Kandel, 1978) to playing with toys in kindergarten children (MacCombie, 1978).

An enduring problem has been to clarify how individual propensities and within-individual behavior organization become melded into a between-individual dyadic organization. There is a correlated issue of how different persons may be synchronized in ways that do not compromise their distinctive personalities and dispositions.

Social Networks. Individuals and dyads are coordinated in larger units which are subsumed by various terms (e.g., "families," "peer groups," "gangs"). In this regard, it has been recognized that such social units may transcend and organize the behaviors of individuals and dyads who are participants in the unit. The actions of the entire group may be mutually supportive and correlated (e.g., Cohen, 1955; Sherif & Sherif, 1953; Thrasher, 1928). Recent evidence indicates that organizing network effects occur in normal groups as well as highly deviant ones (e.g., delinquent gangs). Strong cluster effects have been identified in normal groups of preschool children (Strayer & Noel, 1986), in elementary school classrooms (Cairns, Cairns, Neckerman, Gest, & Gariépy, 1988), and in naturally occurring friendship groups in adolescence (Magnusson, 1988).

The commonalities in values and behaviors are characteristic of groups, not merely individuals. One of the primary dimensions that defines childhood peer groups involves similarities in acting out behaviors and aggressive expression. Aggressive children tend to hang around together, as do aggressive adolescents (Cairns, Cairns, Neckerman, Gest,

& Gariépy, 1988). A correlated matter has to do with the effects of not being in a social group, as indicated by exclusion, rejection, or ostracism (Coie, 1990). How these two effects—social support and social rejection—contribute to aggressive and violent behavior is a matter of significant theoretical and empirical interest.

Internetwork Relations. Interrelations among clusters and social networks provide another distinct unit of analysis. In adolescence, clusters of peers are formed outside the family unit that may rival or gain hegemony over the family system. Social clusters among peers are dynamic and susceptible to change from year-to-year, in that a given adolescent typically shifts in friendship patterns over time. Yet there are continuities of influence across social systems, from peer group-to-peer group and family system-to-peer group. On this count, coercive families may have children who, in turn, affiliate with coercive peer groups. This raises the critical question of how the effects of familial stresses of childhood on adult problem behaviors are mediated over time (e.g., Elder, Caspi, & Burton, 1988; Eron, this volume; McCord, 1979, 1986). Perhaps the constraints imposed by peer affiliations and their sequelae (e.g., in marital choices, in educational-economic status) provide critical links in development.

Other issues arise when there are apparent discrepancies in cluster influence, such as conflicts between the values of the peer groups and those of the family. Adolescents must resolve which of the two (or more) standards will dominate, and when they will dominate.

Cultural-Ecological-Economic Context. The fifth level of analysis addresses economic, subcultural and ecological influences. Shifts in the economy can have a major impact upon the individual's behavior directly and indirectly. In teenagers, for example, job availability may influence whether they drop out of school, how many hours they work while in school, and how much they get shackled with debts. Economic factors also help to determine whether or not both parents have to work, how much the family is disrupted by unemployment (or employment), and the quality of the parent–child relationship, including monitoring and discipline (Bolger, Caspi, Downey, & Moorehouse, 1988). Irritability in the father which is occasioned by unemployment, for example, may produce multiple consequences in the family (Elder et al., 1988). Contemporary adolescents may become involved so heavily in 20–40 hours of employment that school performance becomes less central in their lives than work.

More generally, it seems obvious that individuals and their groups are nested within the values and structure of the society. It seems equally obvious that these influences should not be ignored in a systematic analysis of behavior development. The larger issue is not whether social behavior is determined by multiple factors; it is whether the influences can be studied simultaneously without the research design becoming hopelessly complex.

Endless Levels? Attempts to coordinate this information—whether within levels or between levels—present a formidable challenge for the social sciences. If serious attention is given to the 'multidetermination' of social behavior patterns such as aggression, the interrelations among systems cannot be ignored. Yet most analyses of aggression have assumed that the best way to proceed has been to control, match, or otherwise eliminate the sources of variance that extend beyond one's limited research focus. Although this strategy permits investigators to get on with the business of research, it invites the error of lifting a variable and its effects out of context, thereby distorting its meaning and function. In the case of aggressive behaviors, the hazards are particularly great. Coercive and hurtful behaviors constitute problems of living, and hurtful acts cannot be divorced from the interpersonal and social relationships in which they are embedded. Aggressive behaviors occur in dynamic developmental contexts which determine their meanings, functions, and outcomes. But it is one thing to recognize that aggressive actions are determined by several factors acting together; it is yet another to translate the idea into productive research without getting buried under multiple levels of analysis.

Two Simplifying Assumptions

Making explicit certain assumptions about developmental integration and constraints may permit researchers to simplify the empirical task without compromising its complexity. One assumption concerns the dynamic equilibrium and synchrony that occurs across levels; the other concerns the nature of the constraints that occur as a consequence of development.

Dynamic Equilibrium and Synchrony. The first concept concerns the holistic principle of the developmental model. Critics of this feature of the developmental perspective have dismissed it as (a) a trivial truism (Buss & Plomin, 1984) or, more insidiously, (b) a vague proposition which is a "cop out" and inhibitive of precise empirical analysis because "everything influences everything else" (Hansen, 1968).[1] In an incisive commentary, Magnusson (1988, especially pp. 19–21) demonstrates how such criticism misses the point. A key implication of the assumption is that the levels of influence are coordinated and synchronized in order to promote adaptive functioning. The levels are neither independent nor, typically, are they in competition. Attention is focused on the ways in which the several levels act collaboratively in the support of organized, adaptive behaviors, regardless of whether there are hurtful or helpful consequences for other persons. Rather than inhibiting research, the holistic assumption, properly employed, should facilitate empirical study as well as heighten its accuracy and generalizability.

Developmental Constraints. The principle of developmental constraints is concerned with the processes by which development is directed and channeled. An enduring issue in the developmental sciences concerns the regulation of developmental change. Do outcomes at maturity arise (a) from inherent forces within (whether conceived as an entelechy or as RNA), or (b) from mechanical forces without (whether conceived as biochemical action or as social learning)? The developmental answer rejects both of the two alternatives as inadequate, because directions for development arise during the course of development (Bertalanffy, 1933/1962). Once a subsystem is consolidated, it provides constraints on the organism and the directions in which growth and change can occur in the rest of the system.

A couple of examples from different levels of analysis may illustrate how developmental constraints may help resolve some puzzling features of behavior analysis. Consider, for instance, how an individual's involvement in a social interaction provides inevitable constraints upon that person's behavior as long as she/he remains in the interaction. From microanalyses of behavioral interchanges, we know that the acts of the two persons, A and B, who are involved in the interchange tend to be highly intercorrelated ($r > .85$; Hall & Cairns, 1984). Hostile acts of person A are associated with hostile acts of person B, and under many conditions, there is a mutual escalation in intensity.

A minor dilemma arises because the actions of person A are themselves organized in internally dependent behavior chains. The auto-correlations in most behavior chains tend to exceed $r = .85$. The same applies for person B. How, then, can strong interpersonal organization

[1]From Hansen's (1968) review of Z-Y. Kuo's *The dynamics of behavior development.* A rebuttal was offered in Cairns (1968).

arise in the face of strong internal behavior organization? The answer suggested by the principle of developmental constraints is that the acts of person A constrain the counteractions of person B, and vice versa. But the dyadic constraints must operate within the limits imposed by the internal organization of the behavior of each person. Hence both internal organization and dyadic organization can be maintained, simultaneously, though within limits imposed from within and from without. The direction of the interaction—toward escalation or remediation—is jointly regulated by the nature of the feedback provided by each person and by the internal coherence of their own action patterns. Interactions cease when the conditions of mutual accommodation cannot be met.

Over longer time intervals, intersystem constraints occur in ontogeny. In this regard, genetic selection can rapidly produce selected strains of mice that are identical in appearance but which differ in aggressive behavior and in the key neurobiological systems which affect behavioral inhibition. When differences in inhibition are expressed in dyadic interactions, there is a rapid escalation in the likelihood of violent attacks in one strain, and peaceful, nonaggressive interactions in the other strain (Cairns, MacCombie, & Hood, 1983; Gariépy, Hood, & Cairns, 1988; Hood & Cairns, 1988). Constraints occur not only in development but in subsequent social interactions.

Other research has demonstrated how constraints occur between major levels of analysis in human social behavior. For example, very early maturation at puberty is associated with both changes in physical structure and in social roles for females (Magnusson, 1988). These changes, in turn, influence self-perceptions, behavioral deviance through affiliation with older males and females, and the settings for new social learning. There exists an interdependence among influences on behavior in development, and these influences are coordinated and typically correlated. Forces that arise during development limit the degrees of freedom in other aspects of the organism, and these limits act to align seemingly separate systems.

Order and synchrony arise despite multiple changes—or, more properly, because of multiple changes. It is in this regard that the introduction of developmental constraints may simplify empirical analyses of behavior, not add to their complexity. The mutual constraints that have been shown to operate over development in neurobiological and morphological systems seem likely to hold in dyadic and network systems as well. An individual's entry into a social system presupposes that she/he will adopt some of the distinguishing values, behaviors, and attitudes of all members of that system. The conditions for entry into relationships, networks, and institutions do not wholly predict the eventual outcome of such involvement.

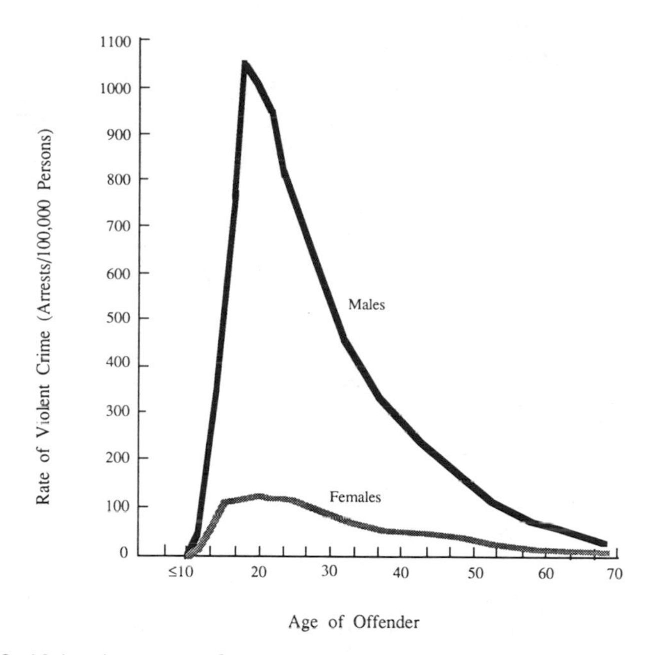

FIG. 10.1. Arrest rates for violent crime by males and females as a function of age, with rape excluded due to bias in statistical reporting. (Data from Crime in the United States [1982] and U.S. Census Report [1980]).

When the concept of developmental constraints is taken seriously, a shortcoming in Table 10.1 becomes apparent. An additional dimension, time, must be added to the table. Moreover, different growth trajectories may be described for the various processes and behavior systems. For instance, the developmental course of behaviors that involve arrests for violent crimes shows a sharp increase for males between 12–17 years of age (Fig. 10.1). This developmental trajectory differs from the developmental course of, say, cognitive growth or empathy.[2] When the arrest curves are compared with normative self-evaluations on aggression, a large discrepancy appears. Self-evaluations on aggressive behaviors—including the self-evaluations of highly aggressive subjects who have been arrested for violent crimes—show a slight decrease rather than a sharp increase in aggression (Fig. 10.2). When the same ages in the two graphs are compared, the curves are orthogonal. Furthermore, there are few reliable differences between males and females at any age in global self-descriptions of aggressive behavior, even though there are large sex differences in criminal violence.

[2]But it parallels the development of sexual dimorphism, as noted in Cairns (1986).

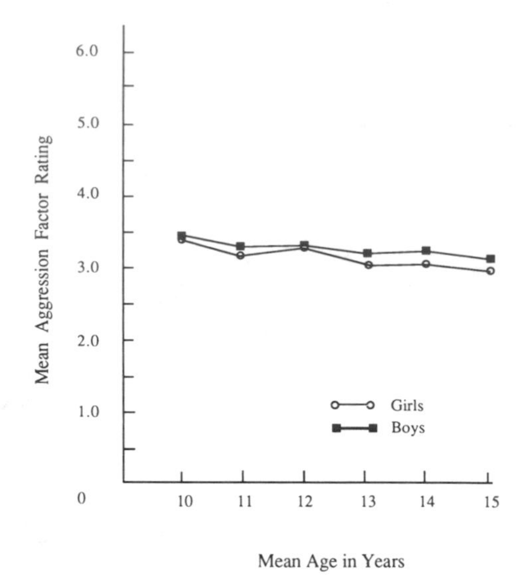

FIG. 10.2. Self reports of aggressive behavior as a function of age in a longitudinal sample of representative girls (N = 116) and boys (N = 104). (Data are from Cairns, et al. [1989].)

Which Level Gains Hegemony? Given the multiple forces that are simultaneously active, which are most influential and which determine the direction of development? Ordinarily, biological sources—including genetic and neurobiological factors—are pitted against social and cultural sources. For example "reductionism" refers to the assumption that neurobiological and genetic sources of influence ultimately will be shown to regulate the course of behavioral development. To achieve balance in the understanding of developmental processes, investigators must go beyond the simplistic assertion that the levels of analysis influence one another, or are bidirectional. For precision and clarity, it is necessary to identify which systems are likely to provide constraints upon which behavior patterns, and how the balance of influence might shift in the course of ontogeny. To obtain this information, attention should be given (a) to the constraints that operate during the course of development and (b) to the issues of behavioral measurement.

AGGRESSIVE BEHAVIORS AND SOCIAL PERCEPTIONS

Are the social and self-perceptions of aggressive children and adolescents more distorted—or more accurate—than those of nonaggressive children and adolescents?

To address this question, it is useful to inquire about the functions of self-perceptions for any person, young or old, aggressive or nonaggressive. The developmental model implies that social perceptions serve at least two masters (Cairns & Cairns, 1988a). One function is to achieve internal integration and dynamic equilibrium with respect to other functions of the organism. The second function is to achieve veridicality and social consensus. Self-cognitions do not always have to be veridical in order to be functional (Cairns & Cairns, 1981; 1988a; see also Epstein, 1973; Greenwald, 1980; Wallwork, 1982). Even if one is old and anxious and poor, there should be reason to get up in the morning (Mills-Byrd & Cairns, 1987). The essential idea is that one's view of oneself may serve different functions from those served by one's view of others.

In the course of living, there are indeed developmental changes in how these functions are fulfilled. The empirical evidence suggests, however, that there is not an across-the-board increase in self–other veridicality. To the contrary, as one's ability to communicate and discern discrepancies increases, so may one's ability to rationalize and create self deceptions. This could be an important buffer against depression and reality, and it may be each person's right to create his or her own world of plans, dreams, and reasons to live.

Among other things, the empirical findings raise questions about the utility of therapeutic strategies which are designed to help children and adolescents achieve self-concepts in line with "reality." If a child is really intelligent, good-looking, influential, respected, and gets along well with peers and adults, it may be all to the better to share in the social consensus in the design of the self-concept. But what if children fall beneath the normative standard on desirable characteristics—as do 50% of the population? To accept automatically consensus social judgments for self evaluations could be tantamount to judging oneself substandard. For those who are autistic or garrulous, shy or aggressive, schizoid or melancholy, or below the average of one's reference group on any dimension of competence, a "looking glass" self may be counteradaptive.

But there are constraints on how far one's self concept can differ from concepts that others hold of the self. There must be a basis for achieving synchrony between individuals as well as within individuals. This suggests that compromises must be forged between the internal self and the public self. On this count, those social concepts and beliefs that are most concrete, public, and salient should be least open to compromise or creative interpretation by the self (Kenrick & Stringfield, 1980). But the more abstract or private the concept, the greater the possibility for personal reconstruction. For example, children tend to have high levels of self–other consensus on some attributes, including their own gender, physical size, and other salient dispositions. There is less agreement on private or abstract qualities of the self, such as one's essential goodness, honesty, altruism, and friendliness.

Social Perceptions of Aggressive Behaviors: Normative Findings

One implication of the above discussion is that negative events are likely to be perceived with greater consistency and clarity than positive events, by virtue of a difference in salience and specificity. In this regard, Boucher and Osgood (1969) refer to the "Pollyanna Law." They found that positive words occur with greater frequency than negative words, regardless of the culture or language analyzed. Other investigators found that positive evaluations were used both more frequently and more ambiguously than punitive or negative evaluations in the classroom (Cairns & Paris, 1971; Paris & Cairns, 1972; see also Levine, Leitenberg, & Richter, 1964, and Buchwald, 1962). More generally, aggressive terms constitute a more vivid, salient, and recognizable class than positive, affiliative terms (Cairns & Lewis, 1962).

It is perhaps for this reason that investigations that compare the correspondence between self-ratings and the ratings of others on global dimensions have shown that aggressive behaviors tend to have higher self–other correspondence than, say, popularity, withdrawn, or affiliative behaviors (Cairns, Cairns, Neckerman, Ferguson, & Gariépy, 1989; Ledingham, Younger, Schwartzman, & Bergeron, 1982). Aggressive acts are more salient and easily classified, for both the self and the observer, than are other terms. But the linkages between the self and others show considerable slippage. Indeed, the agreement among sources outside the self—whether derived from peers, teachers, or direct observations—is consistently greater than agreement between the self and outside sources (Achenbach, McConaughy, & Howell 1987; Alicke, 1985; Cairns et al, 1989).[3]

It may also be expected that the more concrete the event, the more salient it should be and the greater the level of agreement between the self and others. When global ratings of aggression are broken down into component items, the more concrete and discrete items are the ones upon which there is greatest self–other agreement. For example, in a longitudinal study of 695 children and adolescents, we found that the more specific items showed consistently higher levels of self–other agreement than less specific ones (see also Alicke, 1985).

The specificity–generality dimension tells only part of the story. Even when specific and concrete incidents are reported by subjects, not all

[3]And it is not because the self-ratings on a global dimension of aggression are unreliable. To the contrary, the levels of consistency in year-to-year self ratings rival those obtained from year-to-year ratings from outside sources (teachers, peers; see Cairns et al., 1989).

features of their accounts show the same levels of self–other agreement. For example, children who are asked to describe recent conflicts that they have had with other children tend to show high levels of independent agreement on the identity of the other person, and the consequences that the conflict produced. There is virtually no agreement, however, on motivation and intentions. The question, "who started it," rarely yields self-incrimination (less than 10% of the subjects accept responsibility for initiating the conflicts that they report). Because cognitive attributions are usually easier to shift than behaviors, internal synchrony may be efficiently achieved by changing interpretations rather than by changing actions.

Self-Perceptions of Aggressive Children

Now we return to the original question raised on the perceptions of highly aggressive children and adolescents. Do they show lower levels of accuracy in perceptions of self and others than persons who are not at risk for aggressive behavior? At first blush, the data on this matter appear to be discrepant. For example, it has been shown that aggressive children are more likely to attribute hostile intent to others in ambiguous situations than are nonaggressive children (e.g., Dodge, 1986). Furthermore, aggressive children express more aggressive strategies than nonaggressive children when confronted with various problem solving situations. Such data have been interpreted in terms of social information processing deficiencies.

Other lines of research suggest that highly deviant and aggressive adolescents have, if anything, a more reliable view of deviant interactions than normal control adolescents (Bandura & Walters, 1959). Aggressive adolescents are less likely than nonaggressive adolescents to distort or otherwise deny the occurrence of hostile or violent acts (Bandura & Walters, 1959, pp. 302–308). Similarly, no reliable differences appear between highly aggressive and matched control subjects in the magnitude of self–other correlations on global ratings of aggression (Cairns & Cairns, 1988a).

How can these findings on the social perceptions of aggressive adolescents be reconciled? One answer is that the empirical findings are consistent; it is only the interpretations that differ. Consider, for instance, the finding of information processing deficiencies in aggressive subjects (Dodge, 1986). Examination of the scoring systems adopted in social skills inventories suggests that subjects who report aggressive behavior in concrete settings will be classified as deficient in social information processing. Hence endorsement of aggressive behavior as a solution for interpersonal conflict is taken as evidence that the individual (a) is deficient in cognitive skills and/or interpersonal strategies and (b) this deficiency accounts for his/her aggressive behavior. An alternative possibility is that the children were indeed habitually assertive and aggressive, and that they merely reported their likely behavior in that setting.

One other example may be instructive. Aggressive subjects tend, on the average, to rate themselves slightly lower than average when asked to evaluate themselves on such dimensions as academic performance, popularity, and social competence (Harter, 1983; Cairns & Cairns, 1988a). On the basis of such evidence, it has been concluded that highly aggressive children have lower levels of self-acceptance and self-esteem than their nonaggressive counterparts. While it cannot be gainsaid that highly aggressive children and adolescents evaluate themselves lower than matched controls on such measures, it is also the case that outside agents—including peers and teachers—evaluate them even lower. Whether the self-esteem of aggressive subjects is higher or lower depends upon which reference standard is used. If social competence is determined by the evaluations of other persons, highly aggressive subjects err in having too high an opinion of themselves. That is, if their absolute performance is the standard, they may be judged to have low self-esteem. But if the ratings of others are considered, the self-evaluations of aggressive subjects may actually be higher than the consensus evaluation.

Regardless of whether the self-esteem is high or low, it would be a mistake to overlook major sources of difference in the self-attributions of aggressive and nonaggressive children and adolescents.[4] The biggest differences may be in content of the self-concept rather than the process by which it is achieved. That is, the major effects between aggressive and nonaggressive children may lie in the values and standards that have been adopted in the course of living. For example, if a boy is most proud of his "toughness" and his ability to beat up other people, his future may not be very bright, regardless of the accuracy of his perception. Yet studies of extremely aggressive and violent adolescents have found such values to be quite important. An aggressive adolescent studied by Bandura and Walters (1959) illustrates the point:

> Interviewer: Are there things about yourself that you're proud of, and wouldn't want to change?

---

[4]We thank John Coie for his valuable comments in the Carolina Consortium on Human Development meeting on November 8, 1988. He noted that there was only modest evidence to support the proposition that aggressive children had broad-based deficiencies in social perception; their shortcomings seem to appear in specific settings, relationships, and types of encounters.

> Subject: Motorcycle riding.
> Interviewer: Is there anything else?
> Subject: Say, something like you're proud of? You probably won't understand, but "stomping." I'm proud of it because, I don't know, all the guys I hang around with do that. Do you know what "stomping" is?
> Interviewer: No, I don't.
> Subject: Fighting with two feet without using your hands, see. I'm not trying to be conceited or anything, but I know I can use my feet better than all the guys I hang around with, so I wouldn't want to change that. Like my Dad, he said, "If you know how to fight with your feet, it's in your hands, you got it made," or something like that. "You never need be afraid of anybody." (pp. 121–122)

Virtually identical responses were obtained in our more recent study of highly aggressive adolescents (Cairns & Cairns, 1988b). Such values can predispose adolescents to create confrontations in which they eventually become both antagonists and victims. Perhaps the problem with aggressive adolescents is not so much their deviant perceptions as it is their deviant beliefs and values. The beliefs and values are then employed in the organization of their views of relationships, and their instigation of behaviors. The self-esteem of aggressive adolescents may be the same as nonaggressive ones; the problems may lie in what behaviors are esteemed.

Social Perceptions in Aggressive Children

Immediately linked to the problem of self-perceptions are social perceptions, and the degree to which views of the actions and intentions of other persons are distorted by children and adolescents who have been identified as highly aggressive. As Dodge (1986) demonstrated, there is an attributional bias in some ambiguous settings where aggressive subjects tend to project aggressive intent. Whether this is a distortion of the present or an extension of past experiences in similar settings demands further investigation. Given the individual's own characteristics and prior experiences, he/she may be correct in anticipating hostility in return. The "error" in attribution may not be an error at all; it may simply reflect one's past experiences in similar settings. The perception and anticipatory action, as Dodge (1986) indicated, could be self-maintaining by providing further constraints on the actions and attributions of the other individual.

What are the possible limits of such biases in social perception? In this regard, the "errors" (which in fact are non-distorted reports) should be limited to special or borderline situations of provocation, or those which are at the threshold for aggressive expression. But in broader settings, there should be social consensus. For example, virtually all children within a social network should be able to describe most of its salient properties, including the affiliations and subclusters of persons within the network. This includes the reports of children who have been labeled as "aggressive."

In this regard, seventh-grade students may be asked to describe the social groups that existed within their classroom (i.e., "Do any people in your class hang around together?"). Virtually all adolescents have this information readily available for immediate recall. High levels of agreement are usually obtained on which persons are included in particular groups, and which persons are excluded altogether (Cairns, Perrin, & Cairns, 1985). Highly aggressive subjects provide essentially the same descriptions of the social network as matched control subjects. The individual's placement of himself/herself in the social structure seemed to be reasonably consistent with the judgment of others, except for an egocentric bias to name themselves and their own groups first. The ability of children and adolescents to construct social maps illustrates a remarkable skill for perceiving, remembering, accumulating, and organizing concrete social information. These social maps correspond, to a significant extent, to the frequency and types of interchanges that may be observed (Cairns et al., 1985; Cairns, Cairns, Neckerman, Gest, & Gariépy, 1988).

To sum up, there is only modest evidence in support of the proposition that highly aggressive children and adolescents have a more distorted view of themselves than do matched control subjects. Although their global self-evaluations suggest a somewhat lower-than-average standing on desirable social attributes, outside evaluations suggest that the self-evaluations may be more positive than the aggressive subjects deserve. Taken in total, the findings are consistent with a developmental model that emphasizes the dynamic, adaptive properties of self- and social cognitions. The same principles appear to hold for highly aggressive and nonaggressive children and adolescents. A major difference in the self-evaluations of aggressive and nonaggressive adolescents involves the value they place upon aggressive expression, and their acceptance of the behavior as appropriate. In contrast with nonaggressive adolescents, some highly aggressive adolescents express pride in their ability to fight and abuse others.

AGGRESSION: PEER REJECTION OR PEER SUPPORT?

Do adolescents behave aggressively because of their social affiliations; or, alternatively, are they aggressive because they have been alienated and rejected by the social system?

These two alternatives on adolescent aggression are found in both sociology and psychology. In the sociological literature, descriptions of aggressive adolescents as "alienated" (Hirschi, 1969) and "displaced persons" (Yablonsky, 1962) may be contrasted with accounts of aggressive adolescents as members of "gangs" (Cohen, 1955; Thrasher, 1928) and deviant social networks (Giordano, Cernkovich, & Pugh, 1986). Similarly, in developmental psychology, aggressive children have been described as (a) "rejected" or "controversial" (Coie, 1990; Coie & Dodge, 1983; Dodge, 1986), as well as (b) members of deviant peer networks (Cairns, Cairns, Neckerman, Gest, & Gariépy, 1988; Raush, 1965) or coercive family systems (Patterson, 1982). Which view is correct, or are they both correct?

Empirical research may be cited to support either view, depending on the level of analysis adopted. For example, highly aggressive children and adolescents are clearly not as popular with peers in general as are nonaggressive children (see the review of Coie, 1990). It is not difficult to see why they are not held up as models by school personnel. Extreme aggressiveness violates norms for appropriate behavior in school and the classroom, and it inevitably disrupts the organized activities of the school. Unprovoked aggression cannot be tolerated without threatening the basic authority of teachers and social organization in the classroom.

However, it has also been shown that there is both intragroup contagion and intergroup peer support for assertiveness and violence in childhood and adolescence (e.g., Sherif & Sherif, 1953). Recent studies also confirm that aggressive and delinquent adolescents tend to hang around with persons who are like themselves (Elliot, Huizinga, & Ageton, 1985; Giordano et al., 1986). Even in normal school settings, children and adolescents tend to affiliate with others who are similar to themselves with respect to aggression (Cairns, Cairns, Neckerman, Gest, & Gariépy, 1988), drug usage (Jessor & Jessor, 1977; Kandel, 1978), and other problem behaviors.

It may be the case that both descriptions are accurate, but they represent different levels of analysis (Table 10.1). Accordingly, proposals which focus on rejection and alienation refer to the *individual* level of analysis, and to enduring dispositions of the person. In contrast, proposals which focus on social support refer to a *network* level of analysis, and to the dynamics of social regulation and social control.

A step toward the integration of the two perspectives was recently offered by Cairns, Neckerman, and Cairns (1989). It presupposes that the dynamics of social networks are consistent with the principles that govern dyadic interactions. Dyadic interactions, in turn, are regulated by intraorganismic and developmental constraints. The key points of the proposal are as follows:

1. There is a strong bias toward social synchrony at all developmental stages, in that actions and attitudes of other persons are readily enmeshed with the behavioral organization of the child. A necessary byproduct of such reciprocal integration and mutual constraint is enhanced similarity between the action patterns of persons in the interaction. In late childhood and early adolescence, there is a sharp developmental increase in the ability of persons to reciprocate behaviors beyond the dyad, leading to the formation of strong peer clusters. These social clusters promote common values and behavioral similarities that can support—or compete with—those of other social units, including the family and the school.

2. The informal clusters of late childhood and adolescence are in a state of unstable equilibrium due to developmental changes in their members and to dynamic forces within clusters. Sub-alliances shift among members and continuously challenge the integrity of the social organization itself. With the developmental breakdown of old clusters and the formation of new ones through new alliances, a new cycle of differential selection is initiated. At every stage, individuals are changed by their associations, and they carry to the next set of relationships the behavioral residue of the recent past. These changes provide the basis for alliances and a fresh network of supporting relationships. There is a dynamic exchange between enduring behaviors of the self and social relations with others, providing fresh meaning to Baldwin's (1897/1902) assertion that personality is an "ever changing, never completed thing."

3. To promote intracluster synchrony, there are norms for initial acceptance into any social group in adolescence. Such "gate-keeping" criteria help to heighten the likelihood of initial similarity of cluster members with regard to key characteristics (i.e., "bi-selection"). The most salient selection criteria shift as a function of age and the goals and needs of the members. For example, in childhood, gender membership is of basic importance, and most childhood clusters are typically same-sex. What behaviors are valued (or devalued) reflects local standards as well as the age–gender status of the individual. In childhood and early adolescence, one of the more universal behavioral dimensions employed in selection is the occurrence of salient, acting out, aggressive behaviors. In late adolescence, the gender criterion may be relaxed, or reversed, as enduring heterosexual relationships are formed (Dunphy, 1963).

4. Within the clusters of adolescence, strong reciprocal forces operate on all members toward conformity with respect to salient attitudes and behaviors; hence there is "socialization" on various non-conventional behaviors (e.g., Jessor & Jessor, 1977; Kandel, 1978; Magnusson, 1988; Rodgers, Billy, & Udry, 1984). As a consequence, between person sim-

ilarities emerge which extend beyond the similarities required for initial group entry. Once in a group, new patterns of deviance may be adopted and old ones consolidated for the individual and the social cluster. In adolescence, typical forms of nonconventional behavior include substance use (alcohol, tobacco, drugs), sexual behaviors, violence, and criminal activities.

5. Peer social clusters serve not only the prosocial functions of providing for intimacy and helping to define the personal identity of the members, they serve to express individual aggression and control. The tools for aggressive expression include ostracism and character defamation, which are especially effective because they are "hidden" forms of attack and conceal the aggressor from possible counter-responses by the victims. Because the peer clusters of early adolescence are in a state of unstable equilibrium—due in part to shifting alliances and jealousies from within and without—safeguards must be established for the maintenance of synchronized, reciprocal intragroup relations. (from Cairns, Neckerman, & Cairns, 1989, pp. 282–284).

The preceding analysis suggests that many young people encounter problems because of their social affiliations, not because of their disaffiliation. The problem seems to be that they cannot escape from the synchrony of a deviant social system, and they become enmeshed in deviant acts. On this score, Giordano and colleagues (1986) pointed out that delinquency for girls nowadays is not a solitary phenomenon. Similarly, Ann Campbell (1980) argued that delinquent adolescents have plenty of status, but it's with the wrong people. This theme had earlier been expressed in studies of delinquent males (Thrasher, 1928) and the street gangs of Chicago (Cohen, 1955).

Adolescent subjects are able to identify social clusters with high levels of agreement. Recent analyses indicate:

1. Aggressive subjects are as likely to be members of social clusters as nonaggressive subjects.
2. There are few differences between highly aggressive and nonaggressive subjects in the ability to identify social clusters.
3. There are few differences between aggressive and nonaggressive subjects in the accuracy of self-placement in the social system.
4. There is a strong propensity toward bi-selection in aggressive behavior, in that highly aggressive subjects tend to affiliate with other aggressive subjects, and nonaggressive subjects tend to affiliate with nonaggressive subjects (Cairns, Cairns, Neckerman, Gest, & Gariépy, 1988).

Other data suggested that there was indeed some problem in veridicality of social perceptions, but that the problem was not limited to aggressive adolescents. In general, there seems to be a propensity toward self-enhancement in self descriptions, with the more abstract the concept, the greater the discrepancy from social consensus. In the case of social networks, the relationships are quite public and concrete.

The lower levels of general popularity and likability of aggressive adolescents may have obscured the social competencies that permitted these adolescents to survive in difficult conditions (Cairns, Cairns, Neckerman, Gest, & Gariépy, 1988). As noted by Campbell (1980), being popular with the group as a whole may not be the only goal for these adolescents. Hence failure to achieve broad-based popularity in the mainstream should not be taken as evidence of wholesale social rejection. Furthermore, aggressive behaviors and the lifestyles that they index appear to provide a highly salient basis for peer affiliations.

This does not mean that societal rejection and aggression are unrelated. On the contrary, aggressive adolescents may reject conventional society as much as the opposite. Coalitions of aggressive adolescents inevitably come into conflict with adults as well as peers, and adolescent gangs can devastate the authority of adults, whether in the school or the community. Few school administrators and teachers are unaware of this hazard. The implicit rejection of aggressive adolescents by school personnel can, over time, set the stage for their progressive removal from relationships with more conventional peers. Aggressive adolescents are more likely than nonaggressive controls to drop out of school, or to be forced out through suspension and expulsion (Cairns & Cairns, 1988b).

In addition, girls in early adolescence tend to employ indirect techniques of aggressive expression—including social exclusion, character defamation, and ostracism—as opposed to direct confrontational techniques (Cairns & Cairns, 1988a; Feshbach & Sones, 1971). Such manipulation of the opinions and attitudes of one's peers can be essential, and necessary for self-defense. Friendships are necessary for the establishment of individual identity (Youniss, 1986) and for individual protection (Strayer & Noel, 1986). Perhaps this is why the characteristics of "trust" and "honesty" figure importantly in the criteria for friendship in early adolescence (Bigelow, 1977).

To sum up, the evidence on social rejection and social support indicates that both may occur in the lives of highly aggressive children and adolescents. The phenomena are not mutually exclusive in development. Individual propensities qualify persons for entry into distinctive social groups whose members are similar with respect to key behavioral dimensions, including aggressive, acting out behaviors. By virtue of one's participation in a deviant group, both the individual and the group may become at high risk for (a) rejecting the conventional social structure, and (b) being rejected by that structure. Peer evaluations and those of conventional authorities can become intertwined in the school and the community.

THE GROWTH AND DIFFUSION OF AGGRESSION

Extremely aggressive behaviors in childhood are associated with aggressive problems in adolescence and they are predictive of other serious problems in living (e.g., school dropout, suicidal behavior). Why do some highly aggressive children show configurations of internalizing and externalizing problems in later development?

This issue has been less often a matter of debate than it is has been overlooked. Because of the tendency to segregate the study of behavior problems into separate categories, the overlap between aggressive behaviors and other problems in living has often been unrecognized.[5] The close linkage between suicidal behavior and aggression is a case in point. An analysis of all children and adolescents who committed suicide over a 4 year period in England and Wales indicated that about two-thirds of them had had serious problems with aggressive behavior expression (Shaffer, 1974). Furthermore, studies of a state-wide sample of extremely aggressive children and adolescents indicate that a high proportion of them have made serious attempts to commit suicide. Among highly aggressive adolescent girls (white females, 14–15 years of age), 39% have a suicidal history. A similar though less extreme incidence (24% to 29%) was observed among aggressive white males and black females 16–17 years of age. Only aggressive black males showed a significantly lower incidence of suicide attempts (5% to 6%). These rates may be compared with the 1% to 3% incidence of suicidal behavior in unselected samples of children and adolescents in the same age range (Cairns, Peterson, & Neckerman, 1988).

More generally, longitudinal studies indicate that problem behaviors tend to occur as configurations in the lives of adolescents, not as single variables (Jessor & Jessor, 1977; Robins, 1986). On this score, there are linkages between aggression and school failure and dropout (e.g., Hawkins, Doueck, & Lishner, 1988; Cairns & Cairns, 1988b), criminal arrests (e.g., Farrington, 1986, Magnusson, 1988), teenage parenthood (e.g., Cairns & Cairns, 1988b), low popularity among peers (e.g., Coie, 1990; Coie & Dodge, 1983), teenage accidents and death (Cairns & Cairns, 1988b), and, in some samples, delinquency and drug abuse (e.g., Hawkins, Jenson, Catalano, & Lishner, 1988). Robins (1986) observed

[5]But see Jessor and Jessor (1977) and Robins (1986) for notable exceptions.

that early aggression among females is associated with the later occurrence of both internalizing and externalizing disorders.

Explanations for the existence of such configurations fall into one of two different classes: attribution to within-individual factors, and attribution to external factors. Accounts in terms of within-individual factors imply that there are certain enduring and systemic dispositions (or deficiencies) which are reflected in multiple ways. An explanation of the aggression–suicide configuration as reflecting poor impulse control is a case in point (Cairns, Peterson, & Neckerman, 1988). According to this account, persons who act impulsively against others when enraged may, as well, act impulsively against themselves when depressed. As a corollary proposition, persons who take aggressive risks in interpersonal relationships may also take risks with their own physical well-being.

An alternative explanation of the same phenomenon would emphasize the social support and facilitation for deviant behavior. In this regard, persons who are welcomed into particular social groups for one reason—sharing common behavior patterns and interests (such as motorcycle riding or fighting, as in the subject cited previously)—will be likely to adopt other unconventional values that may become dominant in the group. These unconventional values may involve education (relating to school dropout), criminal behavior, drug usage, or specific life-threatening behaviors. That is, the contagion of unconventional behaviors in individual lives may be mediated by the social networks in which persons are embedded.

Within a holistic, developmental model, these two explanations are not mutually exclusive. The individual factors that qualify the person for involvement in aggressive, acting out groups may serve a dual function. Not only does the network have a strong influence on behavior, certain persons may be especially responsive to the influences. Even in the case of suicidal behavior—which is an individualistic act—the group could strongly influence the individual's beliefs and attitudes with respect to the behavior. Our own longitudinal study recently provided an illustration of how such effects can be produced. Four of the five teenage boys who were affiliated in a network of friendships committed suicide over a 2 year span. Since the deaths occurred at different times and there was no evidence of a group pact, the co-occurrence escaped media and community attention. Further information showed that they shared a joint involvement in hard drugs, and, presumably, they shared a diminished inhibition about suicidal risks.

Just as there are configurations of consequences, there are also configurations of determinants. We have already noted that individual effects and group effects are typically not in conflict; on the contrary, there is often codetermination of behavior. Systematic accounts of social groups extend this point to include the over-determination of group influences.

Discussions of "peer group" or "family" effects tend to describe these sources of social influence as being in conflict with each other. On this score, the concept of "youth culture" reflects the idea that children, adolescents, and adults live in different worlds. A different picture emerges from a consideration of developmental constraints. To the extent that peer group membership becomes constrained by family influences, the peer and family influences may be convergent rather than divergent. By the same process, peer group membership creates another form of social inertia. Membership in a peer group in one year helps constrain which peer group the adolescent will enter the next year.

In this regard, families may influence peer groups, indirectly and directly. The indirect influences come about, for example, by where the family chooses to live, which schools the children attend, and the socioeconomic class of the family (e.g., Hollingshead, 1949). Direct influences can occur through parental monitoring, parental intervention, and the encouragement of particular activities and particular relationships. Direct coercive techniques may be resorted to only when indirect ones fail, hence a conventional correlational analysis between parental monitoring and peer group membership may not be especially revealing. In that families may play both indirect and direct roles from year to year, the "invisible hand" of parental influence may extend through childhood, adolescence, and early adulthood.

Similarly, the range of peer groups for which adolescents may qualify is itself constrained. There are major limits on peer group membership by virtue of racial and socioeconomic factors (e.g., Hollingshead, 1949). Although group membership may shift radically from year to year, particular subgroups appear to be generated from a restricted pool of "qualified" candidates. Although year-to-year movement from one group within a pool to another is common, movement to a different pool is rare. The defining characteristics for membership in broader pools are both behavioral and demographic. By high school, the factors of SES and race play important initial defining roles. In addition, salient and distinguishing behavioral characteristics (e.g., cheerleading, attractiveness in females, major sports participation in males; violent, criminal behavior in either sex, studiousness and high academic aspirations) can provide the basis for both cluster formation as well as general pool identification.

By mid-adolescence, male and female groups may share membership in the same general pool even though there is only modest gender overlap in particular group membership (Neckerman, 1990). This point is of special interest in attempts to understand self- and social-imposed restrictions upon dating and romantic involvement. "Going steady" at this age is not an especially enduring state. Boyfriends and girlfriends are switched about from year to year, but the switches are not random. There is a "musical chair" quality to the shifting of partners within a restricted circle. The potential candidates for a new romantic involvement tend to come from the same basic network as prior relationships.

All this is to say that the networks of relationships in which individuals become embedded are themselves correlated over settings and over time. The correlation is mediated not merely by the individual's self selection, but also by the direct and indirect influences of the family, school personnel, prior associations, and the values and behaviors of the individuals themselves. Cross-generational transmission of values and behaviors is thus supported by the persons themselves and by the networks from which there are few avenues of escape.

The identification of these constraints, which take hold in mid-adolescence, brings another perspective to adolescent autonomy and emancipation. Although there is greater apparent freedom, it is just the opposite for most adolescents. It is a stage where correlated constraints imposed by social class, racial membership, peer values, and familial beliefs become manifest. Individual, network, and cultural constraints become consolidated in concrete ways as the person enters adulthood. The influences are embodied in the behaviors and values of their friends, their family, and their marriage partners. Moreover, there is an iron grip upon individual behavior through economic and educational opportunities, and restrictions. Nor are the constraints simply external. There is little evidence to indicate that adolescents want to "escape" the conditions to which they have grown accustomed, even if they had the opportunity. The influences operate upon the individual and they operate upon the social milieu in which the individual is integrated.

In sum, the configuration of difficulties in late adolescence associated with early aggressive behavior reflect the operation of both internal and external constraints. It would be a mistake to overlook either the individual factors or the social constraints. Not only are individuals selectively brought into social networks, the concrete outcomes in behaviors and values reflect the characteristics of other persons in the network. To the extent that networks are themselves correlated over time, the person becomes increasingly constrained in his or her behaviors and choices. On this count, the picture of adolescence as one where there is great freedom of choice and behavior is an illusion for most teenagers. If anything, it is a period when the limitations of choice become manifest.

CONCLUSION

We observed at the beginning of the chapter that the three questions were being considered together because a developmental perspective suggests that the solution to one may help solve the rest. To recapitulate, there is only slender evidence to indicate that highly aggressive children and adolescents have a more distorted view of themselves and their social world than nonaggressive counterparts. The same principles of social–cognitive organization appear to hold for highly aggressive children as for nonaggressive ones. But these two groups differ markedly in the values that they place upon aggressive acts, and upon their acceptability. Moreover, these values tend to be shared by the other persons with whom they associate, whether in the family or in peer groups. Personal dispositions qualify individuals for entry into social groups, and one of the qualifying criteria for children and adolescents appears to be similarity with respect to aggressive, acting out behaviors. Once a person enters a group, reciprocal processes lead to further commonalities in activities, including deviant ones. There is a transmission of values and, for some networks, a contagion of social problems. The entire group may become at risk. To the extent that social networks are themselves correlated with each other, persons become increasingly constrained in choices, values, and behaviors from childhood through adolescence.

Commonsense interpretations have seen adolescence as a period of emancipation, freedom, and individual choice. But for many key behaviors—including patterns of aggressive expression—the stage is one of decreasing autonomy and increasing constraint. By the time children become adolescents, many of their values and social actions are overdetermined by forces from within and from without. One implication for treatment is that strategies for modifying aggressive behaviors should be informed by the several levels of developmental constraints. Natural developmental transitions may then be used to guide therapeutic efforts, and perhaps enhance their effectiveness. Developmental constraints—in the child, in the family, in the community—are ordinarily viewed as obstacles to treatment. In our view, just the opposite should be the case. Once the constraints are identified and their functions understood, they may be employed in timing and initiating therapeutic changes, and in consolidating treatment advances.

ACKNOWLEDGEMENTS

The research reported in this paper was part of the CLS Project, co-directed by Robert B. Cairns and Beverly D. Cairns. It was supported by funds from the Spencer Foundation and (NIMH 45532). Holly J. Neckerman, Tamara R. Flinchum, Scott D. Gest, and Jean-Louis Gariépy have been our collaborators, and we are grateful for their invaluable contributions to this work.

REFERENCES

Achenbach, T. M., McConaughy, S. H., & Howell, C. T. (1987). Child/adolescent behavioral and emotional problems: Implications of cross-informant correlations for situational specificity. *Psychological Bulletin, 101,* 213–232.

Alicke, M. D. (1985). Global self-evaluation as determined by the desirability and controllability of trait adjectives. *Journal of Personality and Social Psychology, 49,* 1621–1630.

Baldwin, J. M. (1902). *Social and ethical interpretations in mental development: A study in social psychology.* (3rd ed.). New York: Macmillan. (Original work published 1897)

Bandura, A., & Walters, R. H. (1959). *Adolescent aggression.* New York: Ronald Press.

Bertalanffy, L. V. (1962). *Modern theories of development: An introduction to theoretical biology.* New York: Harper & Brothers. (Original work published 1933.)

Bigelow, B. J. (1977). Children's friendship expectations: A cognitive-developmental study. *Child Development, 48,* 246–253.

Bolger, N., Caspi, A., Downey, G., & Moorehouse, M. (1988). Development in context: Research perspectives. In N. Bolger, A. Caspi, G. Downey, & M. Moorehouse (Eds.), *Persons in context: Developmental processes* (pp. 1–24). New York: Cambridge University Press.

Boucher, J., & Osgood, C. E. (1969). The Pollyanna hypothesis. *Journal of Verbal Learning and Verbal Behavior, 8,* 1–8.

Bronfenbrenner, U. (1979). *The ecology of human development: Experiments by natural design.* Cambridge, MA: Harvard University Press.

Buchwald, A. M. (1962). Variations in the apparent effects of "Right" and "Wrong" on subsequent behavior. *Journal of Verbal Learning and Verbal Behavior, 1,* 71–78.

Buss, A. H., & Plomin, R. (1984). *Temperament: Early developing personality traits.* Hillsdale, NJ: Lawrence Erlbaum Associates.

Cairns, R. B. (1968). Behavior: A question of influence. *Science, 161,* 522–523.

Cairns, R. B. (1979). *Social development: The origins and plasticity of social interchanges.* San Francisco: Freeman.

Cairns, R. B., & Cairns, B. D. (1981). Self-reflections: An essay and commentary on "Social cognition and the acquisition of self." *Developmental Review, 1,* 171–180.

Cairns, R. B., & Cairns, B. D. (1988a). The sociogenesis of self concepts. In N. Bolger, A. Caspi, G. Downey, and M. Moorehouse (Eds.), *Persons in social context: Developmental processes* (pp. 181–202). New York: Cambridge University Press.

Cairns, R. B., & Cairns, B. D. (1988b). Lifelines: Childhood aggression and adolescent survival. Technical report of the Social Development Laboratory, University of North Carolina at Chapel Hill.

Cairns, R. B., Cairns, B. D., Neckerman, H. J., Ferguson, L. L., & Gariépy, J.-L. (1989). Growth and aggression: I. Childhood to Early Adolescence. *Developmental Psychology, 25,* 320–330.

Cairns, R. B., Cairns, B. D., Neckerman, H. J., Gest, S., & Gariépy, J-L. (1988). Peer networks and aggressive behavior: Social support or social rejection? *Developmental Psychology, 24,* 815–823.

Cairns, R. B., & Lewis, M. (1962). Dependency and the reinforcement value of a verbal stimulus. *Journal of Consulting Psychology, 26,* 1–8.

Cairns, R. B., MacCombie, D. J., & Hood, K. E. (1983). A developmental-genetic analysis of aggressive behavior in mice: I. Behavioral outcomes. *Journal of Comparative Psychology, 97,* 69–89.

Cairns, R. B., Neckerman, H. J., & Cairns, B. D. (1989). Social networks and the shadows of synchrony. In G. R. Adams, T. P. Gullota, & R. Montemayor (Eds.), *Advances in adolescent development* (pp. 275–305). Beverly Hills, CA: Sage.

Cairns, R. B., & Paris, S. G. (1971). Informational determinants of social reinforcement effectiveness among retarded children. *American Journal of Mental Deficiency, 76,* 362–369.

Cairns, R. B., Perrin, J. E., & Cairns, B. D. (1985). Social structure and social cognition in early adolescence: Affiliative patterns. *Journal of Early Adolescence, 5,* 339–355.

Cairns, R. B., Peterson, G., & Neckerman, H. J. (1988). Suicidal behavior in aggressive adolescents. *Journal of Clinical Child Psychology, 17,* 298–309.

Cairns, R. B., & Scholz, S. D. (1973). On fighting in mice: Dyadic escalation and what is learned. *Journal of Comparative and Physiological Psychology, 85,* 540–550.

Campbell, A. (1980). Friendship as a factor in male and female delinquency. In H. C. Foot, A. J. Chapman, & J. R. Smith (Eds.), *Friendship and social relations in children* (pp. 365–390). Chichester: John Wiley.

Cohen, A. K. (1955). *Delinquent boys: The culture of the gang.* Glencoe, IL: The Free Press.

Coie, J. D. (1990). Toward a theory of peer rejection. In S. R. Asher & J. D. Coie (Eds.), *Peer rejection in childhood* (pp. 365–400). New York: Cambridge University Press.

Coie, J. D., & Dodge, K. A. (1983). Continuities and changes in children's social status: A five-year longitudinal study. *Merrill-Palmer Quarterly, 29,* 261–282.

Dodge, K. A. (1986). Social information-processing variables in the development of aggression and altruism in children. In C. Zahn-Waxler, E. M. Cummings, & R. Iannotti (Eds.), *Altruism and aggression: Biological and social origins* (pp. 280–302). Cambridge (UK): Cambridge University Press.

Dunphy, D. C. (1963). The social structure of urban adolescent peer groups. *Sociometry, 26,* 230–246.

Elder, G. H., Jr., Caspi, A., & Burton, L. M. (1988). Adolescent transitions in developmental perspective: Sociological and historical insights. In M. Gunnar (Ed.), *Minnesota symposia on child psychology (Vol. 21)*. Hillsdale, NJ: Lawrence Erlbaum Associates.

Elliot, D. S., Huizinga, D., & Ageton, S. S. (1985). *Explaining delinquency and drug use*. Beverly Hills, CA: Sage.

Epstein, S. (1973). The self-concept revisited: Or a theory of a theory. *American Psychologist, 28,* 404–416.

Farrington, D. P. (1986). Stepping stones to adult criminal careers. In D. Olweus, J. Block, & M. Radke-Yarrow (Eds.), *Development of antisocial and prosocial behavior: Research, theories, and issues* (pp. 359–384). New York: Academic.

Feshbach, N. D., & Sones, G. (1971). Sex differences in adolescent reactions to newcomers. *Developmental Psychology, 4,* 381–386.

Gariépy, J-L., Hood, K. E., & Cairns, R. B. (1988). A developmental-genetic analysis of aggressive behavior in mice: III. Behavioral mediation by heightened reactivity or increased immobility? *Journal of Comparative Psychology, 102,* 392–399.

Giordano, P. C., Cernkovich, S. A., & Pugh, M. D. (1986). *American Journal of Sociology, 91,* 1170–1202.

Gottlieb, G. (1976). Conceptions of prenatal development. *Psychological Review, 83,* 899–912.

Greenwald, A. G. (1980). The totalitarian ego: Fabrication and revision of personal history. *American Psychologist, 35,* 603–618.

Hall, W. M., & Cairns, R. B. (1984). Aggressive behavior in children: An outcome of modeling or reciprocity? *Developmental Psychology, 20,* 739–745.

Hansen, E. W. (1968). Behavior as a continuous process [Review of Z-Y. Kuo, *The dynamics of behavior development: An epigenetic view*]. *Science, 160,* 58–59.

Harter, S. (1983). Developmental perspectives on the self-system. In P. H. Mussen & M. Hetherington (Eds.), *Handbook of child psychology, Vol. 4,* (4th ed.). New York: Wiley.

Hawkins, J. D., Doueck, H. J., & Lishner, D. M. (1988). Changing teaching practices in mainstream classrooms to improve bonding and behavior of low achievers. *American Educational Research Journal, 25,* 31–50.

Hawkins, J. D., Jenson, J. M., Catalano, R. F., & Lishner, D. M. (1988). Delinquency and drug abuse: Implications for social services. *Social Science Review,* 258–284.

Hirschi, T. (1969). Cause of delinquency. Berkeley, CA: University of California Press.

Hollingshead, A. B. (1949). *Elmtown's youth: The impact of social classes on adolescents.* New York: Wiley.

Hood, K. E., & Cairns, R. B. (1988). A developmental-genetic analysis of aggressive behavior in mice. II. Cross-sex inheritance. *Behavior Genetics, 18,* 605–619.

Jessor, R., & Jessor, S. L. (1977). *Problem behavior and psychosocial development: A longitudinal study of youth.* New York: Academic.

Kandel, D. B. (1978). Homophily, selection, and socialization in adolescent friendships. *American Journal of Sociology, 84,* 427–436.

Kenrick, D. T., & Stringfield, D. O. (1980). Personality traits and the eye of the beholder: Crossing some traditional philosophical boundaries in the search for consistency in all the people. *Psychological Review, 87,* 88–104.

Kuo, Z.-Y. (1967). *The dynamics of behavioral development: An epigenetic view.* New York: Random House.

Ledingham, J. E., Younger, A., Schwartzman, A., & Bergeron, G. (1982). Agreement among teacher, peer, and self-ratings of children's aggression, withdrawal, and likeability. *Journal of Abnormal Child Psychology, 10,* 363–372.

Levine, M., Leitenberg, H., & Richter, M. (1964). The blank trials law: The equivalence of positive reinforcement and nonreinforcement. *Psychological Review, 71,* 94–103.

MacCombie, D. J. (1978). *The development of synchrony in children's interchanges.* Unpublished doctoral dissertation, University of North Carolina at Chapel Hill.

Magnusson, D. (1988). *Individual development from an interactional perspective.* Hillsdale, NJ: Lawrence Erlbaum Associates.

McCord, J. (1979). Some child-rearing antecedents of criminal behavior in adult men. *Journal of Personality and Social Psychology, 37,* 1477–1486.

McCord, J. (1986). Instigation and insulation: How families affect antisocial aggression. In D. Olweus, J. Block, & M. Radke-Yarrow (Eds.), *Development of antisocial and prosocial behavior: Research, theories, and issues* (pp. 343–358). New York: Academic.

Mills-Byrd, L., & Cairns, R. B. (1987). Life satisfaction in elderly, poor, widowed, Black women. Unpublished manuscript.

Paris, S. G., & Cairns, R. B. (1972). An experimental and ethological investigation of social reinforcement in retarded children. *Child Development, 43,* 717–729.

Patterson, G. R. (1982). *Coercive family systems.* Eugene, OR: Castalia.

Patterson, G. R., Littman, R. A., & Bricker, W. (1967). Assertive behavior in children: A step toward a theory of aggression. *Monographs of the Society for Research in Child Development, 32,* (Serial No. 113).

Raush, H. L. (1965). Interaction sequences. *Journal of Personality and Social Psychology, 2,* 487–499.

Robins, L. N. (1986). The consequences of conduct disorder in girls. In D. Olweus, J. Block, & M. Radke-Yarrow (Eds.), *Development of antisocial and prosocial behavior: Research, theories, and issues* (pp. 385–414). New York: Academic.

Rodgers, J. L., Billy, J. O. G., & Udry, J. R. (1984). A model of friendship similarity in mildly deviant behaviors. *Journal of Applied Social Psychology, 14,* 413–425.

Sameroff, A. J. (1983). Developmental systems: Contexts and evolution. In P. H. Mussen (Gen. Ed.) & W. Kessen (Vol. Ed.), *Handbook of child psychology, Vol. 1, History, Theory, and Methods* (pp. 237–294). New York: Wiley.

Schneirla, T. C. (1966). Behavioral development and comparative psychology. *Quarterly Review of Biology, 41,* 283–302.

Shaffer, D. (1974). Suicide in childhood and early adolescence. *Journal of Child Psychology and Psychiatry, 15,* 275–291.

Sherif, M., & Sherif, C. W. (1953). *Groups in harmony and tension.* New York: Harper.

Strayer, F. F., & Noel, J. M. (1986). The prosocial and antisocial functions of preschool aggression: An ethological study of triadic conflict among young children. In C. Zahn-Waxler, E. M. Cummings, & R. Iannotti (Eds.), *Altruism and aggression: Biological and social origins* (pp. 107–131). Cambridge: Cambridge University Press.

Thrasher, F. M. (1928). *The gang.* Chicago, IL: University of Chicago Press.

Toch, H. (1969). *Violent men.* Chicago: Aldine.

Wallwork, E. (1982). Religious development. In J. M. Broughton & D. J. Freeman-Moir (Eds.), *The cognitive developmental psychology of James Mark Baldwin: Current theory and research in genetic epistemology* (pp. 335–388). Norwood, NJ: Ablex.

Yablonsky, L. (1962). *The violent gang.* New York, NY: Irvington Publishers.

Youniss, J. (1986). Development in reciprocity through friendship. In C. Zahn-Waxler, E. M. Cummings, & R. Iannotti (Eds.), *Altruism and aggression: Biological and social origins* (pp. 88–106). Cambridge (UK): Cambridge University Press.

Commentary

Social Cognition and Aggression

Jane E. Ledingham
University of Ottawa

The preceding three chapters reflect well the current diversity in the research on social cognition's relevance to aggression. I would like first to address a few points specific to each individual chapter and then attempt to cut across these three very different presentations by raising two issues that I think are important for all three.

Hostile Attributions

Dodge demonstrated that it is important to distinguish between proactive and reactive aggression, and that when children are separated into groups according to whether their aggression is primarily instrumental or affective, differences emerge in their propensity to evaluate the intended hostility of acts directed towards them. Specifically, those children characterized more by reactive aggression are said to overattribute hostile intentions to the actions of others. However, hostile attributions are implicated in other forms of psychopathology such as paranoid thought. What differences, if any, might exist between the hostile attributions of the reactively aggressive child and those of the paranoid schizophrenic? Is the reactive aggressive child at risk for paranoid states in adulthood? Researchers have also recently reinterpreted the literature on the Type A behavior pattern and have suggested that it is actually hostility and anger that are the components of Type A, which are most predictive of later coronary disease (Dembroski, MacDougall, Williams, Haney, & Blumenthal, 1985; Williams, Haney, Lee, Kong, Blumenthal,

& Whalen, 1980). What is different about the hostility implicated in the models developed to explain reactive aggression and risk for coronary disease? Is the reactively aggressive child at risk for later heart disease? Are there important differences between the hostile attributions of deviant individuals and those of normal individuals? The issue here is whether hostile attributions are a characteristic of many types of maladaptive behaviors, but not necessarily causally related to one specific type of psychopathology, or whether they are a necessary condition only for a specific type of aggressive behavior. Barefoot, Dahlstrom, & Williams (1983) reported that high hostility scores predicted death from all causes as well as they predicted death from coronary heart disease, and it may be the case that hostility is equally predictive of generally poorer psychological adjustment as well.

Maladaptive Social Cognition Without Related Behavioral Strategies

Rubin and his colleagues have carefully documented the evidence that aggressive children as a group differ from other children in their social goals, their social strategies, and their social success in meeting goals both in hypothetical–reflective assessments and in their naturalistically observed behaviors. They have also pointed out very elegantly, in a significant test of the social-cognitive model's applicability to the individual case, that highly aggressive children show little similarity in the way in which their hypothetical–reflective social-cognitive characteristics map onto actual observed behaviors. What shall we make of the children judged by their peers and teachers to be highly aggressive who had many social-cognitive characteristics hypothesized to be associated with aggression but who did not demonstrate these social-cognitive patterns behaviorally? The two children who fit this pattern were both girls, and this may not be accidental. The prohibitions against aggression for girls are probably strong enough to enforce behavioral compliance even in the presence of strong cognitive characteristics that pull for aggressive behavior. It seems likely that girls are identified as aggressive on far subtler (perhaps primarily verbal) indications of aggression. It may also be the case, should these girls choose (as Cairns described) a peer group in adolescence that actively encourages or allows aggression, that more significant acting-out behaviors and aggressive strategies may emerge. That is, girls with social–cognitive deficits but no related behavioral patterns may be more likely than similar boys to later have high rates of aggressive behavior as reinforcement patterns of the peer group change.

Nonveridical Self-Perceptions

The Cairns' chapter reminded us that there is a very important distinction to be made in the class of events that we refer to as social cognition, in that our views of ourselves as we relate to and compare ourselves to others differ markedly from and serve a different function than our judgments about other individuals. Self-cognitions, they suggest, work better if they present a rosier view than is actually the case. These authors further argue that there is a developmental increase in our tendency to present ourself to ourself as better than we actually are. Yet is it truly adaptive to lie to ourselves about our abilities and characteristics if we in fact have failings or suffer in social comparison on these attributes? Is it necessary to deceive ourselves that we are excellent in all respects? Since everyone is below average in some way, I would argue that the answer is not self-deception but determining some way of decreasing the weight or the importance given to certain attributes. We may convince ourselves that it is more important to be attractive than intelligent, or vice versa, so that we can discount the importance of a characteristic on which we fail to compare favorably with others. How the salience of different features is established for each individual probably has something to do with the emotional loadings established over a large number of learning experiences.

The Role of Affect in Social Cognition

What is the role of affect in a social–cognitive model of aggression? I think it is noteworthy that Dodge introduced a primarily affective state such as hostility into his analysis of aggression and acknowledged the role of early negative emotion as a historical determinant of later hypervigilance, fear, and rage. However, Dodge's model at the level of the proximal cause explains the hostility and aggressive rage as if they were solely a product of the cognitive appraisal process rather than as representatives of an independent process or one that preceded and influenced the cognitive operations. That is, Dodge's model implies that biased attributional processes give rise to maladaptive affective states. This creates some paradoxical findings. It is puzzling, for example, that the individuals said to be least planful, thoughtful, and cognitively-driven (the reactive aggressives) are also the ones described as having the greatest cognitive influence on their aggression. It is possible to argue that Dodge's results reflect not so much a difference in social-cognition between proactively aggressive boys and reactively aggressive boys, but the primary effect of greater emotional arousal on reactively aggressive boys, with only secondary or resultant differences on social-cognitive variables.

Although emotion as a construct had suffered a period of relative neglect by developmental psychologists prior to 1980 (Campos & Barrett, 1984), there has been a resurgence of interest in its importance in recent years (Bearison & Zimiles, 1986; Cicchetti & Hesse, 1982; Izard, Kagan, & Zajonc, 1984). Researchers have challenged the notion that emotion is a simple epiphenomenon of thought, and have pointed out the unique role that emotion plays as an organizer of cognitive processes. Bower (1981) has described, for example, how affective states have a profound impact on memory encoding and recall operations. Other writers have noted the contribution of emotional expression by the actor to the interpretations made of the meaning of social acts (Sroufe, Schork, Motti, Lawroski, & LaFreniere, 1984). Although most of this work has concentrated on infants or preschoolers, the evidence is compelling that affect is inextricably linked to cognition in the determination of social behavior (Lewis, Sullivan, & Michalson, 1984).

Santostefano and Rieder (1984) demonstrated that the affective tone of stimuli influences the cognitive processing of aggressive and nonaggressive children differently. The children were presented with a series of 60 copies of a drawing of either fighting cowboys or a house. Elements of the drawing were gradually eliminated, and the children were asked to indicate when they had noticed that changes had taken place. Whereas aggressive children noticed equal numbers of actual changes made to both types of stimuli, nonaggressive children noticed fewer actual changes made to the violent stimuli than the aggressive children but the same number of actual changes to the neutral stimuli. Aggressive children also reported fewer imagined changes to the violent stimuli and more imagined changes to the neutral stimuli than did the nonaggressive children. These results suggest that the emotional context of the task determined the depth of processing that was carried out, and influenced it in a different fashion for aggressive and nonaggressive children.

The discussion by Rubin and colleagues makes few references to the impact of emotion, but their data also seem consistent with a primary affective explanation, since differences on dimensions such as self-esteem, described as possibly contributing to the differentiation among the four most aggressive children, probably have significant affective aspects. Finally, in the Cairns' results, it is possible that affective responses to peer rejection may have provided the push for cognitive reappraisals that led older aggressive children to change their primary reference group. Affective factors may also be responsible for making social cognitions about the self different from those about others, because of the child's greater emotional investment in the former. In general, a cognitive–affective model may prove to be a more useful model than a strictly cognitive model to explain aggression. However, to date few investigators have chosen to include measures of type, lability, and intensity of emotional response or to investigate the consequences of this for social cognition.

Developmental Change in Social Cognition

What are the changes that occur over time in social cognition? The results of Dodge and Rubin and colleagues conflict with those presented by Cairns and Cairns in that the first two present a much more pessimistic picture of the social abilities of aggressive children. Can some of these differences be accounted for by the changes that occur between childhood and adolescence? Several investigators (Shantz, 1983; Younger & Boyko, 1987; Younger, Schwartzman, & Ledingham, 1985, 1986) have carried out a number of studies that demonstrate how children's conceptions of social behavior change with age. Children's understanding of social situations and social behavior seems to become increasingly complex and differentiated over time, and these changing conceptions may be the basis for the changes Dodge reported on the decreasing tolerance among peers for instrumental aggression. Vygotsky (1962) theorized that children's thought acquires control over their actions slowly over time, and this may help to account for why Rubin and colleagues find only a tenuous connection between social cognition and its behavioral manifestations.

Changes that occur in the typical social interactions that children have at different ages should also be associated with changes in social cognition. Berndt (1988) reviewed the literature on how intimate friendships grow in importance and change in their nature as children grow older. Along with this, the child has greater independence from parental monitoring of and involvement in social activities. One might expect to find accompanying these changes greater differentiation in expectations for the behavior of friends as opposed to other social partners such as school acquaintances and family members. The release of the young adult from the compulsory associations of the school system may, however, subsequently lead to a reduction in the differentiation of social cognitions to the extent that the individual establishes his or her own niche in a more limited social environment; that is, the more homogeneous one's chosen social network becomes, the less realistic may be one's expectations for occasional social contacts that differ from the norm.

ACKNOWLEDGMENTS

I would like to thank Alastair Younger for reading an earlier draft of this manuscript.

REFERENCES

Barefoot, J. C., Dahlstrom, W. G., & Williams, R. B. (1983). Hostility, CHD incidence, and total mortality: A 25-year follow-up study of 255 physicians. *Psychosomatic Medicine, 45,* 59–63.

Bearison, D. J., & Zimiles, H. (Eds.). (1986). *Thought and emotion: Developmental perspectives.* Hillsdale, NJ: Lawrence Erlbaum Associates.

Berndt, T. J. (1988). The nature and significance of children's friendships. In R. Vasta (Ed.), *Annals of child development,* Vol. 5 (pp. 155–186). Greenwich, CT: JAI Press.

Bower, G. H. (1981). Mood and memory. *American Psychologist, 36,* 129–140.

Cicchetti, D., & Hesse, P. (Eds.). (1982). *New directions for child development: Emotional development, No. 16.* San Francisco: Jossey-Bass.

Campos, J. J., & Barrett, K. C. (1984). Toward a new understanding of emotions and their development. In C. E. Izard, J. Kagan, & R. B. Zajonc (Eds.), *Emotions, cognition, and behavior* (pp. 229–263). New York: Cambridge University Press.

Dembroski, T. M., MacDougall, J. M., Williams, R. B., Haney, T. L., & Blumenthal, J. A. (1985). Components of Type A, hostility, and anger-in: Relationship to angiographic findings. *Psychosomatic Medicine, 47,* 219–233.

Lewis, M., Sullivan, M. W., & Michalson, L. (1984). The cognitive-emotional fugue. In C. E. Izard, J. Kagan, & R. B. Zajonc (Eds.), *Emotions, cognition, and behavior* (pp. 264–288). New York: Cambridge University Press.

Izard, C. E., Kagan, J., & Zajonc, R. B. (Eds.). (1984). *Emotions, cognition, and behavior.* New York: Cambridge University Press.

Santostefano, S., & Rieder, C. (1984). Cognitive controls and aggression in children: The concept of cognitive-affective balance. *Journal of Consulting and Clinical Psychology, 52,* 46–56.

Shantz, C. (1983). Social cognition. In J. H. Flavell & E. M. Markman (Eds.), *Handbook of child psychology: Vol. 3, Cognitive Development* (4th ed., pp. 495–555). New York: Wiley.

Sroufe, L. A., Schork, E., Motti, F., Lawroski, N., & LaFreniere, P. (1984). The role of affect in social competence. In C. E. Izard, J. Kagan, & R. B. Zajonc (Eds.), *Emotions, cognition and behavior* (pp. 289–319). New York: Cambridge University Press.

Williams, R. B., Haney, T. L., Lee, K. L., Kong, Y., Blumenthal, J. A., & Whalen, R. E. (1980). Type A behavior, hostility, and coronary atherosclerosis. *Psychosomatic Medicine, 42,* 539–549.

Younger, A. J., Schwartzman, A. E., & Ledingham, J. E. (1985). Age-related changes in children's perceptions of aggression and withdrawal in their peers. *Developmental Psychology, 21,* 70–75.

Younger, A. J., Schwartzman, A. E., & Ledingham, J. E. (1986). Age-related changes in children's perceptions of social deviance: Changes in behavior or in perspective? *Developmental Psychology, 22,* 531–542.

Younger, A. J., & Boyko, K. A. (1987). Aggression and withdrawal as social schemas underlying children's peer perceptions. *Child Development, 58,* 1094–1100.

Vygotsky, L. S. (1962). *Thought and language.* Cambridge, MA: Massachusetts Institute of Technology.

II

TREATMENT OF CHILDHOOD AGGRESSION

Section 5: Familial Interventions

11

The Clinical Science Vortex: A Developing Theory of Antisocial Behavior

Marion S. Forgatch
Oregon Social Learning Center, Eugene, Oregon

> All growth of knowledge consists in the improvement of existing knowledge which is changed in the hope of approaching nearer to the truth. (Popper, 1972, p. 71).

It is well accepted that scientific progress occurs in small increments as theories are subjected to increasingly rigorous trials. This chapter introduces the vortex as a metaphor to portray that process. As illustrated in Fig. 11.1, the vortex repeats three basic steps as a given theory evolves: generating *hypotheses*, developing *measurement* strategies for the model's components, and conducting *trials* of the hypotheses. Designing and completing trials of competing hypotheses enables the scientist to retain those that survive for more stringent tests and to reject those that fail (Popper, 1972).

The first cycles in the vortex are necessarily rough and exploratory. Hypotheses are broadly defined, measurement strategies are crude, and trials are usually only weak tests of the theory. Rounds within the vortex reflect refinement in each step. Surviving hypotheses are better specified, erroneous hypotheses are eliminated, and alternative hypotheses are posited. Measurement strategies become more accurate and generalizable. Trials of the hypotheses become more crucial tests of the theory. With each iteration, a theory is placed at risk to be disproved. Although confirmatory findings can increase confidence, no theory can be proven true, because knowledge is always incomplete and new information may support competing theories (Popper, 1972). A theory can attain preferred status, however, after it survives repeated efforts to disprove it.

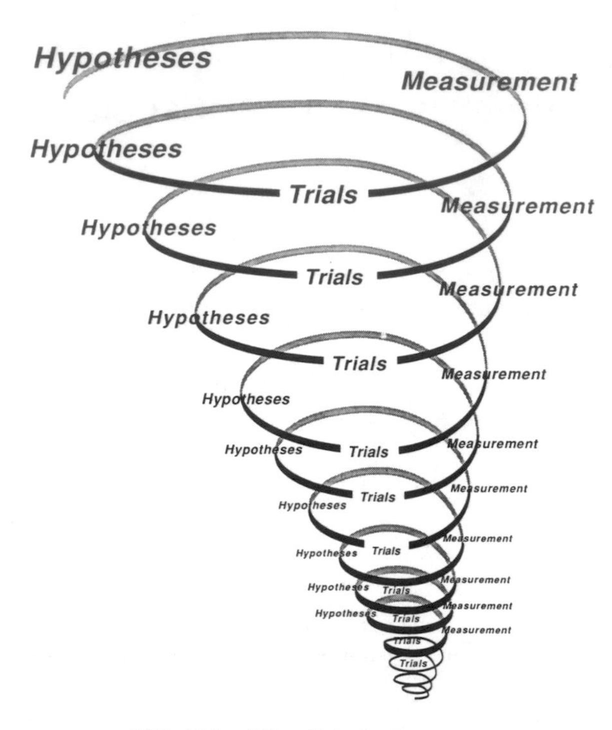

FIG. 11.1. The clinical science vortex.

This chapter illustrates the role of clinical intervention in the scientific process.

Scientific enterprise and clinical application are too often disparate activities, perhaps because each of them is a distinct and complex discipline. In the short run, combining the two may be less efficient than specializing in one; it is certainly time consuming. Yet the effort is worthwhile when the combination expedites the advancement of knowledge. The clinical perspective seems an ideal source of hypotheses to be tested. (The coercive model presented in this report was built as a test of various clinical hypotheses about aggressive children.) In turn, findings from the scientific activities can enrich and refine the therapy. A number of centers that have integrated science and clinical practice are represented in this volume. This chapter presents a brief history of the early cycles in the clinical science vortex at the Oregon Social Learning Center (OSLC) and some of the latest findings in trials of our theory of antisocial behavior in children.

Within the coercion model, one of the ideas is that parental monitoring and discipline practices control antisocial behavior in boys. As a correlational test, new data are presented from three independent samples employing structural equation modeling (Joreskog & Sorbom, 1983) to determine the fit of the idea to the data sets. The correlational model is then subjected to an experimental test in which a parent training procedure is employed as an experimental manipulation.

GENERATING HYPOTHESES

Treatment Informs Hypotheses

Attempts to intervene on a clinical problem with a given population provide a source of hypotheses about its etiology. OSLC studies have focused on the treatment of aggressive and antisocial children of primarily working-class families. Had the treatment problem and population been anorexia in girls of middle-class families, the resulting theory and intervention strategies would most likely have been different. Our clinical experience has taught us that parents of antisocial youngsters have serious deficits in parenting practices (Patterson, 1982). The central hypothesis that has emerged from these efforts is that it is necessary to teach parents effective family management practices to effect lasting reductions in antisocial behavior problems.

The belief that parents have a substantial impact on their children's adjustment now has a solid theoretical and empirical foundation in the parent-training literature (e.g., Forehand & Atkeson, 1977; Patterson, 1985; Wahler, 1975). The OSLC treatment has been described in a number of publications (e.g., Forgatch & Patterson, 1989; Forgatch & Toobert, 1979; Patterson, 1982; Patterson & Chamberlain, 1988; Patterson, Chamberlain, & Reid, 1982; Patterson & Forgatch, 1987; Patterson, Reid, Jones, & Conger, 1975; Reid, Kavanagh, & Baldwin, 1987; Reid & Patterson, 1989). The model involves teaching parents a set of specific parenting practices.

The treatment employs a step-by-step approach; each skill learned forms the foundation upon which a new skill can be laid. Five family management practices are the core components of the OSLC parent-training program: tracking, positive reinforcement, discipline, monitoring, and problem solving. First, parents learn to "track," or pay attention to, specific child behaviors (e.g., compliance versus noncompliance). This enables them to apply contingent consequences. When parents see their children doing something praiseworthy (e.g., complying with a parental request), they learn to respond with positive reinforcement (e.g., with approval, increased privileges, etc.). When parents see their children behaving inappropriately (e.g., with noncompliance), they calmly apply a mild consequence such as Time Out (removal to a boring place for five minutes) or short-term privilege removal (e.g., one hour loss of bike use). We call this "discipline." Parents also learn to "monitor"; that is, to provide close supervision for their children even when the children are away from home. This involves knowing where their children go, with whom, when they will be home, and what they are doing while they are there. Finally, families learn problem solving strategies. This enables them to plan ahead to prevent problems before they arise, and to manage difficulties in a rational manner. It typically requires 20 hours of direct contact with individual families to teach families these basic family management practices.

An alternative to parent training is direct intervention with the child in residential settings. This approach has been studied by other groups. In one in-patient setting, a primarily psychoanalytic treatment program was shown to be effective for antisocial boys, but gains were quickly lost when the youngsters returned to an unchanged social environment (Redl & Wineman, 1957). Another residential program, Achievement Place, used social learning principles in the treatment. The careful evaluation conducted by Jones, Weinrott, and Howard (1981) found that children improved while in the teaching family setting, but again the gains eroded when the youngsters returned to their (untreated) families.

In summary, the hypothesis that has emerged from treatment efforts with antisocial youngsters is: to produce persistent improvements, it is necessary to reprogram the child's social environment by teaching parents effective family management skills.

Observations Inform Hypotheses

One of the inherent advantages in the selection of antisocial child behavior as a problem to treat and understand is that it is readily observable. This makes it possible to generate hypotheses about its sources from direct observations. The importance of studying observable phenomena was introduced by Watson (1913). Barker (1963) challenged investigators to leave their interview rooms and go into the natural environment where the child lives. Patterson and Reid and their colleagues (e.g., Patterson, 1982; Reid, 1978) followed this maxim by visiting the homes of families with aggressive youngsters. In keeping with Barker's (1963) mandate, they recorded sequential behavior observed in the naturalistic environment. Building on the work of Bales (1950), they constructed an a priori code that recorded action/reaction sequences. Field observations with well-designed coding systems have provided evidence that antisocial children do not simply march to their own rhythms. Rather, much of their behavior is in direct response to the stimuli and reinforcing contingencies provided by the behavior of others. Parents, siblings, peers, teachers, and other significant people inadvertantly elicit and maintain the very problem behaviors they find repugnant.

Several scoring systems have been developed that describe social interactional phenomena in a variety of settings: home, school, family problem-solving discussions, treatment sessions, and so forth. These observational systems have been important in the generation of hypotheses about the development and maintenance of deviant processes in families. They are also useful as measures of treatment outcome.

MEASUREMENT DEVELOPMENT

Studies comparing treatment with no-treatment control groups have demonstrated that parents have a bias to report improvement in the behavior of their problem children even when no observable changes have occurred (Clement & Milne, 1967; Patterson & Reid, 1973; Walter & Gilmore, 1973). This has made the development of measures relatively free of bias, yet sensitive to behavioral change essential to treatment outcome studies. Home observational data have become the method of choice to meet this challenge.

The first OSLC observational system was the Family Interaction Coding System (FICS) (Patterson, Ray, Shaw, & Cobb, 1969). This paper and pencil code was used successfully for more than a decade in numerous clinical outcome studies (e.g., Patterson, 1974; Patterson, et al., & Reid, 1982; Weinrott, Bauske, & Patterson, 1979). Its development and use have required that a variety of psychometric problems be examined, such as reactivity, reliability, and observer presence, agreement, bias, and drift, and so forth. Several studies undertaken to address these issues established the psychometric integrity of the FICS (e.g., Jones, Reid, & Patterson, 1975; Patterson, 1982; Reid, 1978).

The most recent home observational system in use at OSLC is the Family Process Code (FPC) (Dishion et al., 1983), based on earlier work with the FICS. The FPC retains the psychometric characteristics of the FICS (e.g., reliability and validity), yet provides new features. For example, interactions are entered directly into hand-held computers. Behavior is scored in real time, providing for analyses of duration. Two new dimensions have been added: (a) *valence,* the coding of positive and negative affect based on tone of voice, gesture and facial expression of the family members; and (b) *context,* the scoring of classes of activity in which the individual is engaged (e.g., work, play, reading, eating). In addition, the FPC provides a more fine-grained detailing of prosocial behavior.

One of the scores from the FPC relevant to this chapter is Total Aversive Behavior (TAB), which has traditionally been used as a treatment outcome measure. TAB reflects the extent to which the target child is observed to engage in noxious behavior in the home. It is composed of nine negative behaviors: noncompliance, verbal attack, general negative verbal, ambiguous threat, clear threat, refusal, negative nonverbal, physical negative, and physical attack. The rate-per-minute of these behaviors serves as the score. TAB has become the "gold standard" of treatment outcome at OSLC over the years because it is thought to accurately describe families' interactional styles, to be sensitive to change, and to be relatively nonreactive to biases.

Our early treatment studies emphasized changing antisocial child behavior. In addition to TAB, other data were collected from parents, including global reports of change, daily reports of specific behaviors, and interviews concerning parenting practices. However, each measure was reported separately. More recently we have begun to employ the multiagent, multimethod approach of combining information from several sources into single construct scores. This strategy, applied to both longitudinal samples and to our most recent treatment study, is described later.

TRIALS OF HYPOTHESES

The first rounds in our clinical science vortex began with a series of treatment outcome studies with families of aggressive and antisocial preadolescents. Parent training was conducted to teach effective family management skills and pre/post levels of child TAB were compared. The series of programmatic studies conducted over a 20-year period has been summarized by Patterson (1985) and is briefly outlined here.

A series of single-case studies in the mid-1960s led to a sequence of group designs in which consecutive cases were treated by the OSLC staff. These early studies showed significant reductions in observed rates of deviant behavior (TAB) for target children and siblings. Follow-up probes at 6 and 12 months showed that the effects persisted (Patterson, 1980, 1982, 1985).

Then a series of random assignment studies were conducted to determine whether improvements in child behavior were due to specific treatment factors or to placebo effects. The first study, by Wiltz and Patterson (1974), used a waiting list control design. The second, by Walter & Gilmore (1973), used a placebo treatment comparison design. Both studies used pre- and posttreatment observation data and random assignment; in both, the parent training group improved and the comparison group showed no change. However, there were numerous methodological problems in both studies (small sample size, poor match on TAB at baseline, a time interval of only 4 or 5 weeks). The next study in the series corrected these flaws. Patterson, et al., (1982) randomly assigned 18 families referred for treatment to OSLC or to community private practitioners. The pre- and postobservation data showed a significant reduction in deviant child behavior (TAB) for the OSLC group and a nonsignificant change for the comparison group. At termination, 75% of the children treated at OSLC were observed to function in the normal range (at baseline, 100% were in the deviant range).

These studies led to the conclusion that the OSLC parent-training treatment is an effective means of reducing antisocial child behavior. The effects persist, they are replicable, and they appear not to be attributed to placebo effects.

Some difficulties in the use of the therapy have been reported. For example, the intervention has failed when time-limited treatment was used (Bernal, Delfini, North, & Kreutzer, 1976; Eyberg & Johnson, 1974), and when the treatment was too narrowly focused on parent training procedures (Eyberg & Johnson, 1974; Fleischman, 1979). Therapists must be experienced and sensitive clinicians who can deal with the numerous family problems that are concomitants of child antisocial behavior (e.g., marital conflict, depression, and alcoholism) (Patterson, 1982).

These early treatment studies provided indirect trials of the theory that parenting practices govern child behavior. The investigators were successful in demonstrating improvements in deviant child behavior using the parent as the agent of change. None of these studies, however, provided a direct test of the hypothesis that it was improvements in parenting that led to the reductions in antisocial child behavior.

Up to this point, the dependent variable employed a single method, direct observation; the independent variables (i.e., the parenting practices) were not assessed. Before more rigorous tests of the theory could be undertaken, fundamental work was required to develop measures of the independent variables and to refine the measurement of the dependent variable. The next section briefly summarizes this stage in the research.

MULTIMETHOD MEASUREMENT

We assume that any single agent or mode of assessment involves some distortion (Feigl, 1956). Thus, while a measure may be highly reliable, it may also be highly biased or distorted. A diversity of relevant and accurate measures embedded in nomological networks that tap the concepts under investigation are required to counter these problems (Cronbach & Meehl, 1955; MacCorquadale & Meehl, 1948). This led us to employ the multiagent/multimethod approach (Campbell & Fiske, 1959) to build latent constructs.

We adopted the following decision rules for measurement of constructs: (a) constructs and their indicators must have face validity; (b) indicators must be reliable; (c) whenever possible, constructs must be measured by at least two different methods; and (d) whenever possible, constructs must be measured by data from at least two different reporting agents.

There are four basic stages in building constructs. First, each item thought to contribute to the definition of the construct is listed. Second, each collection of items (scale) is analyzed to determine whether it is internally consistent. In this stage, items that correlate less than .20 with the corrected total score are dropped. Those scales with Cronbach's alpha greater than or equal to .60 are retained. The third stage uses factor analysis to determine whether the scales load significantly on the factor and whether a unidimensional versus multidimensional interpretation of the construct is appropriate. Those scales with factor loadings of less than .30 are dropped. In the last stage, scales are tested for convergent and discriminant validity by subjecting those to be included in a model to a confirmatory factor analysis. Each scale that survives the rigors of that test may be employed as an indicator for the construct. Several publications describe this measurement strategy (Capaldi & Patterson, 1989; Forgatch, Patterson, & Skinner, 1988; Patterson, 1986; Patterson & Bank, 1986; Patterson & Bank, 1987; Patterson, Reid, & Dishion, in press).

The measurement strategies have been refined over the last two decades, yet they continue to require improvement. The challenge is to design measures that describe relevant behaviors of significant people in the social environment (e.g., target children, sibs, peers, parents, teachers). These measures must also be sensitive to changes, including the gradual changes involved in movement through developmental phases and the more rapid changes inherent in treatment. Each effort to test new hypotheses in the model teaches us the shortcomings of our current strategies and suggests ways to improve.

HYPOTHESIS TRIALS

In 1980, OSLC shifted focus from treatment outcome studies and prepared for a set of longitudinal studies by collecting cross-sectional data from 4th-, 7th-, and 10th-grade boys and their families. A period of measurement development and exploratory hypothesis testing followed. In 1984, the fruits of these efforts came to bear as three interlocking investigations began: two longitudinal studies with children at risk for antisocial behavior problems, and a treatment study with children referred for these problems. All three studies employed the improved assessment procedures. These studies have moved us further into the vortex in our examination of the family processes involved in antisocial problems.

Replications with Correlational Data

The conclusions that could be drawn from the treatment outcome studies were limited, in part because the samples were narrow and the association between the parenting variables and child behavior was not directly tested. The model would gain credibility with path models directly assessing the hypothesized relationships using nonclinical samples. A series of such tests of the model has taken place in recent years, including contrasts between our own and competing models for antisocial behavior in boys (Patterson, et al., in press). Using structural equation modeling, we have tested the fit of the hypothesized models to the data with encouraging results (Patterson, 1986; Patterson & Bank, 1989; Patterson & Forgatch, in press).

Increasingly rigorous tests required replication of the model with samples of differing levels of risk. Failure to replicate could suggest a number of shortcomings: the model is wrong, the measurement of the constructs is faulty, the relationships found in one sample are unique to a developmental stage, or perhaps to a limited or nonrepresentative sample. Such problems with replication would suggest that the hypothesized relationships be re-examined, or other variables heretofore overlooked be included in the model. The next section describes our efforts at replication.

Fig. 11.2 illustrates the model as tested with the three OSLC samples that began in 1984. The hypothesized structural relationship between parental discipline and monitoring practices and child antisocial behavior was tested using structural equation modeling.

This model has come to be known affectionately as Basic Black, because like a black dress, the model is simple, elegant, and is appropriate for most occasions. Over the years, two or three similar models have been given this name (e.g., Patterson, 1986; Patterson & Bank, 1989). The essential nature of Basic Black is that its independent variables are the parenting behaviors thought to determine antisocial behavior in children. The model is that inept discipline worsens parental monitoring,

Basic Black, Risk Sample

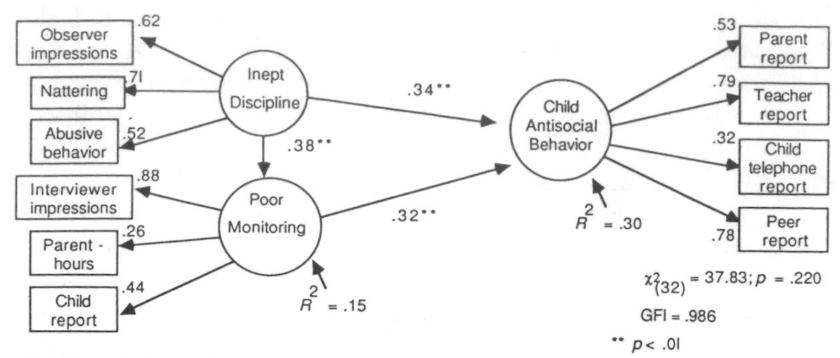

Basic Black, Divorce Sample

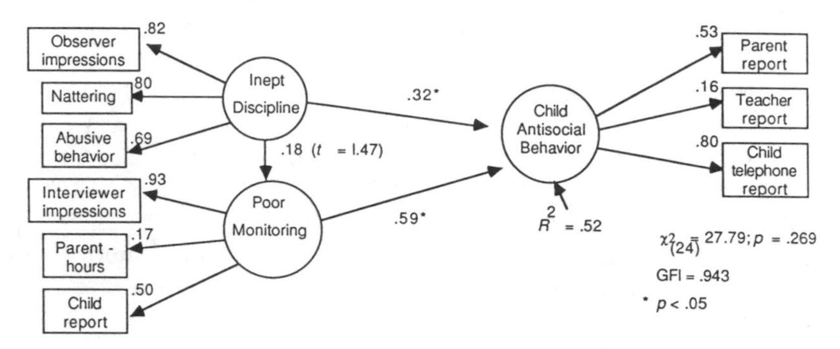

Basic Black, Clinical Sample

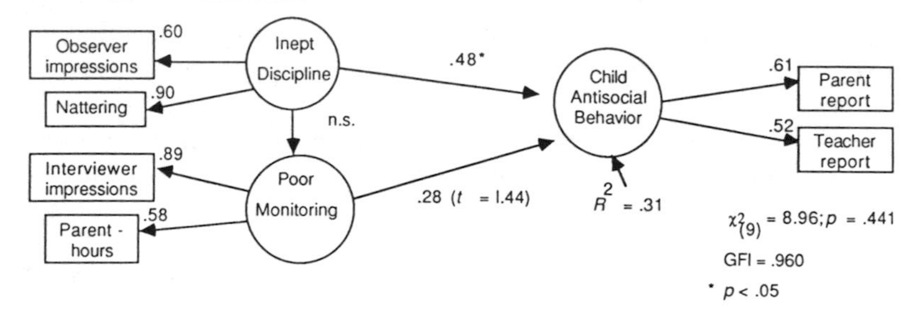

FIG. 11.2. Three aspects of the Basic Black model.

and together inept discipline and poor monitoring result in child antisocial behavior. Although the figure and the language used to describe these relationships imply causal status for certain variables, it should be remembered that these are correlational data and no assumption of causality can be made.

Sample. The first test of the model was conducted with the Oregon Youth Study, a sample of families participating in a 10-year study of the development of antisocial behavior in children. The youngsters (described more fully in Capaldi and Patterson [1989]) were thought to be at risk for delinquency because when they entered the study, the families lived in areas with the highest density of crime in the Eugene/ Springfield, Oregon, metropolitan area. There are two cohorts of boys who were in the fourth grade when they entered the study. The cohorts were combined for this analysis (n = 201).

The first replication of Basic Black was carried out with a sample of children who had experienced their parents' separation in the year prior to study entry. Their participation in a longitudinal study of divorce was solicited through newspaper ads. One hundred ninety-seven families (197 boys; 40 girls) between the ages of 5 and 12 completed the first assessment. The older boys (9 to 12 years old) were included in the present analysis (n = 96). This divorce sample is described more fully in Patterson and Forgatch (in press).

The second replication was conducted with a clinical sample of boys and girls referred for treatment because of high levels of antisocial behavior. This sample is described more fully later in the chapter. Baseline data were employed in the analysis (N = 71).

Constructs. Definition of constructs followed the multiagent/ multimethod guidelines described earlier. For the replication analyses, an effort was made to employ the same items and indicators for each construct used in the original test. The procedures required, however, that some items and indicators be dropped because they did not meet criteria or, as in the case of peer nominations, the measure had not been collected. As can be seen in Fig. 11.2, there was considerable overlap in the measurement of the constructs.

Inept discipline was defined from a set of three home observations using the Family Process Code (Dishion et al., 1983). Each observation session was conducted by a different observer. The indicators were observer impressions, which is a rating of the parent's use of inconsistent and ineffective discipline; nattering, which is the conditional probability that the mother responded with aversive behavior, regardless of the child's behavior; and abusive behavior, a frequency score of high amplitude behaviors (e.g., hitting, humiliation). The abusive behavior indicator was employed with the risk and divorce samples but not the clinical sample.

Monitoring was defined by indicators from three different agents and settings: the impressions of the person who interviewed the parents about their parenting practices, the parents' daily telephone report of time spent with their child, and the child's interview report of parental supervision. The child report of monitoring did not meet the factor loading criterion and was dropped for the clinical sample.

Antisocial behavior was defined by parent report in questionnaires and telephone interviews, teacher report using the Child Behavior Checklist (Achenbach, 1978), child telephone interviews, and peer reports obtained from nominations in the classroom. Peer nominations were obtained for the risk sample only. The child report indicator failed to achieve the factor loading criterion for the clinical sample, and was not included.

Results. For each analysis, there are several questions of importance. Do the data fit the model (as indicated by a nonsignificant Chi^2 and a GFI of more than .90)? Are the hypothesized relationships among constructs found (as shown by significant path coefficients)? Is the amount of variance accounted for in the dependent variable substantial (more than 30%)? Do the construct factor loadings have similar patterns?

As shown by Fig. 11.2, all three structural equation model tests met the first criterion: nonsignificant Chi^2 values and adequate GFI values. Each data set provided an acceptable fit to the a priori clinical model. The implication is that both the factor definitions and the structural relations among constructs may be highly generalizable.

The second important question concerned the magnitude and significance of the hypothesized path coefficients. This particular model required that the two parent practices be significantly related to the child antisocial construct. Since the path coefficients are standard partial beta weights, their relative strengths can be compared. It is noteworthy that the relative contribution of monitor and discipline from one sample to another varied enormously. This suggests that the contribution of parental supervision may vary a good deal from one sample to another, which in turn could have major implications for intervention efforts. Five of the 6 path coefficients were significant; the exception ($t = 1.44$) was of borderline significance. The findings provide a strong base for the hypothesis that discipline and monitor may be significant contributors to antisocial problems. The effect of discipline on parental monitoring accounted for small amounts of variance in the risk (15%) and divorce (3%) samples.

We arbitrarily set 30% of the variance accounted for as the minimum requirement for a satisfactory performance model (Patterson, 1986). The amount of variance explained in the child antisocial construct fulfilled that requirement for all three samples: 30% for the risk and clinical groups and 52% for the divorce sample.

Clearly the Basic Black model is not only generalizable across samples, but it also accounts for a substantial portion of the variance in constructs that define antisocial behavior. Given the differences among samples in the factor structure for the criterion construct, the generalizability of the model is even more noteworthy. The replications provide improved status for the theory.

Longitudinal tests. Replicating the model was a necessary step in advancing its credibility, but more stringent tests can be conducted with longitudinal analyses. The special strength in the longitudinal design lies in its ability to test whether the independent variables predict the dependent variables over time. This requires that the model be stable over time.

Olweus (1979) reviewed several longitudinal studies showing that antisocial behavior has test-retest reliability similar to that found for measures of children's intelligence. Patterson & Bank (1989) showed that the relationships in the Basic Black model are stable over a two year period. Using data from the first cohort of 101 families in the risk sample described earlier, they found the path coefficients for stability to be .80, .73, and .72 for monitoring, discipline, and antisocial behavior, respectively. Multiple regression analyses conducted at Time 1 and two years later showed that both inept discipline and poor monitoring made significant contributions to antisocial behavior. The amount of variance explained each time was 27%. This suggests that the structure of the relationship between these parenting variables and antisocial behavior in children is stable.

Given that the model is stable, it is possible to examine the extent that changes over time in the independent variables predict changes in the dependent variable. If monitoring and discipline control antisocial behavior, then parents who change in their use of these practices should have children who change in their performance of antisocial behavior. Patterson & Bank (1989) recently published data testing these predictions with the first cohort (n = 101) of the risk sample. The assessments were carried out when the boys were in grades 4 and 6. The findings are summarized next, with the results for the monitoring construct shown in Fig. 11.3(a), and the discipline construct shown in Fig. 11.3(b).

Fifteen families improved in monitoring over the two-year period; there was a trend for the predicted decrease in child antisocial behavior, although the decrease was not significant (t = 1.43, p less than .2). In 14 families, a disruption in monitoring occurred, resulting in the hypothesized increase in antisocial behavior (t = 2.71, p less than .01).

The results for parental discipline were somewhat less promising. The group of families in which parents showed improvement over the 2-year period was small (n = 8), and their children obtained rather low antisocial scores compared to the other children at grade 4. Although their scores decreased somewhat over the two years, the small n did not permit a statistical test of the change. For the disrupted discipline group (n = 13), the mean antisocial score showed a modest increase, but these boys

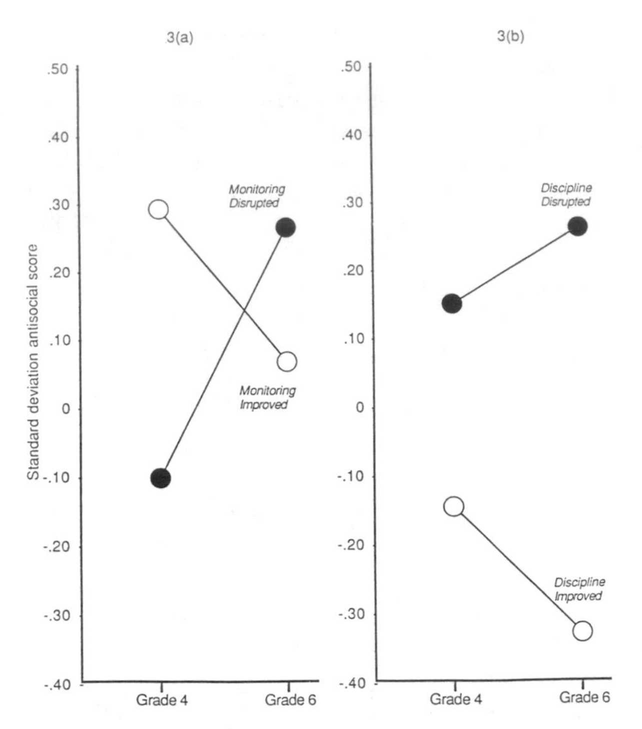

FIG. 11.3. Changes in antisocial behavior as a function of changes in parenting practices. Adapted from figures in Patterson, G. R. & Bank, L. (in press). Some amplifying mechanisms for pathologic processes in families. In M. Gunnar (Ed.), *Minnesota Symposium on Child Psychology*. Hillsdale, NJ: Lawrence Erlbaum Associates.

had somewhat elevated scores at grade 4 and the increase was not significant.

Both sets of data provide consistent support for a causal relationship between parent and child behavior. Changes in parenting practices were accompanied by corresponding changes in child behavior. While this may be presumptive evidence for some kind of causal process, the difficulty is that one does not know which variable is cause and which is effect. The coercion model (Patterson, 1982) strongly emphasizes bidirectional effects for parent/child interactions. In Fig. 11.3(b), the baseline differences in discipline may well represent a stage in a bidirectional process where the coercive child has seriously affected parent discipline practices. As the parent practices deteriorate over time, the child's adjustment worsens. Longitudinal analyses of this kind can provide only indirect, and therefore weak, tests of causal status. A series of experiments was needed in which parent practices were manipulated to determine the effect of child behavior.

REFINING THE MODEL

The early treatment studies demonstrated that antisocial child behavior could be reduced when parents were taught family management practices. The replications of the Basic Black model with correlational data and the longitudinal analyses suggested that monitoring and discipline may have some controlling status for antisocial child behavior. A more crucial test of the theory required an experimental test, pitting alternative theories against each other (Borkovec & Bauer, 1982; Larzelere & Skeen, 1984). Treatment could be used as such a test if the independent variables could be altered in one group and not another. The outcome predicted would be for improvement in the experimental but not the other group. We attempted such an experimental manipulation.

Treatment as an Experimental Manipulation

As mentioned earlier, Patterson & Bank (1989) reported considerable stability in the Basic Black model. The design of the experiment was to alter the stability in monitoring and discipline practices by teaching parents more effective techniques, and thereby disrupt the stability of the child's antisocial behavior (see Fig. 11.4). A random assignment design

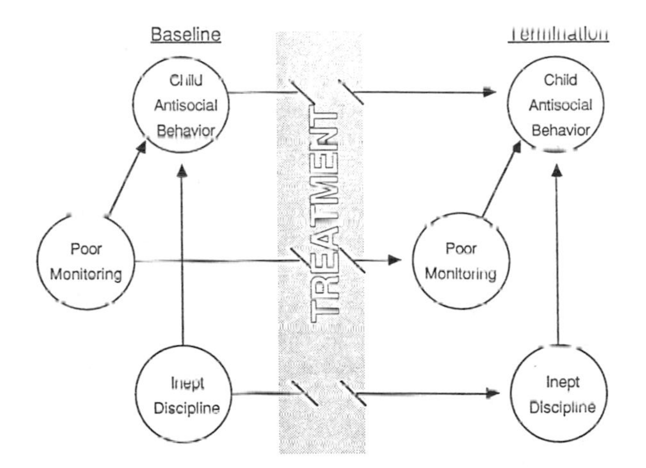

FIG. 11.4. Treatment disrupts continuity of Basic Black model.

was employed in which cases referred for antisocial child behavior received treatment at OSLC or another agency in the community. As the study was originally conceived, we expected that the other agency would take their usual approach to family therapy, which does not include teaching family management practices. As we later discovered in examining the videotapes of treatment sessions, some of the therapists in the comparison treatment taught family management practices. Some families in both groups showed improvement in the crucial parenting variables of monitoring and discipline. For this reason, our test of the model followed a quasi rather than a true experimental approach. The revised design tested the hypothesis that, regardless of treatment condition, parents who made improvements in monitoring and discipline would have children who demonstrated reductions in antisocial behavior.

Sample. Families were referred by schools, community agencies, and parents for problems with child antisocial behavior. Two screening criteria were used to guarantee high levels of the problem: (a) scores at or above one SD of the mean on the externalizing scale of the Child Behavior Checklist (Achenbach, 1978), and (b) .5 SD or more above the mean (for the risk sample) on the measure of TAB when observed at home using the FPC (Dishion et al., 1983). Exclusionary criteria included active psychosis and/or severe mental retardation of parents and/or children. Although families with girls were accepted for treatment, they were excluded from this analysis because many of their patterns were different from those displayed by boys.

There were 50 families with boys who completed pre/post treatment assessment. Target children were between the ages of 5 and 12 at baseline ($X = 8.9$; $SD = 2.18$). The distribution of children in age groups was as follows: 19 children in the 5- to 8-year age range, 18 in the 9- to 10-year age range, and 13 in the 11- to 12-year age range. Twenty-two were single-parent families; 28 were two-parent families.

There were 35 cases treated by OSLC and 15 cases treated by the other agency. The average number of treatment sessions was 19 ($SD = 9.7$; range = 5 to 50). The OSLC treament has already been described. Analyses of videotapes of the treatment sessions showed that the other agency employed an eclectic family approach, including components of brief, structural, and social-learning family therapy.

Constructs. The general strategy for construct design is detailed in Capaldi and Patterson (1989). Constructs were built using raw items to form the indicators. Next, these scales were standardized separately by age group on their baseline distributions. This step was necessary because the age span for the sample (i.e., 5 years to 12 years) covered a variety of developmental stages. Indicators for the constructs at termination were scaled on the distribution of the baseline scores to enable the detection of changes. Constructs were monitoring, discipline, and antisocial child behavior.

Monitoring. This construct was formed from two agents using the same method. Ratings of how well the child was being monitored were obtained separately from the parent and child interviewers. This measure is the interviewer impressions indicator for the clinical sample shown in Fig. 11.2.

Discipline. This construct is exactly that shown for the clinical sample in Fig. 11.2.

Antisocial Child Behavior. This construct is composed of TAB, a parent questionnaire covering the extent to which the child engaged in a wide variety of antisocial behaviors, and a scale obtained from the teacher's CBC (Achenbach, 1978) describing the boy's problematic behavior in school.

Results. The hypothesis was that improvement in parental monitoring and discipline produced during treatment would result in decreases in child antisocial behavior. Tests were conducted separately for each parenting variable, as follows. Families in which parents improved by 30% or more from baseline to termination composed the "improved" group. Those who did not make such gains composed the "unimproved" group. The between-group effects were examined through multivariate analyses of variance (MANOVAs) for repeated measures with the three indicators for child antisocial behavior at baseline and termination as the variates.

The critical test of the theory was in the interaction term for the MANOVA, which described the extent to which improved parenting practices at termination differentiated improvements in child antisocial behavior. For monitoring, the interaction term was significant $F(3,46) = 2.90$, p less than .05, providing support for the hypothesis. Parents who improved their monitoring practices had children with significant reductions in antisocial behavior.

Table 11.1 displays the means and standard deviations for the univariate scores at baseline and termination. These describe the extent to which each variable tested individually contributes to the significant overall effect. The findings for the improved group were consistent across all indicators for the monitor composite. In each case, improved monitoring was associated with improved child adjustment.

The interaction term for the MANOVA testing the effect of discipline

TABLE 11.1
Scores and Comparisons of Indicators for the Antisocial Construct for Improved Versus Unimproved Parental Monitoring Groups

	Improved (N = 8)				*Unimproved (N = 42)*				
	Baseline		*Termination*		*Baseline*		*Termination*		
Indicators for Antisocial construct[a]	*Mean*	*SD*	*Mean*	*SD*	*Mean*	*SD*	*Mean*	*SD*	*Univariate F*
TAB	.66	1.36	−.47	.96	−.14	.85	−.77	.65	1.85
Parent	.09	.69	−1.52	.68	−.15	.92	−.87	1.18	5.58*
Teacher	.07	.99	−.22	1.01	.26	.87	.37	.87	1.45

[a]All positive scores are in deviant direction.
$^*p < .05$.

on the composite for antisocial child behavior was significant, $F(3,46) = 4.15$, $p = .01$. Parental improvements in discipline practices were accompanied by reductions in child antisocial behavior. Table 11.2 displays the means and standard deviations for the univariate scores at baseline and termination for discipline. They reveal that support for the hypothesized causal status of parent discipline is inconclusive. Only the data for the observation indicator showed a significant effect in the predicted direction. Since both the dependent and independent variables were based on the same assessment procedures, even this contribution may be called into question.

We expected that families in which parents improved on both the monitor and discipline variables would experience significant decreases in their youngsters' antisocial behavior. Unfortunately, there were only five families who met this criterion, so it was not possible to conduct a statistical test.

TABLE 11.2
Scores and Comparisons of Indicators for the Antisocial Construct for Improved Versus Unimproved Parental Discipline Groups

	Improved (N = 25)				*Unimproved (N = 25)*				
	Baseline		*Termination*		*Baseline*		*Termination*		
Indicators for Antisocial construct[a]	*Mean*	*SD*	*Mean*	*SD*	*Mean*	*SD*	*Mean*	*SD*	*Univariate F*
TAB	.146	.996	−.823	.783	−.178	.947	−.611	.606	4.18*
Parent	−.199	.655	−.751	1.110	−.016	1.068	−1.197	1.129	5.23*
Teacher	.301	.851	.472	.970	.156	.925	.073	.810	1.14

[a]All positive scores are in deviant direction.
$^*p < .05$.

Discussion. The hypotheses survived the trial. Children who demonstrated the greatest reductions in antisocial behavior were those whose parents improved their performance of monitoring or discipline by at least 30% from baseline to termination. Examination of the univariate scores for each MANOVA showed (with some exceptions) that changes in discipline and in monitoring covaried with the predicted changes in the TAB variable. Both sets of findings were consistent with the idea that changes in parenting influence changes in child behavior. The monitor data gave stronger support for the hypothesis than did discipline.

This experimental test of the theory raised a number of important questions. The first issue concerns a potential bidirectional relationship between parent and child behavior. For example, the data in Fig. 11.3(b) suggested that parents whose discipline practices worsened had children who were acting out more initially; parents whose discipline practices improved had children with lower levels of the problem. It may be that children with extreme problems exacerbate their parents' already poor discipline practices, resulting in yet more problematic child behavior. Perhaps one way to test such a bidirectional relationship would be to study a problem like hyperactivity, which lends itself to improvement with medication. If a medication, such as Ritalin, were used to reduce the hyperactive youngster's activity level, then the effect on parental discipline could be examined to see if a commensurate improvement occurred.

A second problem raised by this study has to do with the differential sensitivity of the indicators measuring change. In part, global report may reflect a positive or negative bias that interferes with the ability to discern measurable change. This was demonstrated in the classic investigation by Wahler and Leske (1973), in which a series of videotapes was shown to parents. Observable improvements were taking place gradually in the behavior of a hyperactive child, but the raters failed to notice the changes unless they were taught to count specific behaviors. The treatment study conducted by Walter and Gilmore (1973) found parents in a placebo group to report improvement in their children's behavior when home observation data revealed a trend for child behavior to worsen. The recent study by Walker and his colleagues (Walker et al., 1983) reported a similar problem with teacher global assessment. Although classroom observations demonstrated significant improvements in child behavior following intervention, teachers did not report a significant change.

TAB has a history of sensitivity to change in home behavior produced during treatment. Studies also demonstrate relatively small effects of observer bias on the molecular data they collect (Patterson, 1982). In addition, the TAB score has been shown to predict later adjustment.

Reid & Bank (1988) collected follow-up data from OSLC treatment studies and found home observation data to predict institutionalization and long-term adjustment. The correlation between child TAB and contacts with police 5 to 20 years laters was .30 (p. less than .01).

A third issue raised by this study concerns the other family management practices thought to be relevant in the treatment of antisocial youngsters. Although the present study found the expected relationship between child behavior and parental monitoring and discipline, changes in positive reinforcement and problem solving did not covary with changes in antisocial behavior. We think that these skills relate more to the development of prosocial behavior than to reductions in deviant behavior. More appropriate tests, therefore, should examine their relationship to variables such as academic achievement, peer relationships, involvement in skill related activities. Because these are rather complex skills, it is likely that they would take some time to develop, and a good time to assess them would be in followup probes. Further studies will be conducted to test these hypotheses.

Finally, the question of which treatment components are related to positive outcomes for the child has yet to be addressed. An emerging plan is to conduct a series of multiple baseline single subject studies. By introducing the parenting variables one at a time, with careful assessment following each stage, it will be possible to use time series analysis to identify which aspects of the treatment are crucial and which are extraneous.

INNER TIERS OF THE VORTEX

Several cycles in the clinical science vortex have been completed. The outcome suggests that the Basic Black model has a preferred status: the hypothesis that parental monitoring and discipline practices control antisocial child behavior has withstood increasingly rigorous trials, including the present quasi-experimental manipulation. The correlational and intervention analyses suggest that discipline and monitoring are both relevant to the model, while the longitudinal analysis suggests that monitoring may be of greater importance. Obviously, there is much yet to be done to clarify these discrepancies.

One of the long-term outcomes of developing a better theory of antisocial behavior would be the ability to prevent its occurrence. The publication by Patterson, Capaldi, and Bank (in press) shows that the model significantly predicts from age 10 to delinquency occurring at age 14 and 15. The next question concerns the generalizability of the model: does it apply outside of Eugene, Oregon? To do this, it will be necessary to first test performance models in stratified probability samples. How much variance can be accounted for with the Basic Black model for different ethnic groups, families living in large metropolitan, or in rural areas? Dr. S. Kellam and his colleagues at Johns Hopkins University are now conducting an epidemiological study that includes measures described here. If the Basic Black model proves to fit a more general population, then it may be possible to develop strategies to make the parent training technology generally available.

ACKNOWLEDGMENTS

The author would like to thank the staff of OSLC over the years the center has been in operation. They have provided the toil and compulsive attention to detail and quality that has made the work possible. The three grants that provided data and support for the present study are also gratefully acknowledged: MH38318, MH37940, MH38730. Finally, there were several people who facilitated this chapter: Jerry, who helped me think my way through the many puzzles; G. R. Patterson and Patricia Chamberlain, who designed the treatment study; John Reid, who makes things work at the Center, and who supervised the therapy; Becky Fetrow, who skillfully conducted the bulk of the data analysis; Judy Ray, who built the constructs and presented the data for final analysis; Kathy Jordan, who scrubbed the data clean; Will Mayer, whose elegant figures made the ideas intelligible; Denise Gilbertson and Mary Perry, who made the manuscript presentable; Miles Yamamoto and Sonny Hays-Ebert, who managed the observational data set, the programming and the computer; the therapy staff; the data collection staff; and Lew Bank, Tom Dishion, Beverly Fagot, Bob Larzelere, Jerry Patterson, and Mike Stoolmiller, who carefully critiqued the manuscript.

REFERENCES

Achenbach, T. M. (1978). The child behavior profile, I: Boys aged 6 through 11. *Journal of Consulting and Clinical Psychology, 46,* 478–488.

Bales, R. F. (1950). *Interaction process analysis.* Cambridge, MA: Addison Wesley.

Barker, R. G. (1963). The stream of behavior as an empirical problem. In R. G. Barker (Ed.), *The stream of behavior* (pp. 1–22). New York: Appleton-Century-Crofts.

Bernal, M. E., Delfini, L. F., North, J. A., & Kreutzer, S. L. (1976). Comparison of boys' behavior in homes and classrooms. In E. Mash, L. Handy, & L. Hamerlynck (Eds.), *Behavior modification and families.* New York: Bruner/Mazell.

Borkovec, T. D., & Bauer, R. M. (1982). Experimental design in group outcome research. In A. Bellack, M. Herson, & A. Kazdin (Eds.), *International handbook of behavior modification and therapy*. New York: Plenum Press.

Campbell, D. T., & Fishe, D. W. (1959). Convergent and discriminant validation of the multitrait and multimethod martrix. *Psychological Bulletin, 56,* 81–105.

Capaldi, D. M., & Patterson, G. R. (1989). *Psychometric properties of fourteen latent constructs from the Oregon Youth Study*. New York: Springer Verlog.

Clement, P. W., & Milne, D. C. (1967). Group play therapy and tangible reinforcers used to modify the behavior of eight-year-old boys. *Behaviour Research and Therapy, 5,* 301–312.

Cronbach, L. J., & Meehl, P. E. (1955). Construct validity in psychological tests. In H. Feigl & M. Scriven (Eds.), *Minnesota studies in the philosophy of science. Vol. I: The foundations of science and concepts of psychology and psychoanalysis* (pp. 174–204). Minneapolis, MN: University of Minnesota Press.

Dishion, T. J., Gardner, K., Patterson, G. R., Reid, J. B., & Thibodeaux, S. (1983). *Family process code*. Unpublished technical report. Oregon Social Learning Center.

Eyberg, S. M., & Johnson, S. M. (1974). Multiple assessment of behavior modification and families: Effects of contingency contracting and order of treated problems. *Journal of Consulting and Clinical Psychology, 42,* 594–606.

Feigl, H. (1956). Some major issues and developments in the philosophy of science of logical empiricism. In H. Feigl & M. Scriven (Eds.), *Minnesota studies in the philosophy of science. Vol I: The foundations of science and concepts of psychology and psychoanalysis* (pp. 3–37). Minneapolis, MN: University of Minnesota Press.

Fleischman, M. J. (1979). *Training and evaluation of aggressive children*. Grant proposal submitted to Center for Studies of Antisocial and Violent Behavior, National Institute of Mental Health.

Forehand, R., & Atkeson, B. M. (1977). Generality of treatment effects with parents as therapists: A review of assessment and implementation procedures. *Behavior Therapy, 8,* 575–593.

Forgatch, M. S., & Patterson, G. R. (1989). *Parents and adolescents: Living together. Part II: Family problem solving*. Eugene, OR: Castalia Publishing Co.

Forgatch, M. S., Patterson, G. R., & Skinner, M. L. (1988). A mediational model for the effect of divorce on antisocial behavior in boys. In E. M. Hetherington & J. D. Aresteh (Eds.), *Impact of divorce, single parenting, and step-parenting on children* (pp. 135, 154). Hillsdale, NJ: Lawrence Erlbaum Associates, Publishers.

Forgatch, M. S., & Toobert, D. J. (1979). A cost-effective parent training program for use with normal preschool children. *Journal of Pediatric Psychology, 4,* 129–145.

Jones, R. R., Reid, J. B., & Patterson, G. R. (1975). Naturalistic observations in clinical assessment. In P. McReynolds (Ed.), *Advances in psychological assessment* (Vol. 3). San Francisco: Jossey-Bass.

Jones, R. R., Weinrott, M. R., & Howard, J. R. (1981). *Final report: The national evaluation of the Teaching Family Model*. Evaluation Research Group, Eugene, OR. Project supported by Grants R01MH25631 and R01MH31018, Center for Studies of Crime and Delinquency, National Institute of Mental Health, U.S. Department of Health and Human Services.

Joreskog, K. G., & Sorbom, D. (1983). *Lisrel VI: Analysis of linear structural relationships by maximum likelihood and least squares methods* (2nd ed.). Chicago: Natural Education Resources.

Larzelere, R. E., & Skeen, J. H. (1984). The method of multiple hypotheses: A neglected research strategy in family studies. *Journal of Family Issues, 5*(4), 474–492.

MacCorquodale, K., & Meehl, P. E. (1948). On a distinction between hypothetical construct and intervening variables. *Psychological Bulletin, 55,* 95–107.

Olweus, D. (1979). Stability of aggressive reaction patterns in males: A review. *Psychological Bulletin, 86,* 852–875.

Patterson, G. R. (1974). Retraining of aggressive boys by their parents: Review of recent literature and follow-up evaluation. *Canadian Psychiatric Association Journal, 19,* 142–161.

Patterson, G. R. (1980). Mothers: The unacknowledged victims. *Monographs of the Society for Research in Child Development, 45* (5, Serial No. 186).

Patterson, G. R. (1982). *A social learning approach to family intervention: III. Coercive family process.* Eugene, OR: Castalia.

Patterson, G. R. (1985). Beyond technology. The next stage in the development of a parent training technology. In L. L'Abate (Ed.), *Handbook of family psychology and therapy* (pp. 1344–1379). Homewood, IL: The Dorsey Press.

Patterson, G. R. (1986). Performance models for antisocial boys. *American Psychologist, 41*(4), 432–444.

Patterson, G. R., & Bank, L. (1986). Bootstrapping your way in the nomological thicket. *Behavior Assessment, 8,* 49–73.

Patterson, G. R., & Bank, L. (1987). When is a nomological network a construct? In D. R. Peterson & D. B. Fishman (Eds.), *Assessment for decision* (pp. 249–279). New Brunswick, NJ: Rutgers University Press.

Patterson, G. R., & Bank, L. (1989). Some amplifying mechanisms for pathologic processes in families. In M. R. Gunnar & E. Thelen (Eds.), *Systems and development: The Minnesota Symposia on Child Psychology* (Vol. 22) (pp. 167–209). Hillsdale, NJ: Lawrence Erlbaum Associates, Publishers.

Patterson, G. R., Capaldi, D., & Bank, L. (in press). An early starters model for predicting delinquency. In D. Pepler (Ed.), *The development and treatment of childhood aggression.* Hillsdale, NJ: Lawrence Erlbaum Associates, Publishers.

Patterson, G. R., & Chamberlain, P. (1988). Treatment process: A problem at three levels. In L. C. Wynne (Ed.), *The state of the art in family therapy research: Controversies and recommendations* (pp. 189–223). New York: Family Process Press.

Patterson, G. R., Chamberlain, P., & Reid, J. B. (1982). A comparative evaluation of parent training procedures. *Behavior Therapy, 13,* 638–650.

Patterson, G. R., & Forgatch, M. S. (1987). *Parents and adolescents living together. Part I: The basics.* Eugene, OR: Castalia Publishing Company.

Patterson, G. R., & Forgatch, M. S. (in press). Mother depression, child aggression and child depression: Three stages of the same process. In G. R. Patterson (Ed.). *Aggression and depression in families: Substantive and methodological issues. Vol. 1. Family Consortium Series.* Hillsdale, NJ: Lawrence Erlbaum Associates, Publishers.

Patterson, G. R., Ray, R. S., Shaw, D. A., & Cobb, J. A. (1969). *Manual for coding of family interactions.* See NAPS Document #01234 for 33 pages of material. Order from ASIS/NAPS, c/o Microfiche Publications, 440 Park Avenue Avenue South, New York, New York 10016. Remit in advance $5.45 for photocopies, $1.50 for microfiche. Make checks payable to Microfiche Publications.

Patterson, G. R., & Reid, J. B. (1973). Intervention for families of aggressive boys: A replication study. *Behavior Research and Therapy, 11,* 383–394.

Patterson, G. R., Reid, J. B., & Dishion, T. D. (in press). *Antisocial boys.* Eugene, OR. Castalia Publishing.

Patterson, G. R., Reid, J. B., Jones, R. R., & Conger, R. E. (1975). *A social learning approach to family intervention. I. Families with aggressive children.* Eugene, OR: Castalia Publishing Company.

Popper, K. R. (1972). *Objective knowledge: An evolutionary approach.* Oxford: Oxford University Press.

Redl, F., & Wineman, D. (1957). *The aggressive child.* New York: The Free Press.

Reid, J. B. (Ed.) (1978). *A social learning approach to family intervention: Vol 2. Observation in home settings.* Eugene, OR: Castalia Publishing Co.

Reid, J. B., & Bank, L. (1988). *Final report: Aggression in families and later antisocial behavior.* Oregon Social Learning Center, Eugene, OR. Project supported by Grant R01MH40024, Center for Studies of Crime and Delinquency, National Institute of Mental Health, U.S. Department of Health and Human Services.

Reid, J. B., Kavanagh, K. A., & Baldwin, D. V. (1987). Abusive parents' perceptions of child problem behaviors: An example of parental bias. *Journal of Abnormal Child Psychology, 15,* 457–466.

Reid, J. B., & Patterson, G. R. (1989). the development of antisocial behavior patterns in childhood and adolescence. *European Journal of Personality, 3,* 107–119.

Wahler, R. G. (1975). Some structural aspects of child deviant behavior. *Journal of Applied Behavioral Analysis, 8,* 27–42.

Wahler, R. G., & Leske, G. (1973). Accurate and inaccurate observer summary reports: Reinforcement theory interpretation and investigation. *Journal of Nervous and Mental Disease, 156,* 386–394.

Walker, H. M., McConnell, S., Walker, J. L., Clarke, J. Y., Todis, B., Cohen, G., & Rankin, R. (1983). Initial analysis of the accepts curriculum: Efficacy of instructional and behavior management procedures for improving the social adjustment of handicapped children. *Analysis and Intervention in Developmental Disabilities, 3,* 105–127.

Walter, H. I., & Gilmore, S. K. (1973). Placebo versus social learning effects in parent training procedures designed to alter the behaviors of aggressive boys. *Behavior Therapy, 4,* 361–377.

Watson, J. B. (1913). Psychology as a behaviorist views it. *Psychological Review, 20,* 158–177.

Weinrott, M. R., Bauske, B., & Patterson, G. R. (1979). Systematic replication of a social learning approach. In P. O. Sjoden, S. Bates, & W. S. Dockens (Eds.), *Trends in behavior therapy* (pp. 331–351). New York: Academic Press.

Wiltz, N. A., & Patterson, G. R. (1974). An evaluation of parent training procedures designed to alter inappropriate aggressive behavior of boys. *Behavior Therapy, 5,* 215–221.

12

Prevention of Aggression and Other Behavior Problems in the Early Adolescent Years

Rex Forehand
University of Georgia

Nicholas Long
University of Arkansas for Medical Sciences

Adolescence can be a difficult time; it has been shown that a number of problem behaviors, including aggression, increase during this age period. The behaviors subsumed under a label of aggression can actually take many forms including arguing, cruelty, demanding, disobedience, fighting, mood changes, and threatening others (Achenbach & Edelbrock, 1981). Not only some of these types of behaviors, but more serious acts of delinquency, increase in adolescence (see Loeber, 1982). Furthermore, Gold and Petronio (1980) reported that over 80% of American adolescents indicated they had engaged in at least one delinquent behavior. Although problems with aggressive behaviors are prevalent during adolescence, problems in other areas have also been noted to appear or are exacerbated during this developmental period. These include depression, eating disorders, suicide, and poor school performance (see Forehand, in press).

The increase in problems during adolescence may be, at least partially, a function of stressors which are unique to this age. For example, the onset of puberty has been associated with an increase in aggression (Inoff-Germain, Arnold, Nottlemann, Susman, Cutler, & Chrousos, 1988). However, it is not only the onset of puberty but its timing which has been associated with problems (Petersen, 1987; Steinberg, 1987). Furthermore, gender appears to serve as a moderating variable as Peterson (1987) reported that a late onset has negative consequences for boys while an early onset has negative consequences for girls. Additionally, transition from elementary to middle school and the timing of this transition can be associated with problems (e.g., Hirsch & Rapkin, 1987).

Finally, Montemayor (1983) reported that, relative to preadolescent years, there is an increase in conflict between parents and children when they reach adolescence. This conflict is reported to be severe in 15% to 20% of families. Of importance, such conflict has been associated with delinquency, running away, and drug use (Montemayor, 1983).

Not only do adolescents experience the unique stressors noted above but Hill (1980) indicated that parental personal distress (e.g., increased marital and job dissatisfaction) usually occurs during the first born child's early adolescent years. Therefore, a young teenager may not have his parents' full resources available to help buffer him/her against the stressors of adolescence.

Although adolescents do experience unique stressors, which are associated with aggressive and other problem behaviors, it is important to note that aggression typically has its genesis much earlier in life. Eron (1988), Olweus (1979), and Loeber (1982) indicated that this behavior pattern starts in the preschool years. Loeber and Schmaling (1985) pointed out that noncompliance to parental commands in the preschool years is the keystone behavior for the development of further aggressive-type behaviors. From a meta-analysis of studies examining antisocial behavior, these authors delineated the sequential development of aggressive-type problem behaviors, beginning with noncompliance and followed by behaviors such as being sassy, blaming others, swearing, and so forth. Furthermore, Patterson (1988) and Forehand and Long (1988) have both outlined the social conditions associated with this sequential development: Noncompliance to parental commands, coercive parent-child interactions, coercive peer interactions, rejection by peers who accept societal norms, rejection of societal norms, and formation of delinquent gangs. Therefore, while certain types of aggressive behaviors and other problems may accelerate during adolescence, such behavior typically has its roots much earlier in life.

If the aggressive behavior pattern has its beginnings in the preschool years and is stable, then a critical question concerns when the treatment of such behaviors should occur. A number of investigators (Eron, 1988; Forgatch, 1988) have recently suggested that earlier intervention is more effective than later intervention. By intervening in the preschool years, noncompliant children who are at risk for later aggression will have had less time to thoroughly develop patterns of such behavior, will be less likely to be in contact with aggressive peers who may help maintain such behavior, and will be less likely to develop other problem behaviors (i.e., poor school achievement) that frequently accompany aggression.

Early prevention measures would appear to be one potentially important method for reducing adolescent aggressive behavior given that aggression is a relatively stable behavior pattern which develops early and later treatment is more difficult than earlier treatment. One research effort described in this chapter involved the delineation of a treatment program for noncompliant preschoolers and the examination of how these children functioned some $7\frac{1}{2}$ years later during early adolescence.

Nevertheless, it obviously is not always possible to intervene in the initial stages of the development of aggression. In these cases one can still implement preventive strategies in the early adolescent years by identifying environmental factors that can serve to buffer these young people against stressors, and, thus potentially reduce the occurrence of aggressive and other problem behaviors. As an example of our efforts in this area, we delineate some of our research findings with adolescents whose parents have recently divorced. Our data suggest that there are family factors which can promote resiliency (i.e., reduce problem behaviors and increase cognitive/academic functioning) in the presence of this stressor.

Before turning to our two research efforts, we should note that, while one of our primary concerns is with aggression, defined in a broad sense, we do not see such behavior as occurring in isolation from other behaviors. Furthermore, we believe that limiting one's efforts to a problem-focused approach in studying children and adolescents is often inadequate. As a consequence, although our focus has been on measures that can be broadly conceptualized as assessing aggression, other problem behaviors, as well as prosocial behaviors, are also examined.

TREATMENT OF EARLY NONCOMPLIANCE TO PREVENT ADOLESCENT PROBLEMS

As noted earlier, noncompliance has been identified as a keystone behavior for the development of other acting out, aggressive types of behaviors (Loeber & Schmaling, 1985; Patterson, 1982). Therefore, noncompliance would appear to be a critical variable that can be targeted for treatment in order to prevent future aggressive type behaviors during the adolescent years.

Once noncompliance has been identified as a treatment target, one is faced with identifying the best possible treatment for this behavior. In a comprehensive review of treatment for antisocial and aggressive behavior, Kazdin (1985) reviewed all available treatment strategies. These included: individual and group therapy, family therapy, behavior therapy, parent-management training, cognitive therapy, and pharmacological intervention. Based on his systematic review, Kazdin concluded that parent-management training is the best documented treatment and the most promising procedure for antisocial behavior. Therefore, based on such evidence, we describe a research effort that examined the use of a parent-training program to modify noncompliance in young children (ages 3–7) who were referred to a clinic for the treatment of noncompliance to parental directions.

We have previously reported substantial data supporting the effectiveness of the treatment program. For example, the children referred for treatment are more noncompliant than nonreferred ("normal") children prior to treatment but after treatment the two groups do not differ (e.g., Forehand, Wells, & Griest, 1980). Furthermore, we have reported data indicating that those who receive treatment improve significantly more than a clinic-referred waiting list control group of noncompliant children (Peed, Roberts, & Forehand, 1977). Of particular importance, with the implementation of our treatment program, there is generalization across siblings, behaviors, and time (up to 3 years) (see Forehand & McMahon, 1981; McMahon & Forehand, 1984, for reviews). In the present research effort, as was noted previously, we examine how children who have previously participated in this program are functioning during their adolescence, an average of 7½ years later.

The assessment and treatment program, which has been described in detail by Forehand and McMahon (1981), includes home observations of the parent–child interactions, parent-completed questionnaires concerning the child's functioning, and use of a 10-session treatment program. In the initial treatment sessions, parents are taught positive reinforcement skills which include attending to the child (without giving commands and asking questions) and learning to praise appropriate behavior. Subsequently, parents are taught skills to utilize in order to ignore minor deviant behaviors (e.g., temper tantrums). Next, they are taught to issue clear, simple, straightforward directions and, when the child complies, to praise such compliance. When noncompliance follows appropriate directions, the parent is taught to use a time-out procedure which involves placing the child in a chair for a brief (3 minutes) period of time.

The skills are taught in a systematic format, which involves explaining each skill to the parent, modelling for the parent how to use the skill, having the parent roleplay the skill with a therapist, and having the parent practice the skill with the child and receive feedback from the therapist. Finally, substantial discussion of ways to generalize the skills to the home occurs.

From the sample of children and parents who had participated in the program, 43 were in the early adolescent age range (11 to 14 years) at the time this follow-up project was undertaken. These adolescents and their parents had completed treatment, on the average, 7½ years earlier (range 4½–10½ years). Of this sample, 21 were contacted and agreed to participate. The reasons for the nonparticipation of the remaining 22 were as follows: (a) letter returned by post office and unable to subsequently locate family ($n = 7$); (b) letter not returned by post office but never heard from family and unable to locate ($n = 6$); (c) contacted but declined to participate ($n = 6$); (d) adolescent in psychiatric hospital ($n = 1$); and (e) agreed only to complete questionnaires through the mail but never returned them ($n = 2$).

Analyses indicated that the participants and nonparticipants did not differ on demographic variables (age of child and socioeconomic status of the family) or pre-treatment measures, such as rate of child compliance and rate of deviant behavior. However, they did differ on one post-treatment measure: The families who participated had children who were more compliant than those who did not participate.

In order to have a comparison sample and to determine whether the previously treated noncompliant children were now functioning in the "normal range," a non-clinic sample was also utilized in the present project. This sample consisted of adolescents who had never been referred for treatment of behavioral/psychological problems and who were matched with the 21 parent-training participants on sex and age of child and socioeconomic status of family.

Participants were assessed on measures designed to examine the functioning of the child in four areas: externalizing problems, internalizing problems, cognitive competence, and prosocial competence. It is important to note that aggressive behaviors are the primary characteristic of externalizing problems. We chose to examine not only this type of problem but the other three categories as well because, as was noted earlier, aggressive behaviors rarely occur in isolation. Not only did we assess four areas of functioning but we assessed these from multiple perspectives, including the mother, father, adolescent, teacher, and behavioral observers. Data from the observers were obtained from a problem-solving situation in which the mother and adolescent attempted to resolve an issue when they identified as being problematic for them.

The measures used in our assessment are presented in Table 12.1[1]. The parent-training participants and the comparison group were compared on each of the measures delineated in Table 12.1 using analysis of variance statistical procedures. The primary findings will be summarized here; the reader interested in more detail should refer to Forehand and Long (1988).

---

[1]All questionnaires utilized in this project are standardized instruments. Information can be obtained about the reliability and validity from the first author. Reliability on the behavioral observation measures was above .85 for adolescent-initiated conflict, for adolescent positive communication, and for adolescent social problem-solving skills.

TABLE 12.1
Measures in Each Area of Adolescent Functioning

Areas	*Instruments*	*Completed By*
Externalizing Problems	Issues Checklist-Number of Issues	Mother, Father, Adolescent
	Issues Checklist-Intensity of Discussion	Mother, Father, Adolescent
	Conflict Behavior Questionnaire	Mother, Father, Adolescent
	Revised Behavior Problem Checklist-Conduct Disorder	Mother, Father, Teacher
	Revised Behavior Problem Checklist-Socialized Aggression	Mother, Father, Teacher
	Revised Behavior Problem Checklist-Attention Problems/Immaturity	Mother, Father, Teacher
	Observational Rating of Adolescent Conflict	Independent Observer
Internalizing Problems	Child Depression Inventory	Adolescent
	Revised Behavior Problem Checklist-Anxiety/Withdrawal	Mother, Father, Teacher
Prosocial Skills	Perceived Competence Scale for Children-Social	Adolescent
	Rating Scale of Child's Actual Competence-Social	Mother, Father, Teacher
	Observational Rating of Adolescent Social Problem Solving	Independent Observer
	Observational Rating of Adolescent Positive Communication	Independent Observer
Cognitive Skills	Perceived Competence Scale for Children-Cognitive	Adolescent
	Rating Scale of Child's Actual Competence-Cognitive	Mother, Father, Teacher
	Grade Point Average	------------------------------------

First, our assessment of externalizing problems, which includes aggressive-type behaviors, can be considered in several different categories: specific parent–adolescent issues (Issues Checklist), global perceptions of the parent–adolescent relationship (Conflict Behavior Questionnaire), specific areas of adolescent psychopathology (Revised Behavior Problem Checklist), and behavior observations of adolescent-initiated conflict. Nonsignificant differences between the parent training and comparison groups emerged for all of the comparisons involving specific parent–adolescent issues. However, when more global perceptions were examined, both mothers and fathers in the parent-training group perceived their relationship with their adolescent as being less satisfactory than did the comparison group. In contrast, the adolescent-completed measure of their relationship with each parent did not differ for the two groups. For the nine comparisons involving specific areas of psychopathology, there was only one significant difference: Teachers reported that adolescents in the parent-training group had more attention problems than did those in the comparison group. Finally, behavior observation measures of adolescent-initiated conflict with his/her mother indicated nonsignificant differences between the two age groups.

Turning to the other three areas of assessment, four comparisons were made involving internalizing problems. Only the teacher-completed anxiety–withdrawal measure indicated a significant difference between groups: The parent training group had higher scores than the comparison group. For the prosocial measures, nonsignificant differences emerged between the two groups for all six of the comparisons. Finally, for the cognitive measures, significant differences emerged for two of the five comparisons: Adolescents in the parent-training group (a) had a lower grade point average and (b) were perceived by their fathers as functioning lower in cognitive competence than the comparison group.

These findings suggest that, with a parenting intervention, noncompliance in an early identified group of problem children did not progress to more serious forms of aggressive behavior in adolescence. In almost all areas of functioning, these young adolescents were doing as well as the nonclinic comparison group, as few significant group differences emerged relative to the number of comparisons which were made. However, the present study does suggest some concern for the adolescents who had been earlier identified and treated for noncompliance.

First, parents who had previously participated in treatment perceived their relationship with their adolescents as poorer than did those in the comparison group. This occurred although there were no differences between the two groups when specific parent–adolescent issues were examined. This finding suggests the need to address parent perceptions as part of parent training. Focusing only on parenting techniques to change child behavior may be insufficient. Second, although only one significant difference emerged for the measures of specific psychopathology, there were nonsignificant differences favoring the comparison group. These differences should, at a minimum, make us cautious about how well the previous participants in parent training are functioning.

Third, the academic differences between the parent training participants and the comparison group are particularly noteworthy. Lower grades, taken in conjunction with the attention problems indicated by the teachers in the measures of specific areas of psychopathology, suggest that parent training specifically for aggressive-type behavior may be insufficient to circumvent problems in some other settings or areas of functioning. Rather, a broader intervention that directly involves the school and that may involve teaching parents how to work with the school and monitor homework and school performance would appear to be needed. In actuality this conclusion is not surprising as our earlier work (Breiner & Forehand, 1981; Forehand, Sturgis, McMahon, Aguar, Green, Wells, & Breiner, 1979) had suggested that parent training effects do not generalize to the school setting immediately after treatment; therefore, generalization to this setting some $7\frac{1}{2}$ years later would probably not be expected.

It is also important to note that there were experimental limitations with the data reported above. The absence of a clinic-referred no-treatment control group (which is not ethical or feasible over a 5–10 year period) and the occurrence of attrition, particularly the selective attrition rate in which follow-up participants were more compliant at post-treatment than nonparticipants, are the most obvious limitations. Also, in reviewing the long term impact of early interventions, Woodhead (1988) recently noted that any conclusions must be limited by the context (e.g., the setting and era) in which the effort occurred. Nevertheless, these shortcomings not withstanding, this study, to the best of our knowledge, represents one of the first attempts to assess the long-term preventive effects of a behavioral program for young children at risk for adolescent aggression.

Based on the data presented above, a primary question is the following: How successful is an early intervention program for young noncompliant children in preventing aggressive and other problem behaviors of young adolescents? The answer, in our opinion, can best be characterized as "moderate" success. Considering the length of time since intervention, the stability of aggressive-type behaviors that is typically reported, and the thoroughness of our assessment across various areas of functioning, we believe this conclusion is basically a positive one.

BUFFERING AGAINST STRESSORS DURING ADOLESCENCE

The second line of preventive research that we have undertaken involves the search for buffers against stressors that young adolescents may experience. One such stress is parental divorce, which has been associated with aggressive-type behaviors and other problems (for reviews see Atkeson, Forehand, & Rickard, 1982; Long & Forehand, 1987). Part of our present research, which is being conducted with 150 young adolescents from intact families and 150 adolescents from recently divorced families (within the past 12 months), is attempting to identify family factors that may prevent or minimize problems when an adolescent's parents divorce. The data thus far suggest two such buffers.

Interparental conflict has been identified as being a primary factor in child and adolescent problems following parental divorce (Emery, 1982; Long & Forehand, 1987). Some of our data suggest that, when divorce is associated with a reduction in parental conflict, adolescents function as well as those from intact families on externalizing or aggressive problems, internalizing problems, and academic grades; however, if a high level of conflict continues from pre- to post-divorce, there is an elevated level of problems in each of these three areas as indicated in Fig. 12.1.[2]

A second factor which has been suggested as a potential buffer against the negative influences of divorce is that a child or adolescent maintain a good relationship with the parents (Camara & Resnick, 1987; Long & Forehand, 1987). Some of our data, as depicted in Fig. 12.2, indicate that, when an adolescent can maintain a good relationship with both parents following divorce, his/her adjustment in terms of externalizing problems, internalizing problems, and cognitive functioning is similar to that of adolescents from intact families where the adolescent has a good relationship with both parents. However, when a poor relationship exists with both parents following divorce, there is a higher level of occurrence of problems in all three areas.

Thus, data from these two research efforts indicate that aggressive type problems, as well as other problems that sometimes accompany aggression, can be minimized during the post-divorce period by the interpersonal relationship between parents and by the relationship between the parents and the adolescent. Each of these two family factors may serve as a buffer (i.e., serve as a specific resource to counter the negative effects of divorce) or, alternately, as a more general marker variable of a source of resiliency during stress. The mechanisms for how these variables operate to protect young adolescents still need to be explored. Also, it is unclear at this time how likely either factor is to exist with or without therapeutic intervention. For example, can parents divorce without conflict? Or, can interventions help parents maintain a good relationship with their adolescent while undergoing the emotional stresses of a divorce?

[2]Further details on the measures and statistical analyses for the data in Figs. 12.1 and 12.2 are available from the first author or may be obtained from the following research reports: Long, Slater, Forehand, and Fauber (1988) and Wierson, Forehand, Fauber and McCombs (1988).

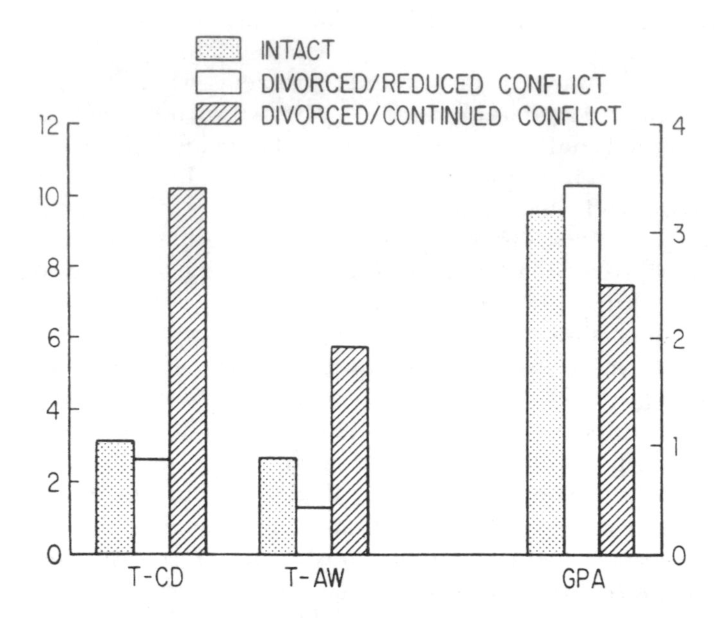

FIG. 12.1. Mean scores for each of three groups (Intact, Divorced with Reduced Interparental Conflict, Divorced with Continued Interparental Conflict) on the teacher-completed Conduct Disorder (T-CD) and Anxiety–Withdrawal (T-AW) scales of the Revised Behavior Problem Checklist and Grade Point Average (GPA). The mean scores for the three groups for the first two measures are reflected on the left horizontal axis whereas those for GPA are reflected on the right horizontal axis. For T-CD and T-AW higher scores reflect greater behavior problems. For GPA higher scores reflect better academic performance (4-point GPA scale).

CONCLUSIONS

As we have noted, early adolescence is a stressful period that can be associated with an acceleration of problem behaviors including aggression. We have presented data from two different research efforts that indicate that aggression and other problems of the young adolescent years can be prevented through the modification of family variables. Our parent-training efforts in the preschool years appear to be encouraging

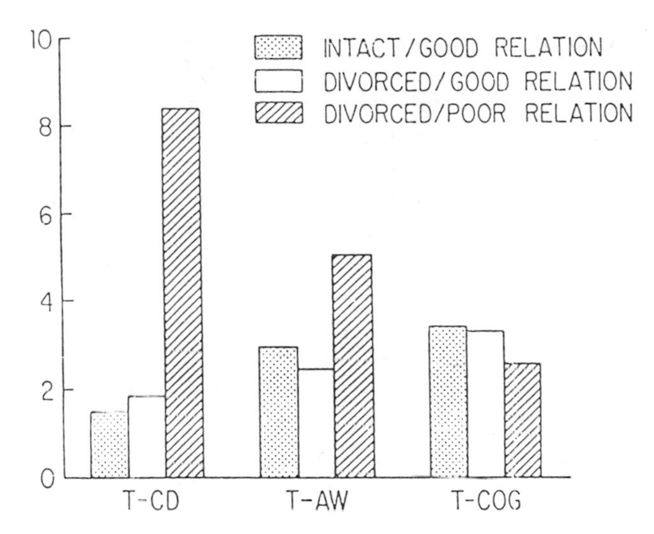

FIG. 12.2. Mean scores for each of three groups (Intact/Good Relation with Both Parents, Divorced/Good Relation with Both Parents, Divorced/Poor Relation with Both Parents) on the teacher-completed Conduct Disorder (T-CD) and Anxiety–Withdrawal (TAW) scales of the Revised Behavior Problem Checklist and the teacher-completed Cognitive subscale (T-COG) of the Rating Scale of Child's Actual Competence. For T-CD and T-AW higher scores reflect greater behavior problems. For T-COG higher scores reflect higher ratings of cognitive competence.

and at least moderately successful in preventing adolescent problems. Because aggressive behavior is relatively stable and becomes more difficult to treat with increasing age, it appears practical and economical to develop intervention programs for application during the preschool years, which may successfully reduce such problem behaviors and thus prevent adolescents from engaging in aggressive and delinquent type behaviors. Considering the cost to society of such behaviors by adolescents, early prevention appears to be both economically important for society as well as desirable for the individual and his/her family. However, one is faced with the dilemma of deciding which children should be identified for such early treatment in the preschool years. Based on the literature now available (e.g., Loeber & Schmaling, 1985), it appears that noncompliance is a key indicator of the need for such early intervention for a particular child.

Nevertheless, many young children who manifest noncompliant behavior will not receive treatment. Furthermore, some other children may not be noncompliant in the preschool years but may begin to demonstrate problems at a later age. Once both of these types of children reach adolescence, it is important to identify factors which may help them overcome some of the stressful events they will face, thus facilitating their functioning. Our second research effort reported in this chapter indicates, at least for one stressor (divorce), that there are family factors that can serve to make the adolescent more resilient. The two factors identified in our efforts, reduced interparental conflict and a good relationship with both parents, appear to be ones that counselors, ministers, teachers, pediatricians, and others who do preventive work with parents and children may wish to include in their efforts with divorcing parents. Also, awareness of the significance of these family factors appears to be important for therapists who develop and implement intervention programs for adolescents from divorced families who are experiencing aggressive problems and other difficulties.

A worthwhile goal for researchers interested in aggression and other problem behaviors of children and adolescents would be to focus on the identification of buffers for other stressors that adolescents experience. Of primary importance is the identification of factors that can potentially be modified. This will hopefully lead to the development of effective intervention programs. With such efforts we then will be in a better position to help our young people cope successfully with some of the difficulties that may be facing them during these formidable years.

ACKNOWLEDGMENTS

The preparation of this chapter was supported, in part, by the William T. Grant Foundation and the University of Georgia's Institute for Behavioral Research.

REFERENCES

Achenbach, T. M., & Edelbrock, C. S. (1981). Behavioral problems and competencies reported by parents of normal and disturbed children aged 4 through 16. *Monographs of the Society for Research in Child Development, 46,* (Serial No. 188).

Atkeson, B. M., Forehand, R., & Rickard, K. M. (1982). The effects of divorce on children. In B. B. Lahey & A. E. Kazdin (Eds.), *Advances in clinical child psychology (Vol. 5)* (pp. 255–281). New York: Plenum.

Breiner, J. L., & Forehand, R. (1981). An assessment of the effects of parent training on clinic-referred children's school behavior. *Behavioral Assessment, 3,* 31–42.

Camara, K. A., & Resnick, G. (1987). Marital and parental subsystems in mother-custody, father-custody and two-parent households: Effects on children's social development. In J. Vincent (Ed.), *Advances in family assessment, intervention and research. (Vol. 4)* (pp. 165–196). Greenwich, CT: JAI Press.

Emery, R. E. (1982). Interparental conflict and the children of discord and divorce. *Psychological Bulletin, 92,* 310–330.

Eron, L. D. (1988). *Relation of parental rejection and nurturance to child aggression.* Paper presented at Earlscourt Symposium on Childhood Aggression, Toronto, Ontario.

Forehand, R. (in press). Early adolescent functioning: Stressors, psychological problems, and the role of family factors. In R. J. McMahon & R. Dev. Peters (Eds.), *Behavior disorders of adolescence: Research, intervention, and policy in clinical and school settings.* New York: Plenum.

Forehand, R., & Long, N. (1988). Outpatient treatment of the acting out child: Procedures, long term follow-up data, and clinical problems. *Advances in Behaviour Research and Therapy, 10,* 129–177.

Forehand, R., & McMahon, R. J. (1981). *Helping the noncompliant child: A clinician's guide to effective parent training.* New York: Guilford.

Forehand, R., Sturgis, E. T., McMahon, R. J., Aguar, D., Green, K., Wells, K., & Breiner, J. (1979). Parent behavioral training to modify child noncompliance: Treatment generalization across time and from home to school. *Behavior Modification, 3,* 3–25.

Forehand, R., Wells, K. C., & Griest, D. L. (1980). An examination of the social validity of a parent training program. *Behavior Therapy, 11,* 488–502.

Forgatch, M. S. (1988). *The relation between child behavior, client resistance, and parenting practices.* Paper presented at the Earlscourt Symposium on Childhood Aggression. Toronto, Ontario.

Gold, M., & Petronio, R. J. (1980). Delinquent behavior in adolescence. In J. Adelson (Ed.), *Handbook of adolescent psychology.* (pp. 495–535). New York: John Wiley and Sons.

Hill, J. P. (1980). The family. In M. Johnson (Ed.), *Toward adolescence: The middle school years* (pp. 31–55). The Seventy-Ninth Yearbook of the National Society for the Study of Education. Chicago: University of Chicago Press.

Hirsch, B. J., & Rapkin, B. D. (1987). The transition to junior high school: A longitudinal study of self-esteem, psychological symptomatology, school life, and social support. *Child Development, 58,* 1235–1243.

Inoff-Germain, G., Arnold, G. S., Nottelmann, E. D., Susman, E. J., Cutler, G. B., Jr., & Chrousos, G. P. (1988). Relations between hormone levels and observational measures of aggressive behavior of young adolescents in family interactions. *Developmental Psychology, 24,* 129–139.

Kazdin, A. E. (1985). *Treatment of antisocial behavior in children and adolescents.* Homewood, IL: The Dorsey Press.

Loeber, R. (1982). The stability of antisocial and delinquent child behavior: A review. *Child Development, 53,* 1431–1466.

Loeber, R., & Schmaling, K. B. (1985). Empirical evidence for overt and covert patterns of antisocial conduct problems: A metaanalysis. *Journal of Abnormal Child Psychology, 13,* 337–352.

Long, N., & Forehand, R. (1987). The effects of parental divorce and parental conflict on children: An overview. *Journal of Developmental and Behavioral Pediatrics, 8,* 292–296.

Long, N., Slater, E., Forehand, R., & Fauber, R. (1988). Continued high or reduced interparental conflict following divorce: Relation to young adolescent adjustment. *Journal of Consulting and Clinical Psychology, 56,* 467–469.

McMahon, R. J., & Forehand, R. (1984). Parent training for the noncompliant child: Treatment outcome, generalization, and adjunctive therapy procedures. In R. F. Dangel & R. A. Polster (Eds.), *Behavioral parent training: Issues in research and practice.* (pp. 298–328). New York: Guilford.

Montemayor, R. (1983). Parents and adolescents in conflict: All families some of the time and some families most of the time. *Journal of Early Adolescence, 3,* 83–103.

Olweus, D. (1979). Stability of aggressive reaction patterns in males: A review. *Psychological Bulletin, 86,* 852–875.

Patterson, G. R. (1982). *Coercive family process (Vol. 3).* Eugene, OR: Castalia.

Patterson, G. R. (1988). *Factors relating to stability and changes in children's aggressive behavior over time.* Paper presented at the Earlscourt Symposium on Childhood Aggression, Toronto, Ontario.

Peed, S., Roberts, M., & Forehand, R. (1977). Evaluation of the effectiveness of a standardized parent training program in altering the interaction of mothers and their non-compliant children. *Behavior Modification, 1,* 323–350.

Petersen, A. C. (1987). Those gangly years. *Psychology Today, 21*(9), 28–34.

Steinberg, L. (1987). Impact of puberty on family relations: Effects of pubertal status and pubertal timing. *Developmental Psychology, 23,* 451–460.

Wierson, M., Forehand, R., Fauber, R., & McCombs, A. (1988). *Buffering adolescents against negative parental divorce influences: The role of good parent–adolescent relations.* Unpublished manuscript.

Woodhead, M. (1988). When psychology informs public policy: The case of early childhood intervention. *American Psychologist, 43,* 443–454.

Commentary

From Simplicity to Complexity: Parent Training Is Coming of Age

Jean E. Dumas
University of Montreal

Parent training is coming of age, as Forehand and Forgatch's work illustrates so clearly. Their chapters reflect the growing maturity of the field of parent training, which has clearly established itself over the past 20 years as a major contributor to the understanding and remediation of childhood behavior problems. When I first read Forehand and Forgatch's papers and began to reflect on this coming of age, I experienced what I can only describe as mixed feelings, something which we were once told behaviorally-oriented researchers and clinicians were not meant to experience (or, at least, should keep to themselves). On the one hand, I felt very positive about the maturity of our field. More specifically, I was amazed by Forehand and Forgatch's tenacity and determination. They and their colleagues have not spent the last 20 years dabbling in different research areas, as dictated by fashion or funding priorities. Rather, they have consistently studied the development and treatment of antisocial behavior, providing us with a good example of the power of very thin intermittent schedules of reinforcement in the control of researchers' behavior. The knowledge that their persistence has brought is clearly reflected in the richness and complexity of their contributions here. On the other hand, I was unable to suppress feelings of disappointment that no more progress had been accomplished in what appears to me to be a very long time. How much have we learned in 20 years about the development and treatment of antisocial behavior? At the risk of offending them, I must ask Forgatch and Forehand: Twenty years of hard work and all you have to show for it is a mathematical model that looks like a black dress, or that parent training may not only serve to treat conduct disorder children but also to prevent the development of delinquency in adolescence? To avoid the easy trap of cynicism, consider where parent training research started and where it may now take us, following the leads provided by colleagues such as Forehand and Forgatch.

Where Did We Start?

Parent training is a generic term that describes a number of empirically-derived therapeutic approaches based on the premise that a child's behavior, whether normal or dysfunctional, cannot be considered as an entity apart from the social system in which he/she interacts, and that the focus of therapy should be at the level of the system itself, rather than at the level of the child alone. More specifically, parent training assumes that a child's dysfunctional behavior is learned and sustained by the positive and negative attention the child receives from social agents, parents in particular; it seeks to establish a shift in social contingencies such that prosocial behaviors obtain positive parental reinforcement and aversive behaviors are consistently punished or ignored (Dumas, 1989).

Parent training was one of the many early therapeutic applications of operant psychology. As is well known, operant psychology is based on the premise that behavior is a function of the contingencies of reinforcement and punishment to which an organism is exposed in the course of daily exchanges with the environment. To quote Skinner: "The simplest contingencies involve at least three terms—stimulus, response, and reinforcer—and at least one other variable (the deprivation associated with the reinforcer) is implied" (1966, p. xii). The three-term contingency provides a means of identifying systematic covariations between a child or a parent's behavior and the environment in which they function and to use these covariations to develop a behavioral intervention.

There is considerable evidence to show that parent training can be effective in changing dysfunctional parent–child interactions in general, and antisocial child behavior in particular (Dumas, 1989; Kazdin, 1987). Specifically, studies that have made use of multiple outcome measures to evaluate effectiveness have shown that positive results of parent training are commonly reflected in records collected by parents at home, standardized questionnaires completed by parents and, to a lesser degree, independent home observations. Despite such evidence, however, several studies have been unable to obtain significant treatment gains or to insure that these gains are maintained over time (e.g., Bernal, Klinnert, & Schultz, 1980; Eyberg & Johnson, 1974; Wahler, 1980). Considerable work conducted in recent years indicates that the effectiveness of parent training may be related to factors that are outside the immediate parent–child relationship, such as a parent's personal or marital adjustment or a family's socioeconomic status or social isolation (Dumas, 1989). This work shows clearly that, although all families are supposed to be equal when it comes to parent training, some families may be more equal than others. Consider the relation that has often been reported between a family's socioeconomic and socioemotional adjustment and its chances of benefiting from parent training.

Dumas and Wahler (1983) reported two identical studies of 67 families who had taken part in a standardized parent training program. Prior to treatment, scores on several measures of socioeconomic disadvantage and social isolation or "insularity" were obtained for each family. These measures formed the basis of two indices of material and social stress. Treatment effectiveness was assessed at a one-year follow-up on the basis of behavioral home observations. In each study, results indicated a steady increase in the probability of treatment failure in the presence of disadvantage, isolation, or both. A discriminant analysis model including the two indices as predictor variables accounted for 49% of the variance in outcome and classified over 80% of the families correctly. These results have since been confirmed in separate studies of different parent training programs (Dumas, 1984; Webster-Stratton, 1985). Comparable results can be found in Wahler (1980) and Wahler and Dumas (1987), who suggested that the association between socioeconomic adversity and treatment outcome may be functional rather than merely correlational. Both studies assessed treatment effectiveness through home observations before and during treatment and at a one-year follow-up. In each, mothers showed significant improvements in their childrearing skills from baseline to treatment. However, in all families, these skills returned to their baseline level at follow-up. In another, apparently conflicting study, Baum and Forehand (1981) reported 1- to 4½-year maintenance of treatment gains in a sample of families who had participated in another standardized program. Although direct comparisons between studies are not possible, it should be noted that only one of the 34 families studied by Baum and Forehand was described as receiving welfare. In contrast, all families studied by Wahler (1980) and Wahler and Dumas (1987) subsisted on extremely low incomes and presented multiple problems besides their children's behavioral difficulties. To illustrate, Wahler and Dumas worked with six families whose incomes averaged $5,400 per year. All of them were coerced into treatment by social service agencies following abuse/neglect charges brought against the parents. Only two mothers were married and one had completed high school. Children ranged in age from 4 to 12. Their referral problems included noncompliance, property destruction, and stealing (six children), physical assault (five children—ranging in severity from fist fights and use of dangerous objects to sexual molestation and killing one person), and drug use (two children). Their mothers described themselves as experiencing frequent depression and anger and reported chronic verbal threats and arguments with extended family members, spouse or boyfriend, social service agents, and neighbors (six mothers), physical violence by spouse or boyfriend (five mothers), and significant health problems (four mothers—including Lupus, cancer, and heart dysfunctions). The fact that these highly disadvantaged mothers did demonstrate significant behavior changes in the course of intervention but a return to baseline at follow-up suggests that their behavior may have been under the control of powerful contextual contingencies that intervention was only capable to override temporarily.

Many therapists who have worked with similar families have experienced the same failure. Looking back, it is easy to see that my colleagues and I must have been naive in our attempts to help these multiproblem families by focusing only on the immediate relationship between mothers and their problem children. Somehow, it was like trying to keep the Titanic afloat with paper tape. So what have we learned from our failures?

Enters Complexity

Consider again Skinner's quote mentioned earlier. As I emphasized elsewhere (Dumas, in press), Skinner illustrated the power of the operant model with relatively simple behavioral contingencies observed under highly controlled laboratory conditions. However, the model does not a priori limit the study of contingencies to simple covariations between easily definable and measurable behaviors that take place in the same setting and follow each other closely in time. It is in several applications of the model, including a large number of parent training studies, that researchers and clinicians have focused almost exclusively on the measurement and manipulation of narrowly defined contingencies and failed to describe and account for the *context* in which these contingencies are embedded. In other words, applied operant research has generally ignored the context in which human behavior is exhibited and, in the process, has acted as if all contingencies involved three terms only. Although Skinner was aware that matters are always more complex when he stated that a fourth term is necessarily "implied" in even the simplest contingencies, Forehand and Forgatch's work illustrates clearly that this fourth term cannot simply be treated as a background variable of secondary importance. It must be made explicit, by becoming an integral part of our studies.

If we allow ourselves to consider the fourth term of the operant contingency, we allow complexity to enter our working models. And not any complexity, but rather one that will radically change the nature of our work. The challenge of the papers prepared by Forehand and Forgatch is that they invite us to embrace complexity in our research and interventions, and, like any good experimenter, to quantify, to measure it.

Consider briefly Forehand's paper. He says most honestly that his preliminary attempts to use parent training as a means of preventing behavioral problems in adolescence has been moderately successful. As is often the case in longitudinal research, interpretation of the results is limited by high levels of subject attrition over time. Important questions obviously remain, such as: What are the contextual effects that allow some families to benefit from the intervention, whereas others apparently do not? The work that Forehand and his colleagues are doing on buffers of stress in adolescence, and the methodology they have developed in their recent studies should provide a useful model to evaluate potential buffers of failure in parent training.

Turning our attention to Forgatch's work, the study she reports sought to rely on a treatment manipulation to obtain experimental evidence that would support the Basic Black model which, although derived from a causal analytic procedure, is essentially correlational in nature. The experimental rationale is clear and logical, and represents an elegant progression from basic descriptive and explanatory research to applied intervention for the purpose of hypothesis testing and model development. The results reported in this study are tentative at this time, however, as the author readily acknowledges. Specifically, I must question the criteria used to define treatment effectiveness. To demonstrate that a treatment procedure is effective, two conditions should be met:

1. Demonstrate that the children who were offered the treatment actually needed it. And this the author does. Children were only selected if they scored above the clinical cutoff on four subscales of the CBCL and obtained a TAB score of .5SD above the normal mean for their age group.

2. Demonstrate that, following treatment, these children were no longer presenting problems of clinical intensity. And this I am not sure the author has shown, as a child was said to have successfully completed the program if he obtained a TAB score at termination that was less than .5SD above the mean. Indeed, one could expect children to move from more to less than .5SD above this mean by chance alone, and not neces-

sarily as a results of treatment, as even a small decrease in TAB (e.g., from .6 to .4SD above the mean) would qualify as a "success".

And then, of course, there is a matter of context, of which I am sure Forgatch is well aware. We need to put the Basic Black model in context, as evidence indicates that a parent's ability to discipline a child appropriately and monitor his/her behavior consistently are themselves influenced by contextual variables that do not involve the child directly, such as maternal social isolation (Dumas, 1986) or depressive symptomatology (Dumas, Gibson, & Albin, 1989).

The two models proposed in Forehand and Forgatch's studies meet two of the most important criteria of scientific acceptability: They are parsimonious yet comprehensive, and they make predictions that are open to empirical investigation. For too long, unfortunately, a third criterion of acceptability has been uncritically followed in the field of parent training, one of simplicity. Forehand and Forgatch's work says it loud and clear: It isn't simple, probably because human behavior is not simple. The first 20 years of parent training have certainly shattered the dream, if there was ever one, of a simple answer to a complex problem. If work in this area is to progress, we will have to adopt complex methodologies such as Forgatch's causal modeling or Forehand's longitudinal bridge building across two different age groups. But beyond increased methodological sophistication, the field of parent training must be willing to question the theoretical assumptions that have guided work in this area for two decades. There are more than three terms to the contingencies that control our behavior or that of dysfunctional families. And so the challenge lies in our ability, not merely to do better what others have already done, but also to examine the assumptions that underlie the manner in which we ask questions and seek to answer them. The comforting thought, if you refuse to be a cynic, is that surely there is enough work for everyone for many years to come.

ACKNOWLEDGMENTS

Preparation of this chapter was supported by grants from the William T. Grant Foundation and the Medical Research Council of Canada.

REFERENCES

Baum, C. G., & Forehand, R. (1981). Long-term follow-up assessment of parent training by use of multiple outcome measures. *Behavior Therapy, 12,* 643–652.

Bernal, M. E., Klinnert, M. D., & Schultz, L. A. (1980). Outcome evaluation of behavioral parent training and client-centered parent counseling for children with conduct problems. *Journal of Applied Behavior Analysis, 13,* 677–691.

Dumas, J. E. (1984). Child, adult-interactional, and socioeconomic setting events as predictors of parent training outcome. *Education and Treatment of Children, 7,* 351–364.

Dumas, J. E. (1986). Indirect influence of maternal social contacts on mother–child interactions: A setting event analysis. *Journal of Abnormal Child Psychology, 14,* 205–216.

Dumas, J. E. (1989). Treating antisocial behavior in children: Child and family approaches. *Clinical Psychology Review, 9,* 197–222.

Dumas, J. E. (in press). Contextual effects in mother–child interaction. Beyond an operant analysis. In E. A. Blechman & M. J. McEnroe (Eds.), *For better or for worse: How families influence emotions and health.* Hillsdale, NJ: Lawrence Erlbaum Associates.

Dumas, J. E., Gibson, J. A., & Albin, J. B. (1989). Behavioral correlates of maternal depressive symptomatology in conduct disorder children. *Journal of Consulting and Clinical Psychology, 57,* 516–521.

Dumas, J. E., & Wahler, R. G. (1983). Predictors of treatment outcome in parent training: Mother insularity and socioeconomic disadvantage. *Behavioral Assessment, 5,* 301–313.

Eyberg, S. M., & Johnson, S. M. (1974). Multiple assessment of behavior modification with families: Effects of contingency contracting and order of treated problems. *Journal of Consulting and Clinical Psychology, 42,* 594–606.

Kazdin, A. E. (1987). Treatment of antisocial behavior in children: Current status and future directions. *Psychological Bulletin, 102,* 187–203.

Skinner, B. F. (1966). Preface to the seventh printing of *The behavior of organisms. An experimental analysis.* New York: Appleton-Century-Crofts.

Wahler, R. G. (1980). The insular mother: Her problems in parent–child treatment. *Journal of Applied Behavior Analysis, 13,* 207–219.

Wahler, R. G., & Dumas, J. E. (1987). Stimulus class determinants of mother–child coercive interchanges in multi-distressed families: Assessment and intervention. In J. D. Burchard & S. N. Burchard (Eds.), *Prevention of delinquent behavior* (pp. 190–219). Newbury Park, CA: Sage.

Webster-Stratton, C. (1985). Predictors of treatment outcome in parent training for conduct disordered children. *Behavior Therapy, 16,* 223–243.

Section 6:
Social-Cognitive Interventions

13

Aggression in Children/Adolescents: Cognitive–Behavioral Treatment Perspectives

Philip C. Kendall
Kevin R. Ronan
James Epps
Temple University

Aggressive, antisocial behavior in youth is a significant problem manifesting itself in several domains of concern to mental health professionals. For example, the symptoms have an unwanted impact on numerous social systems, antisocial youth account for a large percentage of clinical referrals, and multiple child contacts for antisocial activity are predictive of adult psychopathology. Despite the widespread nature and prevalence of the disorder, treatment strategies have generally not proven to be completely effective in eliminating aggressive, antisocial actions.

This chapter holds to the premise that a greater understanding of the cognitive information-processing style of aggressive youth will be an essential basis for a more appropriate and effective intervention. That is, the more we know about how aggressive youth perceive and process their experiences in the world, the more we can adjust the targets of our intervention programs, thereby having the significant impact on aggression that would benefit the children themselves and their society. Accordingly, we first present a cognitive–behavioral conceptualization of childhood aggression, with a special focus on the cognitive information-processing features associated with aggression. We then describe an intervention designed to alter the distorted and deficient cognitive processing of aggressive children and report on an evaluation of its outcomes. Lastly, we examine certain variables that may be involved in the moderation of treatment-produced gains and make suggestions for future research and application.

COGNITIVE AND BEHAVIORAL COMPONENTS OF YOUTHFUL AGGRESSION

Cognitive–behavioral views of aggressive behavior are consistent with Novaco's (1979) view of anger, in that the connection between provoking events and anger arousal is indirect. Angry, aggressive arousal is mediated through the individual's expectations and appraisals. The aggression seen and experienced by outsiders is, in part, the result of the child's internal processing.

An understanding of a cognitive–behavioral paradigm for childhood aggression requires description by terms. A proposed taxonomic system for describing and distinguishing information-processing mechanisms, described in Ingram and Kendall (1986), drew conceptual distinctions between these elements: (a) cognitive structure, (b) cognitive propositions (or content), (c) cognitive processes (or operations), and (d) cognitive products. As described by Ingram and Kendall (1986) and as reviewed in Kendall, Howard, and Epps (1988), cognitive structure may be described as the manner in which information is organized and represented in memory. Based on a history of experiences with the world, individuals develop structured memories. This structure is roughly comparable to the hardware of a system of indexing and filing. Cognitive propositions (or content) refer to the information as represented by and stored within the cognitive structure. The content of ongoing cognitive events are a part of this element of cognition. The combination of these two concepts yields the construct of the schema. Representing the marriage of content and structure, the schema reflects the child's life experiences, and acts as a guideline through which perceptions are filtered and judgments steered. Schemata thereby serve as a point of reference, a template through which the child views himself and the world. Cognitive operations (or processes) are the procedures that the cognitive system utilizes to input, process, and output information. Lastly, cognitive products, as the title makes clear, are the end result of the interaction of information with the above elements of the cognitive system.

A potentially significant distinction can be drawn regarding the type of pathology manifest in cognitive processing/products leading to aggressive behavior: cognitive deficiency versus cognitive distortion (Kendall, 1985). *Cognitive deficiencies* entail an insufficient amount of cognitive activity (e.g., a lack of thinking or problem-solving) in situations wherein more forethought would be beneficial. *Distortions,* on the other hand, refer to dysfunctional thinking processes. To differentiate between these two concepts, consider this example. Impulsivity and aggressive behavior have as cognitive correlates a tendency toward failure to employ verbal mediation and a lack of self-control. The undercontrolled youngster demonstrates a cognitive deficiency—he or she does not seem to follow through on optimal goal-directed cognitive processing, and generates less-than-optimal cognitive products. In contrast, anxious or depressed youngsters tend toward misperception of the demands of the environment, self-criticism, and underappraisal of personal abilities. These children overcontrol themselves, and this overcontrol is characteristic of cognitive distortion. In aggression, both cognitive distortions and cognitive deficiencies have been identified.

In drawing on the works of Dodge (1986), Ingram and Kendall (1986), Novaco (1979), and others, a cognitive–behavioral view of aggression is offered. Cognitive propositions centering about the theme of interpersonal interaction are structured in memory such that schemata result. These schemata reflect the view that: (a) others are provoking and (b) the child is capable of dealing with the provocation only by being more threatening than the stimulus. Thus, though others may be able to see what appears to be a predisposition toward aggression, the child's schema allows him to see his hostility as retaliation rather than "first strike." The deficient and distorted cognitive operations the child utilizes to maintain his posture will be addressed individually, and reflect incomplete utilization of environmental cues, selective attention to aggressive environmental cues, overattribution of hostile intent, and a diminished proportion of effective versus ineffective potential responses to aversive situations. Therefore his cognitive products shape his response behavior, add to his repertoire of negative interpersonal cognitive propositions, and reinforce his cognitive structure. Hence, upon exposure to a similar stimulus event, the schemata are re-enacted readily.

Cognitive Features

Dodge (1986) offers a social information-processing view of aggression which proposes a five-step cognitive process as the antecedent of aggression. These steps are (a) the perception and decoding of environmental cues, (b) the development of expectations of the behavior of others based on attributions of hostile intent, (c) searching for possible responses, (d) deciding which response is appropriate, and (e) enacting the chosen response. Cognitive deficiencies at any one of these processes result in an aggressive response. The framework provides a useful backdrop for discussing these potential deficiencies. As in Gouze (1987), the last three steps listed here will be combined under the rubric of "problem solving" for ease of review.

Use of Environmental Cues. The first of these steps involves the mechanics of transferring cues for behavioral response from the environment to the child's awareness. Deficiencies at this stage of processing are referred to as "cue utilization deficiencies" (Milich & Dodge, 1984, p. 472). Aggressive children seem to use fewer environmental cues to mediate behavior than do nonaggressive children. A study by Dodge and Newman (1981) investigated speed of children's cognitive processing as they relate to biases in interpersonal problem-solving in aggressive children. Drawing on Hochberg's (1970) information-processing theory of perceptual readiness, the authors proposed that aggressive boys may be predisposed through a specific cognitive schema to respond to interpersonal dealings aggressively, and asserted that this would be reflected in the premature impulsive nature of their social judgments. To test this hypothesis, the 45 most aggressive of a sample of 551 kindergarten through fifth-grade boys were matched against the 45 least aggressive. The task involved a "detective" game, wherein the youths were allowed as much information as they requested to determine whether or not a fictitious peer committed a hostile act. Aggressive boys were found to request 30% fewer pieces of information than did their non-aggressive peers. This proportion varied as an interaction of age and level of hostility, with aggressive fifth-graders requesting as little information as non-aggressive first-graders. Other studies by Dodge and his colleagues have uncovered similar findings (e.g., Dodge & Tomlin, 1983; Milich & Dodge, 1984).

In addition, children seem to attend to aggressive environmental cues more than nonaggressive cues. Gouze (1987) utilized a preschool middle- to lower-class male population ($n = 43$; mean age = 53.9 months) to investigate this relationship. In this study, selective attentional bias was measured through tasks designed to assess the children's ability to shift attention away from an aggression-related stimulus (aggressive versus nonaggressive puppet shows), and on freedom from distractibility by aggressive stimuli (aggressive versus nonaggressive cartoon scenes). In both cases the aggressive youth focused more upon aggressive stimuli than nonaggressive stimuli.

A second study by Gouze (1981) investigated differences between aggressive and nonaggressive children in the content of environmental cues upon which they choose to focus. The author's analysis showed that highly aggressive children were more likely to focus on aggressive cues in their environment, while less aggressive children focused on a wider variety of information, including the consequences of aggressive behaviors. The findings from the Gouze studies are consistent, then, with the Dodge and Newman (1981) and Dodge and Tomlin (1983) studies in demonstrating that aggressive children display deficits in ability to perceive and decode environmental stimuli in an unbiased manner.

Attribution of Hostile Intent. The tendency to "assume the worst" regarding the intentions of peers in ambiguous (neither hostile nor benign) situations is referred to as a "hostile attributional bias" (Milich & Dodge, 1984, p. 472). When provoked by a peer, aggressive children seem to draw upon cognitive schemata to overestimate the degree of hostility of intent borne by the provocateur. Dodge (1980) investigated this "cue-distortion" hypothesis with a population of 45 aggressive and 45 nonaggressive, less-advantaged boys. The school-based project had the subjects' efforts toward assembly of a jigsaw puzzle frustrated by a confederate peer who portrayed either a hostile, benign, or ambiguous intent. Although all subjects responded to the hostile and benign conditions in a similar manner (i.e., aggression and restraint, respectively), there were differences between the aggressive and nonaggressive boys within the ambiguous condition. The aggressive boys reacted as though the peer's intentions had been hostile, whereas the less aggressive boys responded as though the peer's intentions had been benign. Further findings by Dodge and his colleagues indicated that: (a) aggressive boys who displayed selective recall of hostile cues also overattributed hostile behavior to a peer, and (b) aggressive subjects who reacted rapidly were more apt to overattribute hostile behavior to peers than were nonaggressive boys.

Similar findings were uncovered by Nasby, Hayden and DePaulo (1980). The pair of studies reported therein studied emotionally disturbed boys in residential treatment (mean age = 13 and 13.4, respectively). The boys were shown still pictures expressing unambiguous affective reactions. In the first study, the boys selected from two accompanying labels portraying two continua: positivity–negativity and dominance–submission. In the second study, the boys received the pictures without the labels, and generated their own labels. Both studies yielded the predisposition toward ascribing negative dominance-oriented labels, holding true across stimulus behaviors. The assertion drawn from these data is that, even in cases wherein stimulus behaviors clearly deserve nonhostile labels, aggressive boys tend to misattribute aggressive intent.

Problem-Solving Deficiencies. The term "response decision bias" has been coined by Milich and Dodge (1984, p. 472) to describe the tendency of aggressive boys to generate a greater percentage of aggressive, incompetent solutions to socially provoking situations than do more sedate boys. The upshot of this bias is that the likelihood of settling on a competent solution decreases as the number of solutions (Spivack & Shure,

1974) and the proportion of competent versus incompetent solutions (Richard & Dodge, 1982) decreases.

Deluty (1981) investigated whether, for aggressive children, there is an underdeveloped ability to generate alternative responses to conflictual interactions. The authors matched 15 highly aggressive children to an equal number of assertive children, and measured the number and type (i.e., "aggressive," "submissive," or "assertive") of responses in the children's repertoire of responses to conflict situations, measured by the Children's Action Tendency Scale (Deluty, 1979). The authors found that aggressive children are capable of conceiving of assertive solutions, but that the percentage of assertive alternatives in their repertoire are few. More than half of the highly aggressive child's responses were aggressive. Therefore, even with the ability to choose between options, it appears likely that the alternative generated will be aggressive. Deluty's conclusion is that aggressive children may benefit from a treatment program that includes increasing the child's assertive alternative-thinking ability.

Richard and Dodge (1982) pursued this hypothesis through a study of the following problem solving skills: generation of a large number of alternative solutions, generation of a high proportion of competent versus incompetent responses, and an analysis of the ability to assess alternatives as competent or incompetent. The results indicated that poorly adjusted (including aggressive) children generated fewer solutions and a higher proportion of hostile, ineffective solutions, than did cooperative children. The conclusion drawn from this study indicates that aggressive boys, when faced with having to choose between a number of alternative responses to conflict situations, may be less skilled than nonaggressive boys. Thus, behavioral problems may ensue when initial solutions are limited and less competent alternative solutions are placed into effect.

Behavioral Features. The Diagnostic and Statistical Manual of Mental Disorders (DSM-III-R; APA, 1987) describes the behavioral correlates of three developmental disorders characterized by disruptive behavior: Conduct Disorder, Oppositional Defiant Disorder, and Attention-deficit Hyperactivity Disorder. Of these, the first two are relevant to this discussion. Children suffering from conduct disorder display a pattern of behavior that violates both societal norms and the rights of others. Overt manifestations of that behavior commonly include self-initiated verbal and physical aggression, cruelty, and property destruction. Covert behaviors may include stealing, substance abuse, early sexual promiscuity, lying, cheating, or running away from home. The child may be prone to sudden and violent outbursts of temper associated with irritability and inability to tolerate frustration. These behaviors commonly occur across a variety of situations, including the home, school, and, in older children, work settings.

Two types of conduct disorders are described by DSM-III-R. The Solitary Aggressive Type is said to display an undersocialized overtly hostile manner. These children are frequently socially isolated and make no attempt to disguise their aggressive behavior. Group Type Conduct Disorder is demonstrated through conduct problems occurring in association with peer group activity. Frequently claiming loyalty to their group, these children may or may not demonstrate physical aggression. A third type, the Undifferentiated Type, represents those children who cannot be identified solely as either Solitary or Group type. This may be the most common case, followed by the Group Type and the Solitary Aggressive Type, respectively.

Oppositional Defiant Disorder holds as its symptoms many of the same behaviors as Conduct Disorder, and is frequently seen as an antecedent to Conduct Disorder. However, the more invasive behaviors infringing on others' rights will not be present (e.g., physical aggression, theft, destruction of property, etc.). Children with this disorder present as negativistic and hostile, frequently defying adult authority and institutional rules. They typically behave in ways that are deliberately annoying, and are prone to frequent temper outbursts and swearing. In comparison to others their age, they are more quick-tempered, "moody," angry, and have lower tolerance for frustration. Substance abuse may be involved. Unlike the Conduct Disorder, the behaviors may be limited to the home setting, or may first be apparent in the home and then spread to other settings.

These descriptions are consistent with a categorization of aggressive behaviors by Rathjen, Rathjen, and Hiniker (1978), which addresses the dimension of respect for the rights of others versus one's own rights. The authors asserted that an aggressive behavioral style reflects a high degree of respect for one's own rights, but that the rights of others are held in low regard.

COGNITIVE–BEHAVIORAL TREATMENT STRATEGIES AND AN EVALUATION

Cognitive–behavioral approaches from the treatment of childhood disorders represent a rational amalgam of cognitive, behavioral, emotive, and developmental strategies. Rewards (and response cost), modelling, role-plays, affective education, homework, self-evaluation, and perspective-taking activities readily combine within the cognitive–behavioral framework (for treatment materials, see Kendall, 1989).

Knowing the need for child motivation, as well as for the acquisition of socialized behavior, treatments benefit from the inclusion of contingency management programs. For example, use of contingent rewards as incentive manipulations can involve the child in the treatment program. Also, given the record of aggressive youth, it is important that they also learn that misbehavior has a cost. Carefully constructed contingency management programs are a part of a cognitive–behavioral program. With this particular sample it is important to outline the rules at the outset, create a sense of trust by being consistent with the rules and rule consequences, and provide a written, if not posted, copy of the full set of rules. To avoid emotional outburst when rules are broken and contingencies are put into operation, it is very valuable to prepare the youth's expectations for contingent outcomes. That is, instead of waiting for the first incident of a misbehavior to explain and follow through with a contingency, it is suggested that the children be given "dry runs" so that they can experience and process the event rationally and hold reasonable expectations for later contingent consequences.

Modelling is an integral component of the cognitive–behavioral perspective. It is incumbent upon the therapist to serve as a valued model for the child. A verbalizing coping model is preferred. As a coping model the therapist does not display socially appropriate and proper behavior on all occasions, but rather makes mistakes, like those in the child's behavioral repertoire, and models a strategy for correcting the misbehavior. Also, the therapist models a strategy to catch the act before it is complete and a strategy to inhibit completing the action. The idea here is that the therapist not be the always-proper adult, but rather the potentially inappropriate self-disclosing model who shares with the child various strategies to prevent misbehavior.

An important aspect of the therapist as model is for the therapist to be a problem-solving model. A problem-solver does not have an answer ready and waiting—the problem solver walks through each situation and seeks various alternative possibilities, evaluates each possibility, and examines the likely consequences of the various alternatives. In so doing, the therapist models a manner to inhibit fast and unthoughtful acts, often aggressive, that do not serve the child's goals or fit within the child's social environment.

Role play activities not only provide excellent opportunities for the child to engage in and practice his new skills, but also present social situations to the child and therapist for their analysis. It is in these role plays that the therapist can assess and modify the child's cognitive processing errors. Perspective taking tasks are very beneficial in this regard. For instance, a difficult social situation is role played with the child playing one role and the therapist playing another. Then, following a discussion of how each person processed the experience, the same situation is role played but with the roles reversed. Now, the child has both experiences and has had a chance to examine how the experience was processed from the two different perspectives. Identification of cognitive processing distortions are facilitated by role play enactments.

Children are not known for their accurate description of emotional states. Far too many youth see themselves as either sad, mad or glad. Creating a "feelings dictionary" and allowing children to learn to identify emotional states in themselves and others helps them to acquire empathy and perspective taking abilities. Often, cartoon sequences with the thought bubbles intentionally left blank can be used to pull the child's self talk in situations like that in the cartoon. Altering certain aspects of the cartoon and determining the child's reactions through his changes in the thoughts placed in the thought bubbles can help to identify misattributions and misperceptions of others' intentions.

Impulsive action lacks forethought and planning. Aggressive action also lacks a retrospective examination of what was done and how each person felt, behaved, and thought about the experience. Using self-evaluation exercises the child is taught to stop and reexamine the activities of a recent past interval of time (e.g., an hour) and consider how the various people in the situation felt and thought about it. Self-evaluation training of this type heightens the aggressive child's sensitivity to the feelings of others.

In an effort to directly modify the deficiencies in careful cognitive processing that have been implicated in aggression, the therapist introduces self-instructions as part of the way that role-play and problem-solving discussion will take place. The child and therapist each talk out loud, stating their view of each problem, suggesting alternatives, providing ideas about what outcomes are most likely, and helping to form a plan of action. Self-instructions can come to inhibit fast action and allow the child to attempt alternatives that were once not considered. Repetitious use of self-guided speech, with the child's own language and with the child's involvement in developing the self-talk steps, is especially beneficial.

Homework is not a sought after activity for children and their follow through is notoriously poor. Nevertheless, the idea of being involved in activities that are therapeutic while outside the therapy itself are desirable. STIC tasks (Show That I Can) (Kendall, Kane, Howard, & Siqueland, 1989) are assignments that allow the child to do an activity outside therapy and report back to the therapist to earn rewards. These assignments are framed as Show That I Can exercises rather than as homework because we have found that compliance is enhanced, though therapist patience is still required.

Although the components of the treatment may seem somewhat diverse, they come together nicely into a treatment program that can run approximately 20 weeks (a copy of the treatment manual and the child's Stop and Think Workbook are available from the first author), though it is often extended in clinical practice. In summary, the cognitive–behavioral approach to the treatment of aggressive youth employs behavioral procedures of demonstrated efficiency but also includes direct and intentional attention to the child's cognitive deficiencies and distortions. Modifications of the child's cognitive information processing style, in addition to behavioral procedures, affective education, and a close and meaningful therapist–child relationship constitute the recommended approach to treatment (see also Feindler, 1991; Lochman, White, & Wayland, 1991).

The demonstrated effectiveness of cognitive–behavior therapy with nonclinical samples of disruptive children (see Kendall and Braswell, 1985) provided the impetus to study further the efficacy of the treatment program with more severely disturbed populations of aggressive children. For example, Kazdin, Esveldt-Dawson, French, and Unis (1987) reported positive findings with a clinical population of children manifesting antisocial behaviors. A treatment program combining cognitive–behavioral therapy (after Kendall & Braswell, 1985 and described above) with interpersonal problem-solving (Spivack, Platt, & Shure, 1976) was found to be superior to a relationship enhancement therapy and an attention placebo condition across parent and teacher reports.

A recent study was designed to expand and evaluate the clinical efficacy of the cognitive–behavior therapy with a population of day-hospitalized, conduct-disordered children (Kendall, Reber, McCleer, Epps, & Ronan, 1990). A 20-session cognitive–behavioral treatment modeled on the Kendall and Braswell program (1985) was compared with the therapeutic modalities currently in place at a local psychiatric facility (i.e., supportive and insight-oriented). Subjects were conduct disordered youth (29 Black and Hispanic children) from the day hospital program of the psychiatric facility. The hospital program provides elementary education and psychiatric treatment to children deemed too disruptive for traditional educational settings. All subjects (26 boys and 3 girls) were screened before treatment utilizing the Diagnostic Interview for Children (DICA; Herjanic & Reich, 1982). Each child received a diagnosis of conduct disorder and 5 received a concurrent diagnosis of attention-deficit–hyperactivity disorder. Subjects were first- to eighth-graders, aged 6- to 13-years (m = 10.7 years).

Subjects were randomly assigned to one of two treatment sequences in a crossover design: (a) cognitive–behavioral treatment followed by the current conditions treatment or (b) current conditions treatment followed by cognitive–behavior therapy. Subjects in both sequences received an average of just over 20 individual sessions lasting 45–55 minutes. Treatment groups were reversed in the weeks following the last session of the initial treatment, thus allowing each child exposure to both therapeutic modalities. Therapy was provided by mental health professionals (psychiatric residents, psychologist, social worker) who provided treatment on the two successive periods within the crossover.

A battery of outcome measures were given to each subject to examine changes on the cognitive, behavioral, and emotional factors implicated in an earlier section as features of childhood aggression. Measures were included to assess not only a reduction in psychopathology, but also to assess gains in cognitive processing and positive social behaviors. The actual measures were of three general types: (a) behavior rating scales, (b) a self-report measure, and (c) a task performance measure. Measures were administered to each subject at three time periods: (a) prior to treatment, (b) following the first treatment sequence, and (c) following the second treatment sequence.

Results indicated the superiority of the cognitive–behavior therapy in producing significant gains across various domains as identified by the following teacher and self-report inventories: self-control as measured by the Self-Control Rating Scale for Children (Kendall & Wilcox, 1979), the Internalizing, Adaptive Functioning, and Appropriate Behavior subscales of the Child Behavior Checklist-Teacher Report Form (CBCL-TRF; Achenbach & Edelbrock, 1983), and the Social Acceptance and Scholastic Competence subscales of the Self-Perception Scale for Children (SPSC; Harter, 1982).

The clinical significance of behavioral improvement—that is, behaviors that bring deviant patients within nondeviant ranges—was addressed by the use of normative comparison (see Kendall & Norton-Ford, 1982; Kendall & Grove, 198). Normative comparisons were used where appropriate norms for the dependent measures were available. On the Self-Control Rating Scale, the subjects were rated at pretreatment more than one standard deviation above a normative mean. After treatment the scores of those children following the cognitive–behavioral treatment were within one standard deviation of the normal mean, whereas the scores of those receiving current conditions treatment were not. Further analysis of the percentage of individuals whose scores improved to within-normal limits confirmed that there was a statistically significant difference between the cognitive–behavioral and current treatment groups. The proportion of children who met the clinically significant criterion was higher following cognitive–behavioral treatment. This same pattern of results was observed on the CBCL Adaptive Functioning subscale. It should be noted, however, that these analyses used mean scores and did not specifically address individual changes. Thus, in this clinic sample of aggressive children, mean scores on measures indicating behavioral deficits in self-control and adaptive functioning were improved to within normal limits as a result of the cognitive–behavior therapy.

The findings described above suggest that significant treatment effects where indicated were positive and largely attributable to cognitive–behavior therapy. Both (a) teacher's blind ratings (of self-control and prosocial behavior) and (b) children's self-reports (of perceived social competence) provided support for the efficacy of the cognitive–behavior program with conduct-disordered children. Other dependent measures, however, did not show this pattern (e.g., improvement seen for all children on the Matching Familiar Figures Test). Nevertheless, the hypothesized improvements were generally focused and the results suggest that the cognitive–behavior program was more effective than the current therapeutic modalities in producing behavioral improvement in a clinical population of disruptive children. The differential improvement seen in the areas of self-control, appropriate and adaptive behavior, and working hard as rated by teachers, and increased self-perceptions of scholastic and social competence suggest both a reduction in emotionality and an increase in socially adaptive interpersonal skills.

Maintenance of treatment effects was not addressed because the crossover design (all subjects received both treatments) precluded the assessment of differential long-term treatment effects. However, data was available 6 months after the first cognitive–behavioral treatment implementation indicating a lack of maintenance effects. These results suggest that improvement produced by cognitive–behavior therapy did not persist beyond the time of the treatment program. Unfortunately, lack of treatment generalization appears to be a pervasive finding when working with highly aggressive target populations of children (see Kendall & Braswell, 1985; Kazdin, 1987).

The documentation of the ability of the program to produce gains, plus the evidence that these gains did not persist beyond the period of the active therapy program, raise the question of how best to modify future treatment delivery to insure that positive therapeutic effects last beyond the confines of an effective operative program. One manner of addressing this issue has been suggested by Copeland (1981, 1982) and Kendall and Braswell (1985)—both emphasize the utility of identifying change-producing or "active" ingredients in empirically documented treatment programs and examining individual factors which may moderate the effects of a therapeutic enterprise.

With these points in mind, Kendall and colleagues, (1990) sought to assess the potential moderating effect on therapy outcome of the experience of the therapist. That is, to what extent does an experienced therapist produce gains that are superior to a novice? It is not experience per se that is of interest here, but experience with the treatment manual. In other words, are limited effects due to a less qualified therapist, with greater gains linked to more qualified/experienced appliers of the treatment manual? Therapists in the study were initially naive to the cognitive–behavior program and were trained for its application just prior to the first treatment sequence. The nature of the crossover design allowed each therapist to apply the cognitive–behavior program in two separate sequences while gaining additional technical expertise in weekly supervision sessions with the first author. Results indicated that for some outcome measures reflecting improvement following cognitive–behavior treatment, greater improvement was observed following the second application of the program. Although these results could be attributable to other influences (e.g., group composition, longer length of stay in the day hospital program), they do support the added benefit of experienced therapists and encourage further empirical documentation of experience with treatments guided by manuals as a moderator of therapeutic efficacy.

Regarding the potential moderating effect of the aggressive youngster himself in cognitive–behavioral treatment, a supplemental study to Kendall and colleagues (1990) sought to assess subject characteristics and the influences that these individual factors have on therapy outcome (Epps, Ronan, & Kendall, 1990). Attributional style, hostility and aggression, and family environment factors were chosen for study because of (a) the salience of these factors in the conduct-disordered child's symptom pattern and (b) their previous identification as potentially having a moderating effect on treatment outcome (e.g., Bugental, Whalen, & Henker, 1977; Dadds, Sanders, Behrens, & James, 1987; Lochman, Lampron, Burch, & Curry, 1985). These factors, of course, also reflect relevant dimensions of cognitive–behavioral theory. As discussed earlier, the term "cognitive–behavioral" is a synthesis of cognitive, behavioral, affective, and social strategies for change (Kendall, 1985; Kendall, Howard, & Epps, 1988; Kendall & Ronan, 1990). As such, the conceptual breakdown of these individual factors reflects the cognitive domain (attributional style), the interactive cognitive–behavioral–affective domain (aggression), and the social context (family environment) of the conduct-disordered child.

The specific measures utilized to tap these dimensions were as follows. Attributional style was assessed prior to treatment utilizing the Multidimensional Measure of Children's Perceptions of Control (MMCPC; Connell, 1985), a self-report scale which measures perceptions of control in children. Various dimensions of hostility and aggression were assessed at pretreatment utilizing the CBCL-TRF Aggression subscale and two self-report inventories: (a) the Hostility–Guilt Inventory (HGI) and (b) the Interview for Aggression (see Kazdin, Esveldt-Dawson, Unis, & Rancuello, 1983). Family context was assessed pretreatment utilizing the Family Environment Scale (FES; Moos, 1974) a measure which looks at the social and environmental structure of family life, examining the relative strengths and weaknesses of dimensions reflecting personal growth, relationship, and system maintenance issues. Pretreatment scores on each of the measures studied were correlated with change scores on those dependent variables rendering significant improvement following cognitive–behavioral treatment.

Results indicated significant relationships between the individual subject factors and improved outcome following cognitive–behavior therapy. Self-reported verbal aggression was negatively correlated with multiple teachers' blind ratings of improvement. Children who rated themselves as highly verbally assaultive were less likely to be judged by their teachers as improved on measures of hyperactivity, social ability, conduct, inattention, appropriate behavior, or externalizing behavior. Several other manifestations of aggression predicted limited teacher-reported improvement. Self-reported suspicion was negatively correlaed with several teachers' measures of improvement. Suspicious children were less likely to show improvement in teacher reports of hyperactivity, social ability, inattention, and learning as a result of the cognitive–behavior therapy. Self-reported resentment was negatively correlated with teacher reports of improvement in hyperactivity, social ability, and inattention. Children high in self-reported resentment were thus less likely to be judged by their teachers' as improved in those behavioral areas.

Interestingly, one reliable positive correlation revealed that children who reported as severely aggressive, suspicious, and irritable reported significantly more progress in reducing their own perception of the severity of aggressiveness following cognitive–behavior therapy. Thus, from the child's perspective, those who at pretreatment described themselves as highly aggressive and hostile were those who received the greatest symptom relief.

With regard to attributional style, results indicated significant relationships between attributions of causality and improved outcome following cognitive–behavior therapy. Specifically, pretreatment scores indicating a more internal attributional style (i.e., high in internal attributions and/or low in unknown or powerful others orientations) were significantly related to positive outcome on teacher's ratings of the following behavioral areas: conduct, inattentiveness, hyperactivity, and social abilities. These results were buttressed by trends in the data indicating a positive relationship between this attributional style and improved teacher ratings of both socialized, appropriate behaviors and internalizing behaviors. Further, there was a significant positive correlation between pretreatment externality and significant improvement towards fewer external attributions at posttreatment. That is, children who initially rated themselves high in perceptions of external control tended to evidence the greatest improvement towards an attributional orientation emphasizing perceptions of personal control capacity following cognitive–behavioral treatment.

Regarding the impact of family environment, one noteworthy pattern of results was indicated. A subscale which examines children's perceptions of the presence of parental control and centralized decision-making in the family was positively correlated with improved outcome on teacher's ratings of the following behaviors: self-control, appropriate behavior, internalizing behavior, learning, adaptive functioning, hyperactivity, social ability, inattention, and tension/anxiety. Thus, children who perceived more active parental management within the family also evidenced more behavior improvement following cognitive–behavior therapy.

The overall findings appear to indicate that in this sample of conduct-disordered children, those lower in perceived levels of hostility and aggression with a more internalized attributional style from families higher in centralized parental decision-making show the greatest improvement on teacher's blind ratings of behaviors following cognitive–behavior therapy. What about treating the seemingly more disturbed children, such as those with higher self-reported aggression and more external attributional? Though our present data are more supportive of treatment for less aggressive, internal youngsters, they nevertheless indicate that the more severe cases can also receive observable benefit from the cognitive–behavioral treatment (e.g., more externally-oriented children becoming more internal in their locus of control).

These findings have implications for the practice of cognitive–behavior therapy with samples of highly aggressive clinic children. Cognitive–behavioral practitioners might best aid their young clients by adjusting the intervention to match the child's pretreatment levels of aggression and perceived control (see also Bugental, Henker, & Whalen, 1977). For example, children who initially exhibit more internalized attributional styles and lower levels of aggression may benefit most from the aspects of the intervention geared towards efficiently utilizing this more empowered, manageable orientation. For example, enhancing self-instructional and interpersonal problem-solving skills while providing objective feedback might be emphasized. On the other hand, children exhibiting more externalized attributional orientations and/or high levels of aggression might benefit most by initially emphasizing the behavioral aspects of the intervention (e.g., social reinforcement, response cost) geared towards producing positive change via a change agent (i.e., therapist) structuring a predictable and safe environment. As the child incrementally begins to understand that his or her behaviors have efficacy within this milieu (i.e., shifting to a more internal perception of personal control and lowered levels of aggression), a gradual shift to emphasizing, for example, self-instructional problem-solving, objective feedback, and self-reinforcement may prove most fruitful. Although some positive evidence for these speculations exists with nonclinical populations (see review by Braswell, Koehler, & Kendall, 1985), more empirical efforts are needed to determine clinical efficacy with more severely disturbed populations of aggressive children.

CONSIDERATIONS AND FUTURE DIRECTIONS

It is worthwhile at the present juncture to recall the oft-used water glass metaphor—"Is it half full or half empty?" Proponents of the cognitive–behavioral conceptualizations and intervention program would see the cup as half full, pointing to the significant gains in self-control and prosocial behavior as compared to those produced from a typical standard practice. Those seeing the cup as half empty would, in contrast, point to the limited evidence of maintenance and the failure of the treatment to turn conduct-disordered youth into "boy scouts." A rational consideration of these issues does not resolve them, but certain matters are raised.

We recognize that eternal optimism may be needed to accept the idea that the treated youth learned something that will have a positive impact on the rest of their lives. Nevertheless, it is possible and worthy of consideration that the children did acquire certain cognitive problem solving skills that they will take with them and use later in life. The treatment may produce "sleeper effects," where the skills acquired are not necessarily demonstrated at this point in time, but may be referred to later in life. An anecdotal case report lends some credence to this idea. A hyperactive girl treated with a cognitive–behavioral program (Kendall & Urbain, 1981) was reported by her mother some 7 to 8 years later, to remember and use the problem-solving steps that she had been taught. She was taught the skills at a young age, but was telling her mother about using them at age 15.

Rational expectations for treatment outcome suggest that the cup is half full. Is it reasonable to expect that 20 one-hour sessions will entirely rearrange a child's perspective and behavior pattern? We think not. Rather, the outcome research employing a 20-session program helps to identify an independent variable (cognitive–behavioral therapy) that has a beyond-chance favorable impact on the recipients. Once the independent variable has been confirmed as active, it can then be integrated into practice. However, truly impressive changes in behavior may require longer interventions with longer term commitments on the part of the youth for booster sessions, and so forth.

A definite positive note is struck when one considers the potential for future research. For instance, what are the effects of parent involvement in the treatment protocol? Would individual child treatment be superior to a cognitive–behavioral program designed for families? Would peer-run groups facilitate the acquisition of cognitive processing styles that are less prone to aggressive action? Although real world constraints do limit research endeavors, there are still many questions that can be asked and answered about the potential of cognitive–behavioral procedures in the remediation of childhood aggression.

REFERENCES

Achenbach, T. M., & Edelbrock, C. S. (1983). *Manual for the child behavior checklist and revised child behavior profile.* Burlington, VT: University Associates in Psychiatry.

American Psychiatric Association. (1987). *Diagnostic and Statistical Manual of Mental Disorders.* (3rd ed.). Washington, DC: Author.

Braswell, L., Koehler, C., & Kendall, P. C. (1985). Attributions and outcomes in child psychotherapy. *Journal of Social and Clinical Psychology, 3,* 458–465.

Bugental, D. B., Whalen, C. K., & Henker, B. (1977). Causal attributions of hyperactive children and motivational assumptions of two behavior change approaches: Evidence for an interactionist position. *Child Development, 48,* 871–881.

Connell, J. P. (1985). A new multidimensional measure of children's perceptions of control. *Child Development, 56,* 1018–1041.

Copeland, A. P. (1981). The relevance of subject variables in cognitive self-instructional programs for impulsive children. *Behavior Therapy, 12,* 520–529.

Copeland, A. P. (1982). Individual difference factors in children's self-management: Toward individualized treatments. In P. Karoly & F. H. Karfer (Eds.), *Self-management and behavior change: From theory to practice.* New York: Pergamon.

Dadds, M. R., Sanders, M. R., Behrens, B. C., & James, J. E. (1987). Marital discord and child behavior problems: A description of interaction during treatment. *Journal of Child Clinical Psychology, 16,* 192–203.

Deluty, R. H. (1979). Children's Action Tendency Scale: A self-report measure of aggressiveness, assertiveness and submissiveness in children. *Journal of Consulting and Clinical Psychology, 47,* 1061–1071.

Deluty, R. H. (1981). Alternative-thinking ability of aggressive, assertive and submissive children. *Cognitive Therapy and Research, 5*(3), 309–312.

Dodge, K. A. (1980). Social cognition and children's aggressive behaviors. *Child Development, 51,* 162–170.

Dodge, K. A. (1986). A social information processing model of social competence in children. In M. Perlmutter (Ed.), *Minnesota Symposium on Child Psychology (Vol. 18).* Hillsdale, NJ: Lawrence Erlbaum Associates.

Dodge, K. A., & Newman, J. P. (1981). Biased decision-making processes in aggressive boys. *Journal of Abnormal Psychology, 90,* 375–379.

Dodge, K. A., & Tomlin, A. (1983). The role of cue-utilization in attributional biases among aggressive children. Unpublished manuscript. Cited in Milich, R. & Dodge, K. A. (1984). Social information processing in child psychiatric population. *Journal of Abnormal Child Psychology, 12*(3), 471–490.

Epps, J., Ronan, K. R., & Kendall, P. C. (1990). *Moderator variables in a cognitive–behavioral treatment for conduct disordered children.* Manuscript in preparation. Temple University.

Feindler, E. (in press). Anger control for children and adolescents. In P. C. Kendall (Ed.) *Child and adolescent therapy: Cognitive-behavioral procedures.* NY: Guilford.

Gouze, K. (1981). Children's initial aggression level and the effectiveness of intervention strategies in moderating television effects on aggression. Cited in Gouze, K. R. (1987). Attention and social problem-solving as correlates of aggression in preschool males. *Journal of Abnormal Child Psychology, 15*(2), 181–197.

Gouze, K. R. (1987). Attention and social problem-solving as correlates of aggression in preschool males. *Journal of Abnormal Child Psychology, 15*(2), 181–197.

Harter, S. (1982). Perceived Competence Scale for Children. *Child Development, 53,* 87–97.

Herjanic, B., & Reich, W. (1982). Development of a structured psychiatric interview for children: Agreement between child and parent on individual symptoms. *Journal of Abnormal Child Psychology, 10,* 307–324.

Hochberg, J. (1970). Attention, organization and consciousness. In D. I. Mustofsky (Ed.), *Attention Contemporary Theory and Analysis.* Biased decision-making processes in aggressive boys. *Journal of Abnormal Psychology, 90,* 375–379.

Ingram, R., & Kendall, P. C. (1986). Cognitive clinical psychology: Implications of information-processing perspectives. In R. Ingram (Ed.), *Information processing approaches to clinical psychology* (pp. 3–21). New York: Academic Press.

Kazdin, A. E. (1987). *Conduct disorder in childhood and adolescence.* Beverly Hills, CA: Sage.

Kazdin, A. E., Esveldt-Dawson, K., Unis, A. S., & Rancuello, M. D. (1983). Child and parent evaluations of depression and aggression in psychiatric inpatient children. *Journal of Abnormal Child Psychology, 11,* 401–413.

Kazdin, A. E., Esveldt-Dawson, K., French, N. H., & Unis, A. S. (1987). Problem-solving skills training and relationship therapy in the treatment of antisocial child behavior. *Journal of Consulting and Clinical Psychology, 55,* 76–85.

Kendall, P. C. (1985). Toward a cognitive–behavioral model of child psychopathology and a critique of related interventions. *Journal of Abnormal Child Psychology, 13,* 357–372.

Kendall, P. C. (1989). *Stop and Think Workbook.* Available from the author, 238 Meeting House Lane, Merion Station, PA 19066, USA.

Kendall, P. C., & Braswell, L. (1985). *Cognitive–behavioral therapy for impulsive children.* New York: Guilford.

Kendall, P. C., & Grove, W. (1988). Normative comparison in therapy outcome. *Behavioral Assessment, 10,* 147–158.

Kendall, P. C., Kane, M., Howard, B., & Siqueland, L. (1989). *Cognitive–behavioral therapy for anxious children: Treatment manual.* Available from the author, Department of Psychology, Temple University, Phila: PA 19122.

Kendall, P. C., Howard, B. L., & Epps, J. (1988). The anxious child: Cognitive–behavioral treatment strategies. *Behavior Modification, 12*(2), 281–310.

Kendall, P. C., & Norton-Ford, J. D. (1982). Therapy outcome research methods. In P. C. Kendall & J. N. Butcher (Eds.), *Handbook of research methods in clinical psychology.* New York: Wiley.

Kendall, P. C., Reber, M., McCleer, S., Epps, J., & Ronan, K. R. (1990). Cognitive–behavioral treatment of conduct disordered children. *Cognitive Therapy and Research, 14.*

Kendall, P. C., & Ronan, K. R. (1990). Assessment of children's anxieties, fears, and phobias: Cognitive–behavioral models and methods. In C. R. Reynolds & R. W. Kamplaus (Eds.), *Handbook of psychological and educational assessment of children: Personality, behavior, and context.* pp. 223–244. New York: Guilford Press.

Kendall, P. C., & Urbain, E. S. (1981). Cognitive–behavioral intervention with a hyperactive girl. Evaluation via behavioral observations and cognitive performance. *Behavioral Assessment, 3,* 345–357.

Kendall, P. C., & Wilcox, L. E. (1979). Self-control in children: The development of a rating scale. *Journal of Consulting and Clinical Psychology, 47,* 1020–1030.

Lochman, J. E., Lampron, L. B., Burch, P. R., & Curry, J. F. (1985). Client characteristics associated with behavior change for treated and untreated aggressive boys. *Journal of Abnormal Child Psychology, 13,* 527–538.

Lochman, J. E., White, K. J., & Wayland, K. K. (in press). Cognitive-behavioral assessment and treatment with aggressive children. In P. C. Kendall (Ed.), *Child and adolescent therapy: Cognitive-behavioral procedures.* NY: Guilford.

Milich, R., & Dodge, K. A. (1984). Social information processing in child psychiatric populations. *Journal of Abnormal Child Psychology, 12*(3), 471–490.

Moos, R. H. (1974). *Family Environment Scale preliminary manual.* Palo Alto, CA: Consulting Psychologist's Press

Nasby, W., Hayden, B., & DePaulo, B. M. (1980). Attributional bias among aggressive boys to interpret ambiguous stimuli as displays of hostility. *Journal of Abnormal Psychology, 89,* 459–468.

Novaco, R. W. (1979). The cognitive regulation of anger and stress. In P. C. Kendall & S. D. Hollon (Eds.), *Cognitive–behavioral interventions: Theory, research and procedures.* New York: Academic Press.

Rathjen, D. P., Rathjen, E. D., & Hiniker, A. (1978). A cognitive analysis of social performance: Implications for assessment and treatment. In J. P. Foreyt & D. P. Rathjen (Eds.), *Cognitive behavior therapy: Research and application.* New York: Plenum.

Richard, B. A., & Dodge, K. A. (1982). Social maladjustment and problem solving in school aged children. *Journal of Consulting and Clinical Psychology, 50,* 226–233.

Spivack, G., & Shure, M. (1974). *Social Adjustment of Young Children.* San Francisco: Jossey-Bass.

Spivack, G., Platt, J., & Shure, M. B. (1976). *The problem-solving approach to adjustment.* San Francisco: Jossey-Bass.

14

A Social-Cognitively Based Social Skills Training Program for Aggressive Children

Debra J. Pepler
York University

Gillian King
Thames Valley Treatment Centre

William Byrd
Temple University

Aggressive children comprise a significant proportion of referrals to treatment centers (Patterson, 1982). Their behavior problems have been resistant to traditional treatment approaches and long term improvements have seldom been demonstrated (e.g., Patterson, 1979; Robins, 1974). Social skills training has been implemented as an alternative approach to the treatment of childhood aggression at Earlscourt Child and Family Centre, a children's mental health center serving children aged 6 to 12. Earlscourt specializes in the treatment of aggressive children and their families through a variety of programs, from highly intensive residential care and the treatment of young offenders to less intensive family services and school-based programs. Social skills training has been selected as a component of interventions at Earlscourt because aggressive children appear to be deficient in many of the social and social-cognitive skills required for successful peer interactions.

In this chapter, we examine the Earlscourt Social Skills Group Program from a social-cognitive perspective, elaborate on research that indicates the social-cognitive deficits of aggressive children, describe elements of our social skills program that address these social-cognitive deficits, and review the research on the effectiveness of the Earlscourt Social Skills Group Program to change both social behaviors and social cognitions.

BACKGROUND OF SOCIAL SKILLS TRAINING FOR AGGRESSIVE CHILDREN

The importance of developing adequate social skills is emphasized by recent findings that a variety of mental health problems, including conduct disorders, have been associated with deficient social performance (e.g., Coie & Kupersmidt, 1983). In addition, there is evidence to suggest that poor social relationships in childhood are associated with mental health problems in adulthood (Parker & Asher, 1987).

Recent research supports the need for social skills training that addresses both the behaviors and cognitions of aggressive children. Observational studies have indicated that aggressive children have failed to develop age-appropriate social behaviors. Their rates of aggressive behavior are comparable to the rates of much younger children and they display low rates of prosocial behavior (e.g., Patterson, 1982). The social cognitions of aggressive children have also been shown to be deficient. Aggressive children, for example, tend to misinterpret ambiguous acts by attributing hostile intent (Dodge & Frame, 1982). Aggressive children also report that it is easy to perform aggression, difficult to inhibit aggressive impulses, and that aggression is likely to produce rewards (Perry, Perry, & Rasmussen, 1986).

Early social skills training programs utilizing single strategies demonstrated limited effectiveness (e.g., Oden & Asher, 1977). Subsequent programs have utilized a variety of behavioral strategies, such as modelling, behavioral rehearsal, coaching, and video feedback to teach social skills. These programs have been found to improve social knowledge and the quality of peer interactions (e.g., LaGreca & Santogrossi, 1980). Early evaluations of social skills training, however, failed to demonstrate generalization and maintenance of treatment gains over time.

Social skills interventions with a cognitive, rather than behavioral, emphasis have also been developed. Although such programs have resulted in improved social problem solving skills, behavioral changes have been limited (e.g., Weissberg, Gesten, Rapkin, Cowen, Davidson, de Apodaca, & McKim, 1981). The findings, therefore, suggest that interventions based solely on social-cognitive strategies have limited effectiveness in producing behavioral change and that both social cognitions and behaviors need to be addressed by social skills programs.

The effectiveness of social-cognitive/behavioral social skills training with aggressive children has been demonstrated in recent studies (e.g., Kazdin, Esveldt-Dawson, French, & Unis, 1987; Lochman, Burch, Curry, & Lampron, 1984). These programs have led to decreases in externalizing and aggressive behaviors. Elements of successful social skills training programs include: social relations training (Coie, Underwood, & Lochman, this volume), prohibition of aggression (e.g., Bierman, Miller, & Stabb, 1987), anger control (e.g., Lochman et al., 1984) and cognitive behavioral problem solving (e.g., Kazdin et al., 1987; Kendall, Ronan, & Epps, this volume). There is some recent evidence that social skill training can be generalized to other settings and that the gains can be maintained over time (e.g., Matson et al., 1987).

Many successful social skills programs have trained aggressive children individually or in dyads (e.g., Matson et al., 1987; Kendall, this volume). For many clinical settings, however, individual social skills training is neither an economically feasible form of service delivery nor the preferred method of intervention. Social skills training may be enhanced by the opportunity to practice newly acquired skills in a supportive peer group setting. In addition, a skilled group leader can use group process to facilitate change. For example, more skilled children can serve as models for others and good group cohesion can enhance motivation to change. The Earlscourt Social Skills Group Program employs a group format for many of the above reasons.

EARLSCOURT SOCIAL SKILLS GROUP PROGRAM

Theoretical Bases. The Earlscourt Social Skills Group Program (ESSGP) is grounded in a blend of two theoretical perspectives: social learning theory and social cognitive theory. These are by no means the only perspectives on aggressive behavior in children, but are the primary ones upon which we have based our clinical practice and research. While the focus of this chapter is on the social-cognitive bases of aggressive behavior, it is important to note that the ESSGP is also deeply rooted in the social learning tradition.

The program was originally drawn from Goldstein's skill streaming techniques, which involve breaking down social skills into component steps (Goldstein, Sprafkin, Gershaw, & Klein, 1980). Goldstein's psycho-educational training approach, called Structured Learning, consists of modelling, role playing, performance feedback, and transfer of training. The ESSGP incorporates all of these components and other social learning principles (such as positive reinforcement and lack of reinforcement for unwanted behaviors) and procedures (such as charting). In addition, some of the program's features and content were derived from the information processing model of aggressive behavior based on the work of Dodge (1986), Perry (Perry, Perry, & Rasmussen, 1986; Perry, Perry, & Boldizar, in press), Rubin and Krasnor (1986) and others.

Program Description. The ESSGP is a didactic, experiential program designed to improve the self-control and social skills of moderately aggressive, noncompliant children between the ages of 6 and 12. These children have trouble getting along with peers or adults, difficulty in exhibiting self-control, and are more aggressive, disruptive, and noncompliant than their peers. ESSGP is a school-based program that serves children in either regular or special education classes. Parent training sessions are also offered as part of the program to help parents acquire more effective child management techniques and to facilitate the children's generalization of the skills. Other efforts are directed to the generalization of the learned skills to the classroom. These include: homework assignments, teacher involvement, and the teaching of a skill to the child's entire class.

The ESSGP is designed to increase prosocial behavior and to address the causes of aggressive behavior. The group leaders take an enhancing view towards the children and intervene on their highest level of functioning to ensure the development of prosocial strategies and behaviors. A positive therapeutic environment is assured by encouraging a fun, club-like atmosphere, by supportive and caring leadership style, and by attention to children's needs for approval and respect. Most children enjoy the groups very much and do not feel stigmatized for being withdrawn from class to attend the ESSGP. Stigmatization is also reduced by: (a) teaching skills or conducting prosocial activities with entire classes to encourage understanding of the program and to enhance the profile of the target child; and (b) regular meetings with teachers to discuss the child's progress, to problem-solve with the teacher and to encourage the transfer of behavior management techniques to the classroom.

Format. The ESSGP employs a group format for five to seven children at a time. Both primary groups (ages 6 to 8) and junior groups (ages 9 to 12) are conducted. Children attend two 75-minute sessions a week for 12 to 15 weeks. Eight basic skills are taught: Problem Solving, Knowing Your Feelings, Listening, Following Instructions, Joining In, Using Self-Control, Responding to Teasing, and Keeping Out of Fights. Each skill is taught using a module format, which involves three sessions. In the first session, the need for the skill is discussed with the children and the components of the skill (the "skill steps") are generated. Sessions two and three involve repeated opportunities for skill acquisition through role-play and rehearsal (often videotaped) and reinforcement activities, such as crafts and games.

Referral Process. Children are referred to the program by their teachers. After a referral form is completed and reviewed by relevant school personnel (such as the principal or school social worker), the school contacts the parent/guardian to discuss the referral. If the parents give verbal approval, then the Social Skills Group Leader is contacted. A classroom visit is scheduled, during which the group leader observes the child and reviews the referral with the teacher. If the child seems suited to ESSGP, the group leader then visits the home to discuss the referral and obtain written consent.

Admission Criteria. In addition to clinical judgments about the suitability of a child for the program, an admission criterion is employed. On the referral form, teachers are asked to indicate how aggressive, disruptive, and noncompliant the target child is in comparison to his/her peers. The child must obtain a minimum score on this measure.

Key Techniques. The ESSGP is a multi-faceted program incorporating the techniques of a number of successful programs. The behavioral techniques include: (a) positive reinforcement; (b) extensive behavioral rehearsal to encourage overlearning of the skills steps; (c) generalization activities to encourage the transfer of the learned skills to the classroom, playground, and home environment; and (d) training parents in child management skills. The social-cognitive techniques include: (a) making children aware of their feelings and helping them understand the role of feelings in triggering their behavior; (b) enhancing children's problem-solving skills; (c) developing children's self-control skills; (d) promoting thinking aloud to assist self-monitoring; and (e) encouraging self-enhancing (rather than self-defeating) cognitions. The skill steps, themselves, also serve as cognitive labels that guide appropriate problem solving.

Social-Cognitive Theoretical Foundation

The recent research on the role of social cognition in aggressive behavior has contributed greatly to our understanding and treatment of aggressive children. This research has shown that these children possess biases and deficits in their social problem-solving, which may lead them to act aggressively.

Dodge and others have examined social problem-solving from an information processing perspective. Dodge (1986) proposed a social information processing model of competent social responding and related it to aggressive behavior in children. The model identifies a sequence of five cognitive operations that are necessary for competent performance in a social problem-solving situation. Others have suggested one additional step, "evaluation," in the social problem-solving process (e.g., Novaco, 1978; Perry, Perry, & Rasmussen, 1986; Rubin & Krasnor, 1986).

Encoding. The first step is the encoding of social cues in the environment. This involves searching for, selecting, attending to, and storing relevant social information (e.g., attending to a peer's facial expressions to gather information about intentions) (Dodge, 1986; Rubin & Krasnor,

1986). Aggressive children search for fewer cues or facts than nonaggressive children prior to determining another child's intentions (Dodge & Newman, 1981, Slaby & Guerra, 1988). This cursory cue search may indicate that aggressive children have a developmental lag in their cue search skills; or it may be that their previous experiences have set up expectancies which limit cue search (Dodge, 1986). Support for the latter explanation comes from data indicating that, compared to nonaggressive children, aggressive children were more likely to cite general expectancies rather than specific cues to justify decisions about another's behavior (Dodge & Tomlin, 1983). Aggressive children tend to exhibit a recency bias; they base decisions on the cues presented last and neglect cues presented earlier (Dodge & Tomlin, 1983). Aggressive children also tend to focus on highly sensational cues (either positive or negative) rather than neutral, subtle, or ambiguous stimuli (Milich & Dodge, in press).

Interpretation. The second step, the interpretation process, involves integrating the encoded cues with memories of past experiences and inferring meaning from the cues attended (e.g., accurately reading a peer's actions as accidental, hostile, or prosocial) (Dodge, 1986; Novaco, 1978; Shaver, 1985). Aggressive boys have been shown to be deficient in role-taking and perspective-taking skills (e.g., Chandler, 1973; Selman, 1976). More specifically, it has been shown that aggressive juvenile delinquents are deficient in affective perspective-taking; specifically, in the recognition of approval and annoyance in others (Argyle, 1981). It follows that with weak abilities in understanding another's situation and affect, the interpretations made by aggressive children would be less competent as compared to children with more developed role-taking skills.

Aggressive children possess a bias toward interpreting the behavior of a peer as hostile (Dodge, 1980; Slaby & Guerra, 1988) which in turn may lead them to respond aggressively. This tendency to perceive hostile motivation even when it may not exist is called "hostile attributional bias." Aggressive children have been found to be as skillful as nonaggressive children in detecting hostile intentions in others, but less effective in detecting prosocial and accidental intentions (Dodge, Murphy, & Buchsbaum, 1984).

Dodge (1986; in press) has suggested both developmental and experiential explanations for the hostile attributional bias of aggressive boys. On the one hand, aggressive children may be inadequately skilled (perhaps due to a developmental lag) in the processes required to make an accurate interpretation of an ambiguous situation. On the other hand, they may have been subject to experiences that have elicited this bias. For example, aggressive children have often experienced chronic aversive and abusive treatment from parents and peers (Patterson, 1982; Perry, Perry, & Boldizar, in press). They may draw on these experiences of hostility to interpret ambiguous behavior in a negative light. The natural response to a situation in which an aggressive child feels threatened by someone perceived as hostile may be to counterattack.

Response Search. The third step, response search, involves divergent thinking to generate possible behavioral responses to the situation (e.g., thinking of active or passive, prosocial or aggressive responses to the social problem) (Dodge, 1986; Rubin & Krasnor, 1986). Aggressive children are deficient in their ability to generate potential behavioral responses to conflict situations. They generate fewer responses to hypothetical story conflicts than less aggressive children (Richard & Dodge, 1982; Slaby & Guerra, 1988) and their responses are more likely to be agonistic than those of nonaggressive children (Krasnor, 1982; Ladd & Oden, 1979; Rubin, 1982; Rubin & Daniels-Beirness, 1983). Even if aggressive children are able to generate a first response that is competent, their subsequent responses are more likely to degenerate to agonistic and ineffective strategies more quickly than those of nonaggressive children (Richard & Dodge, 1982; Slaby & Guerra, 1988). Aggressive children are also less likely than nonaggressive children to generate assertive but nonaggressive solutions to conflicts (Perry et al., 1989).

Response Decision. The fourth step involves considering the possible consequences of the responses generated in the previous step and choosing a response that fits the situation (e.g., a child may choose a prosocial response to a positive peer behavior, but may choose to counterattack to aggression) (Dodge, 1986; Perry et al., 1986; Perry, Perry, & Boldizar, in press; Rubin & Krasnor, 1986). Aggressive children consider fewer consequences for behavior than nonaggressive peers (Slaby & Guerra, 1988).

Since aggressive children are more likely to generate an aggressive response, it follows that in the response search step they are more likely to decide to employ an aggressive strategy to solve a social problem. The likelihood of choosing an aggressive strategy is increased by the tendency of aggressive children to evaluate aggressive responses more positively than their nonaggressive peers (Perry et al., 1986; Slaby & Guerra, 1988). In addition, aggressive children are less inclined to choose an assertive response, as they are less likely to endorse assertive nonaggressive strategies and more likely to endorse passive and aggressive responses as compared to nonaggressive children (Dodge, 1986).

Aggressive children are especially confident that aggression will yield tangible rewards and they believe that aggressive acts will be successful in terminating aversive behavior directed toward them by annoying peers (Perry et al., 1986). Home observations of aggressive children substantiate the expectation of positive outcomes of aggression: these children are reinforced frequently for coercive behavior within the family (Patterson, 1986). Finally, aggressive children may be more likely than nonaggressive children to choose an aggressive response because they indicate less concern or remorse about the suffering of their victims (Perry & Bussey, 1977; Slaby & Guerra, 1988).

Enactment. The fifth step involves the enactment of the response selected as a result of the earlier operations (i.e., following through with a prosocial or aggressive behavior) (Dodge, 1986; Novaco, 1978; Rubin & Krasnor, 1986). Enactment depends on the child having the chosen behavior in his/her repertoire (i.e., the child may decide that questioning the peer's behavior is a suitable response, but if he/she does not have the verbal skills to support this response, the enactment will not be competent).

The ultimate success of children's social problem-solving rests with the ability to perform the chosen response. Aggressive children appear to lack many of the social skills required to achieve their goals through peaceful and prosocial means (Perry et al., 1989) and are, therefore, unsuccessful in their peer interactions. For example, in group entry situations, aggressive children have been rated as less competent and less successful in their behavior as compared to nonaggressive children (Dodge, 1986). In provocation situations, aggressive children have been shown to be less skilled in enacting a competent response and more likely to respond with retaliatory aggression as compared to nonaggressive children (Dodge, 1986).

Evaluation. The final step, evaluation, involves the consideration of the consequences of the chosen response (e.g., assessing the benefit of the chosen response, considering the impact of this response on the self and other) (Novaco, 1978; Perry et al., 1986; Rubin & Krasnor, 1986).

If aggressive children experience deficits at one or more of the steps of social information processing, they will likely be inadequate in reviewing, evaluating and learning from the social problem solving process. This might be conceptualized as "meta-problem-solving." There are only a few studies, however, in which the ability and predisposition of aggressive children to consider the consequences of their problem-solving behaviors have been related. Perry and his colleagues have specifically examined the value that aggressive children place on the outcomes of aggression. Compared to nonaggressive children, aggressive children are less concerned about the negative consequences of aggression such as suffering by the victim, retaliation from the victim, peer rejection, and negative self-evaluation (Boldizar, Perry, & Perry, 1989). Other research also suggests that aggressive children are egocentric and overly concerned about themselves. Gagnon (1988) reported that aggressive boys lack self-awareness: Their self-concepts are overinflated in some domains and do not accurately reflect their skills and capabilities (Gagnon, 1988).

Although the picture is far from conclusive, these data suggest that aggressive children lack the predisposition to reflect carefully on the effectiveness of a problem-solving strategy. This is an area for future research and may have important ramifications for interventions.

Describing Program Features from a Social-Cognitive Perspective

The mapping of the deficits of aggressive children onto the model of social information processing provides direction for the development of interventions with aggressive children. In this section, the components of ESSGP are described as they address the deficits of aggressive children at the various steps of the social problem solving model. The social information processing steps, the deficits of aggressive children, and the program components are summarized in Table 14.1.

Encoding. A number of program features attempt to enhance appropriate encoding. The importance of examining situational and bodily cues is stressed in the instruction of the "Knowing Your Feelings" skill. One step of this skill is "What did it?": children are encouraged to look to the situation for the source of their feelings. In the "Listening" skill and the "Following Instructions" skill, children are instructed to "look" at the person talking and "think" about what that person is saying. This emphasis on the other person is intended to enhance children's attention to other people and to the environment.

Interpretation. Correct interpretations of problems, feelings, and others' behaviors are encouraged in the program. For instance, the "What is wrong?" step of the "Problem Solving" skill encourages children to define the problem in an accurate way. Also, the "Why?" step of the "Self-Control" skill prompts children to consider the reason they feel the way they do, and the "Decide" step of the "Responding to Teasing" skill prompts children to decide whether they are being teased in a friendly or mean way. Lastly, children sometimes first take one role in a role-play scenario and then switch roles with another child to perform

TABLE 14.1
Composite Model of Social Information Processing:
Assessment and Treatment of Aggressive Children

Steps of Model	*Deficits of Aggressive Children*	*Program Features*
ENCODING		
Attention cuing	Cue search	What did it? (Feeling skill)
Perception of cues	Selective attention:	Attention to situational cues (Knowing your feelings)
Examing context cues	Recency bias	Attention to body cues (Knowing your feelings)
	Focus on sensational cues	Look and think (Listening skill)
	Attentional deficits	Listen (Following instructions)
INTERPRETATION		
Attributions of intentionality	Hostile attributional bias	Labeling other's affect (Feelings role plays)
Assignment of blame		What is wrong? (Problem solving)
Labeling of affect		Why? (Using self-control)
		Decide (Responding to teasing)
RESPONSE SEARCH		
Accessing possible strategies based on preceding steps	Fewer alternatives generated	What can I do? (Problem solving)
	Fewer assertive solutions	What are my choices?
		Cool down (Teasing skill)
RESPONSE DECISION		
Decision based on social goals, expectations, and experience	Aggressive valued as effective	Which is best? (Problem solving)
	Failure to think of consequences	"If . . . then . . ." decision making
	Lack of empathy	Cost (Keeping out of fights)
		Who? How? When? (Joining in skill)
ENACTMENT		
Behavioral skills	Limited prosocial behavior repertoire	Do it and learn (Problem solving)
		Self-control Skill
		Role plays
		Mind talk
		Skill-practicing missions
EVALUATION OF OUTCOME		
Consideration of consequences	Lack of self-awareness	Do it and learn (Problem solving)
Coping strategies	Lack of self-evaluation	Mind talk (self-enhancing cognitions)
	Negative response to failure	Encouraging self-evaluation
	Lack of meta-problem solving	Feedback from group leaders

the role play a second time. This role reversal encourages an awareness of the perspective of the other child.

Response Search. Children are encouraged to consider a full range of possible responses through the "What can I do?" step of the "Problem Solving" skill and the "Choices" step of other skills. They are encouraged to think of a number of possible ways to deal with a problem. Children are also encouraged to think of ways to "cool down" when they are being teased by others. In terms of homework assignments, the ESSGP employs four general approaches to promote the transfer of learning. One of these approaches involves having children find out how their parent or other important adult used a particular social skill in the past. This strategy expands the alternatives that a child has when faced with a problem situation and extends the positive modelling of important adults.

Response Decision. The program helps children make effective decisions by encouraging them to consider which of their various options is the best one to choose: the "Which is best?" step of "Problem Solving." In the "Keeping Out of Fights" skill, children consider the cost of getting into a fight. In fact, the consideration of the consequences of various actions is emphasized throughout the program: "If . . . then . . ." decision-making is encouraged and modelled by the group leaders.

Enactment. Prosocial behavior is encouraged through modelling and role play of difficult situations, "mind talk" that accompanies behavioral rehearsal, and homework assignments that involve the practice of the skill outside the group. In addition, the final step of many of the skills is "Do it and learn." The entire "Self-Control" skill focuses on the importance of controlling one's impulsive behavior. Thus, in many ways, the program seeks to expand a child's limited behavioral repertoire so that it contains prosocial alternatives.

Evaluation of Outcome. The evaluation of a behavioral choice is encouraged through feedback from the other group members and from the group leaders. Children are also encouraged to evaluate their own performance and are given the opportunity to view their own performance through videotaping of role plays. Group leaders tell children that the "Do it and Learn" skill step means that they need to evaluate whether their behavioral choice was a good one. If it was not a good choice, children are encouraged to make self-evaluative and coping statements such as, "Oh well, I guess that didn't work. I'll try one of my other choices next time." At the beginning of every session, homework assignments are reviewed: Children are asked to report on their attempts to practice the newly learned social skill, are reinforced for having practiced, and are encouraged to evaluate the success of these attempts.

EVALUATION OF THE ESSGP

The evaluation of the Earlscourt Social Skills Group Program started with a comparison of teacher and parent ratings on the Child Behavior Checklist (Achenbach & Edelbrock, 1983) before and after intervention. The children were rated as significantly improved on teacher and parent ratings of externalized, internalized, and total behavior problems following social skills training. These results were replicated in a subsequent study. These initial, nonexperimental program evaluations indicated that ESSGP was achieving its goal of reducing the behavior problems of aggressive, disruptive children as perceived by both teachers and parents. We were cautious in interpreting these results given the limitations of the preliminary assessments without a control group and, therefore, embarked on a more comprehensive assessment comprising a pre/post control group decision. This study, described in the following section, extended the preliminary research by including measures of social problem-solving and by assessing the maintenance of treatment gains. A waiting list control group was employed.

The hypotheses for this study were as follows: (a) children in the social skills group would improve on behavior problem ratings and in social problem-solving skills following social skills training; (b) children in the social skills group would be better on behavior problem ratings and in social problem-solving skills than children on the waiting list at Time 2; (c) children in the waiting list group would be better on behavior problem ratings and in social problem-solving skills following their participation in social skills training; and (d) children in the social skills group would maintain gains in behavior ratings and social problem-solving for 3 months following treatment (Time 1 vs. Time 3).

Subjects

Participants in the project were 40 children (34 boys and 6 girls) ranging in age from 8 to 12 years with a mean age of 10 years. The children were referred to the ESSGP by their teachers for aggressive, disruptive, and noncompliant behaviors. They were randomly assigned to either a fall or a spring session of social skills training. Children in the spring session served as a waiting list control group.

Measures

Measures were gathered from parents, teachers, and children at Time 1 (before either group had had social skills training), at Time 2 (after the social skills group had been through social skills training and before the waiting list group went into treatment) and at Time 3 (for a 3 month follow-up of those children in the social skills group and at the end of social skills training for children in the waiting list group).

Behavior Problems. As in the preliminary studies, children were rated by their teachers and parents on the Child Behavior Checklist. This instrument assesses the extent of a child's behavioral problems on two scales: externalizing behavior problems (e.g., aggressiveness, delinquency, and hyperactivity) and internalizing behavior problems (e.g., depression, social withdrawal, and somatic complaints). The CBCL also provides a measure of total behavior problems. The children were rated by their teachers on the Teachers' Report Form of the Child Behavior Checklist and by their parents on the standard Child Behavior Checklist at admission and discharge from social skills training. In addition, the social skills group was rated by parents and teachers 3 months after the end of the training period.

Social Problem Solving. The Social Intentionality Problem Solving Interview (SIPSI) (Bream, Hymel, & Rubin, 1986) was administered to the children. In an individual interview with one of the project researchers, children were asked to respond to four stories in which they were to imagine being the recipient of a negative outcome created by a hypothetical peer. After being read each story, children were led through a series of interview questions designed to assess social problem-solving based on the information processing model described above (Dodge, 1986; Rubin & Krasnor, 1986). Specifically, children were asked to project either a positive or negative expected outcome to a social dilemma, to infer either accidental or purposeful intent to the story actor, and to suggest possible behavioral responses to the situation. All of the children's responses were tape recorded and subsequently transcribed for coding.

The behavioral solutions suggested by the children were coded into one of the following content categories: avoidant, prosocial, gain information, assertive, aggressive, adult intervention, or don't know. A quarter of the SIPSI protocols were coded for reliability by an independent rater. Percentage interrater reliabilities for the coding categories ranged from 88% to 96%. The content solutions were tabulated as a proportion of the total number of solutions suggested by each child summed across four stories.

Results

The effectiveness of social skills training was assessed using 2(group) × 3 (time) multivariate repeated measures analyses of variance on the teacher and parent summary ratings of the CBCL and on the social problem-solving measures. One-tailed planned comparisons (Dunn's multiple comparison procedure) were subsequently conducted to test the specific hypotheses outlined above.

Teacher Ratings. There were significant main effects for time and group × time interactions on teacher ratings of externalizing behavior problems. There was a significant group by time interaction for teacher ratings of internalizing behavior problems.

Planned comparisons of teacher ratings of externalizing behavior problems indicated that teachers rated: (a) children in the social skills group as significantly improved following social skills training; (b) children in the social skills group as having fewer behavior problems than those in the waiting list control group at Time 2; (c) children on the waiting list as having fewer behavior problems following their participation in social skills training; and (d) children in the social skills group as significantly different from Time 1 to Time 3 indicating a maintenance of gains for 3 months following treatment.

Teacher ratings of internalizing behavior problems indicated no significant differences on the planned comparisons.

Parent Ratings. There were significant main effects for time on parent ratings of externalizing and internalizing behavior problems. There was also a significant group effect for parent ratings of internalizing behavior problems.

Planned comparisons of externalizing behavior problems indicated that parents rated: (a) no significant improvement for children in the social skills group following social skills training; (b) no significant difference between children in the social skills group and those in the waiting list control group at Time 2; (c) no difference for children in the waiting list group following their participation in social skills training; and (d) a significant improvement for children in the social skills group from Time 1 to Time 3.

Planned comparisons of internalizing behavior problems indicated that parents rated: (a) children in the social skills group as significantly improved following social skills training; (b) children in the social skills group as having fewer internalizing behavior problems than those in the waiting list control group at Time 2; (c) no difference for children on the waiting list control group in internalizing behavior problems following social skills training; and (d) children in the social skills group as significantly different from Time 1 to Time 3 indicating maintenance of treatment gains over 3 months.

Social Problem Solving. The hypotheses that we tested focused on changes in the social problem-solving of aggressive children following social skills training. Specifically, we expected that following treatment, there would be a decrease in hostile attributions, a decrease in the proportion of aggressive solutions, and a corresponding increase in the proportion of prosocial and/or assertive solutions.

The analyses indicated no effects of social skills training on any aspect of social problem-solving of children in the social skills group: There were no significant differences between their social problem-solving scores at Times 1 and 2, nor did they differ from the waiting list control group at Time 2. Additionally, there was no difference in the social problem-solving scores at Times 1 and 3 for children in the social skills group.

The planned comparisons of the social problem solving scores of the waiting list group from Time 2 to Time 3 indicated some effectiveness of social skills training. Following social skills training, children in the waiting list group suggested fewer purposeful or hostile attributions and they also showed the expected decrease in the proportion of aggressive solutions offered to deal with a hypothetical conflict situation. In addition, the waiting list group showed a significant increase in the proportion of assertive solutions they suggested.

The results of this study offer very limited and tentative support for the effectiveness of social skills group training in changing the social problem-solving skills of aggressive children. Although children in the social skills group made no significant changes in their social problem-solving skills, children in the waiting list group did demonstrate improvements with social skills training. The results for the waiting list group are encouraging as they suggest that children in this group, at least, began to change the way they thought about social problems, making fewer hostile attributions and replacing aggressive problem-solving strategies with more appropriate assertive alternatives. These results must be interpreted with considerable caution given the lack of a control group for comparison with the waiting list group and the failure to find change in the social problem-solving skills of children in the fall social skills group.

The social skills group's failure to show significant improvements may be a function of the heterogeneity of this sample of aggressive children. As Dodge (this volume) and Rubin and colleagues (this volume) have pointed out, not all children become aggressive via the same mechanism and not all aggressive children manifest the same social-cognitive deficits. It may be that the ESSGP emphasizes skills that address the deficits of only some of the aggressive children in the present study. An alternative explanation is that there may have been different experiences in the first and second sessions of social skills training. Coie and colleagues (this volume) report that the effectiveness of their social skills training program increased as the "treaters" became more practiced. The ESSGP group leaders may have been more skilled at delivering the social problem-solving components of the program during the second session of the year.

CONCLUSIONS AND FUTURE DIRECTIONS

The assessments of the Earlscourt Social Skills Group Program show some improvements that are maintained over time. The most notable improvements are those in the targeted behaviors (i.e., externalizing behavior problems) by the referring agent (i.e., the teachers). There was evidence of improved social problem-solving skills for one of the two groups of aggressive children in the social skills program. Future research considering the individual problem-solving styles of children in treatment might elucidate the process and extent of change. For this research, there must be a careful selection of measures to assess all steps in the social information processing sequence for a clearer indication of program effectiveness.

Given the three major features of our program: social skills training for the child, parent groups, and generalization activities with teachers and classes, an additional challenge for the associated research is to determine those aspects of the program that contribute most to the improvements in ratings of the aggressive children. In our current research, we are investigating the contribution of the parent training component to the effectiveness of the program in improving both child behavior problems and family interactions. Future plans include further assessments and observations of the peer relationships of the aggressive children. These observations are particularly important to establish that the improvement in teachers' ratings is not merely an effect of their hopes that these aggressive children would improve with the program. In addition, observations will provide information on the actual social problem-solving skills of the children.

Finally, the exercise of mapping the deficits of aggressive children onto the social information processing model (organizing the deficits of aggressive children, programming and measures along a theoretical model of social-cognitive processing) has been beneficial for generating ideas for program development and future research. It has guided our research, helped us look more carefully at the aggressive children we serve, and has encouraged the development of programming that will ameliorate their behavior problems at home, at school, and with their peers. Even if we have come only a short way in this process, we can hope to have prevented the acceleration of aggressive behavior problems for some children and interrupted their slide down the slippery slope toward maladjustment in adulthood.

ACKNOWLEDGMENTS

The research described in this paper was conducted at Earlscourt Child and Family Centre, Toronto, Canada. It was supported by the Laidlaw Foundation, the Ontario Mental Health Foundation and the Ontario Ministry of Health.

REFERENCES

Achenbach, T. M., & Edelbrock, C. (1983). *Manual for the child behavior checklist.* Burlington, VT: Queen City Printers.

Argyle, M. (1981). The contribution of social interaction research to social skills training. In J. D. Wine & M. D. Smye (Eds.), *Social competence.* New York: Guilford Press.

Bierman, K. L., Miller, C. L., & Stabb, S. D. (1987). Improving the social behavior and peer acceptance of rejected boys: effects of social skill training with instructions and prohibitions. *Journal of Consulting and Clinical Psychology, 55* (2), 194–200.

Bream, L., Hymel, S., & Rubin, K. (1986). The social problem solving interview: A manual for administration and scoring. Unpublished manuscript, University of Waterloo, Waterloo.

Chandler, M. J. (1973). Egocentrism and anti-social behavior: The assessment and training of social perspective taking skills. *Developmental Psychology, 9,* 326–327.

Coie, J. D., & Kupersmidt, J. B. (1983). A behavioral analysis of emerging social status in boys' groups. *Child Development, 54,* 1400–1416.

Dodge, K. A. (1980). Social cognition and children's aggressive behavior. *Child Development, 51,* 162–170.

Dodge, K. A. (in press). Attributional bias in aggressive children. In P. C. Kendall (Ed.), *Advances in cognitive-behavioral research and therapy.* New York: Academic Press.

Dodge, K. A. (1986). A social information processing model of social competence in children. In M. Perlmutter (Ed.), *Minnesota Symposia on Child Psychology.* Hillsdale, NJ: Lawrence Erlbaum Associates.

Dodge, K. A., & Frame, C. L. (1982). Social cognitive biases and deficits in aggressive boys. *Child Development, 51,* 620–635.

Dodge, K. A., Murphy, R. R., & Buchsbaum, K. (1984). The assessment of intention-cue detection skills in children: Implications for developmental psychopathology. *Child Development, 55,* 163–173.

Dodge, K. A., & Newman, J. P. (1981). Biased decision making processes in aggressive boys. *Journal of Abnormal Psychology, 90,* 375–379.

Dodge, K. A., & Tomlin, A. (1983). The role of cue-utilization in attributional biases among aggressive children. Presented at the Second Invitational Conference on Social Cognition, Nagshead, North Carolina.

Gagnon, C. (1988). Self-concept of aggressive boys. Paper presented at the University of Waterloo Conference on Child Development, Waterloo.

Goldstein, A. P., Sprafkin, R. P., Gershaw, J., & Klein, P. (1980). *Skill streaming the adolescent: A structured learning approach to teaching prosocial skills.* Champaign, IL: Research Press.

Kazdin, A. E., Esveldt-Dawson, K., French, H., & Unis, A. S. (1987). Problem-solving skills training and relationship therapy in the treatment of antisocial child behavior. *Journal of Consulting and Clinical Psychology, 55*(1), 76–85.

Krasnor, L. R. (1982). An observational study of social problem solving in young children. In K. H. Rubin & H. S. Ross (Eds.), *Peer relations and social skills in childhood.* New York: Springer-Verlag.

Ladd, G., & Oden, S. (1979). The relationship between peer acceptance and children's ideas about helpfulness. *Child Development, 40,* 402–408.

LaGreca, A. M., & Santogrossi, D. A. (1980). Social skills training with elementary school students: A behavioral group approach. *Journal of Consulting and Clinical Psychology, 48,* 220–227.

Lochman, J., Burch, P. R., Curry, J. F., & Lampron, L. B. (1984). Treatment and generalization effects of cognitive behavioral and goal setting interventions with aggressive boys. *Journal of Consulting and Clinical Psychology, 52,* 915–916.

Matson, J. L., Esveldt-Dawson, K., Andrasik, F., Ollendick, T. H., Petti, T., & Hersen, M. (1980). Direct, observational and generalization effects of social skills training with emotionally disturbed children. *Behavioral Therapy, 11,* 522–531.

Milich, R., & Dodge, K. A. (in press). Social information processing patterns in child psychiatric populations. *Journal of Abnormal Child Psychology.*

Novaco, R. W. (1978). Anger and coping with stress: Cognitive-behavioral intervention. In J. P. Foreyt & D. P. Rathjen (Eds.), *Cognitive behavioral therapy: research and application.* New York: Plenum.

Oden, S., & Asher, S. R. (1977). Coaching children in social skills training for friendship making. *Child Development, 48,* 495–506.

Parker, J. G., & Asher, S. R. (1987). Peer relations and later personal adjustment: are low-accepted children at risk? *Psychological Bulletin,* 102–3, 357–389.

Patterson, G. R. (1986). Performance models for antisocial boys. *American Psychologist, 41*(4), 432–444.

Patterson, G. R. (1982). *Coercive family process: A social learning approach, Vol. 3.* Eugene, OR: Castalia Publishing Co.

Patterson, G. R. (1979). Treatment for children with conduct problems: a review of outcome studies. In S. Feshbach & A. Fraczek (Eds.), *Aggression and behavior change: Biological and social processes,* New York: Praeger Publishing Co.

Perry, D. G., & Bussey, K. (1977). Self-reinforcement in high- and low-aggressive boys following acts of aggression. *Child Development, 48,* 653–658.

Perry, D. G., Perry, L. C., & Boldizar, J. P. (in press). Learning of aggression. In M. Lewis & S. Miller (Eds.), *Handbook of developmental psychopathology.*

Perry, D. G., Perry, L. C., & Rasmussen, P. (1986). Cognitive social learning mediators of aggression, *Child Development, 57,* 700–711.

Perry, D. G., Perry, L. C., & Weiss, R. J. (1989). Sex differences in the consequences that children anticipate for aggression. *Developmental Psychology, 25,* 312–319.

Richard, B., & Dodge, K. (1982). Social maladjustment and problem solving in school-aged children. *Journal of Consulting and Clinical Psychology, 50,* 226–233.

Robins, L. N. (1974). Antisocial behavior disturbances of childhood: prevalence, prognosis, prospects. In E. J. Anthony and C. Kaupernick (Eds.), *The child in his family, Vol. 3: Children at psychiatric risk,* (pp. 447–460). New York: Wiley.

Rubin, K. H. (1982). Social skill and social-cognitive correlates of observed isolation behavior in preschoolers. In K. H. Rubin & H. S. Ross (Eds.), *Peer relations and social skills in childhood.* New York: Springer-Verlag.

Rubin, K. H., & Daniels-Bierness, T. (1983). Concurrent and predictive correlates of sociometric status in kindergarten and grade one children. *Merrill-Palmer Quarterly, 29,* 337–352.

Rubin, K. H., & Krasnor, L. R. (1986). Social cognitive and social behavioral perspectives on problem solving. *The Minnesota Symposia on Child Psychology* (Vol. 18). Hillsdale, NJ: Lawrence Erlbaum Associates.

Selman, R. L. (1976). Toward a structural analysis of developing interpersonal relations concepts: Research with normal and disturbed preadolescent boys. In A. D. Pick (Ed.), *Minnesota Symposia on Child Psychology,* (Vol. 10). Minneapolis: University of Minnesota Press.

Slaby, R. G., & Guerra, N. G. (1988) Cognitive mediators of aggression in adolescent offenders: 1. Assessment. *Developmental Psychology, 24*(4), 580–588.

Weissberg, R. P., Gesten, E. L., Rapkin, B. D., Cowen, E. L., Davidson, E., de Apodaca, R. G., & McKim, B. J. (1981). Evaluation of a social problem-solving training program for suburban and inner-city third grade children. *Journal of Consulting and Clinical Psychology, 49,* 251–261.

Commentary

Social-Cognitive Treatment Programs

Linda Rose-Krasnor
Brock University

Social skills programs emphasizing social cognition grew rapidly during the 1970s for at least two reasons. First, treatments based on traditional behavioral techniques often failed to produce generalized and long-lasting effects. Social-cognitive programs, which tended to stress self-regulation of behavior, seemed to offer a better chance for generalization and internalization. Second, the predominantly Piagetian research of this decade provided strong theoretical support.

Social-cognitive interventions seemed especially appropriate for aggressive children. Although early evidence linking aggression and social-cognitive deficits was largely correlational, the results strongly suggested that major causes of aggression could be remediated through social-cognitive means. Early social-cognitive interventions drawn from these studies tended to be based on social problem-solving models (e.g., Spivack, Platt, & Shure, 1976). They were relatively simplistic, short-term, with narrow outcome measures, and overly optimistic in expecting long-term effects (see Denham & Almedia, 1987; Urbain & Kendall, 1980). These early programs also had an intra-individual focus which overemphasized the role of the child's internal cognitive structure in determining aggression. The influence of parents, peers, and other external factors on aggression were correspondingly underemphasized.

The programs presented by Kendall, Pepler, and colleagues illustrate much of the progress made since those early years. Both programs employed multiple outcome measures, included relevant control groups, and used follow-ups to assess maintenance. The post hoc analyses of moderating variables (e.g., subject attributes) begun by these authors holds promise for the future refinement of social-cognitive programs. Neither program, however, directly assessed target behaviors in the natural setting, although both used indirect measures of behavioral change (rating scales, role-play assessments). The lack of such observational measures is common to social-cognitive approaches and represents one of its major current limitations.

Recently, several reviewers have concluded that social-cognitive programs are effective in changing targeted social-cognitive skills in normal and at-risk groups. Corresponding changes in social behaviors, however, have not been consistently demonstrated for high-risk groups (Pellegrini & Urbain, 1985; Rubin & Krasnor, 1986). Evidence for a causal link between changes in social cognition and changes in behavior has been even scarcer (Durlak, 1983; Gresham, 1985). Analyses of aggressive subtypes, well-represented in this volume (e.g., Dodge; Rubin, Bream, & Rose-Krasnor), suggest that only *some* aggressive children will benefit from social-cognitive interventions. In addition, the use of social-cognitive training for primary prevention purposes has not yet been established, since there is little evidence that early social-cognitive deficits actually cause future social problems in nonrisk groups (Durlak, 1983).

These findings highlight the need to reexamine the simplistic model of the relationship between cognition and behavior which underlies many current social-cognitive programs. The original Piagetian and information-processing contexts of many programs supported the idea of people as rational, relatively affectless processors of information. Basically, this direct model can be summarized as "I think, therefore I act." However, there are many children who know about nonaggressive strategies, who talk easily about the negative consequences of aggression, and who *still* aggress. This is inconsistent with a logical model of behavior.

The paradox of many psychopathologies is that although many individuals can think rationally, they often do not exercise this skill (Wenar, 1984). Similarly, Selman (1980) hypothesized that normal and problem children may not differ in their social-cognitive abilities but rather in the likelihood that they will apply these skills in their everyday interactions. There are also many examples of nonaggressive behavior from children who give hypothetical aggressive strategies during testing and/or who do not suggest negative consequences for hypothetical aggression. This cognitive-behavior discrepancy may result from assessment task demands which exceed the child's processing capacity or from the use of automatic but competent social behavior outside the testing situations.

In any case, it appears that social cognition is neither necessary nor sufficient for nonaggression. So what is cognition *doing* in a treatment program? Results from intervention studies indicate that social-cognitive skills can increase the likelihood of socially competent behavior, but only inconsistently. Thus, it is necessary to better specify the variables that mediate social-cognitive influences on behavior before we can effectively incorporate these elements into treatment programs.

In recent years, this search for explanatory variables has taken a systems perspective, emphasizing interrelated systems and feedback processes (Berrien, 1968). A systems approach is consistent with the information processing orientation which forms the basis of the Kendall and colleagues and Pepler and colleagues programs. In such programs, specific social-cognitive steps form the basis of much of the training. Many of these approaches, however, show a relatively static view of social cognition, since the connections between these steps are relatively neglected (Rose-Krasnor, 1988).

From a more dynamic and integrative view, the social-cognitive system would be considered to be smoothly functioning when it was characterized by efficiency, flexible adaptation to changing inputs, and effectiveness. In contrast, poorly integrated social-cognitive processes result in breakdowns in the flow between components. For example, an objective of many social-cognitive training programs is to help the child produce a large number of hypothetical, nonaggressive strategies. This procedure, however, may generate too many potential strategies to handle in the next step (evaluation of alternatives). The process may stop (the child gives up), may discard potentially appropriate strategies in order to reduce them to a manageable number, or use a simple and inadequate evaluation algorithm (e.g., repeat what was done the last time). This system may also break down from a lack of accurate external feedback regarding the effects of an action. The aggressive child is particularly likely to be deficient in feedback processes. Although many social-cognitive programs teach the information-gathering aspects of feedback as a social-cognitive step, relatively few emphasize how that information actually feeds back and alters the ongoing behavioral sequence.

An example of a model for the cognition-behavior systems is presented in Fig. 1. A brief summary of the system will illustrate how such a model might be used to better understand why adequate social cognitions fail to translate directly into adequate social actions. In this model, the steps within the social-cognitive system (SCS) outlined by Kendall, Ronan, & Epps and Pepler, King, & Byrd are represented by the single oval "a." This representation illustrates that systems often consist of smaller subsystems, which themselves receive inputs, process them, and produce outputs. Here, the SCS receives inputs from both external ("b") and internal ("c") sources. Examples of external inputs relevant to aggression include cues indicating others' emotions, the scarcity of resources, or threatening peer behaviors. Internal sources may include

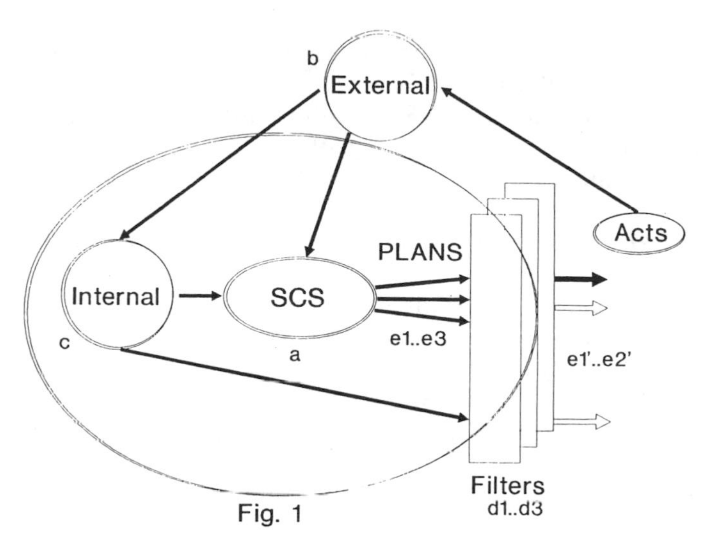

Fig. 1

information from parasympathetic and sympathetic systems, as well as knowledge stored in memory. It is also possible for the SCS to produce outputs which serve as inputs to itself. The social attributions described by Pepler and colleagues, for example, are outputs of a social-cognitive process and have been related to social strategy choices (Dodge, this volume).

The SCS outputs intended actions or plans (E1 . . . E3), corresponding to the hypothetical social strategies assessed in the Pepler and colleagues program. One of the most critical questions for social-cognitive treatments is why these social plans are not directly translated into actions. In this regard, it is helpful to conceptualize these planned actions as having to pass through a series of filters ("d1 . . d3") before they emerge in the "real" world as actions ("e1', e2'"). These intended actions may be blocked or distorted as they pass through the filters. The nature of these filters are of major theoretical and practical significance.

Some of the filters are primarily internal to the child and may include skill deficiencies. For example, a child might decide to hit a home run to impress classmates but lack the necessary physical skills, or a child may intend to explain her actions to an angry friend but not have the relevant verbal skills. External filters include environmental deficits (e.g., no one around to play with) as well as constraints (e.g., interfering peers). Acts emerging from these filters change the child's external environment.

The cognitive-behavioral system requires information regarding these effects to adapt itself accordingly. Overall, the model illustrates the need to consider factors outside the SCS itself in order to understand the role of social cognition in the treatment of aggression. Most of the social-cognitive treatment programs, however, tend to overemphasize the SCS alone.

One advantage of such a model is that it can help identify important clinical or research topics, as well as provide a framework for classifying types of interventions according to their relative emphasis. The form of this model suggests that programs which are predominantly social-cognitive in nature will only be effective with those aggressive children whose deficits are within the SCS oval. Many of these deficits have been well explained in previous chapters and, for example, include difficulties in generating social strategies and inferring others' intentions. Another potential problem is an inability to accurately represent relevant filters inside the SCS. These children will intend actions that have little chance of being successfully implemented and thus will be frequently frustrated. These children could perhaps benefit from social-cognitive interventions specifically designed to monitor internal and external resources and possibilities. In contrast, some children may act without using the SCS at all. They may have adequate social cognitive processing, but fail to engage it in social interaction. Effective treatment for these children should focus on the use of self-generated (e.g., anger) and external (e.g., threat) cues to explicitly engage cognitive processes. These components are present in both the Pepler and Kendall programs, and should result in an increased correspondence between thinking and action as well as less impulsive aggression.

Other treatment approaches focus on the filters themselves. Some children may be unable to translate their nonaggressive intended actions into behaviors because of internal filter problems. Planned actions can only be accomplished if required abilities are present. Simple aggressive acts may slip through the filters more easily than more complex nonaggressive acts. These children may benefit from behavioral treatments, such as those present in both the Kendall and Pepler programs, designed to improve specific physical and verbal skills.

Other children may be aggressive due to external filters (e.g., overly restrictive parents, peers who reinforce aggression). Since social-cognitive processes in these children may be adequate, further training would not be recommended. Ecologically-based therapy would seem most appropriate in loosening the constricting or distorting effects of environmental conditions and increasing the correspondence between adequate social cognitions and behavior.

Other aggressive children may have difficulty in affect regulation, even though their "cold" cognitive processes may be quite normal. Almost all social-cognitive skill training is conducted under cold cognitive conditions. There is strong evidence, however, that emotion may alter the cognitive process itself (e.g., Isen, 1984). For example, negative affect tends to reduce the number of alternative solutions and complexity of evaluation. Training for these children should include control for emotion, so that cold cognitive abilities can be translated into action.

In many ways, the programs described by Pepler and Kendall and their colleagues represent the best of current social skills programs emphasizing social-cognitive principles. However, the field of social-cognitive interventions, especially those based on social problem-solving models, is particularly vulnerable to criticisms regarding the lack of behavioral outcome measures. In addition, there is a clear need for more complex and testable models of the cognitive-behavior relationships to better guide treatment choices for specific target groups.

REFERENCES

Berrien, F. (1968). *General and social systems.* New Brunswick, NJ: Rutgers University Press.

Denham, S. A., & Almedia, M. C. (1987). Children's social problem-solving skills, behavioral adjustment and intervention: A meta-analysis evaluating theory and practice. *Journal of Applied Developmental Psychology, 8,* 391–409.

Durlak, J. (1983). Social problem solving as a primary prevention strategy. In R. Felner, L. Jason, J. Maritsugu & S. Farber (Eds.), *Preventive Psychology* (pp. 31–18). New York: Pergamon Press.

Gresham, F. (1985). Utility of cognitive behavioral procedures for social skills training with children: A critical review. *Journal of Abnormal Child Psychology, 13,* 411–423.

Isen, A. (1984). Toward understanding the role of affect in cognition. In R. S. Wyer & T. K. Srull (Eds.), *Handbook of social cognition: Vol. 3.* (pp. 179–326). Hillsdale, NJ: Lawrence Erlbaum Associates.

Pellegrini, D., & Urbain, E. (1985). An evaluation of interpersonal cognitive problem solving training with children. *Journal of Child Psychology and Psychiatry, 26,* 17–41.

Rubin, K. H., & Krasnor, L. R. (1986). Social-cognitive and social-behavioral perspectives on problem solving. In M. Perlmutter (Ed.), *Minnesota Symposium on child psychology* (Vol. 18, pp. 1–68). Hillsdale, NJ: Lawrence Erlbaum Associates.

Rose-Krasnor, L. (1988). Social cognition. In T. D. Yawkley & J. E. Johnson (Eds.), *Integrative processes and socialization* (pp. 79–95). Hillsdale, NJ: Lawrence Erlbaum Associates.

Selman, R. (1980). *The growth of interpersonal understanding.* New York: Academic Press.

Spivack, G., Platt, J., & Shure, M. (1976). *The problem solving approach to adjustment.* San Francisco: Jossey-Bass.

Urbain, E., & Kendall, P. (1980). Review of social-cognitive problem-solving interventions with children. *Psychological Bulletin, 88,* 109–143.

Wenar, C. (1984). Commentary: Progress and problems in the cognitive approach to clinical child psychology. *Journal of Counselling and Clinical Psychology, 52,* 57–62.

Section 7:
Peer and School-based Intervention

15

Programmatic Intervention with Aggressive Children in the School Setting

John D. Coie
Marion Underwood
John E. Lochman
Duke University

In this chapter we describe a program of intervention activities conducted with aggressive children in several school settings. As the background for this study, we review the alternative intervention models for working with aggressive children, articulating the premises and change dynamics of each model for implementation within a school setting. The project we are reporting on is part of a larger preventive intervention effort with elementary school children who are socially rejected by their peer group (Coie, Rabiner, & Lochman, 1989). Here we describe just the data that pertain to the aggressive subset of this sample. For this reason we describe the relation between aggression and peer rejection in childhood and present a rationale for focussing on this jointly defined risk population.

For those of us whose research interests have been initially directed toward the phenomenon of childhood social rejection, the problem of aggression is hard to ignore, because aggressiveness is the single most important reason for a child to be rejected by peers (Coie, Dodge, & Kupersmidt, 1990). This latter conclusion should not be interpreted as meaning that most or even the majority of children who are rejected by peers can be characterized as highly aggressive. The percentage of rejected children who are highly aggressive ranges from 30% to 40%, with the figures being higher for males. In the samples of low-income Black children that comprised the population to which our intervention was directed, about half of the rejected boys were highly aggressive. In these studies, aggression was measured by peer nominations as "frequently starting fights." A nomination total greater than one standard deviation

deviation above the mean was the cut-point for high aggression. Peer assessments of aggression are positively correlated with teacher ratings of aggression and groups formed on the basis of these scores reflect appropriate differences in unbiased observations of aggressive behavior (Coie & Dodge, 1988).

When the issue is turned the other way around, the relation between aggression and rejection is even stronger. Almost two thirds of highly aggressive boys are rejected, whereas only 20% of nonaggressive boys are rejected. Thus, it is hard to ignore the social consequences of aggressive behavior when considering an intervention for rejected children.

The primary motivation for the larger intervention project was to improve rejected children's social relations with their peers as a way of testing the hypothesized causal relation between rejected peer status and various forms of disorder in adolescence. The longitudinal connection between rejection and disorder has been found to be particularly strong for aggressive rejected children. Parker and Asher (1987) have documented a compelling case for the connection between early aggression and later delinquency. In fact, the predictive ratios of delinquency are at least three to one for aggressive and nonaggressive boys (Magnussen, Statlin, & Duner, 1983; West & Farrington, 1973). Roff, Sells, and Golden (1972) report ratios of $2\frac{1}{2}:1$ for rejected and non-rejected boys, but in one study in which aggression and rejection were compared as predictors (Kupersmidt & Coie, in press), aggression was significantly better in predicting delinquency than rejection. These studies all described predominantly White samples. Some unpublished data from our longitudinal work with a predominantly Black population have revealed some surprisingly different results for conduct disorder in early adolescence.

A sample of 172 sixth graders was administered Elliott and Huizinga's (1983) survey interview on conduct disorder. Their mothers also completed the Child Behavior Checklist (Achenbach & Edelbrock, 1981). These children were randomly selected from a sample of more than 500 third graders who had been screened on sociometric and behavioral assessment measures. Fourth-grade data on these same measures had also been obtained for this sample. Non-orthogonal model comparisons of the predictive power of aggression and peer rejection were applied to these data on conduct disorder for this sample. Peer rejection in third and fourth grade was a significant predictor of both self-reported conduct disorder and maternal ratings of externalized disorder in sixth grade. (The same thing was true for maternal ratings of internalized disorder.) Aggression was a less powerful predictor of conduct disorder than peer rejection and in some cases it was not a significant predictor. Although there were no significant interaction effects for aggression and rejection, the general pattern is for children who are both rejected and aggressive to be at highest risk for conduct problems in adolescence. The significance of rejection as a risk marker in this population may be tied to the relatively higher occurrence of aggression among these elementary school children, making the local standards of peer group adjustment more important as a discriminating factor. These results underscore the value of using both peer rejection and aggression as screening variables for the prevention of adolescent delinquency.

RATIONALE FOR SCHOOL-BASED INTERVENTION

Our intervention program took place within the schools. The screening of subjects for placement in the program was carried out across all the third-grade classrooms in cooperating schools. Lack of parent permission and subject consent were the only conditions precluding involvement. In many of the earlier intervention studies with antisocial and aggressive children, subjects were identified for the program by external agencies such as juvenile authorities. Intervention activities frequently took place in the home or in clinical settings. Because of these differences, it may be useful to discuss some of the implications of basing a prevention program in the schools.

The most obvious advantage of a school-based program is access to the most representative sample of subjects who are aggressive. Referred samples carry with them the potentially biasing factors of any clinic sample. The circumstances that bring a child to the attention of juvenile authorities, or even school counselors, may constrain the sample in ways that are unknown to the investigators. To some extent one might expect to confront the worst cases, yet it is also possible that subjects who are "caught" or found out do things that upset adults more than peers, or are not skilled in avoiding detection and thus constitute a sample of lower social intelligence. Characteristics of parents also may be important. Shepherd, Oppenheim, and Mitchell (1971) noted that when children who have been treated in clinics for behavior problems are matched to children with similar problems, based on teacher ratings of problem behavior, the primary difference in the two groups lies with their mothers. Mothers of clinic-referred children are more anxious and less confident about their ability to deal with their children.

A second advantage of school-based intervention is that access to the children is more uniform and more convenient. The children are in one place and, if they attend school, one is not dependent on their parents remembering to keep appointments.

A third advantage is that school is the major arena for social interaction for most children. By locating the intervention there, one has greater potential access to information on the actual aggressive interactions with peers. This can facilitate the formation of treatment goals and the evaluation of progress in meeting these goals. Peers that are brought in for group activities are the ones with whom real change is desired, so that this type of in vivo practice can lead to real social gains.

The disadvantages of screening subjects in the schools and soliciting participation in the program is that the project staff have to carry the burden of motivation for change. Although this may not be any different than for some clinic-referred cases, the initiative for change is the investigator's. Neither parents nor school staff have requested help and thus cannot be expected to cooperate with the intervention program. This fact can limit the options for the intervention strategy, particularly those that require monitoring or reinforcement activities by the child's caretakers.

Because the primary task of school is academic development, interventions having a social focus, such as reducing aggressive behavior, are often viewed as peripheral and coming at the expense of the basic mission of the teacher. Not all school administrators or teachers feel this way, but in a multiple-site intervention such as ours, this can be a significant source of nonexperimental variance.

For our purposes, the advantages of working in the schools seemed to outweigh the disadvantages, though this decision placed some constraints on our choice of intervention method, as outlined above. The approach that was adopted has an educational cast to it, because the focus was on helping aggressive children develop mechanisms for the internal control of aggressive impulses. This choice did support the goal of testing interventions with the potential for a broad range of applications. If it is possible to help children develop internal controls in this way, the program has the potential for assisting children to master inappropriate aggressive behavior in a wide range of situations not normally accessible to behavior management techniques.

Available Intervention Models

Numerous and varied methods of treatment have been used in attempts to reduce aggressive behavior in children, and a comprehensive review of these is beyond the scope of this chapter. Despite the enormous energy these efforts represent, the record of success in these undertakings is somewhat discouraging. In reviewing the literature on aggression, we have been struck by the extent to which research on the effectiveness of intervention with aggression is so infrequently connected to research on the nature and function of aggression. Oftentimes intervention researchers do not explicitly connect their strategies for intervention to models of aggressive processes. In the following discussion of approaches to aggression intervention, we attempt to articulate the models of aggression which underlie the different methods of treatment. Approaches to intervention with aggressive children seem to fall into five broad categories: (a) behavior management, (b) emotional control strategies, (c) social skill training, (d) social information processing, and (e) cognitive or emotional perspective taking.

The most well-researched model of intervention involves some variant of behavior management techniques. Aggressive behavior is reduced by reinforcing the child's positive behavior, and by using time-out or response-cost procedures as deterrents to negative behavior. These programs typically focus on training parents in behavior management techniques (e.g., Patterson, Chamberlain, & Reid, 1982; Wahler, 1975), but in some investigations, teachers apply these same principles with children in their classrooms (e.g., Patterson, 1974).

Behavior management interventions are based on a model of aggression that comes from social-learning theory. Excessive aggression is taken to be the result of a socialization history in which the instrumental value of aggression has been greater than that which is typical of the larger community. Children have learned to get what they want by means of aversive behavior; sometimes this is the result of observing others, but sometimes the acquisition pattern is more complicated as in the sequence of coercive interactions outlined by Patterson and his colleagues (1982). Aggression is viewed as a bad habit acquired as a result of faulty environmental contingencies. Thus, it is assumed that altering these contingencies can lead to the extinction of this tendency toward excessive aggression.

Some of the best examples of behavior management approaches to intervention with aggressive children are to be found in the parent-training programs developed by Patterson (1974) and Wahler (1975), and the response cost program devised by Forman (1980). All of these have been effective in reducing aggressive behavior. Parent-training programs seem to be effective in reducing aggressive behavior at home and not at school, and teacher-based training programs seem to be effective in reducing aggression at school but not at home (Breiner & Forehand, 1981).

A second broad category of approaches to intervention with aggressive children entails the use of emotional control strategies. Children are helped to control their angry impulses by training them to recognize their own strong negative affect and to control it by the use of self-statements and other cognitive mediation stratagems. The premise of emotional control strategies is that aggression is the result of inadequate impulse control, of faulty anger management. Unfortunately, well-articulated models of emotional development that might provide guidelines as to how and when children learn to handle their strong feelings in socially appropriate ways do not yet exist.

There is a fair-sized literature on the evaluation of programs for teaching emotional control to impulsive or aggressive children (e.g., Meichenbaum & Goodman, 1971; Novaco, 1979; Kettlewell & Kausch, 1983). With one exception, these programs have not been effective in reducing aggressive behavior as observed by teachers or other adults, although they typically lead to changed performance on various cognitive measures. However, Lochman, Burch, Curry, and Lampron (1984) have developed an anger control program that has yielded significant decreases in disruptive and aggressive behavior in the classroom and at home. The essential elements of their program were adopted in the present study and are described later.

Emotional control strategies have the advantage of being well suited to intervening with aggressive children in the school setting. Teaching these strategies in the school allows for a steady exposure to cognitive mediation principles over longer periods of time, as well as ample opportunity to practice emotional control in the types of naturally occurring social situations that aggressive children often find difficult.

A third, more indirect, approach to the reduction of aggression in children has been the use of social skills training, training in positive interaction skills or social problem-solving skills. The goal of these programs is to substitute more appropriate and socially effective behaviors for aggression.

The social skills training approach to intervention assumes that aggression is a less adequate response to difficult social situations. The aggressive child is thought to have an inadequate repertoire of skills for handling difficult social situations, and thus resorts to aggression.

There are several reported studies in which the effectiveness of social skills training for the reduction of aggressive behavior in children has been evaluated. Pitkanen (1974) found that coaching in socially appropriate ways to handle conflict situations resulted in decreased aggressiveness on a variety of lab games and activities. Goldstein, Sherman, Gershaw, Sprajkin, and Glick (1978) found that social skills training with aggressive adolescents resulted in increased negotiations skills in the laboratory. Bierman, Miller, and Staub (1987) compared the effectiveness of social skills training and prohibition in reducing the negative behaviors of boys rejected by other children. Subjects in the prohibition condition showed immediate, stable decreases in aversive behavior, and subjects who received social skills instruction exhibited increased rates of positive social interaction 6 weeks after treatment. This suggests that although social skills training may increase prosocial behavior in aggressive children, prohibition for negative behavior may be necessary for a reduction in aggressive behavior.

Like emotional control training, social skills training seems quite suitable for interventions in the school setting. Reliance on adult caretaker cooperation is quite minimal, the training procedures fit nicely with an academic curriculum, and the opportunity for training and practice in the variety of social situations offered by the school should enhance the effectiveness of this method.

A fourth possibility for intervening with aggressive children is training in social information processing skills. Recent research by Dodge and his colleagues (e.g., Dodge, McClaskey, Brown, & Petit, 1987) has shown that aggressive children have specific deficits in the way they process social cues in ambiguous and frustrating social situations, the way they generate and evaluate appropriate responses to these situations, and in their enactment of effective solutions. As yet, there have been no published examples of intervention programs that are based on this model of aggression, but the research literature in support of the model is so compelling that its existence must be acknowledged.

The assumptions of an information processing model are difficult to enumerate because the problems of faulty social information processing can be construed as involving more than just cognitive errors. Children are seen as behaving aggressively because they make mistakes about the harmful intent of others, they do not select the most socially appropriate response alternatives, or they implement them poorly. Although the social information processing model does not address the issue of emotional control directly, because the emphasis is on cognitive process, motivational priorities may influence either social perception or the response selection process or both. Some children may be more vigilant to interpersonal slights than others, or the importance of letting others know that they cannot get away with things may influence response choices. Unskillful implementation of appropriate social responses might be traced to lack of practice or to social anxiety. It is difficult to disentangle these elements from one another, so that although the most obvious retraining paradigm would be a cognitive training model, in reality an intervention model might not be so easy to articulate.

A last approach to aggression is worth mentioning because it has a developmental tradition that has been elaborated and tested with conduct disorder, although not explicitly with aggressive children. The Piagetian perspective on social development centers on perspective-taking ability as a critical factor in determining social effectiveness. The ability to recognize that other people have a different perspective on social events and to be able to reconstruct that other perspective from the available cues is considered to be a significant cognitive achievement, from the standpoint of social development. Adolescents who are deficient in this ability are thought to be less empathetic than others and more prone to violate their rights. In this spirit, Chandler (1973) trained adolescent delinquents in social role-taking skills and found that this decreased subsequent offenses. There have been no other published studies in which this method was used with aggressive or conduct disordered children. A perspective-taking approach to intervention with aggressive children assumes that aggressive behavior is a result of an egocentric perspective or cognitive style.

DESCRIPTION OF THE TRAINING PROGRAM

The social relations training program we used in our study is actually a composite of several of the approaches mentioned earlier. The goal of this program was to improve the overall social skills of the child. However, social relations training is different from social skills training in that it is not aimed solely at helping children develop skill at prosocial behaviors like cooperation and the negotiation of play activity. The program also emphasized the development of social problem-solving skills, as well as the reduction of aggressive behaviors. The program was made up of four components: (a) social problem solving, (b) positive play training, (c) group entry skill training, and (d) dealing effectively with strong negative feelings. Although the last component of the program, dealing effectively with strong negative feelings, seemed to be most relevant to the modification of aggressive behavior, we also thought that social problem-solving and social skills training might serve to reduce aggression by helping children to generate and enact alternative, more acceptable social behaviors. Thus, the program had four components: some were parts of programs with demonstrated effectiveness, and others were based on research on the determinants of negative peer status.

Social relations training took place during 26 scheduled individual sessions of a half hour in length, and 8 sessions with pairs or small groups of children. Children were seen twice weekly in sessions during the school day from early October until late April.

The program was designed to be flexible, and staff members were encouraged to vary the pacing of various parts of the curriculum to match the particular needs of subjects. The program was divided into four general units on social problem solving, partner play skills, group entry skills, and anger-coping skills. Staff members used videotapes extensively to introduce concepts. In the peer play and group sessions, children were encouraged to make films of themselves in play or negotiation situations in a manner similar to that employed by Bierman and Furman (1984). The children were told that they were making the films for the purpose of teaching college students about what fourth graders are like. The groups practiced situations similar to those for which the rejected children had been given prior training, and the staff member pointed out and praised behavior that illustrated the concept that the children had been taught in order to reward positive social behavior and to create a feeling of successful task performance for the group.

Approximately seven sessions were scheduled for social problem-solving training. The elements of this section were: focusing on identifying problem situations, articulating goals in these situations, inhibiting impulsive reactions, and considering alternative solutions and their consequences. Children were presented with a "social problem-solving ladder," a shorthand representation of the sequence involved in social problem solving, in order to make the process easier for them to remember. An assumption underlying problem-solving training is that once children learn to think of alternative responses, they will be more likely to enact some of the more appropriate responses in their social behavior. As particular types of problematic behaviors became evident for particular children, they were encouraged to practice the more adaptive solutions in role-playing versions of these situations. Specific goals for behavior change were sometimes formulated as behavioral contracts with the children and they and their trainers monitored progress toward these goals. The social problem-solving unit served as an organizing framework for all the subsequent units. Peer play, group entry, and anger-coping units were approached as exemplars of situations in which social problem-solving would be useful.

The second component of social relations training focuses on enhancing skills involved in playing with a partner. Children were assisted in evaluating and working on improving the way they look, the way they sound, the things they say when they initiate contact with others, how they respond to negative reactions from others, and how to get involved with other children using strategies like negotiation and cooperation. The nine scheduled sessions for the partner play unit emphasized skills related to maintaining dyadic relationships with peers. Much of this was based on earlier work by Oden and Asher (1977) and Ladd (1981). The earlier sessions focused on use of nonverbal communication through eye contact, body language, and voice tone. Later sessions emphasized more sophisticated interpersonal skills, such as negotiation, cooperation, and acceptance of rejection. Rehearsal and practice with peers was an important component of this section.

The third component of social relations training was designed to help children in several group-related skills. Research on peer group entry and sociometric status has demonstrated that rejected children are often unsuccessful in their attempts to join groups of children (Putallaz, 1983; Dodge, 1983). Putallaz and Wasserman (in press) propose that the relevance of an entering child's behavior to the ongoing activity of the group may be the determining factor in whether the child is accepted into the group or rejected from joining it. Children were trained to assess the general climate of groups they want to join, to recognize the rules of the group and the leadership structure of the group, and to match their style of entry to the ongoing play and activity of the group. Children were also encouraged to consider which types of approaches are more or less likely to be successful in different types of group situations. This unit on group entry skills consisted of 14 sessions, including practice in small group sessions.

The fourth unit of social relations training, coping with angry feelings, is the component most clearly oriented toward aggression, and therefore this unit was emphasized most for the subjects described in this report. This section of the program was designed to teach children to control strong negative feelings by teaching them how to identify and curtail impulsive responses, to use self-statements to regulate behavior, and by helping them to reframe the ways they think about who "wins" in interpersonal situations. This last unit was scheduled to take place during the last four sessions in the original design of social relations training. However, for the subjects in this study for whom aggression was particularly a problem, the anger control unit was covered right after the social problem-solving unit and was expanded to cover as many sessions as were required. Controlling aggressive behavior was also emphasized in the context of the material presented in the other units on social problem solving, partner play, and peer group entry.

The last component of the anger-control section of social relations, the section on helping children rethink who "wins" and "loses" in various types of social situations, was new to this program and was not part of the Lochman (Lochman et al., 1984) program that was adapted for use in this project. There is a remarkable need for research that addresses the goals and motivations of aggressive children. It seems as though many of these children have an unusually strong need for retaliation. They seem highly motivated not to let other children get the best of them. Retaliation seems to be very important for children; for them "winning" in interpersonal encounters often means having the last word or striking the last blow. Therefore, one goal of social relations training was to help these children reframe their thinking about what it means to win or lose in a social interaction. For example, it was suggested to highly aggressive subjects that when they respond to provocation by becoming angry or fighting, they have been manipulated by others into losing control of themselves. An attempt is made to convince the child that an even better way to "win" in such a situation is to respond in a way that does not allow the other child to think that he can provoke him to behave in ways that get him into trouble, and may make him look bad in front of others.

Academic Skill Training

In addition to social relations training, subjects in the experimental groups who were low in academic achievement received academic tutoring. In a study of the effects of academic tutoring on the social status of low-achieving, socially rejected children, Coie and Krehbiel (1984) found that subjects who received academic skills training showed significant improvement in social status, as well as in academic areas. These children also improved significantly in their ability to stay working appropriately at tasks in the classroom.

THE RESEARCH DESIGN

Each year for three successive years all the third-grade children in 11 elementary schools completed sociometric questionnaires using positive and negative nominations. They also nominated peers who best fit eight behavioral descriptions, including one that read: "This person starts fights with others, hits them, and says mean things." The sociometric nomination totals were combined to identify rejected children in each cohort using a procedure described by Coie, Dodge, and Coppotelli (1982). Children whose aggression nomination totals exceeded the one standard deviation criterion mentioned earlier were categorized as aggressive. Altogether a total of 49 aggressive, rejected children completed the project.

Following these identification procedures in the early spring of the third grade, children in the target population were observed in the school and administered the Harter (1982) self-concept scale, once parent permission was obtained. Each child's classroom teacher completed a behavior checklist that also included items on the child's peer status. Subjects were also screened on the basis of academic achievement scores and assigned a tutoring-eligible condition if their CAT scores were at or below the 35th percentile. Subjects were randomly assigned to intervention or control groups within the tutoring-eligible or noneligible subgroups.

In October of the fourth-grade year, intervention began and continued through April. Those in the low-achievement subset of the intervention group received individualized academic tutoring (Coie & Krehbiel, 1984) in addition to the social relations training program described above. Children met twice a week with intervention staff either individually or in groups of two or three. At the end of the intervention period all subjects were observed, given the self-concept questionnaire, and the sociometric and behavioral assessment measures were administered to the classes in which they were located. Follow-up assessments were conducted in the spring of the following year, when most subjects were in the fifth grade. More complete details on the total project can be found elsewhere (Coie, Rabiner, & Lochman, 1989).

RESULTS OF THE PROJECT

In a project of this complexity, some experience in conducting the intervention activities is necessary. Although there was significant turnover among the intervention staff each year, the principal investigators developed ideas about the implications of their program for a school-based intervention, particularly for the aggressive subjects. One critical factor, which we return to after reporting the outcome results, is the issue of motivation for changing aggressive behavior. As it became clear that there was no one in the day-to-day lives of most of the aggressive subjects who consistently provided them with motivation to become less aggressive, we considered ways to influence the motives of the children themselves. For the most part, the anger-control program did not do this and so in the last year we emphasized the idea of reframing the circumstances of provocation to aggression as they were construed by our aggressive subjects. We also gave the training staff the flexibility to spend more time on the anger-control segment of the program with the aggressive children. For this reason we analyzed the outcome data for the project in two ways, with all three cohorts combined and separately for the last cohort.

The results for the combined cohorts are summarized in Table 15.1. Most of the outcome data used peers as the source of change. Since peers were the source of selection data, this was appropriate. However, teachers rated the subjects on two dimensions of behavior that were especially salient to this project. In the case of teachers, different raters provided preintervention and postintervention ratings since subjects changed classrooms and grade levels between the time of preintervention assessment and the actual conduct of intervention. The teachers who did the postintervention ratings were aware of children who were actually being given the program, did not know the identity of the control subjects, because the list of children they rated at the end of the year contained some names of children who were not involved in the project. To some

TABLE 15.1
Postintervention Adjusted Means for Outcome Measures for All Three Cohorts Combined

	Intervention	*Control*	*F*	*p*<
Peer Social Preference	−0.73	−1.15	1.18	0.28
Peer Acceptance Ratings	−0.61	−0.93	2.52	0.12
Peer Prosocial Ratings	−0.46	−0.41	0.48	0.49
Peer Aggression Ratings	0.92	1.22	0.33	0.57
Teacher Aggression Ratings	3.35	3.61	0.55	0.46
Teacher Rejection Ratings	2.64	2.81		[a]
Harter Self-Concept	2.69	2.77		

[a]For teacher ratings of rejection there was a significant interaction effect ($F = 6.08$, $p < .02$) for Tutoring Condition by Intervention Condition.

	Intervention	*Control*
Tutored	2.99	2.56
Nontutored	1.86	3.16

extent the peer groups also changed from year-to-year. Classmates had less opportunity to know who was in the intervention because many children left the classroom for different purposes during the year.

The data were analyzed by analysis of covariance with preintervention scores serving as the covariate. The tables contain just the adjusted postintervention means. Although the pattern of means reflected in Table 15.1 suggests that intervention subjects were consistently better off than control subjects at postintervention, none of these differences was statistically significant. Only a significant interaction effect for the teacher ratings of peer rejection indicated significant improvement in the nontutored group that received social relations training. It is hard to know whether this represents a possible chance finding given that seven dependent variable effects were tested. It does suggest, if valid, that the intervention may have had differential effectiveness with low-achieving and adequately achieving aggressive children. One possibility is that the low achievers were slower to pick up the cognitive elements of the social problem-solving and anger-control programs than their higher-achieving counterparts and thus did not benefit from the program as much. The peer evaluations did not match this interaction, however, either in the social preference scores or the peer acceptance ratings. The peer evaluations showed differences that favored all intervention subjects generally, but not at statistically significant levels.

More promising results were obtained for the last of the three intervention cohorts. Two of the seven measures reached conventional significance levels and, except for the Harter data, the overall trend was toward greater improvement in the intervention group. The data in Table 15.2 indicate that the aggressive-rejected children in this third cohort improved their social status with peers significantly. One reason for this is that peers perceived them to be engaged in more prosocial behavior. There were also large differences in both peer and teacher ratings of aggression for intervention and control groups at the end of the intervention period, however, these differences did not reach conventional significance levels. The latter results suggest high within-cell variance on changes in aggressiveness. Our explanation for the greater success of intervention with this third cohort is based on a subjective sense that the intervention staff did a better job of getting the aggressive children to consider alternative solutions to anger-arising events. Less emphasis was placed on being less aggressive in order to be good, and more on being under control. Some of this came about because of overall program emphasis, but much of it may be traced to greater experience in working with this population.

The self-concept data are puzzling because they run counter to the rest of the findings. There are several possible interpretations. One is that the intervention sensitized children to their own problem behavior. Many children are reluctant to acknowledge having problems and the social problem-solving unit may serve to make children less defensive about this issue. The risk is that by focusing on difficulties and the importance of developing new solutions to situations that are difficult for them, they may come to hold a less positive view of themselves. On the other hand, there is evidence that children in this population do not respond to the Harter self-concept measure the way white or middle-

TABLE 15.2
Postintervention Adjusted Means for Outcome Measures for Third Cohort

	Intervention $n = 9$	*Control* $n = 10$	F	$p<$
Peer Social Preference	−0.72	−1.56	6.04	0.03
Peer Acceptance Ratings	−0.62	−1.37	2.59	0.13
Peer Prosocial Ratings	−0.35	−0.74	8.13	0.01
Peer Aggression Ratings	0.57	1.31	0.91	0.35
Teacher Aggression Ratings	3.54	4.40	2.95	0.10
Teacher Rejection Ratings	1.93	3.47	2.60	0.17
Harter Self-Concept	2.54	2.79	2.06	0.17

class children do. Whidby (1986) found that popular girls from this same school system rated themselves lower on the social competence scale of the Harter measure than rejected girls. This may be attributable to greater defensiveness on the part of rejected girls or to more self-effacement among socially successful girls. Clearly this is an issue that merits further study.

In some ways what was most impressive was the consistently large size of the differences in means between the intervention and control groups. All of the peer measures are expressed in standard score terms. In comparison with previous studies designed to improve peer status by means of social skill training, these are quite substantial changes. Small sample sizes and within-cell variance obviously limited the statistical significance of some of these comparisons. This latter issue, within-cell variance, was a problem for the project as a whole and can be traced to the lengthy time interval between pretesting and posttesting, approximately 15 months. Given the limits on year-to-year stability of most of these measures ($r = 0.56$ for social performance and 0.52 for peer acceptance, for example), there was a great deal of change in scores within cells of the design and the overall results of the project reflected the tendency of regression to the mean across time (Coie, Rabiner, & Lochman, 1989).

As with many other systematic attempts to intervene with aggressive or antisocial children, the results for the combined cohorts remind us that this is a very difficult undertaking. There are a number of reasons why this should be so. Patterns of family interaction and parental discipline seem to shape the antisocial behavior of aggressive children and reinforce its occurrence (Patterson, 1986; Patterson & Dishion, 1985; Patterson & Stouthamer-Loeber, 1984). There is also evidence that aggression is rewarding in the peer group context itself (Coie, Belding, & Underwood, 1988; Patterson, Littman, & Bricker, 1967). Even though aggression may lead to rejection in the eyes of peers and hence be a source of motivation for change, it is not clear that these children always recognize the social consequences of their aggressive behavior (Parkhurst & Asher, 1987; Williams & Asher, 1987). There is some evidence that the long-range social consequences of this behavior are less important to them than the immediate, instrumental benefits (Crick & Ladd, 1987). Thus, it is not surprising that it is so difficult to convince aggressive children to change their socially offensive behavior.

Before concluding this chapter, there are two dimensions of the problem of treating aggression that we want to discuss because we think they have something to do with the limited success of our efforts to solve this problem. We want to discuss the role of motivation in aggressive processes and the importance of distinguishing among types of aggression. Essentially our thesis is this: There are two major types of aggression, reactive and proactive, and there are reasons to think that some of the existing models for treating aggression make better contact with one type of aggression than the other. Furthermore, we think different types of motives are involved in these different types of aggression. First, we will recount some of the background for our desire to reconsider the role of motivation in treating aggression.

Recall that in considering the various models for treating aggression we opted for a model that emphasized the importance of emotional control strategies and positive social skill training, rather than behavior management or response-cost methods. This was not necessarily an ideological decision, but was based on the recognition that in attempting a school-based intervention we were giving up access to those individuals who control many of the important reinforcement and behavior-shaping opportunities. (Although it is true that teachers can play a useful role in this respect, our experiences in this system led us to conclude that most teachers were too overworked to participate or too resistant to the concepts involved to cooperate with us.)

One strength of the emotional-control and social-skill training models is that they are oriented toward developing the capacities of the child for positive behavior. To the extent that this can be achieved, they hold the promise of greater maintenance and generalization of treatment effects than behavior management strategies have been documented to yield, thus far. Besides being more adaptable for use within the school, they tend to fit well with the educational perspective. It is easy to introduce the program as another type of learning experience. The problem that must be faced in using them is that many children may not be motivated to use the skills that these programs offer, or even to learn them. This is a tricky issue at the level of actual intervention, because most children will give lip service to the idea that they should not fight (many will even deny that they do this very often without clear provocation, but this is still another matter). By relying on this apparent acquiescence to the goals of the program (to stop getting into fights), the training person can fall into several traps. The most obvious is that there is not genuine agreement and hence there is no real motivation for the child to become engaged with the program. The more subtle problem is that in the mind of the child the trainer joins that company of adults from whom any detailed discussion about the real world of peer interaction must be hidden. It then becomes very difficult for the trainer to help the child make effective application of the skills that could be learned in the program.

The question arises as to how best to address this problem of insufficient motivation. Before attempting to respond to this question it is important to outline a distinction among two types of aggression because different motivational concerns may be involved in these two different types of aggression. In a recently published paper, Dodge and Coie (1987) revived a distinction about aggressive behavior that has been used by a number of scholars (e.g., Buss, 1966; Feshbach, 1964, 1970; Hartup, 1974; Moyer, 1976; Rule, 1974; Scott, 1972). Proactive and instrumental aggression is seen as a relatively nonemotional display of force that is aimed at some external goal such as object possession or social dominance. Reactive or hostile aggression is less controlled, involves heightened emotional response, and appears to be in reaction to some provocation or frustration. By these definitions it is obvious that different motives are implicated in these two types of aggression. Reactive aggression suggests a motive to avoid looking weak or to appear as someone who can be pushed around. Children who are overly reactive may be hypervigilant with respect to acts that are intended to give offense. The instrumental flavor of proactive aggression suggest the kinds of motives that are assumed in any behavioral management program, however there is a sense that overly proactive children may have a heightened investment in asserting dominance over others. In this same paper, Dodge and Coie demonstrated that children whose behavior most often reflected reactive aggression showed greater inclination to make a certain kind of social information processing error. This error is the tendency to attribute hostile intent to others under ambiguous circumstances of injury to the self. Children whose aggression is most often proactive are no more inclined to this sort of error than nonaggressive children.

While it is possible that proactively aggressive children are disposed toward other kinds of biased cognitive processes, these have not yet been articulated, and we would argue that the social information processing and emotional control models of aggression make better contact with reactive aggression than proactive aggression. The question is how to engage the motivations of reactively aggressive children so that they can become genuinely involved in training programs that fit these models. In our experience, you cannot argue children out of their social perspectives. They are quite firmly convinced of their attributions about the intentions of others. For this reason we adopted the reframing technique (Watzlawick, Weakland, & Fisch, 1974) as a way of coping with the motivational issue. Lacking hard data to support the point, we can only say that on subjective grounds this seems to be a way to engage aggressive children in thinking about alternative responses to frustrating actions of others. The drawback to this technique, as well as the reason it works so readily, is that it does not transform the basic premise of the reactive, aggressive child, namely that others are hostilely motivated toward oneself. Instead of getting even, they are motivated to thwart the provocative intentions of others, by not letting other children set them off. Our hope is that by not acting aggressively, they begin to defuse the negatively charged social atmosphere between themselves and others. This may lead to more positive interchanges with peers, which, in turn, lead to less hostile attributions on both sides. It is important to search for other solutions to the motivational aspects of reactive aggression, however, because there are limitations to this reframing approach.

Our ideas about dealing with proactive aggression are less well formed. The model that has the most apparent connections with proactive aggression is the behavior management model. The goal of proactive aggression is to obtain material or social advantages and behavior management methods use these same consequences to shape behavior into more socially acceptable forms. This approach is limited in its potential impact on proactive aggression only by the extent to which consequences can be controlled in the lives of aggressive children. The assumption of this model is that once behavior is shaped into less aggressive forms that still attain social desirable outcomes for the children, they will adopt these latter strategies and forsake their old habits even when contingencies change. It is here that one can see the advantages of pairing social-skill training or social problem-solving methods with behavior management methods, as Bierman, Miller, and Staub (1987) have done. Instead of having to depend on children discovering alternative behaviors for reaching their social goals, these latter methods provide systematic instruction and practice in acquiring such behaviors. The trick here is to convince the child that these alternative behaviors are truly as effective in meeting that child's goals as the more direct and aggressive methods. This is where the issue of motivation comes into play, again. Sometimes, as Dodge, Asher, and Parkhurst (in press) have observed, children have multiple goals and these multiple goals have differentially weighted values. One boy simply wants to play with a much sought after electronic game, a second boy may have the same goal but wants to demonstrate to the rest of the group that he controls the access to valued objects. Dealing only with the apparent importance of object attainment in training with the second boy may result in an intervention that does not fully address the motives of this child. What often happens in social-skill or social problem-solving programs is that trainers promote the value of goals such as being well thought of by one's peers. The success of this venture often depends on the ability of the trainer to change some of the priorities in an aggressive child's goal hierarchy.

In the preceding examples, we attempted to illustrate the ways that the motives of aggressive children may vary according to the type of aggression they are engaged in most often. We also argued that some methods for treating aggression make better connection with some of these motives than others. One implication of this argument is that it may be demanding too much of any one method that it be uniformly effective across a broadly sampled population of aggressive children such as that which would be identified in a school-based intervention such as ours. We also contended that some methods are more amenable to implementation in a school setting. These two conclusions would suggest that school-based interventions will be doomed to a certain proportion of failures because of the limitations on methods. A less pessimistic conclusion is that in the future we could set out on preventive interventions such as this by identifying the target population in the school but setting up our intervention plan in ways that make the best possible match between method and subject.

REFERENCES

Achenbach, T. M., & Edelbrock, C. S. (1981). Behavioral problems and competencies reported by parents of normal and disturbed children aged four through sixteen. *Monographs of the Society for Research in Child Development, 46* (1, Serial No. 188).

Bierman, K. L., & Furman, W. (1984). The effects of social skill training and peer involvement on the social adjustment of preadolescents. *Child Development, 55*, 151–162.

Bierman, K. L., Miller, C. L., & Staub, S. D. (1987). Improving the social behavior and peer acceptance of rejected boys: Effects of social skills training with instructions and prohibitions. *Journal of Consulting and Clinical Psychology, 55* (2), 194–200.

Breiner, J. L., & Forehand, R. (1981). An assessment of the effects of parent training on clinic-referred children's school behavior. *Behavioral Assessment, 3*, 31–42.

Buss, A. H. (1966). Instrumentality of aggression, feedback, and frustration as determinants of physical aggression. *Journal of Personality and Social Psychology, 3*, 153–162.

Chandler, M. J. (1973). Egocentrism and antisocial behavior: The assessment and training of social perspective taking skills. *Developmental Psychology, 9*, 326–327.

Coie, J. D., Belding, M., & Underwood, M. (1988). Aggression and peer rejection in childhood. In B. B. Lahey and A. Kazdin (Eds.), *Advances in clinical child psychology*. New York: Plenum Press.

Coie, J. D., & Dodge, K. A. (1988). Multiple sources of data on social behavior and social status in the school: A cross-age comparison. *Child Development, 59*, 815–829.

Coie, J. D., Dodge, K. A., & Coppotelli, H. (1982). Dimensions and types of social status: A cross-age perspective. *Developmental Psychology, 18*, 557–570.

Coie, J. D., & Krehbiel, G. (1984). Effects of academic tutoring on the social status of low-achieving, socially-rejected children. *Child Development, 55*, 1465–1478.

Coie, J. D., Dodge, K. A., & Kupersmidt, J. (1990). Peer group behavior and social status. In S. R. Asher & J. D. Coie (Eds.), *Peer rejection in childhood.* New York: Cambridge University Press.

Coie, J. D., Rabiner, D., & Lochman, J. E. (1989). Promoting peer relations in a school setting. In L. A. Bond, & B. E. Compas (Eds.), *Primary prevention and promotion in the schools.* Newbury Park, CA: Sage.

Crick, N. R., & Ladd, G. W. (1987). *Children's perceptions of the consequences of aggressive behavior: Do the ends justify being mean?* Paper presented at biennial meeting of the Society for Research in Child Development, Baltimore, MD.

Dodge, K. A. (1983). Behavioral antecedents of peer social status. *Child Development, 54,* 1386–1399.

Dodge, K. A., Asher, S. R., & Parkhurst, J. T. (1989). Social life as a goal coordination task. To appear in C. Ames and R. Ames (Eds.), *Research on motivation in education, Vol. 3.* New York: Academic Press.

Dodge, K. A., & Coie, J. D. (1987). Social information processing factors in reactive and proactive aggression in children's peer groups. *Journal of Personality and Social Psychology, 53*(6), 1146–1158.

Dodge, K. A., McClaskey, C. L., Brown, M. M., & Petit, G. (1987). Social competence in children. *Monographs of the Society for Research in Child Development, 51,* (2, Serial No. 213).

Elliot, D. S., & Huizinga, D. (1983). Social class and delinquent behavior in a national youth panel. *Criminology: An Interdisciplinary Journal, 21,* 149–177.

Feshbach, S. (1964). The function of aggression and the regulation of the aggressive drive. *Psychological Review, 71,* 257–272.

Feshbach, S. (1970). Aggression. In P. H. Mussen (Ed.), *Carmichael's manual of child psychology Vol. 2.* (3rd ed.). New York: Wiley.

Forman, S. G. (1980). A comparison of cognitive training and response-cost procedures in modifying aggressive behavior of elementary school children. *Behavior Therapy, 11,* 594–600.

Goldstein, A. P., Sherman, M., Gershaw, N. J., Sprajkin, R. P., & Glick, B. (1978). Training aggressive adolescents in prosocial behavior. *Journal of Youth and Adolescence, 7,* 73–92.

Harter, S. (1982). The perceived competence scale for children. *Child Development, 53,* 87–97.

Hartup, W. W. (1974). Aggression in child developmental perspectives. *American Psychologist, 29,* 336–341.

Kettlewell, P. W., & Kausch, D. F. (1983). The generalization of effects of a cognitive-behavioral treatment program for aggressive children. *Journal of Abnormal Child Psychology, 11*(1), 101–114.

Kupersmidt, J., & Coie, J. D. (in press). Preadolescent peer status, aggression, and school adjustment as predictors of externalizing problems in adolescence. *Child Development.*

Ladd, G. W. (1981). Effectiveness of a social learning method for enhancing children's social interaction and peer acceptance. *Child Development, 52,* 171–178.

Lochman, J. E., Burch, P. R., Curry, J. F., & Lampron, L. B. (1984). Treatment and generalization effects of cognitive-behavioral and goal setting interventions with aggressive boys. *Journal of Consulting and Clinical Psychology, 52*(5), 915–916.

Magnussen, D., Statlin, H., & Duner, A. (1983). Aggression and criminality in a longitudinal perspective. In K. T. Van Dusen & S. R. Mednick (Eds.), *Prospective studies of crime and delinquency.* Hingham, MA: Kluwer-Nijhoff Publishing.

Meichenbaum, D. H., & Goodman, J. (1971). Training impulsive children to talk to themselves as a way of developing self-control. *Journal of Abnormal Child Psychology, 77*(2), 115–126.

Moyer, K. (1976). *The psychobiology of aggression.* New York: Harper and Row.

Novaco, R. W. (1978). Anger and coping with stress: Cognitive behavioral interventions. In J. P. Foreyt & D. P. Rathjen (Eds.), *Cognitive behavior therapy: Research and application.* New York: Plenum Press.

Oden, S., & Asher, S. R. (1977). Coaching children in social skills training for friendship making. *Child Development, 48,* 495–506.

Parker, J. G., & Asher, S. R. (1987). Peer relations and later personal adjustment: Are low-accepted children at risk? *Psychological Bulletin, 102*(3), 357–389.

Parkhurst, J. T., & Asher, S. R. (1987). *The social concerns of aggressive-rejected children.* Paper presented at the biennial meeting of the Society for Research in Child Development, Baltimore, MD.

Patterson, G. R. (1974). Interventions for boys with conduct problems: Multiple settings, treatments, and criteria. *Journal of Consulting and Clinical Psychology, 42*(4), 471–481.

Patterson, G. R. (1986). Performance models for antisocial boys. *American Psychologist, 41*(4), 432–444.

Patterson, G. R., Chamberlain, P., & Reid, J. B. (1982). A comparative evaluation of a parent-training program. *Behavior Therapy, 13,* 638–650.

Patterson, G. R., & Dishion, T. J. (1985). Contributions of families and peers to delinquency. *Criminology, 23*(1), 63–79.

Patterson, G. R., Littman, R. A., & Bricker, W. (1967). Assertive behavior in children: A step toward a theory of aggression. *Monographs of the Society for Research in Child Development, 32*(5, Serial No. 113).

Patterson, G. R., & Stouthamer-Loeber, M. (1984). The correlation of family management practices and delinquency. *Child Development, 55,* 1299–1307.

Pitkanen, L. (1974). The effect of simulation exercises on the control of aggressive behavior in children. *Scandanavian Journal of Psychology, 15,* 169–177.

Putallaz, M. (1983). Predicting children's social status from their behavior. *Child Development, 54,* 1417–1426.

Putallaz, M., & Wasserman, A. (1990). Children's entry behavior. In S. R. Asher & J. D. Coie (Eds.), *Peer rejection in childhood.* New York: Cambridge University Press.

Roff, M., Sells, S. B., & Golden, M. (1972). *Social adjustment and personality development in children.* Minneapolis: University of Minnesota Press.

Rule, B. G. (1974). The hostile and instrumental functions of human aggression. In J. deWit and W. W. Hartup (Eds.), *Determinants and origins of aggressive behaviors*. The Hague: Mouton.

Scott, J. P. (1972). Hostility and aggression. In B. Wolman (Ed.), *Handbook of genetic psychology*. Englewood Cliffs, NJ: Prentice Hall.

Shepherd, M., Oppenheim, B., & Mitchell, S. (1971). *Childhood behavior and mental health*. London: University of London Press.

Wahler, R. G. (1975). Some structural aspects of deviant child behavior. *Journal of Applied Behavior Analysis, 8*, 27–42.

Watzlawick, P., Weakland, J., & Fisch, R. (1974). *Change: Principles of problem formulation and problem resolution*. New York: Norton and Co.

West, D. J., & Farrington, D. P. (1973). *Who becomes delinquent?* London: Heineman.

Whidby, J. M. (1986). *Peer social status and behavior among black preadolescent females*. Unpublished dissertation, Duke University.

Williams, G. A., & Asher, S. R. (1987). *Peer and self-perceptions of peer rejected children: Issues in classification and subgrouping*. Paper presented at the biennial meeting of the Society for Research in Child Development, Baltimore, MD.

16

Bully/Victim Problems Among Schoolchildren: Basic Facts and Effects of a School Based Intervention Program

Dan Olweus
University of Bergen, Norway

Bullying among schoolchildren is certainly a very old phenomenon. The fact that some children are frequently and systematically harassed and attacked by other children has been described in literary works, and many adults have personal experience of it from their own school days. Though many are acquainted with the bully/victim problem, it was not until fairly recently—in the early 1970s—that efforts were made to study it systematically. So far, these attempts have largely been confined to Scandinavia. In the 1980s, however, bullying among school children has also received some public attention also in other countries such as Japan, England, and the USA.

This chapter gives an overview of some recent research findings on bully/victim problems among schoolchildren in Scandinavia. I mainly confine myself to results of the two large-scale studies I was commissioned by the Ministry of Education to conduct in connection with a nationwide intervention campaign against bully/victim problems in Norwegian comprehensive schools. The latter part of the chapter reports some main results on the effects of the intervention program, as evaluated in 42 schools in Bergen, Norway. I also briefly describe the content of the program and some of the principles on which it was based.

A number of findings concerning developmental antecedents of bullying problems, characteristics of typical bullies and victims, and the veracity of some popular conceptions of the causes of these problems are presented only briefly in this context, since these results have been described in detail in previous publications (e.g., Olweus, 1973a, 1978, 1979, 1980, 1981, 1983, 1984, 1986). It should be mentioned, however, that the findings from this earlier research have generally been replicated in several different samples and were obtained with a number of different methods, including peer ratings, teacher nominations, self-reports, grades, projective techniques, hormonal assays, and mother/father interviews about child-rearing practices. Most of these results were derived from my Swedish longitudinal project, which started in the early 1970s and is still continuing (see Table 16.1).

A Historical Thumbnail Sketch

A strong societal interest in bully/victim problems was first aroused in Sweden in the late 1960s and early 1970s (Heinemann, 1972; Olweus, 1973a), and it quickly spread to the other Scandinavian countries.

In Norway, bully/victim problems were an issue of general concern in the mass media and among teachers and parents for a number of years, but the school authorities did not engage themselves officially with the phenomenon. A few years ago, a marked change took place.

In late 1982, a newspaper reported that three 10- to 14-year old boys from the northern part of Norway had committed suicide, in all probability as a consequence of severe bullying by peers. This event aroused considerable uneasiness and tension in the mass media and the general public. It triggered a chain of reactions, the end result of which was a nationwide campaign against bully/victim problems in Norwegian comprehensive schools (grades 1 to 9), launched by the Ministry of Education in the fall of 1983.

BASIC INFORMATION

What is Meant by Bullying?

The word used in Scandinavia for bully/victim problems is "mobbing" (Norway, Denmark) or "mobbning" (Sweden, Finland). This word has been used with several different meanings and connotations. The original English word stem "mob" implies that it is a (usually large and anonymous) group of people who are engaged in the harassment (Heinemann, 1972; Olweus, 1973a). But the term has also often been used when one person picks on, harasses, or pesters another. Even if the usage is not quite adequate from a linguistic point of view, I believe it is important to include in the concept of "mobbing" or bullying both situations in which a single individual harasses another and those in which a group is responsible for the harassment. In many cases, it may not make much difference for the victim whether he or she is bullied by one or by several tormentors. Recent data collected in the large-scale study in Bergen (Olweus, 1985, 1986) showed that a substantial portion of victimized students were bullied primarily by a single student. Accordingly, it is natural to regard bullying from a single student and from a group as closely related phenomena—even if there may be some differences between them.

Bullying can be defined in the following general way: *A person is being bullied when he or she is exposed, repeatedly and over time, to negative actions on the part of one or more other persons.*

The meaning of the expression *negative actions* must be specified further. It is a negative action when someone intentionally inflicts, or attempts to inflict, injury or discomfort upon another—basically what is implied in the definition of aggressive behavior (Olweus, 1973b). Negative actions can be carried out by physical contact, by words, or in other ways, such as by making faces or dirty gestures or by refusing to comply with another person's wishes.

Even if a single instance of more serious harassment can be regarded as bullying under certain circumstances, the definition given above emphasizes negative actions that are carried out "repeatedly and over time." The intent is to exclude occasional nonserious negative actions that are directed against one person at one time and against another on a different occasion.

It must be stressed that the term bullying is not (or should not be) used when two persons of approximately the same strength (physical or psychological) are fighting or quarreling. In order to use the term bullying, there should be a certain *imbalance in the strength relations (an asymmetric power relationship)*: The person who is exposed to the negative actions has difficulty in defending him/herself and is somewhat helpless against the person or persons who harass.

It is useful to distinguish between *direct bullying*—with relatively open attacks on the victim—and *indirect bullying* in the form of social isolation and exclusion from a group. It is important to pay attention also to the second, less visible form of bullying.

In this chapter the expressions "bullying problems" and "bully/victim problems" are used synonymously.

Some Information About the Recent Studies

The basic method of data collection in the recent large-scale studies in Norway and Sweden has been an inventory[1] (questionnaire) that I developed in connection with the nationwide campaign against bullying. The inventory, which can be administered by teachers, differs from several previous inventories on bully/victim problems in a number of respects, including the following:

1. It provides a definition of bullying so as to give the students a clear understanding of what they are to respond to.
2. It refers to a specific time period.
3. Several of the response alternatives are quite specific, such as "about once a week" and "several times a day," in contrast to alternatives like "often" and "very often," which lend themselves to more subjective interpretation.
4. It includes questions about the others' reactions to bullying as perceived by the respondents, that is, the reactions and attitudes of peers, teachers, and parents.

In connection with the nationwide campaign all primary and junior high schools in Norway were invited to take the inventory. We estimate that approximately 85% actually participated. For closer analyses I selected representative samples of some 830 schools and obtained valid data from 715 of them, comprising approximately 130,000 students from all over Norway. These samples constitute almost a fourth of the whole student population in the relevant age range (roughly 8 to 16; first-grade students did not participate, since they did not have sufficient reading and writing ability to answer the inventory). This set of data gives good estimates of the frequency of bully/victim problems in different school forms, in different grades, in boys as compared with girls, etc. In addition, it provides information on how differences between schools in these regards relate to the characteristics of the schools themselves and of the surrounding communities in terms of population density, degree of urbanization, economic resources, percentage of immigrants,

[1]There is an (expanded) English version of this inventory (one version for grades 1–4, and another for grades 5–9 and higher grades). This inventory as well as other materials related to the intervention program (see footnote 2, below) are copyrighted which implies certain restrictions on their use. For more details, please write to Dan Olweus, University of Bergen, Oysteinsgate 3, N-5007 Bergen, Norway.

and similar factors. I report here on some main findings from this study, but a number of more refined analyses remain to be done.

To get more detailed information on some of the mechanisms involved in bully/victim problems and on the possible effects of the campaign, I also conducted a longitudinal project in Bergen. This study comprises some 2500 boys and girls in four adjacent cohorts, originally in grades 4 through 7, from 28 primary and 14 junior high schools. In addition, we obtained data from 300–400 teachers and principals as well as some 1000 parents. We collected data from these subjects at several points in time.

An overview of my main projects on bullying and related problems is given in Table 16.1.

TABLE 16.1
Overview of Studies

	Nationwide Study in Norway (1983)	*Intensive Study in Bergen, Norway (1983 1985)*	*Study in Greater Stockholm, Sweden (1970–)*
Units of Study:	715 schools, grades 2–9 (130.000 boys and girls)	4 cohorts of 2500 boys and girls in grades 4–7 (1983) 300–400 teachers 1000 parents	3 cohorts of boys (900 boys in all), originally in grades 6–8 (1973)
Number of measurement occasions:	one	several	several
Measures include:	inventory on bully/victim problems (aggregated to grade and school level), data on recruitment area of the school: population density, socioeconomic conditions, percent immigrants, etc. school size, average class size, composition of staff	self-reports on bully/victim problems, aggression, antisocial behavior, anxiety, self-esteem, attachment to parents and peers etc. grades, some peer ratings teacher data on characteristics of class, group climate, staff relations, etc.	self-reports and reports by mothers on a number of dimensions, peer ratings, teacher nominations, official records on criminal offenses, drug abuse, etc. for subgroups: interviews on early child rearing, hormonal data, psychophysiological data

One Student Out of Seven

On the basis of the nationwide survey, one can estimate that some 83,000 students, or 15% of the total in the Norwegian comprehensive schools (568,000 in 1983–84), were involved in bully/victim problems "now and then" or more frequently (autumn 1983)—as bullies or victims. This percentage represents one student out of seven. Approximately 9%, or 53,000 students, were victims, and 7%, or 41,000, bullied other students "now and then" or more frequently (see items 1 and 2 in section on "Outcome Variables" below for exact formulations of the two questions). Some 9,000 students were both victims and bullies.

In calculating these percentages, I have drawn the line at "now and then": For a student to be considered bullied or bullying others, he or she must have responded that it happened "now and then" or more frequently (i.e., from "about once a week" to "several times a day").

Analyses from the Bergen study indicate that there are good grounds for placing a cutting point just here. But it can also be useful to estimate the number of students who are involved in more serious bully/victim problems. We find then that slightly more than 3%, or 18,000 students in Norway, were bullied "about once a week" or more frequently, and somewhat less than 2%, or 10,000 students, bullied others at that rate. Using this cutting point, only 1,000 students were both bullies and victims. A total of approximately 27,000 students (5%) in Norwegian comprehensive schools were involved in more serious bullying problems as victims or bullies—about 1 student out of 20.

Analyses of parallel teacher nominations in approximately 90 classes (see Olweus, 1987) suggest that the reported results do not give an exaggerated picture of the frequency of bully/victim problems. Considering that the student (as well as the teacher) inventory refers only to part of the autumn term, it is likely that the figures in fact underestimate the number of students who are involved in such problems during a whole year.

Against this background, it can be stated that bullying is a considerable problem in Norwegian comprehensive schools, a problem that affects a very large number of students.

Bully/Victim Problems in Different Grades

If one draws a graph of the percentage of students in different grades who are bullied at school a fairly smoothly declining curve is obtained for both boys and girls (see Fig. 16.1). The decline is most marked in the primary school grades. Thus the percentage of students who are bullied

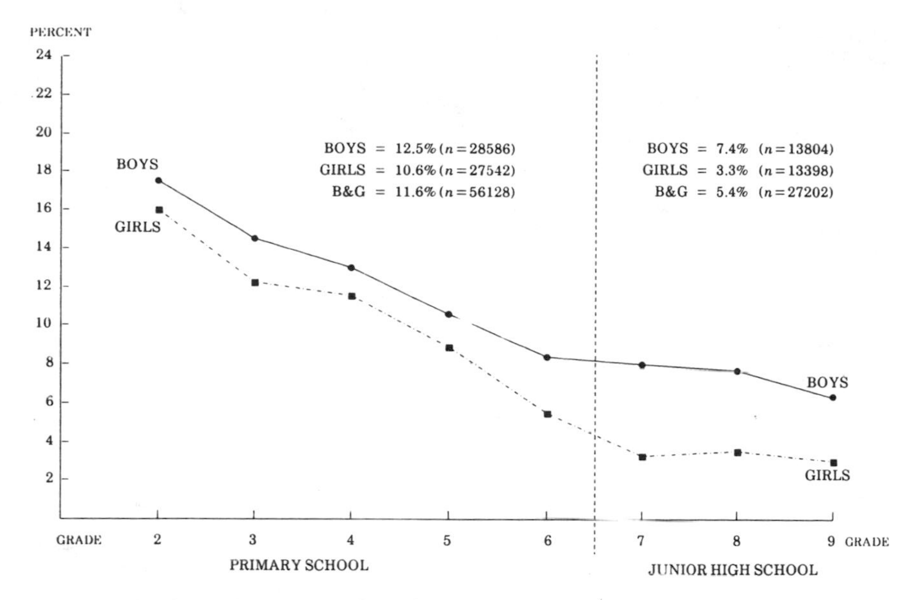

FIG. 16.1. Percentage of students in different grades who reported being bullied (being exposed to direct bullying).

decreases with higher grades. *It is the younger and weaker students who reported being most exposed.*

In junior high school (grades 7 to 9) the curves decline less steeply. The average percentage of students (boys and girls combined) who were bullied in grades 2 to 6 (11.6%) was approximately twice as high as that in grades 7 to 9 (5.4%). With regard to the way in which the bullying is carried out, there is a clear trend toward less use of physical means in the higher grades.

From the Bergen study it can also be reported that *a considerable part of the bullying was carried out by older students.* This is particularly marked in the lower grades: More than 50% of the bullied children in the lowest grades (2 and 3) reported that they were bullied by older students. It is natural to invoke the latter finding as at least a partial explanation of the form of the curves in Fig. 16.1. The younger the students are, the more potential bullies they have above them; accordingly, the inverse relationship between percentage of victims and grade level seems reasonable. More detailed analyses of the factors affecting the shape of the curves will be undertaken in the future, but not in this volume.

As regards the tendency to bully other students, depicted in Fig. 16.2, the changes with grades are not as clear and systematic as in Fig. 16.1. The average percentage for the junior high school boys was slightly

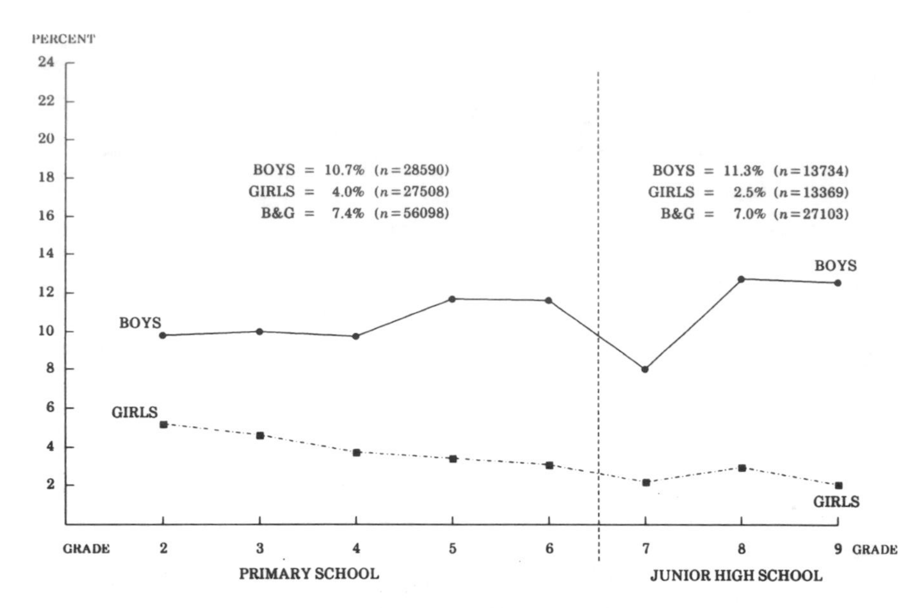

FIG. 16.2. Percentage of students in different grades who reported having bullied other students.

higher (11.3%) than for the boys in the lower grades (10.7%), whereas the opposite was true for the girls (2.5% in junior high vs. 4.0% in the lower grades). The relatively marked drop in the curves for grade 7, in particular for the boys, is probably a reflection of the fact that these students were the youngest ones in junior high school and accordingly did not have "access to suitable victims" in lower grades to the same extent.

The analyses above concern the distributions of victims and bullies across grades. The most remarkable result is that bully/victim problems in primary schools were considerably more marked than previously assumed.

Have Bully/Victim Problems Increased?

Several different methods, including inventories (for overviews in Scandinavian languages, see Pikas, 1975; Raundalen & Raundalen, 1979; Roland, 1983), teacher nominations (Olweus, 1973a, 1978), and peer ratings (Lagerspetz, Björkqvist, Berts, & King, 1982; Olweus, 1978), have been used in previous Scandinavian studies of the frequency of bully/victim problems. The samples have mainly consisted of students in grades 6—9. In summary, it can be stated that the percentages of bullied and bullying students, respectively, were found to be in the vicinity of 5%–10%. By and large, the figures in these studies conducted chiefly in the 1970s are somewhat lower than the percentages obtained in the surveys reported in Figs. 16.1 and 16.2. It should be noted, however, that many of the earlier studies are very preliminary in nature, with small sample sizes and no clear definition of what is meant by bullying (and with nonspecific response alternatives). In addition, the studies were often conducted by undergraduate students with little supervision from more experienced researchers. Against this background it is difficult to ascertain whether the noted discrepancy actually indicates an increased frequency of bully/victim problems in recent years, or whether it reflects methodological differences. There are simply no good data available to directly assess whether bully/victim problems have become more or less frequent in the 1980s. Several indirect signs suggest, however, that bullying both takes more serious forms and is more prevalent nowadays than 10–15 years ago.

Whatever method of measurement is used, there is little doubt that bullying is a considerable problem in Norwegian comprehensive schools, one which must be taken seriously. At the same time, it is important to recognize that 60%–70% of the students (in a given semester) are not involved in bullying at all—neither as targets nor as perpetrators. It is essential to make use of this group of students in efforts to counteract bully/victim problems at school.

Bullying Among Boys and Girls

As is evident from Fig. 16.1, there is a trend for boys to be more exposed to bullying than girls. This tendency is particularly marked in the junior high school grades.

These results concern what was called direct bullying, with relatively open attacks on the victim. It is natural to ask whether girls were more often exposed to indirect bullying in the form of social isolation and exclusion from the peer group. One of the inventory questions makes it possible to examine this issue ("How often does it happen that other students don't want to spend recess with you and you end up being alone?"). The responses confirm that girls were more exposed to indirect and more subtle forms of bullying than to bullying with open attacks. At the same time, however, the percentage of boys who were bullied in this indirect way was approximately the same as that for girls. In addition, a somewhat larger percentage of boys was exposed to direct bullying, as mentioned above. (It may also be of interest that there was a fairly strong relationship between being a victim of direct and of indirect bullying.)

It should be emphasized that these results reflect main trends. There are of course a number of schools and classes in which there are more girls, or as many girls as boys, who are exposed to direct bullying, also in junior high school.

An additional result from the Bergen study is relevant in this context. Here it was found that *boys carried out a large part of the bullying to which girls were subjected.* More than 60% of bullied girls (in grades 5–7) reported being bullied mainly by boys. An additional 15%–20% said they were bullied by both boys and girls. The great majority of boys, on the other hand—more than 80%—were bullied chiefly by boys.

These results lead in a natural way to Fig. 16.2, which shows the percentage of students who had taken part in bullying other students. It is evident here that a considerably larger percentage of boys than girls had participated in bullying. In junior high school, more than four times as many boys as girls reported having bullied other students.

In summary, *boys were more often victims and in particular perpetrators of direct bullying.* This conclusion is in good agreement with what can be expected from research on sex differences in aggressive behavior (Ekblad & Olweus, 1986; Hyde, 1984; Maccoby & Jacklin, 1980). It is well documented that relations among boys are by and large harder, tougher, and more aggressive than among girls (Maccoby, 1986). These differences certainly have both biological and social/environmental roots.

The results presented here should definitely not be construed as implying that we need not pay attention to bullying problems among girls. As a matter of course, such problems must be acknowledged and counteracted, whether girls are the victims of bullying or they themselves perpetrate such behavior. It should be recalled in this connection that girls were exposed to indirect bullying to about the same extent as boys.

How Much Do the Teachers Do and How Much Do the Parents Know?

The students' responses to one of the inventory questions give information on how often the teachers try to interfere when a student is being bullied at school. As a general summary, it can be concluded that *the teachers do (or did in 1983) relatively little to put a stop to bullying at school* according to both the bullied and bullying students. In addition it was found that *parents of students who are bullied and, in particular, who bully others, are relatively unaware of the problem and talk with their children about it only to a limited extent* (see Olweus, 1987, for more details).

Bullying at School and on the Way to and from School

It is fairly often asserted that bullying chiefly takes place on the way to and from school rather than at school. The results from the recent studies clearly show that this view is not valid. There were almost twice (in junior high school, three times) as many students who were bullied at school as on the way to and from school. (There is a fairly strong association here, however: Students who were bullied on their way to and from school tended to be bullied at school, too.) *The school is, no doubt, where most of the bullying occurs.*

The students reported, however, that they got considerably less help from others if they were bullied on their way to and from school. Accordingly, it is important to take effective measures against bullying there as well.

Is Bullying Primarily a Big-City Problem?

It has been commonly assumed that bullying occurs primarily in big-city schools. Results from the nationwide Norwegian surveys show that this is a myth. The percentage of students in Oslo, Bergen, and Trondheim (with populations varying from 450,000 to 150,000 inhabitants) who were bullied or who bullied others were approximately the same as or somewhat lower than corresponding figures from the rest of the country. The "big-city" children and youth were thus better than their reputation in this respect. It was also found that teachers as well as parents in the three cities talked more often with students involved in bullying problems than was done in other parts of the country. These results point to a somewhat greater awareness of the problems in the cities.

The Size of the School and the Class

Another common view, popular especially among teachers, is that bully/victim problems increase in proportion to the size of the school and the class. The data from 10 schools in Greater Stockholm that I presented in the beginning of the 1970s (Olweus, 1973a, 1978) gave no support at all to these hypotheses. Data from these schools in Finland also failed to show any relationship between percentage of bullied or bullying students on one hand and school or class size on the other (Ekman, 1977; Lagerspetz, Björkqvist, Berts, & King, 1982).

The recent Norwegian surveys give new and considerably extended possibilities of testing the validity of these hypotheses. With the available data one can make comparisons among more than 700 schools and several thousand classes. It should be noted, however, that such comparisons must be carried out within the same kind or type of school (e.g., primary schools or junior high schools) in order to be meaningful.

The variations in school and class size among the units compared were quite substantial. For example, the smallest ordinary grade 1–6 school had only 43 students, whereas the largest had 930. With regard to average class size, the range was from approximately 7 to 27 students per class for schools of this kind.

The results were clear-cut: There were no positive relationships between level of bully/victim problems (the percentage of bullied and/or bullying students) and school or average class-size. The international research on the "effects" of class and school size agrees in suggesting that these factors are of no great significance, at least within the ranges of size variation typically found (e.g., Rutter, 1983). We can thus conclude that *the size of the class or school appears to be of negligible importance for the relative frequency or level of bully/victim problems in the class or the school.* Accordingly, one must look for other factors to find the origins of these problems.

It is nevertheless a fact that the *absolute number* of bullied and bullying students is greater on average in big schools and in big classes. It is therefore possible that it is somewhat easier to *do* something with the problems in a small school or a small class. This possibility will be examined more closely in the Bergen study.

Two Popular but Nonsupported Hypotheses

In the general debate it has been commonly maintained that bullying is a direct consequence of competition and striving for grades in school. More specifically, it has been argued that the aggressive behavior of the bullies toward their environment can be explained as a reaction to failures and frustrations in school. A detailed causal analysis of data on 444 boys from greater Stockholm, who were followed from grade 6 to grade 9, gave no support at all for this hypothesis. Though there was an association between poor grades in school and aggressive behavior, there was nothing in the results to suggest that the behavior of the aggressive boys was a consequence of poor grades and failure in school (Olweus, 1983).

Further, a widely held view explains victimization as caused by external deviations. It is argued that students who are fat, are red-haired, wear glasses, or speak an unusual dialect, and so forth, are particularly likely to be the targets of bullying. This explanation seems to be quite common among students.

This hypothesis also received no support from empirical data. In two samples of boys, victims of bullying were by and large found to be no more externally deviant (with regard to 14 external characteristics assessed by means of teacher ratings) than a control group of boys who were not exposed to bullying (Olweus, 1973a, 1978). The only "external deviation" that differentiated the groups was physical strength: The victims were physically weaker than boys in general, whereas the bullies were stronger than the average, and in particular stronger than the victims. This characteristic, however, has generally not been implicated in the hypothesis discussed. In spite of the lack of empirical support for this hypothesis, it seems still to enjoy considerable popularity. Some probable reasons why this is so have been advanced, and the interested reader is referred to that discussion (Olweus, 1978, 1986).

A Sketch of the Typical Victim

The picture of the typical victim emerging from the research literature is relatively unambiguous (see Olweus, 1978, 1986; Olweus & Roland, 1983). Victims of bullying are more anxious and insecure than students in general. They are often cautious, sensitive, and quiet. When attacked by other students, they commonly react with crying (at least in the lower grades) and withdrawal. They have a negative view of themselves and their situation. They often look upon themselves as failures and feel stupid, ashamed, and unattractive.

Further, the victims are lonely and abandoned at school. As a rule, they don't have a single good friend in their class. They are not aggressive or teasing in their behavior; accordingly, one cannot explain the bullying as a consequence of the victims themselves being provocative to their peers (see below). If they are boys, they are likely to be physically weaker than boys in general.

In summary, the behavior and attitude of the victims seem to signal to others that they are insecure and worthless individuals who will not retaliate if they are attacked or insulted. A slightly different way of describing the typical victims is to say that they are characterized by *an anxious personality pattern combined* (at least in the case of boys) *with physical weakness.*

Detailed interviews with parents of victimized boys (unpublished) indicate that these boys were cautious and sensitive already at a young age. Boys with such characteristics (and maybe physical weakness in addition) are likely to have had difficulty in asserting themselves in the peer group.

There are thus good reasons to believe that these characteristics directly contributed to their becoming victims of other children's aggression. At the same time it is obvious that the repeated harassment by peers must have considerably increased their anxiety, insecurity, and generally negative evaluation of themselves.

Data from the same interviews suggest that victimized boys have a closer contact and more positive relations with their parents, in particular their mothers, than boys in general. Sometimes teachers interpret this closeness as overprotection on the part of the mothers. It is reasonable to assume that such tendencies toward overprotection are both a cause and consequence of the bullying.

This is a sketch of the most common type of victim, who I have called the *passive victim.* There is also another, much smaller group of victims, the *provocative victims,* who are characterized by a combination of both anxious and aggressive behavior patterns. See Olweus (1973a, 1978) for more information about this kind of victim.

The Bullies

A distinctive characteristic of the typical bullies is their aggression toward peers; this is implied in the definition of a bully. They are, however, often also aggressive toward teachers, parents, and siblings. Generally, they have a more positive attitude to violence and use of violent means than students in general. They are often characterized by impulsivity and strong needs to dominate others. They seem to have little empathy with victims of bullying.

In contrast to a fairly common assumption among psychologists and psychiatrists, we have found no indications that the aggressive bullies (boys) are anxious and insecure under a tough surface. Data based on several samples and using both direct and indirect methods such as projective techniques and hormonal assays all pointed in the same direction: The bullies had unusually little anxiety and insecurity or were roughly average on such dimensions (Olweus, 1981, 1984). And they did not suffer from poor self-esteem.

These conclusions apply to the bullies as a group. The results certainly do not imply that there may not be (a certain, relatively small proportion of) bullies who are both aggressive and anxious.

It should also be emphasized that there are students who sometimes participate in bullying but who usually do not take the initiative—they may be called *passive bullies,* followers, or henchmen. The group of passive bullies is likely to be fairly heterogeneous and can certainly also contain insecure and anxious students.

In summary, the typical bullies can be described as having *an aggressive personality pattern combined* (at least in the case of boys) *with physical strength.*

Bullying can also be viewed as a component of a more generally antisocial and rule-breaking behavior pattern. From this perspective, it is natural to predict that youngsters who are aggressive and bully others in school run a clearly increased risk of later engaging in other problem behaviors such as criminality and alcohol abuse. Several recent studies confirm this general prediction (Loeber & Dishion, 1983; Magnusson, Stattin, & Dunér, 1983).

In my own follow-up studies we have also found strong support for this assumption. Approximately 60% of boys who were characterized as bullies in grades 6 to 9 had at least one conviction at the age of 24. Even more dramatically, as much as 35%–40% of the former bullies had three or more convictions at this age while this was true of only 10% of the control boys (those who were neither bullies nor victims in grades 6 to 9). Thus, as young adults the former school bullies had a fourfold increase in the level of relatively serious, recidivist criminality.

It may be mentioned that the former victims had an average or somewhat below average level of criminality in young adulthood.

Development of an Aggressive Personality Pattern

In light of the characterization of the bullies as having an aggressive personality pattern, it becomes important to examine the question: What kind of rearing and other conditions are conducive to the development of an aggressive personality pattern? Very briefly, the following four factors have turned out to be particularly important (based chiefly on research with boys; for details, see Olweus, 1980):

1. The basic emotional attitude of the primary caretaker(s) toward the child during early years. A negative emotional attitude, characterized by lack of warmth and involvement, increases the risk that the child will later become aggressive and hostile toward others.

2. Permissiveness for aggressive behavior by the child. If the primary caretaker is generally permissive and "tolerant" without setting clear limits to aggressive behavior toward peers, siblings, and adults, the child's aggression level is likely to increase.

3. Use of power-assertive child-rearing methods such as physical punishment and violent emotional outbursts. Children of parents who make frequent use of these methods are likely to become more aggressive than the average child.

We can summarize these results by stating that *too little love and care and too much "freedom" in childhood are conditions that contribute strongly to the development of an aggressive personality pattern.*

4. Finally, the temperament of the child. A child with an active and hot-headed temperament is more likely to develop into an aggressive youngster than a child with an ordinary or more quiet temperament. The effect of this factor is less powerful than those of the first two conditions mentioned.

The factors listed above can be assumed to be important for both younger and somewhat older children. It can be added that, for adolescents, it is also of great significance whether the parents supervise the children's activities outside the school reasonably well (Patterson & Stouthamer-Loeber, 1984)—what they are doing and with whom.

It should also be pointed out that the aggression levels of the boys participating in the analyses above (Olweus, 1980, 1981) were not related to the socioeconomic conditions of their families, measured in several different ways. Similarly, there were no (or very weak) relations between the four childhood factors discussed and the socioeconomic conditions of the family.

Some Group Mechanisms

When several students jointly engage in the bullying of another student, some group mechanisms are likely to be at work. Several such mechanisms have been discussed in detail in Olweus (1973a, 1978). Because of space limitations, they are only listed here: (a) Social "contagion," (b) weakening of the control or inhibitions against aggressive tendencies, (c) diffusion of responsibility, and (d) gradual cognitive changes in the perceptions of bullying and of the victim.

A Question of Fundamental Democratic Rights

The reported results demonstrate convincingly that bullying is a considerable problem in Scandinavian elementary and junior high schools, that the teachers (in 1983) did relatively little to counteract it, and that the parents knew too little about what their children were exposed to or engaged in. The victims of bullying are a large group of students who are to a great extent neglected by the school. We know that many of these youngsters are the targets of harassment for long periods of time, often for many years (Olweus, 1977, 1978). It does not require much imagination to understand what it is to go through the school years in a state of more or less permanent anxiety and insecurity and with poor self-esteem. It is not surprising that the victims' devaluation of themselves sometimes becomes so overwhelming that they see suicide as the only possible solution.

Bully/victim problems have even broader implications than those suggested in the previous paragraph. They really concern some of our *fundamental democratic principles: Every individual should have the right to be spared oppression and repeated, intentional humiliation, in school as in society at large.* No student should be afraid of going to school for fear of being harassed or degraded, and no parent should need to worry about such things happening to his or her child!

Bully/victim problems also relate to a society's general attitude to violence and oppression. What kind of view of societal values will a student acquire who is repeatedly bullied by other students without interference from adults? The same question can be asked with regard to students who, for long periods of time, are allowed to harass others without hindrance from adults. To refrain from actively counteracting bully/victim problems in school implies a tacit acceptance.

In this context, it should be emphasized that it is also of great importance to counteract these problems for the sake of the aggressive students. As reported above, school bullies are much more likely than other students to follow an antisocial path. Accordingly, it is essential to try to redirect their activities into more socially acceptable channels. And there is no evidence to suggest that a generally "tolerant" and permissive attitude on the part of adults will help bullies outgrow their antisocial behavior pattern.

INTERVENTION

Main Goals and Components of Intervention Program

Up to this point, an overview of what is known about bully/victim problems has been presented, based primarily on my own research. Against this background it is now natural to briefly describe the effects of the intervention program that we developed in connection with the nationwide campaign against bully/victim problems in Norwegian schools. The program was offered to all comprehensive schools (grades 1–9) via the ordinary administrative channels of the Ministry of Education.

The major goals of the program were to reduce as much as possible existing bully/victim problems and to prevent the development of new problems.

The main components of the program, which was aimed at teachers and parents as well as students, were the following:

1. A 32-page booklet for school personnel describing what is known about bully/victim problems (or rather: what was known in 1983) and giving detailed suggestions about what teachers and the school can do to counteract and prevent the problems (Olweus & Roland, 1983). Efforts were also made to dispel common myths about the nature and causes of bully/victim problems which might interfere with an adequate handling of them. This booklet was distributed free of charge to all comprehensive schools in Norway.

2. A 4-page folder with information and advice to parents of victims and bullies as well as "ordinary" children. This folder was distributed by the schools to all families in Norway with school-age children.

3. A 25-minute video cassette showing episodes from the everyday lives of two bullied children, a 10-year old boy and a 14-year old girl. This cassette could be bought or rented at a highly subsidized price.

4. A short inventory of questions (questionnaire) designed to obtain information about different aspects of bully/victim problems in the school, including frequency and the readiness of teachers and students to interfere with the problems. The inventory was completed by the students individually (in class) and anonymously. Registration of the level and nature of bully/victim problems in the school was thought to serve as a basis and starting point for active interventions on the part of the school and the parents. A number of the results presented earlier in this chapter were based on information collected with this inventory.[2]

Another "component" was added to the program as used in Bergen, the city in which the evaluation of the effects of the intervention program took place. Approximately 15 months after the program was first offered to the schools (in early October, 1983) we gave, in a 2-hour meeting with the staff, individual feedback information to each of the 42 schools participating in the study (Manger & Olweus, 1985). This information, derived from the students' responses to the inventory in 1983, focused on the level of problems and the social environment's reactions to the problems in the particular school as related to data from comparable schools obtained in the nationwide survey (October, 1983). At the same time, the main principles of the program and the major procedures suggested for intervention were presented and discussed with the staff.

[2]An updated "package" related to the intervention program against bully/victim problems consists of the inventory for the measurement of bully/victim problems (above and footnote 1), a copy of a small book *Bullying - what we know and what we can do* (Olweus, in press c) aiming at teachers and parents, and a parent folder. (Additional materials are being developed.) For more information, please write to the author at the address given in footnote 1.

Since we know from experience that many (Norwegian) teachers have somewhat distorted views of the characteristics of bullying students, particular emphasis was placed on a discussion of this topic and on appropriate ways of handling bullying behavior. Finally, the teachers rated different aspects of the program, in particular its feasibility and potential efficacy. Generally, this addition to the program, as well as the program itself, were quite favorably received by the teachers, as expressed in their ratings and comments.

Subjects and Design

Space limitations prevent detailed presentation of methodological information including sampling scheme, definition of measuring instruments and variables, and significance tests. Only summary descriptions and main results are provided in this context.

Evaluation of the effects of the intervention program is based on data from approximately 2500 students originally belonging to 112 grade 4 to 7 classes in 42 primary and junior high schools in Bergen (modal ages at Time 1 were 11, 12, 13 and 14 years respectively). Each of the four grade/age cohorts consisted of 600–700 subjects with a roughly equal distribution of boys and girls. The first time of data collection (Time 1) was in late May (and early June), 1983, approximately four months before the initiation of the campaign. New measurements were taken in May 1984 (Time 2) and May 1985 (Time 3).

Because the campaign was nationwide, it was not possible to set up a strictly experimental study with random allocation of schools or classes to treatment and control conditions. Instead, a quasi-experimental design was chosen, making use of "time-lagged contrasts between age-equivalent groups". In particular, for three of the cohorts, data collected at Time 1 (see Fig. 16.3) were used as a base line with which data for age-equivalent cohorts at Time 2 could be compared. The latter groups had then been exposed to the intervention program for about 8 months. To exemplify, the data for the grade 5 cohort at Time 1 (modal age 12 years) were compared with the Time 2 data for the grade 4 cohort which at that time had reached approximately the same age as the base line group. The same kind of comparisons were made between the grade 6 cohort at Time 1 and the grade 5 cohort at Time 2, and between the grade 7 cohort at Time 1 and the grade 6 cohort at Time 2.

Comparisons of data collected at Time 1 and Time 3 permit an assessment of the persistence or possible decline or enhancement of the effects over a longer time span. For these comparisons data for only two of the cohorts could be used as a base line, those of the grade 6 and grade 7

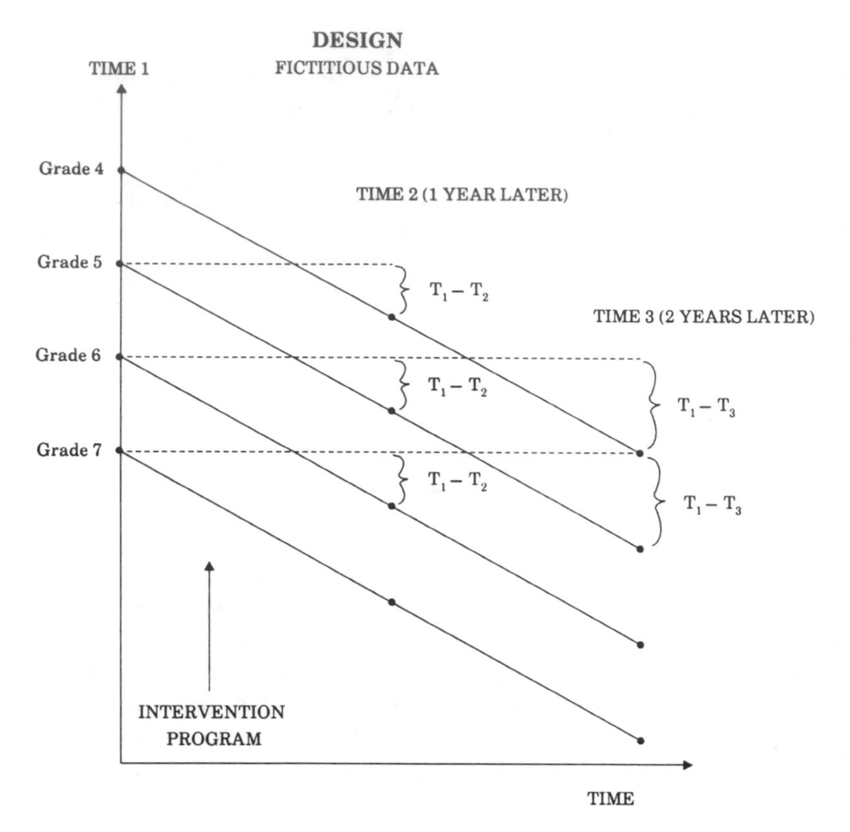

FIG. 16.3. Design for evaluation of effects of intervention program. Fictitious data (which to some extent reflect the general trend of the empirical findings).

cohorts, which were contrasted with data collected at Time 3 on the grade 4 and grade 5 cohorts respectively. The latter groups had been exposed to the intervention program during approximately 20 months at that time.

An attractive feature of the design is the fact that two of the cohorts serve as a base line group in one set of comparisons and as a treatment group in another. This is the case with the grade 5 cohort at Time 1, the data for which are used as a base line in comparison with the grade 4 cohort data collected at Time 2 (after 8 months of intervention). In addition, the grade 5 cohort data obtained at Time 2 serve to evaluate the possible effects of 8 months of intervention when they are compared with the data for the grade 6 cohort at Time 1. The same situation applies to the grade 6 cohort in comparisons with the grade 5 and grade 7 cohorts respectively.

The advantage of this aspect of the design is that a possible bias in the sampling of the cohorts would operate in opposite directions in the two sets of comparisons, thus making it more difficult to obtain consistent "intervention effects" across cohorts as a consequence of such bias. There are, however, no grounds for expecting such bias since the classes/schools were distributed on the different cohorts by a basically random procedure. Accordingly, the cohorts should be essentially equivalent in important respects at Time 1. For certain variables, this assumption can and will be empirically tested. This aspect of the design would provide the same kind of protection against faulty conclusions in case the base line data for one or both of these cohorts were unusually high or low simply as a function of chance.

To avoid erroneous conclusions due to possible selective attrition (more extreme or deviant individuals may be more likely to drop out in longitudinal studies) analyses were restricted to students for whom there were valid data at both time points in a particular comparison (both for the base line and the intervention groups). In this research, however, the results were basically the same whether we controlled or did not control for such attrition.

It should also be noted that since selection of the subjects was not based on some kind of "extreme score" criterion, the problem with "regression toward the mean" which looms large in many evaluation studies, is not at issue in the present research. By the present design the common and serious problem of attempting to statistically adjust for initial differences between nonequivalent groups is also avoided.

Outcome Variables

The main variables on which possible effects of the intervention could be expected to show up, are of course related to different aspects of bully/victim problems. In the present context, only data for the key individual items reflecting these problems will be reported. In later publications analyses of more reliable composites of items will be presented.

The three key items were worded as follows:

1. How often have you been bullied in school? (Being exposed to direct bullying or victimization, with relatively open attacks on the victim.)
2. How often have you taken part in bullying other students in school? (Bullying or victimizing other students.)
3. How often does it happen that other students don't want to spend recess with you and you end up being alone? (Being exposed to

indirect bullying or victimization by means of isolation, exclusion from the group.)

As mentioned in the beginning of the chapter, to avoid idiosyncratic interpretations the students were provided with a detailed but simple "definition" of bullying before answering question 1. And in both the written and the oral instructions, it was repeatedly emphasized that their answers should refer to the situation "this spring," that is, the period "from Christmas until now." All three questions had the same seven response alternatives, ranging from "it hasn't happened this spring" (scored 0) over "now and then" (scored 2) and "about once a week" (scored 3) to "several times a day" (scored 6).

Other items referred to being bullied or bullying others on the way to and from school. Several items also concerned the individual's attitude toward victims of bullying (e.g., "How do you usually feel when you see a student being bullied in school?") and bullying students (e.g., "What do you think of students who bully others?").

With regard to the validity of self-reports on variables related to bully/victim problems, it may be mentioned that in my early Swedish studies (Olweus, 1978) composites of 3–5 self-report items on being bullied or bullying and attacking others respectively correlated in the range .40–.60 (unpublished) with reliable peer ratings on related dimensions (Olweus, 1977). Similarly, Perry, Kusel, and Perry (1988) have reported a correlation of .42 between a self-report scale of three victimization items and a reliable measure of peer nominations of victimization in elementary schoolchildren.

In the present study we also obtained a kind of peer rating in that each student had to estimate the number of students in his or her class who were bullied or bullied others during the reference period. These data were aggregated for each class and the resulting class means correlated with the means derived from the students' own reports of being victimized or victimizing others. The two sets of class means were quite substantially correlated, the average correlations across the grade 5–7 cohorts being .61 for the victimization dimension and .58 for the bullying variable (Time 1). Corresponding coefficients for estimated average *proportion* of students in the class being bullied or bullying others (which measure corrects for differing number of students in the classes) were even somewhat higher, .62 and .68 respectively. There was thus considerable agreement across classes between class estimates derived from self-reports and from this form of peer ratings. These results certainly attest to the validity of the self-report data employed.

Because a link has been established between bullying behavior and antisocial/criminal activities, it was hypothesized that the intervention program against bullying *might* also lead to a reduction in antisocial behavior. To measure different aspects of antisocial behavior in relatively young people, preadolescents and adolescents, a new self-report instrument was developed (Olweus & Endresen, in preparation; Olweus, in press a). This inventory shows similarities with the instruments recently developed by Elliott & Ageton (1980) and by Hindelang, Hirschi, and Weis (1981) but our inventory contained fewer items on serious crimes and more items related to school problems.

The 23 core items of the inventory were selected from two broad conceptual domains. One concerned disciplinary problems and other rule-breaking behavior in school, while the second covered more general and non-school-related antisocial acts such as vandalism, theft, burglary, and fraud. Though it was possible and meaningful to divide the items into two separate scales roughly corresponding to the two conceptual domains, the results to be presented in this context only concern the Total Scale of Antisocial Behavior (TAS) consisting of all 23 items. Psychometric analyses of the inventory have given quite encouraging results indicating that the scales have satisfactory or good reliability, stability, and validity, as well as theoretical relevance.

Finally, it was thought important to assess possible effects on student satisfaction with school life, in particular during recess time. (In Norwegian comprehensive schools, students usually have a break of approximately ten minutes every 45 minutes. In addition, they have a lunch break of 20–30 minutes in the middle of the day.) Because most of the bullying takes place at school (during recess and on the way to and from classes, and not on the way to and from school) the following question was considered particularly relevant: "How do you like recess time?"

Statistical Analyses

Since classes rather than students were the basic sampling units (with students nested within classes), it was considered important to choose a data analytic strategy that reflected the basic features of the design. Accordingly, data were analyzed with ANOVA (analysis of variance) with students nested within classes nested within schools nested within times/occasions (Time 1 versus Time 2, Time 1 versus Time 3). Sex of the subjects was crossed with times, schools (within times), and classes (within schools). Because several of the cohorts figured in two comparisons, the analyses had to be conducted separately for each combination of cohorts (for further information, see Olweus, in press b).

For several of the variables (or derivatives of them such as percentages), less refined (and in some respects, less informative) analyses with t-tests and chi square were also carried out. The findings from these analyses were in general agreement with those obtained in the ANOVAs.

Results

The results for some of the variables discussed above are presented separately for boys and girls in Figs. 16.4–16.9. Because the design of the study is relatively complex, a few words about how to read the figures are in order.

The panel to the left shows the effects after 8 months of intervention, and the one to the right displays the results after 20 months. The upper curves (designated "Before") show the base line data (Time 1) for the relevant cohorts (the grade 5, grade 6, and grade 7 cohorts in the left panel and the grade 6 and grade 7 cohorts in the right). The lower curves (designated "After") display data collected at Time 2 (after 8 months of intervention) in the panel to the left and at Time 3 (after 20 months of intervention) in the right-hand panel for the age-equivalent

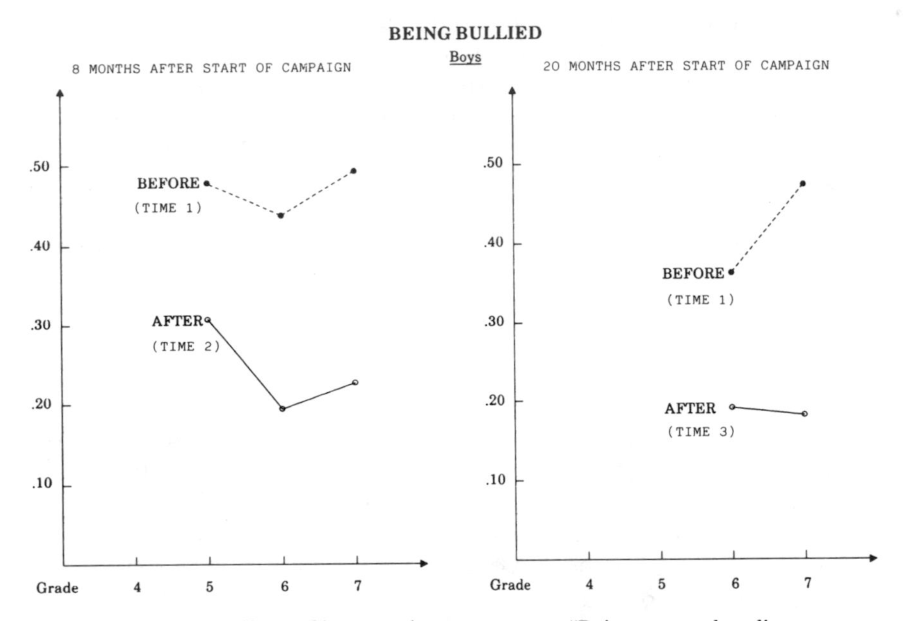

FIG. 16.4. Effects of intervention program on "Being exposed to direct bullying" for boys. Panel to the left shows effects after 8 months of intervention; panel to the right displays results after 20 months of intervention. Upper curves (designated "Before") show base line data (Time 1), and the lower curves (designated "After") display data collected at Time 2 in the left panel and at Time 3 in the panel to the right.

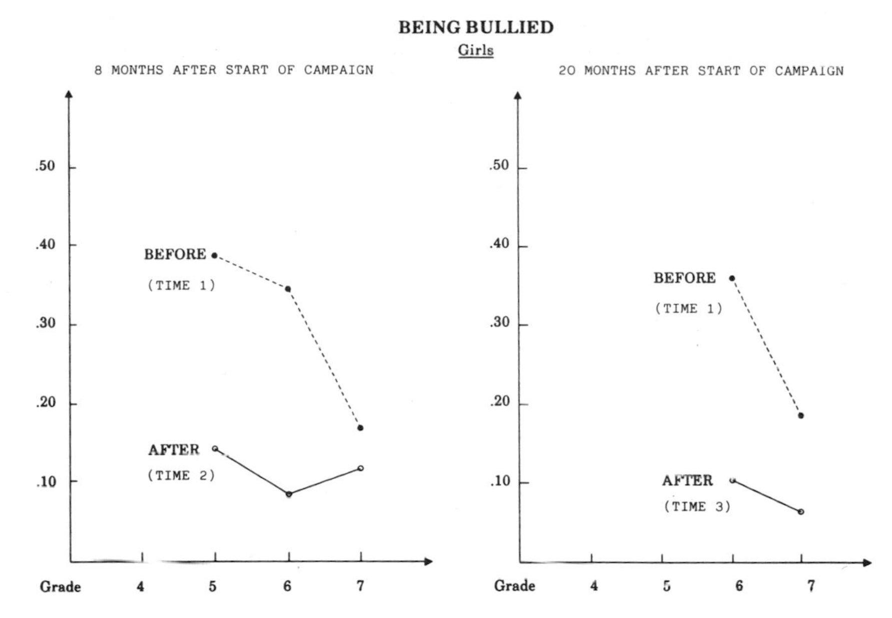

FIG. 16.5. Effects of intervention program on "Being exposed to direct bullying" for girls. See Fig. 16.4 for explanation of the figure.

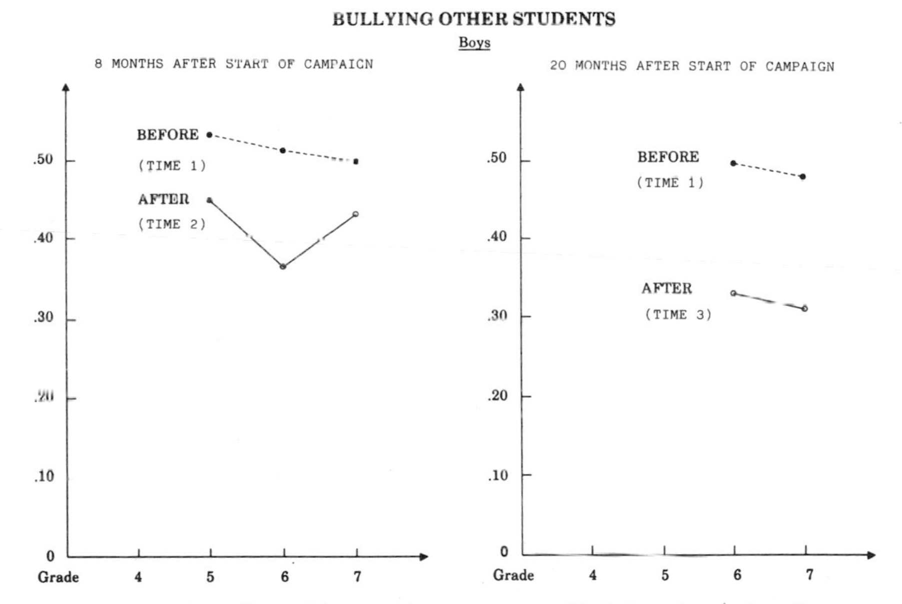

FIG. 16.6. Effects of intervention program on "Bullying other students" for boys. See Fig. 16.4 for explanation of figure.

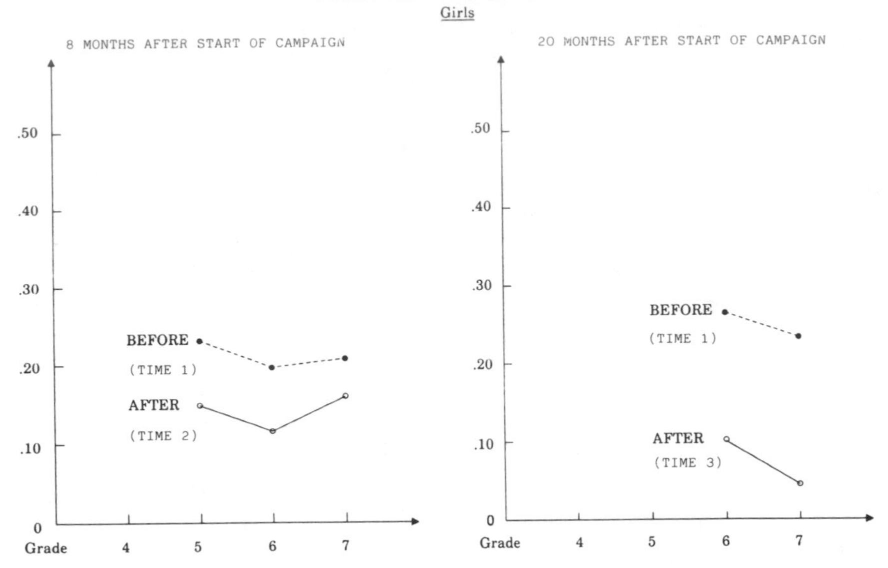

FIG. 16.7. Effects of intervention program on "Bullying other students" for girls. See Fig. 16.4 for explanation of the figure.

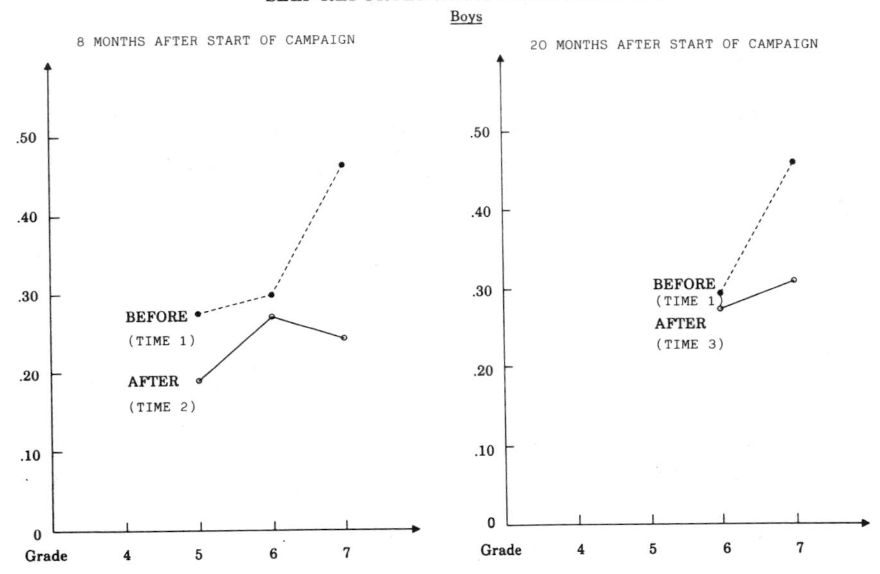

FIG. 16.8. Effects of intervention program on "Total Scale of Antisocial Behavior" (TAS) for boys. See Fig. 16.4 for explanation of the figure.

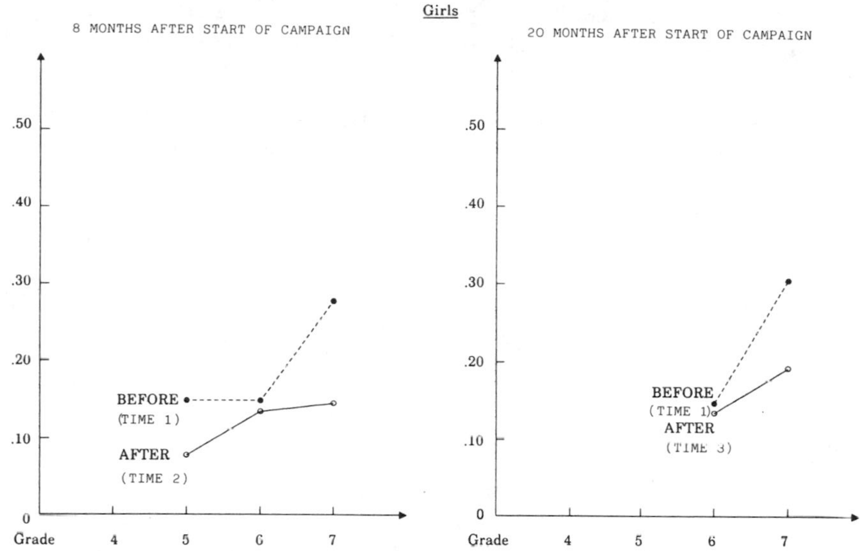

FIG. 16.9. Effects of intervention program on "Total Scale of Antisocial Behavior" (TAS) for girls. See Fig. 16.4 for explanation of the figure.

cohorts (the grade 4, grade 5, and grade 6 cohorts at Time 2 and the grade 4 and grade 5 cohorts at Time 3).

It should be noted that in some of the figures there are minor differences in base line data ("Before") for the grade 6 and grade 7 cohorts when presented in the left and right panels respectively. This is a consequence of the restriction of the analyses to subjects who had valid data at both time points; accordingly, it is not exactly the same subjects who entered the two sets of analyses.

The scales on the Y-axis are in some sense arbitrary, simply reflecting the system used in scoring the variables.

The *main findings* of the analyses can be summarized as follows.

1. There were marked reductions in the levels of bully/victim problems for the periods studied, 8 and 20 months of intervention respectively (Figs. 16.4–16.7). By and large, reductions were obtained for both boys and girls and across all cohorts compared. For the longer time period the effects persisted in the case of "Being exposed to direct bullying" and "Being exposed to indirect bullying" and were strengthened for the variable "Bullying others."

2. Similar reductions were obtained for the aggregated "peer rating"

variables "Number of students being bullied in the class" and "Number of students in the class bullying others." There was thus consensual agreement in the classes that bully/victim problems had decreased during the periods studied.

3. In terms of percentages of students reporting being bullied or bullying others "now and then" or more frequently, the reductions amounted to approximately 50% or more in most comparisons (Time 1–Time 3 for "Bullying others").

4. There was no displacement of bullying from the school to the way to and from school. There were reductions or no changes on the items measuring bully/victim problems on the way to and from school.

5. There was also a reduction in general antisocial behavior (Figs. 16.8 and 16.9) such as vandalism, theft, and truancy. (For the grade 6 comparisons the effects were marginal for both time periods.)

6. At the same time, there was an increase in student satisfaction with school life as reflected in "liking recess time."

7. There were weak and inconsistent changes for the questions concerning attitudes to different aspects of bully/victim problems.

In the majority of comparisons for which reductions were reported above, the differences between base line and intervention groups were highly significant or significant (in spite of the fact that many of them were based on single items).

Discussion of Data and Alternative Interpretations

Because of space limitations I will give only a relatively brief discussion of certain aspects of the study, in particular from the perspective of possible alternative interpretations of the results. I want to begin the discussion by reporting some general conditions surrounding the research that are likely to support my basic interpretation that the findings obtained are a consequence of the intervention program and not a result of "irrelevant" factors.

The students responded to the self-report forms anonymously and the confidentiality of their answers was strongly emphasized on each measurement occasion. Confidentiality was achieved by means of a code system which permitted identification of answer forms across time points but prevented both teachers and researchers from knowing which forms belonged to which students. All of the data collection was administered by research assistants and not by teachers which might have affected the students' willingness to give honest responses. Generally, the research assistants repeatedly stressed the importance of giving sincere responses: We wanted the students to report how they really felt, were treated, and behaved. All of these conditions should have encouraged the subjects to give careful and veridical responses.

In addition, the first wave of data collection took place roughly four months before the launching of the campaign, which, as mentioned, was administered through the ordinary channels of distribution of the Ministry of Education. And the campaign was not much followed up by the Ministry of Education and never in the context of our measuring occasions. Also, media attention was limited and mainly concentrated on the launching of the campaign in early fall, 1983. Accordingly, there are good reasons to believe that the students saw no connection between our research activities and the intervention program. In this way, the subjects should have had very little motivation to try to please (or frustrate) the researchers by giving certain kinds of responses on the different occasions.

Due to the large-scale nature of the study we had to rely heavily on self-report data. Every source of data has its own particular strengths and weaknesses but I want to argue that, by and large, *self-reports are the best single data source for the purposes of this study*, in particular for giving information on different aspects of victimization (see section on the possibility of underreporting of bullying). The usefulness of self-report information is, however, highly contingent on the way it is obtained. In the present study, in which the dependent variables should be *sensitive to changes* in the relevant behaviors, we thought it very important to have a clear definition of the key targeted behaviors, to use as specific frequency alternatives as possible, and to make reference to a delimited and natural time unit, as previously described. An ordinary inventory format designed to tap generalized, habitual reaction patterns is not likely to have been very useful for this aspect of the study (though such items were included in the study for other purposes).

When I emphasize the general appropriateness of self-report data for giving information on victimization, in particular, it is because the victims have first-hand knowledge of what the other students are doing to them and they experience directly "on their own bodies" the harassment, humiliation, and social isolation. Answering anonymously and in an atmosphere characterized by encouragement of sincere responding, they are not likely to underreport the extent of their problems. And judging from the study comparing self-reports with teacher reports (above), there also seems to be relatively little risk of overreporting, by and large. This view of self-report data on victimization as reasonably accurate is supported in a general way by the previously reported findings on the validity of such data, including the results on the aggregated peer rating variables used in the present study. This notwithstanding, one could have wished also to have available data obtained through direct observation in the school setting, at least for a subset of subjects. At the same time, it is an open question whether direct observation can adequately capture more subtle aspects of bully/victim problems as well as the not too infrequent instances of bullying taking place in secluded places such as the bathroom and in the hallways. In addition, it would have been very difficult, if not impossible, to get meaningful incidence and prevalence data (Olweus, in press a) by means of direct observation, unless enormous resources were invested.

It should be noted that the items on antisocial behavior, in conformity with the questions on bully/victim problems, called for quite specific information. The general format of this inventory was as follows: "Have you done (taken part in) this: Purposely destroyed seats in a bus, a movie, or other places?", with three response alternatives: NO, never; YES, in the past but not this spring; YES, about . . . . . times this spring. For the last alternative, the student should fill out the estimated number of times. This questioning format, which avoided vague response alternatives such as "often" and "seldom", should have encouraged the subjects to give precise information and also make it sensitive to possible changes over time. For the present (and many other) purposes it is obvious that self-report data on antisocial behavior are superior to data from other sources, for instance, referrals to the child welfare committee or official records of arrests or convictions, the rate of which would be extremely low for subjects of the present ages.

So far the discussion has mainly focused on the nature and quality of the data in a general way. In considering whether the results can be explained in ways other than as a consequence of the intervention program, three alternatives seem particularly relevant. One concerns the possibility that, due to some kind of social pressure or expectancy, there occurred an *underreporting* (at Time 2 and Time 3) of behaviors that had not changed at all or very little in reality. Another explanation would implicate a *change in attitude* to bully/victim problems, which might show up as a reduction in the measured variables—again without any real changes in the relevant behaviors. Finally, the effects obtained might be a consequence of *repeated measurement* in that the treatment groups had been "tested" more frequently and for longer periods of time than the base line groups.

If the intervention program as implemented in the schools conveyed a certain amount of repudiation of bullying behavior (which it should do), it is quite possible to assume that bullies would like to conceal or underreport (at Time 2 and Time 3) their degree of actual bullying (in spite of anonymous responding and a generally nonconformist attitude on the part of the bullies). There are no grounds for assuming, however, that more "neutral" peers who estimated the number of bullying and bullied students in the class, should react in the same way. And the peers agreed that a reduction in the number of bullies (and victims) had occurred, as may be recalled. Also, and in particular, the victims were not likely to underreport their degree of exposure to bullying and their suffering because of such repudiation. One would rather expect a *sensitization effect* among bullied children, that is, a lowered threshold for perceiving and reporting different forms of harassment, which would thus show up as higher scores on variables related to victimization. Such effects have often been reported in the literature for similar situations where one has suddenly focused attention on a societal problem and maybe also signalled a readiness to do something about it. Furthermore, if there were some validity to the assumption about underreporting, it would be reasonable to expect more marked reductions in bullying behavior than in being exposed to bullying (in particular at Time 2). However, as previously shown (Figs. 16.4–16.7), the empirical findings were quite the opposite, with weaker effects on bullying behavior than on being bullied at Time 2, a fact that further undermines the alternative explanation at issue. (The effects for these two variables were of roughly the same magnitude only at Time 3.)

Another kind of explanation would implicate a *gradual change of attitude* to bully/victim problems to the effect that there had occurred a general increase in tolerance of bullying behavior over time (at Time 2 and Time 3). Such a change would imply use of a more lenient standard of judgment, or a raising of the threshold of detection and reaction, and might apply to both bullies, victims, and "neutral" students. This hypothesis about attitudinal change is derived from the field of social psychology, where it has been observed that it is often easier to change attitudes than behavior.

Some of the arguments presented above are relevant also in considering the reasonableness of this second alternative explanation. In particular, it would seem that sensitization effects are a much more probable outcome than blunting or heightened tolerance when there is increased attention to the targeted problems in the context of an intervention program. This is likely to apply particularly to victims and maybe also, to a somewhat lesser degree, to "neutral" students. In addition, if an attitudinal change had taken place, one would expect this to become evident in the empirical analyses of items tapping attitudes to bully/victim problems. This was not the case, however, as may be recalled. These items, in contrast to the behavioral items, showed no marked and consistent changes. All considered, it must be concluded that *an explanation of the results along attitudinal lines is very unconvincing*. It can be added that both alternative hypotheses suggested above would fall short in explaining the reduction in antisocial problems and the increase in student satisfaction, aspects not specifically targeted in the intervention program.

The third main alternative explanation to be considered implies that there might be some kind of systematic changes in the students' responding as a consequence of *repeated measurement* (saturation, boredom, or sensitization effects or the like). It is by no means obvious that such possible changes would result in reductions rather than increases in the relevant variables but it would nevertheless seem important to test whether alterations did occur and if so, in what direction. This was done by comparing two groups of subjects who responded to a 26-item inventory on bully/victim problems (containing also the three key items, above) in the fall of 1984 (one year after the initiation of the campaign). One group consisted of the majority of the core subjects of the project (*n* approximately 2000 in these comparisons) who had at that time taken part in a total of more than six hours of measurement, and the other group (*n* approximately 2800) contained subjects from parallel classes in the same schools who had been measured only once with the 16-item inventory on bully/victim problems (in connection with the launching of the nationwide campaign in October, 1983). The analyses, restricted to the three key items, were conducted separately for each of the four grade levels and the two sexes. Because the statistical tests were quite sensitive due to the relatively large number of subjects, nine out of 24 comparisons were significant. In five of these comparisons the project group scored higher than the other group and in the remaining four results in the opposite direction were obtained. The majority of the differences were quite small, a fifth or a sixth of a standard deviation. We can thus conclude that *there did not seem to be any systematic interpretable changes in responding due to repeated measurement* (within the range studied) and that the reported reductions in bully/victim problems cannot be accounted for by such changes.

One can possibly think of slightly different versions of the first two alternative hypotheses, in particular, or of some combination of them, but it appears that both conceptual considerations and the empirical results would be at variance with such explanations. It turns out, in fact, to be fairly difficult to come up with alternative explanations that are both conceptually meaningful and in agreement with the empirical findings.

It should also be noted that the present design is in principle sensitive to a "history" interpretation (Cook & Campbell, 1979) implying that some "irrelevant" factor concomitant to the intervention program was in reality responsible for the "effects" observed. We know, however, that during the two year period of the present study there were no systematic changes, besides those related to the intervention program, in the administrative, educational, or other school routines in the local school system to which all participating schools belonged. It is also very difficult to conceive of changes in "irrelevant" factors in the society at large that co-occurred with the program and could be reasonably linked to the reductions in bully/victim problems registered in the schools.

All in all, though several more refined analyses remain to be done (to try to document, for instance, what aspects of the program were particularly effective; see Olweus, in press b), *it can be concluded that the reductions in bully/victim and associated problems are likely to be mainly a consequence of the intervention program and not of some other "irrelevant" factor.*

Basic Principles

Having reported the main goals and components of the intervention program as well as some of its effects, it is now natural to present its underlying principles and major subgoals.

The intervention program is built around *a limited set of key principles* derived chiefly from research on the development and modification of the implicated problem behaviors, in particular aggressive behavior. It is considered important to try to create a school (and ideally, also home) environment characterized by *warmth, positive interest, and involvement from adults* on one hand and *firm limits to unacceptable behavior* on the other. Third, in cases of violations of limits and rules, *nonhostile, nonphysical sanctions* should be consistently applied. Implied in the latter two principles is also a certain degree of *monitoring and surveillance* of the students' activities in and out of school (Patterson, 1986). Finally, *adults* are supposed to *act as authorities at least in some respects.*

It can be seen that the first three of these principles largely represent the opposite of the child rearing dimensions found to be important in the development of an aggressive personality pattern discussed previously: negativism on the part of the primary caretaker, permissiveness and lack of clear limits, and use of power-assertive methods (Olweus, 1980). In a sense, the present intervention program represents an *authoritative adult–child interaction, or child rearing, model (cf., e.g., Baumrind, 1967) as applied to the school setting.*

The principles listed above can be translated into a number of specific measures to be used at the *school, class,* and *individual levels.* It is considered very important to work on all these levels, if possible. Figure 16.10 lists a number of such measures that were recommended in the intervention program (Olweus & Roland, 1983; a few of the measures in Fig.

COMPONENTS TO PROGRAM PACKAGE AGAINST BULLYING

GENERAL PREREQUISITES: AWARENESS + INVOLVEMENT

SCHOOL LEVEL

- School conference day on bully/victim problems
- Better supervision of recess
- More attractive school playground
- Contact telephone
- Meeting staff--parents
- Teacher groups for the development of the "school climate"
- Parent circles (study and discussion groups)

CLASS LEVEL

- Class rules against bullying: clarification, praise, and sanctions
- Regular class meetings
- Cooperative learning
- Meeting teacher--parents/children
- Common positive activities
- Role playing
- Literature

INDIVIDUAL LEVEL

- Serious talks with bullies and victims
- Serious talks with parents of involved children
- Teacher use of imagination
- Help from "neutral" students
- Advice to parents (parent brochure)
- "Discussion" groups with parents of bullies and victims
- Change of class or school

FIG. 16.10. Overview of measures at the school, class, and individual levels presented in the intervention program.m

16.10, including cooperative learning, were not included in the original program). Space limitations prevent a detailed description of the various measures suggested but such an account can be found in a small book designed for teachers and parents (Olweus, 1986, in press, c)[3].

With regard to implementation and execution, the program is mainly based on a *utilization of the existing social environment:* teachers and other school personnel, students, and parents. Nonexperts thus play a major role in the desired *restructuring of the social environment.* Experts such as school psychologists and social workers also serve important functions as planners and coordinators, in counseling teacher and parent groups, and in handling more serious cases.

Additional Characteristics

Further understanding of the program and its way of working can be gained from a brief description of its four major subgoals (this entails some repetition of earlier material):

1. *To increase awareness of the bully/ victim problem and advance knowledge about it,* including to dispel some of the myths about it and its causes. Use

[3]See footnote 2 on p. 23.

of the inventory is an important step in obtaining more specific knowledge about the frequency and nature of the problems in the particular school.

2. *To achieve active involvement on the part of teachers and parents.* This implies among other things that the adults must recognize that it is their responsibility to control to a certain degree what goes on among the children at school. One way of doing this is to provide adequate supervision during recess time. In addition, the teachers are encouraged to intervene in possible bullying situations and give a clear message to the students: Bullying is not accepted in our school. Teachers are also strongly advised to initiate serious talks with victims and bullies, and their parents, if a bully/victim problem has been identified in the class. Again, the basic message should be: We will not tolerate bullying in our school and will see to it that it comes to an end. Such an intervention on the part of the school must be regularly followed up and closely supervised; otherwise the situation may easily become worse for the victim than before the intervention.

3. *To develop clear rules against bullying behavior* such as: (a) We shall not bully others. (b) We shall try to help students who are bullied. (c) We shall make a point to include students who become easily left out. Such a set of rules may serve as a basis for class discussions about what is meant by bullying behavior in concrete situations and what kind of sanctions should be used for students who break the rules. The behavior of the students in the class should be regularly related to these rules in class meetings ("social hour"), and it is important that the teacher make consistent use of sanctions (some form of nonhostile, nonphysical punishment) in cases of rule violations and also give generous praise when the rules have been followed.

4. *To provide support and protection for the victims.* If followed, class rules against bullying certainly serve as support for children who tend to be victimized. In addition, the teacher may enlist the help of "neutral" or well-adjusted students to alleviate the situation of the victims in various ways. Also, teachers are encouraged to use their imagination to help victimized students assert themselves in the class, to make them valuable in the eyes of their classmates. Parents of victims are exhorted to help their children develop new peer contacts and to teach them in detail how to make new acquaintances and to maintain a friendship relation.

It may be added that the present intervention program has been evaluated by more than 1000 Norwegian and Swedish teachers. In short, their reactions have generally been quite favorable, indicating among other things that the teachers see the proposed principles and measures as useful and realistic.

CONCLUSION

Though what has been presented in this chapter about the effects of the intervention program only represents the first stages of analysis, the basic message of our findings is clear: *It is definitely possible to reduce substantially bully/victim problems in school and related problem behaviors with a suitable intervention program.* Thus, whether these problems will be tackled or not no longer depends on whether we have the knowledge necessary to achieve desirable changes. It is much more a matter of our willingness to involve ourselves and to use the existing knowledge to counteract these problems.

ACKNOWLEDGMENTS

The research reported was supported by grants from the William T. Grant Foundation, the Norwegian Council for Social Research, in earlier phases, the Norwegian Ministry of Education, and the Swedish Delegation for Social Research (DSF). Several of the ideas presented were developed while the author was a Fellow at the Center for Advanced Study in the Behavioral Sciences, Stanford, USA. He is indebted to the University of Bergen, the Spencer Foundation, the Norwegian Council for Social Research, and the Center for Advanced Study in the Behavioral Sciences for financial support of his year at the Center in 1986–87.

REFERENCES

Baumrind, D. (1967). Child care practices anteceding three patterns of preschool behavior. *Genetic Psychology Monographs, 75,* 43–88.

Cook, T. D., & Campbell, D. T. (1979). *Quasi-experimentation.* Chicago: Rand McNally.

Ekblad, S., & Olweus, D. (1986). Applicability of Olweus' aggression inventory in a sample of Chinese primary school children. *Aggressive Behavior, 12,* 315–325.

Ekman, K. (1977). *Skolmobbning.* Pro gradu-arbete. Åbo, Finland: Åbo Akademi.

Elliott, D. S., & Ageton, S. S. (1980). Reconciling race and class differences in self-reported and official estimates of delinquency. *American Sociological Review, 45,* 95–110.

Heinemann, P. P. (1972). *Mobbning—gruppvåld bland barn och vuxna.* Stockholm: Natur och Kultur.

Hindelang, M. J., Hirschi, T., & Weis, J. G. (1981). *Measuring delinquency.* Beverly Hills, CA: Sage.

Hyde, J. S. (1984). How large are gender differences in aggression? A developmental meta-analysis. *Developmental Psychology, 20,* 722–736.

Lagerspetz, K. M., Björkqvist, K., Berts, M., & King, E. (1982). Group aggression among school children in three schools. *Scandinavian Journal of Psychology, 23,* 45–52.

Loeber, R., & Dishion, T. (1983). Early predictors of male delinquency: A review. *Psychological Bulletin, 94,* 69–99.

Maccoby, E. E. (1986). Social groupings in childhood: Their relationships to prosocial and antisocial behavior in boys and girls. In D. Olweus, J. Block, & M. Radke-Yarrow (Eds.), *Development of antisocial and prosocial behavior.* New York: Academic Press.

Maccoby, E. E., & Jacklin, C. N. (1980). Sex differences in aggression: a rejoinder and a reprise. *Child Development, 51,* 964–980.

Magnusson, D., Stattin, H., & Dunér, A. (1983). Aggression and criminality in a longitudinal perspective. In K. T. Van Dusen & S. A. Mednick (Eds.), *Prospective studies of crime and delinquency.* Boston: Kluwer-Nijhoff.

Manger, T., & Olweus, D. (1985). Tilbakemelding til skulane. *Norsk Skoleblad* (Oslo, Norway), *35,* 20–22.

Olweus, D. (1973a). *Hackkycklingar och översittare: Forskning om skolmobbning.* Stockholm: Almqvist & Wiksell.

Olweus, D. (1973b). Personality and aggression. In J. K. Cole & D. D. Jensen (Eds.), *Nebraska symposium on motivation, 1972 (Vol. 20).* Lincoln: University of Nebraska Press.

Olweus, D. (1977). Aggression and peer acceptance in adolescent boys: Two short-term longitudinal studies of ratings. *Child Development, 48,* 1301–1313.

Olweus, D. (1978). *Aggression in the schools: Bullies and whipping boys.* Washington, DC: Hemisphere (Wiley).

Olweus, D. (1979). Stability of aggressive reaction patterns in males: A review. *Psychological Bulletin, 86,* 852–875.

Olweus, D. (1980). Familial and temperamental determinants of aggressive behavior in adolescent boys: A causal analysis. *Developmental Psychology, 16,* 644–660.

Olweus, D. (1981). Bullying among school boys. In N. Cantwell (Ed.), *Children and violence.* Stockholm: Akademilitteratur.

Olweus, D. (1983). Low school achievement and aggressive behavior in adolescent boys. In D. Magnusson & V. Allen (Eds.), *Human development. An interactional perspective.* New York: Academic Press.

Olweus, D. (1984). Aggressors and their victims: Bullying at school. In N. Frude & H. Gault (Eds.), *Disruptive behavior in schools.* New York: Wiley.

Olweus, D. (1985). 80 000 barn er innblandet i mobbing. *Norsk Skoleblad* (Oslo, Norway), *35,* 18–23.

Olweus, D. (1986). *Mobbning—vad vi vet och vad vi kan göra.* Stockholm: Liber.

Olweus, D. (1987). Bully/victim problems among schoolchildren. In J. P. Myklebust & R. Ommundsen (Eds.), *Psykologprofesjonen mot år 2000.* Oslo: Universitetsforlaget.

Olweus, D. (in press a). Prevalence and incidence in the study of antisocial behavior: Definitions and measurement. In M. Klein (Ed.), *Cross-national re-*

search in self-reported crime and delinquency. Dordrecht, The Netherlands: Kluwer.

Olweus, D. (in press b). Assessing change in a cohort-longitudinal study with hierarchical data. In D. Magnusson, L. R. Bergman, G. Rudinger, & B. Törestad (Eds.), *Matching problems and methods in longitudinal research.* New York: Cambridge University press.

Olweus, D. (in press c). *Bullying—what we know and what we can do.* Mimeographed.

Olweus, D., & Endresen, J. (in preparation). *Assessment of antisocial behavior in preadolescence and adolescence.* Manuscript.

Olweus, D., & Roland, E. (1983). *Mobbing—bakgrunn og tiltak.* Oslo, Norway: Kirke-og undevisningsdepartementet.

Patterson, G. R. (1986). Performance models for antisocial boys. *American Psychologist, 41,* 432–444.

Patterson, G. R., & Stouthamer-Loeber, M. (1984). The correlation of family management practices and delinquency. *Child Development, 55,* 1299–1307.

Perry, D. G., Kusel, S. J., & Perry, L. C. (1988). Victims of peer aggression. *Developmental Psychology, 24,* 807–814.

Pikas, A. (1975). *Så stoppar vi mobbning.* Stockholm: Prisma.

Raundalen, T. S., & Raundalen, M. (1979). *Er du på vår side?* Oslo: Universitetsforlaget.

Roland, E. (1983). *Strategi mot mobbing.* Oslo: Universitetsforlaget.

Rutter, M. (1983). School effects on pupil progress: Research findings and policy implications. *Child Development, 54,* 1–19.

Commentary

School-Based Interventions for Aggressive Children: Possibilities, Limitations, and Future Directions

Claude Gagnon
Université de Montréal

Because of the heavy burden of suffering it constitutes, childhood aggression deserves research efforts directed toward discovery of effective prevention and treatment techniques. The material reported in this book is a significant demonstration of what is being done in that direction. The two intervention programs described by John Coie and by Dan Olweus are good examples of treatment of aggression based on research results.

The two programs are school-based interventions. One is designed to reduce the incidence of one type of aggressive behavior in school settings, the bully/victim problems, the other identifies subjects in greatest need of help within schools, children rejected by their peers, and focuses intervention efforts on them. Coie, Underwood and Lochman have listed advantages and disadvantages of school-based interventions. One must not underestimate the difficulty of implementing interventions having a social focus, such as reducing aggressive behavior, in a setting where teaching academic skills is viewed as the primary purpose. The Scandinavian project of Olweus is in that sense a good demonstration of the level of involvement of the school personnel that can be achieved when there is a willingness to solve the problem.

Let us consider more closely first Olweus' program to reduce bully/victim problems among school children. Referring either to one's personal recollection of one's own school days or to systematic information, such as the sort collected by Olweus (1978), one has no difficulty in understanding the bullying phenomenon in school settings. Its prevalence seems to be high (one student out of seven being involved "now and then" or more frequently in bully/victim problems); the suffering is great for the victims and the prognosis of the bullies is grim. Any intervention that can produce a decrease in the number of such incidents per year is welcome. Results reported by Olweus are indeed quite remarkable. A decrease of more than 50% of bully/victim problems in the schools during the two years following the implementation of the program, plus a marked drop in antisocial behavior in general (such as theft, vandalism and truancy) seems like a frank success in view of the fact that previous attempts to modify aggressive and antisocial behavior have often met with meager results.

The results are particularly significant also in view of the limited amount of new resources needed to achieve them. The basic ingredient of such an intervention is the willingness to involve all actors in the school—teachers, parents, and students—to become aware of the problem and to clearly establish and enforce rules against bullying behavior in the setting. Nonexperts indeed play a major role in this "restructuring of the social environment." Although more refined analyses of this intervention program are currently underway, from my present vantage point, three additional considerations appear to be worthwhile. First, we need to see efforts to replicate Olweus' success with similar and younger populations. Second, although one can appreciate the quality of the quasi-experimental design employed by Olweus, namely the "time lagged contrasts between equivalent groups," subsequent studies should include a genuine control group. Finally, outcome evaluations by people other than the program participants are needed in order to confirm the validity of the results demonstrated by Olweus. The message of the findings reported here, however, is quite clear: it is possible to significantly reduce bullying incidents in schools with a suitable intervention program.

It is a kind of a paradox, however, that such a success can be achieved with a rather simple approach in comparison to the limited success reported by Coie and colleagues, with a more complex intervention for aggressive children. For an explanation, one would obviously point to the fact that the objectives of the two intervention programs are different, as were the type of children targeted. In one case, the major goal of the intervention was to reduce as much as possible the frequency of bullying incidents in the school setting without much attention to the individuals who engage in these behaviors and with no specific intervention tailored to these individual children. In the other case, based on evidence showing that, apart from the fact of being very disruptive in school, socially rejected children are also at risk of various adjustment difficulties later in life, the main goals of the intervention were to improve the overall social skills of the targeted children as well as reduce their aggressive behaviors.

Because the personal characteristics of the rejected children appear to be relatively stable over time, at least from grade 3 onwards, one wonders if the type of children Coie and others have been working with are not the hard core group who continue to bully other children in spite of the successful school-wide program implemented by Olweus. Isn't it likely that the decrease in the frequency of bullying could be due to greater social control in the school setting, or less social contagion, factors that deter a number of children from bullying others? These desisting children could be the proactive type, referred to by Dodge & Coie (1987), whose aggressive behavior could be modified by behavioral management. If one has to continue efforts though, to reduce serious aggression in the school settings, one has also to focus intervention on children who seem to need more intensive treatment. This is the main characteristic of Coie and colleagues' intervention program.

Focussing on aspects of rejected children's social behavior that contribute to their being disliked, the goals derived for the intervention are quite straightforward: decreasing the amount of antisocial, aggressive behavior, and increasing the amount of prosocial behavior. The program's four components—social problem solving, positive play training, group entry skill training, anger control—as well as academic tutoring, have sound bases in research on the determinants of negative peer status and in programs that have demonstrated some effectiveness. It is a sort of shotgun approach where one uses a large variety of techniques. If this approach does not work, there doesn't seem to be any point continuing in that direction; if it works, it is always possible afterwards to document which aspects of the program were particularly effective. Of course, there is always the possibility that the components might be effective separately and yet not work when thrown together.

Overall results reported by Coie and others show that although the patterns of postintervention measures suggest intervention subjects were consistently better off than control subjects, none of the differences were statistically significant. Results are more promising though for the third cohort, because more time was spent on the anger-control component of the program and especially because the idea of redefining the circumstances of provocation to aggression was emphasized. The improved results of the third cohort may also be an indication that any evaluation of an intervention project should not rely only on the first trial, but rather on the second or the third, when one can be sure that all the program implementation problems have been overcome.

Besides the relative success of Coie's and colleagues' intervention program, what appears to me to be one of the most seminal ideas coming out of the investigators' experience has to do with the observation that these children have no real motivation to become engaged in the intervention program and use the skills the program offers. Hence the suggestion of trying to engage the motivations of aggressive children in training programs according to the type of aggression they are engaged in most often, that is, reactive or proactive. The idea of matching the type of treatment to type of subject is not new (see Sullivan, Grant, & Grant, 1957), but it seems to me that the idea of tackling differentially the motivational issue according to the type of aggression usually displayed by the children is worth a serious trial.

Considering together now the two intervention programs presented here, one cannot refrain from thinking of what an ideal match the two could make for a comprehensive school-based intervention. The successful Scandinavian program is a clear demonstration that all members of a school setting can be involved in the restructuring of the social environment, thus reducing the incidence of aggressive behavior. It is also clear that a certain number of aggressive children need a more intensive intervention. When the cooperation and support of the whole school staff as well as of the parents and of the students is ensured, it is more likely that the proactive aggressive children would have to shape their behavior into more socially acceptable forms, and that the reactive aggressive children could be more closely monitored in their rehearsal of learned social skills in targeted areas. That kind of a comprehensive school-based intervention would be in line with the social development model proposed by Hawkins and Weis (1985), where it is clear that the school, the family, the peers, and the community have to be targeted for effective interventions.

As a concluding comment, I would like to address a related issue, namely our need for an integrated view of the whole spectrum of interventions with aggressive children. Once one has decided to reduce the frequency of aggressive behaviors in a certain population, and to focus intervention on individuals at risk for, or already experiencing significant problems, one has to be aware of the many ways that prevention, treatment, and rehabilitation can be pursued even though one can usually tackle one type of intervention at a time.

For the foreseeable future, there will always be a need for interventions with some adolescents focussing on the reduction of the sequelae resulting from established stable patterns of aggressive behavior. The perspectives of success with this hard core group are still grim. Secondary and primary preventions are more promising (Offord, 1987). School-wide or community-wide interventions, like the one described by Olweus, may achieve good results in reducing the incidence of some aggressive behavior amongst children. Ideally, these large prevention campaigns should include procedures that identify children in greatest need of help and focus efforts on them. Within the realm of primary prevention, programs can be addressed to children at a given age or developmental level or to children that are believed to be at greater risk of developing stable patterns of aggressive behaviors. The issue here is not so much to find out what is the best approach among these, but to discover the links among them in order to establish a sort of continuum along which prevention efforts can be ordered. For example, Coie's and colleagues' intervention program, due to the nature of targeting the children at risk (namely the peer sociometric status), can hardly be implemented before the fourth grade because of the relative instability of rejected status before that age. A too large number of false positives would thus be included in the program, and false negatives left out.

On the other hand, there is ample evidence that some children show serious signs of disruptive/aggressive behaviors before that age (Achenbach, Verhulst, Baron, & Akkerhuis, 1987; Kohn, 1977; McGee, Selva, & Williams, 1984; McGuire & Richman, 1986; Richman, Stevenson, & Graham, 1982). In our Montreal longitudinal study (Tremblay, Charlebois, Gagnon, & Larivée, 1986) teacher ratings were used to identify kindergarten boys who were exhibiting aggressive behaviors. Three years later, 38% of these at-risk boys were already behind a grade or in special class compared to 17% in the normative group. Any intervention starting in the fourth grade would have been too late for these children because they would already have been out of the regular educational system. Within the same longitudinal study, an experimental group received an intervention consisting of parent training, school based social skills training and a supervision of the content of television viewing. The main trend already observed among this group of boys after 3 years is a reduction of grade retention (29% compared to 38% for the control group) and a positive improvement in the peer evaluation of aggressive behavior. If one uses properly chosen marker variables, preventive intervention may be possible earlier (see Schweinhart, 1987; Weissberg & Allen, 1986).

Without necessarily endorsing the argument of "earlier is better", we must mention that in our longitudinal study (Tremblay, et al., 1986), one of the strongest markers associated with a high degree of aggressive/disruptive behavior at kindergarten was the age of the mother when she gave birth to her first child. Children born of teenage mothers are at a higher risk of developing behavior disorders (McAffer, Serbin, Schwartzman, & Azar, 1988). A number of other early predictors of aggressive behavior have also been reported in the research literature (Loeber & Dishion, 1983). Depending on the marker variables one chooses for intervention, the critical period for implementation will vary. In terms of implications for social policy, the point is not so much to find out which period is the most critical for intervention, as to implement a series of dovetailed programs, each appropriate for a particular stage of development—prenatal, infancy and toddlerhood, preschool and the early elementary school years, middle childhood, and adolescence (Rutter, 1987; Ziegler & Bierman, 1983; Ziegler & Hall, 1987).

What has become more recognized from evaluation results of intervention programs is the need to involve the main actors of the child's social environment, namely parents, teachers, and peers. The intervention programs described by John Coie and colleagues and Dan Olweus have these components to different degrees. The next step would be to systematically involve in a given intervention these three socialization agents.

REFERENCES

Achenbach, T. M., Verhulst, F. C., Baron, G. D., & Akkerhuis, M. S. (1987). Epidemiological comparisons of American and Dutch Children: I Behavioral/Emotional problems and competencies reported by parents for ages 4 to 16. *Journal of American Academy of Child and Adolescent Psychiatry, 26,* 317–325.

Dodge, K., & Coie, J. D. (1987). Social information processing factors in reactive and proactive aggression in children's peer groups. *Journal of Personality and Social Psychology, 53*(6), 1146–1158.

Hawkins, J. D., & Weis, J. (1985). The social development model: An integrated approach to delinquency prevention. *Journal of Primary Prevention, 6*(2), 73–97.

Kohn, M. (1977). *Social competence symptoms and underachievement in childhood: A longitudinal perspective,* Washington, DC: Winston.

Loeber, R., & Dishion, T. J. (1983). Early predictors of male delinquency: A review. *Psychological Bulletin, 94,* 68–99.

McAffer, L., Serbin, L., Schwartzman, A., & Azar, S. (1988, June). The intergenerational transmission of high-risk status. Paper presented at the Annual Meeting of the Canadian Psychological Association, Montréal.

McGee, R., Selva, P. A., & Williams, S. (1984). Behaviour problems in a population of seven year-old children: prevalence stability and types of disorder—a research report. *Journal of Child Psychology and Psychiatry, 25,* 251–259.

McGuire, J., & Richman, N. (1986). The prevalence of behavioural problems in three types of preschool group. *Journal of Child Psychology and Psychiatry, 27,* 455–472.

Offord, D. R. (1987). Prevention of behavioral and emotional disorders of children. *Journal of Child Psychology and Psychiatry, 28,* 9–19.

Olweus, D. (1978). *Aggression in the schools: Bullies and whipping boys.* Washington, DC: Hemisphere (Wiley).

Richman, N., Stevenson, J., & Graham, P. J. (1982). *Pre-school to school: a behavioural study.* London: Academic Press.

Rutter, M. (1987). Psychosocial resilience and protective mechanisms. *American Journal of Orthopsychiatry, 57*(3), 316–331.

Schweinhart, L. J. (1987). Can preschool programs help prevent delinquency?

In J. Q. Wilson & G. C. Loury (Eds.), *From children to citizens. Vol. III. Families, schools and delinquency prevention.* New York: Springer-Verlag.

Sullivan, C., Grant, M. O., & Grant, J. D. (1957). The development of interpersonal maturity: applications to delinquency. *Psychiatry, 20,* 373–385.

Tremblay, R. E., Charlebois, P., Gagnon, C., & Larivee, S. (1986). Prediction and prevention of juvenile delinquency in early childhood. The Montreal longitudinal study. Paper presented at the 11th International Congress of the International Association for Child and Adolescent Psychiatry and Allied Professions, Paris.

Weissberg, R. P., & Allen, J. P. (1986). Promoting children's social skills and adaptive interpersonal behavior. In B. A. Edelstein & L. Michelson (Eds.), *Handbook of Prevention.* New York: Plenum Press.

Zigler, E., & Bierman, W. (1983). Discerning the future of early childhood intervention. *American Psychologist, 38,* 894–906.

Zigler, E., & Hall, N. W. (1987). The implications of early intervention efforts for the primary prevention of juvenile delinquency. In J. Q. Wilson & G. C. Loury (Eds.), *From children to citizens. Vol. III, Families, schools and delinquency prevention.* New York: Springer-Verlag.

Author Index

A

B

C

S

Subject Index

A

B

C

O

P

S

T

U, V